HARDPRESS.NET
HOME OF HARD-TO-FIND BOOKS

The Lawyer's and Magistrate's Magazine
by Unknown

Address:
HardPress
8345 NW 66TH ST #2561
MIAMI FL 33166-2626
USA
Email: info@hardpress.net

THE
LAWYER'S
AND
MAGISTRATE'S
MAGAZINE.

IN WHICH IS INCLUDED

An Account of every important Proceeding in the

COURTS AT WESTMINSTER,

DURING THE PRESENT YEAR.

WITH THE DECISIONS OF THE

JUDGES,

IN THEIR OWN WORDS.

VOL. I.

FOR THE YEAR MDCXCII.

—DUBLIN:—

PRINTED FOR W. JONES, 86, DAME-STREET,
AND H. WATTS, CHRIST-CHURCH-LANE.

1792.

PLAN of the WORK.

TO give an immediate, full, and accurate account of every important Decision in the several Courts at Westminster is the primary object of this Publication; the utility of which to every one who practises the law, and still more to those who administer it, is too obvious to be enlarged upon. To the Student also it will be found a source of necessary knowledge, and to the Private Gentleman a fund of useful information.

In the course of the Work, every important object depending before the Legislature will be constantly noticed; and a particular account will be given of all Trials, Criminal or Civil, which involve any important Law point, or materially engage the public attention.

A Publication of this kind seems peculiarly proper at this time, when the newspapers are daily giving undigested and erroneous accounts of Law Cases, which cannot fail to perplex and mislead the Practitioner and the Student; and to betray the people, as circumstances may arise in their own concerns, into mistaken hopes and fears from the Justice of the Country.

It remains only to add, that this Work will be continued Monthly, and no pains or diligence shall be wanting to render it acceptable to the Profession, instructive to the Student, and useful to that most honourable and beneficial of all public characters, the COUNTRY MAGISTRATE.

a 2

C O N T E N T S.

Rex

CONTENTS.

For ALPHABETICAL INDEX see the End of this Volume.

TABLE

OF THE

PRINCIPAL MATTERS.

THE
LAWYER'S
AND
MAGISTRATE'S MAGAZINE.

For FEBRUARY, 1790.

Adjudged Cafes in the Courts at Weftminfter in laft Michaelmas Term.

Rex, v. Hurdis.

THIS was an appeal againft a poor-rate; which rate was confirmed by the feffions, fubject to the following

CASE.

THE appellant objected to the rate, becaufe one Ifaac Wood, gunner of his majefty's fort and battery at Seaford, who was a fervant to his majefty, and not in his own right the occupier of the dwelling-houfe thereto belonging, and who therefore ought not to have been charged in the rate, was inferted therein, and charged as the occupier of the battery-houfe. Wood was taxed for the battery-houfe ten fhillings. At the time of making the rate, he was, and ftill is, a head or mafter-gunner, and acted as fuch in the fort or battery of Seaford. The fort and battery-houfe are the property of the crown. A mafter-gunner is a warrant-officer, appointed and removeable at pleafure by the mafter-general of the ordnance; though his office is ufually confidered as a provifion for life. Wood, being fo employed in the fort, *occupied the whole of the houfe*, except one room, which is allotted to the under-gunner by direction from the ordnance; and the furniture of this houfe belonged to Wood. The inhabitants of the town, port, or parifh, paying to the poor-rate thereof, have a right to vote in the election of

VOL. I.   B   members

members of parliament for the town and port; and the appellant is an inhabitant of that description.

LORD KENYON, C. J.—I shall determine on the ground of positive law, as laid down in 43. Eliz. which subjects every occupier of lands, houses, &c. to be rated to the poor. Now, it is expressly stated, that *Wood was the occupier of the battery-house*; and though it might perhaps have been contended below that he was not the occupier in the legal sense of the word, yet the finding of the sessions precludes that question here. It is not however a general position, that a servant of the crown, occupying a house in respect of his office, is not rateable for it; for I was always rated for the house which I had as Master of the Rolls; and so are the auditors and tellers of the exchequer. Soldiers indeed cannot be said to be the *occupiers* of their barracks; they are no more than mere servants.

ASHHURST, J.—Wherever persons are stated by the sessions to be the *occupiers* of crown-lands or houses, they must be rated; though such property would not be rateable in the hands of the king himself. In the same manner, though hospitals, or lands held for their immediate support, are not rateable, yet if any officer hold part of the hospital lands for his own convenience, then he becomes rateable; as, in the case of *Eyre and Smallpace* (2 Burr. 1059), the comptroller of Chelsea College, residing in the comptroller's apartments, was, held rateable as occupier. Now, Wood was occupier in this case; and though he had not a life-interest, yet it is well known that such persons are never dismissed, unless for misbehaviour; and if he were considered as a mere tenant at will, that will not vary the case.   Order confirmed.

REX, v. JUSTICES OF HEREFORDSHIRE.

An order of removal was made on the 18th of *April,* and the pauper was removed on the 19th to a place twenty miles distant from Hereford, where the quarter-sessions were held on the 22d *following.*—The parish not having appealed at this sessions, the justices refused to receive the appeal at the Midsummer sessions, they not being the *next* quarter sessions after the order.

This was an application for a *mandamus* to the justices to receive the appeal.

LORD KENYON, C. J.—The words of the act 13 and 14 Car. II. cap. 12. § 2. expressly require the appeal to be made at the next sessions after the grievance. Where indeed an order has been made some time before, and only executed

ed a very short time before the sessions, so that there was
no possibility of appealing to those sessions, this court has
granted a *mandamus* to receive the appeal afterwards,
because the "next sessions" must mean the next *possible*
sessions. But here were two intervening days after the
delivery of the pauper before the Easter sessions. And if
there was not time to give reasonable notice of appeal, the
appeal might have been entered and adjourned according to
9 Geo. cap. 7, § 8.

The other judges concurred.

Rule discharged.

REX, v. ST. MATTHEW, IPSWICH.

Edm. Stollery and wife were removed from St. Nicholas
to St. Matthew, in Ipswich. Order confirmed by sessions,
subject to the following

CASE.

About five years ago, the waiter belonging to S. Ribbands, who kept an inn in St. Matthew, being ill, sent for
the pauper, Edmund Stollery (who was then a single man,
and legally settled in St. Nicholas) to assist him at the inn,
where he stayed as *helper to the waiter* about six months,
and then went away. The waiter, being again taken ill,
sent for the pauper *to help him*, which he did; and he continued in the inn as boot-catcher for nineteen months,
during which time he lodged and boarded there, and was
to be satisfied by the gentlemen who came to the house.
Ribbands knew of his being there the night after he came,
but nothing passed between him and the pauper at the
time. The waiter who sent for the pauper continued in
the service of Ribbands till about July in the next year,
when he went away, and the pauper continued there till
the Christmas following; when, Ribbands and the pauper
having some dispute, the former told him to go away;
upon which he asked Ribbands to give him something for
the time he had been there. Ribbands replied he shou'd
not give him any thing, as he had made no agreement
with him; but, on being pressed again to consider his
situation, he not having any thing to help himself, Ribbands
gave him two guineas, and sent him away; and the
pauper then left the house. The pauper considered himself
not as a servant to Ribbands, but as assistant to the
waiter, and thought himself at liberty to go away when

B 2

he

he pleafed: he faw Ribbands fometimes, who, if a gueft wanted his boots, told the pauper to get them, and at other times fent him on errands.

In fupport of the order, it was contended that the hiring and fervice with Ribbands was good; for the waiter acted as the mafter's agent, as appears from Ribbands's feeing him the fecond day. There was no agreement for *wages*; but, as the mafter accepted the fervice of the pauper, he might have demanded recompence. And as he continued in the fervice fix months after the waiter was gone, without any new agreement, a general hiring may be prefumed.

LORD KENYON, ftopping the other fide, faid, a hiring was never prefumed by retrofpect; a *conditional* hiring was held good in the *New-Windfor* cafe (Burrowes's Settl. Cafe 19), but then there was from the firft an exprefs hiring by the mafter. Hiring by the mafter *himfelf* is not neceffary, nor are wages; and if there be an hiring, unlefs the contrary appears, a year will be prefumed.—But the argument here is, that he was Ribbands's fervant, which is contradicted by the Cafe itfelf; for the *waiter* engaged him as *his helper*. But the Cafe muft turn upon his fecond coming—he came again to *help the waiter*; and there is nothing to infer that he was Ribbands's fervant. For the laft fix months, a contract with Ribbands may be implied; and if he had been before in Ribbands's fervice, and then lived under a yearly hiring, the fettlement would have been gained. Where the nature of the cafe implies an hiring, the court will prefume it; but here the manner in which the pauper came excludes an hiring by the mafter.

Rule abfolute.

REX, *v.* THE INHABITANTS OF ST. AGNES.

Two occupiers of rateable property in the parifh of St. Agnes, Cornwall, appeal againft the poor-rate, becaufe certain perfons entitled to *farms of tin* and *toll tin* are omitted to be rated. Seffions quafh the rate, fubject to the following

C A S E.

J. P. Andrews, as truftee of J. Enys, is entitled to a certain difh, or meafure, arifing out of certain lands and tin bounds in St. Agnes, called *toll and farm tin*; which toll is one 15th part of all the tin gotten in the lands of J. Enys, within the parifh of St. Agnes; and which faid *farm tin or due*, is one 12th part, after the faid 15th part is deducted, for

for toll of all such tin so gotten within the tin bounds in the parish; and which said dues or duties are due and payable by the laws and customs of the Stannaries of Cornwall, free and clear of all risk and deduction whatsoever: but they are uncertain, and vary every year; yet for many years last past have produced a considerable sum annually. And N. Donnithorne is entitled to a certain dish, or measure, called *toll tin, or dues,* arising out of certain lands in St. Agnes, and due and payable in the manner before stated; and which toll varies, and is uncertain, but also produces a considerable sum annually.

It was objected that Andrews and Donnithorne should have been made parties to this Case. But the Court said they would not be concluded by the determination, but might appeal themselves, whenever they were taxed for this property.

LORD KENYON, C. J.—said, he approved of the cases of Rowls *v.* Gells, and R. *v.* Maddern (the former of which had been cited at the bar, as concluding the question of want of notice, and the latter as deciding the rateability of this property); though these two persons would not be precluded from objecting to their being charged in any future rate on any ground they might think proper. But they were not parties to this case, and could not make any objection to the order of sessions.

Order of sessions, quashing the rate, confirmed.

REX, *v.* THE INHABITANTS OF SCAMMODEN.

C. Bottomley and wife were removed from Scammoden to Soyland. The sessions quashed the order, subject to the following

CASE.

The pauper being settled in Soyland, in the West Riding of Yorkshire, agreed with J. Harrison for the purchase of an estate in Rishworth for 28 l. and the consideration in the deeds, and in the receipt indorsed, was 28 l. but the appellants produced parole-evidence, to prove that, before the deeds were executed, the vendor declared that, as the agreement was not in writing, he was not bound by it; and, having since had 30 l. offered for the estate, he would not take less; nor would he execute the deeds, unless the purchase-money were made up that sum. Upon which the pauper advanced 1 l. 15 s. more, which, with 5s. owing from Harrison to the pauper, made up the sum of 30 l. but
the

the deeds were not altered, and the consideration therein mentioned was left according to the original agreement, viz. 28l. The counsel for the appellants contended this was a *bona-fide* purchase for 30l. But the sessions were of opinion, that no parole-evidence could be given to contradict the consideration mentioned in the deeds. The estate purchased was the estate of Harrison's wife; and in the deed there was a covenant from Harrison, that he and his wife would levy a fine unto C. Bottomley, in fee, of the premises, at the cost of Bottomley; towards the expence of which fine C. Bottomley left in the hands of his attorney four guineas. The pauper resided above three months upon the premises, and afterwards sold them to his brother J. Bottomley. To this conveyance Harrison and his wife were parties; and it recited Harrison's covenant in the former deed to levy a fine; but, as such a fine had not then been levied, it was agreed that, instead thereof Harrison and his wife should acknowledge and levy a fine of the premises upon Bottomley in fee, which fine was, in Hilary term, 1787, levied accordingly; part of the expence of levying it was discharged by the four guineas, so left in the hands of the attorney by the pauper; and the other part was paid by Bottomley. And the court of sessions, being of opinion that the sum of four guineas was to be considered as part of the consideration under the act of parliament, and, that C. Bottomley, by such purchase, gained a settlement in Rishworth, discharged the order.

Chambre, against the order, said the parole-evidence was properly rejected by the sessions. A *contract* in writing, much more a *deed*, cannot be contradicted by parole evidence; and, in Clarkson v. Hannay (2 P. Wms. 203), parole-evidence was denied to prove other considerations than those mentioned in the deed.

Lord Kenyon, C. J.—Considerations not expressed in the deed may be proved. It is so in all cases of covenants to stand seized to uses. And, in the case of Filmer v. Gott (Brown's Parl. Cases, 70), the deed was set aside, because, upon an issue out of Chancery, the jury found *natural love and affection, mentioned in the deed,* made *no part* of the consideration. Order of sessions affirmed.

REX, v. THE INHABITANTS OF FOLKSTONE.

CASE.

On the 10th of October, 1781, James King, the pauper, hired a house in the parish of Folkstone of the yearly value of of 5l. 5s. of Henry Selden, in which he resided for three years; during which time he paid the land-tax for the house: but, after he had paid three quarterly rates in 1782, he complained to his landlord, that his (the landlord's) other tenants did not pay the land-tax for their houses, and therefore desired him to deduct it. The landlord refused to allow what the pauper had already paid, but agreed to deduct it in future, which he did. There was not any agreement made between the pauper and his landlord which of them should pay the land-tax. The rate for the land-tax was in the following form:

Sum Assessed.	Proprietors Names.	Occupiers Names.	Premisses.	Quarterly payment.
£10 10 0	Henry Selden.	James King.	House.	£0 2 6

The sessions were of opinion that the *landlords were the persons intended to be rated in the rate*; and that the names of occupiers, inserted in the second column, were only meant to distinguish the premisses, and to direct the collectors to whom they were to apply for payment of the rate.

LORD KENYON, C. J.—This is the landlord's tax. And, when the question first came before the court, it was doubted whether a tenant, who was rated to, and paid the land-tax, should gain a settlement by it: but in R. v. Bramley it was observed that "that doubt had been gotten over." But in this case no question can arise: on the rate there is one column of the proprietors, and another of the tenants; but the names of the tenants were only inserted in order to shew for what property the landlords were rated. And the justices in this case have stated (what I think they were bound to do) that the landlord was rated.

BULLER, J.—In R. v. Mitcham, (Cald. 276) R. v. St. Lawrence, (ib. 379), and R. v. Endon, (ib. 374), it was held that, as between the public and the tenant, the land-tax is the tenant's tax, though, as between the landlord and the tenant, it is otherwise; that, if it be doubtful on the rate itself, whether the landlord or the tenant be rated, it must be collected from other circumstances; that the land-tax is *primâ facie* a tenant's tax, and that, if nothing appear to the contrary, the occupier must be presumed to be the person rated. This idea was not adopted in these late cases for the first time, for so long ago as in a case in 30 Geo. II. Foster, J. said " the occupier is the person who is to pay."

But

But whether the landlord or tenant be rated is a question of fact, which should always be found by the justices: here it is stated, and we are precluded, by their opinion, from entering into the question. — Order of sessions affirmed.

REX, v. GUARDIANS OF THE POOR OF CHICHESTOR.

Two Justices in March 1789, adjudged one Lover reputed father of a bastard. Lover appealed to the General Quarter Sessions in April following, where the order of filiation was quashed.

The proceedings now came before the court, not upon a *case*, but by a *certiorari*, and it was moved to quash the order of Sessions, because the statute 18 Eliz. c. 3. gives the appeal to the next General Sessions, for this was a Quarter Sessions, and it does not appear but that a General Sessions might have intervened—and it was so held Rex, v. Shaw. Salk. 483.

LORD KENYON, C. J. said that the case cited did not appear to be one of the most authentic in Salkeld's Reports; but it is a general rule that every intendment shall be made to support an order of Justices, and as it does not appear that the General Quarter Sessions, held on the 22d of April, were not the Sessions next following the 27th March, we will not presume it for the purpose of quashing the order of sessions.   Order of sessions affirmed.

PETRIE AND ANOTHER, EXECUTORS OF PAGE KEEBLE, AGAINST HANNAY, BART.

The testator, Sadlier Petrie, and the defendant, were concerned in large stock speculations on a joint account, the whole of which were illegal, except a transfer of 10,000 l. Having incurred many losses, they settled with Portis, their broker, who had paid the differences; and on that occasion Keeble repaid Portis all the money advanced by him, except 811 l. which was part of the defendant's share of the losses, and for which Keeble drew on him in favour of Portis, which the defendant accepted. N. B. 264 l. being the defendant's share of the loss on the legal transaction of 10,000 l. was included in the 811 l. The defendant not paying the bill when it became due, Portis brought an action, after Keeble's death, against his executors, the present plaintiffs, and recovered the amount, no defence being set up on account of the illegality of the transaction.

The

The prefent action was to re-imburfe the plaintiffs the money fo paid for the defendant's ufe; and they recovered upon it at the fittings before Lord Kenyon.

A rule was obtained, to fhew caufe why the verdict fhould not be fet afide, or, at leaft, reduced to the fum of 264 l.

Bearcroft, Mingay, and Ruffel, now fhewed caufe; and faid, this cafe was not within the ftatute, 7 George II. c. 8, to prevent ftockjobbing, as it was not an action to fatisfy differences of ftock, but to recover money paid to Portis under the defendant's authority; and they refted upon the cafe of Faikney v. Reynous (4 Burrowes 2069), whence the defendant pleaded againft a bond that it was for ftock-jobbing differences, and the court held that the plaintiff was entitled to recover what he had paid, though for an illegal purpofe. At all events they contended they were entitled to recover the 264 l. as that was perfectly clear from any objection arifing under the act.

Erfkine and Wood, *contra*, faid the tranfaction was al-together illegal, and came within the fpirit of the act; and that the 264 l. could not be feparated, the whole being one general fcheme of fpeculation. Thefe parties were *participes criminis*, and one partner cannot call upon another for his contribution to a lofs arifing out of a matter prohibited by law. Suppofe a partnerfhip contract for fmuggled goods, and one pays the whole, he would not be fuffered to recover againft the other.

LORD KENYON, C. J. — As to the 264 l. I have no doubt whatever. It was a fair tranfaction; the ftock actually purchafed, and the transfer made: none of the pro-vifions of the act were infringed; and it is too much to fay that, becaufe the other tranfactions were invalid, this fhall not be binding. But, on the principal queftion, I have not formed a decifive opinion; and I have not heard any ar-gument to convince me that the plaintiffs' demand can be enforced. The great difficulty is to diftinguifh this cafe from that of Faikney v. Reynous; but that does not at prefent appear to me to conclude this queftion. That was an action on a bond; and the whole argument at the bar, and the decifion of the court, proceeded on the ground that they could not take into confideration matter which was not properly introduced by the plea. And they thought that, as nothing illegal between thofe parties was difclofed on the record, the payment of the money could not be refifted. But this is not the cafe of a bond; and, if we confider this

cafe

case *à priori* on the ground of policy, and recollect the infinite mischiefs brought on individuals by means of stock-jobbing, it is to be wished that the remedies offered by the legislature should extend to the whole mischief. Now, I do not see how that can be done so effectually as by saying that no person, who is concerned in such a transaction, shall recover any demand arising out of it in a court of law. The first action which was brought against these plaintiffs was on a bill of exchange, which had been accepted by the defendant on account of the losses. Now, it is clear that that action did not merge the original demand, and the whole transaction may still be brought before the court ; and, if it appear to the court that a bill of exchange is given without any consideration, it is *nudum pactum ex quo non oritur actio* ; or, if for an illegal consideration, the whole matter may be examined. But, in the case of a bond, the consideration cannot always be gone into, as in the instance of a voluntary bond. In this case the testator and the defendant were partners in an illegal transaction, in which Portis the broker acted as agent, knowing it to be contrary to law, since every man is bound to take notice of public laws. Now it is a rule that those, who come into a court of justice to seek redress, must come with clean hands, and must disclose a transaction warranted by law. And I cannot distinguish this case from that of smuggling, put at the bar, where, if one of two partners advance money in a smuggling transaction, he cannot recover his proportion of it against his partner, because the transaction is prohibited ; and yet smuggling is not *malum in se*, as contradistinguished from *malum prohibitum*. If this transaction had been disclosed in the former action, Portis could not have recovered. Now, supposing the bill of exchange puts the plaintiffs in his situation, they are not assisted by it ; or considering them, on the other hand, standing in their own situation, unconnected with Portis, they then appear as partners in a matter prohibited by the laws of the country, and cannot therefore have recourse to those laws to enforce their contract. But at present I speak with great diffidence ; and I shall be glad to correct this opinion, if, on reconsideration, I find I am mistaken. I wish however to have it understood, that I do not mean to disturb the case of Faikney *v.* Reynous ; there the court did not think themselves warranted in saying that sufficient was disclosed on the record to bring the case within the statute : but here the whole transaction may be enquired into, which, on examination, is, I think, prohibited by that act.

ASHHURST,

ASHHURST, J.—I think that this case must be governed by that of Faikney v. Reynous; and, if we were to determine now for the defendant, we must overturn that case. The court did not proceed in that case on the ground that it was an action on the bond, for they permitted a discussion of the facts; but they said, that, even admitting them to be true, still it was no defence to the action; and Lord Mansfield and the whole court proceeded on the ground, that as it was not *malum in se*, but only *malum prohibitum*, and as the plaintiff was not concerned in the use which the other made of the money, it was a fair transaction between those parties. I see no difference between that case and the present.

BULLER, J.—About the 264l. there can be no doubt. But, in order to consider the great question in the case, whether the plaintiffs are entitled to recover the large sum under the circumstances which are disclosed, it is necessary to trace this transaction to its origin, for it very much depends on the light in which this question must have been considered, if Portis had been the plaintiff. We may, I think, infer that the defendant consented, and requested Portis to pay the differences in the stocks. And here I agree that, in the case of an illegal transaction, if one person pay money for another, without an express authority, he cannot recover it back; for there is a wide difference between partners in legal and illegal contracts: in the former, if one of the partners pay the whole of a partnership debt without any express promise from the other, the law gives him a right to recover it back in an action for money paid to the use of that other partner; and it proceeds on this ground, that both are liable to pay. But in the case of illegal contracts, as they are not bound to pay, one of them cannot acquire a right of action against the other by paying the whole without his consent; but he must have the consent of that other. The question therefore here is, whether the court cannot infer from the evidence, that the money was paid with the authority of the defendant; and I think we are bound to draw that conclusion. It appears that the defendant agreed to pay his proportion of the loss, and accepted a Bill drawn on him by Keeble in favour of Portis. How then would the case have stood, if Portis had been the plaintiff? And here I agree with my brother Ashhurst, that, as Portis paid the money with the consent of the defendant, he would be entitled to recover it back again, unless the determination of Faikney v. Reynous be not law. Some light may perhaps be thrown on that case,
from

from confidering the time when it was argued: It came before the court in E. 7 Geo. III. juft at the time when the queftion in pleading, whether a defendant could aver any thing *dehors* the condition of the bond, had undergone much difcuffion in Weftminfter-hall. But it is now fully fettled, that matter *dehors* the bond may be pleaded. And it would be highly inconvenient if it were otherwife; for no perfon who is engaging in an illegal tranfaction would be fo abfurd as to ftate the illegality of it on the bond itfelf. In Faikney *v.* Reynous Lord Mansfield was filent on the queftion of pleading; and he gave his opinion on the general ground, that if one perfon apply to another to pay his debt (whether contracted on the fcore of ufury, or for any other purpofe, it makes no difference) he is entitled to recover it back again. And he did not feem to confider that there was any diftinction, whether the debt arofe on a bond or other fecurity. The three other judges alfo concurred; and faid, "that it remained a good bond on the "face of it, till the obligor fhewed that it was bad." So that the conclufion drawn by them is, that the tranfaction, as difclofed by the plea, did not make it illegal as between thofe parties. Therefore I think that this cafe is governed by that of Faikney *v.* Reynous.

GROSE, J.—I agree clearly as to the fmaller fum; and I cannot diftinguifh this cafe from that of Faikney *v.* Reynous, upon which I give my judgment.

Rule difcharged.

ROLLESTON and others, Affignees of MARGETSON, a Bankrupt, v. HIBBERT and others.

On an action of trover for a fhip, the general iffue was pleaded, and the following cafe referved.

CASE

The bankrupt being indebted to the defendants in 2000 l. on bills, which they had accepted and paid for him, on the 21ft of June, 1788, gave them his promiffory note, payable in three months; and, by way of fecurity, executed to them a bill of fale of the fhip Commerce, and, at the fame time, depofited in their hands the grand bill of fale, and alfo a policy of infurance on the fhip from London to Jamaica, and back again. The bill of fale was *abfolute* on the face of it, and in the ufual form, but it did not contain a recital of the certificate of the regiftry of the fhip, as required by ftat. 26 Geo. III. cap. 60.

§ 17.

§ 17.   But at the time when the bankrupt executed the bill of sale, and deposited that, together with the grand bill of sale and policy, with the defendants, they gave him an *acknowledgment in writing, promising to return the same upon payment of the note.*   On the 21st of June, 1788, the ship was in foreign parts, and did not arrive in England till the 22d of November, 1788.   The bankrupt stopped payment the 3d of July, 1788.   On the 18th of the same month, a commission was issued against him; and on the 8th of August his effects were assigned to the plaintiffs. Immediately on the ship's arrival in England, the defendants took possession of her, and still continue in possession. After the 21st of June, 1788, and before his bankruptcy, the bankrupt paid to his creditors, in the course of his trade, between 3000 l. and 4000 l.   And it was also found by the case, that the bill of sale was not executed by the bankrupt in contemplation of bankruptcy.

Shepherd, for plaintiffs, said, the defendants could not detain the ship either as a *purchase* or a *lien.*   It could not be a sale, because the statute 26 Geo. III. cap. 60, § 17, enacts " that when and so often as the property in any " ship of a British subject shall be transferred to any other " British subject, in whole, or in part, the *certificate of* " *the registry* of such ship *shall be truly recited in the bill, or* " *other instrument of sale, otherwise such bill of sale shall be* " *utterly null and void,* to all intents and purposes."   Therefore the sale of this ship is void, and the bill of sale a nullity.   The defendant cannot have a lien to enable him to retain the ship to satisfy his demand; for, as the bill of sale is void, there is nothing to shew the ship was delivered for any specific purpose.   And if any thing in this transaction could make it binding in a court of law as a lien, *an interest* would be created in the ship, which is expressly provided against by the statute.   Foreigners might claim in the same manner, and the whole policy of the law subverted.

The counsel on the other side spoke very fully; but, as the chief arguments were afterwards recited by the judges, it is needless to give them in this place.

LORD KENYON, C. J.—The question is, whether this bill of sale is an effective instrument to convey the property.   The statute declares, in the most positive terms, such bill of sale to be absolutely void.   In answer to which it was argued, that it was not necessary this property should be conveyed by a written instrument; but certainly, if the parties do so convey, they shall not refer to any other agreement.   And here the title of the defendants being reduced

duced to writing, though it be void, they cannot go into
any other agreement. It is like the case of a bill of sale
without stamps, which could not be produced in evidence;
but the vendor would not be suffered to resort to parole
evidence of the agreement.

It is argued that this statute does not apply to *transfer
of ships at sea*, it being impossible to comply with the act
in that case, because, the certificate being on board the ship,
reference could not be had thereto; but the words of the
27th section are general, and make no exception of such
cases; besides the parties might recur to the registry at the
Custom-house, where a duplicate is kept. Then it is
said, the defendants had a lien on the ship to the amount
of their demand; but that is not so, for the bill of sale
professes to convey the absolute property. And supposing
that the bankrupt had never called for a return of the ship,
from what time can the title of the vendees be said to
accrue? Was it only from the time when the sum of 2000 l.
became due, and was not paid? On payment of that sum
indeed the vendor would have had a right to call for a
return of the ship; but that could not divest the intermediate property of the vendors under the bill of sale. The
law was so with respect to real property, prior to the 14th
Geo. II. cap. 20; before which time conditional surrenders
were made by tenants for life to make good tenants to
the *præcipe* to suffer common recoveries, which surrenders
were to be avoided by the payment of large sums on
particular days, when the surrenderees were to reconvey:
now, if during that interval the whole property did not
pass to the surrenderees, such recoveries would have been
void; but undoubtedly the property did pass in such cases.
So in the case of a mortgage, where a descent is cast before
it becomes absolute, the legal estate must descend according
to the terms of the mortgage, notwithstanding the day of
redemption is not passed. There is nothing in the act of
parliament to warrant our giving effect to this bill of sale.

ASHHURST, J.—If we decide this bill of sale to be good
to a *particular intent*, we should go in direct opposition to
the statute, which renders all bills of sale, which do not
comply with the requisites of the act, *null and void, to all
intents and purposes*. It is said the statute could not be complied with, because the certificate was with the ship at sea
at the time the bill of sale was made; but that is fully answered, as they might have extracted it from the registry
at the Custom-house. Then it is said the defendants have
a lien on the ship, and may retain the possession. That
might

might be an argument againſt the bankrupt himſelf; but, ſince the bankruptcy, all the creditors have an equitable lien on his eſtate; and when two equities meet, the legal title muſt prevail, which is with the plaintiff.

BULLER, J.—It is a hard caſe, that the defendants, who have acted fairly, ſhould loſe the benefit of their ſecurity; but it is impoſſible to get over the ſtatute. It has been contended that this caſe is not within the act; 1ſt, as the ſhip was ſold at ſea; and, 2dly, becauſe the defendants acquired no right to navigate the ſhip, which was the only object of the legiſlature. As to the firſt: I think that the other clauſes of the ſtatute are deciſively againſt it; becauſe the caſe of a ſale of a ſhip, either at ſea or in a foreign port *to a foreigner*, is expreſsly provided for by the 15th ſection; then, if we ſee that in one part of this ſtatute the legiſlature had in view the ſale of a ſhip at ſea or in a foreign port, and made ſpecial proviſions for ſuch a purchaſe by a foreigner, it cannot be argued that the ſelling of a ſhip at ſea in other caſes was not in the contemplation of the legiſlature: but it ſhews that they only intended to make one exception, leaving all other caſes within the general words of the 17th ſection. Beſides, before ſuch an argument ought to be adopted, it ought to appear that, beyond all controverſy, the parties could not comply with the requiſites of the ſtatute, and that this was a *caſus omiſſus*; which is by no means to be collected from the ſtatute.

The ſecond ground of objection is not well-founded, becauſe there is an abſolute transfer of the property by the bill of ſale; whereas, to found that argument, it ought to have been ſhewn that, independently of this act of parliament, the defendants had no right to navigate the ſhip under the title they had acquired. If ſuch an argument could prevail, it would be ſaying that every inſtrument might avail, though expreſsly declared void by ſtatute. It was argued, that the 17th ſection of the ſtatute *cannot extend to all caſes*; but that has always been conſidered as an excepted caſe; and this is a *transfer by the party*. It was then contended, that if the plaintiffs had filed a Bill of Chancery to compel poſſeſſion, they muſt firſt have ſatisfied the demand; but that argument is not applicable here; for, in that court, he who aſks equity muſt firſt do equity; and, if ſuch a bill would have been diſmiſſed, it would be becauſe the demand was unconſcientious; but that would not decide the property of the ſhip. The argument ought to go further, and ſhew that, if the defendants in this caſe had

applied

applied to a court of equity for the ship, that court would have decreed it. I know of no such case. Had this been the practice of a court of equity, it would have had great weight with me; for, in my opinion, nothing can be more unfortunate for the subject, than that different rules respecting property should prevail in the different courts, and in mercantile transactions particularly. If the defendants have a clear, equitable title, we sitting in this court ought not to permit the possession to be taken from them.

GROSE, J. concurred in opinion; and said, this is an absolute bill of sale conceived in the strongest terms; the vendor could not make a more complete title; and the vendee might (if the statute had been complied with), have carried this instrument to market. The acknowledgments signed by the defendants only gave a right of action to the vendor, in case the bill of sale was not returned, but it did not affect the property in the ship.

Postea, for the plaintiffs.

HOLLOWAY, v. BENNETT.

A *qui tam* action had been tried at the assizes for some penalties of 50 l. under the Silk-Weavers Act, 13 Geo. III. cap. 68. § 5. and verdict given for the defendant, with one penalty *generally*; but the plaintiff's counsel chose to apply it to a *particular count*, and the *postea* was indorsed accordingly: the verdict on this count being confessedly bad in point of law, the question now was, whether the finding could be applied to other counts that were good.

LORD KENYON, C. J.—As this is a penal action, and the plaintiff has elected to enter the verdict on one count, he shall not now resort to another. For though the jury would in some cases have no difficulty in giving their verdict on *any* count, yet in others that would not be warranted. And though in this case the verdict was general, the application of it by the plaintiff's counsel to one point must bind them. And it is admitted *this count* cannot be supported, therefore   The judgment was arrested.

REX, v. WITHERS.

The defendant, having been convicted of writing and publishing a libel against Mrs. Fitzherbert, was brought up for judgment.

Erskine, against the defendant, produced, in order to aggravate the sentence, a pamphlet written by the defendant

after

after the trial, and more libellous than that for which he had been convicted.

Dallas, for the defendant, objected, and said, that this second publication might be prosecuted as a new crime, but could not be brought to aggravate the present punishment. It was depriving his client of the advantages of trial; and, as he was liable to be prosecuted for it afterwards, if it was now taken into consideration, he might, in effect, be punished twice for the same offence.

LORD KENYON, C. J. said, the subsequent conduct of the defendant is generally brought to extenuate the offence; but it may also be produced in aggravation, though the court in such case will inflict no greater punishment than the principal offence would warrant; but the defendant should be allowed time to answer the present affidavit.

He was accordingly brought up on a subsequent day, and, producing no affidavits in answer, was sentenced to pay a fine of 50 l. to be imprisoned twelve months in Newgate, and find sureties for his good behaviour for three years.

DAVIES, *v.* COTTLE.

A rule was obtained by the defendant, to shew cause why there should not be the same judgment as in case of non-suit, on the usual affidavit that the plaintiff had not proceeded to trial, after giving regular notice: this rule was afterwards discharged on an affidavit from the plaintiff, that the defendant had agreed to pay 12 guineas, on condition the action was discontinued; and that this agreement took place subsequent to the said notice of trial.

Motion to discharge the second rule, three persons swearing that the plaintiff's affidavit was utterly untrue.

LORD KENYON, C. J.—The court will not go into the subject again on the ground of costs only: the plaintiff may be indicted if he has sworn falsely. The court might perhaps have given time to examine into the matter, if it had been urged, *at the time,* that the affidavit was false.

Rule refused.

WAUGH, *v.* AUSTIN.

Between the interlocutory and final judgment, the plaintiff became a bankrupt, and sued out execution *in his own name,* and charged the defendant in custody of the marſhal.   The queſtion was, whether the aſſignees ſhould not have ſued out a *ſcire facias* to revive the judgment, and then have charged the defendant in execution.

Wood in ſupport of the *execution*, cited Bibbin *v.* Mantel, (2 Wilſon, 358);   where plaintiff became bankrupt after the interlocutory, and executed a writ of enquiry in his own name.

Baldwin, contra, ſaid, that the defendant in this caſe had no opportunity of pleading, and was therefore without remedy, unleſs the court aſſiſted him.

By the court.—The bankruptcy of the plaintiff does not abate the ſuit; and aſſignees frequently continue the bankrupt's ſuit in his name.

Application diſmiſſed.

BARRINGTON, *v.* REX, *in Error.*

Writ of Error to reverſe an Outlawry in Felony.

It was aſſigned for error, *inter alia,*

I. That the writ of *capias cum proclamatione*, alleged to be iſſued, does not require the ſaid G. Barrington *to render himſelf to the ſheriff of* Middleſex, *ſo that the ſaid ſheriff might have his body before the juſtices therein named at the return of the ſaid writ,* as by law it ought to have been done; but, on the contrary thereof, *requires the ſaid* G. Barrington *to be before the juſtices at the return of the ſaid writ,* which is contrary to the law of the land.

II. That the ſaid writ of proclamation does not appear to be iſſued or executed as the ſtatute in that caſe made and provided requires.

III. That it is not alleged, that the ſaid G. Barrington was exacted, or demanded, at the Sheriff's County-Court of Middleſex, holden at the houſe known by the name of the Sheriff's-Office in Took's-Court, Curſitor-Street, and in and for the county of Middleſex, as by law it ought to have been.

IV. That the ſaid G. Barrington is alleged to be a fifth time demanded and outlawed on the 21ſt day of February in the 28th year, &c. when it appears by the ſaid writ of *capias cum proclamatione,* and the ſaid proclamation returned thereon, that he the ſaid G. Barrington had a day given, to be before the juſtices therein named, until the general ſeſſion of the peace next after the 1ſt day of February, in the 28th year, &c. being the 25th day of that month.

LORD

LORD KENYON, C. J.—I am very glad, from the clearness of one of the objections, to be relieved from the necessity of giving any opinion on the others. The proceedings in this case impute to the prisoner, that he has been guilty of disobedience of the law : they require, that he should render himself to the justices at the general sessions of the peace next after the 1st of February then next ensuing ; and that time is ascertained, by another part of the record, to be on the 25th of February : but, before that day arrived, namely, on the 21st of February, the sentence of outlawry is pronounced on him. It is clear that the disobedience of the law, for which he was to be punished, never happened ; for the day was not arrived, on which he was required to render himself. Therefore, on the plainest principles of common sense, without looking after critical objections, I am of opinion, that this outlawry must be reversed.

ASHHURST, J.—of the same opinion.

BULLER, J.—I am glad that we are not called upon to give any opinion on the third objection ; though I confess I have a strong opinion upon it. I do not know that it has ever been determined, that, in any return made by a sheriff, any technical form of words is necessary : certain requisites must be observed ; but, if observed in substance, and the return be not in equivocal terms, a great deal of argument is necessary to convince me that such a return is bad. But the last objection is perfectly clear. The statute, 8 Hen. VI. cap. 10, which has been referred to, has no relation to this case : that act only applies to indictments in one county against offenders residing in another, and only to cases where it appears, on the face of the indictment, that he does reside out of the county. There the legislature have required that a proclamation shall issue with a second capias, and go into the county where the person indicted lives ; and, it is true, in such a case, the writ must require the person indicted to appear before the justices at the return of the writ : but that return is before the time of the outlawry ; for there must be a *pluries capias* before the outlawry can issue ; all those are preparatory steps to the outlawry, and the prisoner's appearance is required in order to prevent the outlawry. But this is a very different case ; for here the writ is returnable after the outlawry is complete. In looking into the precedents on this subject, there is one of The King *v.* Cranstoun, for the murder of Mr. Blandy, which deserves attention, because some of the most eminent gen-

tlemen

tlemen of the profeſſion were employed in it ; and therefore it is natural to ſuppoſe that great care was taken in
ſettling that outlawry ; and in that I obſerve, that the writ
of *capias cum proclamatione* required Cranſtoun *to render himſelf to the ſheriff, ſo that the ſheriff might have his body before
the juſtices at the return,* &c.   The form of outlawry in
civil caſes is alſo material to be conſidered.   The ſtat. 31
El. cap. 3. ſettles the form in *civil* proceedings ; and 4 &
5 W. cap. 22. § 4. extends the proviſions of the former
act to *criminal* caſes, *before judgment.*   For there is a difference in that reſpect, whether the outlawry be *after* or
before judgment ; for, if after judgment, no proclamation
is neceſſary.   And unleſs that diſtinction be attended to in
Wilkes's caſe, that caſe, as reported in Burrow, may miſ-
lead ; for the arguments are not ſtated.   In fact, that was
an outlawry *after* conviction, and therefore it did not
come within the ſtatute of W. & M.   But that ſtatute extends the proviſions of the 31 El. to criminal caſes before judgment ; and therefore that, which has prevailed
in civil caſes, is a fair rule in this caſe.   Now, in civil
caſes, the writ of *capias cum proclamatione* univerſally requires the perſon indicted *to render himſelf to the ſheriff, ſo
that the ſheriff may have his body before the juſtices at the return,* &c.   Therefore it ſeems to me, that this is a deciſive
objection, and that the outlawry muſt be reverſed.

GROSE, J.—I am glad not to be obliged to give any
opinion on the other objection ; for the laſt appears to be
deciſive.   It ſeems abſurd to pronounce a judgment of
outlawry againſt a perſon on the 21ſt of February, for not
appearing on the 25th of the ſame month.

Outlawry reverſed.

Priſoner remanded for trial, and reſtored to his former
rights.

He was accordingly tried in the December ſeſſions, 1789,
at the Old Bailey.

Trial of GEORGE BARRINGTON.

George Barrington was indicted for felonouſly ſtealing,
on the 19th of January, in the 29th year of his preſent
Majeſty's reign, at the pariſh of St. Martin in the Fields, a
ſilk purſe value 2d. and twenty-three guineas, value 24l. 3s.
and one half-guinea, value 10s. 6d. the property of Havilard
Le Meſurier, Eſq. privily from his perſon.

Before the Jury were ſworn, the priſoner ſaid, ' I beg
leave to challenge them.   I own that I am acting under the
influence

influence of a report which is, perhaps, very untrue.—I mean no reflection;' upon which the second Middlesex Jury was put in the place of the first.

Havilard Le Mesurier. I was at the play-house in Drury-lane, on the 19th of January, 1787; I saw the prisoner there; it was at the end of the play: I left my party to meet my servants. As I came into the lobby, I observed it was excessively crowded: a circumstance then struck me of having a great deal of money in my purse, which led me to be extremely on my guard. When I got into the lobby, I put my watch-chain very deep in my fob, and put my left hand down to guard my pocket. I went along, pressing through the crowd to get to my servants; I felt my purse move, and, on feeling my purse move, I immediately got a hand up in this manner with my right hand, and with my left I turned round to seize the person whose hand I had. I seized the prisoner's hand close to my pocket, and with the other hand I turned round and seized his person. I did not say any thing to the prisoner; my aim and wish was to recover my purse, which I thought was in his hand. I had not time to seize upon him; for a clergyman, Mr. Adean, stept up and said, Sir, you are right, I saw him do it. Mr. Adean is now abroad. There were people all round: on Mr. Adean's stepping up to me, on my having his hand up still, a gentleman from the other side called out, Sir, here is your purse; and delivered me my purse. It was instantly on feeling my purse move that I caught the hand; there was no interval whatever; neither the prisoner's hand, or any hand, was ever in my pocket; my breeches pocket was never unbuttoned; my purse, although it contained twenty-three guineas and a half, which is a weight, got through my pocket without being unbuttoned; and, on examining my breeches afterwards, I found that my breeches was cut through. No hand was in my pocket; Mr. Adean and myself kept possession of the prisoner's person; after having recovered the purse, I had the care of it, and it being known there was money in it, I got hold of his person with my left hand; there was a great deal of trouble; we were shoved about. But I ought to state, that the prisoner on my seizing him, and on Mr. Adean's assisting me, said, What do you mean? I am a gentleman; consider, Sir, what you are doing, I am a gentleman; only consider the consequence of this, for God's sake consider. The prisoner was extremely pale and confused; I kept asking him, who are you? to which he gave me no answer, only saying he was a gentleman. We called out for a constable, and after some fome time a conftable came; we afked the conftable, who was the unfortunate Blandy, if he knew him; he looked at him very hard, and faid, No, I do not know the prifoner. After a great deal of difficulty he was had to the Brown Bear, where I delivered him to the cuftody of Blandy. I attended the next day at the office in Bow-ftreet, but the prifoner was not there. It was a ftriped filk purfe, with twenty-three guineas and a half. It was merely the lining of the pocket that was cut, perhaps a couple of inches through the upper part of the pocket. When the conftable faid it was not Barrington, Mr. Adean faid, I faw him take it, and I will lay down my life on the occafion. I believe I faid in Bow ftreet, that I feized a perfon's hand near to my pocket, which hand appeared to be the defendant's, and that I there-fore believed and fufpected that the defendant was the per-fon that robbed me.

Queftion from the Jury.—When you feized the prifoner, was he on your right hand or the left?—He was behind me; the perfon that gave me the purfe was on one fide. I was ftanding in this manner: I had the prifoner's hand, and the firft idea I had was, it belonged to the perfon that was before me, but jerking it up, I found that it belonged to the prifoner.

Court. You fay the prifoner was behind you?—Yes.

Where was the hand?—The hand was clofe to my pocket, and he was behind me.

Jury. Did you keep faft hold of him by the hand till you laid hold of him with the other hand?—Yes.

Why had you any doubt in Bow-ftreet?--I had no doubt; my idea was, the hand belonged to the man that was before me, and I wanted to know to whom the hand belonged, and, jerking it up, I found it belonged to the prifoner.

Yes, but you faid in Bow-ftreet, that it *appeared* to be-long to the prifoner, and you *fufpected* it was him that robbed you?—That word *appeared* I never meant; and if I made ufe of it in Bow-ftreet, I never meant it.

Prifoner's Defence.

May it pleafe your Lordfhip, and you Gentlemen of the Jury; the benignity and candour which mark the judicial proceedings of this country, of which I have recently met a diftinguifhed proof, induce me to hope, with the utmoft humility, that the indulgent attention of the Court will not be withheld on the prefent occafion; but that it will be ex-tended, not through the merit of any thing I may urge, but from the generous and impartial impulfe of your own minds

minds towards every one who is so unhappy as to stand here, the subject of accusation; and if ever there was a case which called for the calm, I will not say the compassionate, consideration of your Lordship and the Gentlemen of the Jury, it is perhaps the present, as well from the heavy affliction I have sustained for many months before I could obtain a trial, as from the newspaper calumny that has been levelled against me, even under the pressure of a long imprisonment, and to the very hour of my trial.

It is but too true, that I had the misfortune to be at the play about the time mentioned in the indictment; I had sometimes an opportunity to obtain an order for the play, through the medium of a respectable though no very intimate friend; and it is unnecessary for me to say, that the part of the house is not thought material in general when an order is given. I was going through the box-passage on my way home, when some one said it is certainly Barrington, and almost at the same instant I was addressed by a person who requested me to tell my name; I asked his reason for the enquiry; he turned from me, and said, Mr. Le Mesurier, is this the person? The prosecutor said he had lost his purse, and that I was near him, but no more; the passage was extremely crowded, and this conversation excited the general attention: some of the bystanders requested I would give my name. I told them I should decline giving my name there, the matter being of an unpleasant nature; but that, if there was any charge against me, I had no objection to go before a magistrate. Some gentlemen close to the prosecutor observed, that such a step would be quite unnecessary, if I would call on any gentleman present; while others said that my name was Barrington: the prosecutor in the mean time was no way active on the occasion, or like a man that was at all convinced in his own mind; and an altercation merely about my name continued, I may venture to say, pretty near half an hour; when the approach of the constable was announced, the crowd was so great it was with great difficulty they could come near; and then being asked concerning me, he said he could not recollect me, or words to that effect. Some gentlemen continued to suggest the propriety of my calling on some person that knew me, which they said would entirely do away all imputation; while others said, Mr. Le Mesurier, you should go before Sir Sampson Wright. Mr. Le Mesurier then absolutely replied, What is the use of my going there? I am not sure; I can say nothing to affect him. This, Gentlemen of the Jury, was really the language of Mr. Le Mesurier then, however it may have been forgot ; however it may have been changed fince, to anfwer the prefent purpofe : fome little altercation further continued about my name, when fome one faid, Here is Townfhend of Bow-ftreet, he perhaps knows fomething of the prifoner, let us hear what he fays. When he mentioned my name, fome gentleman faid, I told you how it was ; when feveral other gentlemen obferved that my name was then quite immaterial from the declaration that Mr. Le Mefurier had made ; that, if Mr. Le Mefurier had been convinced of the fact in his own mind, I ought to have been taken before a magiftrate, who-ever I was, or whatever my name was ; but that, as he had declared he was by no means certain, it was neither fair nor reafonable that a man fhould be criminated becaufe his name was Barrington. This, Gentlemen of the Jury, was the opinion of many gentlemen ; fome of whom, I am fatis-fied, Mr. Le Mefurier well knows to be fuch, and the ma-jority of the company concurred in that opinion. The al-tercation ftill continued about my name ; and it may appear ftrange, perhaps incredible, that I, who about half an hour before was accufed with a breach of the peace, and as an offender, fhould be then actually employed as moderator in endeavouring to appeafe the generous impulfe that prevailed in my favour, by requefting that the matter might have a legal hearing : fuch, however, Gentlemen was the fact. I was conveyed to the publick-houfe, the Brown Bear in Bow-ftreet ; and however the unhappy circumftance of my withdrawing from thence may have hitherto operated to my difadvantage, I truft, that when the circumftances of the cafe are duly and candidly confidered, it will lofe that effect. I found myfelf there under a charge that I clearly perceived looked up to fomething for its fupport, beyond facts and circumftances ; I had juft feen a ftriking proof what prejudice may be attached to a name ; and it was impoffible for me to fay how far it might not extend. Under apprehenfion, at once natural and alarming, an opportunity occurred to enable me to withdraw, and I embraced it — unfortunately embraced it I I broke no gaol nor watch-houfe on the occafion ; no ju-dicial profecution, or commitment, had taken place ; and I truft that it may fairly be conftrued rather as a retreat from prejudice, than as a flight from accufation ; in leav-ing that place, gentlemen, I neither ufed violence or pe-cuniary influence, whatever has been fuggefted to the con-trary ; and here it is impoffible for me to forbear moft fo-lemnly declaring, in the prefence of the court and the world, that the unhappy man who was convicted for fuf-

fering

fering me to escape, was neither wilfully, or wittingly, consenting thereto: if I was of a disposition to rejoice at the calamity of a fellow-creature, I perhaps had some reason for it there; for this poor man, instead of doing me any kindness, was perhaps one of the greatest enemies I had in the world, so far, gentlemen of the jury, as bringing up my name constantly in the minds of the public every night at the play-house; and if I was two hundred miles from London, if I was at any part of the universe, it was immaterial to him; this was still done; it was his constant rule. It is true, that the unhappy man was convicted on evidence; for Townshend swore that he must know of my retreat. Gentlemen of the jury, this poor man was a tradesman, and a shopkeeper; this took up his attention in the day, and in the evening he attended his duty as constable; and he was, beside that, an old infirm man; and perhaps, in the best of his days, he never possessed that keeness of sight which they do who are runners by profession; and I trust, gentlemen, that some little attention will be paid to what I say on this occasion; I have now no longer any interest from it; and he, poor man, can bear no part of it; he is freed now from the strife of life, and not entangled with the perplexities of justice; but it is a tribute due to the memory of an unfortunate man, and I think myself bound to pay it, whatever my own case may be. And, gentlemen of the jury, it is with very great concern indeed, that I find myself under the necessity to say any thing which perhaps may appear invidious or impertinent; I wish not to say any thing that may look like a reflection on the conduct of the prosecutor; and if his memory had not been of the strange nature that I know it to be, I certainly would not say any thing on the occasion; but it is a memory of the most convenient nature; for it can forget circumstances which happened, because they were in my favour; and can fancy others which never did happen, and it can remember only those which may injure and tend to convict me: I therefore, gentlemen, am compelled to say something about the conduct of the prosecutor; the veneration I feel for the wisdom and beneficence of the court, whose judgment restored me to the dearest privilege of the subject, the trial by jury, will not permit me to say any thing concerning the law itself, and but little concerning the prosecution; yet thus much I hope I may be allowed to say without incurring the displeasure of the court; that outlawry is the greatest possible

ad-

advantage that can be taken by the law of this country, that it sets aside the invaluable privilege of the subject, the trial by jury, and condemns a man to death unheard; that it was an advantage which the prosecutor derived from real ignorance on my part; that the prosecutor, if he had been the most vindictive, and the most cruel man that ever lived in this country, could not have attempted to do more against the blackest traitor, or the most foul murderer that ever appeared in the shape of human nature. Gentlemen of the jury, I am very far from attempting to extenuate the offence I am charged with; I am conscious of its enormity; I never will commit it; but I hope I may be allowed to say, that there is an immutable distinction in crimes; that policy and humanity demand the preservation of that distinction; if I had been the most violent, if I had been the most inhuman man that ever lived, it was impossible that Mr. Le Mesurier could have proceeded to greater extremity than he has done with respect to me. Gentlemen of the jury, if Mr. Le Mesurier had wished to have impressed you with an idea of his candour, he might effectually have done it, by waving that advantage which ignorance on my part gave; and had he, instead of calling an unfortunate fellow-creature before the judgment-seat, to demand sentence of death against him, and to urge it with all the rigour that a furious mind could dictate: had he omitted this in a moment when the most liberal and humane sentiments seemed to prevail in every part of the world; had he done this, you might have had some opinion of his candour; it would not have tarnished the lustre of his beneficence, or diminished the fame of his moderation and modesty. The language of Mr. Le Mesurier, the counsel, I will not much mention; I am convinced it speaks for itself, and will operate more in my favour in any liberal mind, than any thing I can say against it: and perhaps he has been led to such vehemence, by being at once the brother and counsel of the prosecutor: and I wish, I wish, gentlemen of the jury, that Mr. Le Mesurier may not have been advised to such extremity from a quarter, where, of all others, it ought not to have proceeded: public justice is a good and necessary thing, but there is something due to individual justice; and a persecuting spirit should never be suffered to overpower the sacred rights of truth and humanity. And permit me humbly to observe, that the question is not now, what the private opinion of individuals concerning George Barrington may be, but whether there is, or is not,

not, that full, clear, and unequivocal evidence which the wisdom of ages has established as the criterion for jurors to decide by, and which ought never to be departed from, in any man's cafe whatever. To ftrain a point to acquit, may proceed from Godlike motives; and perhaps men of the moft vindictive tempers muft refpect, in others, the benevolent impulfe; but to ftrain a point to condemn, is repugnant to juftice, to confcience, and to humanity.

Here the learned Judge ASHHURST *fummed up the evidence, and added the following obfervations:* He faid, there are fome facts arifing from Mr. Le Mefurier's evidence, which feem to apply pretty clofely to the cafe of the prifoner; there is one fact particularly, which came out upon the crofs-examination, which may be material for your confideration; that is, that Mr. Le Mefurier told you, at the time he felt his purfe move, the prifoner was ftanding behind him, but his hand was clofe to his pocket: now to be fure, in the natural pofition one would expect for a man who ftood behind another perfon, it is not very probable that his hand could be fo far advanced before Mr. Le Mefurier as to be at his breeches-pocket; therefore that obfervation, in point of probability, feems to apply very hard againft the prifoner; he tells you further, that, the moment he felt his purfe moving in his pocket, he inftantly took his hand from that part which was over his purfe, and caught hold of the wrift of fomebody that was near his breeches-pocket; that fomebody, whoever it was, to be fure, in point of probability, does appear the moft likely perfon to whom we could attribute it; he kept hold of the hand, and turned round, and with his other hand he feized on the perfon to whom the hand belonged, which proved to be the prifoner at the bar: thefe, gentlemen, to be fure, are ftrong circumftances; it has been imputed to Mr. Le Mefurier, that he had, at the time he went to Bow-ftreet-office, faid, when he was told he muft go to the office, It is to no purpofe for me to go to the office, I know nothing about it; but he pofitively denies that he held any fuch language; he fays, as near as he can guefs, what he faid was this, that he feized a perfon's hand near his pocket, which appeared to be the prifoner's, and therefore he believed him to be the perfon. Therefore, gentlemen, it is for you, on the whole of this evidence, to confider whether the prifoner is, or is not, guilty of the crime that is now imputed to him: as to any general knowledge you may have of the prifoner, or of his character, that you are to lay totally out of the cafe on the prefent occafion; for every caufe muft be tried by its

own

own circumstances; therefore you are to consider now only of the particular evidence, and how it must apply. Now, if you believe the account given by the prosecutor, that at the time the purse moved in his pocket, he immediately took hold of the prisoner's hand close by his breeches-pocket; and more particularly, if you believe that the prisoner was standing behind him at the time with his hand near his pocket, I am sorry to say it does amount to very strong circumstantial proof, in regard to the prisoner's being guilty of the fact: there has been no evidence called to contradict the account that he has given. Gentlemen, it is your duty to consider on the whole evidence; if you are satisfied that the prisoner is not guilty of the crime, then certainly you ought to acquit him; but if, from all the circumstances laid together, you think they do so strongly apply to the prisoner, that he is guilty; in that case you will find him so. Gentlemen, there is one thing that I ought to inform you of; indeed, it was given up by the counsel, which is the capital part of the charge; for it was laid to be stolen privily from his person. Now there have been determinations, that, whenever the person is sensible of the thing at the time, that that takes off the capital part; therefore the capital part you will acquit him of; but it is still open to the larceny, though the capital part is given up by the counsel on the opening.

Verdict of the Jury.   NOT GUILTY.

PETRIE, *v.* BENFIELD.

A rule was obtained to shew cause why the bill in an action on the bribery-act for 60,000 l. which was filed in the office at the time, but now either lost or taken off the file, should not be supplied by an attested copy; the same having before been allowed in the case of Petrie v. Macpherson, two years ago.

It was objected against the rule, that this was a penal action, that the copy comes from the plaintiff's hand, and is not even attested by the attorney who prepared the original.

LORD KENYON, C. J.—It is highly expedient to grant this application; dangerous consequences might otherwise ensue.

BULLER, J.—Great enquiry was made in the case of Macpherson respecting the loss of these bills; and there was reason to suspect that they had been surreptitiously taken off the file.   Rule absolute.

HAN-

HANCOCK AND OTHERS, ASSIGNEES OF EDENSOR,
A BANKRUPT, v. ENTWISLE AND OTHERS.

The bankrupt was a broker, and had purchased for the
defendants some cotton, by which they were considerable
losers : in consequence of which, an agreement was entered
into between the defendants and the bankrupts, that he
should reimburse them their loss, which exceeded the sum
of 1900 l. but which, for the sake of accommodation, was
settled at that sum, and no more ; that in payment of this
sum, the bankrupt should from time to time, in the
course of four years, recommend parcels of cotton to the
defendants for their purchase : and the bankrupt undertook
that the clear profits of such sale should, in the space of
four years, discharge the said sum of 1900 l. but, if the
same should not be paid in that time, the bankrupt, in case
he should be living, was to pay the difference.

The question now arose upon an action on a bill of exchange, whether the defendants were entitled to a set-off
upon this agreement. Lord Kenyon, on the trial, was of
opinion, that the defendants were not entitled to a set-off,
and the plaintiffs obtained a verdict.

On a rule to shew cause why a new trial should not be
granted,

Law, in support of the rule, was desired to begin :
he contended, that these were liquidated damages by the
agreement, and therefore not like the case of Howlet v.
Strickland (Cooper 56). The defendants might have
proved the 1900 l. under the commission, and may now
set it off in this action ; for it became a debt on the bankruptcy, the party being incapable of performing the contract.

LORD KENYON, C. J.—Without the deed, the defendant's claim could not have been set off, because it rested
in damages merely, and must have been settled by action.
But the deed liquidated the damages, and a certain recompence was to be made in the course of four years. If a
certain sum of money had been payable by instalments,
and one of the payments due before the bankruptcy, the
whole might have been proved under the commission.
But the bankrupt is not discharged by his bankruptcy from
the deed ; for, after his certificate, he may perform the sti-
pulations of it. Then if he were not discharged by his
certificate, this debt could not be proved, nor can it be
set off ; for it had no existence as a debt at the time of the
bank-

bankruptcy. The diſtinction is, if the demand be payable *at all events*, though at a future day it may be proved; but where it depends on a *contingency* whether it will be paid or not, it cannot be proved, unleſs it be ſecured by a penalty which is *forfeited at law* (Atkins, 115, 116.) But in this caſe there was no legal demand at the time of the bankruptcy.

Rule diſcharged.

BOLDERO AND OTHERS v. MOSSE AND OTHERS.

Defendants were arreſted by a *latitat* for 423 l. directed to the Chamberlain of the County Palatine of Lancaſter; but afterwards proceedings were ſtayed on payment of debt and coſts. The Maſter in taxing the bill refuſed to allow a charge of two pounds for each arreſt paid to the Sheriff's officer, one guinea only being the uſual charge in other counties.

The Quarter Seſſions of the county of Lancaſter had ſettled a table of fees in 1767, in which bailiffs were allowed in arreſts for debts from 200 l. to 500 l. 2 l. for each arreſt; and this ſum had been actually paid to the bailiff in the preſent inſtance. The ſeſſions made this table by virtue of the act 32 Geo. II. cap. 28, which orders the Juſtices to regulate the charges for lodging, &c. of perſons under arreſt; and it was urged, that though this clauſe may apply only to expences after arreſt, yet as the table had remained ſo many years, and as the guinea uſually allowed by the Maſter was greater than that fixed by the ſtatute 23 H. VI. they ought to be reimburſed the money *bonâ fide* paid.

BY THE COURT. Motion refuſed. The Seſſions have no authority to fix fees for this court. If bailiffs exact *in future* more than the uſual ſum, they may be indicted for extortion.

JOHN PARSLOW, ESQ; *against* FRANCIS SYKES, ESQ;

Counſel for Plaintiff, Mr. Erſkine and Mr. Shepherd. For Defendant, Mr. Bearcroft.

Mr. Erſkine on the part of the plaintiff began this.——Gentlemen of the Jury, the plaintiff is an officer in one of the regiments of the King's dragoons, a gentleman of ſlender fortune. The defendant, Mr. Sykes, is an officer of the ſame regiment, the only ſon of Sir Francis Sykes, Bart. a gena gentleman who has acquired great wealth in India. The plaintiff and defendant had become acquainted with each other in consequence of their being together in the service, and as brother officers their friendship began. They were both officers in the army; and as officers it was natural to expect in them that natural gallantry which distinguishes the character of military life, which to the honour of that most honourable profession he was happy to say, and he took this favourable opportunity to do so, having once been of that class himself, that speaking in general terms, the gallantry of officers to the fair sex was not more distinguishable than that heroic gallantry which has so well and so laudably been employed in the service of their country, and the state. The defendant, however, as far as his character could be involved in the description, formed a complete and striking contrast of the officer, the man of honour, and of all that is to be expected of a man of openness, candour, and integrity; for instead of that manliness of spirit, and unwillingness to trifle with the happiness of others, he had discovered himself to be of so selfish a disposition, that he was ready to sacrifice all the comforts of his dearest friend to the gratification of his own desires. All the civilities which a man of polite life could possibly expect, or receive from another, were experienced by the defendant from the plaintiff: they were brother officers, and those offices of friendship which that condition of life particularly affords were not omitted by the plaintiff; sorry am I to say, that the defendant made so bad, so ungenerous, and so unprincipled an use of these advantages, that at the moment he received them, he expressed himself in terms of the most shocking brutality, against him; for he had not been of the mess with Mr. Parslow three weeks before he formed a resolution to dishonour that man, whom, by all the laws of humanity, he ought to reverence; he had seen the plaintiff's wife, who was a virtuous, beautiful, and accomplished woman; he formed a system of seduction, and said, in the presence of officers of the mess, " I should like to debauch that woman;" this, when compared with his subsequent conduct, would explain the extreme depravity of his heart.

The plaintiff, ignorant of this design, interchanged visits and civilities, and lived in habits of the most friendly intimacy with the defendant, without having the most distant suspicion that any dishonourable intentions were harboured in Mr. Sykes's mind, for he deported himself with so much decorum, decency, and respect to Mrs. Parslow, and so much apparent friendship for her husband, that it was

im-

impoffible to entertain fufpicions. The conduct of Mr. Parflow towards his wife was founded in indulgence and love. She vifited her relations and her friends; he did not think of keeping her aloof from fociety, for he had no fufpicion that fhe was expofed to temptation. He was tender and affectionate, but he did not fhew that affection by locking his wife up like a Spaniard.

The ladies who kept company with Mrs. Parflow, the officers who vifited the family, (characters by no means deficient in penetration), never entertained the leaft particle of doubt of the honour of Mrs. Parflow, and of the fincere friendfhip of Mr. Sykes towards her hufband. Thus fituated, the plaintiff little thought, that under this mafk of friendfhip, Mr. Sykes was fupplanting him in the affections of his wife; it was true that Mr. Sykes and Mrs. Parflow were often together, but nothing happened, or in the moft remote degree tranfpired, which could induce any human being to fufpect the intentions of Mr. Sykes, nor was a doubt entertained upon the fubject until the very evening they eloped.

In July laft, on a Sunday afternoon, Mr. Sykes called, in his phaeton, at Ipfwich, at Mr. Parflow's houfe, and as Mrs. Parflow had in the morning expreffed a defire to take an airing, it was propofed that fhe fhould ride out in Mr. Sykes's phaeton; to this propofal Mr. Parflow affented, and fo little did he fufpect what was then intended by Mr. Sykes, that with the utmoft affection he took his wife by the hand to the carriage in the moft engaging manner, wifhed her the advantage and benefit of an airing, and anticipated her fafe return; little did he think that he faw her for the laft time! Night came on—but fuch a night—the power of words fail me—torn with anxiety for the fate—fearful of the danger—diftreffed and diftracted for the fafety—the honour—the virtue—the life of the dear object of his love! he fufpected, trufted, hoped, confided—the hour of midnight came, but not the tender partner of his joys—it might be faid of him, in the language of the almoft-infpired poet—

    " But, O what damned minutes tells he o'er,
    " Who doats, yet doubts; fufpects, yet ftrongly loves !"

When he was afterwards informed that his wife was feen in the carriage with Mr. Sykes many miles off, and driving with great rapidity towards London, yet even this would not entirely extinguifh the flame of his love; he determined to follow his wife; but the artifice of Mr. Sykes eluded the vigilance of Mr. Parflow and Mr. Wallace, who bore him company. Mr. Parflow now finding that his affection was

be-

betrayed, and bed dishonoured, did not follow Mr. Sykes, as the first impulse of anger had directed; he did not seek revenge in the manner which, perhaps, the blunt sensations of honest nature might dictate; he did not seek the life of the man who, under the mask of friendship, had been the foulest and the meanest enemy; he did not chuse to be the avenger of his own wrong, he came to a jury of his country, he came to twelve honest men and laid his case before them; he calls not for reparation, for that is beyond the power of an earthly tribunal to measure; he calls for that sort of attention to his case, which the law enables jurymen to bestow.

I shall shew you, gentlemen, by the evidence, that the defendant practised a deliberate scheme and system of seduction; that the reserve and respect which he always observed towards Mrs. Parslow, was nothing but well-acted hypocrisy. He cannot plead those causes which, unhappily for human-nature, are sometimes irresistible, and unavoidable in their effects; he cannot plead the impulse of a momentary passion; he cannot plead the combination of those circumstances, and the importunity of appetite under the influence of their union, which sometimes defy and baffle the most determined and well-regulated principles of morality; he cannot say that he was suddenly driven off the poise of reason, suddenly assaulted and subdued by the effect of enchanting beauty: No! his was a cold, deliberate, unfeeling infamy; he was methodically mischievous, a seducer by system; his guilt was such as the jury could better feel than the advocate describe; on the feelings of the jury, therefore, we must draw for the deficiency of expression!

There is every reason to believe, that but for the intrusion of this defendant, many children would have blessed the parents, and adorned the family—Children, at once the care and happy fruits of the nuptial bed—Children, whose blooming aspect give vigour to declining age, and whose engaging manners sweeten the most bitter drops of the cup of affliction!—It is for them we toil and endure the hardships of the roughest life!—It is for them we labour beyond the period at which it is natural to seek repose in retired life! It is for them the female beauty fades without regret, and contemplates her own decay, while, smiling, she views her beauty, commencing, in her daughter, a blooming and a new life! These are the consolations of declining age, and without them the most splendid ornaments of life avail us nothing—These he has lost for ever.

Compensation, gentlemen, in this case is out of all question; double the damages here laid are nothing when opposed to the injury which the plaintiff has sustained. But, you will remember, you are cloathed with power, and as citizens you are armed with duty, to use all your offices in support of the injured plaintiff; a man, who had sustained upon his mind a load too much for human fortitude to bear, and upon the honour of his family a stain that can never be erased.

Evidence for the Plaintiff.

The marriage proved, in May 1785.

Captain Williams. I was abroad with Mr. and Mrs. Parslow. I always understood them to be a happy pair. Mr. Parslow behaved with the utmost tenderness and affection to his wife.

Three weeks after he joined the regiment, he said in my presence at the mess, that it would give him great pleasure to debauch Mrs. Parslow. Mr. Parslow was not present.

Mrs. Parslow did not shew any levity, or any partiality to Mr. Sykes the defendant.

Nor did any thing pass to my knowledge, that ought or could alarm the suspicion of Mr. Parslow.

Mr. Sykes continued to visit Mr. and Mrs. Parslow above three months; afterwards went away and again visited them at Reading, to which place the regiment was removed for a short time, and again removed to Sudbury and continued for one month: at this place there were no lodgings for the ladies, the town being very full; the plaintiff, Mr. Parslow, was therefore, and on that account, compelled to be absent a short time from his lady.

Cross-examined by Mr. Bearcroft.

I rebuked Mr. Sykes for his observation at the mess, but do not recollect that he made any reply; we were both sober. I thought no more of it, and took no notice of it to Mr. Parslow, because I was confident it must have produced very serious consequences.

Major Callow. I believe Mr. and Mrs. Parslow lived on terms of the very best love and affection. I am married, and Mrs. Parslow frequently visited my wife. I never heard or suspected any thing improper respecting Mrs. Parslow; for had there been any doubt of the honour of Mrs. Parslow, her visits to the ladies of the regiment would not have been received.

Captain Watson. The behaviour of Mr. Parslow to his lady was proper and becoming; indeed, he was exceedingly affectionate; the least doubt was never entertained of the honourable character of Mrs. Parslow.

Colonel

Colonel Gwynn. I commanded the regiment of which Mr. Parflow was Captain at Sudbury, where Captain Parflow's attendance was indispensably requisite; and the town was so full that the ladies could not be accommodated.

Captain Parflow always spoke of his lady with a great deal of feeling and affection.

Mr. Sykes looks more, but is not above one or two and twenty; his manner was very young, particularly at the mess; his behaviour was not what I always liked.

I saw Mrs. Parflow and Mr. Sykes together in a phaeton at Ascot races, which I thought an impropriety.

Mr. McMahon. I am surgeon to the regiment. About three years ago, Mrs. Parflow's health was indifferent. I advised her to go out in an open carriage often, but not to ride on horseback, because it was too violent an exercise; I afterwards advised her to try the air of France.

Captain Parflow was very affectionate and indulgent to his lady; he took her to the Continent according to advice, but when she returned her health was worse.

I frequently saw Mr. Sykes at Mr. Parflow's, but saw no difference in his behaviour to Mrs. Parflow from that of any other officer who frequently visited the family; I saw no behaviour that could or might alarm a husband.

Captain Wallace. I have been married to the sister of Mrs. Parflow about four years, and reside now at Windsor. Mrs. Parflow came there on a visit, and went in my carriage to Ascot races. I saw Mr. Sykes on the race ground in his phaeton. I went upon the stand, and left the ladies in my carriage, and after the first heat I saw a gentleman talking to the ladies; they told me it was Mr. Sykes. I saw Mr. Sykes about half an hour afterwards, and Mrs. Parflow took a view of the amusement of the race in Mr. Sykes's phaeton. I did not object to it, because Mrs. Parflow told me Mr. Sykes was the particular friend and brother officer of her husband; she then returned to my carriage to her sister, and went home.

I saw Mr. and Mrs. Parflow at Ipswich together loving and affectionate as usual. Mr. Sykes at this time visited Mr. and Mrs. Parflow frequently, and continued to do so until the time that he carried her off, which was eight days afterwards.

At no one time in my knowledge did Mrs. Parflow and Mr. Sykes go out together—nor was their behaviour so particular as to excite the least suspicion.

Mr.

Mr. Parslow behaved to his lady with the utmost affection and tenderness of a husband; and she behaved excessively well; even on the very day on which the elopement happened, not the least suspicion had been entertained.

On the Sunday of the elopement, Mr. Sykes came to the house of Mr. Parslow, in the morning; and it was agreed, that in the afternoon he should call with his phaeton to take Mrs. Parslow out for an airing, she having complained she was not well; she did not appear quite restored to health.

Between five and six o'clock, Mr. Sykes came in his phaeton, and Mr. Parslow attended his lady and assisted her into the carriage, and then they drove off. I had not, nor had any other person, the least suspicion of what was intended by Mr. Sykes, at least I could not tell that any body suspected; I had no suspicion till ten at night; I then began to suspect, as they did not return; and at this time Captain Parslow appeared very unhappy; I never saw a man more unhappy, distressed, and agitated in my life; he appeared the whole of the next day quite distracted, and incapable of knowing what to do; but on the Tuesday he became able to listen to advice: and then Captain Parslow and myself set off for London, in pursuit of Mrs. Parslow and Mr. Sykes, but could not come up with them.

Before this, I believed Mr. and Mrs. Parslow to be the happiest couple in the world; they had a beautiful child of four years of age.

Mr. Sykes had some conversation with Mrs. Parslow the day of the elopement; but nothing was perceived which conveyed the least suspicion.

Captain Pye. I saw Mrs. Parslow and Mr. Sykes on the day of the elopement—saw them in the dusk in a phaeton, on the road about twelve miles from Ipswich; I went up and spoke to them, and they appeared confused; Mrs. Parslow asked how far it was to Ipswich; I answered, about twelve miles; she then said to Mr. Sykes, " Turn round " and go home as soon as you can;" to which he answered, " That he would turn in the town," and then drove on.

Margaret Kemp. I am chambermaid of the George inn at Thetford; July 19, at a quarter past twelve at night, Mr. Sykes and Mrs. Parslow came to the inn; the lady ordered a room to be got ready, which was immediately done: the lady went into bed, and ordered me to inform the gentleman that she was in bed; and the gentleman came up stairs into the room, put out the candle, and bid the chambermaid call him at nine the next morning.

Letitia

Letitia Fletcher, chambermaid at Ofborne's Hotel in the Adelphi, fwore, that Mr. Sykes, in July laft, came to their houfe with a lady, and ftaid one night—they had two bed-chambers---but---they flept in one bed. I faw them in bed together.

The Rev. Mr. Methat. I knew the defendant at college; in July laft I faw the defendant at the Mount Coffee-houfe; he afked if I had heard any news from Ipfwich, and what they faid of him; I made no anfwer: then the defendant faid, " I met Parflow and Wallace, and if Par-
" flow has any call on me, I am determined to fight him—
" I am ready for him. I am come to town with Mrs.
" Parflow---my journey to Ipfwich has anfwered my pur-
" pofe; I have got her in Bennet-ftreet, where I fhall
" be glad to fee you.---Will you dine with me to-mor-
" row?"

This was partly addreffed to Mr. Methat, and partly, by way of boafting, to the company in the coffee-room, who were about forty in number; ten at leaft being at that table.

DEFENCE.

Mr. Bearcroft faid, he was ready to confefs, he was oppref-fed with a cafe which, he was ready to own, called for the ferious attention of the jury. The oppreffion was two-fold. The firft part of it was the picture of eloquence which had been painted in fuch glowing colours by Mr. Erfkine's elo-quence, which, if the founds of it had ceafed to vibrate in the ears of the jury, the effect, he was fure, ftill clung to their hearts;---fecondly, the difficulty of the cafe itfelf, indepen-dent of this glowing picture; he faid, it was not eloquence alone that had marked the conduct of Mr. Erfkine on this trial; he conducted the caufe with infinite prudence and confummate judgment; he had called witneffes to eftablifh his cafe, but did not ftop here, for he had endeavoured to weaken the defence by anticipating its effect:---in the mode of examining his own witneffes, he had put to every one of them the queftion, " Whether Captain Parflow
" was not affectionate and attentive to his wife?" And by all of them, undoubtedly, was anfwered in the affirma-tive---but Mr. Bearcroft was inftructed to ftate, that Mr. Parflow had been extremely negligent of his wife, not at Sudbury only, but at other places; that he had been guilty of grofs negligence to her, particularly when it was con-fidered that fhe was a woman of fuch enchanting beauty,

and

and furrounded as she was by young officers, and men of gaiety and fashion; he did not, however, impute to Captain Parflow any dishonourable views, such as often happen in cases of this sort, of connivance with a view to get rid of a wife of whom the husband is tired; or a conspiracy between the husband and wife, for the purpose of bringing an action for large damages; those things, although in actions of this description they often occurred, were not imputed here; all that he was instructed to state on the part of the defendant was, that Captain Parflow had really been guilty of very gross negligence and inattention to Mrs. Parflow; this, if proved, must considerably diminish the damages.

To augment the damages, it has been said, if a man cannot pay in his *purse*, he must pay in his *person*; he felt himself intitled to appeal to the noble and learned judge, whether that doctrine was not solely and exclusively applicable to *criminal proceedings*, and not in the least degree to govern the case of an *action for damages*; if, therefore, the jury gave great and very high damages, they might be beyond the ability of the defendant to pay, and they might be more than his father shall chuse to advance; the confequence will be, a perpetual imprisonment of the defendant; this would be in diametrical opposition to one of the most wife maxims of the law of England, " *No* " *man shall be charged with the payment which is beyond his* " *capacity to pay.*" There was no proof before the jury, that the prefent defendant was worth a guinea; on the contrary, it could be very easily proved, that, exclusive of his dependance on his father (which is an uncertain allowance), he is many pounds worse than being worth nothing!

He should not state that the plaintiff, Mr. Parflow, had acted criminally; but he was instructed to state, that he had acted very improperly, and very indiscreetly, in suffering his beautiful wife to ride with the defendant in a phaeton; nay, he should prove, at least he was so instructed, that the plaintiff constantly allowed his wife to ride out with Mr. Sykes, and that, when she was not attended with any other person; that he permitted her to dance with Mr. Sykes at different balls, and other places of public amufement; constantly and invariably appearing careless of the consequences of such blameable negligence and indiscretion.

Evi-

Evidence for the Defendant.

Charles Wren. I was servant to Mr. Sykes, who came to join the regiment in the year 1788. Mr. Sykes used to travel with four horses in a phaeton; Mrs Parslow frequently used to ride out with him unattended. I frequently carried messages from Mrs. Parslow to Mr. Sykes, that she would ride with him; at other times from Mr. Sykes to Mrs. Parslow, inviting her to ride.

In the way from Weymouth, Mrs. Parslow went in her chariot, and Mr. Sykes in his gigg; but from Blandford to Salisbury they both went in the gigg, and Mr. Parslow saw them going, but did not object. I have seen Mr. Sykes at Mrs. Parslow's, so much in liquor, that I have been obliged to lead him home.

That Captain Parslow said, when Mr. Sykes and Mrs. Parslow were in the gigg, "there they go, they do very "well."

On his cross-examination, he said, he rode all the way behind, while Mr. Sykes and Mrs. Parslow went in the gigg, from Blandford to Salisbury; and as they were drawn by *hackney horses*, he could not tell but that it might be to the *horses* that Mr. Parslow alluded, when he said, "there "they go, they do very well."

William Broadway. I was servant to Mr. Sykes; Mr. Sykes frequently visited Mrs. Parslow, at Dorchester, and once in particular they were left alone in the parlour; I saw them together the night I went to my master to ask whether I should provide horses to go to Bath the next day. Mr. Sykes and Mrs. Parslow were at that time sitting together in the dining-room; this was about twelve at night; they were frequently together in this manner---but I saw them thus no more than once. I recollect Mrs. Parslow once coming to Mr. Sykes's lodgings, half an hour before all the officers came; who afterwards spent the evening together, and for that half hour Mrs. Parslow and Mr. Sykes were together. Mr. Sykes frequently used to send presents to Mrs. Parslow; he sent once a *dozen pair of shoes.* By messages and compliments, Mrs. Parslow and Mr. Sykes used to spend evenings often together; they frequently met in the streets. Mrs. Parslow and Mr. Sykes went together in Mr. Parslow's carriage from Weymouth to Dorchester: Mr. Parslow got out of his own chariot, and desired Mr. Sykes to go into it, and he did so with Mrs. Parslow, while Mr. Parslow rode in a hackney post-chaise, behind and alone.

Mr

Mr. Erſkine croſs-examined this witneſs. Mrs. Parſlow had not the appearance of a perſon out of health. Mr. Sykes treated Mrs. Parſlow as his friend. He never ſaw Mr. Sykes and Mrs. Parſlow together more than once in the dining-room; and he would not ſwear that Mr. Parſlow was not in the houſe at that time. Mr. Parſlow generally placed Mr. Sykes at Mrs. Parſlow's ſide, while Mr. Parſlow was at the bottom of his own table.

When Mr. Sykes got into the chariot to Mrs. Parſlow, at the requeſt of Mr. Parſlow, *Mrs. Parſlow's ſiſter was with her.*

Mr. Erſkine, in reply, ſaid, my indignation has been riſing, ſtep by ſtep, from the commencement to the concluſion of this defence; but it has at laſt melted into compaſſion for the defendant; for there is a ſtage of depravity in human-nature, to which nothing but compaſſion is applicable: of that deſcription is the defence ſet up upon the preſent trial; ſo monſtrous, ſo inhuman, ſo much againſt the very ſpirit and eſſence of juſtice, was the conduct of this trial upon the part of the defendant, that it might be ſtated as a caſe which was entirely out of the ordinary courſe of human life; ſuch a complicated ſcene of vice and iniquity has never, perhaps, before exiſted; the defendant no ſooner ſaw the plaintiff's wife, but the reſolution is taken to encompaſs her deſtruction; and this reſolution is not once checked, until the infamous deed is done: he no ſooner looks at the happineſs of his friend in the love, ſociety, and affection of his wife, but he determines to deſtroy it: this beautiful woman becomes inſtantly, not the object of his admiration, but the object of his luſt; at once he determines to violate all the laws of honour, humanity, friendſhip, and nature; he coolly and deliberately ſays to himſelf, " I ſee you are happy; I will deſtroy that happineſs; I ſee you are now the envy of the world for the bliſs you participate from mutual love, but I will make you miſerable, for it is my choice it ſhall be ſo---I look on that child, that beautiful innocent, whom every night I ſee you careſs, as the proof and remembrance of your former endearments, and pledge of your future joy; I will change it into a ſerpent, when hereafter you take it to your boſom; that genuine ſource of your virtuous love ſhall become your curſe, and not your conſolation." This did he ſpeak to himſelf when firſt he meditated this unparalleled miſchief; this was evident from the whole tenour of the defence, which, indeed, was not according to the advice of the counſel for the defendant;

his

his good fenfe induced him to hint and allude to, rather than feem to make, a regular defence; he was, from his great experience, well aware of the effect of fuch a mode of defending a cafe of this extraordinary nature; and notwithftanding the great difcretion and extraordinary abilities of Mr. Bearcroft, they were altogether unable to hide the infamy of the defendant's cafe. His *own domeftics* are brought to defend him through his career of infamy. After the moft grievous injury that can poffibly be done to man, it is to be entirely forgotten, becaufe the delinquent's menial fervants approve of the conduct of their mafter; the adulterer looks around to his dependants, bids them try if they can fee any negligence in the hufband, or fuch as may appear to them to be negligence and inattention to his wife. Good God!---are we in England! in the face of magiftracy! in a country where every man is intitled to freedom and protection! in a land where morality, honour, and religion are revered!---Or in a defert, inhabited by wild beafts and favages, where no rights are acknowledged and poffeffed, but thofe derived from ftrength and cunning!---According to this defence, every man in England muft not only lock up his wife like a Spaniard, but he muft alfo keep a journal of the minutes of his own life, or elfe the adulterer will excufe himfelf, by thus proving the negligence of the injured hufband.

With refpect to the principle upon which Mr. Bearcroft had contended, that no man ought to be charged with a fum which was beyond his power or ability to pay; I anfwer, that the extreme infamy of the defendant's cafe entitles him to no favour, and there is a probability he will fome time be able, if not at prefent.

It fhould not be forgot, that the defendant had at laft become fenfible of the injury which he had done, and offered certainly to make a complete compenfation, he had offered to *cut the plaintiff's throat!* he had offered to add murder to adultery! but this was kind and relenting, for as he knew that the plaintiff muft be miferable while he remained on earth, he offered to fend him to a happier ftate.

I entreat you, gentlemen, to reflect on the plaintiff's fituation, and that of his unprotected and deferted child. How can he look upon this lovely infant without the keeneft anguifh! How can he behold its lovely face without the moft mournful throbs of heart-felt forrow, while it exhibits to his mind the memory of the once-loved mother, whofe endearments produced it! How can he

rear

rear this tender plant, and daily behold it, without exclaiming, O mayst thou always preserve the virtue which thy mother once possessed! Mayst thou have her enchanting and lovely beauty, but God protect thee from her fate!

CHARGE.

Lord KENYON observed to the jury, from the attention they had paid to this cause, he was sure the material points were deeply impressed upon their minds.

This was a cause which called for the most serious attention of the jury, not from any difficulty they would meet in its discussion, but on account of the enormous conduct that had been imputed to the defendant, and also on account of the very great and heavy injury of which the plaintiff complained, and for which he sought justice in their verdict.

Two questions, his lordship said, presented themselves to the jury——Whether the fact of which the plaintiff complained was proved.——And, if proved, what damages he was entitled to receive.

The adultery beyond all doubt was proved: the seduction was proved by clear and precise evidence; they would therefore naturally turn to the second consideration, namely, the amount of the damages which should be given to the plaintiff.

Causes of this nature had great variety of distinction. Instances there were, where the adultery was clearly proved, and yet the plaintiff was entitled to small or no damages: where it appears that the husband himself takes part in the seduction, he shall not be entitled to any damages ——Where (as one may say) he puts his wife in bed with the adulterer, and himself places the pillow under their heads, the law will say, " You have received no " injury by that act to which you have consented, and " therefore no attention shall be paid to your complaint." Guilt, in a moral view, certainly must always attend adultery; but if the husband consents to it, he shall not be permitted by the law to complain.

Another case is; where a husband has wilfully neglected his wife, has been carelessly and shamefully inattentive to her, he shall not recover damages to a large amount, because he is in a great degree the cause of the moral transgression. The jury, in the present case, should attentively consider, whether there had been a trap laid by the plaintiff

tiff to catch the defendant; and also, whether the plaintiff had been inattentive and negligent towards his wife; in these confiderations, nothing but the evidence could fairly lead the jury to a determination. His lordship faid, that this was the province of the jury, they were to find out the merits of the defendant's caufe; as to himfelf, he confefed, that he did not fee that the defence difclofed circumftances which could poffibly, in fair reafon, operate in his favour. What was the defendant's cafe? He comes into the regiment very uninformed, as appeared by unqueftionable evidence, and young. He comes as a brother officer into the company of the plaintiff, a gentleman into whofe family he is introduced and received, and it might have been of great advantage to the defendant to have had the friendfhip of fuch an officer. The defendant, inftead of making a proper ufe of this advantage, difgraces himfelf by purpofing almoft immediately to abufe it; for he had not joined the regiment a fortnight, before he is heard to utter the moft deteftable fentiment; he has the hardened wickednefs to fay of a lady, whom it was his duty to refpect as his friend's wife---"It would give me great pleafure to debauch that lady."

He conftantly partook of that hofpitality, which, it feems diftinguifhed Captain Parflow's houfe; thither he is permitted to repair when he has no other employment for his time; and which, as it ultimately appears, he employs in the deftruction of the happinefs of his friend; he follows Captain Parflow to Ipfwich, where he puts in practice what he had before faid he wifhed to do; he then comes to London, and in an open Coffee-room has the audacity to boaft of his conduct inftead of being covered with fhame and confufion for his guilt; and then fays, he is ready to fight the plaintiff; fo that if the plaintiff is not contented to be filent about the injury, *his throat is to be cut*. This part of the defendant's conduct went a great way to affift the jury in their determination upon this cafe, becaufe it fhewed that the defendant was well aware, that he ran away with the lady againft the confent of the plaintiff.

Courts of juftice in this country did not exhibit on their records a cafe more aggravated than this. The defendant had difcovered that he had long meditated this fcheme; that he went to Ipfwich with a deliberated and fixed purpofe to commit it, and afterwards gloried in the completion of it, and the crime of adultery might have been followed up by the crime of murder. If any thing cou could aggravate this, it is, that the plaintiff, after being deprived of all domestic happiness, and after being compelled to drag the defendant into a court of justice, is to have an attempt made to add to the injury, by an endeavour, on the part of the defendant, to stain his honour, by endeavouring to shew, that the plaintiff in this cause was the guilty person---that he had laid a trap to catch the defendant, to procure large and inflamed damages.

His lordship said, the jury, in their sober discretion, are the only persons who have a right to govern entirely all considerations of damages; and they would not run wild in assessing (although in this case, that was not very easy) the damages, and allow their passions to subdue their judgment; but if large damages are not given, the jury would fall short of that justice which they owed to their country. They stand in a double capacity; they are as much the guardians and protectors of virtue, as they are the punishers of vice; and he was sure their own good sense would guide and direct them to do justice between the parties,

Verdict for the plaintiff. Damages 10,000l.

Trial of JOHN STOCKDALE for a Libel against the HOUSE of COMMONS, before Lord KENYON, in the Court of King's Bench.

The information charges that he (John Stockdale), being a seditious and ill-disposed person, did publish in a pamphlet, intituled, *A Review of the principal Charges against Warren Hastings, late Governor General of Bengal*, a certain false and malicious libel concerning the Impeachment of Warren Hastings, and concerning the Commons of Great Britain in Parliament assembled.

The several offensive passages are then set forth; but, as they are repeated in Mr. *Erskine's argument, we do not recite them here.*

Mr. ATTORNEY GENERAL *addressed the court and jury in an elegant and most candid speech, in which he explained the motives of the prosecution, and then said,* The offence which I impute to the defendant, is that of calumniating the House of Commons, not in its ordinary legislative capacity, but when acting in its accusatorial capacity, conceiving it to be their duty on adequate occasions to investigate the conduct of persons in high stations, and to leave their conduct to
be

be judged of by the proper conftitutional tribunal, the Peers in Parliament affembled.

After due inveftigation, the Commons of Great Britain thought it their duty, as is well known, to fabmit the conduct of a fervant of this country, who governed one of its moft opulent dependencies for many years, to an enquiry before that tribunal. One fhould have thought, that every good fubject of this country would have forborn imputing to the Houfe of Commons motives utterly unworthy of them, and of thofe whom they reprefent; inftead of this, to fo great a degree now has the licentioufnefs of the prefs arifen, that motives the moft unbecoming that can actuate even any individual, who may be concerned in the profecution of public juftice, are imputed to the Reprefentatives of the people of this country in a body; no credit is given to them for meaning to do juftice to their country, but, on the contrary, private, perfonal, and malicious motives are imputed to the Commons of Great Britain.

When fuch an imputation is made upon the very firft Tribunal that this country knows, namely, the Inqueft of the Nation, the Commons in Parliament affembled, carrying any fubject, who they may think has offended, to the bar of the houfe of lords——I am fure you will think this an attack fo dangerous to every Tribunal, fo dangerous to the whole adminiftration of juftice, that if it be well proved, you cannot fail to give it your ftigma, by a verdict againft the defendant.

The Attorney General here read the libellous paffages charged in the information (vid. p. 49 feq.) *and then concluded thus:*

I do not chufe to wafte your time, and that of my Lord, in fo plain a cafe, with much obfervation; but, hacknied as it may be, it is my duty, upon every one of thefe occafions, to remind you, gentlemen, that the fecurity of the prefs confifts in its good regulation—if it is meant that it fhould be preferved with benefit to the public, it muft be from time to time lopped of its exceffes, by reafonable and proper verdicts of juries, in fit and clear cafes.

EVIDENCE *for the* PROSECUTION.

The Solicitor of the Treafury proved, from the Journals of Parliament, that there was an impeachment, &c.

William Gotobed produced the pamphlet, and faid, he bought it at Mr. Stockdale's fhop; a boy ferved him with
it.

it. Mr. Stockdale was in the shop, and the boy acted as his servant.

This was the whole evidence for the prosecution; and Mr. Erskine, counsel for the defendant, thus addressed the jury in his

DEFENCE.

Gentlemen of the Jury,

Mr. Stockdale, who is brought as a criminal before you for the publication of this book, has, by employing me as his advocate, reposed what must appear to many an extraordinary degree of confidence; since, although he well knows that I am personally connected in friendship with most of those whose conduct and opinions are principally arraigned by its author, he nevertheless commits to my hands his defence and justification.

A trust apparently so delicate and singular, vanity is but too apt to whisper an application of to some fancied merit of one's own; but it is proper, for the honour of the English Bar, that the world should know such things happen to all of us daily, and of course; and that the defendant, without any sort of knowledge of me, or any confidence that was personal, was only not afraid to follow up an accidental retainer, from the knowledge he has of the general character of the profession.

Happy indeed is it for this country that, whatever interested divisions may characterize other places of which I may have occasion to speak to day, however the Councils of the highest departments of the state may be occasionally distracted by personal considerations, they never enter these walls, to disturb the administration of justice: Whatever may be our public principles, or the private habits of our lives, they never cast even a shade across the path of our professional duties.

If this be the characteristic even of the Bar of an English Court of Justice, what sacred impartiality may not every man expect from its Jurors and its Bench?

As, from the indulgence which the Court was yesterday pleased to give to my indisposition, this information was not proceeded on when you were attending to try it, it is probable you were not altogether inattentive to what passed on the trial of the other indictment, prosecuted also by the House of Commons; and therefore, without a re-statement of the same principles, and a similar quotation of authorities to support them, I need only remind you of the law
appli-

applicable to this fubjeâ, as it was then admitted by the
Attorney General, in conceffion to my propofitions, and
confirmed by the higher authority of the Court, viz.

Firft, that every information or indiâment muft contain
fuch a defcription of the crime, that the defendant may
know what crime it is which he is called upon to anfwer.

Secondly, that the Jury may appear to be warranted in
their conclufion of guilty or not guilty.

And, laftly, that the Court may fee fuch a precife and
definite tranfgreffion upon the record, as to be able to apply
the punifhment which judicial difcretion may diâate, or
which pofitive law may infliâ.

It was admitted alfo to follow as a mere corollary from
thefe propofitions, that where an information charges a writing to be compofed or publifhed of and concerning the
Commons of Great Britain, with an intent to bring that
body into fcandal and difgrace with the public, the author
cannot be brought within the fcope of fuch a charge, unlefs
the Jury, on examination and comparifon of the whole
matter written or publifhed, fhall be fatisfied that the particular paffages charged as criminal when explained by the
context, and confidered as part of one entire work, were
meant and intended by the author to vilify the Houfe of
Commons as a body, and were written of and concerning
them in Parliament affembled.

Thefe principles being fettled, we are now to fee what
the prefent information is.

It charges, that the defendant, ' unlawfully, wickedly,
' and malicioufly devifing, contriving, and intending to
' afperfe, fcandalize, and vilify the Commons of Great
' Britain in Parliament affembled; and moft wickedly
' and audacioufly to reprefent their proceedings as corrupt
' and unjuft, and to make it believed and thought, as if
' the Commons of Great Britain in Parliament affembled
' were a moft wicked, tyrannical, bafe, and corrupt fet of
' perfons, and to bring them into difgrace with the public—'
The defendant publifhed—*What ?*---*Not* thofe latter ends
of fentences, which the Attorney General has read from his
brief, as if they had followed one another in order in this
book;---*Not* thofe fcraps and tails of paffages which are
patched together upon this record, and pronounced in one
breath, as if they exifted without intermediate matter in
the fame page, and without context any where.----*No*---
This is not the accufation, even mutilated as it is. For the
information charges, *that with intention to vilify the Houfe of*
Commons,

Commons, the defendant published the whole book, describing it on the record by its title:

" A Review of the Principal Charges against Warren
" Haftings, Efq. late Governor General of Bengal ;"

*In which amongft other things, the matter particularly felected is
to be found.* Your enquiry therefore is not confined to, Whether the defendant published *thofe felected parts of it*, and whether, looking at them as they are diftorted by the information, they carry in fair conftruction the fenfe and meaning which the inuendos put upon them; but whether the author of the *entire work,* I fay the author, fince, if he could defend himfelf, the publifher unqueftionably can—whether the author wrote the volume which I hold in my hand, as a free, manly, *bona fide* difquifition of criminal charges againft his fellow citizen: or whether the long eloquent difcuffion of them, which fills fo many pages, was a mere cloak and cover for the introduction of the fuppofed fcandal imputed *to the felected paffages* ; the mind of the writer all along being intent on traducing the Houfe of Commons, and not on fairly anfwering their charges againft Mr. Haftings.

This, gentlemen, is the principal matter for your confideration ; and therefore, if after you fhall have taken the book itfelf into the chamber which will be provided for you, and read the whole of it with impartial attention ;---if, after the performance of this duty, you can return here, and with clear confciences pronounce upon your oaths, that the impreffion made upon you by thefe pages is, that the author wrote them with the wicked, feditious, and corrupt intentions, charged by the information ; you have then my full permiffion to find the defendant guilty. But if, on the other hand, the general tenor of the compofition fhall imprefs you with refpect for the author, and point him out to you as a man miftaken perhaps himfelf, but not feeking to deceive others :---if every line of the work fhall prefent to you an intelligent animated mind, glowing with a Chriftian compaffion towards a fellow-man, whom he believed to be innocent, and with a patriot zeal for the liberty of his country, which he confidered as wounded through the fides of an oppreffed fellow-citizen; if this fhall be the impreffion on your confciences and underftandings, when you are called upon to deliver your verdict ; then hear from me, that you not only work private injuftice, but break up the prefs of England, and furrender her rights and liberties for ever, if you convict him.

Gentlemen,

Gentlemen, to enable you to form a true judgment of the meaning of this book, and of the intention of its author, and to expose the miserable juggle that is played off in the information, by the combination of sentences, which in the work itself have no bearing upon one another——I will first give you the publication as it is charged upon the record, and presented by the Attorney General in opening the case for the Crown; and I will then, by reading the interjacent matter, which is studiously kept out of sight, convince you of its true interpretation. The information, beginning with the first page of the book, charges, as a libel upon the House of Commons, the following sentence:

" The House of Commons has now given its final decision
" with regard to the merits and demerits of Mr. Has-
" tings. The Grand Inquest of England have delivered
" their charges, and preferred their impeachment ; their
" allegations are referred to proof; and from the appeal
" to the collective wisdom and justice of the nation in
" the supreme tribunal of the kingdom, the question
" comes to be determined, whether Mr. Hastings be
" guilty or not guilty?"

It is but fair, however, to admit, that this first sentence which the most ingenious malice cannot torture into a criminal construction, is charged by the information rather as introductory to what is made to follow it, than as libellous in itself; for the Attorney General, from this introductory passage in the first page, goes on at a leap to page *thirteenth*, and reads almost without a stop, as if it immediately followed the other,

" What credit can we give to multiplied and accumulated
" charges, when we find that they originate from mis-
" representation and falsehood?"

From these two passages thus standing together, *without the intervenient matter which occupies thirteen pages*, one would imagine that, instead of investigating the probability or improbability of the guilt imputed to Mr. Hastings; instead of carefully examining the charges of the Commons, and the defence of them which had been delivered before them or which was preparing for the Lords : the author immediately, and in a moment after stating the mere fact of the impeachment, had decided that the act of the Commons originated from misrepresentation and falsehood.

Gentlemen, in the same manner a veil is cast over all that is written *in the next seven pages :* For knowing that the context would help to the true conſtruction, not only of the paſſages charged before, but of thoſe in the ſequel of this information; the Attorney General, aware that it would convince every man who read it that there was no intention in the author to calumniate the Houſe of Commons, paſſes over by another leap *to page twenty*; and in the ſame manner, without drawing his breath, and as if it directly followed the two former ſentences *in the 1ſt and 13th pages*, reads from page 20th---

" An impeachment of error in judgment with regard to the
" quantum of a fine, and for an intention that never was
" executed, and never known to the offending party,
" characteriſes a tribunal of inquiſition rather than a
" Court of Parliament."

From this paſſage, by another vault, he leaps over *one-and-thirty pages more, to page fifty-one*; where he reads the following ſentence, which he mainly relies on, and upon which I ſhall by-and-by trouble you with ſome obſervations.

" Thirteen of them paſſed in the Houſe of Commons, not
" only without inveſtigation, but without being read;
" and the votes were given without enquiry, argument,
" or conviction. A majority had determined to im
" peach; oppoſite parties met each other, and *juſtled in
" the dark*, to perplex the political drama, and bring the
" hero to a tragic cataſtrophe."

From thence, deriving new vigour from every exertion, he makes his laſt grand ſtride *over forty four pages*, almoſt to the end of the book, charging a ſentence *in the ninety-fifth page*.

So that out of a volume of *one hundred and ten pages*, the defendant is only charged with a few ſcattered fragments of ſentences picked out of *three or four*. Out of a work, conſiſting of about *two thouſand five hundred and thirty lines*, of manly ſpirited eloquence, *only forty or fifty lines* are culled from different parts of it, and artfully put together, ſo as to rear up a libel out of a falſe context by a ſuppoſed connexion of ſentences with one another, which are not only entirely independent, but which, when compared with their antecedents, bear a totally different conſtruction.

In this manner the greateſt works upon government, the moſt excellent books of ſcience, the ſacred ſcriptures themſelves, might be diſtorted into libels; by forſaking the
                                                          general

general context, and hanging a meaning upon selected parts:
——Thus, as in the text put by Algernon Sidney,

" The fool has said in his heart there is no God;"

The Attorney General on the principle of the present proceeding against this pamphlet, might indict the publisher of the Bible for blasphemously denying the existence of heaven, in printing

" *There is no God.*"

For these words alone, without the context, would be selected by the information; and the Bible, like this book, would be *underscored* to meet it. Nor could the defendant in such a case have any possible defence, unless the Jury were permitted to see, by the book itself, that the verse, instead of denying the existence of the Divinity, only imputed that imagination to a fool.

Gentlemen, having now gone through the Attorney General's reading, the book shall presently come forward and speak for itself.

But before I can venture to lay it before you, it is proper to call your attention to how matters stood at the time of its publication; without which the author's meaning and intention cannot possibly be understood.

The Commons of Great Britain in Parliament assembled had accused Mr. Hastings, as Governor General of Bengal, of high crimes and misdemeanors; and their jurisdiction for that high purpose of national justice was unquestionably competent. But it is proper you should know the nature of this inquisitorial capacity.——The Commons, in voting an impeachment, may be compared to a Grand Jury finding a bill of indictment for the Crown: neither the one nor the other can be supposed to proceed, but upon the matter which is brought before them; neither of them can find guilt without accusation, nor the truth of accusation without evidence.

When, therefore, we speak of the *accuser* or *accusers* of a person indicted for any crime, although the Grand Jury are the accusers *in form*, by giving effect to the accusation; yet in common parlance we do not consider them the responsible authors of the prosecution. If I were to write of a most wicked indictment, found against an innocent man, which was preparing for trial, nobody who read it would conceive I meant to stigmatize the Grand Jury that found the bill; but it would be enquired immediately who was the prosecutor, and who were the witnesses on the back of

it.

it. In the fame manner I mean to contend, that if this book is read with only common attention, the whole fcope of it will be difcovered to be this.

That, in the opinion of the author, Mr. Haftings had been accufed of malicious adminiftration in India, from the heat and fpleen of political divifions in Parliament, and not from any zeal for national honour or juftice; that the impeachment did not originate from Government, but from a faction banded againft it, which, by mifreprefentation and violence, had faftened it on an unwilling Houfe of Commons; that, prepoffeffed with this fentiment, (which, however unfounded, makes no part of the prefent bufinefs, fince the publifher is not called before you for defaming individual members of the Commons, but for a contempt of the Commons as a body,) the author purfues the charges, article by article;——enters into a warm and animated vindication of Mr. Haftings, by regular anfwers to each of them; and that, as far as the mind and foul of a man can be vifible, I might alfo fay, embodied in his writings, his intention throughout the whole volume appears to have been to charge with injuftice the private accufers of Mr. Haftings, and not the Houfe of Commons as a body; which undoubtedly rather reluctantly gave way to, than heartily adopted, the impeachment.

This will be found to be the palpable fcope of the book; and no man who can read Englifh, and who at the fame time will have the candour and common fenfe to take up his impreffions from what is written in it, inftead of bringing his own along with him to the reading of it, can poffibly underftand it otherwife.

But it may be faid, that admitting this to be the fcope and defign of the author, what right had he to canvafs the merits of an accufation upon the records of the Commons; more efpecially while it was in the courfe of legal procedure. This, I confefs, might have been a ferious queftion; but the Commons, *as Profecutors of this information*, feem to have waved or forfeited, their right to afk it.

Before they fent the Attorney General into this place, to punifh the publication of *anfwers* to their charges, they fhould have recollected that their own want of circumfpection in the maintenance of their privileges, and in the protection of perfons accufed before them, had given to the public *the charges themfelves*, which fhould have been confined to their own journals.——The courfe and practice of Parliament might warrant the printing of them for the ufe of their own Members, but there the publication fhould

have

have ſtopt, and all further progreſs been reſiſted by authority.

If they were reſolved to conſider *anſwers to their charges* as a contempt of their privileges, and to puniſh the publication of them by ſuch ſevere proſecutions, it would have well become them to have begun firſt with thoſe printers who, by publiſhing *the charges themſelves* throughout the whole kingdom, or rather throughout the whole civilized world, were anticipating the paſſions and judgments of the public againſt a ſubject of England upon his trial, ſo as to make the publication *of anſwers* to them, not merely a privilege, but a debt and duty to humanity and juſtice.

The Commons of Great Britain claimed and exerciſed the privileges of queſtioning the innocence of Mr. Haſtings by their impeachment ; but as, however queſtioned, it is ſtill to be preſumed and protected, until guilt is eſtabliſhed by judgment, he whom they had accuſed had an equal claim upon their juſtice, to guard him from prejudice and miſrepreſentation until the hour of trial.

Had the Commons, therefore, by the exerciſe of their high, neceſſary, and legal privileges, kept the public aloof from all canvaſs of their proceedings, by an early puniſhment of printers, who, without reſerve or ſecrecy, ſent out *the charges* into the world from a thouſand preſſes in every form of publication, they would have then ſtood upon ground to-day, from whence no argument of policy or juſtice could have removed them ; becauſe nothing can be more incompatible with either, than appeals to the many upon ſubjects of judicature, which by common conſent a few are appointed to determine, and which muſt be determined by facts and principles, which the multitude have neither leiſure nor knowledge to inveſtigate. But then let it be remembered, that it is for thoſe who have the authority to accuſe and puniſh, to ſet the example of, and to enforce this reſerve, which is ſo neceſſary for the ends of juſtice.

Courts of Law, therefore, in England never endure the publication of *their* records : and a proſecutor of an indictment would be attached for ſuch a publication ; and upon the ſame principle, a defendant would be puniſhed for anticipating the juſtice of his country, by the publication of his defence, the public being no party to it, until the tribunal appointed for its determination be open for its deciſion.

Gentlemen, you have a right to take judicial notice of theſe matters, without the proof of them by witneſſes ; for

jurors

jurors may not only without evidence found their verdicts on facts that are notorious, but upon what they know privately themselves, after revealing it upon oath to one another; and therefore you are always to remember, that this book was written when the *Charges* against Mr. Hastings, *to which it is an answer*, were, to the knowledge of the Commons, (for we cannot presume our watchmen to have been asleep) publicly hawked about in every pamphlet, magazine, and newspaper in the kingdom.

Gentlemen, you well know with what a curious appetite these Charges were devoured by the whole public, interesting as they were, not only from their importance, but from the merit of their composition; certainly not so intended by the honourable and excellent composer to oppress the accused, but because the commonest subjects swell into eloquence under the touch of his sublime genius.

Thus by the remissness of the Commons *who are now the prosecutors of this information*, a subject of England, who was not even charged with contumacious resistance to authority, much less a proclaimed outlaw, and therefore fully entitled to every protection which the customs and statutes of the kingdom hold out for the protection of British liberty, saw himself pierced with the arrows of thousands and ten thousands of libels.

Gentlemen, before I venture to lay the book before you, it must be yet further remembered (for the fact is equally notorious), that under these unauspicious circumstances, the trial of Mr. Hastings at the bar of the Lords had actually commenced long before its publication.

There the most august and striking spectacle was daily exhibited, which the world in any age of it ever witnessed. A vast stage of justice was erected, awful from its high authority, splendid from its illustrious dignity, venerable from the learning and wisdom of its judges, captivating and affecting from the mighty concourse of all ranks and conditions which daily flocked into it, as into a theatre of pleasure; there, when the whole public mind was at once awed and softened to the impression of every human affection, there appeared, day after day, one after another, men of the most powerful and exalted talents, eclipsing by their accusing eloquence the most boasted harangues of antiquity; rousing the pride of national resentment, by the boldest invectives against broken faith, and violated treaties, and shaking the bosom with alternate pity and horror, by the most glowing pictures of insulted nature and humanity. Ever animated and energetic, from the love of fame, which

is

is the inherent paffion of genius; firm and indefatigable, from a ftrong prepoffeffion of the juftice of their caufe.

Gentlemen, when the author fat down to write the book now before you, all this terrible, unceafing, exhauftlefs artillery of warm zeal, matchlefs vigour of underftanding, confuming and devouring eloquence, united with the higheft dignity, was daily, and without profpect of conclufion, pouring forth upon one private unprotected man, who was bound to hear it, in the face of the whole people of England, with reverential fubmiffion and filence.

Gentlemen, I do not complain of this as I did of the publication of the Charges; becaufe it is what the law allowed, and fanctioned in the courfe of a public trial; but when it is remembered that we are not angels, but weak fallible men, and that even the noble Judges of that high tribunal are cloathed beneath their ermines with the common infirmities of man's nature, it will bring us all to a proper temper for confidering the book itfelf, which will in a few moments be laid before you.

Gentlemen, it was under all thefe circumftances, and amidft the blaze of paffion and prejudice, which the fcene I have been endeavouring faintly to defcribe to you might be fuppofed likely to produce, that the author, whofe name I will now give to you, fat down to compofe the book which is profecuted to-day as a libel.

The hiftory of it is very fhort and natural.

The Rev. Mr. Loggan, Minifter of the Gofpel at Leith in Scotland, a clergyman of the pureft morals, and as you will fee by-and-by of very fuperior talents, well acquainted with the human character, and knowing the difficulty of bringing back public opinion after it is fettled on any fubject, took a warm, unbought, unfolicited intereft in the fituation of Mr. Haftings, and determined, if poffible, to arreft and fufpend the public judgment concerning him. He felt for the fituation of a fellow citizen, expofed to a trial which, whether right or wrong, is undoubtedly a fevere one; a trial, certainly not confined to a few criminal acts, like thofe we are accuftomed to, but comprehending the tranfactions of a whole life, and the complicated policies of entire nations; a trial, which had neither vifible limits to its duration, bounds to its expence, nor circumfcribed compafs for the grafp of memory or underftanding; a trial, which had therefore broke loofe from the common form of decifion, and had become the univerfal topic of difcuffion in the world, fuperfeding not only every other grave purfuit, but every other fafhionable diffipation.

Gen-

Gentlemen, the question you have therefore to try upon all this matter, is extremely simple ; it is neither more nor less than this : at a time when the charges against Mr. Hastings were, by the implied consent of the Commons, in every hand, and on every table ; when, by their Managers, the lightning of eloquence was incessantly consuming him, and flashing in the eyes of the public ; when every man was with perfect impunity saying, and writing, and publishing, just what he pleased of the supposed plunderer and devastator of nations ; would it have been criminal in *Mr. Hastings himself* to have reminded the public that he was a native of this free land, entitled to the common protection of her justice, and that he had a defence in his turn to offer to them, the outlines of which he implored them, in the mean time, to receive, as an antidote to the unlimited and unpunished poison in circulation against him ?

Gentlemen, this is, without colour or exaggeration, the true question you are to decide. For I assert, without the hazard of contradiction, that if Mr. Hastings himself could have stood justified or excused in your eyes, for publishing this volume in his own defence, the author, if he wrote it *bona fide* to defend him, must stand equally excused and justified ; and if the author be justified, the publisher cannot be criminal, unless you had evidence that it was published by him with a different spirit and intention from those in which it was written. The question therefore is correctly what I just now stated it to be : Could *Mr. Hastings* have been condemned to infamy for writing this book ?

Gentlemen, I tremble with indignation, to be driven to put such a question in England. Shall it be endured, that a subject of this country, instead of being arraigned and tried for some single act in her ordinary courts, where the accusation, as soon at least as it is made public, is followed within a few hours by the decision, may be impeached by the Commons for the transactions of twenty years, that the accusation shall spread as wide, as the region of letters, and the accused shall stand day after day, and year after year, as a spectacle before the public, which shall be kept in a perpetual state of inflammation against him ; yet that he shall not, without the severest penalties, be permitted to submit any thing to the judgment of mankind in his defence. If this be law (which it is for you to day to decide), such a man has no trial ; that great hall, built by our fathers for English justice, is no longer a

court,

court, but an altar; and an Englishman instead of being judged in it by GOD AND HIS COUNTRY, is a VICTIM AND A SACRIFICE.—Gentlemen, you will carefully remember, that I am not presuming to question either the right or the duty of the Commons of Great Britain to impeach; neither am I arraigning the propriety of their selecting, as they have done, the most extraordinary persons for ability which the age has produced to manage their impeachment. Much less am I censuring the Managers themselves, charged with the conduct of it before the Lords, who were undoubtedly bound by their duty to the House, and to the public, to expatiate upon the crimes of the person whom they had accused.

None of these points are questioned by me, nor are in this place questionable. I only desire to have it decided, whether if the Commons, when national expediency happens to call in their judgment for an impeachment, shall, instead of keeping it on their own records, and carrying it with due solemnity to the Peers for trial, permit it without censure and punishment to be sold like a common news-paper in the shop of my client, so crowded with their own Members, that no plain man, without privilege of Parliament, can hope even for a sight of the fire in a winter's day; every man buying it, reading it, and commenting upon it; the gentleman himself who is the object of it, or his friend in his absence, may not, without stepping beyond the bounds of English freedom, put a copy of what is thus published into his pocket, and send back to the very same shop for publication a *bona fide*, rational, able answer to it, in order that the bane and antidote may circulate together, and the public be kept straight till the day of decision.

Gentlemen, if you think that this common duty of self-preservation in the accused himself, which Nature writes as a law upon the hearts of even savages and brutes, is nevertheless too high a privilege to be enjoyed by an impeached and suffering Englishman; or if you think it beyond the office of humanity and justice, when brought home to the hand of a brother or a friend, you will say so by your verdict of GUILTY——The decision will then be *yours*; and the consolation *mine*, that I laboured to avert it. A very small part of the misery which will follow from it is likely to light upon *me*; the rest will be divided amongst *yourselves and your children*. Gentlemen, I observe plainly, and with infinite satisfaction, that you are shocked and offended at my even supposing it possible you should pronounce

nounce such a detestable judgment; and that you only require of me to make out to your satisfaction (as I promised) that the real scope and object of this book is a *bona fide* defence of Mr. Hastings, and *not a cloak and cover for scandal on the House of Commons.* Gentlemen, I engage to do this, and I engage for nothing more; I shall make an open manly defence. I mean to torture no expressions from their natural constructions; to dispute no inuendos on the record, should any of them have a fair application; nor to conceal from your notice any unguarded intemperate expressions, which may perhaps be found to chequer the vigorous and animated career of the work. Such a conduct might, by accident, shelter the defendant; but it would be the surrender of the very principle on which alone the liberty of the English press can stand; and I shall never defend any man from a temporary imprisonment, by the permanent loss of my own liberty, and the ruin of my country. I mean therefore to submit to you, that though you should find a few lines in page thirteen, or twenty-one, a few more in page fifty-one, and some others in other places, containing expressions bearing on the House of Commons, even as a body, which, if written as independent paragraphs by themselves, would be indefensible libels; yet that you have a right to pass them over in judgment, provided the substance clearly appears to be a *bona fide* conclusion, arising from the honest investigation of a subject which it was lawful to investigate; and the questionable expressions, the visible effusion of a zealous temper, engaged in an honourable and legal pursuit. After this preparation, I am not afraid to lay the book in its genuine state before you.

Here Mr. Erskine compared, with wonderful ingenuity, the several passages of the book, and endeavoured to shew, that the whole work was a bona fide *defence of Mr. Hastings; and that the terms of obloquy were directed against the individual accusers of him, and not against the House of Commons. He then proceeded,*

Here, gentlemen, said he, we must be permitted to pause together a little; for in examining whether these pages were written as an honest answer to the charges of the Commons, or as a prostituted defence of a notorious criminal, whom the writer believed to be guilty, *truth becomes material at every step.* For if *in any instance* he be detected of a *wilful* misrepresentation, he is no longer an object of your attention.

Will the Attorney-General proceed then to detect the hypocrisy of our author, by giving us some detail of the
proofs

proofs by which these personal enormities have been establilhed, and which the writer muft be suppofed to have been acquainted with? I afk this as the defender of *Mr. Stockdale*, not of Mr. Haftings, with whom I have no concern. I am sorry, indeed, to be fo often obliged to repeat this proteft; but I really feel myfelf embarraffed with thofe repeated coincidences of defence which thicken on me as I advance, and which were, no doubt, overlooked by the Commons when they directed this interlocutory enquiry into his conduct.

I afk then, *as counfel for Mr. Stockdale*, Whether, when a great ftate criminal is brought for juftice at an immenfe expence to the public, accufed of the moft oppreffive cruelties, and charged with the robbery of princes and the deftruction of nations, it is not open to any one to afk, Who are his accufers? What are the fources and the authorities of thefe fhocking complaints?—Where are the ambaffadors or memorials of thofe princes whofe revenues he has plundered?—Where are the witneffes for thofe unhappy men in whofe perfons the rights of humanity have been violated?—How deeply buried is the blood of the innocent, that it does not rife up in retributive judgment to confound the guilty! Thefe furely are queftions, which, when a fellow-citizen is upon a long, painful, and expenfive trial, Humanity has a right to propofe; which the plain fenfe of the moft unlettered man may be expected to dictate, and which all hiftory muft provoke from the more enlightened.

When Cicero impeached Verres, before the great tribunal of Rome, of fimilar cruelties and depredations in *her* provinces, the Roman people were not left to fuch enquiries. All Sicily furrounded the forum, demanding juftice upon her plunderer and fpoiler with tears and imprecations. It was not by the eloquence of the *orator*, but by the cries and tears of the miferable, that Cicero prevailed in that illuftrious caufe. Verres fled from the oaths of his accufers and their witneffes, and not from the voice of Tully; who, to preferve the fame of his eloquence, publifhed the five celebrated fpeeches which were never delivered againft the criminal, becaufe he had fled from the city, appalled with the fight of the perfecuted and the oppreffed.

It may be faid, that the cafes of Sicily and India are widely different; perhaps they may; whether they are or not, is foreign to my purpofe. I am not bound to deny
the

the poffibility of anfwers to fuch queftions; I am only vindicating *the right to afk them.*

Gentlemen, another paffage, arraigned by the information, is this:

" An impeachment of *error* in *judgment* with regard to the
" *quantum* of a fine, and for an *intention* that never was
" *executed,* and never known to the offending party,
" characterifes a tribunal *inquifition,* rather than a Court
" of Parliament."

Gentlemen, I am ready to admit that this fentiment might have been expreffed in language more referved and guarded; but you will look to the fentiment itfelf, rather than to its drefs; to the mind of the writer, and not to the bluntnefs with which he may happen to exprefs it. It is obvioufly the language of a warm man, engaged in the honeft defence of his friend, and who is brought to what he thinks a juft conclufion in argument, which perhaps becomes offenfive in proportion to its truth. Truth is undoubtedly no warrant for writing what is reproachful of any *private* man; for if a member of fociety lives within the law, then if he offends it is againft God alone, and man has nothing to do with him; and, if he tranfgrefs the laws, the libeller fhould arraign him before them, inftead of prefuming to try him himfelf. But as to writings on *general fubjects,* which are not charged as an infringement on the rights of individuals, but as of a feditious tendency, it is far otherwife.

When, in the progrefs either of legiflation or of high national juftice in Parliament, they who are amenable to no law, are fuppofed to have adopted through miftake or error a principle which, if drawn into precedent, might be dangerous to the public; I fhall not admit it to be a libel *in the courfe of a legal and* bona fide *publication,* to ftate that fuch a principle had *in fact* been adopted; for the people of England are not to be kept in the dark, touching the proceedings of their own reprefentatives. Let us therefore coolly examine this fuppofed offence, and fee what it amounts to——

Firft, Was not the conduct of the Right Honourable Gentleman, whofe name is here mentioned, exactly what it is reprefented? Will the Attorney-General, who was prefent in the Houfe of Commons, fay that it was not? Did not the Minifter vindicate Mr. Haftings in what he *had done;* and was not his confent to that article of the impeachment

peachment founded on the intention of levying a fine on the Zemindar for the service of the state, beyond the quantum which he the Minister thought reasonable?

What else is this but an impeachment of error in judgment in the quantum of a fine?

So much for the first part of the sentence, which, regarding Mr. Pitt only, is foreign to our purpose; and as to the last part of it, which imputes the sentiments of the Minister to the majority that followed him with their votes on the question, that appears to me to be giving handsome credit to the majority for having voted from conviction, and not from courtesy to the Minister. To have supposed otherwise, I dare not say, would have been a more *natural* libel, but it would certainly have been a greater one—The sum and substance therefore of the paragraph is only this: that an impeachment for an error in judgment, is not consistent with theory or the practice of the English Government.—So SAY I.

I say, without reserve, speaking merely in the abstract, and not meaning to decide upon the merits of Mr. Hastings's cause, that an impeachment for an error in judgment is contrary to the whole spirit of English criminal justice, which, though not binding on the House of Commons, ought to be a guide to their proceedings. I say that their extraordinary jurisdiction of impeachment, ought never to be assumed to expose error, or to scourge misfortune, but to hold up a terrible example to corruption and *wilful* abuse of authority by extra legal pains.

If public men are always punished with due severity, when the source of their misconduct appears to have been *selfish, corrupt, and criminal*, the public can never suffer when their errors are treated with gentleness; for no man from such protection to the magistrate can think lightly of the charge of magistracy itself, when he sees, by the language of the saving judgment, that the only title to it is an honest and zealous intention.

Gentlemen, if at this moment, or indeed in any other in the whole course of our history, the people of England were to call upon every man in this impeaching House of Commons, who had given his voice on public questions, or acted in authority civil or military, to answer for the issues of our councils and our wars, and if honest single intentions for the public service were refused as answers to impeachments, we should have many relations to mourn for, and many friends to deplore. For my own part, gentlemen, I feel I hope for my country as much as any

man

man that inhabits it : but I would rather see it fall, and be buried in its ruins, than lend my voice to wound any Minister, or other responsible person, however unfortunate, who had fairly followed the lights of his understanding and the dictates of his conscience for their preservation.

Gentlemen, this is no theory of mine ; it is the language of English Law, and the protection which it affords to every man in office, from the highest to the lowest trusts of Government.

In no one instance that can be named, foreign or domestic, did the Court of King's Bench ever interpose its extraordinary jurisdiction, by information against any Magistrate for the widest departure from the rule of his duty, without *the plainest and clearest proof of corruption.* To every such application, not so supported, the constant answer has been, Go to a Grand Jury with your complaint. God forbid that a Magistrate should suffer from an error in judgment, if his purpose was honestly to discharge his trust. We cannot stop the ordinary course of justice ; but wherever the Court has a discretion, such a Magistrate is entitled to its protection. I appeal to the noble Judge, and to every man who hears me, for the truth and universality of this position. And it would be a strange solecism indeed to assert, that in a case where the Supreme Court of criminal justice in the nation would refuse to interpose an *extraordinary* though a legal jurisdiction, on the principle that the ordinary execution of the laws should never be exceeded, but for the punishment of malignant guilt, the Commons in their judicial capacity, growing out of the same constitution, should reject that principle, and stretch them still further by a jurisdiction still more *eccentric.*——Many impeachments have taken place, because the law *could not* adequately punish the objects of them ; but who ever heard of one being set on foot because the law upon principle *would not* punish them ?—— Many impeachments have been adopted for a higher example than a prosecution in the ordinary Courts, but surely never for a different example.———The matter therefore, in the offensive paragraph, is not only an indisputable truth, but a truth in the propagation of which we are all deeply concerned.

Whether Mr. Hastings, in the instance, acted from corruption, or from zeal for his employers, is what I have nothing to do with ; it is to be decided in judgment ; my duty stops with wishing him, as I do, an honourable deliverance.——

liverance.—Whether the Minister or the Commons meant to found this article of the impeachment on mere error without corruption, is likewise foreign to the purpose. The author could only judge from what was said and done on the occasion. He only sought to guard the principle which is a common interest, and the rights of Mr. Hastings under it; and was therefore justified in publishing, that an impeachment, founded in error in judgment, was to all intents and purposes illegal, unconstitutional, and unjust.— Gentlemen, it is now time for us to return again to the work under examination.

The author, having discussed the whole of the first article through so many pages, without even the imputation of an incorrect or intemperate expression, except in the concluding passage, the meaning of which I trust I have explained, goes on with the same earnest disposition to the discussion of the second charge, respecting the princesses of Oude, which occupies eighteen pages, not one syllable of which the Attorney-General has read, and on which there is not even a glance at the House of Commons; the whole of this answer is indeed so far from being a mere cloak for the introduction of slander, that I aver it to be one of the most masterly pieces of writing I ever read in my life: from thence he goes on to the charge of contracts and salaries, which occupies five pages more, in which *there is not a glance at the House of Commons, nor a word read by the Attorney-General.*—He afterwards defends Mr. Hastings against the charges respecting the opium contracts. *Not a glance at the House of Commons; not a word by the Attorney-General.* And, in short, in this manner he goes on with the others to the end of the book.

Now is it possible for any human being to believe, that a man, having no other intention than to vilify the House of Commons (*as this information charges*), should yet keep his mind thus fixed and settled as the needle to the pole, upon the serious merits of Mr. Hastings's defence, without ever straying into matter even questionable, except in the two or three selected parts out of two or three hundred pages. This is a forbearance which could not have existed, if calumny and detraction had been the malignant objects which led him to the enquiry and publication. The whole fallacy therefore arises from holding up to view a few detached passages, and carefully concealing the general tenor of the book.

Having now finished most, if not all of these *critical* observations, which it has been my duty to make upon this

unfair

unfair mode of prosecution; it is but a tribute of common justice to the Attorney-General, (and which my personal regard for him makes it more pleasant to pay,) that none of my commentaries reflect in the most distant manner upon him; nor upon the Solicitor for the Crown, who sits near me, who is a person of the most correct honour; —far from it. The Attorney-General, having orders to prosecute in consequence of the address of the House to his Majesty, had no choice in the mode; no means at all of keeping the prosecutors before you in countenance, but by the course which has been pursued; but so far has he been from enlisting into the cause those prejudices, which it is not difficult to slide into a business originating from such exalted authority, he has honourably guarded you against them; pressing indeed severely upon my client with the weight of his ability, but not with the glare and trappings of his high office.

Gentlemen, I wish that my strength would enable me to convince you of the author's singleness of intention, and of the merit and ability of his work, by reading the whole that remains of it. But my voice is already nearly exhausted; I am sorry my client should be a sufferer by my infirmity.

Gentlemen, if this book contain a wilfully false account of the instructions given to Mr. Hastings for his government, and of his conduct under them, the author and publisher of it deserve the severest punishment, for a mercenary imposition on the public. But if it be true that he was directed to make the safety and prosperity of Bengal the first object of his attention, and that under his administration it has been safe and prosperous; if it be true that the security and preservation of our possessions and revenues in Asia were marked out to him as the great leading principle of his government, and that these possessions and revenues, amidst unexampled dangers, have been secured and preserved; then a question may be unaccountably mixed with your consideration, much beyond the consequence of the present prosecution, involving perhaps the merits of the impeachment itself which gave it birth; a question which the Commons, as prosecutors of Mr. Hastings, should, in common prudence, have avoided; unless that, regretting the unwieldy length of their proceedings against him, they wished to afford him the opportunity of this strange anomalous defence.—For although I am neither his counsel, nor desire to have any thing to do with his innocence, yet, in the collateral defence of

my

my client, I am driven to state matter which may be considered by many as hostile to the impeachment. For if our dependencies have been secured, and their interests promoted, I am driven, in the defence of my client, to remark, that it is mad and preposterous to bring to the standard of Justice and Humanity the exercise of a dominion founded upon violence and terror. It may and must be true, that Mr. Hastings has repeatedly offended against the rights and privileges of Asiatic Government, if he was the faithful deputy of a power which could not maintain itself for an hour without trampling upon both : he may and must have offended against the laws of God and Nature, if he was the faithful viceroy of an empire wrested in blood from the people to whom God and Nature had given it : he may and must have preserved that unjust dominion over a timorous and abject nation, by a terrifying, overbearing, insulting superiority, if he was the faithful administrator of your Government, which, having no root in consent or affection, no foundation in similarity of interests, nor support from any one principle which cements men together in society, could only be upheld by alternate stratagem and force. The unhappy people of India, feeble and effeminate as they are from the softness of their climate, and subdued and broken as they have been by the knavery and strength of civilization, still occasionally start up in all the vigour and intelligence of insulted Nature. To be governed at all, they must be governed with a rod of iron ; and our Empire in the East would over and over again have been lost to Great Britain, if civil skill and military prowess had not united their efforts to support an authority which Heaven never gave by means which it never can sanction.

Gentlemen, I think I can observe that you are touched with this way of considering the subject ; and I can account for it. I have not been considering it through the cold medium of books, but have been speaking of man and his nature, and of human dominion, from what I have seen of them myself amongst reluctant nations submitting to our authority. I know what they feel, and how such feeling can alone be repressed. I have heard them in my youth from a naked savage, in the indignant character of a prince surrounded by his subjects, addressing the governor of a British colony, holding a bundle of sticks in his hand, as the notes of his unlettered eloquence. " Who " is it," said the jealous ruler over the desart encroached upon by the restless foot of English adventure ——" Who

" is it that caufes this river to rife in the high mountains,
" and to empty itfelf into the ocean? Who is it that caufes
" to blow the loud winds of winter, and that calms them
" again in the fummer? Who is it that rears up the fhade
" of thefe lofty forefts, and blafts them with the quick
" lightning at his pleafure? The fame Being who gave to
" you a country on the other fide of the waters, and gave
" ours to us; and by this title we will defend it," faid
the warrior, throwing down his tomohawk upon the
ground, and raifing the war-found of his nation. Thefe
are the feelings of fubjugated man all round the globe;
and, depend upon it, nothing but fear will controul, where
it is in vain to look for affection.

Thefe reflections are the only antidotes to thofe ana-
themas of fuperhuman eloquence which have lately fhook
thefe walls that furround us; but which it unaccountably
falls to my province, whether I will or no, a little to ftem
the torrent of; by reminding you that you have a mighty
fway in Afia, which cannot be maintained by the finer
fympathies of life, or the practice of its charities and affections. What will they do for you when furrounded by
two hundred thoufand men with artillery, cavalry, and
elephants, calling upon you for their dominions which you
have robbed them of? Juftice may, no doubt, in fuch a
cafe, forbid the levying of a fine to pay a revolting foldiery:
a treaty may ftand in the way of increafing a tribute to
keep up the very exiftence of the government; and delicacy for women may forbid all entrance into a Zenana for
money, whatever may be the neceffity for taking it.—All
thefe things muft ever be occurring. But under the preffure of fuch conftant difficulties, fo dangerous to rational
honour, it might be better perhaps to think of effectually
fecuring it altogether, by recalling our troops and our merchants, and abandoning our Oriental Empire. Until this
is done, neither Religion nor Philofophy can be preffed
very far into the aid of reformation and punifhment. If
England, from a luft of ambition and dominion, will infift
on maintaining defpotic rule over diftant and hoftile nations, beyond all comparifon more numerous and extended
than herfelf, and gives commiffion to her viceroys to govern them with no other inftructions than to preferve them,
and to fecure permanently their revenues; with what colour of confiftency or reafon can fhe place herfelf in the
moral chair, and affect to be fhocked at the execution of
her own orders; adverting to the exact meafure of wickednefs and injuftice neceffary to their execution, and complaining

plaining only of *the excess of the immorality*; confidering her authority as a difpenfation for breaking the commands of God, and the breach of them as only punifhable when contrary to the ordinances of man?

Gentlemen, fuch a proceeding begets ferious reflections. It would be better perhaps for the mafters and fervants of all fuch governments, to join in fupplication, that the Great Author of violated humanity may not confound them together in one common judgment.

Gentlemen, I find, as I faid before, I have not fufficient ftrength to go on with the remaining part of the book. I hope, however, that; notwithftanding my omiffions, you are now completely fatisfied, that whatever errors or mifconceptions may have mifled the writer of thefe pages, the juftification of a perfon whom he believed to be innocent, and whofe accufers had appealed to the public, was the fingle object of his contemplation. If I have fucceeded in that object, every purpofe which I had in addreffing you has been anfwered.

It only now remains to remind you, that another confideration has been ftrongly preffed upon you, and, no doubt, will be infifted on in reply.——You will be told, that the matters which I have been juftifying as legal, and even meritorious, have therefore not been made the fubject of complaint; and that whatever intrinfic merit parts of the book may be fuppofed or even admitted to poffefs, fuch merit can afford no juftification to the felected paffages, fome of which, even with the context, carry the meaning charged by the information, and which are indecent animadverfions on authority.

Gentlemen, to this I would anfwer (ftill protefting as I do againft the application of any one of the innuendos), that if you are firmly perfuaded of the finglenefs and purity of the author's intentions, you are not bound to fubject him to infamy, becaufe, in the zealous career of a juft and animated compofition, he happens to have tripped with his pen into an intemperate expreffion in one or two inftances of a long work. If this fevere duty were binding on your confciences, the liberty of the prefs would be an empty found, and no man could venture to write on any fubject, however pure his purpofe, without an attorney at one elbow, and a counfel at the other.

From minds thus fubdued by the terrors of punifhment, there could iffue no works of genius to expand the empire of Human Reafon; nor any mafterly compofitions on the general nature of Government; by the help of which, the

great

great commonwealths of mankind have founded their esta-
blishments ; much less any of those useful applications of
them to critical conjunctures, by which, from time to
time, our own constitution, by the exertion of patriot citizens, has been brought back to its standard.

Under such terrors, all the great lights of science and
civilization must be extinguished : for men cannot communicate their free thoughts to one another with a lash held
over their heads.

It is the nature of every thing that is great and useful,
both in the animate and inanimate world, to be wild and
irregular ; and we must be contented to take them with
their alloys which belong to them, or live without them.
Genius breaks from the fetters of criticism ; but its wan-
derings are sanctioned by its majesty and wisdom, when
it advances in its path ; subject it to the critic, and you
tame it into dulness. Mighty rivers break down their
banks in the winter, sweeping away to death the flocks
which are fattened on the soil that they fertilize in the
summer : the few may be saved by embankments from
drowning, but the flock must perish for hunger. Tem-
pests occasionally shake our dwellings, and dissipate our
commerce ; but they scourge before them the lazy ele-
ments, which, without them, would stagnate into pesti-
lence.

In like manner, Liberty herself, the last and best gift of
God to his creatures, must be taken just as she is ; you
may pare her down into bashful regularity, and shape her
into a perfect model of severe scrupulous Law ; but she
will be Liberty no longer ; and you must be content to die
under the lash of this inexorable Justice which you have exchanged for the banner of Freedom.

If it be asked where the line to this indulgence and impunity is to be drawn; the answer is easy. The Liberty
of the Press *on general subjects* comprehends and implies as
much strict observance of positive law as is consistent
with perfect purity of intention, and equal and useful society ; and what that latitude is, cannot be promulgated
in the abstract, but must be judged of in the particular
instance, and consequently upon this occasion must be
judged of by you, without forming any possible precedent
for any other case ; and where can the judgment be possibly so safe as with the members of that society which alone
can suffer if the writing is calculated to do mischief to the
public ?

You

You muſt therefore try the book by that criterion, and ſay whether the publication was premature and offenſive; or, in other words, whether the publiſher was bound to have ſuppreſſed it, until the public ear was anticipated and abuſed, and every avenue to the human heart or under-ſtanding ſecured and blocked up.

I ſee around me thoſe, by whom, by-and-by, Mr. Haſtings will be moſt ably and eloquently defended *; but I am ſorry to remind my friends, that, but for the right of ſuſpending the public judgment concerning him till their ſeaſon of exertion comes round, the tongues of angels would be inſufficient for the taſk.

Gentlemen, I hope I have now performed my duty to my client; I ſincerely hope that I have; for, certainly, if ever there was a man pulled the other way by his intereſts and affections,—if ever there was a man who ſhould have trembled at the ſituation in which I have been placed on this occaſion; it is myſelf, who not only love, honour, and reſpect, but whoſe future hopes and preferments are linked from free choice with thoſe who, from the miſtakes of the author, are treated with great ſeverity and injuſtice.—— Theſe are ſtrong retardments; but I have been urged on to activity by conſiderations, which can never be inconſiſtent with honourable attachments, either in the political or ſocial world; the love of juſtice and of liberty, and a zeal for the conſtitution of my country, which is the inheritance of our poſterity, of the public, and of the world.

Theſe are the motives which have animated me in de-fence of this perſon, who was an entire ſtranger to me; whoſe ſhop I never go to; and the author of whoſe pub-lication, as well as Mr. Haſtings, who is the object of it, I never ſpoke to in my life.

One word more, gentlemen, and I have done. Every Human Tribunal ought to take care to adminiſter juſtice, as we look hereafter to have juſtice adminiſtered to ourſelves. Upon the principle which the Attorney General prays ſen-tence upon my client——God have mercy upon us!——In-ſtead of ſtanding before him in judgment with the hopes and conſolations of Chriſtians, we muſt call upon the mountains to cover us; for which of us can preſent, for omniſcient examination, a pure, unſpotted, and faultleſs courſe?—But I humbly expect that the benevolent Author of our being will judge us as I have been pointing out for your example.—Holding up the great volume of our lives

* Mr. Law, Mr. Plumer, and Mr. Dallas.

in

in his hands, and regarding the general scope of them; if he discovers benevolence, charity, and good-will to man, beating in the heart, where he alone can look;—if he finds that our conduct, though often forced out of the path by our infirmities, has been in general well directed; his all-searching eye will assuredly never pursue us into those little corners of our lives, much less will his justice select them for punishment, without the general context of our exist-ence; by which faults may be sometimes found to have grown out of virtues, and very many of our heaviest of-fences to have been grafted by human imperfection upon the best and kindest of our affections. No, gentlemen, believe me, this is not the course of Divine Justice, or there is no truth in the Gospels of Heaven.—If the general tenor of a man's conduct be such as I have represented it, he may walk through the shadow of death, with all his faults about him, with as much cheerfulness as in the common paths of life; because he knows, that, instead of a stern accuser to expose before the Author of his nature those frail passages, which, like the scored matter in the book before you, chequers the volume of the brightest and best-spent life, his mercy will obscure them from the eye of his purity, and our repentance blot them out for ever.

All this would, I admit, be perfectly foreign and irrele-vant, if you were sitting here in a case of property between man and man, where a strict rule of law must operate, or there would be an end in that case of civil life and society.

It would be equally foreign, and still more irrelevant, if applied to those shameful attacks upon private reputation which are the bane and disgrace of the press; by which whole families have been rendered unhappy during life, by aspersions cruel, scandalous, and unjust. *Let* SUCH LI-BELLERS *remember, that no one of my principles of defence can at any time, or upon any occasion, ever apply to shield* THEM *from punishment*; because such conduct is not only an in-fringement of the rights of men, as they are defined by strict law, *but is absolutely incompatible with honour, honesty, or mistaken good intention.*

On such men let the Attorney General bring forth all the artillery of his office, and the thanks and blessings of the whole public will follow him. But this is a totally different case. Whatever private calumny may mark this work, it has not been made the subject of complaint; and we have therefore nothing to do with that, nor any right to consider it.

We

We are trying whether the public could have been considered as offended and endangered, if Mr. Hastings himself, in whose place the author and publisher have a right
to put themselves, had, under all the circumstances which
have been considered, composed and published the volume
under examination. That question cannot in common
sense be any thing resembling *a question of* LAW; but is a
pure question of FACT, to be decided on the principles
which I have humbly recommended. I therefore ask of the
Court, that the book itself may now be delivered to you.
Read it with attention; and as you find it, pronounce your
verdict.

Lord Kenyon's Charge to the Jury.

Gentlemen of the Jury,

I DO not feel that I am called upon to discuss the nature of this libel, or to state to you what the merit of the
composition is, or what the merit of the argument is; but
merely to state what the questions are, to which you are to
apply your judgment, and the evidence given in support of
this information.

It is impossible, when one reads the preface to this information, which states that the libel was written, to asperse
the House of Commons, not to feel that it is a matter of
considerable importance; for I don't know how far a fixed
general opinion, that the House of Commons deserves to
have crimes imputed to it, may go; for men that are governed will be much influenced by the confidence reposed
in the governors. Mankind will never forget that governors
are not made for the sake of themselves, but are placed in
their respective stations to discharge the functions of their
office for the sake of the public; and, if they should ever
conceive that the governors are so inattentive to their duty
as to exercise their functions to keep themselves in power,
and for their own emolument, without attending to the
interests of the public, government must be relaxed, and
at last crumble to dust; and therefore, if the case is made
out which is imputed to the defendant, it is no doubt a
most momentous case indeed; but though it is so, it does
not follow that the defendant is guilty; and Juries have
been frequently told, and I am bound, in the situation in
which I stand, to tell you, that, in forming your judgment upon this case, there are two points for you to attend
to; namely,

Whether

Whether the defendant, who is charged with having published this, did publish it; and,

Whether the sense which the Attorney General, by his innuendos in this information, has affixed to the different passages, is fairly affixed to them.

From any consideration as to the first of these points you are delivered, because it is admitted that the book was published by the defendant; but the other is the material point to which you are to apply your judgment. It has been entered into with wonderful abilities, much in the detail; but it is not enough for a man to say, I am innocent; ---it belongs to the Great Searcher of Hearts to know whether men are innocent or not; we are to judge of the guilt or innocence of men (because we have no other rule to go by) by their overt-acts, from what they have done.

In applying the innuendos, I accede entirely to what was laid down by the Counsel for the Defendant, and which was admitted yesterday by the Attorney General, as Counsel for the Crown, that you must, upon this information, make up your minds, that this was meant as an aspersion upon the House of Commons——and I admit also, that, in forming your opinion, you are not bound to confine your enquiry to those detached passages which the Attorney General has selected as offensive matter, and the subject of prosecution.

But let me, on the other side, warn you, that though there may be much good writing, good argument, morality, and humanity, in many parts of it; yet, if there are offensive passages, the good part will not sanctify the bad part.

Having stated this, I ought also to tell you that, in order to see what is the sense to be fairly imputed to those passages that are culled out as the offensive passages, you have a right to look at all the context; you have a right to look at the whole book; and, if you find it has been garbled, and that the passages selected by the Attorney General do not bear the sense imputed to them, the man has a right to be acquitted; and God forbid he should be convicted!

It is for you, upon reading the information (which if you go out of Court you will undoubtedly take with you), comparing it with this pamphlet, to see whether the sense the Attorney General has affixed is fairly affixed; always being guided by this, that, where it is truly ambiguous and doubtful, the inclination of your judgment should be on the side of innocence; but if you find you cannot acquit him without distorting sentences, you are to meet this

case,

case, and all other cases as I stated yesterday, with the fortitude of men, feeling that they have a duty upon them superior to all leaning to parties; namely, administering justice in the particular cause.

It would be in vain for me to go through this pamphlet which has been just put into my hand, and to say whether the sense affixed is the fair sense or not. As far as disclosed by the information, these passages afford a strong bias, that the sense affixed to them is the fair sense; but of that you will judge, not from the passages themselves merely, but by reading the context of the whole book, so much at least as is necessary to enable you to ascertain the true meaning of the author.

If I were prepared to comment upon the pamphlet, in my situation it would be improper for me to do it; my duty is fulfilled, when I point out to you what the questions are that are proposed to your judgment, and what the evidence is upon the questions; the result is yours and yours only.

> The Jury withdrew for about two hours, when they returned into Court with a Verdict finding the Defendant NOT GUILTY.

THE KING *against* THE DEAN OF ST. ASAPH.

The very interesting question, of the Right of Juries to judge of the LAW as well as FACT in the Case of LIBEL, is so largely discussed in the following speech of Earl Mansfield, when he delivered the judgment of the court in the Case of the Dean of St. Asaph, that it cannot fail of being acceptable to our readers. The Dean had been tried at Shrewsbury before Judge Buller for a Libel; and the Judge said, there were two objects only for their consideration, namely, the fact of the publication, and the truth of the *innuendos*; the verdict of the jury was, Guilty of publishing, but whether a libel or not they did not find. A motion was made in Michaelmas Term, 1784, for a new trial on the score of a misdirection to the jury, when EARL MANSFIELD delivered the judgment of the court as follows:

This motion to set aside the verdict, and to grant a new trial, for the misdirection of the Judge, supposes that, upon the verdict, either as a general, or as minutes of a special one, to be reduced into form, judgment may be given; for if the verdict were defective, and omitted finding any thing within the province of the jury to find,

no

no judgment could be given, and there muſt be a *venire de novo*; conſequently this motion would be improper.

Four objections have been made to the direction of the Judge. The firſt, peculiar to this caſe ; and therefore I begin with it, that he did not leave the evidence of a lawful excuſe or juſtification to the jury as a ground for acquitting the defendant. Circumſtances merely of alleviation, or aggravation, are irrelevant upon the trial ; they are immaterial to the verdict ; and they may be made uſe of when judgment is given, to increaſe or leſſen the puniſhment. Circumſtances which amount to a lawful excuſe, or juſtification, are proper upon the trial, and can only be uſed then. Upon every ſuch defence, there ariſe two queſtions ; one of law, the other of fact ; the firſt to be decided by the Court, the ſecond by the jury. Whether the fact alleged, ſuppoſing it true, be a legal excuſe, is a queſtion of law ; whether the allegation be true, is a queſtion of fact ; and according to this diſtinction the Judge ought to direct, and the jury ought to follow the direction ; though, by means of a general verdict, they are intruſted with the power of confounding the law and the fact, and follow the prejudices of their affections or paſſions.

The circumſtances urged in defence are, the letter of the 24th of January to Mr. Edwards, and the advertiſement, and what is ſaid by Mr. Jones of the converſation with the defendant on the 7th of January. Upon this part of the caſe we muſt ſuppoſe the paper ſeditious or criminal ; then the defendant, *knowing it had been ſtrongly objected to*, publiſhed it with an advertiſement, avowing and juſtifying the doctrine. The next circumſtance is from the evidence of Edward Jones ; that the defendant knew the paper was objected to, as having a ſeditious tendency, and might do miſchief, if tranſlated into *Welch* ; and therefore that deſign was laid aſide. This he knew on the 7th of January, and ſent it to be printed on the 24th ; and it was read at a county meeting with a rope about his neck (as he ſaid), and that it was *not ſo bad*. We are all clearly of opinion, that if the writing be criminal, thoſe circumſtances are aggravation, and ought not to have been left as any excuſe. What was meant by ſaying the affidavit ſhould have been ſet out in the indictment, I do not comprehend ; much leſs that blaſphemy may be charged in the Scripture, by ſtating half the ſentence. If any part of the context qualify what is ſet forth, it may be given

in

in evidence *. Every circumstance which tends to prove the meaning, is every day given in evidence; and the jury are the Judges, and must find the meaning.

The second objection is, that the Judge did not give his own opinion, whether the writing was a libel, or seditious, or criminal.

The third was, that the Judge told the jury they ought to leave that question upon the record to the court, if they had no doubt of the meaning and publication.

And the fourth, that he did not leave the defendant's intent to the jury.

The answer to these objections is, that by the constitution the jury ought not to decide the question of law, whether such a writing, of such a meaning, published without a lawful excuse, be criminal: and that they cannot decide it against the defendant, because, after a verdict, it remains open upon the record: therefore it is the duty of the Judge to advise the jury to separate the question of fact from the question of law; and as they ought not to decide the law, and the question remains entire for the Court, he is not called upon to tell them his own opinion. It is almost peculiar to the form of a prosecution for a libel, that the question of law remains entirely open for the Court upon the record, and that the jury cannot decide it against the defendant; so that a general verdict, that the defendant is guilty, is equivalent to a special verdict in other cases. It finds all which belongs to the jury to find, and finds nothing as to the question of law. Therefore, when the jury are satisfied of every fact within their province to find, they have been advised to find the defendant guilty, and in that shape to take the opinion of the Court upon the law; and no case has been cited of a special verdict, in a prosecution for a libel, leaving the question of law upon the record to the Court; though to be sure it might be left in that form: but the other is more simple and better. A criminal intent from doing a thing in itself criminal, without a lawful excuse, is an inference of law. Where an innocent act is made criminal, when done with a peculiar intent, there the intent is the material fact to constitute the crime. The subject-matter of these three objections has arisen upon every trial for a libel since the Revolution, now near 100 years ago. In every reign there have been many such trials both of a private and public nature. In every

* Vid. R. v. Bear. Salk. 417.

reign there have been several defended with all the acrimony of party animosity, and a spirit ready to contest every point, and to admit nothing. But during all this time, as far as it can be traced, one may venture to say, that the doctrine of every Judge has been consonant to the doctrine of Mr. Justice Buller; and no counsel has complained of it by an application to the Court. Counsel for the Crown to remove the prejudices of the jury, and to satisfy the bye-standers, have expatiated upon the enormity of the libel. Judges, with the same view, have sometimes done the same thing: both have done it wisely with another view, to obviate the captivating harangues of defendants' counsel to the jury, that they can and ought to find that in law the paper is no libel. But the formal direction of every Judge, under which every lawyer has so far acquiesced as not to complain of it to the Court, seems to me, ever since the Revolution, to have been agreeable to the direction given in this case. It is difficult to cite cases; the trials are not printed; unless a question arises, notes are not taken: nobody takes a note of a direction of course not disputed. We must, as in all cases of tradition, trace backwards, and presume from the usage, which is remembered, that the preceding usage was the same. The Craftsman was a celebrated party paper *, written in opposition to the Ministry of Sir Robert Walpole, by many men of high rank and great abilities; the whole party espoused it. It was thought proper to prosecute the famous Hague Letter; I was at the trial; it happens to be printed in the 9th vol. of St. Tr. 255. There was a great concourse, great expectation, and many persons of high rank were present to countenance the defendant. Mr. Fazakerly and Mr. Bootle were the leading counsel for the defendant; they started every objection, and laboured every point: and when the Judge over-ruled them, he usually said, " if I am wrong, you know where " to apply." The Judge was Lord Chief Justice Raymond, who had been eminent at the bar in the reign of Queen Anne, Solicitor and Attorney-General in the reign of George the First, and intimately connected with Sir Edward Northey; so that he must have known what the ancient practice had been. The cause was so blended with party passion, that it required his utmost attention; yet, when he came to sum up and direct, he did it as of

* *Vid. R. v. Tutchin*, 1704. 5 *St. Tr.* 532.

course,

course, juft as Mr. Juftice Buller did on this occafion.
Fazakerly and Bootle, very able lawyers, and connected
in party with the writers of the Craftfman, never thought
of complaining to the Court.   The other trials before Lord
Raymond are not printed ; nor to be found in any notes ;
but, to be fure, his direction in all was to the fame effect.
I recollect one, where the Craftfman was acquitted, from a
ballad made by Mr. Pulteney :—

> For Sir Philip well knows that his innuendos
>   No longer will ferve him in verfe or in profe ;
> For twelve honeft men have decided the caufe,
>   Who are judges of fact, tho' not judges of laws.

There are no notes of the trials before Lord Hardwicke,
or Lord Chief Juftice Lee., before 1752, when the cafe of
the King v. Owen came on before Chief Juftice Lee.—It
happens to be printed in the *State Trials* †.   I attended as
Solicitor General ; Lord Chief Juftice Lee, the moft fcru-
pulous obferver and follower of precedents, directed, as
of courfe, in the fame manner as was done in this cafe.
When I was Attorney General, I profecuted for fome libels ; one I remember was the King v. Nutt.   He was
convicted under the fame direction by Lord Chief Juftice
Ryder.   In the year 1756, I came into the office I now
hold, and, upon the firft profecution for a libel which ftood
in my paper, I think it was the cafe of the King v. Sheb-
beare, I made up my mind as to the direction I ought to
give ; and I have uniformly given the fame almoft in the
fame form of words.   No counfel ever complained of it to
the Court.   Upon every defendant being brought up for
judgment, I have always ftated the direction I gave, and
the Court has always affented to it.   The defence of a lawful excufe never exifted in any cafe before me : therefore I
told the jury, " if they were fatisfied with the evidence
of the publication, and that the meaning and innuendos
were as ftated, they ought to find the defendant guilty ;
the queftion of law was upon the record for the judgment
of the Court."   The direction being as of courfe, and no
queftion raifed concerning it in the Court, though I have
had the misfortune to try many libels in very warm times
againft defendants moft obftinately and factioufly de-

† 10 *St. Tr. Ap.* 196.

fended,

fended, there are no notes or reports of what paffed. In one cafe, the King v. Woodfall, on account of another kind of queftion, there is a report; and there the direction is adopted by the whole Court as right, and the doctrine of Mr. Juftice Buller laid down in exprefs terms. Such a judicial practice in the precife point from the Revolution, as I think, down to the prefent day, is not to be fhaken by general theoretical arguments of popular declamation. Every fpecies of criminal profecution has fomething peculiar in the mode of procedure; therefore general propofitions, applied to all, tend only to complicate and confound the queftion. No deduction or conclufion can be drawn from what a jury may do from the form of the procedure to what they ought to do upon the fundamental principles of the Conftitution, and the reafon of the thing, if they will act with integrity and a good confcience. The fundamental definition of trials by jury depends upon an univerfal maxim, without an exception, *ad quæftionem*. Where the queftions can be fevered by the form of the pleadings, the diftinction is preferved upon the face of the record, and the jury cannot encroach upon the jurifdiction of the Court. But where by the form of pleading the two queftions are blended together, and cannot be feparated upon the face of the record, the diftinction is preferved by the honefty of the jury. The conftitution trufts that, under the direction of the Judge, they will not ufurp a jurifdiction which is not their province. They do not know, and are not prefumed to know, the law; they are not fworn to decide the law; they are not required to do it. If it appear upon the record, they ought to leave it there; or they may find the facts fubject to the opinion of the Court upon the law. But, upon the reafon of the thing, and the eternal principles of juftice, the jury ought not to affume the jurifdiction of law: they do not know, and are not prefumed to know, any thing of the matter; they do not underftand the language in which it is conceived, or the meaning of the terms; they have no rule to go by but their paffions and wifhes. It is faid if a man give a right fentence upon hearing one fide only, he is a wicked Judge, becaufe he is right by chance only, and has neglected taking the proper method to be informed: fo a jury who ufurp the judicature of law, though they happen to be right, are themfelves wrong, becaufe they are right by chance only, and have not taken the conftitutional way of deciding the queftion. It is the

duty

duty of the Judge, in all cafes upon general iffues, to tell the jury how to do right, though they have it in their power to do wrong, which is a matter between God and their own confciences. To be free, is to live under a Government by law. The liberty of the prefs confifts in printing without any previous licence, fubject to the confequence of law. The licentioufnefs of the prefs is *Pandora's* box, the fource of every evil. Miferable is the condition of individuals, dangerous is the condition of the State, if there is no certain law, or (which is the fame thing) no certain adminiftration of law to protect individuals, or to guard the State. Jealoufy of leaving the law to the Court, as in other cafes, is, *now*, in the prefent ftate of things, puerile rant and declamation. The Judges are totally independent of the Minifters that may happen to be, and of the King; their temptation is rather to the popularity of the day; and I agree with the obfervation cited at the bar from Mr. Juftice Fofter, that a popular Judge is an odious and pernicious character. The judgment of the Court is not final: In the laft refort it may be reviewed in the Houfe of Lords, where the opinion of all the Judges is taken. In oppofition to this, what is contended for? that the law fhall be in every particular caufe what any 12 men, who fhall happen to be the Jury, fhall be inclined to think; liable to no review, and fubject to no control, under all the prejudices of the popularity of the day, and under all the bias of intereft in this town, where thoufands, more or lefs, are concerned in the publication of newfpapers, paragraphs, and pamphlets. Under fuch an adminiftration of law no man could tell, no counfel could advife, whether a paper were or were not punifhable. I am glad that I am not bound to fubfcribe to fuch an abfurdity, fuch a folecifm in politics; but that, agreeably to the uniform judicial practice fince the Revolution, warranted by the fundamental principles of the conftitution of trials by jury, and upon the reafon and fitnefs of the thing, I am of opinion this motion fhould be rejected, and the rule difcharged.

But the judgment was afterwards arrefted on a defect in the indictment.

SHERRINGTON *and* BULKLEY'S CASE.

The prisoners were indicted on the statute 21 Geo. III. cap. 68, for stealing a quantity of lead affixed to the WORK-HOUSE of the Poor of the Old Artillery-Ground ; and the property was laid to belong to " *the Trustees of the Poor of the Old Artillery-Ground.*"

By an act of Parliament passed 14 Geo. III. cap. 30. certain persons therein named, and their successors, to be elected and appointed under and by virtue of the said act, are appointed Trustees for putting in execution all the powers thereby given for providing a work-house, and for employing and maintaining the poor of the said Old Artillery-Ground, or any matter or thing concerning the same ; and all *fixtures*, furniture, and other things bought or provided for the use of the poor, are vested in the said Trustees and their successors, for the purposes of the act. And then it goes on in these words : " And the said Trustees are " hereby empowered to prefer or order the preferring of " any bill or bills of indictment against any person or per- " sons who shall steal, take, or carry away any or any part " of such things ; and the monies and things which shall " be so stolen, taken, or carried away, shall, in every such " indictment, be laid and deemed, and taken to be the pro- " perty of *the Trustees of the Poor of the Old Artillery-Ground.* " And every indictment so preferred shall be held good in " law to all intents and purposes."

The question was, Whether the indictment had well laid the property? And the Court held that it had not ; for as the Act of Parliament had not incorporated the Trustees, and by that means given them collectively *a public name*, the property should have been laid as belonging to A. B. C. &c. by their proper names, and the words " *Trustees of the Poor of the Old Artillery-Ground*" subjoined as a description of the capacity in which they were autho-rised by the legislature to act.

THE

THE
LAWYER'S
AND
MAGISTRATE'S MAGAZINE.
For MARCH, 1790.

Adjudged Cafes in the Courts at Weftminfter in Michaelmas Term.

HIGH COURT OF CHANCERY, MICH. 29 GEO. III.

Fox *againſt* MACKRETH, DAWES, *and* GARFORTH, *Eſqꝛs*.

A truſtee for the ſale of eſtates for payment of debts who pur-
chaſes himſelf, and, previous to the completion of his contract,
ſells the eſtate at an advanced price, is a truſtee for the original
vendor for the produce of the ſecond ſale.

C A S E.

THE plaintiff Fox, being ſeiſed in tail of an eſtate in
Surrey, ſubject to an eſtate for life, in ſome parts
thereof, to his mother for her jointure, and likewiſe ſeiſed of
copyhold and leaſehold eſtates in the ſame county, and alſo
entitled to ſeveral other eſtates in expectancy or for life only,
had, before he came of age, embarked in a very expenſive
courſe of life, and was reduced to great diftreſſes, and, under theſe circumftances, had procured money by granting
annuities; and engaging his friends, who were of age, in
bonds and judgments, for ſecuring the payment of them,
his friends propoſed that, as ſoon as might be after he
ſhould attain his age of 21 years, he ſhould ſuffer a recovery
of the Surrey eſtate, which ſhould be conveyed to truſtees to
be ſold, for the payment of his debts, and redeeming the an-

VOL. I.   G   nuitie

nuities for which he and his friends had engaged.   He attained his age of 21 in August 1777, and was, very soon afterwards, introduced to the defendant Mackreth, and, on account of the plaintiff's inability to make a security by mortgage, as a recovery could not be suffered till Michaelmas Term, it was agreed, that the defendants, Mackreth and Dawes, should supply the plaintiff with the sum of 5,100l. upon the plaintiff's granting two annuities of 500l. and 350l. each for his life.   Dawes, on the 23d of September, advanced the 5,100l. for which the following securities were executed.   A bond of that date by the plaintiff, in the penal sum of 6000l. for securing to the defendant Dawes an annuity of 500l. for the life of the plaintiff, a warrant of attorney of even date to confess judgment on the said bond, and an indenture *tripartite*, between the plaintiff on the 1st part, Dawes of the 2d part, and Garforth, of the 3d part, whereby lands in the county of York, of which the plaintiff was seised for life, were conveyed to Garforth, for securing the payment of the annuity of 500l. to Dawes. The annuity of 350l. was secured by a similar bond of the same date, warrant of attorney to confess judgment thereon, and a similar conveyance of the same lands to Garforth, for better securing the same.   In the annuity of 500l. Mackreth admitted he was interested with Dawes, but denied that he was so in that of 350l.   In Michaelmas Term 1777, a recovery was suffered of the freehold part of the Surrey estates, by which they were vested (subject to the mother's estate for life in a part thereof) in Oliver Farrer, in trust to convey the same in such manner as the plaintiff should direct, Mr Farrer having agreed to act as a trustee for the purpose of selling the same and discharging the debts, under the direction of two of the plaintiff's friends (which appear to have been Lord Ligonier and Lord Grantley), if they could be prevailed upon to accept the trust.   In December 1777, the plaintiff, being threatened with an arrest for the sum of 2000l. applied to the defendant Mackreth, who agreed to lend the plaintiff 3000l. on mortgage of the Surrey estate; upon which the mortgage-deeds, dated 22d and 23d of this month, were accordingly prepared and executed. At the time of the execution of these deeds, it was proposed that defendant Mackreth should be a trustee with Farrer, for payment of the debts and redeeming the annuities, when the defendant Mackreth proposed the defendant Dawes for that purpose, as being, from the course of his business, well acquainted with many of the persons who had purchased the plaintiff's other annuities, and could assist in purchasing them at a cheaper rate than Mr. Farrer; which was

af

affented to by the plaintiff, upon an affurance that nothing fhould be done without Mr. Farrer being confulted, and approving thereof. In the fame month the plaintiff delivered to the defendant Mackreth, a particular or rental of the eftate in Surrey, made by Thomas Jackman; by which it appeared, that the rents of the houfes and cottages on the premiffes amounted to 283 l. 1 s. and thofe of the lands to 979 l 14 s. (fubject to the mother's jointure, which was ftated at 240 l. a year); and the timber was valued in the rental at 4000 l. and the whole was valued at 45,000 l. It was alfo in evidence, that Mackreth fent down a man, of the name of Hampton, to view the eftate, who was there a week; but what valuation he made, or whether the fame was communicated to Mackreth, did not appear. A truft-deed was prepared by Garforth, reciting the mortgage, by which the eftates were conveyed to Mackreth and Dawes (fubject to Mackreth's mortgage and the annuity to Dawes), in truft to fell or mortgage the fame, and to pay the debts, and redeem the annuities granted by the plaintiff. Thefe deeds being fent to Mr. Farrer, he made fome objections thereto, on account of the fums advanced, as the prices of the annuities, not being fcheduled as grofs fums carrying intereft at 5 *per cent.* and alfo on account of the truftees being impowered to fell or mortgage the eftates without the intervention of Mr. Fox. And it being afterwards agreed, that Mackreth fhould pay off Dawes, and advance fome further fums, a deed-poll was prepared, calculated for execution on the 16th of January, 1778, and indorfed on the mortgage-deed, to fecure fuch further fum of 7000 l. (confifting of 5,100 l. the confideration-money for the annuities granted by the plaintiff to Dawes, with 212 l. 10 s. intereft thereon, for the quarter's arrear due 23d December, 1777, but which was not paid by Mackreth to Dawes until 16th Jan. 1778) and 51 l 14 s. 9½ d. 23 days arrear of the faid annuities from 23d December to faid 16th January, and 1635 l. 15 s. 2¼ d. paid to the plaintiff on that 16th January, 1778; a new truft-deed was alfo prepared, in which this deed poll was recited, and the 3000 l. and 7000 l. made the firft charges on the eftates. On the 16th January, 1778, the plaintiff Fox and the defendant Mackreth dined together at the houfe of the defendant Garforth, for the purpofe of executing thefe deeds; and, after dinner, and before the plaintiff had executed the deeds, a converfation arofe, in which it was propofed that the defendant Mackreth fhould become the purchafer of the eftate; and Jackman's valuation of 45,000 l was mentioned by the plaintiff as a fair price, which was objected to by Mackreth, confidering the value put thereby upon the houfes and lands ; upon which the defendant made a calculation of the houses at fourteen years purchase, and the lands at thirty; together with the houshold furniture, valued at 500 l. and the timber at 4000 l. (on which last two articles they agreed) amounting to 37,853 l. 14 s. The plaintiff afterwards offered to sell the estates to the defendant for 42,000 l. upon which the defendant said, he would split the difference, and give 39,500 l. for the same, but would not give more ; and, the plaintiff not agreeing to accept the terms, the trust-deeds were then executed by the plaintiff. After the deeds were executed, the conversation was renewed ; and the plaintiff expressing some concern with respect to his mother's jointure, in case he should accept the defendant's terms, the defendant offered the 39,500 l. and to subject himself to the payment of the plaintiff's mother's jointure, in case she should survive him ; upon which the parties agreed; and the defendant Garforth (who had been absent during the greatest part of the treaty) was called in, and drew up a memorandum of such agreement, by which the money was to be paid on or before the 25th of March next, till which time the plaintiff was to receive the rents and profits, and then convey the estate to the plaintiff; and about 12 o'clock at night, this memorandum was signed by the plaintiff, upon which the trust deed was cancelled. On the 28th of the same month, articles for the purchase were executed by both parties. On the 24th April following, the plaintiff, and Anna Fox his mother, on the 2d of May, executed conveyances of the estates to the defendant, in consideration of 39,500 l. ; 11,097 l. of which was retained by the defendant, in payment of the above mortgage of 3000 l. the 7000 l. secured by the deed-poll, and some other sums charged by the defendant, as advanced to the plaintiff, and the defendant gave the plaintiff, as a security for the residue, being 28,408 l. a common accountable receipt; and afterwards, on the objection of the plaintiff, to this as the only security for the money, the defendant wrote on the same piece of paper, which contained the said accountable receipt, the following charge, " 25th April, 1773, I do hereby charge " all my estates in the county of Surrey, with the payment " of the above sum of 28,403 l and interest." At the time of signing the above, the defendant had no estates in the county of Surrey, but those purchased by him of the plaintiff. And the defendant gave to the plaintiff no other security for the residue of the money, than the receipt and charge. In the interval between the execution of the articles and that of the conveyances, Mackreth had treated with Thomas Page, Esq. for the sale of the whole of the said

estate ;

eftate; and on the 21ft March, Mr. Page agreed to give 50,500 l. for the fame, but no article was entered into between him and the defendant till the 30th April following; immediately after, Page was let into poffeffion, and was to receive the rents and profits from Lady-day then laft. The treaty with Page was totally unknown to the plaintiff, when he executed the conveyance to the defendant. The plaintiff drew upon the defendant for feveral fums, on account of the purchafe-money; and in October, 1778, having fent for an account, the defendant drew one out, by which he made a balance remaining in his hands of 773 l. 18 s. 9 d. but admitted in his anfwer that he had therein charged monies unpaid, as the fuppofed amount of two annuities and the arrears thereof then unredeemed; and that, afterwards, in May, 1779, having then fettled the faid annuities, he fent the plaintiff another account, in which he made the balance 616 l. 17 s. above the other balance of 773 l. 18 s 9 d. In June, 1779, the plaintiff, being again in diftrefs, applied to the defendant, when he advanced him 2,100 l. a year, for plaintiff's life, fecured by a bond, in the penal fum of 4,200 l. and warrant of attorney to enter up judgment.

Upon difcovery of the fale to Page, under the circumftances as ftated above, the plaintiff filed his bill, infifting that the defendant Mackreth being a truftee for him under the truft deed for payment of debts, it was his duty to fell the fame for the advantage of the plaintiff.

The defendant, Mackreth, by his anfwer, infifted on the fairnefs of the tranfaction; and that the price at which he bought the eftate was an adequate price, though he expected to have fome benefit by felling it out in parcels; but that the purchafer, Mr. Page, having an eftate in the neighbourhood, gave a larger price than it was worth to other perfons.

The caufe was heard at the Rolls, before Sir Lloyd Kenyon; when his Honour was pleafed to make his decree, that undue advantage was taken, by the defendant Mackreth, of the confidence repofed in him by the plaintiff Fox; and that therefore the defendant Mackreth ought to be confidered as a truftee to all the eftates and interefts comprifed in the conveyance of the 23d and 24th days of April, 1778, for the faid plaintiff Fox, after the execution of the faid deeds; and ordered it to be referred to the Mafter to take an account of the money received by the defendant Mackreth, from Page, and to compute intereft thereon at 5 l. per cent. from the time of receiving the fame, and to take an account of the money paid by defendant Mackreth to Dawes, on account of the annuities of 500 l. and 300 l. and alfo an

account

account of the money advanced by Mackreth, on account of the annuity of 350 l. in 1779, and an account of money received by Mackreth, on account of the mortgage in 1778, and under the contract for the purchase of the estate, and compute interest on the same; and that the defendant Mackreth should pay the plaintiff the costs of the suit, in respect of his insisting on the conveyance of the 23d and 24th of April, 1778, as a conveyance for his own benefit; and granted an injunction against the defendant Mackreth, to restrain him from proceeding at law, touching any matter in question in the cause; and reserved further consideration.

From this decree, the defendant appealed to the Lord Chancellor, before whom the Case was fully argued, and his Lordship delivered his opinion as follows:

The doubt I have is, whether this case affords facts from which principles arise to set aside this transaction, which will not, by necessary application, draw other cases into hazard. And, without insisting upon technical morality, I don't agree with those who say that where an advantage has been taken in a contract, which a man of delicacy would not have taken, it must be set aside; suppose, for instance, that *A.* knowing there to be a mine in the estate of *B.* of which he knew *B.* was ignorant, should enter into a contract to purchase the estate of *B.* for the price of the estate, without considering the mine, could the Court set it aside? Why not, since *B.* was not apprised of the mine, and *A.* was? Because *B.* as the buyer, was not obliged, from the nature of the contract, to make the discovery. It is therefore essentially necessary, in order to set aside the transaction, not only that a great advantage should be taken, but it must arise from some obligation in the party to make the discovery. The court will not correct a contract, merely because a man of nice honour would not have entered into it; it must fall within some definition of fraud; the rule must be drawn so as not to affect the general transactions of mankind. His Honour has referred a great number of accounts to the Master. If the account in the present case is necessary to lead to the judgment, the latter should have been suspended till the former was taken. I shall state the case merely as it stands on the transaction upon the day of the sale; I shall also consider that there are certain terms which I must find in analogy to the character of a juryman. In the first place, I must find the value of the estate to be the sum for which it was sold to Page; for it will be in vain to argue that there was any confidence reposed in Mackreth, or fraud committed by him, if no loss accrued to Fox. If the value of the estate be that which Mackreth gave, it would on that side

put an end to the dispute. If the value be such as now
represented, that does not make an end of the matter, unless the advantage was procured by some of those frauds
which the court has taken notice of. The Master of the
Rolls has decreed the defendant to be a trustee for Fox. He
becomes such by consequence; for if it be true that he has
cheated Fox, though the legal estate passed to him, the equitable claim is Fox's. But this argument does not turn from
the mere circumstances of value, for suppose the estate to
have been worth 50,000 l. on the 16th January 1778, and
that Mackreth bought it by fraud for 40,000 l. whereby Fox
was cheated of 10,000 l. and suppose, by cross events, the
value had sunk more than one-fifth, and Mackreth had sold
it, according to the then market-price, at 40,000 l. or even so
low as 30,000 l. would it not be equally true, that he ought
to be decreed to pay 50,000 l. for the sum due, in respect
of what Fox lost by the fraud of Mackreth? And if you
can ever establish in a court of equity, that a contract has
been fraudulently made, and that a party to that contract
has lost by that fraud, in the common case, whatever the
conveyance be, the party will have that money to pay.——
Therefore his Honour went upon the ground, that the value
of the estate at the time of the sale was 50,000 l. that Mr.
Fox was consequently cheated, and, the contract being to
be set aside, the sale made afterwards was a sale made for him
who had in point of equity a right to it. Taking this as the
point on which it turns, I wish to go through the facts.
Fox's distresses began about four years before he came of
age: he had involved himself and his friends in annuities
upon the harshest terms. When he came of age, as a man
of honour, he was under a duty of imperfect obligation, to
relieve the friends he had involved. In this situation, which
was observed by his friends, before he became of age, a plan
was proposed, to sell such part of his estate as was dis-
posable. When he came of age, he had an estate of about
1260 l. a-year, in Surrey, that was an estate tail, capable consequently of being disposed of when the time for cutting off
the intail should arrive. He had also an estate in Yorkshire,
of about 11,000 l. a-year for life, and one in Ireland, for
life, of which he was in possession of about 6000 l. a-year.
His friends had resorted to a man of character in the profession to conduct the disposal of the Surrey estate. On the
23d August, 1777, no steps had been taken, even to get in
the amount of the debts, or negociating with the annuitants
for an accommodation of their demands; though it must occur to every body, that before he came of age would have
been the best time for arranging those contracts, and conversing

versing with the annuitants about arranging that circumstance. He came of age in August, and, upon the 23d of
September, it appears he had been introduced to Mackreth;
the terms they were then upon were not confidential.   Fox
applied to Mackreth to raise 3000 l. and informed him of his
situation, and that no security could be made him, till the
next term, when a recovery might be suffered.   Mackreth
then proposed an annuity at six years purchase (something
near half less than the actual value); after that, a man cannot talk of any delicacy without the bars of the court of
justice.   If a court of justice is bound to affirm such transactions, it is not from its approbation of them, but because
it would be impolitic and distressful to the general affairs of
mankind to cut them down.   When that situation was disclosed to Mackreth, a mortgage of that estate would have
been an effective lien upon it; and the way to have made
a security would have been, to have insured his life till the
end of next Michaelmas Term.   Under that species of contract, the merciful and just manner of relieving his distress
would have been, to have advanced the money on such
mortgage.   On the other hand, it ought to be observed
that though Mackreth took a different course with him, it
seems to have been (if there is not too much levity in saying it) in *the course of his business*, for it is in evidence that
Mackreth dealt in this way, on the distresses of mankind.
On the 6th of November a recovery was suffered of the
Surrey estate to Farrer, to such uses as Fox should direct,
but nothing was then done towards getting rid of the debt.
On the 24th of December, Fox sends to borrow a sum of
money; Mackreth lent him 3000l. and took a mortgage by
way of security.   Great pains have been taken to impute
great generosity to Mackreth on this occasion.   I see no reason to say so; neither do I see that there was at that time
any plot; on the contrary, I consider that as a very fair
transaction; and it would be an extravagant conjecture for
a Court of Justice to suppose that the object of lending him
that, was to get the legal estate into his hands, to tamper
with it afterwards, to the prejudice of Mr. Fox.   When
once one gets beyond the evidence that is before the Court,
there is no end to conjecture.   Mackreth then acquiesced
with the project of delivering Fox from his distresses, and
industriously offered himself and Dawes as trustees, for that
purpose, I do not agree, that, by that, there was any plot
to get him into bad hands.   There are no better men for
trustees, on such an occasion, than those who will do the
business.   And though Lord Ligonier and Lord Grantley
were proposed on the part of Fox, yet the others, as men of
bu-

bufinefs, might be quite as proper. When Mackreth propofed himfelf as a truftee, I think he meant what he faid,
and that there was a real act of friendfhip intended, to make
the moft of the eftate, and to deal to the beft advantage with
the annuitants. An aukward circumftance is, that himfelf
and Dawes were of that number, Mackreth himfelf to the
amount of 250l. and Dawes of 600l. a-year; thefe being
850l. and I fuppofe there being five or fix times that quantity on the whole. When he undertook to deal with thefe
annuitants at large, and himfelf in the number, he certainly took upon himfelf a very delicate charge. The manner in which he dealt for this annuity, was to confider the
arrears which had been incurred, from the 23d September
to the 23d December gone, as due to the annuitant, and
then he was to take up that fum at the original price, fo
that nothing more was to be paid for the annuity but an arrear that had been incurred after the rate of 850 l. a-year,
which was a little more than 200l. to take up that, and,
when he had done fo, that annuity was to be difcharged.——
I do not approve of that——Who can poffibly fuppofe Mr.
Mackreth, recommending himfelf to Mr. Fox as a man
who would deal more vigilantly with annuitants than another, and, in the firft inftance, allowing the annuity to ftand
for an arrear which had gone only for a quarter, I think he
fhould have confidered it as a loan from the beginning.——
So of Dawes's fhare of the annuity, it fhould have been
confidered as difcharged on the 24th December: he bought,
however, on the part of Mr. Fox, but with his own money.
Upon the 16th of January, inftead of confidering it as an
annuity difcharged on the 24th of December, he confiders
it as bought up for his own ufe, and therefore he was to
continue an annuitant of Fox, after he had bought it of
Dawes, to the 16th of January. It is impoffible to fay he
has not in this gone a little further than that fpecies of indelicacy which a court will look at; for he fhall not have the
annuity till January, it fhall be confidered as difcharged in
December; and yet, from the manner in which he has
dealt with the annuitant, in general, it feems to me as if he
thought this a fair way of dealing between man and man
in that market, and I fhould have thought fo univerfally,
had I not obferved that in regard to one of the annuities,
he has compromifed it at a lower rate than that; and inftead of regarding the annuity as due, as to the principal
fum, and the arrears due, which is the manner he charged
it in October, 1778, it turns out that he had bought it below that rate, although he had charged Fox, in October,
1778, up to the rate as if he had made the bargain fairly
with

with the annuitant.—In thefe two inftances his conduct muft be refcinded, and he has acted unfairly in the execution of the truft he had taken upon him. Mr. Fox, the plaintiff, has therefore the advantage of finding Mr. Mackreth dealing with him refpecting himfelf, as a man who would ferve him with fidelity, though he had an intereft himfelf, and acting unjuftly in a manner which a court of juftice muft refcind. From hence, till the 16th January, I confider him as a truftee, and whatever confequences arife from that relation, muft belong to this bufinefs. He fends down an agent (Hampton) to value the eftate, and he has managed fo as to prevent the court from looking much at what was done in confequence of the orders which were given to Hampton. Courts of juftice are to act temperately; but muft confider what is the refult from the feveral parts of a tranfaction. On one fide it is faid that he fent down the agent to value the eftate, as meaning to treat himfelf: but I think the fair conftruction is, that he fent him in the character of a truftee. He was beginning to act as fuch with an intention to fell the eftate at the beft advantage, therefore it was part of the execution of the truft. Hampton's knowledge was Fox's knowledge. But wherever a truftee gains intelligence as a truftee and fervant to the *ceftui que truft*, and conceals the circumftances he fo gains knowledge of from the *ceftui que truft*, he may have the hands of a Court of Juftice laid upon him as a fraud. I find myfelf at a lofs as to what paffed between Mackreth and Hampton; he went down twice; the firft time he was there a week, the latter time longer; but the refult of the intelligence he got the fecond time, could not be of any ufe. The intelligence he got the firft time, was communicated to Mackreth. In thefe circumftances he begins to deal with him, and there alfo he remains in the character of a truftee. Fox had a valuation of the eftates, by Jackman, not a long one, but fuch as afforded general terms, fuch as the naming a grofs value of the eftates, and the number of years value fet upon them. This Fox had in his hands, and, with this valuation *in medio* Fox infifts that the value of the eftate is 45,000l. Mackreth reafons, and afferts firft, that the houfes are valued too high, that he would only give $\frac{14}{28}$ of the value, he offering 14 years purchafe for them—That he will not give 30 years purchafe for the land; he will only give 28 or 29 years purchafe; that he looked upon the valuation of the copyhold part of the Horfely eftate as much too high. He argues upon them, and haggles Fox down, till, either from conviction, or from the confideration of his circumftances, they meet at 39,000l. The queftion arifing on this

is,

is, whether the character of truftee fhall vary Mackreth from a ftranger; for it is not argued that in the cafe of a ftranger treating in the fame manner, the tranfaction muft be cut down. If a truftee treats with a ftranger as a truftee for himfelf, ever fo fairly, the vendee would be a truftee for the firft *ceftui que truft*, and the Court will not confider whether the confideration was fair or not, which muft be by reafon of the confidence which the accident of their relation introduced; then the queftion is, whether I can find, as a juryman, that Fox agreed to the propofal in confidence of Mackreth's knowledge and integrity. If a ftranger had faid to Fox, I will deal fairly with you, and, afterwards, mifreprefented the value, I fhould hold that to be an abufe of a confidence which he was bound to obferve. Was that the cafe here? I confefs I am in doubt; I do not fee that I have facts from which to draw that inference. But if Mackreth had not the character of truftee, he might retain that of confidential friend. I am at a lofs to find that. They feem to have dealt as men ufually do, each endeavouring to reprefent the cafe as makes beft for his own intereft. There are two facts to be fettled: firft, what was the real value: nobody will think Mackreth's criticifms on Jackman's valuation unnatural or unfair. There is evidence that Jackman would have given the money at which he eftimated the eftate, if he had had it; that it was fold to Page for more, which is ftrong evidence to fhew that the value was more. Suppofe it to be allowed, that the real value was what Page paid; let us fee what followed: on the 16th of January, Garforth put the agreement into writing, and it was figned by both parties. This ftruck me as fhewing an eagernefs to have the matter fixed; but, from the evidence, it appears that the article for the fale was not entered into till the day after, when they carried it to one degree more of formality. It ftands upon the articles till the 24th of April. In the mean time, Mackreth had fold the eftate. No man of delicate honour would have carried the contract into execution on the 24th of April, after he had fold the eftate on the 20th of March, and have kept that tranfaction a fecret. He was obliged, by every call of honour, to confider himfelf as a truftee; but I fear that if I fhould lay down the rule, that the court will compel whatever a man of ftrict honour would do, I fhould go too far, and might lay down a rule which would be inconvenient in other cafes. Obfervations are made on the note given by Mackreth to Fox; it was an accountable receipt, bearing 5 *per cent*. intereft. Fox had not the money. I think this, as Mackreth was to apply it in the payment of annuitants, was fair. The fecurity,

curity, being only that of an equitable lien, does not afford any inference of fraud being intended; and, in fact, the money has been paid. The method of making up the account has been urged as a mark of confidence. It is true, it is so; but the question is, whether it was a confidence that he would give him a fair value. As to the confirmations, they follow so naturally from the occasions, that they cannot be said to have been sought for by way of obtaining confirmations.—With regard to confirmations, they have been confidered different ways. In Chefterfield v. Janssen, it turned upon Spenser doing the acts with his eyes open.—There he ftood liable to the former bond; but there is another way in which confirmations operate, that the party looks upon himfelf to have been dealt fairly with. In January, Fox did not confider himfelf as having had an unfair advantage taken of him. In that view it goes further, for there was no complaint till 1781. It is fair to infer, that fo large a difference of value was not expected in fo long a time. When would a transaction of this fort be at an end, if not after three years? And it would have lafted in the fame way till 1800, had not the difcovery been made of the fubfequent fale. It goes much to the queftion of the real value, that it could not be fixed till a fubfequent fale. If the price paid by Page was accidental, no man could argue from that to there being a fraud in Mackreth. It muft be afcertained what was the real value of the eftate at the time of the fale. Evidence of this has been given only on one fide, Mackreth having been advifed to fhew that contract, which leads to a confideration how far it would be conducive to the queftion to have that part further enquired into; it would put an end to the queftion on one fide, on the other it would leave it open. I have been defirous of ftating my doubts, becaufe poffibly I may think it neceffary to have this undergo a further confideration. After converfing with his Honour, and near half the Judges, a doubtfulnefs and difference of opinion has arifen as to the policy of laying down the rule, either of law or evidence to the extent now contended for I own I hefitate to lay down any fuch rule on the fubject. It is of no ufe to lay down the rule of law, if the rule of evidence is left indefinite. Two ways have ftruck me; one, to let this matter go to a further enquiry; the other, to which I have been more inclined, to have it re-heard, with the affiftance of thofe who will furnifh me with the means of laying down the rule which may fet men at eafe for their property, that, when they obferve a transaction for the fale of an eftate cut down for inadequacy of value, after it

has

has been affirmed by conveyances, and acquiesced in for three years and a half, I may know how I can state such a case as mankind shall understand, without putting them in fear with respect to the regulation of their property.

The Lord Chancellor on a following day said :—I have considered of the case of Fox *v.* Mackreth, and have examined it very much; I have read over all the arguments; my opinion is not varied since I spoke of it at large; I cannot see that the decree is wrong, and therefore it must be

Affirmed.

But the defendant has appealed to Parliament.

GOODRIGHT *on the Demise of* HALL *against* RICHARDSON.

This was an ejectment tried in Surrey, where a verdict was found for the lessor of the plaintiff, subject to the opinion of the Court; and the question was, whether a lease granted of the premises " *for and during the full end and term* " *of three, six, or nine years,* from the Feast of St. Thomas " next ensuing the date, and to be fully complete and ended " on the said Feast of St. Thomas, *which shall be determinable* " *in the years* 1788, 1791, 1794," is to be considered as a lease for *nine* years, determinable on proper notice at the end of three and six years.

It was argued for the plaintiff, that *certainty* was essential to the existence of every Term; and though this lease was good as to the first three years, it was void for the rest, from the uncertainty. And Lord Mansfield, in the Case of *Ferguson* and *Cornish* *, which was the case of a lease for seven, fourteen, or twenty-one years, said it was a good lease for the seven years, whatever might be the validity of the two eventual terms.

LORD KENYON, C. J.—There is no doubt of what Lord Mansfield's opinion would have been in *Ferguson* v. *Cornish,* as to the validity of the lease, beyond the first seven years. In these cases, the intention of the parties ought to prevail, if it be not contrary to law. It is true that there must be a certainty in the lease, as to the commencement and duration of the term: but that certainty need not be ascertained at the time; for if in the fluxion of time a day will arrive which will make it certain, that is sufficient. As if a lease be granted for twenty-one years after three lives in being; though it is uncertain at first when that term will

* (*Burroughs,* 1034.)

com-

commence, becaufe thofe lives are in being ; yet, when they die, it is reduced to a certainty ; and *id certum eft quod certum reddi poteft :* and fuch terms are frequently created for raifing portions for younger children. Now in this cafe, it is impoffible to form any doubt refpecting the intention of thefe parties. It was intended that this leafe fhould take effect for three years, at all events; and that it fhould be in the election of either of the parties to put an end to it at that time, or at the end of fix years, giving reafonable notice to the other. It is like a leafe for a year, and fo from year to year ; where, if the leffee wifh to determine it at the end of the year, he muft give reafonable notice to the other party. And though here either of the parties might have determined the leafe at the expiration of the firft three years, yet when the time elapfed, at which notice ought to have been given for that purpofe, the leafe could not be determined till the end of the next three years. Confequently, the leffor of the plaintiff is not entitled to recover.

ASHHURST, J.—All that is required is either that the term fhould be certain in itfelf, or reducible to a certainty. Now that is the cafe here ; for it is for three, fix, or nine years, as the cafe may happen ; the parties having agreed that it fhould be determinable in the years 1788, 1791, 1794. It is therefore a leafe for three years certain, or for fix, or nine years, unlefs the parties determine it fooner.

BULLER, J.—This is a leafe for nine years, determinable by either of the parties at the end of the firft three or fix years ; for it is ftated in the cafe that it is *determinable in the years* 1788, 1791 1794. But if it were not determined at either of thofe periods, the party firft giving reafonable notice, it was to continue for the nine years.

GROSE, J.—Of the fame opinion.

Poftea to the defendant.

ELLIS *again ft* HUNT, *and alfo againft* DAWES, *Affignee of* MOORE, *a Bankrupt.*

THIS was an action of trover, in which a verdict had been taken for the plaintiff, fubject to the opinion of the Court ; the Cafe was :

Moore, before the bankruptcy, ordered goods from the plaintiff at Sheffield ; the goods were fent by the carrier, and arrived at the carrier's inn in London, two days after Moore became bankrupt ; on their arrival there, the goods were attached by procefs of foreign attachment, out of the Mayor's Court of London, by a creditor of the bankrupt. The Meffenger

of

of the Commissioners, two days after, demanded the goods of the carrier, and put his mark upon them, but did not take them away. The plaintiff, then hearing of the bankruptcy, wrote to the carrier not to deliver the goods to the bankrupt, and, soon after, made a formal demand of them. The carrier refused to deliver them to the plaintiff, and afterwards, on the attachment being withdrawn, gave them up to the assignees of Moore.

It was contended, on the part of the plaintiff, that in case of insolvency, the consignor has a right to stop goods any time before they get into actual possession; that the letter to the carrier was a countermand of the delivery, and the bankruptcy is of itself a countermand, and these goods were never once out of the possession of the carrier.

LORD KENYON, C. J.—If any case had been decided to the extent of the plaintiff's argument, namely, that bankruptcy is of itself a countermand, the plaintiffs here would be entitled to recover: but that has never yet been decided. The doctrine of stopping goods *in transitu* is bottomed on the case of Snee *v.* Prescot, where Lord Hardwicke established a very wise rule, that the vendor might resume the possession of goods consigned to the vendee before delivery, in case of the bankruptcy of the vendee: on this all the other cases are founded. There have indeed been cases, where nice distinctions have been taken on the fact, whether the goods had or had not got into the possession of the vendee; but they all profess to go on the ground of the goods being *in transitu*, when they were stopped. As to the necessity of the goods coming to the " corporal touch" of the bankrupt; that is merely a figurative expression, and has never been literally adhered to. For there may be an actual delivery of the goods, without the bankrupt's seeing them; as a delivery of the key of the vendor's warehouse to the purchaser. In order to decide this case, it is material to attend to the dates; on the 24th of November, the provisional assignment was made to Wells, who, on the same day, demanded the goods in question of the defendant Hunt, *and put his mark on the cask.* Now it is said that this should have been done by the bankrupt himself; but by the assignment he was stripped of all his property, which was then vested in the provisional-assignee. Therefore, if a corporal touch were necessary to defeat the right of the vendors, it took place here. It is true that the provisional assignee did not alter the situation of the goods; but they were then arrived at the end of their destined journey, and deposited in a place where they would have remained till the bankrupt could

have

have carried them to a warehouse of his own. All this happened on the 24th of November; and it was not until the 28th of that month that the vendor wrote to countermand the delivery of the goods: but that was too late; for the goods were no longer *in transitu*; they were then in the possession of the party to whom they were configned, or of those who reprefented him. In cafes of this fort, we cannot but feel for the fituation of the manufacturer; but it is fuch as they are neceffarily fubject to from their mode of dealing: however, the feverity of the cafe cannot induce us to break through the rule of law.

ASHHURST, J.—The leaning of my mind would be in favour of the plaintiff; but the law will not allow him to be in a better fituation than the reft of the bankrupt's creditors. The general rule is, that the confignor has a right to flop the goods, if he can, before they get into the actual poffeffion of the bankrupt. But here, before the plaintiffs thought of countermanding the goods in queftion, the provifional affignee, who then flood in the place of the bankrupt, had actually taken poffeffion of them, and put his mark on them.

BULLER, J.—I am not difpofed to difturb or to leffen the authority of any of the cafes that have been decided on this fubject: but none of them could juftify the vendor in this cafe in taking back the goods. In the former cafes, the line has been precifely drawn; and they all turn on the queftion, whether or not there had been an *actual* delivery to the bankrupt. It is of the utmoft importance to adhere to that line; for if we break through it, we fhall endanger the authority of the cafes that have been already decided, and fhall fritter away the rule entirely. In one of the cafes cited, Lord Mansfield took the diftinction between an *actual* and a *conftructive* delivery to the vendee. There may be cafes where, as between the buyer and feller, if no bankruptcy or infolvency happen, the goods are confidered in the poffeffion of the buyer the inftant they go out of the poffeffion of the vendor: as if A. order goods from B. to be fent by a particular carrier at his own rifk, the delivery to the carrier is a delivery to the vendee to every other purpofe; but ftill, if he become a bankrupt before the carrier actually deliver them to him, I fhould hold that the vendor might feize them; becaufe that is only a *conftructive delivery* to the vendee: but an *actual delivery* is neceffary to deveft the vendor's right of ftopping the goods *in transitu*. It is clear that bankruptcy itfelf does not put an end to the contract; and if not, the right of the vendor to feize goods *in transitu* is founded only on equitable principles. It is a right, with
which

which he is indulged on principles of justice, originally
established in courts of equity, and since adopted in courts
of law. But, in order to avail himself of it, he must stop
the goods before they get into the actual possession of the
vendee. But in this case there is the strongest evidence of
the consignee's taking actual possession of the goods, by his
assignee putting his mark on them. It was said by the plaintiff's counsel, that the carrier would have been liable in an
action by the vendor: but he would not have been liable in
the character of carrier, for the goods had got to the end of
their destined journey; but he would have been liable only
as a warehouse-keeper, in respect of the recompence which
he was to receive for warehouse-room. But the instant the
provisional assignee put his mark on the goods, the ware-
house-man became the agent or servant to the bankrupt.

GROSE, J.—The general rule is perfectly clear that the
consignor may seize the goods in transitu, in case of the insolvency of the consignee, before they actually reach him.
The question therefore here is, whether, on the facts of this
case, the goods were, or were not, in transitu, when the
plaintiffs wrote to countermand the delivery of them. Now
it is stated as a fact, that before this letter arrived, the provisional assignee had put his mark upon the cask; and this
distinguishes it from the cases cited. When the goods were
marked, they were delivered to the consignee as far as the
circumstances of the case would permit; the assignee could
not then take them away, because they were at that time
under an attachment. After the mark was put on them,
they were no longer in transitu; and consequently the plaintiff's right to seize them was devested.

Postea to the defendants.

THE KING, v. IRELAND.

The statute 5 W. and M. cap. 11. § 3. enacts, that if a
defendant removing an indictment by *certiorari* into the
Court of King's Bench, shall be convicted thereon, the
Court shall give costs to the prosecutor; who, for the recovery of such costs, shall, *within ten days* after demand made,
and refusal of payment by the defendant, have an attachment
against him. The question in the present case was, Whether
the ten days must elapse before the attachment can be granted,
or whether the prosecutor is entitled to it immediately after
demand and refusal.

THE COURT said, the statute must be construed to mean that ten days must elapse after the demand made before an attachment be granted; otherwise the indulgence which the Legislature appears to hold out, could not exist.

Attachment refused.

BIGGS and others, v. LAWRENCE.

This was a rule to shew cause why there should not be a new trial. *Buller*, J. who tried the cause in *Cornwall*, reported that the action was for goods sold and delivered; the plaintiffs were partners, one of whom lived in *Guernsey*, the rest in England. The defendant, who lived in Cornwall, sent an order to the partner in Guernsey, for some brandy to be delivered to *Wood*, the master of a smuggling-vessel; and the goods were delivered in small casks fit for smuggling. Two questions arose on the trial:

1st. Whether Wood's written receipt for the goods was evidence of the delivery to the defendant.

2dly, Whether the plaintiffs could recover in this action, they being subjects of this country, and the contract made in contravention of the laws, namely with a view of smuggling the goods into England. Upon this ground, the plaintiffs were nonsuited.

It was now contended in favour of the rule, that the contract being completed in Guernsey, where such a contract was not illegal, brought it within the case of *Holman* v. *Johnson*, Cowp. 341.

And that the subsequent use made of the transaction will not affect the original contract, according to the case of *Robinson* v. *Bland*, 2 Burroughs, 1077.

LORD KENYON, C. J.—If the decision of this case had the least tendency to overturn that of *Holman* v. *Johnson*, I should certainly pause a little before I gave any opinion which might shake it. But I wish to leave the authority of that case unquestioned, because I approve of it. To the case of *Robinson* and *Bland* I also give my assent. The former of those cases was on a contract entered into by foreigners, bound by no allegiance to this country: and the latter was a contract made in France, which, being warranted both by the laws of that country and this, was carried into execution here. But in this case it is admitted, and the plaintiff's counsel was obliged to make the admission, that this must be considered as a contract made in England. But it has been insisted that no adjudged case is to be found, in which it has been determined that persons, standing

ing

ing in the situation of these plaintiffs, shall not recover. But similar cases have frequently occurred at *nisi prius*; and the reason why no solemn decisions are to be met with on the subject is, because the *nisi prius* determinations were thought too clear to be questioned. Where a contract is made for smuggled goods, a party cannot come into a court of justice to recover on it. A person suing in a court of law, must disclose a fair transaction; and it must not appear, from his own shewing at least, that he has infringed the laws of his country. Now here three of the plaintiffs lived in England; and it is clear that they knew, either personally, or (which is the same) by their agent, the other partner living at Guernsey, that the contract, which they had entered into, was made in direct contravention of the laws of their country; for the goods came under more than suspicious circumstances, since they were sent in slings, and half ankers, ready for smuggling: and it requires much argument to convince me that a contract thus made can be carried into execution in England. There is no *dictum* in favour of the plaintiff's right of action; and the whole string of cases, by analogy, is against it. Therefore I am of opinion that the non-suit ought to stand.

ASHHURST, J.—I form my opinion on this circumstance, that three of the plaintiffs lived in England; and therefore though the partner, with whom the contract was made, lived abroad, this case must be considered in the same light as if all the partners lived here. It is not necessary to determine whether a person, who sells goods in England, which are afterwards to be applied to an illegal purpose, can recover the price of them here. For, in this case, the goods were sold and delivered, not in England, but in Guernsey, and packed too in such a manner as to shew that they were intended for the purpose of smuggling. The plaintiffs were agents to the very act of smuggling; they were *participes criminis*, and therefore cannot avail themselves of the laws of this country in order to enforce a contract made in direct opposition to them.

BULLER, J.—This case must be considered as if it were a contract made between the plaintiffs and the defendant, all residing in this country, for the delivery of goods in Guernsey, for the purpose of smuggling them into England. And I use the latter expression because it is clear, from the manner in which they were packed at the time when they were delivered, that they were intended to be smuggled: that was the act of the plaintiffs. And I cannot say in a Court of Justice, that the plaintiffs, so offending against the law of

H 2 the

the land, shall be permitted to recover on such a contract. None of the cases cited apply to the present. That of *Holman* v. *Johnson*, went on the ground of the plaintiffs being foreigners, which materially distinguishes it from this; because the subjects of one country residing there are not bound to take notice of the revenue laws of any other. That maxim has been long since adopted here, and recognized by Lord Mansfield in *Holman* and *Johnson*. But this is the case of one of the king's subjects making a contract directly against the statute laws of this country. Neither has the case of *Petrie* v. *Hannay* any relation to the present: here the contract, on which the action is founded, is illegal; which was not so there. And in order to make this case like that, it is necessary to shew that these plaintiffs were not concerned in the original transaction, but afterwards paid money for the use of the defendant, which they wished to recover back; for there the money was paid to a person, who was not a partner in the original transaction; and the action was founded on the subsequent contract, and not on the stock-jobbing transaction.

GROSE, J. of the same opinion.

Mr. J. BULLER then said, that another objection had been made at the trial, that the plaintiffs ought not to be nonsuited, and that it should have been left to the jury to consider whether the plaintiffs knew the goods were to be smuggled; but that he had been of opinion that, as the counsel on both sides had fully argued the question of law on the admission of facts, the plaintiffs ought not to be at liberty to go to the jury on the same facts, when they found his opinion against them in point of law; to which the Court assented.

Rule discharged.

SOUTHALL, v. LEADBETTER.

This was a replevin for rent; and the action was brought with a view of trying the single question, whether the lessee of a repairing lease for 21 years, of a house at a peppercorn rent for the first half year, and at a rack-rent for the remaining term, having afterwards assigned his lease for a small *premium*, was liable to pay the moiety of the expence of a party-wall between this house and one adjoining, which wall was re-built by virtue of the statute of the 14th Geo. III. cap. 78, § 41; or whether the landlord who granted the lease is bound to pay the same.

The

The Jury found a verdict for the plaintiff, subject to the opinion of the Court on the question above-mentioned. The words of the statute are, " that the owner who shall be " intitled to *the improved rent* of the adjoining building shall " pay a proportion of the expence of rebuilding any party-" wall."

LORD KENYON, C. J.—The *improved rent* mentioned in this Act of Parliament stands contra-distinguished from *some other rent* ; but here no other rent was reserved but that at the granting of the lease. But it is said that the lessee received from his assignee *a sum in gross*, as the consideration for the purchase, which is equivalent to an *improved rent* : if indeed a large sum were paid for the purchase of a lease, though no improved rent were reserved to the original lessee, I think he would be liable to pay this expence within the act of parliament. But that is not the present case. For when Winter, the landlord, granted this lease, he reserved the best rent which could be procured for it at that time, since this rent exceeds the rent formerly reserved by 10 l. *per annum*, and the whole of the land-tax ; and the case ought not to be varied by the circumstance of the estate's gradually increasing in a small degree. Where the parties contract for a lease at rack-rent, the landlord is the person who ought to bear the expence of the party wall. Then it was contended that the full rent was not reserved originally, because it was stipulated that the tenant should lay out a considerable sum of money in improving the estate ; but it must also be remembered that, in consideration of that, the lessee was to pay no rent for the first half year ; which might have been considered at the time as commensurate with the sum to be laid out in the repairs. Neither is the lessee concluded by the covenant to pay the taxes, assessments, impositions, &c. for that only extends to the *land-tax*, and all other taxes *ejusdem generis :* but this is not a tax. Therefore the plaintiff in replevin is entitled to judgment, because he has overpaid the rent distrained for.

ASHHURST, J.—The Legislature intended to throw this burden on the lessees of building leases, by whom the value of the estates is considerably improved, and who afterwards make under leases, reserving improved rents. But here it does not appear that any greater rent was reserved to the first lessee than there was at the time of granting the lease.

BULLER, J.—The case which the Legislature had in view was where a small sum is reserved, as a ground-rent, on a long building lease ; and the lessee, in consequence of the improvement, underlets, reserving an improved rent. But here

here the plaintiff and defendant stand in the relation of landlord and tenant ; and in *Stone* v. *Greenwell*, Lord Mansfield
said, as the parties stood in the relation of landlord and tenant, the former was liable, under this Act of Parliament,
to pay this expence.

GROSE, J.—It does not appear to me that the statute is
merely confined to building leases ; the words of the act are
so framed as to comprehend other cases. The statute says,
that the owner of the *improved rent* shall pay : but in this
case there is only *one* rent reserved, and that is payable to
Winter ; he therefore is liable to pay this expence.

Postea to the plaintiff.

WRIGHT on the Demise of ANNE BURRIL and MARY BURRIL, v. KEMP.

On trial of an ejectment at the last York Assizes, a verdict
was taken for the plaintiff, subject to the opinion of the
Court on the following

CASE.

Samuel Burril, who was seised in fee according to the
custom of the manor of Skipsea of the estate in question,
on 1st of February, 1743, made a voluntary surrender of it
to the use of himself for life, and from and after his decease to the use of Elizabeth his wife during her widowhood ; and after his decease, and upon the marriage of Elizabeth, then to the use and behoof of William Wallis, son
to Elizabeth, for his natural life ; and from and after his decease to the use of the issue of his body lawfully to be begotten ; with a proviso that *in case William Wallis should die in
the life-time of the surrenderor, or without issue of his body,
then and thereupon all the surrendered premises should go to the
right heirs of the surrenderor* for ever. W. Wallis was the
natural son of S. Burril by E. Wallis, whom he afterwards
married ; and he and Elizabeth Burril both died in the life-
time of the surrenderor ; William Wallis left issue, the lessors
of the plaintiff, who have been admitted tenants ; and he
bequeathed the tuition and guardianship of the persons and
estates of the lessors of the plaintiff to his brother, J. Burril, by will dated 25th of April, 1767, and died in the
same year. S. Burril died the 3d of April, 1774. John,
who was the eldest legitimate son of his father Samuel, was
admitted tenant of the premises, as heir to his father, on
the 15th of May, 1775 ; under whom the defendant claims

as a purchafer for a valuable confideration, though with notice of the claim by Wallis's children, under the furrender
in February, 1743, and he has been alfo admitted.

LORD KENYON, C. J.—The queſtions here are, what was
the intention of the parties to the furrender, whether they
have expreſſed it in legal terms; and if fo, whether any
rule of law will be violated in giving effect to it?　There is
no doubt but that a furrender is confidered as a common law
conveyance, and is not entitled to the fame favourable conſtruction as a will.　And therefore, unlefs the furrenderor
in this cafe has uſed the language which will confer a legal
eſtate, it cannot be conferred.　In deeds, certain legal phrafes
muſt be uſed, in order to create certain eſtates; as the word
" heirs" to create a fee; and " heirs of the body" to create
an eſtate in tail.　But beyond that I would fay, with Lord
Hardwicke, that there is no magic in particular words, further than as they fhew the intention of the parties.　Now
here it is impoſſible to entertain any doubt: S. Burril furrendered the eſtate to the uſe of himfelf for life, then to his
wife during her widowhood; *then*, that is, in cafe her eſtate
for life is put an end to by doing this act, which he meant
to guard againſt, to his fon W. Wallis for life, and after
his deceaſe to the iſſue of his body.　Therefore I cannot
accede to what was faid by the defendant's counfel, that this
was a contingent remainder in W. Wallis; for it was
veſted: though I cautiouſly avoid faying what the limitation
to his iſſue is.　The furrender then proceeds to ſtate a provifo, that, in cafe W. Wallis fhould die in the life-time of
the furrenderor, *or* without iſſue of his body, the eſtate
fhould go to the right heirs of the furrenderor: and here
the queſtion arifes on the word " *or*."　Now there is no
doubt on the intention of the parties: and where fenfe requires it, there are many cafes to fhew that we may con-
ſtrue the word *or* into *and*, and *and* into *or*, 2 *Str.* 1175.
and 3 *Atk.* 390, in order to effectuate the intent of the parties.　Here, therefore, in order to give effect to the intention of the furrenderor, we muſt fay, that, when he uſed
the word *or*, he meant *and*.　And there is no cafe, in which
any difference has been made, as to this point, between a
will and a deed; when the Court are confidering how the
intention of the parties can be effected.　Then, without
deciding what intereſt the leſſors of the plaintiff have, at
all events they have a fufficient title to maintain this ejectment.

ASHHURST, J—The intention of the furrenderor muſt
prevail, unleſs it be contrary to any rule of law.　We muſt
collect

collect the intention of the parties in deeds as well as in
wills; to give effect to which the word or they in both cases
be equally construed into and.

BULLER, J.—In addition to the cases mentioned by my
Lord, there is another to the same effect in *Moor* 422,
where the words are, " if he die without issue or before
21, then over." The manifest intention of the surrenderor
was to reserve a life-estate to himself, then to his widow,
during her widowhood, and then to his son W. Wallis and
his issue: then the limitations must be moulded if possible,
to answer that intent.

GROSE, J.—There was also a like case of *Gubb* v. *Gubb*,
arising on a devise which came from Exeter; and, on a motion for a new trial, it was given up as a settled point.

Postea to the plaintiff.

DOE on the Demise of HELEN COMBERBACH and others, v. PERRYN, KNT.

A verdict on this ejectment was taken for the plaintiff,
subject to the opinion of the Court on the following

C A S E.

James Comberbach, being seised in fee, by will, dated
the 21st of May, 1756, (after bequeathing a leasehold estate
to R. Perryn, during his term and interest therein, and all
his personal estate in the manner therein mentioned,) de-
vised the premises in question to his niece Dor. Comberbach, wife of his nephew James Comberbach, for life, for
her separate use, with a power of leasing for any term not
exceeding seven years in possession, reserving the most improved rent; remainder to trustees to preserve contingent
remainders, remainder to all and every the children of Dor.
Comberbach, begotten, or to be begotten, on her body by
his nephew James Comberbach, and their heirs for ever, to
be equally divided between and among such children (if
more than one) share and share alike; but if only one child,
then to such only child and his or her heirs for ever,; and
for default of such issue to James Comberbach for life,
with power of leasing as before; remainder to trustees to preserve contingent remainders, and from and after the decease
of the survivor of James Comberbach and Dor. his wife,
without issue as aforesaid, to and among all and every the
children of his nephew Roger Comberbach, and of B. Perryn, respectively begotten, or to be begotten by them, on
the

the body or bodies of their respective wives, and to his
niece Eliz. Adams, and to the heirs of such children of E.
Adams respectively, in manner following; namely, one-
third part or share thereof (the same to be divided into three
equal shares or parts) to the child or children of his nephew
R. Comberbach, who should be living at his [the devisor's]
decease; and, if more than one, to be divided among them
equally share and share alike, and to the heirs of such child
and children respectively; one other third part thereof to
the child and children of his nephew B. Perryn, and who
should be living at the time of his [the devisor's] decease,
and to be divided among them (if more than one) share
and share alike, and to the respective heirs of such child and
children of the said B. Perryn; and the other remaining
third part to his niece Eliz. Adams, and the heirs of her
body lawfully to be begotten; remainder to his own right
heirs for ever; with like power of leasing to R. Comberbach
and B. Perryn during the minority of their children, and to
Eliz. Adams respectively, as they should be in actual possession, as was before given to Dorothy Comberbach; remainder to his own right heirs for ever. The will also
contained a devise of other premises specifically, and of all
other the real estate of the devisor to his nephew J. Adams
for life; remainder to trustees to preserve contingent remainders; remainder to all and every the children of James Adams,
equally to be divided between them (if more than one) share
and share alike, and to their heirs respectively; but if only
one, then to such only child, and to his or her heirs; and
for default of such issue to and among all and every the
children of his nephews R. Comberbach and B. Perryn, by
their respective wives, and to his niece Eliz. Adams, and
to the heirs of R. Comberbach's and B. Perryn's children, and his niece Eliz. Adams respectively, in manner
following; one third part to the child and children of R.
Comberbach, who should be living at the time of his [the
devisor's] decease, and to the heirs of such child and children respectively; one other third part to the child and
children of B. Perryn who should be living at the time of
his [the devisor's] decease, and to the respective heirs of
such child and children of B. Perryn, and the remaining
other third part to Elizabeth Adams, and *the heirs of her
body* lawfully to be begotten; remainder to the devisor's
right heirs for ever; with similar powers of leasing to James
Adams, when in possession, and to R. Comberbach and B.
Perryn during the minority of their children respectively,
and to Elizabeth Adams, when they should respectively
come

come into poſſeſſion ; and a deviſe of the reſidue and remainder of his eſtate real and perſonal to R. Comberbach, B. Perryn, and Elizabeth Adams, ſhare and ſhare alike.

The deviſor died in 1737, leaving Roger Comberbach his nephew, and heir at law ; who was alſo the heir at law of J. Comberbach and of the children of James and Dorothy Comberbach ; and under him the leſſors of the plaintiff claim. James Comberbach and Dorothy his wife were married in the life-time of the deviſor, but had not any iſſue at the time of his death: though in 1739 they had a daughter, who died in 1740 ; and in 1741 another daughter, who died in 1761, without iſſue ; and a ſon in 1742, who died in 1761, without iſſue. James Comberbach died in 1784, and Dorothy in 1786. Elizabeth Adams died ſoon after the deviſor, without having been married, and without doing any act to deſtroy the eſtate-tail limited to her by the will. The defendant claimed as one of the children of B. Perryn.

This ejectment was defended only for an undivided third part of the eſtates deviſed by James Comberbach to Dorothy Comberbach, with the remainders over in the will. And the queſtion reſerved for the opinion of the Court was, whether the plaintiff was entitled to recover that third part.

LORD KENYON, C. J.----After ſtating the will, and obſerving that the ſecond remainder to the right heirs of the deviſor had no meaning, proceeded thus ; The grounds on which this caſe has been argued on the part of the defendant, are thoſe on which we proceed in giving our judgment, namely, what is the general intention of the deviſor, and whether he has uſed words ſufficient in law to carry that intent into execution. In doing this, we are not to proceed on conjecture, but on the words of the will ; from the whole of which we are to endeavour to extract the fair meaning. There is no doubt but that legal formal words may be controlled by the context of the will ; but we ought not to reject the legal meaning of thoſe words, unleſs we are clear that, in ſo doing, we give effect to the deviſor's intention. Two points have been made for the defendant ; 1ſt, that the limitation to the children of Dorothy Comberbach only created an *eſtate tail* ; and, 2dly, but even if it gave them a *fee*, it was not to veſt in thoſe children on their reſpective births, but to remain in ſuſpenſe till the death of the ſurvivor of James and Dorothy Comberbach. And if the defendant be right in either of theſe points, he is entitled to our judgment.

In-

In the firſt place, then, do theſe words confer an eſtate-tail, or a fee, on Dorothy's children? The words are, " To all and every the children of Dorothy, begotten, or to be begotten, on her body by James Comberbach, *and their heirs for ever ; and for default of ſuch iſſue,* &c. then over." Now words more emphatical cannot be uſed to create a fee, than " to *A.* and his heirs for ever." Undoubtedly thoſe words may be controlled by ſubſequent ones ; and were properly ſo in the caſe of *Ives* v. *Legge,* cited by the defendant's counſel ; becauſe there the limitation was to his daughter, and the children of her begotten, and their heirs, and afterwards to a perſon who might by poſſibility have been heir to thoſe children. That ſufficiently explained the intention of the deviſor, becauſe there could not be a failure of heirs general, while the remainder-man, or any of his deſcendants, were living. But that caſe differs from the preſent, becauſe there the limitation over was " in default *thereof,*" namely, *heirs* ; and here " in default of *iſſue,*" which is referable to *children.* And we may expound one part of the will by another : now this deviſor knew what words were proper to convey an eſtate-tail ; becauſe, in creating the limitation to Elizabeth Adams, he uſed a form of technical expreſſion peculiar to the creating of an eſtate-tail. And if this expoſition wanted any further argument in aid of it, it may be drawn from the clauſe giving the power of leaſing. The power of leaſing given by the ſtatute to tenants in tail, only continues during the exiſtence of the eſtate-tail, and does not bar the remainder-man or reverſioner. Now here the deviſor intended to give a power of leaſing which ſhould govern the whole eſtate ; and therefore, during the infancy of the children of R. Comberbach and of B. Perryn, the power is given to their parents, and to Elizabeth Adams herſelf ; but no ſuch power is given to the children of Dorothy, becauſe it was not neceſſary. This ſhews that he intended to give a larger eſtate to Dorothy's children than to the other two ſets of children : but I do not rely much on that minute circumſtance. Then it was ſaid that the children of Dorothy were the primary objects of the deviſor's bounty, and that the other deviſees ſhould not take till there was a failure of thoſe children : but the defendant's conſtruction does not meet that idea ; for if they took only an eſtate-tail, and ſome of theſe children had died without iſſue, their ſhares would have gone over to the remainderman, that is, would have gone away to the reſt of the children, as there is nothing in the deviſe to create croſs remainders between them. Therefore I think it is infinitely too much for us, in conſtruing this will, to ſay that theſe

wor

words only gave an estate-tail to Dorothy's children; if we were to say so, we must proceed on conjecture only, against the express words of the will.

Then, if they took a fee, is there any thing in the will to limit it to such as were living at the time of the death of the survivor of Dorothy and James? And here I again refer to the language which the devisor has used in other parts of the will. The devise to the children of Dorothy is, *to them and to their heirs for ever:* but in other parts of the will, where he intended that the limitations should be confined to such children as were living at any particular time, he used express words to that effect. The case of *Else* v. *Osborn*, which was cited by the defendant's counsel, does not apply to the present; for that only decides that, where there is a limitation to *A.* for life, and afterwards to an uncertain number of persons who might come *in esse*, that remainder shall only be vested in those who are in existence at the determination of the particular estate. Then it was said by the defendant, that if the estate vested in a child of Dorothy, born in the devisor's life-time, the limitations over could not take effect at all: but it is found by the Case, that Dorothy had no child, either at the time of making the will, or of the devisor's death. So that there is nothing to distinguish this case from that cited from Douglas, and that of *Lodington* v. *Kime*. The clear intent of the devisor was, that the children of Dorothy, if any, should take a fee; and if she had no children, then that the remainders over should take effect: but Dorothy had children, by which the limitations over were defeated. Therefore the title is properly derived to the lessors of the plaintiff. As to what the devisor would have said, had he looked to the event of Dorothy's children dying in the life-time of their parents, it is unnecessary to consider.

ASHHURST, J.—Wherever a fee is created by positive words in a will, it can only be defeated by subsequent words equally plain, or by necessary implication. The operation of this will is, that the limitation to Dorothy's children was contingent till they were born; but it became vested on the birth of the first child, subject however to be diminished in quantity as other children of Dorothy should be born: and, on the birth of Dorothy's first child, the subsequent limitations were defeated. Then the only question is, whether there is any thing in the will to shew that the children of Dorothy must necessarily be confined to *children living at the time of the decease of their parents:* but no words are used in the will, from which such an inference must necessarily be drawn; and it is clear by the subsequent parts that, if

such

such had been the devisor's intention, he knew how to express himself.

BULLER, J.—In this will the devisor has used the words *heirs, heirs of the body, children* and *issue*; and having used them all, we are bound to say that he understood the meaning of each; and we cannot substitute one for the other, unless by unavoidable and necessary construction in order to make sense of the will. But no such necessity exists in this case. *Children* and *issue*, in their natural sense, have the same meaning: but not so the word " heirs:" and unless we are compelled, in order to make sense, to say that " children" and " heirs" are synonymous, we are bound to say that " heirs" do not mean " children." It has been argued from different parts of the will that *heirs* must mean *heirs of the body*; because a remainder is limited to the devisor's right heirs, after the limitation to the children of R. Comberbach and B. Perryn, and their heirs, and to Elizabeth Adams, and the heirs of her body; and that the word *heirs*, in the limitation to Dorothy's children, must have the same meaning as the word " heirs," in the limitation to the other two sets of children. But the limitation to the children of R. Comberbach and B. Perryn, and to Elizabeth Adams in tail, is, to them respectively *in manner following*, namely, as to two-thirds to the children *and their heirs* generally; and as to the other third part to Elizabeth Adams, and *the heirs of her body*; and the remainder to the devisor's right heirs must mean the remainder expectant on the determination of the estate given to Elizabeth Adams in tail; and cannot refer to the other two-thirds, which were given in fee. The remainder to the right heirs of the devisor, which is given a second time, applies to nothing; it conveys no idea; nor can it explain any other part of the will. In the case of *Ives* v. *Legge*, the words, after the first limitation, were " in default thereof;" which distinguish it from the present, where the words are " for default of *such issue*," which mean the same as " for default of *such children*." Then it was contended that the word " *such*" might be rejected: where indeed a word is absurd and nonsensical, and cannot be read in the sense in which it is written, we ought to read it in such a manner as to make it intelligible; but the Court cannot reject any word, which has sense in the place where it stands. That question was fully discussed in *Denn d. Briddon* v. *Page*, and another, where the devise was to the son of T. Nash for life, remainder to his first and other sons in tail-male, and for default of such issue to the daughters of T. Nash (without words of limitation,) and for default of *such* issue, remainder over; there

it

it was contended that the word *such* ought to be rejected, and then the daughters would take an estate-tail; but the answer given by the Court was, that they could not say that *such* had no meaning, for *daughters* were before named, to whom *such* was referable; and it was held that the daughters only took an estate for life. So here the words " such issue" are sensible if they mean *children*; and therefore the Court cannot reject either of them. Then it was said by the defendant's counsel that the limitation over might take effect, either if Dorothy had no children, or, if she had, if they died in the life-time of their parents. The words " dying without issue" have been frequently held to mean " without issue *at the time of the death* of the party," in cases of personal property, but not in limitations of freehold estates. In *Fonnereau* v. *Fonnereau*, Lord Mansfield asked whether there was any such determination in the case of real property, and the counsel agreeing that there was none, the judgment of the Court in that case proceeded upon that ground. The reason why this has not been decided in limitations of freehold estates is, that courts of law always lean in favour of the vesting of estates; and therefore, on such a limitation as the present, they have said that the estate shall vest on the birth of a child, and without waiting for the death of the parents; which rule is not attended with any inconvenience to the children, because where the estate is limited to a number of children, it shall vest in the first, and afterwards open for the benefit of those who shall be born at a subsequent period. But if this were held not to vest till the death of the parents, this inconvenience would follow, that it would not go to grand-children: for if a child were born, who died in the life-time of his parents, leaving issue, such grand-child could not take, which could not be supposed to be the intention of the devisor. The case of *French* v. *Caddell*, went on a different ground; that was not an executory devise, but a devise to take effect in possession at the devisor's death; for though the devisor said " in default of issue male and female of his own body," yet the contingency must be known at the time of his death. The case of *Wellington* v. *Wellington* proceeded on the same ground. But the case of *Keene* dem. *Pinnock* and wife v. *Dickson*, is nearly similar to the present: there the devise was to G. Pinnock for life, remainder to her first and other sons in tail *general, and for default of such issue* MALE, remainder over; and it was contended at the bar that the word *male* might be rejected, but the Court said they could not do it, but held that the remainder over was a contingent devise only on the event of there never being a son, and if there
were

were a fon ever born, though he died, the remainder over was void. In that cafe a fon was born, who died during the life of G. Pinnock; on the birth of whom, the eftate vefted in him, and the limitation over was void.

GROSE. J.—added, that he perfectly agreed with the Court in the reafons given for their judgment, which it was unneceffary for him to repeat.

Poftea to the plaintiff.

HAYNE *and another* v. MALTBY.

The plaintiffs were affignees of one Taylor, who had obtained a patent for a machine to be ufed in the ftocking manufactory. The defendants obtained permiffion to ufe this machine under certain reftrictions mentioned in articles of agreement entered into between the parties; for a breach of covenant in which articles, this action was brought.

The defendant pleaded, *inter alia*, that the patent was void, is never having been enrolled; that it was not a new invention; and that the patentee was not the inventor.

The plaintiff demurred; and it was contended that the defendant was eftopped in this action, by his covenant, from pleading in bar that the patent was void: it is not a void confideration; befides, a Court of *Law* will not avoid a deed.

LORD KENYON, C. J.—The facts of this cafe are fhortly thefe: the plaintiffs, pretending to derive a right under a patent, affigned to the defendant part of that right on certain terms; and notwithftanding the facts now difclofed fhew that they have no fuch privilege, they ftill infift that the defendant fhall be bound by his covenant, though the confideration of it is fraudulent and void. This is not to be confidered as a covenant to pay a certain fum in grofs at all events; but to ufe a machine in a particular way, in confideration of the plaintiffs having conferred that intereft on the defendant, which they profeffed to confer by the agreement. Now, in point of confcience, it is impoffible that two perfons can entertain different ideas upon the fubject. But it is faid that, though confcience fails, the defendant is eftopped in point of law from faying that the plaintiffs had no privilege to confer. But the doctrine of eftoppel is not applicable here. Where indeed an heir apparent, having only the hope of fucceffion, conveys, during the life of his anceftor, an eftate, which afterwards defcends upon him, although nothing paffes at that time, yet when the inheritance defcends upon him, he is eftopped to fay that he had no intereft at the time of the grant: there an eftoppel is

founded

founded on law, conscience, and justice: but what is the case here? Who is estopped? The person, supposed to be estopped, is the very person who has been cheated and imposed upon. In the case of *Oldham* v. *Langmead*, the patentee had conveyed his interest in the patent to the plaintiff; and yet, in violation of his contract, he afterwards infringed the plaintiff's right, and then attempted to deny his having had any title to convey: but I was of opinion that he was estopped by his own deed, from making that defence. But there is no similarity between that and the present case. Neither does this resemble the case of landlord and tenant; for the tenant is not, *at all events*, estopped to deny the landlord's title; the estoppel only exists *during the continuance of his occupation*: and if he be ousted by a title paramount, he may plead it.

ASHHURST, J.—This is a good plea; and the defendant is not estopped from disclosing any of the matters contained in it. This is not like the case of landlord and tenant: as long as the latter enjoys the estate, he shall not be permitted to deny his landlord's title, for he has a meritorious consideration; but when he is expelled by a person having a superior title, he may plead it. But this is a case of a very different kind. The plaintiffs use this patent as a fraud on all mankind; and they state it to be an invention of the patentee, when in truth it was no invention of his. The only right conferred on the defendant by this agreement was that of using this machine, which was no more than that which he, in common with every other subject, has without any grant from the plaintiffs.

BULLER, J.—In the construction of all covenants and agreements, the Court has universally considered the intention of the parties. Now here the plaintiffs asserted that they had an exclusive right to a particular machine; and, if they had, they might convey it to any other person. They then came to an agreement with the defendant, by which they covenanted that he should be at liberty to use the patent machine, of which they were then in possession, provided he would use it in the manner therein specified; in consideration of which, he covenanted not to use any other machine. But it is now discovered that they had no such right, and therefore the defendant has not the consideration for which he entered into this covenant; and, notwithstanding which, they insist that he is still bound. I think that the case of landlord and tenant is not unlike this; for the facts in this case, disclosed by the pleas are equivalent to an
eviction

eviction of the tenant.   As long as the tenant holds under the leafe, he is eftopped from denying his landlord's title: but when he is evicted, he has a right to fhew that he does not enjoy that which was the confideration for his covenant to pay the rent, notwithftanding he has bound himfelf by the covenant.

GROSE, J.—Declared himfelf of the fame opinion.
Judgment for the defendant.

CATES *qui tam v.* KNIGHT, and *v.* MELLISH.

This was a Rule to fhew caufe why judgment fhould not be arrefted in the following

CASE.

By the ftatute 25 Geo. III. cap. 51, it is enacted, that all penalties thereby inflicted of the amount of 50l. fhall be fued for in the Courts at *Weftminfter*; the ftatute then provides " that it fhall and may be lawful for any Juftice re-" fiding near the place where the offence fhall be committed, " to hear and determine any offence againft this Act, which " fubjects the offender to any pecuniary penalty not amount-" ing to 50l." and afterwards enacts that the Juftice may mitigate the penalties.   An action was brought to recover penalties under this ftatute, fome of 50l. with other counts for penalties of 10l. and verdict was given for the plaintiff on the 10l. counts only.   The queftion now was, Whether the fuperior Courts have any jurifdiction over the penalties *under* 50l. or whether it be not oufted by the claufe above-recited.

LORD KENYON, C. J.—In general, the popular argument that a penalty fhall not be incurred without the intervention of a Jury, and which preffes on the minds of the Court, is urged on the part of the defendant: but in this cafe, the reverfe of that argument ought to prevail.   For it is clear that the Legiflature inferted this claufe for the benefit of the profecuted; and they enacted that, when a party fhould incur one of the fmaller penalties of the act, he fhould be fued before a Magiftrate, in order to prevent his being faddled with the unmerciful cofts of a mercilefs profecutor.   Therefore I think that we are acting up to the full intent of the Legiflature, in faying that thefe penalties can only be recovered before a Magiftrate.   For though I agree that in general the jurifdiction of this Court is not to be oufted but by exprefs words, and where no particular mode

is pointed out, by which a penalty is to be recovered, the proceeding must be by action in the superior Courts, yet there is another maxim equally clear, *expressum facit cessare tacitum.* Now by the 59th section of this statute, which is subsequent to that which directs that the 50l. penalties shall be sued for and recovered in the superior Courts, it is provided, that " it shall and may be lawful to and for any Jus-
" tice of the Peace residing near the place, &c. to hear and
" determine any offence against this act, which subjects the
" offender to any pecuniary penalty, not amounting to 50l."
And the words " shall and may" have been held in many cases to be imperative. If this were not the true construction of this clause, the 63d section, which enables the Magistrate to mitigate the penalties, might be rendered nugatory. Therefore I am of opinion that, according to the intention of the Legislature, and the fair construction of this Act of Parliament, all the penalties inflicted by it, not amounting to 50l. can only be recovered before a Justice of the Peace.

ASHHURST, J.—Generally speaking, this Court cannot be ousted of its jurisdiction but by express words, or by necessary implication, any more than an heir at law of his inheritance : the *necessary implication,* in both instances, is ingrafted on the general rule. Nothing can be clearer than the intention of the Legislature in this instance : the greater penalties must be sued for in the superior Courts, but the smaller offences may be enquired into by a Justice of the Peace. And there seems to be a good reason for the distinction ; for the latter has the power to mitigate the penalties. And it would have been absurd to have said, that the Justices should have a concurrent jurisdiction with this Court, and that they should have the power of mitigating the penalties, and that we should not ; for if it were optional in the prosecutor to sue where he pleased, he would of course institute his suit before that jurisdiction, by whom the penalties could not be mitigated.

BULLER, J. and GROSE, J.—Of the same opinion.

Rule absolute.

GLOVER,

GLOVER, v. LANE, Clerk.

The plaintiff obtained a verdict at the last *Stafford* Assizes, for that he being seised of part of *Sutton Colfield* waste, within the manor of *Perry Bar*, in his demesne, as of fee, built and inclosed a house, and approved the same, into which the defendant of his own wrong broke and entered, &c.

The defendant had pleaded that he was Rector of the parish where that part of the common lay, in which he was seised in his demesne as of freehold, and had common of pasture there, in the enjoyment of which he was prevented by the erection of this house.

It was now moved to arrest the judgment, upon the ground that *none but the Lord of the Manor could approve.*

LORD KENYON, C. J.—It has been insisted, in support of this motion, that the party approving must in strictness appear to be the Lord of the Manor: but, if that were so, half of the wastes in the kingdom could not have been approved. For many of the places that are called manors would not be found to be such in point of law, if the matter were strictly examined. To constitute a manor, it is necessary not only that there should be two freeholders within the manor, but two freeholders *holding of the manor, subject to escheats.* After this motion was made, I looked into the second Institute on this subject, where I found every passage supporting the approvement in this case. Lord Coke even doubted whether at common law the Lord could not approve; for which he cites, Tr. 6 Hen. III. And though in the statutes of Merton and Westminster 2, only the Lord is mentioned; yet, in those days, there was a paucity of expression in Acts of Parliament; and the *Lord of the Manor* is put as the *owner of the soil,* where they stand in the same predicament. And a contrary decision, in this case, would be ruinous indeed, and extremely prejudicial to the public. Therefore I am of opinion that there is no pretence to arrest the judgment.

ASHHURST, J.—It would be a very narrow construction on these Acts of Parliament to say that only the Lords of Manors can approve. We are to consider the policy of those statutes; they were not made merely for the benefit of the Lord, but of the Public. If there be more than a sufficiency of common, the Public ought not to be deprived of the advantages that may be made of the wastes; for it was intended that they should be benefited by the encrease of culture.

BULLER,

BULLER, J.—I have looked into the precedents, and they are as has been stated by the defendant's counsel: but that cannot decide this question. For if in point of fact all those precedents have been of cases where the Lord of the Manor has approved, it does not follow from thence that none but the Lord of the Manor can approve. The only doubt (if there be any doubt at all) is whether those statutes extend to wastes that are not wastes of a Manor: but it is not necessary to decide that question here; for the replication states that this is a large waste within a Manor. Now it appears from the cases, that if the part be severed from the Manor, it does not prevent its being approved. "If the Lord grant over the waste, the alienee may approve." This is the present case. It is not necessary to go farther for the determination of this question; but if it were, I should have no difficulty in saying that at Common Law the Lord might have approved as much in cases of common by grant as of common appendant. Lord Coke indeed seems to have been of a different opinion: but I find no reason for that opinion. And if a Lord of a Manor, having 1000 acres, grant away a few of them to a freeholder, it is too much to say that he may not approve any part of the rest. I should require the most explicit authority before I could accede to so absurd a proposition.

GROSE, J.—declared himself of the same opinion.

Rule discharged.

DEWAR, v. SPAN.

On the sale of a West India estate, a bond was taken by the plaintiff's father for the purchase money, bearing the interest of the island, namely 6 *per cent.* which bond was afterwards cancelled, and another executed in England in lieu thereof, in which the same interest was reserved. Upon an action of debt on this bond, Lord Kenyon non-suited the plaintiff on the ground of usury.

It was now urged, to set aside this non-suit, that by the statute 14 Geo. III. cap. 79, " all securities executed *here* of " or concerning any lands, &c. in the *West Indies,* or *Ire-* " *land,* shall be valid, provided no greater interest than is " allowed in those places, be secured." The first bond was therefore certainly legal, and the second being given in consequence of it, and it being part of the agreement at the time of the sale of the estate that this purchase-money should remain on bond, this is in the same situation.

LORD

LORD KENYON, C. J.---The queſtion is, Whether a bond given by one perſon to another, both reſident in this country, is valid, though it reſerve a greater intereſt than is allowed by the laws of this country. The ſtatute 14 Geo. III. cap. 79. (which, it has been argued, protects this Caſe) is an enabling act, extending to particular caſes therein mentioned, and does not reach any others. Now it enacts, that mortgages and other ſecurities reſpecting lands in Ireland and the Weſt Indies, reſerving intereſt allowed in thoſe countries, ſhall be valid, though executed in England: but it does not extend to *perſonal* contracts. And if the preſent attempt were to ſucceed, it would ſap the foundation of the ſtatutes of uſury.

The three other Judges concurring,

Rule diſcharged.

CASES in the COURT OF COMMON PLEAS, in Hilary Term, 30 GEO. III.

TOUCH, *on the Demiſe of* WARD, *v.* WILLINGALE.

This was a motion to ſet aſide a non-ſuit in the following Caſe; viz. The defendant rented certain premiſes from year to year, and had regular notice from the plaintiff to quit. But, not quitting purſuant to the notice, the plaintiff diſtrained for the rent due at the time the notice expired, and alſo for a quarter's rent which had afterwards become due for the time the defendant held over ſince the expiration of the notice. The plaintiff was non ſuited at the trial of the ejectment, on the ground that diſtraining for rent which accrued after the expiration of the notice to quit, was a waiver of the notice.

Now upon cauſe ſhewn, the Caſe of *Doe* v. *Batten* (Cowper, 243) where the acceptance of rent after the expiration of notice to quit, was held not to be a waiver of the notice but a queſtion for the Jury to find the intention of the parties upon, was inſiſted on as analogous to the preſent.

LORD LOUGHBOROUGH ---There could be no queſtion of intention left to the Jury, as the taking a diſtreſs was an act not to be qualified, and an expreſs confirmation of the tenancy.

GOULD,

GOULD, J.---In the mere acceptance of rent, the *quo animo* is to be left to the Jury, agreeable to Lord Mansfield's doctrine in the cafe in Cowper. But I agree with my Lord Chief Juſtice, that the diſtreſs was, in this cafe, an act not to be qualified, and amounted to a confirmation of the tenancy.

WILSON, J.---I am of the fame opinion. In *Doe v. Batten*, there was a defign to deceive the landlord; and a queſtion, I remember very well, was made, whether he ſhould be bound by the terms of the receipt in which the money was called *Rent* for that direct purpoſe; which was the ground of Lord Mansfield's ſaying, that the queſtion *quo animo* ſhould be left to the jury. The mere acceptance of money is equivocal; it may be in ſatisfaction for the trefpaſs, or it may be for rent: and in an action of trefpaſs for mefne profits, accord and ſatisfaction may be pleaded in bar if rent has been accepted. There would be no doubt but that the plaintiff would not have been precluded by taking a diſtreſs, if, inſtead of the year and a quarter, it had been only for rent due at Michaelmas, becauſe the ſtatute ſays, that a diſtreſs may be taken within ſix months after the determination of a leafe, provided the intereſt of the landlord, and the poſſeſſion of the tenant continue: the law in this reſpect being altered ſince the time of Lord Coke, when the old notion prevailed, that a diſtreſs could not be taken, unleſs the fame relation ſubſiſted between the parties.

Rule diſcharged.

PARSONS *v.* THOMPSON.

C A S E.

The plaintiff was a maſter-joiner in one of the King's Dock-Yards; the defendant, having a view of ſucceeding him, entered into a written agreement to allow him, in cafe he ſhould procure himfelf to be ſuperannuated, and the defendant ſucceed to his appointment, his *extra-pay* from the yard-books, excluſive of the ſuperannuation-money paid by Government, during his life.

An action of aſſumpſit was brought for the *extra-pay*; and now upon ſhewing cauſe why the verdict ſhould be ſet aſide, and a non-ſuit entered,

LORD LOUGHBOROUGH delivered the judgment of the Court. On the trial of this cauſe two points were made, one, whether the agreement was legal, the other, what was the meaning of *extra* pay. The ſecond queſtion is immaterial,

terial, if the firft be againft the plaintiff.   But it is to be obferved, that if the conftruction be as the plaintiff contends,
that all which the defendant could receive as mafter-joiner
would be 2 s. 6 d. a-day, the objection to the validity of the
agreement is ftill more apparent ; becaufe it would have this
effect, that no exertion of the defendant, for which *extra*
pay would be due, would be beneficial to himfelf, which
might produce public mifchief.   But taking the agreement
on this point in a reftrictive fenfe, that it means a certain
ftated and fixed allowance, beyond 2 s. 6 d. a-day, underftanding it to be a defined known fhare of perquifites, we
are all of opinion that it does not afford a juft caufe of action.
Every action on promifes muft reft on a fair and valuable
confideration, which it is for the plaintiff to make out.
What is the confideration ftated here ? That the plaintiff reprefented himfelf as unfit for future fervice, and entitled to
a penfion for the paft.   This he did at the requeft of the
defendant, on the promife from him of a certain allowance.
Now the reprefentation was either true or falfe.   If true,
there was no ground for any bargain with the defendant :
the plaintiff did nothing for the defendant ; all he did was
for his own eafe and advantage.   If falfe, the public is deceived, the penfion mifapplied, and the fervice injured.   It
is not ftated that the plaintiff procured the appointment for
the defendant, (which would clearly have been brocage of
office and bad), but that he made way for the appointment.
But from thence no valuable confideration can arife.   Had
the tranfaction paffed with the knowledge of the Admiralty,
judging of the cafe, and applying at their difcretion the allowance they are bound to make, poffibly it might have
ftood fair with the public : I fay poffibly only ; to be fure
the ground of deceit on the public would be done away.
But this cafe refts on a private unauthenticated agreement
between the officers themfelves, which cannot admit of any
confideration fufficient to maintain an action.   If it could
be proved that it was to be meafured by money fo as to
form a valuable confideration, it muft be in refpect to the
time when it was made, when the plaintiff was prevailed
upon to retire in favour of the defendant.   In this view it
certainly would approach very near to brocage ; it would
differ very little in effect from felling the intereft itfelf,
though there would be a difference in the conduct of the
party, who in the one cafe would be paffive, in the other
active.   But his paffive merit, if I may ufe the expreffion,
would not avail him, where his active exertion would be a
demerit.   The cafe cited from 1 *Vern.* 98, I think, may be
supported.

supported.   It was of the purchafe of a commiffion in the
army, which the Duke of Ormond refufed to ratify, on the
ground, that the plaintiff had bought, without the other
party having leave to fell, who had not bought.   I fhould
rather fufpect, from the ufual inaccuracy of the cafes in Vernon, that the plaintiff got the commiffion by fucceffion, and
fet up this defence againft the payment of the bond.   There
is fomething very like it in the reafoning of the Court, who
held there was no relief againft the bond.   The queftion of
the confideration did not occur to them ; and they feem to
have holden that where commiffions were generally faleable,
there was nothing unfair in fuch a tranfaction.   The next
cafe in 2 *Vern.* 308, if true, is a decifion undoubtedly contrary to what we now decide, and, I think, contrary to an
evident principle of law.   On the ftate of the report, the
bonds are directly and plainly given for brocage of an office
of truft and profit, which is not an object of fale.   I have
therefore no difficulty to fay that I hold that cafe to be extremely ill-determined, if the note of it be at all correct.
The cafe of *Ive* v. *Afh*, *Prec. Chanc.* 199. I think rightly
determined ; there was a purchafe of a commiffion allowed
to be fold ; the commiffion was given up, and the purchafer
wanted to get rid of the bargain, and be free from the agreement.   He objected that a commiffion in the marines could
not be fold ; but it turned out, upon examination, that the
fale of fuch commiffions was permitted, not being looked
upon as within the ftatute.   I therefore hold that cafe to
be well adjudged : for the queftion whether an office is faleable or not, is a matter of public regulation, and not a
queftion for a court.   If by public regulation, right or wrong,
certain offices are faleable, the Court cannot fet afide the
tranfaction for their fale ; the Court is not to make the regulation.   Whether by the general police of the country an
individual office is faleable or not, is not a matter of law.
But in the prefent cafe there is no ground to fay, that the
defendant's office was fold under any regulation, or that the
tranfaction between the parties was carried on under any
authority, or with the confent of their fuperiors.   This
agreement refting on private contract and honour, may
perhaps be fit to be executed by the parties, but can only
be enforced by confiderations which apply to their feelings,
and is not the fubject of an action.   The law encourages no
man to be unfaithful to his promife, but legal obligations are, from their nature, more circumfcribed than moral
duties.

Judgment for the Defendant.

It

It may not be improper here to insert the Judgment of this Court on a question similar to the above, delivered in Michaelmas Term, 27 Geo. III. in the Case of GARFORTH *v.* FEARON, where the Plaintiff had procured the Defendant to be appointed to the office of *Customer of the Port of Carlisle*, and had taken from him a declaration that the office was held in trust for the Plaintiff, and a promise to appoint such deputy as he should nominate, and also that the Plaintiff should receive all the fees, profits, and salaries, to his own use. The question before the Court was, Whether a non-suit should be entered on an action for the fees and profits?

LORD LOUGHBOROUGH delivered the Judgment of the Court as follows:—On full consideration of all the arguments used in this cause, I am of opinion that the transaction which is the foundation of the action is illegal, and the agreement void. This transaction concerns a public office, deemed by law to be a place of public trust, prohibited to be sold; and even the deputation of which, where such deputation may be made, cannot be an object of sale. The transaction is, that Fearon being appointed by the recommendation of Garforth, shall not interfere in the office, but shall appoint such deputies as Garforth shall nominate, and pay to him the profits. The effect of this is, that to all profitable purposes, and as to all the exercise of the office except as to signing a receipt for the salary, Garforth is the real officer, but is not accountable for the due execution of it; he may enjoy it without being subject to the restraints imposed by law on such officers, for he does not appear as such officer; he may vote at elections, he may exercise inconsistent trades, he may act as a magistrate in affairs concerning the revenue, he may sit in parliament, and will be safe if he remains undiscovered. If extortion be committed in the office by those appointed, the profits of that extortion redound to him, but he escapes a prosecution; for not being the acting officer, he does not appear registered upon the records of the Exchequer, and is not liable to the disabilities imposed by the statute on officers guilty of extortion, who are incapacitated to hold any office relating to the revenue. Whether a trust can be created in such an office, is for the consideration of the Court in which the suit was originally brought: the only question in this Court is, Whether the agreement springing out of such a transaction can support an action?

The written agreement of the 25th of February 1773, was for two purposes; one, to appoint such deputies as the Plaintiff should name; the other, to pay over to him all the profits

fits of the office. Though this Cafe has been argued very fully and very ingeniously by the Counfel on both fides, I do not recollect any argument ufed in fupport of the firft promife, namely, to appoint, at the nomination of another, deputies, for whom the perfon appointing is in point of Law anfwerable, and whofe places he is not allowed to fell or bargain for. The argument and doctrine laid down in the Cafe of *Smith* v. *Colefbill* 2 *And.* 55. which is fimilar to this, are, that if one part of the agreement were bad, no action could be maintained on any other part which might be good. But it is not neceffary to reft on this point, becaufe I am of opinion that the agreement is bad in both parts. If it be without any confideration in a Court of Law, no action will lie upon it ; it is but *nudum pactum.* What then is the confideration upon which this agreement proceeds ? It is that Fearon is appointed on the application of Garforth, in truft for him ; this is the confideration. Now what is this but in plain terms this propofition ; *viz.* that the Public is abufed, and the King deceived in the application ? I fhould therefore not find much difficulty to conclude, if there were nothing more in the Cafe, that the Common Law would not fupport an *affumpfit* on fuch an agreement.

But I think it is clearly void by pofitive law refpecting this office. The appointment of any cuftomer by any means contrary to the ftatute 12 *Ric.* II. *cap.* 2. is a mifdemeanor. That ftatute, though very ancient, is certainly not obfolete ; it is the ftatute under which they are fworn in the Exchequer. It not only prohibits the appointment, but goes on to fay that " none that purfueth by him or by others, privily or " openly to be in any manner of office fhall be put in the " fame office or in any other," and the 5 & 6 *Ed.* VI. *cap.* 16. makes void all promifes, bonds, and affurances, as well on the part of the bargainor, as the bargainee. It is faid that this was no fale of the office, that no money has paffed on the part of Fearon to obtain it. But the ftatute does not ftop there. It is neither confined in its expreffion nor its intent. In the cafe where a perfon obtaining an office gives money, the words of the act are extremely general, and according to their obvious conftruction without any enlargement neceffarily require that all bargains for money concerning thofe offices which are mentioned in the ftatute, are and fhall be prohibited. Now is it not clear that the Plaintiff has bargained with the Defendant ? would the Defendant have had the office without that bargain ? The promife which is the ground of this action is, that the Plaintiff fhall have

all

all the profits. By the words of the ftatute any profit, however fmall, would have affected the tranfaction; but here there is a bargain for the whole. Courts of Law have very properly confidered this as a remedial ftatute, and have conftrued it liberally where the validity of fuch a tranfaction has been brought before them.

The cafe of Sir Arthur Ingram has been cited, and there it is clear that the tranfaction was not immoral; it was no otherwife wrong than as it was prohibited by a pofitive ftatute. It was a bargain between Sir Edward Vernon and Sir Arthur Ingram, for a furrender of the office of cofferer of the houfehold; on the furrender of Vernon, Ingram was appointed, and a bond given to account for the profits. This was holden to be within the ftatute, becaufe he had charge of the king's money to pay the houfehold. In that cafe the king was not deceived, the tranfaction was public and notorious, and the crown was difpofed to have re appointed the officer with a *non obftante*; but the queftion being referred to the Chancellor and twelve Judges, whether the king could by a *non obftante* give the right of receiving the appointment to Ingram, their opinion was, that the Cafe was within the ftatute, and therefore that Ingram was difabled from taking the office, and could not by a *non obftante* be made capable of holding it. In the Cafe of *Godolphin* v. *Tudor*, 6 *Mod.* 234. which is alfo in 2 *Salk.* 251. which was mentioned in the argument, the tranfaction was between the principal and the deputy; and the agreement was, that the deputy executing the office fhould pay to the principal, out of the profits, a certain fum. The Court there held, that where the agreement was to pay out of the profits a certain proportion of the profits, it was not within the ftatute; and the reafon given is very plain, and carries its own authority with it, namely, that the principal is entitled to all the perquifites and fees of the office, and the deputy to recompence, as it were, on a *quantum meruit* for the labour he has in the execution of it. All the effect therefore of fuch an agreement is, to afcertain the fhare which the deputy fhould have for the execution of the office. But it is remarkable with what ftrictnefs the Courts have holden that propofition, and how careful they have been to guard againft any tranfaction that might give any colour to the principal's receiving a grofs fum out of the profits of an office executed by a deputy. For in this cafe, as it is reported in 6 *Mod.* the agreement was that Tudor fhould pay Godolphin 200l. a-year, and it appeared upon record that the profits of the office amounted to 329l. 10s. every year in which it had been executed by Tudor; but

but as the stipulation was to pay 200 l. a-year absolutely without any reference to the profits of the office, the Court thought themselves bound to give judgment for the Defendant. Now that was a transaction perfectly fair, the mistake in stating the manner of the agreement was an innocent one; but the Court would not permit the Plaintiff to recover on an agreement, where it was not stated on the agreement itself, that the payment should be only of a portion of the profits, and not an absolute one of the whole.

Courts of Equity, in setting aside securities supposed to be valid at law, have gone by the same rule, and have been just as careful not to permit by any construction any breaches to be made in the provisions of the statute. The Case of *Lockner* v. *Strode,* 2 *Chan. Caf.* 48. was quoted as a determination, where the Court of Chancery held a looser rule with respect to giving a bond for the payment of a certain sum to the principal appointing a deputy. But that case is, as most of the others are in the same Book, grossly misreported: no such determination was made, and both the state of the Case and the decision are perfectly mistaken. I have a copy of it from Lord Nottingham's notes, from which it appears, that the Defendant, being sheriff, made John Lockner his under-sheriff; and the Plaintiff, who was the brother of John Lockner, gave a bond as a temporary security till the common security was given. John gave a bond in the usual form from an under-sheriff to his principal, for performance of the covenants in the indenture; but the first bond was not given up. Strode, after he was out of office, arrested the Plaintiff on it, who was obliged to give bail to Sir Francis Rolle, the succeeding sheriff in 600 l.; and to be relieved was the object of the bill. The Defendant pleaded a special agreement, that the bond was to secure him 400 l. by quarterly payments for the under-sheriff's place. This the Plaintiff denied, and also insisted that such an agreement was illegal, and contrary to the statute 23 *Hen.* VI. *cap.* 9. The Chancellor being under doubts, a trial was directed, and the point reserved. So that no opinion was given by him on the validity of the transaction. The date of that Case is also mistaken; it is stated in the report to have been Feb. 9, 1680, but it was in fact in Hilary Term, 21 *Car.* II. But in a subsequent Case, Lord Nottingham very plainly intimated what would have been his opinion, if the agreement had been found good in law. That was the Case of *Juxton* v. *Morris,* which is in the same book and also misreported. By Lord Nottingham's notes it appears that a bishop's Registrar made a deputation of his office, rendering thereout 90 l.

per

per annum; the Plaintiff exhibited a bill for an account, and the Defendant pleaded that it was within the statute of 5 & 6 *Ed.* VI. and that there ought to be no account. It was answered, that this was only a reservation of part of the profits, and the principal being intitled to the whole, it was not illegal; which (says Lord Nottingham) " seemed specious." But, upon looking into the bill, it charged an express covenant to pay 90 l. a-year, without reference to the profits of the office. The plea was therefore allowed, and the bill dismissed. These cases connected, shew that the opinion of the Court of Chancery at that time, in considering how far these securities were liable to be avoided as contrary to the provisions of the statute, was, that between principal and deputy there might be a reservation out of the profits (though Lord Nottingham did not expressly so determine); but if otherwise, the security was clearly bad. In the case of *Law* v. *Law,* Lord Talbot set aside a bond, supposing it to be good in a Court of Law, the consideration of which differed very little from the present. On the part of the Plaintiff, the case of *Bellamy* v. *Burrow* was relied on, as an authority to shew that a Court of Equity will permit a trust to be created of an office, clearly within the statute of *Ed.* VI. and on reading that case with attention, I admit it is a determination full to the point for which my brother Adair cited it; and undoubtedly as such a determination it is of very considerable authority, both in respect to the learning and the known integrity of Lord Talbot. But it is fit to be observed, that in the same case there stands very fully delivered the opinion of Sir Joseph Jekyll to the contrary; and it rests upon an opposition between two very learned and upright men. Either opinion is probable, when there is such authority for its support. I will not enter into the consideration of that case; nor is it necessary to give an opinion here, whether a trust can in any instance be created in such on office. I do not take upon myself to say, without other consideration than the present circumstances can afford, that there is no possible case in which a trust fit to be executed may not be created in offices within the statute of *Ed.* VI. This is not a case of the execution of a trust, the cognizance of which is peculiar to a Court of Equity. Perhaps, if the Master of the Rolls had fixed on Fearon the character of a trustee, a Court of Law might not think itself at liberty to question the authority of the determination. But the whole question for a Court of Law to determine is simply, whether there appears a good consideration on which an *assumpsit* can be supported? And I am of opinion, for the reasons I have

stated,

stated, both on the principles of the common law, and because the transaction is in defiance of the statutes which have been made to guard against evils of the same nature, that the consideration of the promise in this case is bad, that consequently it will not support an *assumpsit*, and therefore that a verdict must be entered

For the defendant.

CASES in the KING'S BENCH, in HILARY TERM, 30 GEO. III.

REX, *v. Guardians of the Poor of the Hundreds of* TUNSTEAD *and* HAPPING, *in Norfolk.*

By the 25th Geo. III. cap. 27. any *occupier* of lands or tenements, within the hundreds above-mentioned, are *compellable* to take apprentices at the requisition of the Guardians of the Poor. A poor child was so bound to J. Reynolds, who appealed to the sessions; and the sessions determined, subject to the opinion of this Court, that Reynolds, not being an *inhabitant* of the district, but an occupier of lands only, was not bound to receive the apprentice.

It was now argued that the statute 20 Geo. III. cap. 36, (which says no person shall be compelled to take an apprentice unless he shall be an inhabitant *and* occupier of the parish) must be taken *in pari materia* with this of the 25th of Geo. III. And that the Case of the *King v. Clapp*, being determined on the 43d of Eliz. cap. 2. does not affect this Case.

LORD KENYON, C. J.—This Case is not to be distinguished on principle from that of *R. v. Clapp*; and we see no reason to depart from the opinion which we gave in that Case. It would require very strong words to convince me, that this particular district should be governed by a different law from the generality of parishes throughout the kingdom: if indeed the Legislature had used imperative words, we must have been bound by them; but there are none such in this statute. Here great stress has been laid on the proviso in 20 Geo. III. which has the words " inhabitants *and* occupiers." Now the statute 43d Eliz. uses the word " inhabitants," which has been held not to be confined to *resiants*: and Lord Coke, in his reading on the 22d Hen. VIII. cap. 5.
relative

relative to the repairing of bridges by the *inhabitants* of counties, says, that the word " *inhabitants*" includes those who occupy lands in the county, though they do not reside there. For some purposes " *inhabitants*" and " occupiers" are synonymous terms. Where a person derives a benefit from property which he occupies in a parish, he is liable to contribute to the ease of it; and in *Rex* v. *Clapp*, we observed that this was one of the modes by which he was to contribute to the ease of his parish. If indeed the Legislature had added the word " resiants" to " inhabitants" in this Act of Parliament, that would have confined this burden to persons actually residing within the parish.

The three other Judges concurring,

Order of sessions quashed.

Rex, *v. Inhabitants of* BRIDGEWATER.

Thomas Bastard's children were removed, by order of two Justices, from *Cardiff* to *Bridgewater*.

The sessions confirmed the order.

C A S E.

T. Bastard was rated at Cardiff, as tenant in the land-tax-book (in which book the landlord also was named) but before any tax had been paid, he absconded. At the request of the landlord, and to save him from the payments, the Collector went to distrain Bastard's goods. A child of Bastard's, about thirteen years old, who was in the house, begged them not to distrain; but went with them to a neighbour, who paid the Collector the money, and took the change and a receipt. The landlord was present at the whole transaction.

The COURT said, the money was raised for Bastard's use, and an action would lie against him for it. If this friend had not interfered, Bastard's goods would have been taken.

Both orders quashed.

REX,

REX, v. *Inhabitants of* WALTON *in the* DALE.

R. Cunliffe was removed by order of two Justices from Walton to Kirkham. The sessions, upon appeal, quashed the order.

CASE.

The pauper had an original settlement in *Kirkham*; but afterwards bound himself apprentice by indenture, under which he served two years in *Walton*. By the indenture, the pauper covenanted to provide himself in provision, lodging, apparel, and physic, during the term; and the master was to pay him five shillings a week for the first three years; six shillings a week for the two next years; and seven shillings a week for the remaining time. The indenture was written on a proper stamp, but no additional duty was paid, according to the statute 8 Anne, cap. 9. (which voids any indenture where a duty *ad valorem*, on the apprentice-fee or any *thing* in lieu thereof, has not been paid.) The appellants produced this indenture in proof of the settlement in *Walton*, which, the respondents contended, was inadmissible evidence, and in itself void; but the sessions, upon the appeal, admitted it in evidence, and quashed the order of two Justices.

LORD KENYON, C. J.—The principal question, relative to the additional stamp-duty, cannot be decided on this case, as it is now stated. I believe it is the practice at the stamp-office to set a value on these sorts of benefits, as a matter of course, when the indentures are carried to them. Now here the apprentice stipulated to provide himself with certain things, which, it is said, the master is bound by law to provide for him, and for which it is contended an additional stamp duty ought to have been paid, because it is a benefit to the master: but, on the other hand, the master was to make certain weekly payments to the apprentice. Then how can we say that these payments were not an equivalent for the maintenance, &c.? I believe they are much more. But, before we can decide the material question, the Justices must find the fact, whether these payments were, or were not, an equivalent. I therefore studiously avoid giving any opinion on the general question: and it is enough for me to say at present, that it does not appear but that the master gave an equivalent for the benefit which he received.

BULLER,

BULLER, J.—I do not fee any thing like a benefit to the mafter, for which an additional duty ought to have been paid. The mafter covenanted to pay the apprentice fo much *per* week; that clearly is not within the ftatute. Then it was provided that, in cafe the apprentice fhould be ill, and unable to perform his bufinefs, or neglect to do it, he fhould not receive any wages: but this was no benefit to the mafter; it was only an agreement that he *fhould not pay*, but not *that he fhould receive any thing.*

Order of feffions confirmed.

REX, v. COOK.

The defendant, who is poft-mafter at Kingfton-upon-Thames, was convicted before a Juftice, under the 26th of Geo. III. cap. 51, for letting a horfe to travel poft, without a ftamp-ticket; and alfo for not inferting an account of the fame in his weekly account. He appealed to the feffions, who affirmed the conviction, fubject to the opinion of the Court. The chief circumftances of the cafe were as follows: a letter was forwarded to the poft-houfe at Kingfton, with the following way-bill, figned by the Poft-Mafter-General: " *For his Majefty's fpecial fervice, to the feveral* " *deputy-poft-mafters, between Portfmouth and London, with* " *the utmoft expedition.*" The defendant immediately difpatched it, by a man and horfe, to the poft-houfe in London. The letter was from the Governor of Portfmouth to the Secretary of State, and wholly related to the public concerns of the kingdom, and to no private matter whatever. The defendant was allowed three-pence a mile for this conveyance, in his account with the Poft-office. No ftamp-ticket was delivered to the poft-boy with the horfe, at the time he went, and no account of the letting fuch horfe was inferted in the weekly account, which, under his licence to let poft-horfes, the defendant is required, by the ftatute, to keep. The cafe alfo ftated, that the King's Meffengers, going on the public fervice, always pay the poft-duty for horfes hired; and that letters to the public offices, though on government-fervice, are always paid for at the Poft-office.

LORD KENYON, C. J.—Generally fpeaking, in the conftruction of acts of Parliament, the king, in his royal character, is not included, unlefs there be words to that effect. This has been likened to feveral cafes to which I cannot, by any means, affimilate it: it has been faid, that if the duty be not paid for fuch an exprefs as the prefent, becaufe it related to public business, the excise-duties will not be paid at the public offices; but exciseable commodities are things *promiscui usus*, on which the duty is payable before it is known by whom they are to be consumed. It was very properly decided in *Rex v. Webber*, that a conveyance by express is not exempt from the payment of the duties imposed by this act of parliament, if there be an immediate subject on whom the tax will fall. But this is the case of a public express, on the service of Government. The stat. 25 Geo. III. cap. 51. §. 4. enacts " that for and in respect of every horse hired by the mile or stage, to be used in travelling post, there shall be charged a duty of 1½d. for every mile such horse shall be hired to travel post;" and the 15th section enacts, " that the post-master shall ask, demand, and receive of and from the *person, or persons, hiring the same* the sum of 1½d. *per* mile, &c. Now in this case, who can be said to be the person hiring the horse? The packet was sent for the use of Government; and it passed through the hands of the different post-masters, who forwarded the express in consequence of an official duty incumbent on them. But they cannot be said to be the persons hiring the horses within the meaning of the act. My opinion proceeds on the ground that this was on the service of Government; and the case states, in express terms, that the packet contained a letter directed to one of the principal secretaries of state, *and that it was not on any private business whatever, but wholly related to the public concerns of this kingdom*. Now although there is no special exemption of the king in this act of parliament, yet, I am of opinion, that he is exempted by virtue of his prerogative, in the same manner as he is virtually exempted from the 43 Eliz. and every other act imposing a duty or tax on the subjects. And I understand that the horses, carrying the mail, were never deemed liable to the post-horse duty.

The three other Judges concurring,

Order of sessions quashed.

REX v. JOTHAM.

The trustees of a dissenting meeting at Bradford invited John Lloyd to become their minister, which he accepted, and officiated as such for two years, when he received a dismissal, signed by part of the congregation; and the doors have since been shut against him. There is an endowment for

for the minister of this meeting; and Lloyd conceived himself appointed for life, unless he should misbehave.

On shewing cause why a *mandamus* should not go to restore him, it was stated that he had behaved improperly in many instances; had slandered his congregation from the pulpit; that he had not obtained a licence as by law required; nor complied with the regulations of the Toleration-Act.

It was argued *contra*, that these forms need not be stated to obtain a *mandamus*; and that in the case *Rex v. Barker*, (3 Bur. 1265) the *mandamus* was granted upon shewing the endowment; the election; and the removal.

LORD KENYON, C. J.—There is no doubt but that a *mandamus* lies in these cases, where there is an endowment, if a proper case be made out. But it is necessary for a party applying for a *mandamus* to be restored to any office to make out a *primâ facie* title to such office, and shew at least that he has complied with all the forms necessary to constitute his right. Here it does not appear that the party applying has gone through all those ceremonies which the particular sect of which he is a member has made necessary. I am inclined also to think that the party applying should have shewn his compliance with the requisites of the Toleration-Act.

ASHHURST, J.—I think this application not sufficiently founded; it is not enough for the complainant to state his *supposition* that he was elected for life; he ought to have shewn the grounds of it. And in opposition to this, the other party has shewn an instance in which the congregation exercised the right of removing the minister.

BULLER, J.—The *King v. Barker*, was the case of a *mandamus to admit*: and there is a great deal of difference between that and a *mandamus to restore*. The former is granted merely to enable the party to try his right, without which he would be left without any legal remedy. But the Court have always looked much more strictly to the right of the party applying for a *mandamus* to be restored. In these cases he must shew a *primâ facie* title; for if he had been before regularly admitted, he may try his right by bringing an action for money had and received for the profits. Therefore, in order to entitle himself to this extraordinary remedy, he must lay such facts before the Court as will warrant them in presuming that the right is in him; whereas here no facts have been stated to shew the ground of his title. Therefore I am clearly of opinion, that this *mandamus* ought not to be granted.

GROSE, J. of the same opinion.

Rule discharged.

K 2   CURRY

CURRY v. EDENSOR.

The defendant purchafed cotton for the plaintiff, as his broker, and engaged for half per cent. to guarantee him againft lofs on the re-fale; fome time after, the cotton was re-fold at a great lofs, but, for feveral days after the goods were bought and guaranteed as above, the market-price was confiderably higher than at the time of the firft purchafe.

Upon an action to recover the lofs fuftained by the re-fale, a verdict was given to the plaintiff for the amount. Two queftions arofe on the trial, 1ft, Whether a written minute of the firft purchafe, which proved the guarantee, ought to be admitted in evidence, the fame not being ftamped, as required by ftat. 23 Geo. III. cap 58. 2dly, Whether the fubfequent rife of price did not exonerate the defendant's guarantee. Thefe queftions now came for the confideration of the Court upon a motion for a new trial.

Lord Kenyon, C. J.---When the firft objection was made at the trial, I thought that it was not taken without fome ground; but, on looking into the Act of Parliament, I am of opinion that this is not fuch an agreement as is required to be ftamped. For it was made at the time of the original contract of fale of thefe goods, and *related to the fale of them*. But the ground, on which I proceed, is on the merits of the caufe. I do not impute to the plaintiff any mifconduct, but that, being a fpeculator in cotton, he was not fatisfied with the moderate profits which he might have gained, but waited for a ftill higher rife in the market; and, having waited too long, he now wifhes to be indemnified at the expence of the defendant. But I think, on the fair conftruction of the contract of indemnity, that the defendant is difcharged under the circumftances which have happened; for the fair import of the contract is, that the defendant fhould guaranty to the plaintiff that he fhould be enabled to make a profit of the cotton; and there was evidence to fhew that there had been a gradual rife in the market for three weeks afterwards, during which time the plaintiff might have made confiderable profits if he had chofen to avail himfelf of the opportunity. And having loft that opportunity, I think he cannot now have recourfe to the defendant. If the agreement had been that the defendant was bound to give the plaintiff information refpecting the time when thefe goods could be re-fold to the greateft advantage, there would have been fome ground for the plain-

plaintiff's argument: but that was not neceffary; and indeed it appears that the plaintiff muft have been fully apprifed of the gradual rife of the market, as he was in the habit of attending it. If this were not fufficient to fatisfy the contract of indemnity, no other line could be drawn. Therefore I am of opinion that there fhould be a new trial.

ASHHURST, J.—I agree with my Lord on both points. As to the firft: this is within the exception in the 23 Geo. III. cap. 58. This was not indeed a contract for the fale of goods, but arifing out of a contract for the fale of them; therefore it is *relating to the fale* of them. But, on the other ground I am of opinion that a new trial fhould be granted; for it does not follow that, provided the plaintiff acted *bonâ fide*, he was at liberty to keep the goods as long as he pleafed; he ought to have taken advantage of the rife of the market, and could not indulge himfelf in any further fpeculation at the expence of the defendant. It would be unjuft to put fuch a conftruction on the contract; for then there would be no limits to the defendant's rifk, and the advantage would be all on the fide of the plaintiff.

BULLER, J.—In anfwering the firft objection, the counfel for the plaintiff have taken two different grounds; 1ft, contending that this was a mere parol agreement only, and was not affected by the written evidence; and, 2dly, that if this written entry muft be taken as evidence of the contract, it need not be ftamped. As to the firft, I am clearly of opinion that it muft be confidered as a contract in writing, and that there exifted but one contract in writing between thefe two parties. If the plaintiff had relied on the parol evidence only, the witnefs, who was called to prove it, would have been afked, on his crofs-examination, whether or not it was reduced to writing; and if he had anfwered in the affirmative, no parol evidence could have been given of it. This was all one entire contract, the foundation of which was the defendant's agreement to indemnify the plaintiff againft any lofs which might arife on the re-fale of thefe goods. But, notwithftanding this, I think that this entry need not be ftamped: and this appears from the manner in which I have already confidered the contract. For this was a contract directly for the fale of goods, or at leaft it was a contract *relating to the fale of them*. If the contract of indemnity had not exifted, there would have been no contract whatever between the plaintiff and the original vendors of the cotton.

But, on the merits, the defendant is entitled to a new trial. The meaning of the guarantee feems to me to be this: " I will engage (faid the defendant) that you *may* fell the

the cottons for as much as you gave for them." That is the full extent of the contract: if so, it remains to be enquired whether the plaintiff could have sold the goods at an advanced price, and whether or not he has been guilty of negligence in not having so done. There is no doubt upon the evidence, but that he might have re-sold them at a considerable advance. But it is objected that it does not appear that the plaintiff knew of the rise of the market, and that the defendant was bound to give him notice of it. To this it may be answered, that the plaintiff, having engaged in a mercantile transaction, and having speculated on the rise and fall of the market, was bound to take notice of the true state of it. In such a case as this, where there was a continued advance in the price for three weeks, it was not necessary for the defendant to call on the plaintiff to re-sell the goods. If indeed there had been a sudden rise in the market for a few hours, or for one morning, and that was known to the defendant and not to the plaintiff, the former would not have been discharged, unless he had informed the latter, who then neglected to take advantage of it. But here it is clear, upon the evidence, that the plaintiff might have made some gains, if he had chosen to avail himself of the opportunity. He neglected, however, to take that opportunity, and chose to speculate still further, but that he could not do at the defendant's risk; for if he *might* have profited by a re-sale of his goods, and did not, that is sufficient to discharge the defendant.

GROSE, J.—It does not seem necessary to determine whether or not this contract was in writing; if it were, I should be inclined to differ from my brother *Buller*. I rather think it was a contract *by parol*, founded indeed on a contract in writing. The agreement, on which this action is brought, was a contract of indemnity; of which the written contract between the original parties formed no part. However, I am clearly of opinion that, whether this was so or not, this writing was admissible in evidence, though not stamped, as it *related to the sale of goods*. On the other ground, I think that the contract of indemnity cannot be construed to continue in force *at all events*, till the goods should be sold, be that time when it might. But the construction put upon it by my brother *Buller*, is the true one, that the defendant engaged that the plaintiff *might* re-sell the goods to advantage: and as there is no doubt on the evidence, but that that might have been done, I think the defendant is discharged, and that there ought to be a new trial.

Rule absolute for a new trial.

MASON

MASON v. LICKBARROW, In the Exchequer-Chamber, In Error.

Judgment of the Court of Error in this Caufe, was delivered in the Exchequer-Chamber, Feb. 11, 1790, by the Lord Chief Juftice of the Court of Common Pleas, as follows:

LORD LOUGHBOROUGH.—This Cafe comes before the Court, on a demurrer to the evidence ; the general queftion therefore is, Whether the facts offered in evidence by the Plaintiffs in the action are fufficient to warrant a verdict in their favour ?

The facts are fhortly thefe. On the 22d of July 1786, Meffrs. Turings fhipped on board the fhip Endeavour, of which Holmes was mafter, at Middleburgh to be carried to Liverpool, a cargo of goods by the order and directions, and on the account of Freeman of Rotterdam, for which, of the fame date, bills of lading were figned on behalf of the mafter, to deliver the goods at Liverpool, fpecified to be fhipped by Turings, to order or to affigns. On thefame 22d of July, two of the bills of lading were indorfed in blank by Turings, were tranfmitted by them, together with an invoice of the goods to Freeman at Rotterdam, and were duly received by him, that is, in the courfe of the poft, one of the bills being retained by Turings. I take no notice of there being four bills of lading, becaufe on that circumftance I lay no ftrefs. On the 25th of July, bills of exchange for a fum of 477 l.; being the price of the goods, were drawn by Turings, and accepted by Freeman, at Rotterdam, and Freeman on the fame day tranfmitted to the Plaintiffs in the action, merchants at Liverpool, the bills of lading and invoice, which he had received from Turings, in order that the goods might be fold by them on his account; and of the fame date drew upon them bills to the amount of 520 l. which were duly accepted, and have fince been paid by them; and for which they have never been reimburfed by Freeman, who became a bankrupt on the 15th of Auguft following. The bills accepted by Freeman for the price of the goods fhipped by Turings, had not become due on the 15th of Auguft, but on notice of his bankruptcy, they fent the bill of lading, which remained in their cuftody, to the Defendants at Liverpool, with a fpecial indorfement, to deliver to them and no other; which the Defendants received on the 28th of Auguft 1786, together with the invoice of the goods, and

and a power of attorney. The ſhip arrived at Liverpool on the 28th of Auguſt, and the goods were delivered by the maſter, on account of Turings to the Defendants, who on demand and tender of freight, refuſed to deliver the ſame to the Plaintiffs.

The Defendants in this Caſe are not ſtake holders, but they are in effect the ſame as Turings, and the poſſeſſion they have got is the poſſeſſion of Turings. The Plaintiffs claim under Freeman, but though they derive a title under him, they do not repreſent him, ſo as to be anſwerable for his engagements, nor are they affected by any notice of thoſe circumſtances, which would bar the claim of him or of his aſſignees. If they have acquired a legal right, they have acquired it honeſtly, and if they have truſted to a bad title, they are innocent ſufferers. The queſtion then is, Whether the Plaintiffs have a ſuperior legal title to that right which on principles of natural juſtice, the original holder of goods not paid for, has to maintain that poſſeſſion of them, which he actually holds at the time of the demand?

The argument on the part of the Plaintiffs aſſerts that the indorſement of the bill of lading by the Turings, is an aſſignment of the property in the goods to Freeman, in the ſame manner as the indorſement of a bill of exchange is an aſſignment of the debt. That Freeman could aſſign over that property, and that by delivery of the bill of lading to the Plaintiffs for a valuable conſideration, they have a juſt right to the property conveyed by it, not affected by any claim of the Turings, of which they had no notice. On the part of the Defendants it is argued, that the bill of lading is not in its nature a negotiable inſtrument; that it more reſembles a *choſe in action*, that the indorſement of it is not an aſſignment that conveys any intereſt, but a mere authority to the conſignee to receive the goods mentioned in the bill; and therefore it cannot be made a ſecurity by the conſignee, for money advanced to him; but the perſon who accepted it muſt ſtand in the place of the conſignee, and cannot gain a better title than he had to give. As theſe propoſitions on either ſide ſeem to be ſtated too looſely, and as it is of great importance than the nature of an inſtrument ſo frequent in commerce as a bill of lading, ſhould be clearly defined; I think it neceſſary to ſtate my ideas of its nature and effect.

A bill of lading is the written evidence of a contract, for the carriage and delivery of goods ſent by ſea, for a certain freight. The contract, in legal language, is a contract of bailment, 2 Lord *Raym.* 912. In the uſual form of the con-
traⱶ,

tract, the undertaking is to deliver to the order or assigns of the shipper. By the delivery on board, the ship-master acquires a special property to support that possession which he holds in the right of another, and to enable him to perform his undertaking. The general property remains with the shipper of the goods, until he has disposed of it by some act sufficient in law to transfer property. The indorsement of the bill of lading is simply a direction of the delivery of the goods. When this indorsement is in blank, the holder of the bill of lading may receive the goods, and his receipt will discharge the ship-master; but the holder of the bill, if it came into his hands casually, without any just title, can acquire no property in the goods. A special indorsement defines the person appointed to receive the goods; his receipt or order would, I conceive, be a sufficient discharge to the ship-master; and in this respect I hold the bill of lading to be assignable. But what is it that the indorsement of the bill of lading assigns to the holder or the indorsee? A right to receive the goods, and to discharge the ship-master, as having performed his undertaking. If any farther effect be allowed to it, the possession of a bill of lading would have greater force than the actual possession of the goods. Possession of goods is *primâ facie* evidence of title; but that possession may be precarious, as of a deposit; it may be criminal, as of a thing stolen; it may be qualified, as of things in the custody of a servant, carrier, or a factor. Mere possession without a just title gives no property; and the person to whom such possession is transferred by delivery, must take his hazard of the title of his author. The indorsement of a bill of lading differs from the assignment of a *chose in action*, that is to say, of an obligation, as much as debts differ from effects. Goods in pawn, goods bought before delivery, goods in a warehouse, or on ship-board, may all be assigned. The order to deliver is an assignment of the thing itself, which ought to be delivered on demand; and the right to sue, if the demand is refused, is attached to the thing. The case in 1 Lord *Raym.* 271. was well determined on the principal point, that the consignee might maintain an action for the goods, because he had either a special property in them, or a right of action on the contract: and I assent to the dictum, that he might assign over his right. But the question remains, what right passes by the first indorsement, or by the assignment of it? An assignment of goods in pawn, or of goods bought but not delivered, cannot transmit a right to take the one without redemption, and the other without the payment of the price. As the indorsement of a bill of lading is an

assignment

affignment of the goods themfelves, it differs effentially from the indorfement of a bill of exchange: which is the affignment of a debt due to the payee, and which, by the cuftom of trade, paffes the whole intereft in the debt fo completely, that the holder of the bill for a valuable confideration without notice, is not affected even by the crime of the perfon from whom he received the bill.

Bills of lading differ effentially from bills of exchange in another refpect.

Bills of exchange can only be ufed for one given purpofe, namely, to extend credit by a fpeedy transfer of the debt, which one perfon owes to another, to a third perfon. Bills of lading may be affigned for as many different purpofes as goods may be delivered. They may be indorfed to the true owner of the goods by the freighter, who acts merely as his fervant. They may be indorfed to a factor, to fell for the owner. They may be indorfed by the feller of the goods to the buyer. They are not drawn in any certain form. They fometimes do, and fometimes do not, exprefs on whofe account and rifk the goods are fhipped. They often, efpecially in time of war, exprefs a falfe account and rifk. They feldom, if ever, bear upon the face of them any indication of the purpofe of the indorfement. To fuch an inftrument, fo various in its ufe, it feems impoffible to apply the fame rules as govern the indorfement of bills of exchange. The filence of all authors treating of commercial law is a ftrong argument that no general ufage has made them negotiable as bills. Some evidence appears to have been given in other cafes, that the received opinion of merchants was againft their being fo negotiable. And, unlefs there was a clear, eftablifhed general ufage, to place the affignment of a bill of lading upon the fame footing as the indorfement of a bill of exchange, that country which fhould firft adopt fuch a law, would lofe its credit with the reft of the commercial world. For the immediate confequence would be, to prefer the intereft of the refident factors and their creditors to the fair claim of the foreign confignor. It would not be much lefs pernicious to its internal commerce; for every cafe of this nature is founded in a breach of confidence, always attended with a fufpicion of collufion, and leads to a dangerous and falfe credit, at the hazard and expence of the fair trader. If bills of lading are not negotiable as bills of exchange, and yet are affignable, what is the confequence? That the affignee by indorfement muft inquire under what title the bills have come to the hands of the perfon from whom he takes them. Is this more difficult

than

---

than to enquire into the title by which goods are fold or affigned? In the cafe of *Hartop* v. *Hoare*, jewels depofited with a goldfmith were pawned by him at a banker's. Was there any imputation, even of neglect, in a banker trufting to the apparent poffeffion of jewels by a goldfmith? Yet they were the property of another, and the banker fuffered the lofs. It is received law, that a factor may fell, but cannot pawn, the goods of his confignor. *Patterfon* v. *Tafh*, 2. *Str.* 1178. The perfon therefore who took an affignment of goods from a factor in fecurity, could not retain them againft the claim of the confignor; and yet, in this cafe, the factor might have fold them, and embezzled the money. It has been argued, that it is neceffary in commerce to raife money on goods at fea, and this can only be done by affigning the bills of lading. Is it then nothing, that an affignee of a bill of lading gains by the indorfement? He has all the right the indorfer could give him; a title to the poffeffion of the goods when they arrive. He has a fafe fecurity, if he has dealt with an honeft man. And it feems as if it could be of little utility to trade, to extend credit by affording a facility to raife money by unfair dealing. Money will be negotiable, in every cafe where there is a fair ground of credit: but a man of doubtful character will not find it fo eafy to raife money at the rifk of others.

The conclufions which follow from this reafoning, if it be juft, are, 1ft, That an order to direct the delivery of goods indorfed on a bill of lading is not equivalent, nor even analogous, to the affignment of an order to pay money by the indorfement of a bill of exchange. 2dly, That the negotiability of bills and promiffory notes are founded on the cuftom of merchants, and pofitive law: but as there is no pofitive law, neither can any cuftom of merchants apply to fuch an inftrument as a bill of lading. 3dly, That it is therefore not negotiable as a bill, but affignable; and paffes fuch right, and no better, as the perfon affigning had in it.

This laft propofition I confirm by the confideration, that actual delivery of the goods does not of itfelf transfer an abfolute ownerfhip in them, without a title of property; and that the indorfement of a bill of lading, as it cannot in any cafe transfer more right than the actual delivery, cannot, in every cafe, pafs the property; and I therefore infer, that the *mere indorfement* can in no cafe convey an abfolute property. It may however be faid, that, admitting an indorfement of a bill of lading does not, in all cafes, import a transfer of the property of the goods configned; yet, where the goods when delivered would belong to the indorfee of the bill,
and

and the indorsement accompanies a title of property, it ought in law to bind the consignor, at least with respect to the interest of third parties. This argument has, I confess, a very specious appearance. The whole difficulty of the case rests upon it; and I am not surprised at the impression it has made, having long felt the force of it myself. A fair trader, it is said, is deceived by the misplaced confidence of the consignor. The purchaser sees a title to the delivery of the goods placed in the hands of a man who offers them to sale. Goods not arrived are every day sold, without any suspicion of distress, on speculations of the fairest nature. The purchaser places no credit in the consignee, but in the indorsement produced to him, which is the act of the consignor. The first consideration which affects this argument is, that it proves too much, and is inconsistent with the admission. But let us examine what the *legal* right of the vendor is, and whether, with respect to him, the assignee of his bill of lading stands on a better ground than the consignee from whom he received it. I state it to be a clear proposition, that the vendor of goods not paid for may retain the possession against the vendee; not by aid of any equity, but on grounds of law. Our oldest books consider the payment of the price (day not being given) as a condition precedent implied in the contract of sale; and that the vendee cannot take the goods, nor sue for them, without tender of the price. If day had been given for payment, and the vendee could support an action of trover against the vendor, the price unpaid must be deducted from the damages, in the same manner as if he had brought an action on the contract, for the non-delivery. *Snee* v. *Prescot*, 1 *Atk.* 245. The sale is not executed before delivery : and, in the simplicity of former times, a delivery into the actual possession of the vendee or his servant was always supposed. In the variety and extent of dealing which the increase of commerce has introduced, the delivery may be presumed from circumstances, so as to vest a property in the vendee. A destination of the goods by the vendor to the use of the vendee; the marking them, or making them up to be delivered; the removing them for the purpose of being delivered, may all entitle the vendee to act as owner, to assign and to maintain an action against a third person, into whose hands they have come. But the title of the vendor is never entirely devested, till the goods have come into the possession of the vendee. He has therefore a complete right, for just cause, to retract the intended delivery, and to stop the goods *in transitu*. The cases determined in our courts of law have con-

confirmed this doctrine, and the same law obtains in other countries.

In an action tried before me at Guildhall, after the last Trinity Term, it appeared in evidence, that one Bowering had bought a cask of indigo of Verrulez and Co. at Amsterdam, which was sent from the warehouse of the seller, and shipped on board a vessel commanded by one Tulloh, by the appointment of Bowering. The bill of lading were made out, and signed by Tulloh, to deliver to Bowering, or order, who immediately indorsed one of them to his correspondent in London, and sent it by the post. Verrulez, having information of Bowering's insolvency before the ship sailed from the Texel, summoned Tulloh, the ship-master, before the Court at Amsterdam, who ordered him to sign other bills of lading, to the order of Verrulez. Upon the arrival of the ship in London, the ship-master delivered the goods, according to the last bills, to the order of Verrulez. This case, as to the practice of merchants, deserves particular attention; for the judges of the Court at Amsterdam are merchants of the most extensive dealings, and they are assisted by very eminent lawyers. The cases in our law, which I have taken some pains to collect and examine, are very clear upon this point. *Snee* v. *Prescot*, though in a Court of equity, is professedly determined on legal grounds by Lord Hardwicke, who was well versed in the principles of law; and it is an authority, not only in support of the right of the owner unpaid, to retain against the consignee, but against those claiming under the consignee by assignment for valuable consideration, and without notice. But the case of *Fearon* v. *Bowers*, tried before Lord Chief Justice Lee, is a case at law, and it is to the same effect as *Snee* v. *Prescot*. So also is the case of the *Assignees* of *Burghall* v. *Howard*, before Lord Mansfield. The right of the consignor to stop the goods, is here considered as a legal right. It will make no difference in the case, whether the right is considered as springing from the original property not yet transferred by delivery, or as a right to retain the things as a pledge for the price unpaid. In all the cases cited in the course of the argument, the right of the consignor to stop the goods is admitted as against the consignee. But it is contended, that the right ceases as against a person claiming under the consignee for a valuable consideration, and without notice that the price is unpaid. To support this position, it is necessary to maintain that the right of the consignor is not a perfect legal right in the thing itself, but that it is only founded upon a personal exception to the consignee,

signee, which would preclude his demand as contrary to good faith, and unconscionable. If the consignor had no legal title, the question between him and the *bonâ fide* purchaser from the consignee would turn on very nice considerations of equity. But a legal lien, as well as a right of property, precludes these considerations; and the admitted right of the consignor to stop the goods *in transitu* as against the consignee, can only rest upon his original title as owner, not devested, or upon a legal title to hold the possession of the goods, till the price is paid, as a pledge for the price. It has been asserted in the course of the argument, that the right of the consignor has, by judicial determinations, been treated as a mere equitable claim, in cases between him and the consignee. To examine the force of this assertion, it is necessary to take a review of the several determinations.

The first is the Case of *Wright* v. *Campbell*, 4 *Burr.* 2046, on which the chief stress is laid. The first observation that occurs upon that Case is, that nothing was determined by it. A Case was reserved by the Judge at *Nisi Prius*, on the argument of which the Court thought the facts imperfectly stated, and directed a new trial. That Case cannot therefore be urged as a decision upon the point. But it is quoted as containing in the report of it an opinion of Lord Mansfield, that the right of the consignor to stop the goods cannot be set up against a third person claiming under an indorsement for value and without notice. The authority of such an opinion, though no decision had followed upon it, would deservedly be very great, from the high respect due to the experience and wisdom of so great a Judge. But I am not able to discover that his opinion was delivered to that extent, and I assent to the opinion as it was delivered, and very correctly applied to the Case then in question. Lord Mansfield is there speaking of the consignment of goods to a factor to sell for the owner; and he very truly observes,—1st, That as against the factor, the owner may retain the goods; 2dly, That a person into whose hands the factor has passed the consignment with notice, is exactly in the same situation with the factor himself; 3dly, That a *bonâ fide* purchaser from the factor shall have a right to the delivery of the goods, because they were sold *bonâ fide*, and by the owner's own authority. If the owner of the goods entrust another to sell them for him, and to receive the price, there is no doubt but that he has bound himself to deliver the goods to the purchaser; and that would hold equally, if the goods had never been removed from his warehouse. The question on the right of the consignor to

stop

stop and retain the goods can never occur, where the factor has acted strictly according to the orders of his principal, and where, consequently, he has bound him by his contract. There would be no possible ground for argument in the Case now before the Court, if the Plaintiffs in the action could maintain, that Turings and Co. had sold to them by the intervention of Freeman, and were therefore bound *ex contractu* to deliver the goods. Lord Mansfield's opinion, upon the direct question of the right of the consignor to stop the goods against a third party, who has obtained an indorsement of the bill of lading, is quoted in favour of the consignor, as delivered in two Cases at *Nisi Prius*; *Savignac* v. *Cuff*, in 1771, and *Stokes* v. *La Riviere* in 1785. Observations are made on these cases, that they were governed by particular circumstances; and undoubtedly, when there is not an accurate and agreed state of them, no great stress can be laid on their authority. The Case of *Caldwell* v. *Ball* is improperly quoted on the part of the Plaintiffs in the action, because the question there was on the priority of consignments, and the right of the consignor did not come under consideration. The Case of *Hibbert* v. *Carter* was also cited on the same side, not as having decided any question upon the consignor's right to stop the goods, but as establishing a position, that by the indorsement of the bill of lading, the property was so completely transferred to the indorsee, that the shipper of the goods had no longer an insurable interest in them. The bill of lading in that Case had been indorsed to a creditor of the shipper; and undoubtedly if the fact had been as it was at first supposed, that the cargo had been accepted in payment of the debt, the conclusion would have been just; for the property of the goods, and the risk, would have completely passed from the shipper to the indorsee; it would have amounted to a sale executed for a consideration paid. But it is not to be inferred from that Case, that an indorsement of a bill of lading, the goods remaining at the risk of the shipper, transfers the property so that a policy of insurance upon them in his name would be void. The greater part of the consignments from the West Indies, and all countries where the balance of trade is in favour of England, are made to a creditor of the shipper; but they are no discharge of the debt by indorsement of the bill of lading; the expence of insurance, freight, duties, are all charged to the shipper, and the net proceeds alone can be applied to the discharge of his debt. That Case therefore has no application to the present question. And from all the Cases that have been collected, it does not appear

pear that there has ever been a decifion againft the legal right of the confignor to ftop the goods *in tranfitu*, before the Cafe now brought before this Court. When a point of law which is of general concern in the daily bufinefs of the world is directly decided, the event of it fixes the public attention, directs the opinion, and regulates the practice of thofe who are interefted. But where no fuch decifion has in fact occurred, it is impoffible to fix any ftandard of opinion, upon loofe reports of incidental arguments. The rule therefore which the Court is to lay down in this Cafe, will have the effect, not to difturb, but to fettle the notions of the commercial part of this country, on a point of very great importance, as it regards the fecurity, and good faith of their tranfactions. For thefe reafons, we think the judgment of the Court of King's Bench ought to be reverfed.

REX *v.* DOWNS and GOWAN, Efqrs.

The Defendants, being Juftices of the Peace for the city and liberty of Weftminfter, convicted *R. Turner*, by virtue of the Statute 5 *Geo* III. *c.* 46. in the penalty of 40s for felling Gin and Rum, being excifeable Liquors, without being duly licenfed fo to do. The Seffions upon Appeal quafhed the Conviction fubject to the opinion of the Court.

CASE.

Turner, at his houfe in St. James, Weftminfter, fold Gin by retail. He produced a regular *Excife-office* licence to fell *fpirituous* liquors; and alfo an ale-houfe licence from two Juftices of Weftminfter (R. B. Sheridan and G. Reid Efqrs.) in the ufual form, to fell beer, ale, and *other excifeable* liquors, dated Sept. 20, 1788. But no notice was given by the High Conftable of any meeting of Juftices to grant licences on the day this licence was granted, nor any orders given by the Juftices for that purpofe. On the 29th of Auguft, 1788, regular orders were given to the High Conftable, to give notice of a *general meeting* of Juftices to grant licences in the parifh of St James, on the 11th of September following; in purfuance of which the Defendants and feveral other Juftices met and granted licences; but no application was made by Turner for any licence at that meeting.

A ftatute, paffed in 27 *Eliz.* ordained certain regulations for Weftminfter, namely, a divifion of the *City or Borough* into wards; an annual appointment of burgeffes, to

act

act as aldermen's deputies act in the city of London; but no magiftrates were appointed, nor were the inhabitants incorporated. 'This act is ftill in force. In the reign of *Cha.* II. Juftices were affigned under the great feal, and from time to time fince have been affigned to keep the peace within the liberty of the dean and chapter of the collegiate church of Saint Peter, Weftminfter, the *city, borough, and town,* of Weftminfter in the county of Middlefex, and Saint Martin's Le Grand, London; and certain letters patent iffued under the great feal, dated 5th of Auguft, in the 23d year of the prefent reign, directed (amongft others) to the defendants and the two Juftices, who granted the ale-houfe licence, affigning them to keep the peace within the liberty, &c. as above.   The *city* and liberty of Weftminfter is locally fituate in the county of Middlefex.   It has been cuftomary fince the ftatute made in the 26th year of the reign of *Geo.* II. c. 31. in *many* divifions of the faid *city* and liberty of Weftminfter, to grant licences at *other times than at* the time prefcribed by that ftatute as well as at the time and under the regulations of it.

Counfel in fupport of the Order of Seffions for quafhing the Conviction, Mr. *Pigot* and Mr. *Garrow.*

In fupport of the Conviction, Mr. *Erfkine* and Mr. *Shepherd.*

It appears by the Cafe above ftated, that the conviction was made upon a prefumption that the licenfe granted to Turner by the two Juftices, Sheridan and Reid, was *void,* not being granted at a general meeting convened and notified in the manner directed in the ftatute of the 26 *Geo.* II. c. 31.

Mr. *Pigot,* in fupport of the order of Seffions upon which this Conviction was quafhed, ftated, 1ft, that the ftatute 5 *Geo.* III. c. 46. under which this conviction was made, extends only to felling ale, beer, &c. but not to *diftilled fpirituous* liquors; and 2dly, that *Turner* having an ale licenfe (which he contended was legally granted) and alfo an excife licenfe, he had juftly incurred no penalty whatever.   The COURT directed him to begin with the 2d objection firft. He then faid, after premifing that the Stat. 2 *Geo.* II. c 28. § 11. enacts that no licenfe fhall be granted but at a general meeting of the juftices of the divifion where the perfon lives, on the 1ft of Sept. or within 20 days after, or at any *other* general meetings of the Juftices of the divifion: but there is a *proviso*, that nothing in that act shall extend to *alter the method or power* of granting such licences in *any city* or town corporate. And that the 26 *Geo.* II. *c.* 31. *s.* 4. confines the time of holding the general meetings to the first 20 days of September; and the 16th section provides that nothing in that act shall extend to alter the *time or times* of granting such licences in *any city* or town corporate.

The second objection I have to state is on these acts of the 2d *Geo.* II. and the 26th *Geo.* II. neither of which apply to the City of Westminster, *city* being expressly within the exception of those acts. The act of 26th had originally that provision which relates to this question; and it might be matter of considerable doubt whether the exception in it is not confined to the time or times of granting licences only, and whether the other part of the provisions could not equally extend to towns corporate and other places; but your lordship observes this act of the 26th is only supplementary to the 2d of *Geo.* II. and does not repeat the words concerning the method and power of licensing, but only speaks as to the time.

The act of the 2d of *Geo.* II. says, " Whereas many in-
" conveniencies had arisen from persons being licensed to
" keep ale-houses by Justices of the Peace, who living re-
" mote from the places of abode of such persons, might
" not be truly informed as to the occasion or want of such
" ale-houses; or the character of persons applying for licences,
" to keep the same."

It is obvious that the city of Westminster is not within the inconvenience meant to be provided against by this clause; for in Westminster, the commission of the peace stated in this Case shews it is a local magistracy with no jurisdiction beyond the city and liberty. Is there any particular magic in a corporate office, as a Burgess, Jurat, or Justice of the Peace? They are assigned by the Crown to keep the peace within the limited jurisdiction, and as local Magistrates they licence, and are not within the inconvenience before mentioned; magistrates for Westminster only, answer no part of the description of magistrates living at a remote distance, who consequently could not be acquainted with the character of persons desiring to be licensed. This is not within the mischief intended to be provided against. This act provides, " That no licence shall be granted to any
" person but at a general meeting of the Justices of the
" Peace, acting in the division where the said person dwells,
" to be holden for that purpose on the 1st day of September
" yearly, or within twenty days after." And adds, " Or
" at

" at any other general meeting of the said Justices, to be
" holden for the division wherein the said person resides."
Then comes the Act of the 26th *Geo.* II. which makes no
alteration in the law; nor altering it in any respect, except
by repealing the clause of the 2d *Geo.* II. which says that the
license may be granted at *any other* general meeting; but the
clause remains still in force in which there is this provision,
" Provided nothing therein shall extend to alter the method
" or power of granting licences in any city or town corpo-
" rate."

Now, if the construction of the Court upon this provision
is, that it must be a city or a town corporate, having a local
magistracy, it is intended to be said truly, your lordships are
to supply the word corporate after city, and it must be a city
corporate or a town corporate—You are to supply the word
corporate, and to extend it to city as well as town.   It can
only be material in this Case, that there is a magistracy, with
a local jurisdiction, acting in that city or town corporate.—
But why, because a magistrate is an alderman or burgess,
he must be better qualified to grant licences, and better acquainted with the character of those who apply, it is impossible to supply a reason.   All the mystery that can be in this
clause is this: any city or town corporate, though in that
city there should be no corporate magistrates, if there be a
local magistracy, most undoubtedly the Case is not within
the mischief intended to be prevented.

Then the question is, Whether this exception extends to
Westminster, which is called a city in all acts and charters,
and which was made a Bishopric by Henry VIII. which
most writers have considered as part of the definition of a city.

LORD CHIEF JUSTICE.—Every Bishopric is not a
city.

Mr. *Pigot.*— I do not apprehend it is.

LORD CHIEF JUSTICE.—In South Wales, there are four
Bishoprics, and neither of them a city.

Mr. *Pigot.*—Westminster, if no Bishopric, yet is a city:
and it is clear that the city of Westminster is not within the
mischief intended to be provided against, and falls within the
expression, as well as within the meaning and policy of the
law.   By the 2d *Geo.* II. the Justices might license in September, or at any other *general meeting.*   By the 20th of *Geo.* II.
the legislature says, it has been found inconvenient to license at any after meeting; and therefore you shall now
no longer license at any subsequent general meeting, but
on the 1st of September only, or within twenty days after.
All the 26th of Geo. II. altered, was the time, fixing it to

the

the 1st of September, or within twenty days after, and excluding the general meeting. Not meaning any part of this should extend to towns corporate;—all that was necessary to the alteration then making, was to say, this should not extend to alter the time or times of licensing in cities and towns corporate; because there is no inconvenience in licensing where there is a local magistracy, the case stands in such places exactly as it did in the 2d of Geo. II.

I hope the Court will allow me to mention the other objection which I first took, and which is fatal to this conviction; it is founded upon the 5th of Geo. III. and no other statute; it is a conviction, in the sum of forty shillings and the expences of conviction, which no other statute gives them power to assess and apportion with the penalty. I confess it appears to me so clear, that it requires only shortly to review the Acts to prevent retailing spirituous liquors without licenses, and compare them with other laws upon the subject. The Act of the 5th of Geo. III. does not introduce any new penalty, but it is a commutation of all the preceding pecuniary and corporal punishments. The Act says, the penalties and punishments of this Act are in lieu of all former ones. But the 9th Geo. III. sets up again the old penalties for selling spirituous liquors, and supersedes the Act of the 5th so far as it affects this offence.

The fact is, this Act, under which *Turner* has been convicted for selling gin, applies only to persons selling *ale, beer, or other exciseable* liquors, but not to distilled spirituous liquors; and it is clear the Justices have proceeded upon this statute of the 5th of Geo. III. only, for they have used the summary form prescribed in this statute, and they have awarded costs in the conviction which no other statute authorises them to do.

Mr. *Garrow.*---My Lord, I am on the same side with Mr. Pigot. In the first place, as to the question whether Westminster is to the purposes of this Act, what from the time of passing the 26th of Geo. II. it has been understood to be, and acted upon as such: that is, whether Westminster continues still to be a city in the sense of the statute, there seems to me no great doubt, when the terms come to be considered, of the licensing acts together. It cannot be doubted when the Acts of the 26th of Geo. II. and the 2d of Geo. II. passed, the Legislature had it in contemplation to provide for the manner of granting licenses in large extended counties. If you attend to the preamble which states the evil that has arisen, and is to be cured by it, if the enacting

clauses

claufes are attended to, it cannot be mifunderftood.   This
cafe is not like a queftion lately before the Court, between
the Magiftrates of the City of Carlifle and thofe of a more
extended jurifdiction, that fay they have a concurrent jurifdiction in the city or town corporate, and have a right to
come into that city and town corporate, and exercife jurifdiction; but this queftion is, whether the Magiftrates who
granted this licence to Turner, and who were appointed by
the Crown for fome purpofe or other, may not exercife their
powers in their own local jurifdiction for the benefit of the
public.   In this cafe they are Magiftrates by Letters Patent
from the Crown, and exercifing their functions precifely in
the way all Magiftrates have carried them on fince the 25th
of Geo. II. under the provifions in the Act, taking it downwards in an uninterrupted courfe to the time of this conviction.   Though I do not contend that is an argument to
bind the Court, it is neverthelefs a weighty confideration
upon the expofition of a doubtful ftatute.   At the time the
Act paffed, thofe that attended as witneffes to induce the
Legiflature to make thofe provifions, were good judges whether it extended to their city; they found, from that moment, the provifions extended in terms to counties, and
which are in terms excluded from a city and town corporate.   The cotemporary arguments were, that Weftminfter
was not included in the enacting claufes, but was in the
exception to be found in the Act of Parliament.   It has
been faid that Weftminfter is not a city; I own I was much
furprized to hear that afferted.   To prove that Weftminfter
is a city, I fhall refer to *Coke's Littleton* 109, tranfcribed by
Mr. Juftice Blackftone in his Commentaries 114, who fays,
" A city is a town incorporate, which is, or has been the
" See of a Bifhop; and though the Bifhopric be diffolved,
" as at Weftminfter, ftill it remaineth a city."

LORD KENYON.---I believe that is hardly a definition, as
it never was incorporated.

Mr. *Garrow*.---Mr. Juftice Blackftone fays, as Weftminfter
is, though the Bifhopric be diffolved, ftill it remaineth a city.
He fays a city is a town incorporate.

LORD KENYON.---That is not the cafe of Weftminfter;
it is not incorporated.   There is no incorporation; there
never was.

Mr. *Garrow*.---There is a note in *Hargrave's* Edition of
Coke upon this paffage, which implies, that unlefs a borough is incorporated, it could not be a city.   He fays, " If
" this is Lord Coke's idea, it is not quite accurate; though
" the defcription may be true, it is not univerfal."   I can
                                                        prove

prove that Weftminfter is a city, from the 6th of Edward VI. There is a return of members to ferve in parliament for Weftminfter, from the 5th of January of that year, and downwards from that time the returns always fpeak of them as citizens, burgeffes, and inhabitants; and the writs conftantly are directed to them by that defcription, of the City of Weftminfter. It fhould feem to be a very forced conftruction upon the terms of this Act to fay, befides being a city, it muft be a town-corporate to render it entitled to the exception. The Court are afked to alter the terms of the Act of Parliament to expunge " *or*", and fubftitute " *and*," and not read it as the words oblige them to read it, *City and Town Corporate*, but you are to alter the meaning and force of the words in the Act, and fay nothing can entitle any place to be within the exception, unlefs it be, a city and town corporate. The words of the Act are, " if a city or " town corporate, it fhall be entitled to thofe exceptions." The 2d of Geo. II. fays, nothing in the Act fhall extend to alter the method or power of granting licenfes in cities or towns corporate. As the 2d and 26th of Geo. II. are upon the fame fubject, it is fair to conclude, that the Legiflature, in paffing the 26th of Geo. II. had in contemplation the preceding Act. And when we look at the two Acts together, and find one fpeaking of power and method, and the other fpeaking of time, as not affected by the general provifions of the Act, it is fair to fay nothing in thofe Acts extends to the time, power, or method of granting licenfes before practifed in this City.

I muft contend that the terms of the Act does not alter the method, the power, or the time. If I fatisfy the Court, the method, power, and time ufed in cities and towns corporate, are not to be affected by general provifions of the Act, and thofe provifions only extend to counties, I have fucceeded in fupport of the prefent licenfe, and, of courfe, it will quafh the conviction.

LORD KENYON.----The Act fays, there fhall be a general notice of the time the Juftices mean to do it. It appears in this very cafe of Weftminfter, that the other Magiftrates did on fuch a day iffue their warrant appointing a day for licenfing for this divifion.

Mr. *Garrow*.----It is fo; but your Lordfhip obferves upon the face of this cafe, that uniformly from the 2d of Geo. II. to this time, the Juftices thought they might grant it either way.

Mr. *Erfkine, contra*. May it pleafe your lordfhip to favour me in fupport of this conviction. Mr. Shepherd and
I have

I have looked with attention over all thefe ftatutes and taken much pains in examining them, and we both agree there is not the leaft room for doubt upon thofe acts I am going to refer to.

The firft ftatute in point of time is the 2d of Geo. II. c. 28, the common licenfing act, which fays:

" Whereas inconveniences have arifen from perfons being
" licenfed by Juftices who, living remote from the places of
" abode of fuch perfons, may not be truly informed as to
" the occafion or want of fuch houfes, or the character of
" the perfons applying for licenfes to keep the fame: be it
" therefore enacted that no licenfe fhall be granted, but at
" the general meeting of the Juftices of the Peace acting in
" the divifion where the perfon dwells, to be holden for that
" purpofe in September yearly, or at any other general meet-
" ing of the Juftices to be holden for the divifion wherein
" the faid perfon refides; and all licenfes to the contrary fhall
" be null and void."

The next ftatute in point of time fubfequent to the 2d of Geo. II. is the 9th of Geo. II. c. 23.

Your lordfhip will obferve that the parliament had two diftinct objects in view: one of the regulation of police, the other the revenue; and befides the regulation of police and the revenue, they had an annexed object, which was the prefervation of the human fpecies; fuppofing them to be much affected by the indifcreet fale of fpirituous liquors of any fort, they inflicted a penalty upon perfons felling under two gallons without firft taking a licenfe.

The 9th of Geo. II. fays, there fhall be no fpirituous li- quors of any fort fold in lefs quantity than two gallons with- out an Excife Office licenfe. To enforce this law there is a penalty of one hundred pounds for retailing fpirituous li- quors without fuch licenfe, and the fame act, for the pur- pofes ftated in the preamble, namely, to prevent vice, and to prevent the immoderate ufe of fpirituous liquors, inflicts a penalty of 5 l. upon any perfon who fhall fell any fpiri- tuous liquors or ftrong waters, though he has fuch *Excife Office* licenfe, unlefs he has alfo the Juftices Licenfe to keep an ale-houfe.

The next ftatute is the 16 Geo. II. c. 8. which enacts, that no perfon fhall retail any diftilled fpirituous liquors without an excife licenfe under the penalty of 10 l.; that no fuch excife licenfe fhall be granted to any perfon that has not an Ale licenfe; and then follows the provifo, that fuch excife licenfe fhall not enable any perfon to retail fpi- rituous liquors, unlefs he be alfo licenfed by the Juftices to

fell

fell ale, beer, or other excifeable liquors. The 29 Geo. II. c. 46, reftrains the commiffioners of excife from granting the licenfe for fpirituous liquors, to any one who has not the Juftices Ale licenfe. Then comes the 5 Geo. III. which fays this: " Whereas, by the laws now in force, perfons " felling ale, or other excifeable liquors by retail, without " licenfe, are liable and fubject by different laws to dif- " ferent penalties and punifhments, which has occafioned " much confufion (this applies to the Juftices licenfes, there " was no confufion in the excife laws); every perfon law- " fully convicted of felling ale or beer, or other excifeable " liquors, by retail, after that day, without being duly li- " cenfed, fhall inftead and in lieu of the feveral pecuniary " and corporal punifhments, forfeit for the firft offence 40s. " 4 l. for the fecond, and fo on." And then there is given the form of the conviction under which a man is convicted.

Now the diftinction always to be kept in view is, that where the Legiflature fpeaks of licenfes to fell *fpirituous* li- quors, they mean the *Excife-Office* licence; and by the li- cence to fell ale and other *excifeable* liquors, the *Juftices* li- cence is always meant. Now the confufion alluded to in the preamble of the 5th of Geo. III. was occafioned by the ftatutes of the latter clafs; and the 5th of Geo. III. ex- prefsly fays " that in lieu of the penalties inflicted by former Acts on retailers of ale and other excifeable liquors, with- out licenfe, they fhall forfeit 40s. &c. Now your Lordfhip will obferve what produced the ftatute of the 9th of Geo. III. the very thing Mr. Pigot ftates, the very confufion which was quoted; for it was doubted after the 5th of Geo. III. whether perfons having a *Juftice's* licence, could be pro- fecuted for felling fpirituous liquors without an *excife* licence. To remedy thefe doubts, the 9th of Geo. III. declares, that all penalties relating to the fale of *fpirituous* liquors (except a penalty of 100 l. impofed by the 9th of Geo. II.) might be levied and recovered, notwithftanding the ftatute of the 5th of Geo. III. The fum therefore of thefe two ftatutes is, that in lieu of the penalties which might before have been inflicted on retailers of *fpirituous* liquors without a Juftice's licenfe, though they had an excife licenfe, the penalty of 40s. and cofts is inflicted; but the Juftice's licenfe is not hereby rendered the lefs neceffary; and the excife licence, where the holder of it has no Juftice's licenfe, is in the fame predicament, fince the paffing this ftatute, as it was be- fore. For the ftatute 9 Geo. III. fays: in order to put an end to doubts, " be it enacted and declared, that all and every the

the powers, authorities, penalties, forfeitures, claufes, &c. fince the 8th of Geo. II. relating to the felling *fpirituous* liquors by retail, without licenfe, except the penalty of 100 l. in the 9th of Geo. II. may be recovered; fo that every one Act of Parliament which remains upon the record to punifh perfons felling fpirituous liquors without an excife licenfe remains in force, and the 100 l. would have been levied upon this man *Turner*, had he not that excife licenfe the cafe found him to have.

LORD KENYON.—Suppofe the 2d of George II. cap. 28, which gives the Juftices power to grant licenfes to fell ale and brandy, was the only Act of Parliament that required a licenfe till the excife-law; fuppofe it required a penalty of 5 l. which is more than 40s. By the 5th of Geo. III. would that 5 l. be inflicted upon a perfon that fhould fell fpirituous liquors? Could it, or could it not, notwithftanding the 5th of Geo. III.? The 9th of Geo. III. fays, all penalties fhall be levied. Now could that penalty of 5 l. (I put it for exemplifying it) could that penalty of 5 l. be levied upon a perfon felling fpirituous liquors.

Mr. *Erfkine.*---Undoubtedly it could not; the Act fubftituted 40s. in lieu of that. The 5th of Geo. III. is applicable to a Juftice's licenfe only.

LORD KENYON.—The queftion I mean to put is this: Suppofe a penalty larger than 40s. inflicted on perfons felling ale, &c. without a Juftice's licenfe; would this Act of the 5th of Geo. III. expounded as it is by the 9th of Geo. III. have left the perfon felling fpirituous liquors, fubject to that penalty of 5 l.

Mr. *Erfkine.*---No. Your Lordfhip obferves, as I put the cafe, there was a penalty of 5 l. for felling beer and ale, or fpirituous liquors, without a Juftice's licenfe. By the 9th of Geo. II. cap. 23, there is a particular form of conviction given for it. Though you have an excife licenfe, which prevents your being liable to 100 l. ftill if you do not take out a licenfe for the fale of ale and fpirituous liquors from two Juftices, you fhall forfeit 5 l. Now there is an end of that penalty; for the 5th of Geo. III. changes it, and puts an end to the 9th of Geo. II. which relates to the Juftices licenfes.

LORD KENYON.---I take it for granted this form of conviction is to ftand or fall upon the 5th of Geo. III. as applicable to this cafe. Is it not?

Mr. *Erfkine.*---Yes. It gave two convictions; one for not having an excife licenfe, and another of 5 l. for want of the Juftice's licence, having over and above it an excife licenfe.

cenfe. Your Lordſhip ſees upon the 9th of George II. there are two penalties, one for ſelling liquors without an excife licenſe, for which there is the forfeiture of 100 l. and one for ſelling without the licenſe of Juſtices, for which there is a form of conviction that is changed by the 5th of Geo. III. from 5 l. to 40s. Then doubts ariſe upon ex-cifeable liquors going along with ale; that begets a doubt whether this was not the only Act of Parliament to have any force, both as to the ſale of ſpirituous liquors, and as to the ſale of ale; that brought forward the 9th of Geo. III.

LORD KENYON.—What penalties was he liable to prior to the 5th of Geo. III. for ſelling without a Juſtice's li-cenfe?

Mr. Erſkine.---5 l. penalty.

LORD KENYON.—The argument upon the other ſide is, he is ſubject to that very penalty, and may be proceeded againſt upon that Act.

Mr. Erſkins.---I take the Act to be repealed by the 5th of Geo. III.

LORD KENYON.---Perhaps it would, if that ſtatute ſtood alone---but is it not ſet up by the 9th of Geo. III?

Mr. Erſkine.---No---The 9th of Geo. II. is repealed by the 5th of Geo. III. and not ſet up by the 9th of Geo. III.

Your Lordſhip obſerves in the 9th of Geo. II. the words are theſe:---when they ſpeak of excife licences, they always ſay ſpirituous liquors alone.----Your Lordſhip will obſerve the only thing the 9th of Geo. III. ſets up, is with reſpect to ſpirituous liquors, but it leaves the 5th of Geo. III. where it ſtood, with reſpect to the 5 l. penalty.

The 9th of Geo. II. cap. 23, ſays, You are to take out a licenſe for ſpirituous liquors by itſelf———" No perſon or " perſons ſhall preſume.".—Now this is the Act which gives the 5 l. penalty for ſelling without licenſe from the Juſtices, and gives 100 l. at the ſame time for not having an excife li-cenfe.———It ſays " No perſon or perſons ſhall preſume " to retail ſpirituous liquors without taking out ſuch li-" cenfe."———There is a penalty of 100 l. the exception of which is in the 9th of Geo. III. which ſays, they ſhall be all in force except this 100 l.———Though you are diſabled from ſelling without the excife licenſe, you are not en-abled to ſell without the aid of all the licenſes.——— The 9th of Geo. II. cap. 20, ſays, " Provided, and it is hereby de-" clared, that nothing in this Act ſhall be conſtrued to en-" able any perſon or perſons to ſell any ſpirituous liquors " or ſtrong waters by retail, unleſs ſuch perſon or perſons " be firſt licenſed by two or more Juſtices of the Peace; then " it

" it gives a penalty of 5 l. and afterwards the form of con-
" viction."————Your Lordſhip will obſerve the words, for
the more eaſy and expeditious means of ſuppreſſing the houſes
of ſuch perſons that ſhall preſume to ſell any beer, ale, wine
and other liquors by retail without a licenſe; when they
come to give the 5 l. penalty, it is for ale, beer, cyder, and
all *ſpirituous* liquors, and though you muſt take out an exciſe licenſe, which muſt be producible under the penalty of
100 l. you are not enabled to ſell ſpirituous liquors without the Juſtices licenſe too; for the ſtatute ſays, if you
ſhall preſume to ſell ſpirituous liquors, &c. without a licenſe from two or more Juſtices of the Peace, then you are
to be convicted in 5 l. and the form of the conviction is ſet
up.

Then comes the 5th of Geo. III. which is a poſitive repeal of that ſtatute as far as relates to the 5 l. It ſays,
" Whereas by the laws now in force, perſons ſelling ale and
beer, and other exciſeable liquors, are liable to ſuch and
ſuch puniſhments, which have occaſioned much confuſion;
for the prevention thereof, be it enacted that from and after
the 5th of July, every perſon lawfully convicted of ſelling
ale or beer, or other exciſeable liquors, without licenſe,
ſhall forfeit 2 l. inſtead and in lieu of all penalties by former
acts." Then is not there an end of all the 5 l. penalty?
Is it a thing in doubt? Can it be ſaid, after reciting that nothing in that Act ſhall extend to enable one to ſell ſpirituous
liquors without an ale licenſe, and if you do ſhall forfeit 5 l.
and you might have ſuffered corporal puniſhment under another Act, and other penalties under a third, that this relates
to the exciſe licenſes? Doubts ariſe. What were they?

LORD KENYON.—I am completely converted. You
need not go on any further---I was ſtrongly impreſſed with
my opinion; but upon looking into all the Acts, I have a
clear reaſon to alter it.

Mr *Erſkine.*---Then I will trouble your Lordſhip upon the
other part of the caſe, which I apprehend may be ſtated in
very vew words. I firſt mean to ſay, that Weſtminſter is
not within the exception of any act of Parliament, either of
the 2d or 26th of Geo. II.

Firſt, it is not a city; at leaſt, it is not corporate, which
it muſt be, to be within the meaning of the Act of Parliament. Then ſuppoſing it were a town corporate (which it
is not), the Juſtices are bound, under the 26th of Geo. II.
to purſue a different mode than in this inſtance; ſuppoſing,
I ſay, in the exception of the Act. In reſpect to the firſt,
Lord Coke is right in his law, as he generally is; but I
never

never heard Lord Coke cited to support a fact which was given up. Lord Coke says, in his definition, a city is a town corporate, which is at prefent, or hath been, the fee of a bifhop; in which he is followed by Mr. Juftice Black-ftone, which has been ftated from the text of his Commen-tary. If I agree with Lord Coke, that it is fo in law, the fact is not with him. Suppofe Lord Coke faid, a city is a town corporate, which is or hath been the fee of a bifhop, will that make it a city, or any other place a city? But you would fay, this great man, that knows what goes to confti-tute a city, is unfortunate in this inftance; becaufe it does not fall in the fcope of his definition. It is clear this was not a city. There was an ecclefiaftical jurifdiction till the time of Elizabeth—fhe erects no fort of corporation; but gives powers to the Dean and High Steward, without the power of government or fucceffion, or any thing that belongs to a corporation; and it has been given up and allowed, that Weftminfter is not in that refpect a city. It is a city by mere courtefy.---Then what is the objection? The 2d of Geo. II. has for its object to remedy the inconvenience found by the 5th of King Edward VIth. which enables any two Juftices to licenfe an ale-houfe; and enacted, that no li-cenfe fhould be granted but at a general meeting after public notice in September, or at *any other general* meeting. That was found extremely inconvenient. After the licenfing day marked out, thofe that had any thing on their characters, and durft not appear at that time, lay by for fome jobb to be done at a fubfequent packed meeting. The 26th of George. II. was made to cure that imperfection, and a ge-neral licenfing time was fettled to be obferved throughout all England by all Magiftrates; and Juftices have been fubject to criminal juftice for granting licenfes in other places, or at any other time.

It has been contended by both my learned friends, that this man's licenfe was good though not granted at the gene-ral meeting, becaufe there is an exception of cities and towns corporate. The meaning of the Legiflature is this: Where a town is incorporate, it has Juftices of its own, and an in-ternal Magiftracy. By its own bye-laws it might have a great number of wholefome regulations for its internal po-lice; and we do not mean, by this general regulation, to de-ftroy the internal police of any Magiftrates, which under the bye-laws they have means to make. My learned friend then cites Lord Coke and Mr. Juftice Blackftone, to prove that a city is in its definition a town corporate; differing in no other refpect, but as it is or has been the fee of a bifhop: then,

then, for courtesy, it is put down as a city. The Act did not mean it for compliment of any place that had been a fee of a bishop. It would be abfurd to fuppofe that all vice was to be brought down by the fhade of the bifhop hovering over the place where he once had a fee. That was not the meaning of the Act of Parliament. The Legiflature did not mean to interfere with cities and towns corporate; but I fhould apply the adjective Corporate to both the fubftantives. I put this inftance: Suppofe depredations had been made on the perfons and properties of men in any city or place, by perfons coming in to plunder the inhabitants; and by the law made to prevent it in future there fhould be regulations for fuch towns, and a provifion it fhould not extend to cities or towns forfeited, having walls that might keep out thofe ftragglers---could it mean, that cities which had not walls, but had a bifhop, that that was fufficient fortification for them, and were therefore not in the exception? So in this cafe we muft underftand cities corporate and towns corporate.

My argument in fhort is this. If Weftminfter is not within the exception of the ftatute, not being a corporate city; then I fay the licenfe was not granted in the form required by the Act. But allowing that it is a city within the exception; yet that exception only goes to the *time* of licenfing, and the other regulations of the ftatute muft be complied with in all places. This licenfe therefore not being granted at a general meeting convened by public notice, the licenfe is void, and the conviction of courfe muft be held good.

LORD KENYON, C. J.--On hearing the argument againft this conviction, I thought the ftatute 9 *Geo.* III. *c.* 6. was a parliamentary expofition of the 5 *Geo.* III. *c.* 46. fo as to exempt all perfons who fold fpirituous liquors by retail from the operation of the latter, on which this conviction is founded. But I am now clearly of a different opinion, on the argument urged in fupport of the conviction, that there is a difference in the whole purview of thefe ftatutes between *the Juftice's licenfe* and *the licenfe from the excife*. The ftatute 5 *Geo.* III. *c.* 46. applies to all thofe inftances where a licenfe for ale, beer, or *other excifeable liquors* is required; and the conviction of the party offending againft that act may be in the compendious form there pointed out, and adopted in this Cafe. And I am of opinion that that ftatute remains in force, notwithftanding the 9 *Geo.* III. *c.* 6. as to all the objects of the *licenfe* to be granted by the *Juftices of the Peace*. For the doubts, which the Legiflature wifhed

to

to remove, when they paffed the 9 *Geo.* III. were relative to the *excife licenfe* for retailing fpirituous liquors. I did not know till it was pointed out at the bar that the Juftices of the peace had the power of granting licenfes for felling fpirituous liquors; but I am now fatisfied that they have under the 2 *Geo.* III. *c.* 26. As to the other point; if it depended on the queftion whether or not Weftminfter be a city, I am not prepared to give any opinion on it. But the ground on which I rely is, that, whether it be a city or not, all the regulations prefcribed by the 26 *Geo.* II. *c.* 31. muft be complied with, except fo much of them as comes within the fubfequent *provifo.* Now that *provifo,* on which fo much ftrefs has been laid, only extends to the *time or times* of granting the licenfes in thofe particular diftricts. Such is the conftruction which the very words of the exception exprefs; and which is a conftruction highly advantageous to the Public. For it is of importance to the Public that licenfes of this fort fhould be granted openly, and not by ftealth, in order that they may have an opportunity of objecting to the granting of thefe licenfes to particular perfons on the ground of unfitnefs. Inafmuch therefore as the regulations of that ftatute were not complied with in this inftance, this licenfe having been granted at a *private meeting* of two Juftices, which was holden too after the general meeting was paffed, I am of opinion that the licenfe is illegal, and that it cannot protect the perfon to whom it was granted from the penalties of the 5 *Geo.* III. *c.* 46.; and that the prefent form of conviction may be fupported.

ASHHURST, J.----The principal queftion is involved in fome intricacy; but all the Acts of Parliament appear reconcileable by confidering that the ftatute 5 *Geo.* III. *c.* 46. folely and purely relates to *licenfes granted by the Juftices of the Peace,* and not to licenfes granted by the *excife.* But fome doubts having arifen on the conftruction of this act, the 9 *Geo.* III. was paffed, nor to repeal any part of the former act, but to declare that the 5 *Geo.* III. was not intended to, and did not, do away the operation of any of the former laws relating to *excife licenfes,* and that they fhould remain in the fame force as they did before the 5 *Geo.* III. but with refpect to *Juftices licenfes,* the 5 *Geo.* III. was intended to repeal all former penalties, by fubftituting a penalty of 40s. in their ftead, and prefcribing a general form of conviction. As to the other point; I entirely concur in the opinion which has been given by my Lord. I think it would be a moft mifchievous expofition of the ftatute 26 *Geo.* II. to fay that Juftices of the Peace even in fuch places as fall within
the

the meaning of the exception might grant licenses *privately*, and without giving any public notice of their intention to grant licenses on any particular day.   For though perhaps it was not neceffary that fuch magiftrates fhould be limited to *the time* mentioned in the Act for granting licenses, yet as the Public are fo much interefted in the fubject, the Legiflature thought it proper to include *all places* in the general provifions of the Act; fo that in no place whatever can the Juftices grant a license but at a *public meeting*, though in places within the exception of that Act *the time* of that meeting is not confined to the 20 firft days of September.

BULLER, J.—It is neceffary that a perfon fhould have two licenses to enable him to fell fpirituous liquors; and therefore it is material to afcertain with precifion the terms which the Legiflature have ufed in fpeaking of both thefe; and when the terms are afcertained, there is an end of the queftion.   From the argument which has been urged in fupport of the conviction, it is clear that when the Legiflature fpeak of a license to fell *ale, beer, or other excifeable liquors*, they mean a *Juftice's license*: when they mentioned a license to fell *fpirituous liquors*, or *diftilled liquors*, they mean an *excife license*.   If fo, the license to fell ale, beer, or *other excifeable liquors*, mentioned in the 5 *Geo*. III. means a *license by the Juftices*; and the 9 *Geo*. III. which fpeaks of *licenses to fell fpirituous liquors*, leaves the *Juftices' license* untouched, and only declares that the Legiflature did not intend in paffing the 5 *Geo*. III. to interfere with the *excife license*; and confequently the penalty of 40s. given by the 5 *Geo*. III attaches on perfons who retail fpirituous liquors without a license from the Juftices.

The next queftion is, Whether Weftminfter be or be not a city within the meaning of the exception of the 26 *Geo*. II.; for it is not neceffary to determine generally whether it be a city or not.   But fuppofing it to be a city, I think it is clearly not within the meaning of this *provifo*.   For in common grammatical conftruction, if there be two fubftantives, and one adjective, which may apply to both, it muft be taken as referring to both.   Or if this be confidered on the reafon of the thing, the queftion is equally clear.   If king Charles the Second had never granted a commiffion of the peace for Weftminfter, the licenses there muft have been granted by the Middlefex Juftices; and then Weftminfter would have been precifely within the mifchief which the Legiflature were defirous of remedying by the 26 *Geo*. II.; for Juftices living at any diftant part of the country might

have

have granted licenses for this place. Then what is the charter of Charles the Second? It is not a commission to city Justices; but to enable certain persons to act in the commission of the peace "within the liberty of the dean and chapter of the collegiate church of Saint Peter, Westminster, the city, and borough, and town of Westminster in the county of Middlesex, and Saint Martin's le-grand, London." These therefore are not *city magistrates*. On the fair construction of the *proviso* in the 26 *Geo.* II. it appears that the Legislature did not wish to interfere with cities and towns corporate, which are governed by regulations of their own, as to *the time* of granting licenses.

Grose, J.—This conviction may be supported under the 5 *Geo.* III. *c.* 46.; for the 9 *Geo.* III. enacts and declares that all penalties, &c. imposed on persons retailing spirituous liquors without license might have been, notwithstanding the 5 *Geo.* III. and may be (except as herein after mentioned) for the future recovered, &c. This seems to me to be a declaratory law; saying that the excise licenses were to remain as they did before that act; and that the only alteration which the 5 *Geo.* III. *c* 46. made was with respect to the licenses granted by the Justices. And this is confirmed by the subsequent *proviso*, which says that all the powers and authorities by the former acts to the Justices of the Peace and the commissioners of excise respectively given, of transporting or whipping persons convicted of retailing spirituous liquors without license, shall cease and be no longer put in force. Now that *proviso* directly points to the powers which *the magistrates* had relative to the licenses for selling spirituous liquors. Therefore it is clear that the statute 9 *Geo.* III. *c.* 6. did not mean to interfere with the *Justices licenses*. And the distinction which has been taken between the licenses by the Justices and the licenses by the commissioners of excise, as applied to these Acts of Parliament, renders the question more clear. With respect to the other point: I cannot think that Westminster is a city within the *proviso* in the 26 *Geo.* II.; which only means such a city or town corporate as by virtue of its incorporation had a power of doing that which the Magistrates for the county at large had within the body of the county. But even supposing this to be a city within the *proviso*; still the magistrates of such a place must pursue the regulations of the 26 *Geo.* II. except as to *the time* of granting such license: and the objection to this license is not to *the time*, but to the *manner and place* in which it was granted.

Order of Sessions quashed, and the conviction affirmed.

THE

THE
LAWYER'S
AND
MAGISTRATE'S MAGAZINE.

For APRIL, 1790.

Adjudged Cafes in the Courts at Weftminfter in the laft Term.

TATE v. WELLINGS.

THIS was an action of debt on a bond; but the debt
having arifen out of a loan of money, the produce of
ftock fold at the time for the purpofe of this loan; and the
borrower being bound to replace the ftock in 12 months, or
afterwards to repay the money advanced, together with fuch
intereft as the dividends on the ftock would, in the mean
time, have produced; the dividends, in point of fact,
amounting to more than the legal intereft of the money advanced, the defendant craved oyer of the bond, and alfo of
the condition. The cafe ftated, that the defendant having
occafion for money, applied to his uncle, (fince deceafed, and
to whom the plaintiff is executor) to lend it; which the
uncle complied with, but told him, as he muft difpofe of
74 l. 10s. fhort annuities, he fhould expect the fame annuity as they now produced, and that the ftock fhould
be replaced in one year; and, if not replaced at that time,
the defendant was to repay 912 l. 12s. 6d. the fum at which
the ftock was fold for the purpofe of this loan; to this the
defendant agreed, and alfo to pay the above-mentioned annuity during the time, which amounted, in fact, to 8½ *per
cent*. upon the fum advanced. The ftock was not tranf-
ferred to the defendant, but the uncle gave orders to his

broker to fell it, which was done; and the exact produce
paid the fame day to the defendant.

After the death of the uncle, the defendant not having
fulfilled his agreement either of replacing the ftock at the
expiration of the year, or of repaying the money on a fubfequent day named in the bond; his executors confolidated
the account of principal and intereft, deducting a legacy of
200 l. left by the uncle to the defendant, and took this bond
for the balance. Upon which fecond bond this action was
brought; and the queftion was, whether the original tranfaction was ufurious or not.

Upon the trial, Lord Kenyon had left it to the Jury to fay,
whether this was intended *bonâ fide*, as a loan of ftock, or
whether that part of the tranfaction was a mere colour for
taking more than the legal intereft. The Jury found it a fair
loan of ftock, and gave their verdict for the plaintiff.

Erfkine, againft the rule for a new Trial, faid, that a loan
of ftock to be again replaced, if the intereft taken was no
more than the dividends would have produced, though it
might be greater than legal intereft for the money the ftock
happened to be fold for, ftill it was a legal tranfaction;
becaufe the lender ran the rifk of any fubfequent fall of the
ftocks, or, in other words, his principal was at hazard.
The only ground therefore on which this tranfaction could
be impeached was, that the affair of the ftock was a mere colour and device for getting an exorbitant intereft; the contrary of which the Jury have found by their verdict. He
further urged, that this application for a new trial muft fail
on another ground, namely, that the plea ftated the forbearance to be until the expiration of the firft year when the
ftock was to be replaced, whereas it fhould have ftated the
alternative time at which the money was to be paid, in cafe
the ftock was not fo replaced; elfe the evidence does not
agree with the record. And though there is another plea
ftating the forbearance to be until the time fixed for the re-
payment in money, yet as that plea neither has ftated the alternative, the defect is not cured.

It was contended, on the other fide, in fupport of the
rule, that though the loan of ftock was legal, and the Jury
had found, by their verdict, that the tranfaction was not a
mere colour for the ufury in the firft inftance, yet as the
plaintiff was, after the expiration of the time that the ftock
might have been replaced, receiving more than the legal intereft of the money while his principal was fubject to no
contingency or hazard, this part of the tranfaction was clearly
ufurious.

LORD

LORD KENYON, C. J.—It has been argued by the plaintiff's counsel that we are precluded from considering whether or not the first contract were usurious, because, admitting it to be so, it was merged in the second bond. But as the former bond was the consideration of this, on which the present action is founded, if that were void, as being given for an usurious consideration, most undoubtedly this second bond would be also void. The principal question therefore seems to be, whether the original transaction were or were not usurious. With respect to one part of the argument, that there was no loan of stock to the defendant, there is no doubt whatever. It is true that there was no actual transfer of stock to the defendant *in fact*, though there was *in substance*. For it appeared by the evidence that the stock was sold on the first of September, and that the produce was paid to the defendant himself on the same day. The transfer of the stock itself was never in the contemplation of the parties, and would not have answered the end proposed; but it must be virtually considered as a loan of stock. Now it is admitted that a mere loan of stock is not usurious, nor the payment of the dividends in the mean time, though they exceed the legal rate of interest. In this case it is clear that the loan was originally a loan of stock during the first year, because the party borrowing it had it in his power to re-place the stock itself, if he had chosen. During that period, therefore, there was nothing illegal in the transaction. But I have had some doubt in my mind, in the course of the argument, whether, as the defendant had no power to re-place the stock after the expiration of the year, it did not become a loan of money from that time, with a reservation of usurious interest, and that the pretence of transferring the stock, was merely a colour for the usurious transaction. But my doubt is now removed; for this case ought not to have a colour imputed to it, which is expressly negatived by the finding of the jury. If then this transaction were legal during the first year, is there any thing superadded to make it usurious? I think not. The whole appears to have been a fair transaction.

I am also of opinion that the objection on the ground of the variance has great weight. One of the pleas states it as an *absolute* forbearance till the first of September 1785: but this is not a true narrative of the transaction between the parties; for in one event indeed it was a forbearance till that day, but in another event, at the defendant's option, it was till a subsequent day. The same observation also applies to the other plea, which states the forbearance till the first of

January, 1786: whereas it was not an absolute forbearance either till the one day or the other, but in the alternative. Therefore on this ground also I think the plaintiff is entitled to retain his verdict.

ASHHURST, J.—The question is, whether this transaction was merely colourable, and intended as a loan of money, upon which usurious interest was to be taken, or a loan of stock. It appeared from the evidence that in substance this was a loan of stock. The agreement was, that the defendant should have the use of the money, which was the produce of the stock, paying the same interest which the stock would have produced, with liberty to re-place the stock on a certain day, till which time the lender was to run the risk of the fall of the stocks; but he stipulated that, if it were not re-placed by that time, he would not run that risk any longer, but would be re-paid the sum advanced at all events. And from this contract he derived no advantage, for he was only to receive, in the mean time, the same interest which the stock would have produced. Now though this might have been used as a colour for usury, it was a question for the consideration of the Jury, and they have negatived it.

BULLER, J.—If the defendant fail either in the manner in which he has charged the usury, or on the merits, the plaintiff must succeed. Now I think he has failed in both. As to the first, the contract is in the *alternative*: in both the pleas it is stated to be an *absolute* forbearance till *a certain day*; but the proof is only of an *eventual* forbearance till *either* of those days. On the principal question also I think the plaintiff is entitled to retain his verdict. This has been assimilated to an action on the statute for usury: but I think it is different. Here the defence set up is, that the contract itself was illegal; and in order to support it, it must be shewn that it was usurious at the time when it was entered into; for if the contract were legal at that time, no subsequent event can make it usurious. Now here we are precluded by the finding of the Jury; they were to consider whether or not this was a mere cloak for usury, and they have drawn their conclusion, which I think on the circumstances of this case is the right one. This is not like the case cited from Cro. Jac. where the principal was at all events secure; for here the testator might have been a loser in the event of the stock rising after the first year.

Rule discharged.

UTTER

UTTERSON v. VERNON, *Assignee of* ELIZABETH TYLER, *a Bankrupt.*

This was an issue out of Chancery; and upon the trial before Lord Kenyon, a verdict was found for the plaintiff, subject to the opinion of the Court. The Case was,

The plaintiff lent the bankrupt 10,000 l. 3 *per cent.* annuities, which she engaged to replace, but at no fixed time, and to pay the amount of the dividends in the mean time. About five years after she became a bankrupt, never having replaced the stock; the question was, whether the plaintiff could prove under the Commission the price of the stock, and at what time the price should be taken, the value being on the day the act of bankruptcy was committed 57½, and at the time the commission was issued 70⅛.

LORD KENYON, C. J.----This is a question of some novelty, and of considerable difficulty; and, though I do not say but that some doubt may be formed on it, I am of opinion with the plaintiff. This is an issue directed out of the Court of Chancery, to try whether the bankrupt was indebted to the plaintiff in any, and what sum of money, in respect of some stock which the plaintiff gave her a power of attorney to sell out of the funds. The produce of that stock increased the property of the bankrupt. And the question is, whether or not this created a debt to the plaintiff, so as to be capable of being proved under the commission. Now where it is perfectly contingent whether or not a debt will become due, or where the demand arises on account of some tortious act, in neither of those cases can the debt be proved. But the rule with regard to demands payable at all events on a future day, though the amount of them is uncertain, falls under a different consideration. Where a father covenants that he will make a provision for his wife and children, and becomes a bankrupt, that cannot be proved as a debt under the commission, though the amount of it be specified, *unless* he has stipulated to do it within a reasonable time, and given *a bond* for the performance of it, which *is forfeited at law*: for then, uncertain as the sum is, the Court of Chancery, proceeding on the rules of law, will order a part of the effects to be set apart to secure it; therefore *the mere uncertainty* of the sum, provided there be a *legal remedy* before the bankruptcy happens, will not deprive the creditor of relief under the commission. The case of *Dutch v. Warren*, though different in one respect from the present, goes a great way to support the plaintiff's argument. It

differs

differs indeed in this respect, that in that case *a specific day was mentioned* on which the stock was to be transferred; but that case answers the argument urged on the ground of uncertainty, for the amount of the damages in that case was not more certain than in the present; they both depend on the same denomination of property. I cannot forbear alluding to, and laying considerable stress on, the statute 7 Geo. I. cap. 31, though it does not meet this very case. That act, after reciting that doubts had arisen whether bills, bonds, &c. payable at a future day, could be proved under the commission, enacted and *declared* that they might. Now it is to be observed that the word *" declare"* is always inserted in acts of parliament with great caution, and it does not occur in any other of the bankrupt laws. This therefore was declaratory of the common law; and the common law would probably have been held to apply to this case as well as to those mentioned in the statute, if it had been clear what the common law was. For here (not money indeed, but) money's worth was lent by the plaintiff to the bankrupt, to be recovered on the ground of the contract, and not in a tortious action. The plaintiff had a cause of action which he might have enforced when he chose, and not at the option of the bankrupt. I am therefore of opinion that in this case the plaintiff has a right to come in under the commission for a satisfaction; and the only remaining question is, what shall be the amount of that satisfaction, which depends on the time when the price of the stock is to be taken. Now I have no difficulty in saying that it ought to be computed on the day of the bankruptcy, which was the last possible time; and it is found by the case, that the value of the stock on that day was 5,750 l. Therefore it seems to me, without making any innovation on any of the principles of law, that the plaintiff is entitled to prove that sum under the commission; and there appears to be no ground for deciding this to be usurious, as was argued, the whole being a *bonâ fide* contract for the loan of stock. This is not like the case put at the bar, of an action for not performing a contract for the delivery of goods; for that sounds merely *in damages*, and there is nothing to guide the judgment of the Court: but here the price of the stock is the criterion, and it is capable of being reduced to a certainty.

ASHHURST, J.—Although the inclination of my mind would induce me to say that debts, which ought in justice to be proved under a commission of bankrupt, might be so proved, yet I have great doubt on admitting the present.

I have

I have always underſtood it to be a general rule that nothing is proveable under a commiſſion that cannot be recovered in the form of an *indebitatus aſſumpſit*; and that wherever it is neceſſary to have recourſe to a *ſpecial action on the caſe, or treſpaſs, to recover damages*, the party cannot come in under the commiſſion.   As to the action for meſne profits, though *in form* it is an action of *treſpaſs*, yet *in effect* it is to recover the *rent*, which is at leaſt as certain in its nature as the ſtock in this caſe.   It is true there may be ſome caſes where the Jury are not bound by the amount of the rent, but may give extra damages.   But why may not the plaintiff in that caſe wave the extraordinary damages, if he pleaſe, and reſt content with the rent alone?   and yet, in ſuch a caſe, he cannot come in under the commiſſion.   The form of the action then, in which this demand was to be recovered, ſeems material in this caſe as well as in that.   I cannot therefore at preſent bring myſelf to think that the plaintiff ought to be permitted to prove his demand under the commiſſion.

BULLER, J.—I cannot by any means agree that the form of the action can decide this queſtion which ariſes on the bankrupt laws.   The form of the action very properly decided the caſe of *Goodtitle* v. *North*; but that has no application to the queſtion in this ſtage of it.   There the action was brought to recover damages, and there were no means by which the Court could aſcertain the amount of them; they were uncertain in their nature, depending on a variety of circumſtances to be ſubmitted to the conſideration of a Jury, who alone could aſcertain them.   And therefore there is great weight in what Lord Mansfield ſaid; for he thought that the only difficulty aroſe from the nature of the action which the plaintiff had brought, *which was for damages*. But the rule is this, if the creditor wiſh to prove a debt under a commiſſion of bankrupt, it is neceſſary that he ſhould be able to aſcertain the amount of it without the intervention of a Jury: and if it be ſo certain that he can ſwear to it, he is entitled to prove it under the commiſſion.   In ſome caſes the form of the action is material, in others not.   If money be levied by the ſale of goods under an execution, and the execution be afterwards ſet aſide, there if the party, whoſe goods have been ſeized, inſiſt on contingent damages for keeping him out of his goods and ſelling them, it cannot be proved as a debt under the commiſſion: but if he demand only the value of the goods, he may come in under the commiſſion, becauſe the debt is capable of being aſcertained, and he may ſwear to the amount of it.   So, the caſe put at the bar, of an action for not delivering goods according

cording to an agreement, admits of the fame diftinction; if the party has actually paid for the goods, there he may recover the precife value in cafe of non-delivery, and confequently may prove it as a debt under the commiffion: but if he will not be content with recovering the precife value of them, but goes for contingent damages, arifing from the fluctuation of the market, he cannot come in under the commiffion, becaufe thofe damages are uncertain. There is alfo another cafe, which fhews that the form of the action is not the criterion. Suppofe money has been lent on intereft, and the principal has been paid, and the only point in difpute be on the intereft, *indebitatus affumpfit* will not lie for it *eo nomine* as intereft, but the party muft have recourfe to a fpecial action on the cafe to recover it; and yet, as the amount of the intereft is a matter of computation, he may prove it as a debt under the commiffion. Befides which, I am alfo of opinion that this cafe falls within the principle and good fenfe of the ftatute 7 Geo. I. cap. 31, though not within the very words of it. The object of that act was that all demands, that exifted prior to the time of the bankruptcy, though not payable till a future day, might be proved under a commiffion of bankrupt, *provided they were capable of being afcertained.*

GROSE, J.—I have had confiderable difficulty in forming my opinion on this cafe, becaufe it is perfectly new: but, on confidering the juftice of this cafe, and the principles of former decifions, my doubts are removed. Where a demand refts merely in damages, and is not capable of a clear certain liquidation, it cannot be proved under a commiffion of bankrupt: but I confider this as a contract to do a fpecific act, which the bankrupt is rendered utterly incapable of performing by the bankruptcy; and his incapacity to perform it is attended *with a certain damage* to the plaintiff. The value of the ftock is mixed in the general mafs of the bankrupt's property, of which the affignees and the other creditors are poffeffed; and there is no reafon why in fubftantial juftice the plaintiff fhould not have the fame advantage which the reft of the creditors have, efpecially as the amount of his demand is capable of being afcertained. Several cafes have been mentioned, the principles of which fully warrant us in deciding in favour of the plaintiff. I perfectly concur with my Lord Chief Juftice in the obfervations which he has made on the cafe of Dutch and Warren, and in thofe made by my brother *Buller* on that of *Goodtitle* v *North.* Much has been faid refpecting the form of the action; but I do not, by any means, think it conclufive;

clufive; it may illuftrate, but cannot decide, the queftion. On the whole, I am of opinion that, this being a cafe of clear liquidated damages for the not performing a fpecific act, which the bankruptcy has rendered impoffible to be done, the plaintiff may come in under the commiffion, and the time of the bankruptcy is the time when the amount of it is to be afcertained by the price of the ftock on that day.

By the Court. Enter the verdict for the plaintiff for the price of the ftock on the day of the bankruptcy.

JACKSON *v.* DUCHAIRE.

The defendant took a houfe of the plaintiff, in which there were goods which fhe got a friend to lay down the money for. This friend bargained with the plaintiff to buy the goods at 70 l. and took a bill of fale of them to himfelf. But the defendant made a private agreement, unknown to the friend, to pay 30 l. more than he had agreed for, and for this money fhe gave notes of hand to the plaintiff. Upon thefe notes the action was brought.

LORD KENYON faid upon the trial, that he thought the plaintiff was not entitled to recover, becaufe the agreement upon which thefe notes were given, was a fraud upon the friend who had advanced the 70 l. to the defendant in confidence that it was the whole confideration. But the Jury, notwithftanding, gave a verdict for the plaintiff.

This was a motion to fhew caufe why the verdict fhould not be fet afide.

ASHHURST, J.---I perfectly concur in the opinion given by my Lord at the trial. It is clear both on the principles of law and equity that when any friend advances money to relieve another perfon from the preffure of his neceffities, and the parties interefted enter into a private agreement over and beyond that with which the friend is acquainted, fuch agreement is void in law, as being a fraud on fuch friend. This cafe is fimilar in its principle to one, which was determined in this Court not long ago. Here it is to be obferved that Welch, (the perfon who advanced the money) who was defirous of benefiting his friend, agreed to advance 70 l. which he underftood to be the *full purchafe money*? for fuch was the reprefentation made to him, and 70 l. is expreffed in the bill of fale to be the confideration. But now it turns out that the defendant was to give two promiffory notes for a further fum, under a private agreement between her and the plaintiff, to which Welch was not
privy,

privy, and which, if he had known, he would not probably have advanced his money. This therefore was a fraud on him; and the principles of analogous cases go to shew that this private agreement between the plaintiff and the defendant cannot be enforced. It has been attempted to distinguish this case from them by saying that Welch had a consideration for his money in the goods: but that does not vary the case; for he did not wish to make a bargain for himself, but acted solely for his friend. And even if it be considered that Welch has purchased goods for himself of greater value than 70 l. and has only paid 70 l. himself, then it appears that the defendant had *no consideration* whatever for her notes.

BULLER, J.---As the Jury have only given a verdict for 15 l. this comes within the rule which the Courts have long established, that they will not grant a new trial, unless it can be done without compelling the party applying for it to pay the costs. It is clear that in this case there was no misdirection at the trial: but that is not the only case in which the Court will award a new trial *without costs*. For if the verdict be manifestly against the justice of the case, and the Judge's direction, it is fit that a new trial should be granted without costs: and this verdict is of that description. Here it appears that the plaintiff has been privy to a gross fraud on Welch in this transaction; and then the rule applies, *ex dolo malo non oritur actio*. The plaintiff wished to get 100 l. for the goods, which sum the defendant could not advance; but the scheme was that the goods should be apparently sold to Welch for 70 l. and that the defendant should pay the rest under a private agreement unknown to Welch: now that was a gross fraud on him, in order to induce him to advance his money; and as this fraud was practised by the plaintiff, he cannot recover.

BY THE COURT,

Rule absolute, without costs.

WRIGHT v. REED.

By the Annuity Act, 17 Geo. III. cap. 26, it is enacted, that in every deed by which any annuity shall be granted, the consideration really and *bonâ fide* (which shall be in *money only*) shall be fully and truly set forth and described in words at length, or the same shall be void. In the present Case, part of the consideration was paid in *money*, and part in *Bank Notes*, but the deed named the whole as being paid in *money*.

Upon

Upon an application to the Court that this deed fhould be cancelled, the confideration not being truly defcribed; the queftion arofe whether Bank Notes were money in a legal fenfe.

LORD KENYON, C. J.—Bank Notes are confidered as money to many purpofes. They were fo held by the Court in the Cafe of *Miller v. Race* (1 Burroughs, 452).

ASHHURST, J.—The Annuity Act was paffed for the purpofe of guarding againft fictitious confiderations: but it cannot be contended that the payment in this cafe is within the mifchief which that ftatute intended to remedy. Bank Notes are money to all intents, and in this inftance were taken as fuch.

BULLER, J.—This Court has never yet determined that a tender of Bank Notes is, *at all events,* a good tender: but if they have been offered, and no objection has been made *on that account,* this Court has confidered it to be a good tender; and very properly fo, for Bank Notes pafs in the world as cafh. In a cafe on the other fide of the Hall, the Lord Chancellor once fuggefted a doubt whether thefe kind of notes were money; but here we have always been inclined to confider them as fuch, though the queftion has never yet been directly determined.

Per Curiam,   Rule difcharged.

YEARDLEY v. ROE.

This was an application to change the venue from Shropfhire to Middlefex, upon the fcore of privilege, the defendant being an Attorney.

The Court faid, that it was fully fettled in the Cafe of *Pope v. Redfearne,* (4 Burroughs, 2027) that when an Attorney is *defendant,* he has no privilege to change the venue to Middlefex, but only when he is plaintiff.

Rule difcharged with Cofts.

REX

REX *v.* SMITH.

The defendant was duly elected Mayor of Nottingham, but not having taken the Sacrament in the year before his election, according to the Corporation Act, 13 Ch. II. st. 2, cap. 1. an information in the nature of a *quo warranto* was applied for against him.

LORD KENYON, C. J. said, The rule under which the defendant attempts to shelter himself from the present application, namely that the relators having concurred in his election, ought not to be suffered now to impeach it, holds very properly in cases where the relators concur in the election of the defendant, knowing of a defect in the form of conducting it : but this is a different case; here the defect is a latent one, arising from the omission of an act, which the Legislature have positively required to be done before any person is elected into a corporate office.

Per Curiam,   Rule absolute.

RAWLINSON *v.* SHAW, *Executor of* WOODHOUSE.

Woodhouse, being indebted to the plaintiff in a sum of money, which was the subject of this action, appointed him one of his executors, but he never proved the will, or acted in any way whatever as executor; but having brought his action against the acting executor for his debt, it was argued in demurrer, that not having actually *renounced* the executorship, his *legal* remedy was suspended.

LORD KENYON, C. J.—It is impossible to entertain the least doubt in this case. The argument is, that if *A.* owe *B.* a sum of money, and chuse to make him his executor, though *B.* will not act, his legal remedy is extinguished. The proposition is too monstrous to admit of any argument. If indeed the creditor had accepted of the executorship, and acted, there might perhaps have been something in it. But the facts disclosed by the replication, positively negative that; for it is there averred that he never proved the will, nor took upon himself the burthen of the execution thereof, nor in any manner whatsoever accepted of the supposed appointment to be an executor, nor ever administered, &c. And, notwithstanding this, he is now told that he cannot enforce the payment of his debt in a court of law. I should have
been

been extremely forry to have found myfelf bound by authorities to accede to fuch a pofition : and I am glad that none are found to warrant it, and that there is one direct authority againft it.   There is no pretence therefore for this demurrer; and even if it could have been fupported, it would be difhoneft in the extreme.

BULLER, J.—The argument in fupport of this demurrer is fully anfwered by the plain words of the replication.   The foundation of the argument is, that this is an action in refpect of property, and that the plaintiff has poffeffion of that property : but the replication pointedly ftates that he never proved the will, nor in any manner whatever acted as executor, nor adminiftered.   Then if he has not the poffeffion of the property of the teftator, he ftands in the fame fituation as any other ftranger, and may equally fue the perfon who has the legal poffeffion of that property.

GROSE, J—It is laid down univerfally in all the authorities on this fubject, from the Year-books down to the prefent time, that a defendant, who is fued as executor, cannot plead that another perfon is alfo executor with him, unlefs he aver that that other has adminiftered.   The cafe of *Swallow* v. *Emberfon*, is directly in point.   The only difference is, that here the defendant fays that the plaintiff himfelf is one of the executors, but that does not vary this cafe for the reafons already given.   I lament that the fame practice does not obtain here that prevails in the Court of Common Pleas, where feveral pleas are not permitted to be pleaded without the fpecial leave of the court.   It is attended with infinitely good confequences to the fuitors, as it frequently prevents unneceffary expence to the parties, in introducing improper pleas.   If that were the practice here, this expence would never have been incurred.

Judgment for the plaintiffs.

REX v. the Inhabitants of GAMLINGAY.

This was a rule to fhew caufe why judgment fhould not be arrefted in an indictment tried at the Cambridge Affizes, where the defendants were convicted for not repairing the highway.   The indictment defcribed the road as *leading from Hatley, towards and unto the Parifh of Gamlingay.*   The indictment afterwards ftated that a certain *part of the fame highway, fituate in the Parifh of Gamlingay, is in great decay.*

It was argued againft the rule, that though the word *from* muft be conftrued exclufively, yet the word *unto* may include

the

the parish; besides, if this part of the indictment was rejected, the latter part, where the parish is expressly included, will warrant the verdict.

Lord Kenyon, C. J.—We are not called upon in this case to say whether or not the indictment could have been supported, if it had not described the places *to* and *from* which the road leads; but here the prosecutor has undertaken to describe the road; and the question is, whether the parish of Gamlingay are bound of common right to repair the road which is described. Now they are only so bound, if the road lies within their parish. But the road is described as leading *from Hatley unto Gamlingay*, which excludes *Gamlingay*. I remember a similar question arising on the construction of a turnpike-act some years ago, respecting the road leading through *Battle to Hastings*, 1 *Bur*. 376, when this Court held that the words " from" and " to" were both exclusive. And though it is to be lamented that a judgment is to be arrested on account of the insufficiency of the indictment, after a verdict has been obtained against the defendant, yet we ought not to countenance any negligence in those whose business it is to draw indictments; and if a defect in an indictment of this sort were to be overlooked, it might be expected that the same indulgence should be extended to all others. The case of *Pugh* v. *the Duke of Leeds*, which was cited, (where the words, in a lease, *from* the day of the date, was held to be *inclusive*), is not applicable to the present; for that was determined on the ground of there being no fraction of a day; and it must be remembered that though, I believe, that case was rightly decided, the contrary determination had before been made by all the judges.

Ashhurst, J.—The case of *Pugh* v. *the Duke of Leeds*. (*Cowp.* 714), was properly decided: but that turned on the construction of a contract between two persons, where their intention was to be considered. But greater certainty is required in indictments than in contracts of that kind. Now the whole of the road described by the former part of the indictment is excluded by the terms " from" and " unto;" and the latter part is a contradiction in terms to the former allegation.

Grose, J.—of the same opinion.

Rule absolute.

Cases in the Court of Common Pleas, in Hilary Term, 30 Geo. III.

KIRKMAN v. PRICE.

This was an application to set aside a bond, &c. entered into to secure an annuity, the consideration not being specifically set forth, as required by the Annuity Act, 17 Geo. III. cap. 26. The memorial, enrolled pursuant to the statute, stated that the consideration was 160 l. paid by the plaintiff to the defendant; but the fact was, that the plaintiff had several notes of hand of the defendant's to the amount of near 100 l. for money formerly advanced to him, which were given up at the time of this transaction, and the difference only paid in money.

The COURT said, the statute required the consideration to be *fully and truly* set forth and described, and therefore made the

Rule absolute for cancelling the securities.

COMPTON v. COLLINSON.

This was a reference from the Court of Chancery for the opinion of this Court, on the following

C A S E.

Michael Collinson, ten years after his marriage with Jane Banastre, entered into articles of separation, (to which her father was also a party) and covenanted that she should enjoy all estates, both real and personal, that should come to her during her coverture, and that he would join in the necessary covenants to limit them to such uses as she should appoint.

Some years afterwards her father died, and certain copyhold lands descended to her, and the husband again entered into like articles that he would join in surrendering the same to such uses as she should appoint. Soon afterward she was admitted to the copyholds, and surrendered them to the uses of her will; she afterwards made a will, giving these copyholds to John Willis and his heirs; and, a few days after,

after, July 15, 1772, made an abfolute furrender of them
to him and his heirs, and John Willis was, at the fame time,
admitted thereto. Michael Collinfon the hufband, *did not*
join or concur in any of thefe furrenders made by his
wife.

Jane Collinfon foon after died, her hufband furviving, and
her fon C. S. Collinfon being her heir at law, and her heir
by the cuftom of thefe manors.

The queftion referred to the Court was, whether *John
Willis* took any and what eftate under the furrenders or
will?

LORD LOUGHBOROUGH delivered the judgment of the
Court.—The queftion in this cafe is, whether John Willis
took any, and what eftate under the furrenders, will, and
codicil of Jane Collinfon, or under either, and which of
them? The fubject of difpute being copyhold lands, it is
evident that unlefs the furrenders be valid, no eftate can pafs
at law. No fpecial cuftom is ftated, and therefore the furrenders muft be judged of by the general law of copyhold
eftates. The feveral furrenders on the face of them, are the
furrenders of Jane Collinfon as a feme fole: for it is not
ftated that fhe was privately examined, nor is any notice
taken of her being a feme covert, nor is there any affent,
or evidence of affent, on the part of the hufband accompanying the furrenders. She is ftated by the cafe, to have
been in truth the wife of Michael Collinfon, feparated from
him, firft, by articles renouncing all his right to whatever
eftates, real or perfonal, might come to her during the coverture; and fecondly, by deed after the copyhold eftates
had defcended to her, covenanting that fhe fhould enjoy the
fame to her own ufe; and that he would join in making a
furrender of fuch eftates, and in limiting them to fuch ufes
as fhe fhould appoint. By force of thefe articles, and of
this deed, all the right of the hufband is barred. The queftion therefore is, whether the furrenders of Jane Collinfon,
her hufband not having joined, fhall bar her heir? There
are two diftinct furrenders of each copyhold: the firft made
May 26 and June 3, 1771, to the ufe of her will; the fecond July 14 and 15, 1772, abfolute furrenders to John
Willis, on which he was admitted, and which he on the
fame day furrendered to the ufe of *his* will. If Jane Collinfon had a full power to make a valid furrender, the laft
furrenders have paffed all her eftate at law to her furrenderee.
Thefe furrenders took effect immediately, fhe could not
herfelf have avoided them, nor could the hufband againft
his own covenant. If fhe had fued jointly with her hufband

band to avoid them, it would have been incongruous to have alledged as a defect in the surrender, the omission of that which the husband had covenanted to do; and which it was in her power to procure; and if she had sued as a feme sole against her own surrender, it would have been still more preposterous.   If therefore Jane Collinson could not have avoided these surrenders, it is difficult to conceive how her heir should be in a better condition with respect to an absolute surrender binding upon her, whatever claim he might have against a surrender to the use of her will.   It cannot be more necessary that the husband should join with his wife in the surrender of her copyhold, than in levying a fine of her freehold estates. But it has been settled ever since the case in the 17 Ed. III. that if a fine be levied by a feme covert without her husband, it shall bind her and her heirs, if it be not avoided by the husband; and both Rolle and Comyns seem to intimate, that the law would be the same as to a recovery.   Had the present case been of a freehold estate conveyed by the wife by fine, without her husband, it would clearly have bound her heirs, and the husband being estopped by his deed, the estate of the conusee would have been indefeasible at law.   The modes of conveying freehold and copyhold estates are different, but there is surely a fair argument from analogy, that a copyhold estate transmissible under the same circumstances as a freehold, should be governed by the same rules.   Both are public conveyances, and, from the nature of copyholds, there is more reason to support the surrender of a feme covert, where the interest of the husband is not affected by it, than there is to make a fine effectual without his joining.   Of a freehold estate the husband is *seised* in right of his wife, of a copyhold he has a mere *possession*.   He is not admitted in her right; she is the actual tenant; and when a copyhold descends to a married woman, the new grant of the lord is to her, and not to the husband.   In opposition to this reasoning, two cases were cited at the bar, which were supposed to have denied the application of any argument drawn from the case of a fine, to the validity of a surrender; and to have asserted the absolute nullity of a surrender by a feme covert, without the concurrence of her husband.   The first of these cases is *Taylor v. Philips*, 1 *Vez.* 229.   Now all that can be inferred from that report of Lord Hardwicke's opinion is, that if the fact had been fully before him, he would have made a case for the opinion of a court of law upon this very question, whether a surrender by a feme covert without her husband's joining, but with his assent, was

an effectual surrender? But as there was some reason to suppose there might be a special custom to warrant that surrender, he directed a trial. It is evident then, that Lord
Hardwicke was of opinion, that a custom for a feme covert
to surrender without her husband joining, might be a good
custom, for otherwise the trial would have been idle, and
he would have directed at once a case for the opinion of the
judges. This observation will also materially apply to the
next case, which is *Stephens* v. *Tyrell* 2 *Wils.* 1, where, according to the report, the Court of Common Pleas held,
that a custom for a feme covert to surrender without her
husband's joining, is contrary to law, and bad. In this
case it is said, that the Chief Justice observed, that it was
not stated whether the husband was to consent, though he
did not join, and therefore it must be taken to be without
his consent. Now the natural inference from thence is,
that the consent of the husband, though he did not join,
would have made the surrender effectual. The Chief Justice there censures an inaccuracy in 2 *Danvers' Abridgment*,
439, *pl.* 10. cited in support of the custom, and the remark
is just. But when one looks into the cases referred to in *Danvers*, it is evident that they furnish an authority in support
of a surrender without the husband's joining in the act of
the surrender. The first is an anonymous case in *Moore*,
123, where a custom for a married woman to devise her copyhold lands, with the assent of her husband, was holden
to be good. The next are 3 *Leon.* 81. *Godb.* 14 & 143,
and 2 *Brownl.* 218, which all treat of the same case, viz.
Skipwith's case. There were two parts of the custom alledged in that case, the one that a married woman might
devise, the other that she might surrender in the presence of
the steward and six of the tenants. The state of the case in
Leonard shews that the will was made in favour of the
husband, in the presence of the steward and six of the tenants, and at the next court the surrender to the use of the
will, was also in the presence of the steward and six of the
tenants. The custom seems to have been holden good in
substance, and it is probable that it was so from the ci-
tation in 2 *Brownl.* 218. This is therefore an authority,
that a surrender without the husband's joining, though certainly in a case where his assent might be presumed, is good.
The reasoning of the Chief Justice, according to *Wilson's*
report, proceeds upon a supposition, that the custom stated
excludes the husband entirely, because it does not expressly
require his consent, and that it would therefore enable the
feme covert to dispose of her estate against his consent. But
this

this is by no means a neceffary conclusion. A furrender without the hufband, may be a good difpofition againft all but him, and his right to avoid it is not inconfiftent with fuch a cuftom. The reafons therefore on which the cuftom in *Wilfon* is condemned, do not appear quite fatisfactory; and it has always appeared to me fomewhat arbitrary, to condemn a cuftom, becaufe it is not conformable to the general law and policy of the nation. That eftates fhould be holden in fome manors, by an heirefs independent of her hufband, is not more fingular, than in others that the eftate fhould veft abfolutely in the hufband by the intermarriage, which is the cafe in fome manors in Weftmoreland. This cafe then goes no further than an opinion, that a furrender, in which the hufband neither joins nor affents, cannot be good; but if that opinion were well founded, it would not affect the prefent cafe. In both *Vezey* and *Wilfon*, the obfervation made on the analogy of a fine is, that it works by eftoppel. In the cafe in *Vezey*, Lord Hardwicke is fpeaking of the fine of a tenant in tail, where no intereft paffes, which, he fays, will be good againft the heir by eftoppel, and the phrafe is there correctly ufed. But as to a feme covert levying a fine, where it conveys an intereft, it fhall bind her and her heirs, if the hufband does not enter and avoid it, becaufe, fays Lord Coke, fhe was *examined, and has power over the land*, 10 *Rep.* 43. *a.* The fine there paffes the eftate, and when it is faid that fhe is eftopped by it, the expreffion is ufed in the fame loofe manner, as when it is applied to any other perfon contending in oppofition to his own deed, by which he has paffed away the intereft and eftate which he would claim.

It was objected in the argument, that no cuftom is ftated in the cafe, and that a furrender by a feme covert, even with the hufband's joining, can in no cafe be good but by the particular cuftom of a manor. No authority was cited for this pofition, but it was argued that from the feveral cafes, viz. *Dyer* 363, *b.* Cro. *Eliz.* 717, and *Litt. Rep.* 274, (in which the validity of a cuftom for a feme covert being feparately examined, and her hufband joining, to make a furrender, is affirmed), it was ftrongly implied that fuch a furrender would not be good by the general law of copyholds. This objection refts on a fuppofed defect in the ftatement of the cafe. But the Court will intend that the furrender by the wife feparately examined with the hu nd joining, would have been good. The cafe could not otherwife have been made, and even if the argument had been upon a fpecial verdict, the objection would not prevail. For

it

it would be contrary both to law and reason, that the copyhold of a woman should become unalienable by her marriage, and it is against the nature of copyhold estates, that they should not be surrendered back to the lord, by the act of all the persons having any interest in them, and having a disposing power.

Lord Coke says, "This is the general custom of the realm, that every copyholder may surrender in court, and need not to alledge any custom therefore," *Co. Litt.* 59. *a.* and in *Combe's* case, 9 *Rep.* 75, it is holden to be a necessary consequence of this, that every copyholder may surrender by attorney, as a thing incident by the common law; and in the pleadings of that very case, a surrender by a feme covert and her husband is pleaded, without any custom being alledged. *Co. Entries* 576. The cases which are said to afford a negative implication, that without a custom, the surrender by a husband and wife of the copyhold of the wife would not be good, cannot be so construed. The case in *Dyer,* 363, *b.* arose upon a question whether a custom in the will of *Denbigh,* that a feme covert with her husband, by surrender and examination in court might alien her land, was taken away by the statute of *Wales,* 27 *Hen.* VIII. cap. 26, and the opinion of *Dyer & Wray* was, that such custom was not abrogated, because it was reasonable and agreeable to the custom of England, for the assurance of purchasers. The case in *Cro. Eliz.* 717, states a question, whether the examination of a feme covert out of court by two tenants be good, without a special custom; and it is holden that it is not, because it is a judicial act more proper to be done in court; admitting, at the same time, that a surrender on a sole examination in court would bind her by the custom, *i. e.* by the *general* custom; for though the state of the facts does not appear by the report, it is fairly to be collected, that no special custom for a feme covert to surrender in court, was given in evidence. The short note in *Litt. Rep.* 274, seems more to favour the argument, than the two preceding cases, which, attentively considered, rather make against it. But it may easily be discovered, why in the case in *Littleton,* the defendant chose to alledge a custom, rather than to rely on the general law. He makes use of terms much more extensive than the general law. He pleads a custom that *quælibet fœmina viro co-operta,* (*including infants*) may surrender; the plaintiff replies that every woman of full age may surrender without traversing the custom that *quælibet fœmina, &c.* and the court holds the replication bad, for he ought to have traversed the custom alledged by the

the defendant. It might be a queftion, whether by fpecial cuftom, a feme covert infant could not furrender, though it is contrary to the general law, and therefore it is pleaded that *every* feme covert may furrender: but fuch a cafe affords no inference that it was neceffary to alledge a cuftom for the general pofition, that a feme covert with her hufband, might furrender.

For thefe reafons, this objection ought not to prevail even fo far as to induce the Court to defire a fuller ftate of the cafe; which would be the only effect it could have; for the cuftoms of moft manors being confonant to this general law, there is little doubt but fuch a cuftom might be truly ftated in any cafe, where it were neceffary that it fhould be particularly alledged.

The general objection to the validity of the furrenders, viz. that by the common law, a feme covert is incapable of difpofing of her lands without the concurrence of her hufband, has been in part already confidered; but it may be fit to examine this pofition more particularly. It certainly is, generally fpeaking, a true one, though perhaps not quite correctly expreffed; for a feme covert has no power to convey with her hufband, except by fine or recovery. It would be more accurate to ftate the law to be, that a married woman can make no conveyance of her lands, except by fine or recovery; and that a fine levied by her alone, is avoidable only by her hufband. It is equally a general rule of law, that a feme covert cannot fue or be fued without her hufband, and that fhe can make no contract to bind herfelf. Thefe rules are eftablifhed on the principle (partly religious, and partly political,) that fhe has entered into an indiffoluble engagement, by which fhe is placed under the power and protection of her hufband, given up to him all perfonal property in her actual poffeffion, and the right to receive all fuch as may be reduced into poffeffion. To thefe general rules, there have been, in the procefs of the law, various exceptions allowed, where the principle of the rules could not be applied to the circumftances of the cafe. In the cafe mentioned in *Co. Litt.* 132, *b.* and ftated at large in *Ryley Plac. Parliam.* 19 *Ed.* l. p. 66, the hufband having abjured the realm for felony, the wife was permitted to fue and had judgment to recover feifin of an eftate, of which fhe was jointly enfeoffed with her hufband for life, againft the lord, who after fatisfaction made to the king for the year, day, and wafte, claimed to have the land by efcheat. In the 31 *Ed.* I. it was holden, that the wife of one who had abjured the realm, could make a feoffment by deed, with
warranty

warranty of her land, and should be bound by it. *Fitz. Abr. cui. in vitâ pl.* 31. In the 10 *Ed.* III. a *quare impedit* was brought for the King against the Lady Maltravers; she pleaded coverture, and upon the replication for the King, that her husband was exiled for a certain cause, she was ruled to answer. In the 1 *Hen.* IV. the same point was determined in the case of the Lady *Bellknap,* whose plea of coverture was over-ruled on a replication, that her husband was exiled: and in the following year, 2d of *Hen.* IV. the same lady sued in her own name, and her suit was allowed. Lord *Coke* does not take notice of a circumstance mentioned in the Year Book, and in *Brooke's Abridgment,* that some of the justices said, she sued as farmer of the king; which seems to strengthen the authority, for it shews that during the exile of the husband, she acted as a feme sole, holding an interest under a grant from the king, by which she might both sue and be sued alone.

A feme covert may convey in execution of a power, Sir *W. Jones,* 137, and *Latch* 39, and 134, and though in that case, there is much debate in the Court, and a difference in opinion, whether the wife had any estate, and whether she could convey in execution of a trust, without her husband, yet all agreed that her feoffment without her husband, was a valid act. A feme may execute a power to sell lands without her husband, and may sell them to him. *Co. Litt.* 112, *a.* A feme covert may act in *auter droit* as an executrix, without her husband; and it is said, that she may administer, or prove the will, notwithstanding his refusal. *Com. Dig. Administration* (D). In the three instances last-mentioned, the law supports the act of the wife alone, because the husband has no interest in the execution of it; and, in all the former instances, she is enabled to act by herself, because she cannot have the authority of her husband, whose exile or abjuration, though it does not dissolve the marriage, suspends the marital power.

Cases of separation, and in consequence of the relinquishment of the marital rights by the agreement of the husband, were not likely to have often occurred in the simplicity of ancient times. But there is a case in the Year-book 47th of *Ed.* III. cap. 18, which shews that they were not then totally unknown in the law. " An action of account was brought against one as bailiff of the plaintiff's land, to which the defendant pleaded, that there was a debate between the plaintiff and his wife, on which, by the accord of their friends, the plaintiff assigned to his wife, for her maintenance, the land of which the account was demanded, and

and that the wife leafed thefe lands to him for a term of years. The plaintiff infifts, this is no plea, and amounts merely to a denial of the defendant being bailiff; but the Court held, that he muft anfwer the plea. And then the plaintiff traverfes the leafe alledged to be made by his wife." This cafe feems to prove, that a feme covert might difpofe of the profits of lands allotted for her maintenance, and make a leafe of them, without the hufband joining in the leafe. In *Croke Charles* there are two cafes, on bonds given to fecure the difpofal of a fum of money by a married woman. The firft of them was in the 5 *Car. I. Cro. Car.* 219. It was an action upon a bond given by a man after marriage, conditioned to permit his wife to make a will, and difpofe of a fum not exceeding 50l. in legacies: the defendant pleaded that the wife did not make any will, and on that plea iffue was joined. It was found fpecifically, that fhe did make a will, and difpofed of divers legacies not exceeding 50l. but that fhe was covert at the time of making the will. Judgment was given for the plaintiff; for though by law a feme covert could not make a will without her hufband's affent, yet it was a will within the meaning of the condition. The other cafe was in the 10 *Car. I. Cro. Car.* 376. It was an action on a bond conditioned to pay 300l. after the death of the wife by the hufband, in cafe he furvived, for fuch afes as fhe fhould appoint by any writing under her hand and feal, in the prefence of two witneffes. The defendant pleaded that fhe did not appoint. The plaintiff replied, that fhe by her will in writing, fealed and publifhed in the prefence of two witneffes, did will and appoint fuch fums to be paid; to which the defendant demurred, and judgment was given for the plaintiff. The argument feems to have been upon the pleading this writing as a will, and not as an appointment. But the Court held it to be fufficient, for though it was not properly a will, being made by a feme covert, yet it was a writing in the nature of a will.

Courts of law then had at this period recognized the power of a married woman authorifed by her hufband, to make in effect a teftamentary difpofition of perfonal property.

The cafe of *Munby v. Scott*, 1 *Lev.* 5. decided foon after the Reftoration on an action which had been commenced during the Ufurpation of Cromwell, gave rife to a very large difcuffion of the rights of hufbands and wives. It feemed then to be the opinion of the majority of the Judges, that the hufband could not be fued for any debt contracted by

the

the wife without evidence of his assent; consequently for no debt contracted by her when wilfully separated from him. Hale held the rule so strict, that in a case reported, 2 *Levinz*, 16, some years after the judgment in *Manby* v. *Scott*, he non-suited the plaintiff, in an action brought by a gaoler against a husband for the diet and lodging of his wife. It appeared in the case, that the husband had left his wife in the country, and come up to London, where he married another woman. The former wife caused him to be indicted; and coming to London to prosecute, was, by his contrivance, arrested, and sent to gaol. The husband was convicted on the prosecution. Yet Hale would not allow this peculiar case of the husband's procuring the arrest, to be an exception to the rule, which required his assent to the debt. Subsequent cases however relaxed the extreme rigour of this rule, as where the husband turns the wife out of doors, he gives her credit wherever she goes, according to Holt's opinion, *Salk.* 118. But still in the case of a wilful separation of the wife, the law was understood to be, that the husband was not liable to be sued for her debts. It seems very certain, that the Judges who argued the case of *Manby* v. *Scott*, did not conceive that an action could be brought against the wife. It was equally the supposition of those who maintained that the husband was not chargeable, as of those who held the contrary, that the wife was incapable of having any property, could acquire no credit on her own account, and must either subsist on charity, or starve, unless she could obtain an alimony from Chancery or the Ecclesiastical Court. On the one side, this situation of the wife separated from her husband, is argued as a strong argument to support the conclusion that the husband is liable to an action for necessaries; while they who argue on the other side contend, that the distress in which the wife is placed, is a just and expedient consequence of her separation from her husband, from which the law ought not to relieve her. It does not seem to have occurred to any of the Judges at that time, that a wife separated from her husband may, in fact, possess property, that she will obtain credit by means of her apparent property, and that the consequence of her debts not being recoverable either against her or her husband, would only be prejudicial to the unwary but honest tradesman.

The first case which appears, after this determination of *Manby* v. *Scott*, of an action brought against a married woman, is that of the *Duchess of Mazarine*, 1 *Salk.* 116. Lord *Raym.* 147, *Comb.* 402, in which the Court avoid the question,

tion, though she was holden liable to the action. The Reports say, it may be intended she was divorced, or her husband an alien enemy; and perhaps it may be like the Lady *Bellknap's* case, whose husband was exiled. The only notes of the case are very short, and the point appears to have been made upon a motion for a new trial, in which the Court felt what the justice of the case required, and were not pressed to explain the grounds of their opinion. It would however have been a strange situation, if the Duchess of Mazarine, a woman enjoying a considerable fortune of her own, and for many years a large pension from the Crown of England, had been protected from every legal demand, by a rule of the law of England, that no action could be brought against her, because she had a husband whose person and fortune were utterly unknown, and could not be attached by any one with whom she dealt. The only two grounds hinted at for the decision, could not have stood examination. She neither was nor could be divorced, the law of France not permitting a divorce; and though in the term when the motion for a new trial was denied, the treaty of peace had not been signed, and a Frenchman was then an alien enemy, yet that argument would not have been applicable in the next term. The question whether a married woman, separated from her husband, and enjoying, by his agreement, a separate provision, shall be liable for her debts, has come before the Courts in several cases. In that of *Ringstead* v. Lady *Lanesborough, Hil.* 23 *Geo.* III. the point was directly brought before the Court of King's Bench upon the record, and judgment given that she was liable. In that case the husband was stated to be out of England. But in *Hil.* 24 *Geo.* III. the same question was brought before the Court, the husband being in England, and the same judgment given. In *Mich.* 26 *Geo.* III. the same question was again stated upon the record, in the case of *Corbet* v. *Poelnitz,* with this difference only, that in that case the contract was for money, in the others, for goods; and the judgment was the same. About the same period, *East.* 16 *Geo.* III. the question was agitated in this Court, first, in the case of *Hatchett* v. *Baddeley,* 2 *Blackst.* 1079, where the Chief Justice and my brother *Gould* took a distinction on the pleadings, which neither stated a separation, nor a separate maintenance, but that the wife had eloped and lived separately from her husband; which distinction has certainly great weight. But the other two Judges held that the action would not lie, merely on the ground of the defendant being a married woman. In *East* 18 *Geo.* III. the question was again submitted to this Court,

Court, in the cafe of *Lean v. Schultz,* 2 Bl. 1195, on pleadings, which diftinctly ftated a feparation and feparate maintenance; but the queftion itfelf then received no determination, the Court having given judgment merely on a point of form, namely, that the hufband ought to have been joined for conformity.

From this ftate of the decifions, it cannot be concluded, that it is a fettled point, that an action may be maintained againft a married woman feparated from her hufband by confent, and enjoying a feparate maintenance. But fuppofing the law to be according to the three laft determinations of the Court of King's Bench, it feems to be a neceffary conclufion, that a married woman, whofe feparate property confifts of a copyhold eftate, fhould have a power to furrender it, for otherwife the law would compel her to pay, without allowing her to ufe the means of paying, and enable the creditor to recover a demand, without the power of making that demand effectual. This is certainly an argument from inconvenience alone, and therefore not altogether conclufive; but it has great weight when no poffible inconvenience can be oppofed on the other fide. The intereft of the hufband is entirely out of the queftion; the intereft of the lord is not hurt by the furrender; the expectancy of the heir is not an intereft, and, flight as it is, cannot be fet up as a claim in juftice, to take the eftate without paying the debts.

But the main and fubftantial ground of the cafe is, that the wife is the tenant of the copyhold, and not the hufband; that the eftate can be forfeited or furrendered only by her acts, not by his; that the authority which he acquires by his marital rights, to direct and controul her acts, is by his covenant, in the prefent inftance, annulled, or at leaft fufpended; and there is then no impediment to the validity of an act, paffed in the court of the manor, between her and the lord.

"We are therefore of opinion, that John Willis took an "eftate to him and his heirs, according to the feveral cuftoms "of the manors of Banftead and Ryegate, under the furren-"ders and admittances of the 15th of July, 1772."

Loughborough.
H. Gould.
J. Wilfon.

ROUSE

ROUSE v. BARDIN.

This was an action of trefpafs to try a right of way over Brompton-Heath, in Middlefex. The defendant's juftification ftated, that there had been, from the time whereof the memory of man is not to the contrary, a common foot-way from the highway leading from Knightfbridge to Earl's-Court, through the clofe called Brompton-Heath unto the Highway leading from London to Fulham. But it appearing upon the evidence that the foot-way in queftion over Brompton-Heath, led into another foot-way called Church-Lane, before it reached the road from London to Fulham, Lord Loughborough, who tried the caufe, directed a verdict for the plaintiff, on account of this variance in the *terminus ad quem.*

Now upon a motion for a new trial, the Court gave judgment.

GOULD, J.—This cafe arifes on pleadings of confiderable length, ftating that the trefpafs was committed in a place called Brompton-Heath, with feveral variations in point of defcription. The defendants fay, that from time whereof the memory of man is not to the contrary, there has been a common public highway, for all the liege fubjects of this kingdom, to pafs and repafs on foot, from a certain other common public highway leading from Knightfbridge to Earl's Court, in, through, over, and upon the faid clofe called Brompton-Heath, unto a certain other common highway leading from London to Fulham, and back again, in, through, and over the *locus in quo.* I underftand, that at the end of this clofe leading towards the Fulham road, that is, in the line of the way, you do not immediately iffue into what is called the Fulham road, but into another common highway, called the Church-Lane, and from thence over a very fhort fpace, you enter into that which is properly called the Fulham road. Now my apprehenfion always has been, that in cafes of this fort, the intermediate fpaces, either before the entrance into a field, or at the exit out of it before you reach the *terminus ad quem,* are immaterial. This is the cafe of a common public highway, and there have been very confiderable doubts, whether in a common highway, any *termini* at all need be fet forth. There was a cafe mentioned at the bar, of an indictment for ftopping a highway at Kenfington, in which it was holden, that the way was fufficiently defcribed, without

ftating

stating from what place, to what place it led; and among
other things, a reason was given for that opinion, because a
highway runs from the sea across the whole island. But nevertheless, if a defendant will state the *termini* in his justification, he is bound to prove them. There are many instances, which must occur to every one, where things are
not necessary to be alledged in pleading, yet if they be alledged, they must be proved. Such as the description of a
public act of Parliament; the day when the sessions were
holden; and the like. So where an officer justifies under
process of execution out of a court, it is unnecessary for
him to state a judgment, yet if he will state it, he is bound
to prove it as described. These are common cases, and
many more might be adduced. The question then in the
present case is, what the terms of this plea require to be
proved, and whether they necessarily import that the way
in dispute was *adjoining* to the Fulham road? Now that is
not the case; the way is described to go, *in, through, over*, and
along Brompton-Heath, *unto* the Fulham road. But there
is an intervening space between that and the Fulham road.
If it had been described to be *adjoining* to the Fulham road,
I have already given my opinion as to the proof. But it is
stated to lead *unto* the Fulham road; which in my apprehension, is nothing more than this; a common highway
which is one entire thing, leads over this field to the Fulham road; and so it does, notwithstanding there is an intervening piece of ground. The case cited at the bar from
Ventris, comprehends this idea. It is there said to be sufficient to state the places from which, and to which the way
leads, though the mesne passages should be mistaken. It
will be material to advert to ancient pleadings in justification.
I find in *Rastal's Entries*, 617, *b.* a right of way pleaded as
follows: a man was seised of a messuage in *S.* and prescribed
for a way for all those whose estate, &c. both for horse and
foot " *from the messuage to the parish church of E. and the
market town of M.* with all his carriages *ultrà clausum præ-
dictum.*" Now it would be productive of infinite uncertainty, to require an exact description of the line of the
way, to say that it went so many yards to the North, then
turned to the West, and then to the East, in that irregular
manner. Such justifications as these would then be clogged
with insuperable difficulties in point of proof. And I think
it would be totally unnecessary; the usage defines the way.
I mention this as occurring to me from the books and
pleadings; and with regard to experience, I have always understood that the intermediate spaces are disregarded, both

as

as to the approach to a field and the quitting it. It is fufficient to anfwer the trefpafs, and juftify under a right to pafs over the clofe. I therefore think this is not a material variance from the plea.

WILSON, J.—I am of the fame opinion. Where the way is a public highway, it is in no fort neceffary to ftate either the *terminus à quo*, or the *terminus ad quem*; where it is a private way, it is neceffary to ftate them, becaufe private ways are given for particular purpofes. But it is different with regard to a public highway, becaufe all his Majefty's fubjects have a right to ufe that way, for all purpofes, and at all times. The reafon given in the ancient cafes, why a highway muft be particularly defcribed, is not a very good one, namely, that it muft be ftated to lead to a market town, in order to fhew that it is a highway. Lord *Hale* fays, whether it be a highway or not, depends much on reputation. I am therefore of opinion, that in juftifying a trefpafs, becaufe the place in queftion is a highway, it is not neceffary to ftate the places to which, and from which it leads. If that be fo, the next queftion is, whether thofe places being ftated in the plea, they are fufficiently proved? With refpect to that, the way in difpute is ftated to be a highway leading from one highway to another highway. I think it cannot be doubted, but that this is a fufficient defcription. But it is impoffible to ftate the fpecific line of the road under that defcription, which can only be, that it leads from one point to another. What the line is on which the highway paffes, muft be a matter of evidence. The objection in this cafe is, that the way is ftated to lead to the Fulham road, but that before it reaches the Fulham road, it goes for a little fpace on another highway. But I do not conceive that to be a material variance. I underftand the allegation to import no more than this, namely, that there is a highway over the clofe, on which you may go from the Fulham road to the Kenfington road; but not that the Fulham road joins to the clofe over which the highway leads. But even if that were the import of the allegation, I fhould have confiderable doubts whether this were a variance. But clearly the allegation means no more than this; there is a highway over the clofe, leading from the Fulham road to the Kenfington road, which I think was fufficiently proved by the evidence.

LORD LOUGHBOROUGH.—My brother *Heath* has informed me, that he is of the fame opinion with my brothers *Gould* and *Wilfon*. I therefore certainly feel that the authority of the Court ought to govern my opinion. But on the beft confideration I have given the queftion, I have not been

able

able to bring myself to agree with them. I still retain the opinion I first had at the trial, and think, that in all cases, where a real difference in opinion exists, it is right to avow it, and state the grounds on which we differ. What weighs with me in the present case, is the positive authority of 2 *Rolle's Abridgment*, 81, in which it is said, that in an indictment for an obstruction, or nuisance, near a highway, it is necessary to set out the *terminus à quo*, and the *terminus ad quem*; a case in 15 *Car.* I. is referred to where an indictment was quashed for this reason, which was said to be a common exception, and divers indictments had been quashed on the same account. Against that authority, a case in *Latch,* 123, and some subsequent cases were cited: But that case, in my apprehension, tends rather to confirm than weaken the authority of *Rolle's Abridgment*, for it shews that a much nicer objection was allowed by all the Court. It was stated in the indictment, that at Kensington the defendant obstructed the King's highway from London to Kensington, and the Court two several times held this to be bad, because they said, the manner of describing the way excluded Kensington. The indictment was then drawn in a third form, and the way described to be, the King's highway in Kensington; this was holden to be sufficient, first by Jones, and afterwards by Dodderidge and Whitlock, and the reason given is, because a highway leads from the sea through all England. But that reason I do not conceive to be a fair one: the obvious reason is, that a highway stated to be in a town is sufficiently certain. And in that case, Jones distinguishes a common way, in which the *termini* must be set out, from *alta via regia*. The case in 3 *Keble* 89, is not applicable to the present; it was of a presentment on a view by a jury, on an annoyance in a cloth fair, which the Court, after verdict, held good. I think the case in *Andrews,* 137, before Lord Chief Justice *Lee,* was rightly determined on its own grounds. One question there was, whether the description of the river Thames at Fulham, was sufficient, without stating the places to which and from which it flowed. But it would be absurd to require abuttals of navigable rivers, in that case it was holden sufficient to say the river Thames at Fulham; and both Probyn and Chapple say, it was not necessary to set out the *termini*, for the Court would take notice of the river Thames. But admitting that in an indictment for a nuisance in not repairing, it was sufficient to state a highway generally, yet it seems to me that the same rule is not to be applied to a plea in bar of an action of trespass; because every man has *primâ facie* a right

to

to exclude all others from coming over his land, and the justification must be set out with due certainty, and notice to the plaintiff of the way claimed over his soil.   There may be many ways claimed, and the occupier of the field ought to know which is insisted upon; he may admit one, and deny the other; he has a right to reply *extra viam*, which he cannot do, unless the way is explained with defining the term where it commences and ends.   In the case before the Court, the plaintiff might have admitted the road to the Church-lane; he is deceived by the plea, for he knows there is no road over his field which directly terminates in the Fulham road.   But whether the defendant was or was not obliged to describe the way so particularly, he has undertaken to do it, and has not done it truly; a way terminating in the Church-lane, and a way terminating in the Fulham road, are not only distinct, but it is physically impossible they can be the same.   If the road were a line drawn from the Knightsbridge to the Fulham road, the line actually taken into the Church-lane, must of necessity be *extra viam*, and so *vice versâ*.   To state generally a right to cross a field without any given direction, seems to me so uncertain, that it is impossible to meet it with precision, either in a replication, or on traverse of the plea.

Rule absolute for a new trial.

GUNNIS *v.* ERHART.

The defendant bought an estate at an auction, which, in the printed particulars of sale, was stated to be free from all incumbrances; but there being a charge of 17 l. a-year on the estate, he refused to take it, and this action was brought.

Upon the trial the plaintiff was non-suited, Lord Loughborough refusing to admit evidence that the auctioneer declared publicly to the company at the sale, that the estate was thus incumbered, no proof being offered that the defendant had express personal information given to himself of it.

And now, upon motion for a new trial, the COURT agreed in his Lordship's opinion.

Rule refused.

COLLIS,

COLLIS, *and others, v.* EMMETT.

This was an action against the drawer of a bill of exchange, brought by the indorsers; and a special verdict having been found, it now came for the consideration of the Court.

The verdict stated, that John Emmett, who was partner with Livesay, and Co. at Clithero, wrote his name upon a piece of blank paper, duly stamped, and gave it to Livesay, and Co. for the purpose of drawing a bill of exchange, at such time, for such sum, and to such persons, as they should think fit.

That afterwards the said Livesay, and Co. drew on the said paper, above the name of the said John Emmett, *a certain writing directed to the said* Livesay, and Co. in the words and figures following, viz. " *Clithero, April 5th,* 1788, " £. 1,551, three months after date, pay to Mr George " Chapman, or order, fifteen hundred and fifty pounds, " value received as advised, John Emmett." That the occasion and manner of giving the said paper writing was as follows, viz. That on the said 5th of April, 1788, the said Livesay, and Co. were indebted to Thomas Jeffery, in the sum of 1,512*l.* 9*s.* upon a bill of exchange, which became due that day, and which had been previously given for goods sold by Jeffery to them. That one Richard Collis, clerk to the said Jeffery, on that day applied at the house of Livesay, and Co. in Cheapside, for payment of the said Bill; that on such application, he saw the said Anstie, one of the said partners, who informed the said Richard Collis, that he could not conveniently then pay the same, but requested the said Richard Collis to take a bill on the said house of Livesay, and Co. for the said sum of 1,512*l.* 9*s.* at three months date, including the interest thereof in the mean time, and gave to him the said *blank paper* above-mentioned, with the name of the said John Emmett written thereon, to be filled up by one of the clerks of the said Livesay, and Co.

That one Ludlow, a clerk of the said Livesay, and Co. filled up the said writing for 1,551*l.* being the amount of the said bill, and interest, in manner and form as above set forth, except the acceptance and indorsement thereof as hereinafter mentioned; and that, immediately afterwards, the said paper writing was carried to Andrew Goodrick, another clerk of the said Livesay, and Co. and who was authorised by the said Livesay, and Co. to accept the same, and which the said Andrew Goodrick accordingly did, in the name of the said Livesay, and Co. *That with the authority of the said Livesay,*
and

and Co. *the name of George Chapman was then indorsed in the said paper writing,* and that the said paper writing, so filled up, accepted and indorsed, was then delivered to the said Richard Collis, and the said Richard Collis thereupon delivered up the bill for 1,512*l*. 9*s*. to the said Livesay and Co. That the said Thomas Jeffery afterwards negotiated the said paper writing with the plaintiffs, and *received the full amount thereof from them,* deducting a discount at 4¼*l*. *per cent*. and delivered the same to the said Plaintiffs. That the same was duly presented for payment to the said Livesay and Co. who refused to pay the same, whereof the said John Emmett had due notice.—That there was no such person as the said George Chapman, the supposed payee of the said paper writing, but that the said George Chapman was *merely a fictitious person :* that Emmett gave no *further, or other authority than as aforesaid,* and *knew nothing of this transaction.* That the Plaintiffs had *then no knowledge that the said George Chapman was a fictitious, person,* or. of the circumstances under which the said paper writing was drawn, accepted, and indorsed, but that the said Thomas Jeffery *had full knowledge of the whole of the said transactions.*

LORD LOUGHBOROUGH.—We have taken the whole of this case into our consideration, and the result of our opinion is, that the plaintiff is intitled to recover. The special count in the declaration, stating the whole of the transaction, would have afforded a ground, upon which I have thought that judgment might have been very properly pronounced in his favour. But it appears upon the record, that the case stated on the special count differs from the finding on the special verdict in two or three circumstances; that count therefore would clearly not support a judgment in favour of the plaintiff. The circumstances are not very material, but as the count and the verdict at present stand inconsistent with each other, a judgment for the plaintiff on the first count would undoubtedly be erroneous. We must therefore look into, the declaration, to see if there be any count on the record, on which the plaintiff may support a judgment. And it appears to us, that it may fairly be supported on the second count, stating the bill to be a bill *payable to bearer.* It is certainly not *literatim* payable to bearer, it is drawn payable to *George Chapman* or order. Upon a fact set forth in the special verdict, it appears that by the permission at least, if not something more than the permission of the defendant, a power was given to Livesey and Co. to frame bills of exchange, binding him in any manner they thought proper, within the limits of that power. There is no doubt they might, within those limits, have drawn a bill in terms payable to bearer; the bill they have chosen to draw, is a bill payable to Chapman or order: and it is found on the verdict that there is no such person as Chapman. Now the consequence of this seems naturally and justly to be, that when a security is negociated, on which, by the terms of it, the party receiving it apprehends he has a clear right to recover, and by the insertion of the name of a fictitious person, his recovery is impeded (it being impossible to prove the order of a person who has no existence), it should seem in point of law precisely the same in effect, as if it had been made payable to bearer. A bill of exchange is an authority to pay pursuant to the order of the payee; and it is also an undertaking to pay pursuant to that order. But if there be no person who by an impossibility can give such order, the engagement must be to pay the bill. If the order of the person cannot be procured, and with the knowledge and privity of the parties who make the bill, such a name is put in as cannot give an order, it is in effect, and in point of law, the same thing as if they had made it payable to the person who held the bill, namely the bearer. The determination of the court of King's Bench, has approved the same rule and we think that a right determination.

Judgment for the plaintiff on the second count

BOUCHIER v. WITTLE.

Upon an objection that there was not 15 days between the Teste and Return upon a Capias. The court allowed the Teste to be amended.

MEARS

MEARS v. GRENAWAY

By the statute 22 C. II. st. 2. it is enacted, that, in actions of trespass, assault and battery, &c. where the damages are under 40s. the plaintiff shall recover no more costs than damages, *except where the judge shall certify that the assault and battery was fully proved.* This was an action for assault and battery, stating, that the defendant then and there tore and destroyed the plaintiff's clouths of the value of 20l. so that they became of no use. The jury gave 5s. damages, and the judge did not certify, but the prothonotary allowed full costs to the plaintiff. This was a motion to shew cause why the prothonotary should not revise his taxation.

LORD LOUGHBOROUGH.—There is no doubt in this case, that the same question might have been left to the jury, which my brother Grose asked them in the case of *Cotterill* v. *Tolly*, namely, whether the tearing of cloaths were part of the same act for which they gave 5s. damages; if they had answered that it was so, there would have been no question. But it is the same thing if it appears on the face of the declaration; which, after stating the beating, goes on to state that the cloaths of the plaintiff were spoiled, and then specifies each particular article, his coat, waistcoat, hat wig, shoes, stockings, &c. Now I can only conceive one case, in which, by any reasonable probability, these acts can be considered as wholly distinct; and that is, by supposing that the defendant had first beat the plaintiff, then stripped him stark-naked, and spoiled his cloaths. But it is evident that one act was in consequence of the other; and the law is not to be evaded by a device of pleading.

GOULD, J.—There are two courses marked out for judges in cases of this kind, one by the stat. 43 *Eliz.* the other by 22 & 23 *Car.* II. The first and best determination is in 3 *Keble*, but that has been open to a great deal of subtle reasoning and distinction. Yet I think that the best construction, which best answers the end of the legislature, and puts a stop to all frivolous actions, by restraining more costs than damages from being allowed in the cases specified. If therefore the declaration states the tearing of the cloaths to be done at the same time with the beating, the court will construe it so as to accomplish the object of the statute, and will hold

O 2   the

the tearing to be part of the same act, and a consequence of the battery. It was well determined in Walker's case in 4 *Co.* that the words *adtunc & ibidem*, united and coupled all together.

HEATH, J.—Whatever difference of construction there was formerly on the statute of *Car.* II. it is now settled, that it must either appear on the face of the declaration, or be found by the jury, that the tearing the cloaths was in consequence of the beating. But after a general verdict it is to be intended that it was so found; and this may be without violence to the cases determined in the King's Bench.

WILSON, J.—The plaintiff is not intitled to his full costs. The cases rest on the form of the declaration. If, in an action of this kind, the party choose to forego the *tort* to his person, and only goes for the injury to his cloaths, he would have his full costs. But if he will combine both together in one count, the case is within the statute of *Car.* H. because the principal injury is the battery; and the judge may certify.

Rule absolute.

CLAY *v.* WILLAN.

The defendant, who was a common carrier, advertised, by a printed bill, that he would be answerable for no *cash*, *plate*, &c. above 5l. value if lost, unless entered and paid for as such, namely, one penny for every pound value, as insurance.

This was an action to recover the value of a parcel of light guineas, sent by this carrier to London, and lost. It being proved on the trial that the person who delivered the parcel knew of the above conditions, and did not declare the contents, or pay for it as valuable, the plaintiff was non-suited.

Now, upon motion to set aside this non-suit,

The court said the parcel ought to have been entered, and paid for as valuable, according to the printed conditions, and therefore

Discharged the rule.

TRE-

Trelawney v. Thomas.

In the late election at Bristol the plaintiff was employed by the defendant (who was a member of a committee for conducting Peach's election) as an agent in the interest of Peach and Cruger; and this was an action for labour, &c. and also money advanced in that service.

On the trial two witnesses, Lediard and Ewbank, were called, who having given Mr. Peach bonds of indemnity against the expences of the election, were rejected by Lord Loughborough as interested, inasmuch as Peach might be liable to this debt, if the defendant was discharged of it on the ground of being his agent; and a verdict was given to the plaintiff, with interest for the money advanced.

It was contended, on a motion for a new trial, that no interest should have been allowed; and also that the evidence above-mentioned should have been admitted. Upon which the court gave the following judgment:

GOULD, J.—It would be an exceedingly hard case, if the plaintiff Trelawney was not intitled to recover against the defendant Thomas, considering, from the state of the evidence, the active share and part which he took in this business. For my own part, if I had been present on the spot, and observed his conduct, I should have looked upon him as a person supporting the credit of Cruger, and putting himself forward as a stake to be responsible to every body. With respect to the committee, it is clear that Thomas was a member of it, and supposing the money to come from that committee, and having said nothing to give the plaintiff a better right against any other person, he shall not be permitted to turn the plaintiff round. With respect to the objection to the witnesses, I take it, that unless a witness is interested in the event of a cause, the objection will not go to repel him; it will not go to his competency, but only to his credit. In this case, it seems to me from the statement of it by my lord-chief-justice, that there was an interest in these two witnesses, as they were liable to that sum of money which would follow a verdict in point of costs: they appear therefore to me interested to procure a non-suit if they possibly could for the plaintiff, or a verdict against him. As to the last question, relating to the interest on the money,

ney, I remember a cafe extremely well, where, on a writ of inquiry, the jury, on affeffing damages, found intereft for money lent; my brother Whitaker applied to fet afide that inquifition, on the ground that the giving intereft was not warranted by any precedent: a cafe was then cited from Bunbury's reports (119), in which the court were of opinion, that, for money lent, intereft fhould be recovered; and Whitaker's motion was refufed.   Now money laid out for the ufe of another, and money lent to him, feem to ftand precifely on the fame ground with refpect to reafon, juftice, and equity.   As far therefore as intereft was affeffed with refpect to the liquidated fum, I think the verdict perfectly right, and ought to be fuftained; as to the fum for a day's wages, certainly in my apprehenfion, no intereft ought to be allowed; and this diftinction is made in the cafe in Bunbury, that for goods fold and delivered, or work and labour, no intereft ought to be allowed; otherwife of money lent.   But there is a known and ufual method of remitting damages of this kind.   I am therefore of opinion, that there ought not to be a new trial.

HEATH, J.—I am in the fame opinion with my brother Gould, on the firft point.   I think it clear that Thomas has made himfelf liable; he was one of the acting committee, and the only perfon the plaintiff can fue.   As to the queftion concerning the witneffes who were examined on the *voir dire*, one fays he has entered into a written agreement, the other that he gave a bond for the payment of money; and one fays the money was to be made ufe of in defraying the expences of the election.   If the party were fued on the bond, though in point of law perhaps it could not be pleaded that only fuch a fum was really advanced; yet in equity, no more would be recovered.   Then the queftion is, Whether they are interefted in the event of this fuit? Now it appears clearly, that Cruger and Peach were joint candidates; it alfo appears that there was a committee formed for the intereft of both, and that the defendant Thomas was a member of that committee.   When therefore the two witneffes were called to be examined, and to non-fuit the plaintiff, who brings his action to recover the expences of the election, they fpeak moft materially in refpect to their own intereft; becaufe the money to be recovered by this verdict, will be part of the money, for the fecuring payment of which, the agreement was entered into, and the bond was given.

WILSON,

WILSON, J.—With respect to the first question, it is evident that the Jury might have found either way; there being evidence on both sides, they might very well find for the plaintiff, which they have done. With respect to the other question of the two witnesses, I entertain very great doubts. I am not prepared to go the length of saying their testimony ought to be rejected. All that one of them says is, that he gave a bond to Mr. Peach, conditioned for the payment of money; and that he understood Peach was to apply it to defray the expences of the election. Now, it does not at all appear that Peach would be answerable to the defendant Thomas, because, if the committee undertook the election at their own expence by their own subscription, the candidate was not answerable to them; and if they were merely agents, they were not themselves personally answerable. There is no evidence, therefore, that Thomas could have compelled this money from Peach; and unless that was clearly established, I am of opinion that there is not a shadow of interest in the witness Ewbank. With regard to Lediard, I should also doubt whether he had an interest in this case, which must be shewn, though they might have a common cause. Yet, even if the objection were to hold, it would go only to the credit of the witness. Now these persons are not to pay over to the defendant either the damages or costs of suit which he might incur; but there is a chance that Peach may call upon them. It is also very likely that Lediard might be mistaken; when he was giving an account of a written engagement, he might not recollect exactly what it was, it might be a bond having some recitals in it, or something relating to the election; but we do not know what it was. But I think it is too much to reject the evidence of witnesses, unless there is a positive and direct proof either out of their own mouths, or by record (but out of their mouths it should be), that they are interested in the event of the cause. In the present case it ought to be shewn, that Thomas was employed by Peach, and that Peach was liable to him, when he made himself liable for the money.

GOULD, J.—I remember a case in Strange, where the witness answered to the *voir dire*, that though he was not under any legal obligation to bear out the costs, yet he considered himself under an obligation in point of honour, and that repelled him.

LORD LOUGHBOROUGH—In this case there was no evidence at all of there being any committee, who had money
of

of their own, contributing to pay towards the expence of the election; on the contrary, the evidence on the part of the defendant proved the negative of that propofition. There was a committee managing the election for the abfent candidate, Mr. Cruger; and Mr. Peach, one of the candidates, has an engagement on the part of Mr. Ewbank to pay fimply a fum of money, but Ewbank declares that the confideration on which he had given that bond, and what would make the real debt between Peach and him, was the application of fo much of that fum as fhould be neceffary towards the expences of the election, in relief of Peach, the partner of Cruger. The other witnefs, Lediard, entered into an agreement, which he ftates to be exactly of the fame effect, for the payment of money which he underftood to be for the expences of the election. Now, they feem to me to have the moft direct intereft in the event of the caufe: not that the verdict could be evidence on which the money would be demandable of them, but in the perfuafion of their own minds, that the difference of the caufe was juft fo much to them in the proportion of the cofts. It is certainly fufficient, from the cafe in Strange, that the witnefs thinks himfelf interefted, though in point of law there could be no recovery againft him. Now if he difclofes the nature of his intereft, and honeftly fays what that intereft is, according to his own conception of it, and it is an intereft which by immediate and neceffary confequence muft fubject him to the cofts in the action, it would be ftrange to fay that it was indifferent to him whether the defendant or plaintiff recovered. Certainly, in point of law, thefe witneffes muft pay the money due on their agreements, but it is equally certain that Peach could have execution for no more than he could ftate to be paid by him for the expence of the election. The 44l. due to the plaintiff Trelawney is money advanced towards the expence of the election. In cafe he recovers, the obligation to pay the 44l. and all the cofts of this, and the other action attaches, which, in that refpect, become part of the expences of the election. If the plaintiff had been non-fuited, they might have tendered the two fums to Peach, and thrown on him the cofts. With regard to the queftion, how far collateral intereft in the fame caufe will affect the parties, fo as to reject their evidence, I am at a lofs for a fettled and known rule. The cafes have differed very widely upon it; it has appeared in feveral cafes, that where the witnefs has ftood precifely in the fituation as either party to the caufe, with refpect to another action, it

was

was better to hold it to be an objection that went to his competency rather than his credit. But I know that opinion is combated by very great authority. Yet it was so ruled in the time of Lord Chief Justice Parker by all the Judges of England. The case is in Fortescue 246, Lock v Hayton, where an action was brought on a policy of insurance, and the plaintiff having proved the policy and premium, the master of the ship was called to prove the loss and damages, who admitted that he himself made an insurance on some goods of his own on board; an objection was taken to his competency, which the Chief Justice reserved for the consideration of the Court: and afterwards on a communication with all the Judges it is stated by Fortescue, who was himself a Judge at that time, to be their unanimous opinion, that it was a sufficient objection to repel the witness. But this in the present case goes beside the point, as I take it here, there was a direct interest in the costs of the cause.

Rule difcharged.

CROWN CASES.

The appearance of a monster in human shape, who has lately gone about the streets of London, and wounded several women in the most brutal manner, having carried the public attention to the laws against maiming, the following Cases lately determined on the COVENTRY ACT, not being noticed in *Burn's Juftice*, or the other books of that kind, cannot fail of being acceptable to our readers.

WILLIAM LEE'S CASE.

At the Old Bailey July Sessions, 1763, William Lee was indicted on the COVENTRY ACT, 22 and 23 *Car*. II. cap. 1, before Lord Chief Baron *Parker*, present Mr. Justice *Bathurst*, and Mr. Justice *Wilmot*, for that he, contriving and intending Agnes his wife to maim and disfigure, on purpose and of malice aforethought, by lying in wait, did make an assault with a certain razor, and the neck of the said Agnes did cut, &c. with intent to maim and disfigure.

The facts were, that the prisoner returned home one night, after his wife and two children were abed and asleep and cut his wife's throat with an old razor which he had concealed in his stocking, making a wound about three inches in length, and quite acrofs; but providentially it was not mortal.

The words of the Act of Parliament are, " That whoever fhall on purpofe, and of malice aforethought, and by
" lying in wait, unlawfully cut out, or difable the tongue,
" put out an eye, flit the nofe, cut off a nofe or lip, or cut
" off or difable any limb or member, &c. fhall fuffer death
" without clergy:" and it was fubmitted to the Court, that the evidence did not prove any offence within the ftatute.

THE COURT were of the fame opinion; and the prifoner was accordingly acquitted.

BARNEY CARROLL'S CASE.

At the Old Bailey in July Seffions, 1765, Barney Carroll was indicted before Lord Chief Baron *Parker*, on the 22 and 23 *Car.* II. cap. 1. § 7, for that " he did on purpofe,
" and of malice aforethought, and by lying in wait, felo-
" nioufly and unlawfully make an affault upon Cranley Tho-
" mas Kirby, Efq; with intention to maim and disfigure
" him; and with a certain knife did on purpofe, and of his
" malice aforethought, and by lying in wait, unlawfully and
" feloniously *flit the nofe* of the faid Cranley Thomas Kirby,
" with intention in fo doing to maim and disfigure him;
" AND THAT William King, at the time of the committing
" of the faid felony, was prefent, counfelling, aiding, and
" abetting the faid Barney Carroll to commit the felony
" aforefaid."

The profecutor had apprehended a young pickpocket near Somerfet-houfe in the Strand; and upon threatening to take him before a Magiftrate, the prifoner Carroll, who appeared to have been lurking under the fide of the New-Church, immediately came up, and followed the profecutor while he was conducting the boy towards Temple-bar, walking fometimes before, and fometimes behind them, until they came to the top of Arundel-ftreet, when he ftruck the profecutor a violent blow acrofs the nofe and eyes with a razor-bladed knife, faying, " Damn you, fir, let the boy go;" and it was proved by an accomplice, that four of them had that evening gone out to pick pockets, under an agreement to ftrike on flafh, or cut the nofe and eyes of any perfon who ftopped them. The wound bled profufely; and upon examination

amination it appeared that the two great blood-veffels on Mr. Kirby's forehead were divided; that there was a large tranf-verfe wound acrofs the nofe, fo wide open that the bone was vifible. It began from the right, and went acrofs the eye-lid, and acrofs the nofe. The two mofcles of the nofe were cut through. It proceeded to the left eye-lid, and ter-minated at the temple. A nerve was cut.

It alfo appeared in evidence, that in many old authors who have written on Surgery, fuch wounds are called *flits*, but that *flit* is a word not made ufe of now. The word *flit* is underftood as fynonymous to the word *cut*; but the idea which was formerly conveyed by the word *flit* is now ex-preffed in fpeaking technically by the word *divided*.

The Jury found the prifoners guilty; but it was quef-tioned, Whether fuch a cut was a *flitting* within the letter of the Act, the wound not having perforated to the noftril. It was accordingly referred to the confideration of the Judges; and they were of opinion, That the offence defcribed in the indictment was properly proved, and the conviction legal.

Both the prifoners were executed.

TICKNER's CASE.

At the Old Bailey in February Seffion, 1778, Thomas Tickner and Thomas Adams were indicted on the ftatute 22 and 23 Car. II. cap. I. commonly called the *Coventry Act*; Thomas Tickner, for making an affault on William Jacob with a bill-hook, and flitting his nofe, with intention in fo doing to maim and disfigure the faid William; and Thomas Adams, for being prefent, aiding, and abetting in the faid felony.

The profecutor was fervant to a Mr. Cole, of Twicken-ham, within about a quarter of a mile of whofe houfe the prifoner lived. About twelve o'clock at night, on the 16th of January, 1778, the profecutor difcovered the prifoners in a field belonging to his mafter, where Tickner was pull-ing up turnips. The profecutor went up to Tickner, and fpoke to him; but inftead of making any reply, Tickner immediately ftruck him on the nofe with a fharp inftrument fixed into a ftick of wood, and hanging loofe, fomething like a flail. The blow knocked him to the ground, and he received feveral blows after he was down, which rendered him fenfelefs for fome time. He was carried to St. George's Hofpital, and upon examination, a fmall fuperficial wound was found upon the right fide of his nofe; a very large

wound

wound upon his neck, immediately under the lower jaw; a cut upon his hand; a small one in the right brow; and eight wounds on the top of his head. The cut upon the nose had divided the *exteguments* of the nose in an oblique direction; but did not go through the bones of the nose. There is very little but skin covers the bones of the nose, and it went to the bone, but did not penetrate into the nostril. It was rather a cut or a scratch than a slit; but it was sufficient to leave a mark visible for a long time.

The evidence did not sufficiently affect the prisoner Adams to put him upon his defence; but Mr. Justice Gould (present Mr. Justice Ashhurst, and Mr. Baron Perryn,) told the Jury, that he thought the evidence against Thomas Tickner, if they believed it to be true, sufficient in law to convict him of the charge in the indictment; for that he conceived it was not necessary that either the malice aforethought, or the lying in wait, should be expresly proved to be on purpose to maim or disfigure. The prisoner was engaged in a criminal matter; he was prepared with a weapon to defend himself against any opposer, and to support himself in his unlawful design of stealing the turnips, and therefore was answerable for the consequences which happened in the prosecution of his felonious intent. As to the slitting of the nose, it had been adjudged in the case of one *Kirby*, that a separating of the flesh was sufficient to bring the offender within the meaning of the Act of Parliament, and that in the present case the cut had reached the bone.

The Jury found the prisoner guilty; but on his receiving judgment, Mr. Serjeant *Glynn*, RECORDER, ordered the execution of the sentence to be respited, until the opinion of the Twelve Judges could be procured, Whether this conviction was proper within the meaning of the statute? the words of which are, " That if any person shall on purpose, " and of malice aforethought, and by lying in wait, unlaw- " fully cut out or disable the tongue, put out an eye, *slit* " *the nose*, cut off a nose or lip, or cut off or disable any " limb or member, of any subject of his Majesty, with in- " tention in so doing to maim or disfigure, in any the mat- " ters above-mentioned, such his Majesty's subject; the per- " son so offending, his counsellors, aiders, and abettors, " knowing of and privy to the offence as aforesaid, shall be " felons, and suffer death without the benefit of clergy."

The Judges were of opinion, That the conviction was right.

JOHN

JOHN MILLS'S CASE.

In April Seffion, 1783, John Mills was tried upon this ftatute before Lord Chief Baron Eyre, for maiming on purpofe, and of malice aforethought, and by lying in wait, one Thomas Brafier.

The COURT faid, a perfon who intends to do this kind of mifchief to another, and by *deliberately watching an opportunity*, carries that intention into execution, may be faid to *lie in wait on purpofe*. It is not neceffary that a man fhould plant himfelf in any particular concealment, and effect the mifchief by rufhing from his lurking-place, to bring the offence within the meaning of the ftatute. If, having formed an intention to maim, he comes unawares behind the perfon he intends to maim, and takes a convenient opportunity of deliberately doing the injury, it is a *lying in wait*, although he does not take any particular length of time, or appear to ufe any extraordinary degree of preparation to perpetrate the mifchief.

MISCELLANEOUS CROWN CASES.

WOODCOCK'S CASE.

At the Old Bailey January Seffion, 1789, William Woodcock was tried before Lord Chief Baron Eyre, (prefent Mr. Juftice Afhhurft, and Mr. Serjeant Adair), for the wilful murder of Silvia Woodcock, his wife.

It appeared in evidence, that fhe was found lying in a ditch, in a narrow lane, called Robinfon's-lane, in the vicinity of Chelfea, in the county of Middlefex. She had received eight wounds about the head, face, and neck, which feemed to have been inflicted with the end of a blunt inftrument; and was fo exhaufted with the lofs of blood, as to be apparently dead. The body was taken to Chelfea poorhoufe, put into a warm-bed, and by medical affiftance reftored to life. In the courfe of eight hours, fhe recovered her fenfes to fuch a degree, as to be enabled to give a credible relation of the circumftances by which this cataftrophe had

had happened. The overseers of the parish, therefore, thought it expedient to desire the attendance of a magistrate, for the purpose of taking her information in legal form.

Mr. Read, a Justice of the Peace for the county, attended at the poor-house accordingly. He found the informant, who was a baptized Mulatto, and native of the East-Indies, in a state of perfect recollection. He told her, that he was a magistrate come to take her examination, and admonished her to speak the truth; and as she appeared sensible of the impiety and dangers of falsehood, he administered an oath to her, and received her information, which he reduced, in her own words, into writing. He afterwards read it over to her with great deliberation, and gave it to her to sign; and she made her mark on the paper in approbation of its contents. The magistrate then signed it himself; and being proved on the trial, it was read in evidence.

It also appeared, from the evidence of the surgeons, that she died in about eight and forty hours after the examination had been taken, and that it was impossible from the first moment that she could live long; but that although she retained her senses to the last moment, and repeated the circumstances of the ill usage she had received, she never expressed or seemed ~~sensible of her approaching~~ dissolution. The evidence, independent of the *information* or *declarations* of the deceased, was of a very pressing and urgent nature against the prisoner.

Under these circumstances a question arose with the COURT, Whether the evidence which had been obtained from the deceased could legally be left with the Jury? The learned Judge therefore stated the case to them, independent of that evidence; and then stated his opinion of the admissibility of the examination to the following effect.

LO. CH. BARON EYRE.—If I was satisfied that the case was quite full, without the circumstances which the deceased has disclosed, I should willingly omit to state them as evidence against the prisoner, because there is some difficulty as to the legality of their admission. Great as a crime of this nature must always appear to be, yet the enquiry into it must proceed upon the rules of evidence. The most common and ordinary species of legal evidence consists in the depositions of witnesses taken on oath before the Jury, in the face of the Court, in the presence of the prisoner, and received under all the advantages which examination and cross-examination can give. But, beyond this kind of evidence, there are also two other species which are admitted
b/

by law: the one is the dying declaration of a person who has received a fatal blow: the other is the examination of a prisoner, and the depositions of the witnesses who may be produced against him, taken officially before a Justice of the Peace, by virtue of a particular Act of Parliament, which authorizes Magistrates to take such examinations, and directs that they shall be returned to the Court of Gaol Delivery. This last species of deposition, if the deponent should die between the time of examination and the trial of the prisoner, may be substituted in the room of that viva voce testimony which the deponent, if living, could alone have given, and is admitted of necessity as evidence of the fact.

In the present case a doubt has arisen with the Court, to which doubt I entirely subscribe, whether the examination of the deceased, taken in writing at the poor-house by Mr. Read, the magistrate, is an examination of the nature I have last described? It was not taken, as the statute directs, in a case where the prisoner was brought before him in custody; the prisoner therefore had no opportunity of contradicting the facts it contains. It was not in the discharge of that part of Mr. Read's duty, by which he is, on hearing the witnesses, to bail or commit the prisoner; but it was a voluntary and extrajudicial act, performed at the request of the overseer, and although it was a very proper and prudent act, yet being voluntary, and under circumstances where the Justice was not authorised to administer an oath, it cannot be admitted before a Jury as evidence; for no evidence can be legal, unless it be given upon oath, judicially taken.

But although we must strip this examination of the sanction to which it would have been intitled, if it had been taken pursuant to the directions of the Legislature: yet still it is the declaration of the deceased, signed by herself, and it may be classed with all those other confirmatory declarations which she made after she had received the mortal wounds, and before she died. Now the general principle on which this species of evidence is admitted is, that they are declarations made in extremity, when the party is at the point of death, and when every hope of this world is gone; when every motive to falsehood is silenced, and the mind is induced by the most powerful considerations to speak the truth: a situation so solemn, and so awful, is considered by the law as creating an obligation equal to that which is imposed by a positive oath administered in a Court of Justice. But a difficulty also arises with respect to these declarations; for it has not appeared, and it seems impossible to find out, whether the deceased herself apprehended that she was in such a state of mortality as would

would inevitably oblige her foon to anfwer before her Maker for the truth or falfehood of her affertions. The feveral witneffes could give no fatisfactory information as to the fentiments of her mind upon this fubject. The furgeon faid fhe did not feem to be at all fenfible of the danger of her fituation, dreadful as it appeared to all around her; but lay, fubmitting quietly to her fate, without explaining whether fhe thought herfelf likely to live or die. Upon the whole of this difficulty, however, my judgment is, that inafmuch as fhe was mortally wounded, and was in a condition which rendered almoft immediate death inevitable; as fhe was thought by every perfon about her to be dying, though it was difficult to get from her particular explanations as to what fhe thought of herfelf and her fituation; her declarations, made under thefe circumftances, ought to be confidered by a Jury, as being made under the impreffion of her approaching diffolution; for, refigned as fhe appeared, fhe muft have felt the hand of death, and confidered herfelf as a dying woman. She continued to repeat the facts fhe difclofed rationally and uniformly, from the moment her fenfes returned, until her tongue was no longer capable of performing its office. Declarations fo made are certainly intitled to credit; they ought therefore to be received in evidence: but the degree of credit to which they are entitled muft always be a matter for the fober confideration of the Jury, under all the circumftances of the cafe.

The prifoner was convicted, and executed.

JOHN COGAN's CASE.

At the Old Bailey in May Seffion, 1787, John Cogan was indicted on the ftatute 2 Geo. II. c. 25, for uttering and publifhing as true a certain forged will and teftament, purporting to be the laft will and teftament of James Gibfon, &c.

The will produced in evidence began thus: " James Gib- " fon do hereby," &c. leaving out the pronoun of the firft perfon. The will recited in the indictment began with the pronoun, " I James Gibfon do hereby," &c.

The Court held this variance fatal to the validity of the indictment, and the prifoner was of courfe acquitted.

In the July Seffion following he was again indicted before Mr. Juftice Wilfon (prefent Mr. Serjeant Adair, then Recorder), for falfely uttering and publifhing as true a certain falfe, forged, and counterfeited will and teftament, with a certain mark thereto fet, purporting to be the laft will and

teftament

testament of James Gibson, late a seaman on board the Vigilant, &c. which said false, forged, and counterfeited will and testament is in the words and figures following; that is to say, " James Gibson do hereby," &c. leaving out the pronoun " I," and reciting a fac-simile of the will.

The prisoner being put to the bar, on his arraignment, pleaded *autre fois acquit.* The plea was taken *ore tenus,* and recorded by the Clerk of the Arraigns; who replied to it, on the part of the Crown, *nul tiel record.*

To prove the plea the record of the prisoner's acquittal in May Session was produced. On comparing it with the present indictment, it appeared, as above stated, that the prisoner had been acquitted of uttering a forged will, beginning, " *I* James Gibson do hereby," &c. but that he was now indicted for uttering a forged will, beginning, " James Gibson do hereby," &c. The question therefore was, whether this record was legal evidence of his having been acquitted of the same offence? And after argument by the prisoner's Counsel, in which he chiefly relied upon Lord Hale's construction of Vaux's case, as reported by Lord Coke, the Court rejected the proof as insufficient; and the prisoner pleaded the general issue, over to the felony, and the Jury found him guilty of the offence.

During the course of the trial, James Gibson, the supposed testator of the forged will, was produced and sworn as an evidence on the part of the crown. Upon this circumstance a doubt arose, whether the prisoner had been legally convicted; the indictment charging him with having uttered or published as true a certain *Will and Testament,* and there being no such instrument, in contemplation of law, as the *Will and Testament* of a man who is living, for until the death of a testator, his will cannot exist, either in fact or in law; and upon this doubt the judgment was respited, and the case referred to the consideration of the *judges.*

In the June Session, 1778, the prisoner was put to the bar, and Mr. Justice Wilson delivered the opinion of the *judges* to the following effect.—The instrument which the law takes notice of under the name of *a will,* is in a man's own power during his life, and therefore no instrument or writing is considered as a last will until the testator is dead. Upon the trial of this indictment it appeared that James Gibson, whose will was charged to be forged, was alive, and produced as a witness, and I was in some doubt, whether, under these circumstances, an instrument bearing the similitude of a last will could be considered within the meaning of the statute upon which the indictment is founded.

VOL. I.   P   The

The cafe was laid before *twelve judges*, and, on mature deliberation, they have decided that the doubt was without foundation.

The fact of the prifoner's having uttered this will, knowing it was forged, was very clearly proved at the trial. He told the Proctor that James Gibfon, the fuppofed teftator, was dead, and produced a letter to the fame effect, to corroborate the affertion. By this means he obtained a probate as the executor named in the will; and the judges are all of opinion, that if a forged inftrument, *purporting* to be a laft will and teftament, be uttered and publifhed as a true laft will and teftament, under circumftances manifefting an intention to defraud, it is equally within the meaning of the Act of Parliament, whether the fuppofed teftator be in fact alive or dead. This opinion is founded on the authority of feveral cafes.

In the year 1753, Timothy Murphy was tried in this Court for forging a feaman's will; and though the man whofe will was forged was alive, he was convicted and executed.

In the year 1773, *John Stirling*, a ftudent in the Temple, was tried in this court for forging a will in the name of his laundrefs, by which means he obtained a confiderable fum of money which was invefted in her name in the public funds; and he was convicted and executed, though the laundrefs was then alive.

In the year 1754, Anne Lewis was indicted upon this ftatute for uttering and publifhing as true a forged power of attorney from Elizabeth Tingle, adminiftratrix of her father Richard Tingle, deceafed, a marine on board the Hector. It appeared that Richard Tingle had died childlefs; and a doubt was conceived, whether, fince there never was fuch a perfon as Elizabeth, the daughter of Richard Tingle, the offence was forgery within the meaning of the ftatute? And *eleven* of the *judges* were of opinion, that as the inftrument forged wore the appearance of a power of attorney, it was within the Act, notwithftanding the deed which fhe had publifhed, was impoffible to be true.

There is alfo another cafe, the *King v. Bolland*, who was indicted in this court for forging the indorfement on a promiffory note in the name of "James Banks," whom he reprefented as a wine and brandy merchant, living in Rathboneplace; but in fact no fuch perfon ever exifted; and, upon the opinion of the judges being taken, Bolland was executed.

In

In confequence of this determination the prifoner received judgment of death.

MARGARET CAROLINE RUDD'S CASE.

In the month of March, 1775, it was difcovered, that three bonds had been forged in the name of William Adair, Efq; of Pall-Mall. The firft, dated in October, 1774, for 3300l. A fecond, dated in December, 1774, 5300l. And a third, dated in January, 1775, for 7500l. Sufpicion fell upon Robert Perreau of Golden-Square, upon his brother Daniel Perreau of Harley Street, and upon Mrs. Rudd, who lived with Daniel Perreau. On the 15th and 17th March Mrs. Rudd made information before Sir John Fielding and two other Juftices, by which fhe confeffed that fhe had figned the bond of 7,500l. under very particular folicitations from Robert Perreau; and that he and Daniel Perreau, holding a penknife to her throat, had violently threatened her life in cafe fhe refufed, and, by that means, forced her to comply. The magiftrates conceiving this to be a confeffion of her own guilt, admitted her in the character of an accomplice, as a general witnefs for the crown as to *all* the forgeries; telling her that if fhe would fpeak the whole truth, not only in refpect to the bond in queftion, but of *all other forgeries*, that then fhe fhould be fafe: but fhe denied having any knowledge of, or concern in, any of the other bonds. On the 1ft June, 1775, Robert Perreau was convicted for *uttering* the bond of 7,500l. knowing it to be forged, and Daniel Perreau was convicted of uttering the bond of 3300l. It appeared upon Robert Perreau's trial, from the evidence of Mr. Drummond, that Mrs. Rudd had confeffed to him that fhe was guilty of forging the bond of 7,500l. and that Robert Perreau was innocent. Upon this information the court iffued a warrant againft her, by virtue of which fhe was committed to anfwer all fuch matters and things as fhould be objected againft her touching the faid felony and forgery. On the 7th June a detainer was lodged againft her upon the oath of Sir Thomas Frankland, for forging the bond of 7,500l. and on the 3d July another detainer was lodged againft her on the oath of Robert Perreau's wife, for having forged the bond of 7,500l. Under thefe circumftances fhe obtained a Habeas Corpus to the Court of King's Bench, with a view to be admitted to bail, and the above commitments were accordingly returned to the Court.

P 2　　　　　　　　　　　Mr.

Mr. *Davenport*, for the defendant, contended, that as she had been admitted an evidence for the crown by the Justices of Peace, and had, under the faith and confidence of that admission, made a disclosure of the facts she was acquainted with, it would be a breach of public faith to deprive her of the benefits she was thereby led to expect. He also urged the circumstances of the defendant's health being such as might, in all probability, be endangered by the confinement, if she was remanded.

LORD MANSFIELD. It appears by the return to this writ, that the prisoner is detained in custody by two orders of the court of sessions and gaol delivery at the Old Bailey, for the forgery of two several bonds. It appears also, that she is further detained by a warrant from a Justice of Peace for uttering one of these bonds knowing it to be forged: therefore, though this Court has undoubtedly a discretionary power to bail in all cases whatsoever, yet as the sessions are so near, and the offence committed by the prisoner is of such a magnitude as that of repeated forgery, there is no colour for the present application upon the ground of that general discretion. As to the next allegation, that her state of health is such as to be endangered by the confinement, it is not of itself a sufficient circumstance, in such a case, to induce the Court to interpose in her behalf.

A third ground which has been urged in support of the present application is this: that the prisoner has been drawn in by promises and assurances to answer to an examination, and to swear to it on oath, which she would not have done, but from a confidence that those promises and assurances would have been kept and performed.

The instance has frequently happened, of persons having made confessions under threats or promises: the consequence as frequently has been, that such examinations and confessions have not been made use of against them on their trial. But it has been urged, that the prisoner in this case is an accomplice who has been admitted to give evidence; that she has already given evidence, and is further ready to give evidence, to convict her partners in the business; and therefore, that she is entitled by law to the king's pardon, and to a pardon which would operate in bar of her own crime. If she had such a right, we should be bound *ex debito justitiæ* to bail her. If she had not such legal right, but yet came under circumstances sufficient to warrant the Court in saying that she had a title of recommendation to the king for a pardon, we should bail her for the purpose

pose of giving her an opportunity of applying for such pardon.

There are three ways in law and practice which give accomplices a right to a pardon; and there is one mode which entitles them to a recommendation to the king's mercy.

The three legal ways are, first, in the case of approvement, which still remains a part of the common law, though, by long discontinuance, the practice of admitting persons to be approvers is now grown into disuse: secondly, the case of persons who come within the statutes 10. and 11. of Will. III. c. 23. f. 5. and 5. Ann. c. 31. f. 4. and thirdly, the case of persons to whom the king has, by special proclamation in the Gazette or otherwise, promised his pardon.

Approvers have a right to a pardon, persons within the statutes of William and Anne have a right to a pardon, and the other class of offenders who come in under the royal faith and promise have a right to a pardon; and in all these cases the Court will bail them, in order to give them an opportunity of applying for a pardon.

There is, beside, a practice which indeed does not give a legal right; and that is, where accomplices having made a full and fair confession of the whole truth, are in consequence thereof admitted evidence for the Crown, and that evidence is afterwards made use of to convict the other offenders. If in that case they act fairly and openly, and discover the whole truth, though they are not entitled of right to a pardon, yet the usage, the lenity, and the practice of the Court is, to stop the prosecution against them, and they have an equitable title to a recommendation for the king's mercy.

The statutes of William and Anne are to be laid out of this case: first, because they are confined to the discovery of particular offences only, of which forgery is not one: secondly, because they relate only to persons who are at large; beside which, to entitle themselves to a pardon, they must actually convict two offenders at least; for if their confession be such on their trial as the jury gives no credit to, they are liable to prosecution. These statutes are therefore quite foreign to the present case, as are likewise all promises of pardon from the Crown by proclamation.

There remains, therefore, only the equitable practice which gives a title to recommendation to the mercy of the Crown.

The

The law of approvement (in analogy to which this other practice has been adopted, and so modelled as to be received with more latitude) is still in force, and is very material.

A person desiring to be an approver, must be one indicted of the offence, and in custody on that indictment: he must confess himself guilty of the offence, and desire to accuse his accomplices: he must likewise upon oath discover, not only the particular offence for which he is indicted, but all treasons and felonies which he knows of: and after all this, it is in the discretion of the Court, whether they will assign him a coroner, and admit him to be an approver or not: for if on his confession it appears that he is a principal, and tempted the others, the Court may refuse and reject him as an approver. When he is admitted as such, it must appear that what he has discovered is true; and that he has discovered the whole truth. For this purpose, the coroner puts his appeal into form; and when the prisoner returns into Court, he must repeat his appeal, without any help from the Court, or from any by-stander. And the law is so nice, that, if he vary in a single circumstance, the whole falls to the ground, and he is condemned to be hanged: if he fail in the colour of a horse, or in circumstances of time, so rigorous is the law, that he is condemned to be hanged; much more, if he fails in essentials. The same consequences follow if he does not discover the whole truth: and in all these cases the approver is convicted on his own confession. See this doctrine more at large in *Hale's Pleas Crown*, vol. II. p. 226 to 236. *Staunf. Pl. Crown*, lib. II. c. 52 to 58. 3 *Inst.* 12
—A further rigorous circumstance is, that it is necessary to the approver's own safety, that the Jury should believe him; for if the partners in his crime are not convicted, the approver himself is executed.

Great inconvenience arose out of this practice of approvement.—No doubt, if it was not absolutely necessary for the execution of the law against notorious offenders that accomplices should be received as witnesses, the practice is liable to many objections. And though, under this practice, they are clearly competent witnesses, their single testimony alone is seldom of sufficient weight with a Jury to convict the offender; it being so strong a temptation to a man to commit perjury, if, by accusing another, he can escape himself.

Let us see what has come in the room of this practice of approvement: a kind of hope, that accomplices who behave fairly and disclose the whole truth, and bring others to justice, should themselves escape punishment, and be pardoned. This
is

is in the nature of a recommendation to mercy. But no authority is given to a Justice of the Peace to pardon an offender, and to tell him he shall be a witness against others. The accomplice is not assured of his pardon; but gives his evidence *in vinculis*, in custody; and it depends on the title he has from his behaviour, whether he shall be pardoned or executed. A Justice has no authority to select whom he pleases to pardon or prosecute, and the prosecutor himself has even a less power, or rather pretence, to select than the Justice of Peace.

It rests therefore on usage, and on the offender's own good behaviour, whether he shall be prosecuted or not. And if, in a proper case, an application was to be made to this Court, by an accomplice, to be bailed; that is, in the case of a person properly within the usage, and who has fully complied with the requisite conditions; I should have no difficulty in bailing him, in order that he might apply for the King's pardon.

I am apprised of the case of an accomplice upon a trial before Mr. Justice Gould, the circumstances of which were as follow: An accomplice made a fair and full discovery to the satisfaction of Mr. Justice Gould, who tried the other offenders. The other witnesses who were called upon the trial proved the identity of the accomplice by the description of his person, but failed as to the identity of the other offenders; and the Jury, because they doubted of the guilt of the others, acquitted them. The counsel on the part of the prosecution then contended, that the accomplice ought to be tried: but Mr. Justice Gould, under the circumstances of the case, was of a contrary opinion, and I think very rightly.

These being the general rules, let us see how far the present case is applicable to them, or in any degree falls within the reason of them. A bond is detected to have been forged: three persons are apprehended on suspicion; the two Perreaus and the prisoner. The Justices by their affidavit say, they admitted the prisoner as an evidence against the Perreaus, and swear they considered her as an accomplice: and they say they told her, " that if she would speak the truth, and the " whole truth, not only in respect of the bond in question; " but of all the other forgeries, that then she should be safe; " if not, she would be prosecuted." And the truth is, that in point of law she was liable to be prosecuted for all.

What is the disclosure she makes? It is this: " That Da-" niel Perreau came with a knife to her throat, and threat-" ened to kill her if she did not forge one of the bonds in " question; that under the terror of death she forged it; " and that Robert Perreau brought the bond before ready
" filled

" filled up."   On this information she is no accomplice; she has confessed no guilt, if the fact is true that she was under the fear of immediate death; for it is the will that constitutes a crime. She comes therefore in the character of a person injured, in the character of one to whom this violence has been done. Instead of being a party offending, she is a party offended, as much as a man who has been robbed on the highway.——Further, the Justices do not treat her as an accomplice; for they ought to have kept her in custody if she had been an accomplice; but they discharged her, and they did right, there being no charge against her. But still they say, in their affidavit, they did consider her as an accomplice. Suppose they did really think her guilty, she is not the more or less on that account an accomplice. But what is most material is, that her information is flatly contradicted by herself: for, on a voluntary confession of her own, she took the whole guilt upon herself; said that she alone forged the bond for 7500l.; and that Robert Perreau was an innocent man. If the Justices had known of this confession, they could not have admitted her as an evidence: because by that confession she makes herself not only a principal, but the only person guilty.

One of the bonds, for which she is now detained, is dated three months prior to the bond in which Robert Perreau was concerned. Of this bond she is totally silent, and denies any knowledge of the other two. Her information is, therefore false, and the conditions offered to her by the Justices not complied with.

I agree with Mr. Davenport, that if she had made a fair and full disclosure of all that she knew, and the Justices had deceived her, under a promise or assurance or hope of a pardon from them, she would be entitled to a recommendation to mercy: and in that case I should have been of opinion to bail her, though the Justices had in strictness no right to make such a promise, or give her such assurance. If any evidence or confession has been extorted from her, it will be of no prejudice to her on the trial.

The three other Judges concurred; and Mrs. Rudd was accordingly remanded.

At the Old Bailey in September, 1775, Mrs. Rudd was put to the bar, on an indictment for forging the bond of 5300l. But Mr. Davenport contended, that, having been admitted as an evidence for the Crown, she ought not to be put upon her trial. Mr. Bearcroft submitted to the Court, that the condition upon which she was admitted an evidence was, That she should discover *all* the forgeries of which she

per-

persons and herself had been guilty, but that she had knowingly suppressed that for which she was at present indicted. The Judges differed in their opinions upon this subject, Mrs. Rudd was remanded, and the question submitted to the confideration of the Twelve Judges.

Mrs. Rudd was again put to the bar, on the first day of December Session following, and Mr. Justice Aston delivered the opinion as follows:

Margaret Caroline Rudd, at the last September Session, upon your being brought to the bar, to plead to several indictments found against you for forgery, it was insisted upon by your Counsel, that in point of law you ought not to have been put upon your trial at all, as you had confessed yourself to be an accomplice before the Justices of Peace for the county of Middlesex, and had been by them admitted as an evidence for the Crown, against your companions in guilt Robert and Daniel Perreau. The ground of that claim was founded upon the supposed merit of the discovery you had made: that being admitted to give evidence as an accomplice, and having performed your engagement to the publick, by being examined before the Grand Jury, and being ready to have given evidence upon the trial, if called upon, you was entitled to pardon; or not to have been prosecuted, that you might have time to apply elsewhere: that the constant practice in regard to accomplices becoming the King's evidence was, That they should not be prosecuted for the offence they had confessed, or such like offences: that a contrary conduct would be a breach of faith with you, and would discourage the future discovery of criminals, if after such disclosures they were nevertheless to undergo prosecutions for their offences. To this it was answered, that the discovery meant by law or practice to entitle an accomplice to favour, must be a full, ample, and true discovery; and that it would never discourage the making such discoveries if criminals offering themselves as witnesses, were made to understand, that to entitle themselves to mercy or favour, they are to make a full discovery of all the offences about which they were questioned, and of all their accomplices in guilt. And it was farther insisted, that you had not made a fair disclosure, at the time of your examination, of all you knew relative to the forgeries which had been committed and published, but that you stood charged by the Grand Jury with several other forgeries which you had denied the knowledge of. Upon the debate of this matter before the Bench of Gaol Delivery, the Judges present not all concurring in one opinion, and it being judged a point of

great

great weight and importance in the criminal law, fit to be fully confidered and finally fettled, how far, under what circumftances, and in what manner, an accomplice, received as a witnefs, ought to be entitled to favour and mercy; the farther confideration of the matter was then deferred, in order that the opinion of all the Judges might be taken upon the point of law.

Eleven of the Judges have accordingly met, the Lord Chief Juftice of the Common Pleas being abfent through indifpofition; and have maturely and deliberately confidered of the matter, under all the circumftances; and it falls to my fhare to deliver, in your prefence, to the public, the fubftance of their reafons upon the occafion, that the ground of their refolves may be rightly underftood. All the Judges were of opinion, that in cafes not within any ftatute, an accomplice, who fully and truly difclofes the joint guilt of himfelf and of his companions, and truly anfwers all queftions that are put to him, and is admitted by Juftices of the Peace as a witnefs againft his companions, and who, when called upon, does give evidence accordingly, and appears under all the circumftances of the cafe to have acted a fair and ingenuous part, and to have made a full and true information, ought not to be profecuted for his own guilt fo difclofed by him, nor perhaps for any other offence of the fame kind, which he may accidentally, and without any bad defign, have omitted in his confeffion; but he cannot by law plead this in bar to any indictment againft him, nor avail himfelf of it upon his trial; for it is merely an equitable claim to the mercy of the Crown, from the Magiftrates exprefs or implied promife of an indemnity, upon certain conditions that have been performed; it can only come before the Court by way of application to put off the trial, in order to give the prifoner time to apply elfewhere. Nine of the eleven Judges were of opinion, That all the circumftances relative to a prifoner's claim of indemnity, in fuch a cafe, not only may, but *ought* to be laid before the Court, to enable them to exercife their difcretion, whether, upon the grounds before them, the trial fhould be put off, and confequently have intimation given that the prifoner ought not to be profecuted; for the difcretionary power exercifed by the Juftices of the Peace in admitting accomplices to be witneffes, founded in practice only, cannot controul the authority of the Court of Gaol Delivery, and exempt, at all events, the accomplice from being profecuted. Upon every motion made, upon collateral equitable grounds, the Court will fee and examine into the whole truth, and confequently ought

ought to be informed of all the circumstances affecting the case.

The affidavit of the Justices, therefore, must in this case be necessarily taken into consideration, to see upon what ground they admitted the prisoner as a witness. For if the Court looked no farther than the prisoner's own information, in the present case, they could not have learnt from thence that she had ever been considered as an accomplice at all, and as such have been admitted as a witness against the Perreaus, in either of the prosecutions. Upon their affidavit it appears that the public faith was not engaged but conditionally, and that there was an express admonition given to the prisoner, not to conceal any part of the truth.

The same nine Judges also were of opinion, that if the matter stood singly upon the two informations of the prisoner, compared with the indictments against her, that she ought to have been tried upon all or any of them; for from the prisoner's information, she is no accomplice; she has not confessed herself guilty of any offence at all. By their representation, the share she has had in these transactions is perfectly innocent; but she exhibits a charge against Robert and Daniel Perreau, the one soliciting her to imitate the hand of William Adair, from a paper he produces; the other forcing her to do the fact of forgery, under the threat and fear of death. Her two informations are contradictory, and every indictment that is preferred against her, proceeds upon a falsification of the account she has given; for she answers to the Justices' interrogation, that she did not know of any other forgeries; so she does not confess, make any discovery, or become a witness concerning these offences; and if she has suppressed the truth, and not made a full and fair disclosure, she forfeits all equitable claim to favour and mercy. But if she has *told the truth, and the whole truth,* she cannot be convicted. On the other hand, taking the affidavit of the Justices, and all the case into consideration, if she is guilty of the charge contained in the indictments preferred by Sir Thomas Frankland, the Judges are of opinion, as her informations before the Justices have no relation to these charges, they can in no light be applied to mitigate her offences.

Upon the whole, whether the prisoner is guilty or not guilty, is a fact still to be tried by a Jury upon legal evidence only, without prejudice to the prisoner from any thing which has been insisted upon in point of law by her Counsel, to exempt her from any trial at all: for it would be hard indeed upon the subject, who has a right to advice and as-

sistance

fiftance of Counfel in all matters and points of law that may arife upon his cafe, if the eventual decifion of the 'Court againft the points of law infifted upon in his behalf, fhould prejudice the fubfequent trial of the facts, which is ultimately to be governed by the rule of evidence, and to be decided by the verdict of the Jury. I hope and truft, the facts will be tried without the leaft attention to, or even a remembrance of, any one matter or thing whatever, which has either made its appearance in print, or been the fubject of common converfation. I fhall only add, that an accomplice, who defires his trial may be put off, that he may apply for mercy under all the moft regular pretenfions before laid down, confeffes the guilt ; but, under the circumftances of this cafe, if the prifoner confeffes thefe indictments, fhe has no promife of mercy, and no claim to favour, for the reafons aforefaid. The Judges therefore are of opinion, That the trial ought to proceed ; and I have authority to fay, that the Lord Chief Juftice of the Common Pleas concurs in that opinion.

In confequence of this determination Mrs. Rudd was tried by Mr. Juftice Afton, prefent Mr. Baron Burland, and Mr. Serjeant Glynn, Recorder, for forging a certain paper writing, purporting to be a bond figned, fealed, and delivered by William Adair, Efq. in the penal fum of 10,600l. conditioned for the payment of 5300l. with lawful intereft to Robert Perreau, on the 23d of March, 1775, with an intention to defraud, 1ft, William Adair, 2dly, Sir Thomas Frankland, Baronet. There were alfo other counts for uttering it with the like intention.

The firft witnefs produced on the part of the profecution was Henrietta Alice Perreau, the wife of Robert Perreau, who was then under fentence of death for having knowingly uttered the bond of 7500l. Mr. Serjeant Davy, the prifoner's Counfel, afked her, " Is it not your opinion, that " the fate of your hufband will depend on the conviction " of Mrs. Rudd?" To which Mrs. Perreau anfwered, " I " am not clear of that." He then afked, " Do you not " hope, or expect, that the conviction of Mrs. Rudd will " be a means of obtaining your hufband's pardon ?" To which Mrs. Perreau anfwered, " I have nothing but the " truth to fay." On being preffed to anfwer the queftion directly, fhe faid, " I don't hope for the conviction of Mrs. " Rudd, I hope Mr. Perreau's innocence will clearly ap- " pear." She was then afked, " Whether fhe did not ap- " prehend that Mrs. Rudd's conviction would contribute to

" pro-

" procure her husband's pardon?" To which she answered,
" If Mrs. Rudd is found guilty, I suppose it will. I hope
" it may be the means of procuring Mr. Perreau's pardon."

Upon this evidence it was submitted to the Court, that
Mrs. Perreau was an *incompetent* witness; and the point was
elaborately argued by the Counsel on each side. But the
COURT were of opinion, That it was not an objection
that would go to her *competency*, though it would go very
strongly to her *credit*; and her testimony was accordingly
received.

After a very long trial, the Jury brought in their verdict,
" *According to the evidence before us*, NOT GUILTY."

SESSIONS CASES determined in the COURT OF KING'S
BENCH, subsequent to the Publication of the last
Edition of BURN'S JUSTICE.

THE KING *v. the Undertakers of the* AIRE *and* CALDER NAVIGATION.

The defendants were assessed to the poor at the rate of
1000l. per annum for their tolls, and 27l. per annum for
their lands. They appealed against the former part of the
assessment which the Sessions affirmed, subject to the opinion of the Court on the following:

CASE:

" That the said rivers Aire and Calder were made navigable by an Act of Parliament of the 10th and 11th of
Will. III. which act hath been amended by a subsequent act
in the 14th *Geo.* III. cap. 96, under both which acts the
undertakers are entitled to receive certain tolls and duties
therein mentioned for all goods, &c. carried upon the said
rivers or cuts therein mentioned, according to the distance
which such goods shall be carried. The whole length of
the navigation from Leeds to Wheeland measures 29 miles,
of which 2790 yards in length, and no more, lie within the
local limits of the township of Leeds. The whole tolls and
duties arising upon the whole length of the navigation from
Leeds to Wheeland, or Selby, from the 1st of January, 1785.

to the 1ft. of January, 1786, amounted to 8234l. 6s. 2d. exclusive of the tolls and duties arising from the said navigation from Wakefield to Wheeland and Selby, and the average amount thereof for three years before the 1ft of January, 1786, was 7628l. 7s. The proportion of the tolls arising from the 2790 yards, part of the length of the said navigation, and lying within the local limits of the township of Leeds, amounted to 403l. 1s. 10d. *per ann.* and though upon the face of the affessment the undertakers stand only affessed at and after the rate of 1000l. *per ann.* yet as the houfes and buildings within the township of Leeds are, by the said affessment, rated only at one moiety of the actual rents or real value, the undertakers stand actually affessed at and after the rate of 2000l. *per ann.* The said undertakers of the said navigation had, in a year commencing in July, 1785, and ending July, 1786, divided the fum of 17,000l profits; but that fum was made of many articles befides the tolls and duties. The tolls and duties have been regularly and uniformly rated at the towns of Leeds and Wakefield from the year 1713, and at Wakefield from the year 1759, at the annual value of 1200l. *per ann.* the length of the navigation within the local limits of Wakefield, being 1189 yards, and the tolls and duties arising upon that branch of the navigation from Wakefield to Selby, or Wheeland, being more than that which arifes upon the navigation from Leeds to Selby, or Wheeland. The mills, warehoufes, and other real property of the said undertakers, have been rated from time to time in the townships or places where fuch property lies. But the tolls and duties have not been rated in any of the townships through which the navigation runs between Leeds and Wheeland or Selby, or between Wakefield and Wheeland, or Selby, except at the towns of Leeds and Wakefield. From the year 1752, the said undertakers have been invariably affessed for the tolls and duties, to the maintenance of the poor in the town of Leeds, at the value of 600l. *per ann.* and they, or their leffees, have paid the affessments according to that value. The tolls and duties arising upon the whole length of the navigation have never in any one year during that fpace of time, amounted to the annual fum of 8234l. 6s. 2d. but in feven years during that time, they have been confiderably under that annual fum. In the year 1740, upon an appeal to this Court, it was ordered that the undertakers fhould stand affessed at the value of 500l. *per ann.* In every land-tax act from the year 1709, is contained a claufe that the undertakers fhall not be affessed to the land-tax in any other part, township, or place, places through which the said navigation runs, but at the towns of Leeds and Wakefield; and the undertakers have been uniformly affessed at Leeds at the same annual sums for which they have been rated to the poor rates, and in the above-mentioned Act of Parliament of the 14th of his present Majesty is contained a clause, which enacts " that the rivers or any of the cuts under the authority of that act shall not be subject or liable to the payment of any taxes, rates, or affessments, save and except such taxes, rates, and affessments, as had been and then were usually charged and affessed thereon."

LORD KENYON, Ch. J.—With respect to an objection which has been taken by Mr. Fearnley, that it does not appear by this case that the rate in question was regularly published in the church: if the question were whether an action of trespass could be supported by the persons whose goods were distrained for non-payment of the rate, there is no doubt but that the publication of the rate under the statute of the 17th *Geo.* II. c. 3. must be proved: but the parties here come upon facts ascertained by the court of sessions, on which they ask for the opinion of this court as to the question of law arising upon those facts; therefore it would be wandering from the point to seek objections which were never intended to be referred. Then it was said at the bar, that a custom, commencing in the year 1709, cannot controul the express provisions of an act of parliament: that is true; but contemporary usage in such a case would give some affistance in the construction of an act of parliament. The observation which was made at the bar on the statute 14 *Geo.* II. c 26, namely, that it prohibited any increase in the rate which existed at that time, does not appear to be well founded. On the fair construction of that act of parliament, it might, perhaps, be decided that no other kind of rate than those which were affessed at that time should be imposed; as for instance, if an highway rate, or church rate, or county rate, had not been collected before, the legislature meant that no such new rate should be imposed for the future: but the *quantum* of the rates, which had been imposed, must necessarily vary according to the exigencies of the case. For supposing at that time the land-tax had been at 2s. in the pound, it would be doing great violence to the words of the act of parliament to say that it never should be raised in any future exigency. The remaining question, and indeed the great one in this case, is, whether the rate in question on this property has been affessed in a larger proportion than it ought. It is admitted, generally, that this

species

species of property is rateable; it is also admitted that the Justices at the sessions are the proper judges respecting the equality or inequality of the rate. In the case of the king v. Bregrave, the Court said they could not enter into the inequality of the rate, unless it manifestly appeared to be unequal; and this rule appears to have been laid down with great wisdom by the Judges who sat in the Court at that time. It has been argued that, as the whole extent of this navigation is many miles, of which that which lies in Leeds forms but a small part, the rate in question exceeds its due proportion: but that is not the rule by which those proportions are to be ascertained. It is well known that the duke of Bridgewater's navigation at Manchester extends thirty or forty miles, within three miles of the end of which the grand trunk empties itself, and of course the tonnage in that part of the navigation exceeds beyond all comparison the proportion in any other part of it. So that it is most probable that the part of this navigation which comes into the town of Leeds is of greater value than any other part. However, I disclaim forming my opinion upon any conjecture of this sort, though it is probably well founded; it being enough for me to say, what was said by this Court in the case reported in Burrow, that we cannot enter into the inequality of the rate, unless it be manifestly unequal upon the face of it. Therefore, without entering into any discussion of more points which are open to it, I am clearly of opinion that this rule ought to be discharged.

ASHHURST, J.—The greatest part of the argument used by the counsel, who have argued in support of this rule, is founded upon a supposition that every parish between the extremes of this navigation receives an equal benefit. But that in all probability is contrary to the fact; for most likely many barges are navigated near the town of Leeds which do not pass any other part of the navigation. So that the proportion for which the profits of this canal have been rated in this parish does not necessarily exceed the *quantum*. The case then before us is extremely simple; for this Court never interferes in a question of inequality of a rate, unless it manifestly appears on a rate itself to be unequal: now that does not so appear in this case; and therefore I am of opinion that it must be confirmed.

BULLER, J.—If the objection which was taken by one of the counsel, that the rate does not appear to have been published in the church, would hold, it would destroy every case of this sort which comes before the Court. But the distinction between orders of Justices and special verdicts has

has been long established; in the latter, where it concludes generally, the whole case must appear upon record; but the very reverse is the rule which obtains in the case of orders of Justices: for the Court will intend every thing to be right, which does not appear to be otherwise, and they will not entertain any doubt upon a subject upon which the Justices did not. Here the Court of Sessions have said that the rate was duly made; they made no question about the publication of the rate, and they did not intend to leave any question upon that head to the Court; then it becomes necessary to consider those facts in this case upon which the law arises: and it is material to observe, that it is not stated that the tolls are collected at any other place than Leeds and Wakefield; for if there were any other houses in different parishes at which the tolls are collected, it would make a difference; but on this state of the case we are bound to take it, that all the tolls are collected at these two places. Taking that fact therefore as clear, I think the case which has been decided in this court must govern the present. It is material to consider at what place the toll becomes due. I agree that, if a person has property in Yorkshire, and receives the profits of it in London, he shall not be rated for it in London; for a toll must be considered to be paid at the place where it becomes due. It is impossible to adopt the argument used at the bar, that the toll becomes due at the end of every mile for that mile; for it is an entire contract to carry the goods the whole distance intended, and the hire is payable at the place to which by that contract they are to be carried. The case of Putney-bridge (Douglas 305), is an illustration of the present; where the bridge is rated in Putney and Fulham parishes at 700l. a year in each, there being gates at each end; formerly there was no gate at the Putney end, and then the bridge was not assessed in Putney at all. With respect to the last objection on the act of the 14 Geo. II. c. 96, if that argument has any weight, it must go the length of saying, that the legislature intended that a certain sum should be raised at all events, neither more nor less: but that would be doing great injustice; for it is stated, that the tolls in Leeds amounted only to 400l. per annum, and yet at that moment they were rated at 600l. a year; and if the rates should be reduced, it would be manifest injustice to say that the proprietors of this navigation should be still rated at 600l. per annum.

GROSE, J.—This case is abundantly too clear to require any farther comment.

Rule discharged.
The

The KING *againſt the Inhabitants of* FILLONGLEY.

John Glover, his wife, and their ſix children, were removed from Fillongley to Kinwalſey, in Warwickſhire. The ſeſſions quaſhed the order, and ſtated the following caſe:

The pauper, John Glover, on the 1ſt January, 1786, and for ſome years before, rented, and reſided on, a tenement in the pariſh of Fillongley, of the yearly value of 10l. and upwards, and continued there until the 29th April in the ſame year, when he was removed by an order of removal from the pariſh of Fillongley to the hamlet of Kinwalſey: and on the ſame day on which he was delivered with the ſaid order of removal, he returned back to the tenement in the pariſh of Fillongley, where he reſided without making any new contract with his landlord for the ſame, and without any interruption, for about three quarters of a year, and then was removed by the preſent order to the ſaid hamlet of Kinwalſey. An appeal againſt the ſaid order of removal of the 29th April, 1786, was entered, but was not proſecuted.

LORD KENYON, Ch. J.—This caſe is abundantly too clear to raiſe any ſerious doubt. Nothing can be better eſtabliſhed, than that the order of removal unappealed from is concluſive as to the pauper's ſettlement at that time; but there is nothing in the order which prevents the pauper's return, provided he does not return in a ſtate of vagrancy. It is alſo clear, that it is not in the power either of the two magiſtrates who remove the pauper, or of the Juſtices at their ſeſſion on an appeal, to put an end to a contract between the parties reſpecting the taking of a tenement. As far as reſpects the ſettlement of the perſon removed, they may determine, but no farther. And that diſtinguiſhes this caſe from the King and Kenilworth: that was a caſe of maſter and ſervant, and there the Juſtices have a power of putting an end to the contract. But here, at the time of the firſt removal, the Juſtices had no right to put an end to the contract, nor can we ſee on what ground the pauper was removed; for it is ſtated that he rented and reſided on a tenement of 10l. *per annum*, which infers a contract. That contract was moſt clearly not diſſolved by the adjudication of the Juſtices, and then the pauper cannot be conſidered as returning in a ſtate of vagrancy. And though he did not return under a new contract, yet that was not neceſſary, for
the

the old contract remained; and then by refiding at Fillongley forty days after the removal, he gained a fettlement. It has been faid that the court may prefume fraud in the firft taking: but there is no rule better eftablifhed than that fraud is never to be prefumed: and, I believe, in a cafe for the opinion of this Court which was pregnant with fraud, they would not prefume fraud, becaufe it was not ftated.

AsHHURST, J. — The firft order of removal could not poffibly refcind the prior legal agreement between the pauper and a third perfon. And though an order is conclufive as to the fettlement at the time when it is made, that is merely technical, and fo far we are bound; therefore in this cafe it muft be taken that the pauper had not gained a fettlement in Fillongley at the time of the firft removal. But when he returned, it was under the old contract, which had never been refcinded. Then he did not return as a vagrant; but he came to the parifh of Fillongley to fettle on a tenement of 10l. *per annum,* and he there acquired a fettlement by a refidence for more than forty days. It is not neceffary to determine here what would have been the effect of his refiding in Fillongley for a fhorter fpace of time than forty days after the firft order of removal. The cafe cited from Ca decott does not apply to the prefent; for it is there ftated, that the pauper refided on the premifes againft the confent of the landlord; but, in this cafe, the pauper refided under a contract.

GROSE, J. — This cafe is diftinguifhable from that of The King and Kenilworth for the reafons given. I think, if we could proceed on fuppofition, that the real tranfaction was this: after the appeal againft the firft order was made, the Juftices difcovered that he was wrongfully removed, and then they agreed that he fhould be at liberty to return to Fillongley on his dropping the appeal. However, we are to determine on the facts ftated. And, for the reafons given, I am of opinion, that the contract was not diffolved by the firft order; that the pauper had a right to return to the parifh of Fillongley; and, by refiding there more than forty days, he gained a fettlement in Fillongley.

Rule for quafhing the order of feffions difcharged.

The KING *v.* ST. NICHOLAS, NOTTINGHAM

The pauper, Charles Howell, fettled in St. Nicholas in the town of Nottingham, which is a county of itfelf, was,

by

by indenture dated December, 1787, by the overseers of St.
Nicholas, by the consent of the Mayor and an Alderman of
Nottingham, bound apprentice unto Joseph Birch, of Basford, in the county of Nottingham, until 21 years of age.
This indenture is under the hands and seals of the church-
wardens and overseers of St. Nicholas, and allowed by the
said Justices, and signed by Joseph Birch the master, but is
not executed by the pauper; under which indenture the pauper
served in Basford five months, when he was legally discharged under the statute of 20 Geo. II. cap. 19, by two
Justices, from his apprenticeship, on account of ill treatment
by the master. The boy then became a charge to Basford,
and was removed to St. Nichola's Nottingham, as the place
of his legal settlement; and, on appeal to the Sessions, the
Court confirmed the order, being of opinion, that the overseers, with the consent of the justices of one county, cannot, under the act of the 43d. of Eliz. put out a parish
apprentice from one county into another county, unless the
apprentice execute the indenture: but subject nevertheless to
the opinion of the Court of King's Bench, whether the
pauper, by the service in Basford under the said indenture,
and the circumstances of this case, gained a settlement in
Basford.

LORD KENYON, C. J.—This case is of very great importance; because many poor children are bound apprentices
into manufacturing counties, from counties where no ma-
nufactories are established. It seems to me that the case of
St. Margaret, Lincoln, has decided this; because, on reading that case, no doubt can be entertained but that the indenture was there executed by the church wardens and overseers only; for no question would have arisen as to the legality of the binding, if the apprentice himself had executed
the indenture. If this were to be determined on the words
of the statute 43 Eliz. alone, they are extensive enough to
warrant such a binding as the present; they are to bind apprentices "where the Justices shall see convenient;" and
whether in or out of the parish is not specified; they are
not to be limited by any other rule than the propriety of
the measure itself. But the great difficulty arose in my mind
on another statute, namely, the 8 &9 Wil. III. cap. 30. § 5.
That statute, after reciting that doubts had arisen, whether
persons to whom poor apprentices were to be bound were
compellable to receive them, declares that they shall be compellable to receive them under certain penalties. Now if this
Act of Parliament be commensurate with that of the 43d
of Elizabeth, and the one cannot be extended beyond the
                                                        other,

other, it is a powerful reftriction of the former ftatute; for perfons refiding in one parifh cannot be punifhed for not receiving apprentices bound from any other parifh. But I have folved that difficulty in this way; if the mafter do not reject the binding, but affent to it, then there is the concurrence of all the parties neceffary to give validity to the indenture: and if no objection be made to the binding before the apprentice has refided forty days under it, he thereby gains a fettlement. However, it is the wifeft way to abide by former decifions; and that of *Rex* v. *St. Margaret, Lincoln*, has determined this point: and that decifion fhould be the more readily adopted, becaufe a contrary rule would be attended with infinite inconvenience to the publick. The legiflature feeing that there were many poor perfons who had not the benefit of a parental education, and judging very wifely and humanely that fomebody fhould take care of them, directed (by the 43 of *Eliz.*) that they fhould be under the management of the churchwardens and overfeers of the poor, who were fuppofed to have the beft opportunity of knowing the fituation of the poor children, and required the interference of the Juftices of the Peace as a check on the conduct of the churchwardens and overfeers. So that it feems the legiflature did all that human wifdom could do, by directing the Magiftrates, with the churchwardens and overfeers, to do that for the poor children which their parents could not do for them.

ASHHURST, J.—However doubtful it may be, whether under the 43 *Eliz.* the churchwardens and overfeers, by the confent of the Juftices, have not a compulfory power of binding out of the parifh, under the provifion of the act, which fays, they fhall bind " where they fhall fee convenient;" at all events there can be no doubt but that they have the power of making fuch a binding with the confent of all the parties. Now here the mafter confented by receiving the pauper, and the affent of the pauper may likewife be inferred from the whole of this cafe. It is not ftated negatively that he diffented; he did not object to the binding, but lived under the indenture five months; that implies his confent; and it was only on the fubfequent illtreatment of his mafter that he applied for a difcharge: now that very application is an acknowledgement on his part that the indenture was binding. The pauper then having ferved more than forty days under the indenture, ought to have the benefit of the fervice. If any objection could be fupported againft this binding, on account of the pauper's being bound out of the county, it would be productive of great inconvenience; for many children, living in parifhes where

where there is no manufacture, would thereby be deprived of an opportunity of being instructed in beneficial trades, and be confined to the stations of day labourers. The case of St. Margaret, Lincoln, governs this.

GROSE, J.—I consider that all the parties in this case consented to the binding. If the apprentice had dissented from it, he might have appealed,—so might the parish into which the pauper was bound; and by not having appealed, they must be taken to have consented. Then this case falls within the determination of St. Margaret, Lincoln. And it would be productive of great confusion and inconvenience, if that decision should be departed from in a case like the present, and in which so many persons are concerned. I therefore consider my self as bound by that determination.

Rule absolute, and both orders quashed.

The KING v. MARY WESTPORT.

Two Justices removed Thomas Pretty, and family, from Bradford to St. Mary's Westport, both in the county of Wilts; on appeal the order was confirmed, subject to the opinion of the Court.

C A S E.

Edward Pretty (the grandfather of the pauper) together with his wife and family, went to reside in Bradford, under a certificate from the parish of St. Mary, Westport, in Malmsbury, dated June 21, 1714, acknowledging them to be legal inhabitants of St. Mary, Westport, and promising, for themselves and their successors, the churchwardens and overseers of the poor for the time being, that they would receive the said Edward Pretty, with his wife and family, when they should be thereto requested, unless they, or either of them, should obtain a legal settlement else where. The paupers resided together in Bradford under the certificate till removed by the present order. Thomas, the elder son of the pauper Thomas Pretty, some years ago married, took a house in the same parish, and resided a-part from his father's family. He is since dead, and has left an infant son, John, who now lives with his mother in Bradford, and is under

the

the age of feven years. The paupers named in the order of removal, never afked or received any relief from Bradford, or became perfonally chargeable, unlefs the pauper Elizabeth, under the circumftances hereinafter ftated, can be fo confidered : but Thomas Pretty, the fon, after the feparation above-mentioned, afked and received relief from Bradford during ficknefs ; and fince his death his infant fon has not been maintained by his grandfather, the pauper ; but relief has been applied for by his mother for him, and occafionally granted by Bradford for his fupport. Thomas, the grandfather, knew that relief was fo adminiftered. The pauper, Elizabeth, at the time of her removal, was pregnant with a baftard child, of which fhe has fince been delivered in St. Mary, Weftport.

LORD KENYON, Ch. J.—Although this certificate is not in the ufual form, yet, as far as it relates to the queftion now before us, it muft be confidered as a common certificate. And the fingle queftion is, whether thefe perfons, who have been removed, can, in the fair fenfe of the words, be faid to have been actually chargeable to the parifh of Bradford. Now it is negatived by the cafe that any of thefe parties received relief in perfon. But it is contended that they were virtually relieved, becaufe the fon and the grandfon both received relief. But it muft be obferved, that, at that time, they were not members of the family of the *pater-familias* now removed ; they lived apart from him, and formed another family of themfelves. Then it has been faid that a burthen has been thrown upon the parifh by the relief of the fon and grandfon, and therefore the grandfather was virtually chargeable, becaufe the 43 Elizabeth requires fathers and grandfathers to fupport their children and grandchildren. But the propofition haftens to a conclufion too foon; for by that ftatute they are not in all events to maintain their grandchildren, &c. but only when they are of fufficient ability. Now the Juftices are the proper judges of that ability ; and the grandfathers, &c. are only to be called upon by an order of Juftices. There is another fection in the certificate act, which throws fome light upon this fubject ; that directs, that every perfon who receives relief, and the wife and children of fuch perfons cohabiting in the fame houfe, fhall wear a badge on the fhoulder : this therefore is a ftrong legiflative interpretation of what is meant by the word " family" in that act ; and it would be a very harfh conftruction of the law to fay that the grandfather, when his fon and grandfon, who lived in a different houfe from
him,

him, received relief, could have been badged, or, as mentioned in the latter part of the same clause, sent to the workhouse. So that, on the fair construction of this act of parliament, none of the persons removed by this order can be said to have been chargeable. And even if we could exercise any discretion upon the subject, we should not be inclined to restrain the operation of the certificate act. The case of Walton v. Spark is very distinguishable from the present: there the condition of the bond, which was to indemnify the parish against the person therein-named, and his children, was broken. Then, as to the circumstance of the daughter being with child, it is universally settled, that that is not a sufficient ground for the removal of a certificate person. Perhaps it is rather a hard case, and we might wish the law to be otherwise in some instances. But indeed it is to be considered that, though the woman was pregnant, non constat, that the child would be a bastard; and though it was probable, yet it was not certain, that any burthen would have fallen on the parish, for she might have been married before she was brought to bed.

ASHHURST, J.—No doubt arises from the particularity of this certificate; for the promise, by the certifying parish to receive the paupers when they shall be thereto requested, can only be taken to mean when they should be legally requested. Now the persons mentioned in the certificate had a right to reside in Bradford under it till they became chargeable, when only the certifying parish could legally be requested to receive them. Then the question is, whether or not any of the persons removed actually became chargeable in such a way as to warrant the parish of Bradford in removing them: now it does not appear that any of them fall within that description. For as to the pregnancy of the daughter, it has been repeatedly determined, that a certificate person cannot be removed as being likely to become chargeable, but such person must be actually chargeable; and in such an instance as this the charge may be prevented by marriage. Then as to the relief which was given to the son and grandson, it seems to me that that was not a sufficient ground to remove the grandfather and his family living under a separate establishment. But it has been said, that the grandfather was bound to maintain his son and grandson: that is true under circumstances; but then he must be of sufficient ability and called upon by an order. Now here the relief was not given on the application of the grandfather; and, in order to extend the consequences of this relief to him, the parish should have first called upon him, when, if he had refused, alleging his inability, it might have perhaps
been

been tantamount to a relief of the grandfather. But, as it appears here, we cannot say that it was a necessary act of the parish; it was a voluntary one; and perhaps the grandfather, if he had been applied to, might have relieved the son and grandson.

GROSE, J.—The first question arises on the effect of the certificate. Although that is different from the common form, yet I have no doubt in saying that it can have no other operation than what it derives from the 8th and 9th W. III. ch. 30. If it had, it would go a great way to defeat that statute. For that act directs that a certificate, given in the terms therein prescribed, shall oblige the parish, granting it, to receive the persons therein mentioned when they shall become chargeable; and that then they shall be removed. But this is an undertaking to receive the persons mentioned in it, when they should be thereto requested; which is directly contrary to the statute. Therefore I think this is void, unless it be considered as a certificate within the act. The next question is, Whether that which is stated in the order of removal be true, namely, that the paupers were actually chargeable? Now, that is negatived by the case, which states, that they were not in fact chargeable, unless we can say that they were so in law. Although this question has never been expressly decided, I agree with the opinion delivered by Mr. J. Aston, who was particularly conversant with this branch of the law. And, notwithstanding it was extrajudicial, I cannot help paying a great respect to the opinion of so able a Judge. If the whole of a certificated family were removeable, because one of them only became actually chargeable, it would be attended with great inconvenience; as for instance, if there were three or four young men in the family who were able, by their industry, to procure a competent maintenance, and their sister became chargeable, it would be against the spirit of the act to make that a ground for removing them all. And I think the intent of the act will be fully answered by determining that, when any one of the certificated family becomes chargeable, he only shall be removed: any other determination would defeat the true purposes of the act. Then, as to the pregnancy of the daughter, no case has been cited to shew that a person under such circumstances can be removed; and I think she was not removeable on that account.

Both orders quashed.

REX v. ANDREW TOOLEY.

The defendant was convicted under the 25th George III. c. 51. for letting to hire a horse to travel post, from Totness to Ashburton, and back again, not having a license from the

com-

commiffioners of the ftamp office.   He appealed to the Seffions, where the conviction was quafhed.

CASE.

On the 4th of October, 1788, Richard Gee went to the
appellant, a butcher of Totnefs, and hired a horfe to go from
thence to Afhburton, and back again ; the price to be paid to
the appellant for fuch hire amounted to one fhilling and fix-
pence ; and Richard Gee was to return with the horfe to
Totnefs the fame day ; and it alfo appeared that the appellant
was not a perfon licenfed to let horfes for travelling poft.

The ftatute fays, that every poft-mafter, who fhall let to
hire any horfe for the purpofe of travelling poft by the mile,
or from ftage to ftage, fhall pay 5s. for a licence ; the duties
are put under the management of the commiffioners of the
ftamp-duties ; and adds, that every horfe, hired by the mile
or ftage, fhall be deemed to be hired to travel poft within the
meaning of the act, although the perfon hiring the fame do
not go or travel feveral ftages upon a poft-road, or change
horfes ; and although at the ftage or place, at or to which
fuch horfes fhall be hired, there fhall not be any poft-houfe ;
and although there fhall not be any poft fettled or eftablifhed
on the road upon which fuch horfes fhall be hired to go.

LORD KENYON, Ch. J.—The argument which has been
urged againft the order of Seffions (namely, that going the
ftage, and back again, was equivalent to travelling two ftages)
would be well founded, if the act had ftopped at the words
" that every horfe, hired by the mile or ftage, fhall be deemed
" to be hired to travel poft."   For, if the Legiflature had
only intended to fubject every horfe fo hired to the duty, they
would not have fubfequently added fo many nugatory words :
but the act goes on to fay, " that fuch fhall be travelling poft
within the meaning of the act, although the perfon hiring the
fame do not travel feveral ftages, or change horfes, and although there be not any poft-houfe, or eftablifhed poft-road."
This provifo is adapted to cafes which exift in various parts
of the kingdom, and particularly in the road from Chefter to
Bath, great part of which is not that which is termed a poft-
road ; there perfons do not travel from poft-houfe to poft-
houfe ; but they travel *quafi* poft. If a perfon be, in the popular fenfe of the words, travelling poft, he is within the
meaning of the act of parliament.   The popular fenfe of the
words is to be retained ; and, when that is fatisfied, the 42d
fection provides that the circumftances there mentioned fhall
not exempt the perfon from paying the duty.   But the perfon, in this cafe going on his bufinefs to a market-town and
back again, cannot poffibly be faid to be travelling poft either
                                                        within

within the spirit or the words of this act of parliament, which was evidently not intended to extend to every case of hiring a horse; and, unless it did, this case is not within it.

ASHHURST, J.—This cannot be a hiring to travel post either within the spirit or letter of this Act of Parliament. There is a great deal in what the counsel for the defendant said, that this sort of hiring is, in effect, a hiring for a day, with a restriction that the hirer shall not go further than such a place. One neighbour lets his horse to another, to go from Totness to Ashburton, and back again, which cannot be said to be travelling post within the popular sense of the words; and such was the meaning of the Legislature.

GROSE, J.—If the Legislature had intended that every person, who lets horses to hire for any purpose, should take out a licence, the words " travelling post" need not have been inserted in the act of parliament. Those words must have meant something; and they must be confined to their popular sense, except in those cases which the Legislature has pointed out in the 42d section; in the exposition of which I perfectly agree with my Lord Chief Justice. I do not know what the practice may be; but, if the argument used in favour of the tax were to prevail, the consequence would be, that every clergyman, within either of the universities, who hires a horse for the purpose of attending his church, would be equally liable to the duty for travelling post: but we cannot suppose that the Legislature meant to extend it to such cases.   Order of Sessions confirmed.

REX v. JOHN WEBBER.

The defendant was convicted for letting post-horses without licence, and the Sessions quashed the conviction.

CASE.

Jonathan Green, post-master for Exeter, when any expresses were delivered to him to be forwarded to London, uniformly caused them to be conveyed from Exeter to Honiton, being the first stage, and 16 miles distant, by the defendant, who lets horses for that purpose. Such expresses have been, in every instance within the knowledge of the said defendant, carried on horseback by a boy and horse provided by the defendant: and Green hath always paid the defendant three-pence a mile, and six-pence for the boy. The defendant may send whom he pleases, or go himself with the expresses. On the 25th of February last, a waiter from the Oxford Inn brought an express to Green, directed to the duke of Northumberland, to be immediately forwarded to London. Green inclosed it to the post-master-general in
London,

London, which is the cafe of all expreffes, and delivered it to Webber's boy, with directions to forward it immediately to Honiton; and has fince paid Webber 4s. 6d. for conveying this exprefs to Honiton. The horfe upon which the boy rode in carrying this exprefs was the property of the defendant. Green pays the defendant once a quarter for carrying the expreffes; and he was paid the faid 4s. 6d. in the laft account fettled at Lady-day.

LORD KENYON, Ch. J.---This queftion depends on the conftruction of a fhort claufe in the act of parliament. And it is true that under that act every letting to hire is not a letting to hire for the purpofe of travelling poft. We were of this opinion in the cafe of the King v. Tooley, in the laft term; but, as we wifhed that our judgment fhould be fatisfactory, we gave leave to the crown-officers to argue it again in cafe they had any doubts upon the fubject; and I am happy to find now that no doubt is entertained about it. And I have alfo had an opportunity of knowing, fince that determination, that our opinion coincides with that of the gentlemen who drew the act. Now, it has been argued here, that this defendant did not let a horfe for the purpofe of travelling poft, according to the popular fenfe of thofe words: but it is on that very ground that my opinion is formed; and I think that a horfe, let to carry a letter by exprefs, is in common *parlance* let for the purpofe of travelling poft. And, if we look back to the hiftory of former times, we find that this mode of conveyance was called, not an exprefs, but flying-poft. Perhaps, if this had appeared to be an exprefs fent by the orders of government on public fervice, it might have been otherwife: but I give no opinion on that queftion. However, as it is not ftated in this cafe, that it was a government exprefs, it is impoffible to entertain the leaft doubt on this queftion. Then it was objected, that the defendant was not bound to pay this duty, becaufe the horfe was ridden by his own fervant; but that would equally apply to almoft all cafes of travelling poft, where the driver is the fervant of the owner of the horfes.

ASHHURST, J.--It has been argued, that we muft prefume this exprefs was fent on the account of government: but it is incumbent on the party, who claims the exemption, to prove that he comes within it. Therefore we cannot prefume it from the facts here ftated; and the reverfe of it appears. This cafe then falls within the words of the act of parliament; and if we confider that this was a tax on accommodation and luxury, and that every perfon fending expreffes is fuppofed to be of ability to pay it, it comes alfo
within

within the meaning of the statute; for it is in the popular sense a travelling post.

Order of sessions quashed.

The KING v. *the Inhabitants of* MACCLESFIELD.

CASE.

The pauper George Deane, being settled in Wildboarclough, was hired about fifteen years ago by F. Beswick, of Macclesfield, for 11 months, at 10 guineas wages: at the end of 11 months the master and the pauper settled his wages for 11 months; and his master gave half-a-guinea over, saying, that he had been a good servant, and added, " You may as well stay on an end in your place; the place " suits you, and you suit the place." The pauper's answer was, " Very well, Sir, I have no objection." And the pauper continued to follow his master's business near three years. The pauper, being at Birmingham with his master's cart, was taken ill, and stayed there some time, which occasioned him to lose his service. His master used to give him money during his service; but the pauper kept no account. A few days after the pauper's return from Birmingham, his master settled with him; the pauper did not know in what manner, but supposed the money was right: he thought his wages would come to about four shillings a week. It did not appear to the Court, that the pauper or his children had gained any settlement in any other place.

Two Justices removed the said Geo. Deane and his family from Macclesfield to Wildboarclough; the Sessions on appeal quashed the order, subject to the opinion of the Court.

LORD KENYON, Ch. J.—It is clear that there must either be an express or an implied contract for a year, in order to give the servant a settlement. An express hiring for 11 months will not confer a settlement, unless the Sessions find that it was fraudulent, and that a year's service was intended, though only 11 months were expressed; as in a case, which I remember, where there was an hiring for 11 months, with an agreement to give in another month's service. Now, in this case the first hiring for 11 months was not sufficient to confer a settlement: but, when that time was elapsed, the master told the pauper, that he might as well stay on an end; which, in that part of the country, means an indefinite time. This second hiring, therefore, must be considered as a general hiring, which the law construes to be an hiring for a year. As to this expression, referring to the time for which the pauper was originally hired, it is too refined: it only referred

to

to the nature of the service in which he was before engaged. Then if we confider the wages for which the pauper ferved under the fecond agreement, it negatives the idea, that the parties contracted for another 11 months for the fame definite fum which the pauper received under the firft agreement ; for it is ftated, that he received about four fhillings *per* week, which does not amount to the fame apportionment of wages. Order of Seffions confirmed.

The KING *against the Inhabitants of* OFFCHURCH.

Two Juftices removed Henry Weft, and Martha his wife, from Thurlafton to Offchurch, both in the county of Warwick ; which order was affirmed by the feffions on appeal, fubject to the opinion of the Court on the following

C A S E.

J. Weft, the father of the pauper H. Weft, in January, 1765, and for the two next following years, rented and refided upon a tenement of 100l. a-year in Offchurch, and was fettled there. In January, 1767, the wife of J. Weft, who was mother of H. Weft the pauper, died; and in June, 1767, J. Weft married again with one Jane Lockley, with whom he lived in Offchurch until the year 1770, when they both went to, and refided at, Southam in the faid county, for three years, without doing any act to gain a fettlement there. In 1773, they removed to Ladbroke, in the faid county, to a houfe which was vefted by a fettlement in truftees to the feparate ufe of the wife; with the ufual claufe that her receipt fhould be a difcharge to the truftees for the rents and profits ; and that the rents fhould not be fubject to the hufband's debts. Weft and his wife lived in the houfe from 1773 to the prefent time. The pauper H. Weft was born in Offchurch in January 1765, and refided there with his father until 1770. On his father's leaving Offchurch, the pauper was left with one R. F. Leefon at Offchurch, to be taken care of, his father paying for his lodging and board. The pauper continued at Leefon's at Offchurch for two years, and then went to, and refided with, his uncle H. Haddon, who alfo lived at Offchurch, and continued to refide with his faid uncle for about two years; during the whole of which time his uncle provided him with board, cloaths, lodging, and pocket-money, and he worked with his uncle Haddon, but he received no wages, and was not hired as a fervant. At the end of two years the pauper went to his father's at Ladbrok, and ftaid
there

there a week; and then went to refide with another uncle, William Salmon, of Wefton, with whom he lived fix years, as he had done at his uncle Haddon's; his uncle Salmon providing him with board, cloaths, lodging, and pocket-money; he working for his uncle Salmon, without having been hired as a fervant, or receiving any wages. On leaving his uncle Salmon, he went and lived three weeks with his father at Ladbroke. The pauper has never done any act to gain a fettlement.

LORD KENYON, C. J.——Two queftions arife in this cafe: and the firft which I fhall confider is, whether the fon continued to be part of his father's family during the time his father refided at Ladbroke, fo as to be intitled to the benefit of his father's fettlement. This is the weakeft cafe of emancipation that was ever attempted to be made out. When the father left the parifh of Offchurch, the fon was only five years old: now it cannot be pretended that at that time he was emancipated, and yet he then ceafed to refide in his father's family. It is alfo ftated, that about two years afterwards, when he was about feven or eight years old, and paft the age of a nurfe-child, he went to live with his uncle Haddon. Then, was he emancipated at that time? Ordinarily fpeaking, one of thefe things muft happen before the fon can be faid to be emancipated; either he muft have obtained a fettlement for himfelf, or have become the head of a family, or at moft he muft have arrived at that age when he may fet up in the world for himfelf. But here the fon does not fall within either of thofe defcriptions: no time can be ftated when the emancipation may be faid to have commenced.—— For when he went to live with his uncle Haddon, he was only eight years old at the moft: and he could gain no fettlement either by living with that uncle, or his other uncle Salmon, as a fervant, becaufe the cafe ftates, that he was not hired as a fervant by either of them. Now, during all this time the father had a right to the cuftody of the fon, and might have obtained him by *habeas corpus*; for the parental care was not then done away. It is not neceffary in thefe cafes of derivative fettlements that the child fhould remove with the father from place to place; for the fettlement of the father will be communicated to the child. Otherwife children, who are fent out into the world for education, and are of courfe feparated for a time from the father, might lofe the benefit of their father's fettlement, and when they were about to return home would find themfelves excluded from parental care, if their parents had in the mean time gained a new fettlement. How long the power of communicating

monicating a derivative fettlement may continue, it is not neceffary to determine; for in this cafe it certainly remained longer than till the child was nine or ten years old; and that is fufficient for the determination of this queftion. Then, 2dly, it remains to be confidered, whether the father gained a fettlement in Ladbroke? and certainly the queftion has fome novelty in it. Where a perfon refides on his own property, he gains a fettlement by it; it having been confidered as an excepted cafe out of the acts of parliament. Lord Macclesfield, fol. 257, firft held, that, as a man cannot be diffeifed of his freehold, he is irremoveable from it, and refiding 40 days on an eftate of his own irremoveably, and gaining a fettlement are fynonymous terms. That indeed does not hold in all cafes now; for, by the 9th Geo. I. c. 7. a purchafer of an eftate for lefs than 30l. fhall not acquire a fettlement for any longer time than he refides upon it. Then here, if this had been the father's own eftate, the fettlement would clearly have devolved on the fon. But it is faid, that this is only the equitable eftate of the wife. Now, fuppofing it had been the wife's legal eftate, the hufband would have gained a fettlement. Then muft it be a legal eftate, in order to confer a fettlement? Certainly not. That was not doubted in South Sydenham and Lamerton, or in any of the other cafes. The queftion in that was, Whether the next of kin without adminiftration had any eftate whatever? and it was held that he had not. In *Rex v. Cold Afton*, a doubt was made, whether a next of kin, having the fole right of adminiftration, could not gain a fettlement without taking out letters of adminiftration. That fhews that an equitable eftate is fufficient to give a fettlement. And indeed this pofition is confirmed by many other cafes, and there are none in oppofition to it. Then it is faid, that this is going ftill farther, becaufe this is only the equitable eftate of the wife; and that even the wife herfelf had no right to refide upon it without the confent of the truftees. But fhe might beyond all doubt, if fhe had chofen, have elected to take the *efplees* with her own hands, and that the truftees could not have prevented. The objection then againft the hufband's gaining a fettlement here is too refined, for the wife had a right to refide on her property, and to communicate it to the hufband. And although there is no cafe directly like the prefent, yet the principles of the decided cafes go the length of determining this.

         Both orders quafhed.

              THE

THE
LAWYER'S
AND
MAGISTRATE'S MAGAZINE.

For MAY, 1790.

Proceedings againſt JOHN FRITH for HIGH TREA-
SON, at the OLD BAILEY, April 17, 1790, before
LORD KENYON, Chief Juſtice ; Mr. JUSTICE
HEATH, and Mr. BARON HOTHAM.

THE Priſoner was indicted for High Treaſon in com-
paſſing the Death of the King ; he having thrown a
large ſtone with great violence towards his Majeſty's perſon,
as he paſſed in the State Coach to the Parliament Houſe,
but which fortunately ſtruck only againſt the ſide of the
coach window.

Counſel for the Crown,
Mr. ATTORNEY GENERAL, Mr. SOLICITOR GENERAL.

Counſel for the Priſoner,
Mr. SHEPHERD and Mr. GARROW.

The Priſoner being put to the bar, Mr. Shepherd, one of
his Counſel, addreſſed the Court.

Mr. Shepherd. My Lord, Mr. Garrow, and myſelf, are
Counſel for Mr Frith : and though we are furniſhed with
what we think a ſufficient defence, yet there is ſome very
important evidence which might be procured before the next
Seſſions, on behalf of Mr. Frith : and, on that account, we
apply to the humanity of the Attorney General, to beg he
would conſent to the poſtponing this trial to the next Seſ-

fions. In this cafe we exercife our duty as counfel: Mr. Frith is entitled to the beft of our judgment: whether he will chufe to be guided by that, is certainly a confideration for his own mind. But, Mr. Attorney General we do hope will confent.

Court. This application is made on your judgment.

Mr. Garrow to Mr. Frith. Mr. Frith, we have been applying to the Court, or to Mr. Attorney General, to permit your trial to ftand over till next Seffions, upon our judgment; it appearing to us that your defence will be better arranged.

Prifoner. I object to it, on account of my health being in a bad ftate through long confinement. I fhould rather meet it now: it is depriving a fubject of his liberty, and endangering his health.

Mr. Attorney General. Notwithftanding what this unhappy gentleman has faid, I am given to underftand that there may be fome circumftances in his fituation; and likewife that he is not very well able, in point of pecuniary concerns, to be fo ready in the collection of materials for his defence, as many other prifoners are: therefore if my friends are of opinion that he muft go to his trial now under great difadvantages, poffibly arifing from the laft caufe, as well as the other, I fhall have no objection to give the gentlemen fuch time as will enable them to collect fuch evidence as they may chufe.

Prifoner. Then I fhall make an application to fome Member of Parliament, or the Legiflature. I therefore totally appeal againft fuch power of putting off the trial any further; and whoever dares to oppofe me in that refpect, I will reprefent him to the Legiflature, or fome Member of Parliament; either to General North, or fome gentleman whom I have the honour of knowing.

Mr. Garrow. My Lord, we are put into an arduous fituation. But for one, I feel it to be my duty to take upon myfelf, in oppofition to the Prifoner, for the Prifoner's benefit, to pray that the Attorney General will confent to poftponing this trial.

Court. Mr. Attorney General has conducted himfelf on this occafion, as he always does, exceedingly liberal and proper; and is ready to give all indulgence that humanity calls for; therefore it muft ftand over till next Seffions.

Prifoner. I do not admit of it. And I fhall make an application to Parliament, that I have been here three months in difagreeable confinement; and the King has broke the mutual obligation between him and the fubject: and the affault is of fuch a fimple kind of manner; and what I have

met

met with is of such a nature, that I desire to speak by way of extenuation, and to plead guilty or not guilty to the facts. I shall then make an application as being illegally detained in prison, that you will not admit a British subject to plead to the indictment: I therefore shall make an application to the Legislature, that you are violating the laws of this kingdom. I will not put it in the power of the gentlemen that are employed for me to put it off.

Court. It is impossible for the most inattentive observer not to be aware that there may in this case be a previous enquiry necessary: such is the humanity of the law in England, that in all stages, both when the act is committed, at the time when the prisoner makes his defence, and even at the day of his execution, it is important to settle what his state of mind is, and at the time he is called to plead, if there are circumstances that suggest to one's mind that he is not in the possession of his reason, we must certainly be careful that nothing is introduced into the administration of Justice, but what belongs to that administration. The justice of the law has provided a remedy in such cases; therefore I think there ought now to be an enquiry made, touching the sanity of this man at this time; whether he is in a situation of mind to say what his grounds of defence here are. I know it is untrodden ground, though it is constitutional; then get a jury together to enquire into the present state of his mind: the twelve men that are there, will do.

Prisoner to Mr. Garrow. I beg the favour to speak to you.

Mr. Garrow. By all means, Sir.

Prisoner. The Privy Counsel were pleased to send the King's Physician to me, after I had appeared before my Lord Kenyon, on the 22d of January. I was examined at the Privy Counsel by Lord Camden; and they sent the King's Physician to me. I made dates and memorandums of the Physician's visits, likewise remarks that I spoke to him at various times; and of the Apothecary's visits also; they persevered in my being in perfect health, fit to meet my trial; and I have put down the conversations.

Mr Justice Heath. The Jury will take notice of that.

The Jury sworn as follows:

" You shall diligently enquire, and true presentment make, for, and on behalf of our Sovereign Lord the King, whether John Frith, the now prisoner at the bar, who stands indicted for High Treason, be of sound mind and understanding, or not, and a true verdict give according to the best of your understanding. So help you God."

R 2

Mr.

Mr. Shepherd.   Mr. Frith, you are aware that the Gentlemen of the Jury, that have been juſt ſworn, are going to inquire whether you are in a fit ſituation to plead at this time, and to be tried.   Now I wiſh you to ſtate to theſe gentlemen what reaſons you have to induce them to think you are; and to produce any memorandums.

Priſoner.   I have had a phyſician attending me two months paſt.   On the 22d of January I came into theſe circumſtances: and they were pleaſed to ſend the king's phyſician to examine me, whether I was perfectly in my ſenſes: I perſevered in being ſo, and would take no drugs from the Apothecary.   I begged him to attend as a friend to me, to protect me from inſult, ſuppoſing there was any poſſibility that I could be inſulted in this great priſon: but if I had not been well, I would have had my own phyſician, Dr. Heberden, who attended my father formerly, when living: I looked upon him as a friend attending me, to prove that I was in my ſenſes, or any thing elſe.   I made memorandums of his viſits, and the various converſations that we had together.   I made memorandums likewiſe of letters: a letter which I wrote to Meſſ. Cox and Greenwood; and I have a copy of it, and one that I wrote about the 24th of February, during the time that the laſt Seſſions was here, when I thought I might be tried; I then re-copied it again.   I then mentioned that a diſagreeable thing had happened, that General Clarke is coming home in diſgrace.   To hide that infamy that has happened, they wiſhed to give it out that I was out of my ſenſes.   The agents who had immediately freed me from the inconveniences I was under, they were ordered to deny the ſubject the liberty of drawing on his agent on the houſe where he had money to anſwer his bills.   They acknowledged me to have been perfectly in my ſenſes at the time when I firſt came to England; I drew on them, and I have totally freed myſelf from the inconvenience I was under, from being improperly detained in Cheſhire.   I was writing a letter of what was publickly given out concerning the ſubject: I then wrote to Meſſ. Cox, Cox, and Greenwood, to beg they may ſend down ſome gentlemen here, to prove how the liberty of the ſubject was invaded in 1787, in June, and ſuch letters will prove, that the 24th of laſt February, I was right in my mind then; and that now I re-copied it again about a fortnight ago: and it went through my attorney, to Meſſ. Cox, Cox, and Greenwood's houſe: that will prove the eſtate of my mind at that period of time.

                                                      Mr.

Mr. Garrow. Will you have the goodness, Mr. Frith, to state to the Jury the circumstance that took place on your arrival at Liverpool, about the Clergyman.

Prisoner. When I first arrived at Liverpool, I perceived I had some powers like those which St. Paul had; and the sun that St. Paul gives a description of in the Testament: an extraordinary power that came down upon me, the power of Christ; in consequence of my persecution and being ill used, the publick wanted to receive me as a most extraordinary kind of a man; they would have received me in any manner that I pleased. When I went to St. Thomas's church I was there surprised to hear the Clergyman preach a most extraordinary Sermon upon me, as if I was a God: I found my friends wanted me to support that kind of fanaticism in this country; this Sermon was printed afterwards by Eyre, the printer at Warrington. When I came to London to the King concerning some military business, I told him nothing about any supernatural abilities, or the power of God; when I went to the Infirmary over Westminster-bridge, to the Asylum, I was surprised to hear General Washington's late Chaplain, Mr. Duché; he said, I remember the words, he said, "See him cloathed in Grace," pointing to me; there were some supernatural appearances at that time, therefore I could with the Privy Council, when I came to England, or the Parliament, might be witnesses that I did not want to set up any kind of powers to the publick; but there are such extraordinary appearances that attend me at this moment, that it is singular; and all I do daily is to make memorandums, daily to prove myself in my senses; some friends in Cheshire wanted me to set up some kind of fanaticism, some new branch of religion.

Mr. Garrow. Would you be so good, Mr. Frith, to inform the Court, as you have an opportunity now, of the complaint you made to me of the effect your confinement has upon you, and the pain in your ear?

Prisoner. In respect to the body of people, St. Paul when he was at Jerusalem, the same kind of power then came down on the publick; there is both a kind of good and evil power which we are all liable to in this world; in consequence of that I feel myself in a particularly disagreeable situation in confinement; I am under a state of suffocation almost, the divine ordinances weighing so very low down that I am entirely reduced to a shadow almost, that is all to me as if it was a death seemingly, I am so in a state of confinement.

The

The Rev. Mr. VILLETTE sworn.

Mr Garrow. I believe, Sir, you have had an opportunity of conversing with this gentleman since he has been in custody. State the impressions that such conversations made on your mind?

Mr. Villette. The first time I saw him I really thought from the appearance he had, that he was deranged in his mind; I took notice so to the man that had the care of him; some time after he sent for a Bible; I sent him one; then we had some conversation; and he told me he had a pocket volume of that book, but that they took it from him when he was before the Privy Counsel; he said, I am much obliged to you: I went to him a few days ago; he was reading; he said, it was the Psalms; I then talked about his trial; and he then entered into such conversation as you have heard about St. Paul and Christ.

Prisoner. I said it was when I was landed at Liverpool, and was giving a narrative.

Mr. Garrow. From the whole of your intercourse with him, did it appear to you that he was insane?—I really thought so.

You think so now?—I do.

RICHARD AKERMAN, Esq. sworn.

Mr. Garrow. State from the conversation you have had with the prisoner, what was his conduct on the whole.

Mr. Akerman. I have heard such conversation as you have heard in Court.

Prisoner. I have been very silent and close for many reasons, and to protect my person; I have read the psalms, my Lord, as I had no other books.

Mr. SHERIFF NEWMAN sworn.

Mr. Shepherd. Have you had any conversation with Mr. Frith since he has been in custody?

Mr. Newman. Very frequently; I went the second day after he was in Newgate: I went entirely out of curiosity; I found him a subject of great compassion: he began talking to me very deranged for the first ten minutes; I asked him why he went over to Holland? He said, he went eastward in pursuit of the light; I said, what light? He said, why you have read the scriptures? I said, yes; says he, the same light that fell upon St. Paul when he went to Damascus. I said, what brought you back; Why, says he, when I got there, I found the light was in the West as well as in the East.

Eaft. He defired to have the liberty of walking in the yard; and I confulted Mr. Akerman: and he faid, there was an order concerning him. I found him every time in the fame way: I was there once when Dr. Millan came down; I met him there; he for the firft five minutes had doubts, but before he went away he was perfectly fatisfied the prifoner was infane; I have not the leaft doubt, nor poffibly can have a doubt; I frequently found him reading in the Book of Kings, and he told me he was learning the art of war, and he fhould come to be a general, and he fhould like to underftand the art of making war as the ancients did.

Prifoner. I do not remember fpeaking about that, and I made memorandums of my converfations with Mr. Newman. I never fpoke about particular lights; I faid, when I went over to Holland, as the Minifters neglected doing their duty to me as a fubject, in not protecting me from the infults of the body of people; ftirring up licentioufnefs, aiming at me; they drove me out of the kingdom; I went to Holland to fhelter myfelf from the body of the people; but I do not remember faying any thing of following the light.

To Mr. Newman. Do you think it was abfolute incapacity of mind, or feigned or affumed?

Mr. Newman. I believe abfolutely that he is totally deranged, and not in the ufe of his fenfes for ten minutes together; every day I faw him he was fo, and of that there is not a doubt; I went at different times merely to make obfervations.

Mr. Garrow. Mr. Frith, are you acquainted with Mr. Burnfell the auctioneer?

Prifoner. Yes: he took an extraordinary liberty in putting into the Public Advertifer, the third of February, a letter, dated the firft, declaring me infane; a moft extraordinary liberty; I thought it prudent to keep a copy: I have made memorandums, but they have been taken from me by Colonel Amherft, the fame as Mr. Wilkes's papers were feifed, a kind of alteration of the laws of the land, a kind of fcheme to make a man appear infane; to totally difguife; to undo the liberty of the Britifh fubject; in fact, it is fuch a concealed evil that I do not know where it will end.

M. Garrow. Mr. Burnfell had no ill-will to you?

Prifoner. He was only employed to hide the mutiny that thofe applaufes of the Clergymen had occafioned; he went to a perfon that lives with Mrs. Dowdfwell, in Upper-Brook-ftreet; he had a letter, and was perhaps feed; the Clergyman declared me as a God, the body of the people as a man infane; myfelf applying to the King merely to get my
birth

birth again; when I went to my friend Mr. Burnfell, I spoke of no powers of God or Christ.

Mr. Garrow.   Was that before the complaint that you was afflicted with in your ear?

Prisoner.   Before that, the pain in my ear; shall I finish with respect to Mr. Burnfell?

Mr. Garrow.   If you please.

Prisoner.   I found he wished to suppose me not right in my senses, and that he could produce no proof; he has declared in the public papers, that I behaved in such a violent manner, in his house, as totally to prove myself out of my senses; I have the facts now on one side put down, and I can find no one circumstance of the kind, as to put such a letter into the news paper; if they wish to make a man appear infane, he should be taken before the Lord Chancellor, and there make a general declaration, some way or other; but it is done to interfere with the liberty of the subject.

Mr. Garrow.   Mr. Frith, how long was you afflicted with that complaint in your ear?

Prisoner.   I indured it: I supposed it merely as a trifling thing; but that complaint arises from a power of witchcraft, which existed about a hundred years ago, in this country; there is a power which women are now afflicted with; there is a power that rules now, that women can torment men, if they are in a room---over your head, they may annoy you by speaking in your ear; I have had a noise in my ear like speech; it is in the power of women, to annoy men publickly, even throughout the whole continent.

Mr. Garrow.   Could you satisfy one of the Jury, that such a noise exists in your ear at this time?

Prisoner.   That there is a noise in my ear at this time? No, I am free from it now; but it is the power and effects of what they call witchcraft; or some kind of communication between women and men; but I have remained such a chaste man for these four years, that it has fallen upon me particularly; and the Physician, by leaving me a month ago, and visiting me as a friend, will totally speak to the fact; the last time he visited me, was on the 19th of March; says he, I hope you will be restored, and fit to take your trial; but I know my friend Mr. Hogarth, I have seen him, and some people that are in Court, will be able to declare me in my senses: I have said little or nothing at all lately, and been totally silent, so that it is impossible for me to be in that state.   Shall I beg the favour to address my Lord.

Lord Chief Justice.   If you please, Sir.

Pri-

Prisoner. Do you recollect me ; in the year 1773, when I applied to you in person, on a case of some landed property, between me and one Entwisle, at Cheshire; when you was a counsel, and was one of my counsel, with one Mr. Hughes, knowing me then, and likewise in October, at the Assizes, respecting some contested property, some landed property I have in Cheshire ; now that circumstance may corroborate my declaration of the state of my mind.

Lord Chief Justice. I do not recollect it.

MR. FULLER *sworn.*

I have frequently seen Mr. Frith since he came from the East Indies ; I have had opportunities of conversing with him at particular times.

Mr. Shepherd. Do you recollect any thing particular in his conversation that induced you to take notice of the state of his mind?

Mr. Fuller. Yes, several times ; on Christmas Eve was two years I spent four hours with him ; I conversed with him for three hours before I knew any thing was the matter with him ; and upon asking him a question, respecting the matters he had mentioned before, concerning his ill treatment by Major Amherst, and Ensign Steward in the West-Indies ; he declared then the reason he was ill-treated, was, that he wished to reveal what the government wished to conceal ; for that he saw a cloud come down from Heaven, that it cemented into a rock, and out of that sprang a false island of Jamaica ; and because he wished to reveal it, he had, he said, been confined one hundred and sixty-three days ; and they had taken different means ; that he had taken an oath of this before Sir Sampson Wright ; a copy of which he gave me, and he wanted to have it published, but Woodfall, the printer, refused ; and he said, he hoped, that I, as one of his friends, would make it a conversation, in hopes it would reach the ears of the King ; I thought that the speech of a madman ; and he said, that he had wrote to the King and to Sir George Young, the Secretary of War, and could receive no redress, and that they had reduced him to half pay : I understood that a Gentleman of the name of Garrow was employed as his counsel, and I sent the copy of this oath, enclosed in a letter to inform him of it. I last Christmas-day, by chance, went into the same friend's house, at No 22, in Frith-street ; where I drank tea with Mr. Frith ; he then told me, he was worse used than common, that he was persecuted, and that they wanted to set him up as Anti-christ, or a fourth person in the God-

head,

head; and that he looked upon to be blaſphemy, or elſe he might have a good living; that and many other inſtances I can prove if neceſſary.

Queſ. Did you believe him to be in his ſenſes?

Mr. Fuller. No, upon my oath, and upon that one ſubject of his conceiving himſelf to be in his ſenſes, and ill-treated, and particularly by government. This happened about a month before the circumſtance for which he was taken up; there were four people more that heard it.

LORD KENYON.----Gentlemen of the Jury, the enquiry which you are now called upon is, not whether the priſoner was in this unfortunate ſtate of mind when the accident happened, nor is it neceſſary to diſcuſs or enquire at all what effect his preſent ſtate of mind may have, whenever that queſtion comes to be diſcuſſed; but the humanity of the law of England falling into that, which common humanity, without any written law, would ſuggeſt, has preſcribed, that no man ſhall be called upon to make his defence, at a time when his mind is in a ſituation not capable of ſo doing; for, however guilty he may be, the enquiry into his guilt muſt be poſtponed to that ſeaſon, when, by having his intellects entire, he ſhall be able ſo to model his defence, as to ward off the puniſhment of the law; it is for you, therefore, to enquire whether the priſoner is now in that ſtate of mind; and inaſmuch as artful men may put on falſe appearances, I think the counſel for the priſoner have judged extremely proper for your ſatisfaction and the publick's, not to ſuffer your judgment to proceed on that which he has now ſaid, though that is extremely pregnant with obſervation; but they have called witneſſes, and gone back to the earlier period of his life, and ſtated his condition of mind to you at the time the two letters were written, which you have heard: this ſeems to me to leave no doubt on any man's mind; therefore, the queſtion the Court propoſes to you now, is, Whether he is at this time in a ſane or an inſane ſtate of mind?

Priſoner. Permit me to ſpeak; the Phyſician is the moſt principal perſon, who has viſited me as a friend, he can tell more than from any other private perſon's declarations whatever. I appeal as a Britiſh ſubject.

Jury. My Lord, we are all of opinion that the priſoner is quite inſane.

Court. He muſt be remanded for the preſent.

Priſoner. Then I muſt call on that Phyſician, who ſaid, on the 19th, I was perfectly in my ſenſes.

The priſoner was then removed from the bar.

CROWN

CROWN CASES.

The KING *against* JUDD.

In the KING's BENCH, HILARY TERM, 1788.

Henry Judd was committed to Hertford gaol, by a warrant under the hands and seals of eleven Justices of that county, on the oath of George Sworder and others, charging him " with giving two guineas to one Daniel Wright (which D. Wright stands convicted of a burglary in the dwelling-house of the said George Sworder), to disturb the dwelling-house of the said George Sworder. And also--with giving to Nathaniel Rand, about a fortnight after harvest last, a guinea and a half, to *keep on* with the said George Sworder as the said N. Rand had then begun ; and to do him the said George Sworder all the mischief he could except killing him.----And for being accessary with the said N. Rand, who was committed to Hertford gaol on the oaths of the said George Sworder and others, as well as upon his own confession, in wilfully and maliciously setting fire to a parcel of unthreshed wheat, in the night, the property of the said George Sworder ; and which he the said N. Rand hath confessed he did at the request of the said Henry Judd."

On Monday February 4, 1788, the prisoner was brought up to this Court from Hertford gaol by Habeas Corpus to be bailed ; and his commitment being read, it was contended by Mr. Silvester and Mr. Fielding for the prisoner, that the warrant contained no charge of felony, and therefore he was entitled to be bailed or discharged, by virtue of the statute 31 *Car*. II. cap. 3.

Mr. Erskine, Mr. Mingay, and Mr. Garrow, for the Crown, admitted that the first two charges in the warrant did not contain such a description of felony as would intitle them to expect that the prisoner should be remanded ; but that the third charge contained a full and sufficient description of an accessary *at common law* to the felony, created by the statute 9 *Geo*. I. cap. 22, which enacts, " That if any person or persons shall set fire to any house, barn, or outhouse, or to any hovel, cock, mow, or stack of corn, straw, hay, or wood ; or shall by gift, or promise of money or other reward, procure any of his Majesty's subjects to join him or them in any such unlawful act, every person

so

so offending shall be guilty of felony, without benefit of clergy.

The prisoner's Counsel replied, that accessaries at the common law, unless there was a strong presumption of their guilt, arising from an indictment having been found against them, were entitled to be bailed; that the warrant only charged the principal " with wilfully and maliciously setting fire to a parcel of unthreshed wheat ;" and no such offence was made felony by the statute ; and admitting it was an offence within the meaning of the statute, yet the warrant would be defective, in not charging it to have been done *feloniously*.

Mr. JUSTICE ASHHURST.----However improper the defendant's conduct appears to have been upon the proceedings before the Justices, yet unless it appears upon the face of the commitment itself that the defendant is charged with a felony, we are bound by the *Habeas Corpus Act* to discharge him ; taking such bail for his appearance to take his trial as we in our discretion shall think fit, according to the circumstances of the case : the question therefore is, Whether there is specified in this commitment such an offence as amounts to felony ? It is admitted that neither of the first two charges amount to felony. The last charge is, that the defendant was an accessary with Rand in *wilfully* and *maliciously* setting fire to a *parcel* of unthreshed wheat, without alledging that the offence was done *feloniously*: and although it is not necessary that the word " *feloniously*" should be used in the commitment, yet it ought to appear on the facts stated to be in law a felony, and within the description of the Act. Now the statute has only made it felony to set fire to a *cock, mow, or stack of corn,* and the defendant is not charged with either of these. We must suppose, that the Legislature well knew the meaning of the words they have used , and if a Justice of the Peace uses the same words, we are bound to suppose that he intended them in the same sense ; but if he makes use of other words, he must be more precise. Now here, a *parcel* of unthreshed wheat is too loose a description. It does not come within the description of the Act. We cannot say how much is meant by the word *parcel.* Twenty ears of wheat may be called a *parcel*; but can never be construed either a *cock, mow, or stack.* I am therefore of opinion, that as the warrant of commitment does not charge the defendant with a felony, we are bound to bail him. With regard to the *quantum* of the bail, although the nature of the defendant's crime is not very accurately stated, yet as sufficient appears on the depositions returned with the commitment

mitment to shew that he has at least been guilty of an enormous offence, I think we ought to take ample security for his appearance, and that he himself should be bound in 1000l. and four sureties in 500l. each.

Mr. JUSTICE GROSE.—It is not necessary that the act should be charged in the warrant of commitment to be done *felonice*; it would be sufficient, if on the facts stated we could not but see that the act was feloniously committed. If therefore a *parcel* of wheat *ex vi termini* described a *cock*, *mow*, or *stack* of corn, I should be of opinion that a felony was sufficiently charged in this commitment: but I think that it does not; for if in the act of removing a stack of corn from a farmer's yard to his barn, a small parcel dropped by accident, the setting fire to that parcel would not be an offence within the Act of Parliament. As to the sureties which we in our discretion should require, I am of opinion, that the security mentioned by my brother *Ashhurst* ought to be given, since we cannot but see that the defendant has been guilty of a most atrocious act.

The defendant was bailed accordingly.

HICKMAN'S CASE.

The prisoner was tried before Mr. Justice Buller at the Old Bailey in July Session, 1783, for a robbery upon John Miller.

The prosecutor was servant to Mr. Lewis, table-decker to the Chaplain's room in St. James's Palace, and had an apartment, in which he alone slept, in a court called the Board of Green Cloth. The prisoner was a centinel on guard at the Palace, and had been one night treated by the prosecutor with some bread and cheese and ale in this room. About a fortnight afterwards, very late in the evening of the day laid in the indictment, the prosecutor, on going up stairs, heard somebody stepping almost upon his heels. On turning round, he discovered it was the prisoner, who said, "It is me." The prosecutor replied, "What brought you here at this time of the night?" The prisoner answered, "I am come for satisfaction; you know what passed the other night; you are a Sodomite; and if you do not give me satisfaction I will go and fetch a serjeant and a file of men, and take you before a Justice; for I have been in the Black Hole ever since

I was

I was here laft, and I do not value my life." The profecutor afked him what money he muft have? The prifoner
faid, " I muft have three or four guineas." The profecutor
accordingly gave him two guineas, which was all he had,
and promifed to give him another guinea the next morning.
The prifoner took the two guineas, faying, " Mind, I don't
demand any thing of you." The next morning he came
again, and received the other guinea ; and in a few days after, upon making an application for more money upon the
fame pretence, he was apprehended. The profecutor fwore,
that he was very much alarmed when he gave him the two
guineas, and did not very well know what he did ; but that
he parted with his money under an idea of preferving his
character from reproach and not from the fear of perfonal
violence.

The learned Judge ftated to the Jury the feveral ingredients which the law required to conftitute the crime of
robbery ; and particularly, as applicable to this fpecies of it,
the determination of the JUDGES in the cafe of *the King and
Donnally* ; remarking the difference, that in *Donnally's cafe*
the profecutor had fworn, that he delivered his money under an apprehenfion of perfonal danger, as well as from the
fear of lofing his character ; but that, in the prefent cafe,
the profecutor had fworn he parted with his money for the
fake of his character only, and not from any apprehenfion of
danger to his perfon.

The Jury thought that the profecutor parted with his
money againft his will, through a fear that his character
might receive an injury from the prifoner's accufation ; and
they therefore found the prifoner GUILTY. But as this
was only the fecond cafe of the kind, and as fome doubt
had prevailed with refpect to *Donnally's cafe*, becaufe he was
not executed, the judgment was refpited, and the cafe fubmitted to the confideration of the TWELVE JUDGES, upon
the difference before mentioned between the two cafes.

In February Seffion, 1784, the prifoner was called to the
bar, and Mr. Juftice Afhhurft delivered the opinion of the
Judges to the following effect :—Some doubts having been
entertained as to the opinion of the TWELVE JUDGES in
the cafe of *Patrick Donnally*, the learned Judge who tried
the prifoner thought it proper that the prefent cafe fhould
likewife be referred to their confideration. They have accordingly conferred upon it ; and they are of opinion, That
it does not *materially* differ from the cafe of *Donnally* ; for
that the true definition of ROBBERY is the ftealing, or the
ftealing or taking from the perfon, or in the prefence of

auanother, property of any amount, with such a degree of *force* or *terror*, as to induce the party *unwillingly* to part with his property ; and whether the terror arises from real or expected violence to the person, or from a sense of injury to the character, the law makes no kind of difference ; for to most men the idea of losing their fame and reputation is equally, if not more terrific than the dread of personal injury. The principal ingredient in robbery is a man's being *forced* to part with his property ; and the JUDGES are unanimously of opinion, That upon the principles of law, and the authority of former decisions, a *threat* to accuse a man of having committed the greatest of all crimes, is, as in the present case, a sufficient *force* to constitute the crime of robbery by putting in fear.

The prisoner received sentence of death, and was executed.

FISHER'S CASE.

Old Bailey. January Session, 1785.

The prisoner was indicted, before Mr. Justice *Heath*, for burglariously breaking and entering the dwelling-house of Benjamin Ward, and stealing therein four gold watches of a considerable value ; to which indictment he had pleaded *Not Guilty*.

The prosecutor proved that the burglary had been committed, and that the watches were stolen ; but there was no evidence whatever to bring the charge home to the prisoner, except a confession of the fact, which he had freely and voluntarily made before a Justice of the Peace on his examination, but it was not reduced into writing.

The COURT. It is an established rule of law, that the mere confession of a crime, without any one single circumstance to corroborate it, is not sufficient to convict a prisoner, unless he should again confess the fact, by pleading *Guilty* to the indictment.

GIB-

GIBSON, MUTTON and WIGGS'S CASE.

At the Surrey Lent Affizes, 1785, for Kingfton, the prifoners were convicted before Mr. BARON PERRYN, for burglary in the dwelling-houfe of T. S. and ftealing goods therein, the property of John Hill.

It appeared in evidence, that there was a fhop built clofe and adjoining to the dwelling-houfe mentioned in the indictment; but there was no internal communication whatever between the houfe and fhop, and no perfon flept in the fhop. The only door to the fhop was in the courtyard before the houfe and fhop, which court-yard was inclofed by a brick wall three feet high. In the wall was a wicket which ferved as a communication to both the houfe and fhop. The burglary was committed in the fhop. The *fhop* was let by T. S. to John Hill, together with fome apartments in the *dwelling-houfe*, from year to year, at fix guineas *per annum*.

It was objected by the Counfel for the prifoner, that the fhop could not be confidered as any part of the dwelling-houfe of T. S. and upon this objection the judgment was refpited, and the cafe referved for the opinion of the TWELVE JUDGES.

Mr. BARON EYRE, at the Summer Affizes for the fame county at Croydon, 1785, ordered the prifoners to the bar; and informed them, that the JUDGES had confidered of this cafe, and that they were unanimoufly of opinion it was a proper conviction.

The prifoners received fentence of death, and were executed purfuant to fuch fentence.

SESSIONS CASES determined in the COURT OF KING's
BENCH, subsequent to the Publication of the last
Edition of BURN's JUSTICE.

YOUNG, RANDAL, MULLINS, and OSMER, v. the
KING, in Error.

This was an indictment on the 30th *Geo.* II. cap. 24,
for obtaining money on false pretences, removed by Writ
of Error from the Sessions at Bristol, where the defendants
had been found guilty, and sentenced to transportation for
seven years.

The indictment stated, that the defendants did falsely
pretend to W. Thomas, that John Young had made a bet
of 500 guineas on each side with a Colonel of the Army
then at Bath, " That W. Lewis would run on the high-
road leading from Gloucester to Bristol ten miles within one
hour ;" and that Young and Mullins did go 200 guineas each
in the said bet, and Randal the other 100 guineas, and did,
under colour and pretence of such bet, obtain from Thomas, as a part of such pretended bet, 20 guineas of the
500 guineas, with intent to cheat and defraud him thereof ;
whereas in truth and in fact no such bet had been made, &c.
A second count stated that the defendants did falsely pretend
to the said Thomas that Young had made a bet of 500
guineas on each side with Osmer, that Lewis would run, &c.
as aforesaid, by means of which false pretence the defendants did unlawfully obtain from Thomas the said 20 guineas, with intent to cheat and defraud him of the same, &c.
There were two other counts, charging the defendants
with having obtained 20 guineas from Thomas by false
pretences, without stating what those pretences were. It
was argued in objection to the indictment; 1st. That this
transaction was not subject to criminal prosecution, as the
false pretence must either be accompanied by some false
token, or otherwise be of such kind, as common prudence
cannot guard against ; 2dly, That this charge is not stated
with sufficient certainty, inasmuch as the Colonel's name
should have been set forth ; 3dly, The four defendants
should have been charged severally, and the false pretence ex-

VOL. I.   S   pressed

preffed in words being a feparate act of the perfon ufing them ; 4thly, The fecond count of the indictment charges a diftinct offence, namely, a pretended bet with Ofmer, and fhould have therefore been a feparate indictment.

LORD KENYON, C. J.—This indictment being founded on the ftatute of 30 *Geo.* II. cap. 24. is different from a common law indictment. When it paffed, it was confidered to extend to every cafe where a party had obtained money by falfely reprefenting himfelf to be in a fituation in which he was not, or any occurrence that had not happened, to which perfons of ordinary caution might give credit. The ftatute of the 33d *Hen.* VIII. cap. 1, requires a falfe feal, or token, to be ufed in order to bring the perfon impofed upon into the confidence of the other ; but that being found to be infufficient, the ftatute 30 *Geo.* II. cap. 24. introduced another offence, defcribing it in terms extremely general. It feems difficult to draw the line, and to fay to what cafes this ftatute fhall extend ; and therefore we muft fee whether each particular cafe, as it arifes, comes within it. In the prefent cafe four men came to the profecutor, reprefenting a cafe as about to take place, that William Lewis fhould go a certain diftance within a limited time ; that they had betted upon the event, and they fhould probably win : he was perhaps too credulous, and gave confidence to them, and advanced his money ; and afterwards the whole ftory proved to be an abfolute fiction. Then the defendants, morally fpeaking, have been guilty of an offence. I admit that there are certain irregularities which are not the fubject of criminal law. But when the criminal law happens to be auxiliary to the law of morality, I do not feel any inclination to explain it away. Now this offence is within the words of the act ; for the defendants have, by falfe pretences, fraudulently contrived to obtain money from the profecutor ; and I fee no reafon why it fhould not be held to be within the meaning of the ftatute. The fecond objection is, that the charge is imperfectly ftated ; but that is anfwered by the record. If the indictment did not inform the defendants what charge they were called upon to anfwer, the objection would be well founded. But it holds out to them fufficient intelligence of the offence imputed to them. It ftates the wager to be with " a Colonel at *Bath* ;" perhaps his name was not mentioned, fo that he could not have been defcribed in the indictment with greater accuracy. But if fuch a wager had been actually depending, it was competent to the defendants to have proved it in their defence. As to the 3d objection : this cafe is extremely different

ferent

ferent from that of perjury, to which it has been compared ; becaufe that depends on the very words which the perfon charged, individually ufes in a Court of Juftice: and the words fpoken by one cannot poffibly be applied to another as falfely uttering thofe very words. I do not fee how that could ever have been doubted. But in this cafe all the defendants went together to the profecutor, and thus carried a greater degree of credit; and they all joined in the relation as of a thing within their own knowledge. If they were all prefent, each acting a different part in the fame tranfaction, no rule of criminal proceeding will be violated by adjudging them guilty of the impofition *jointly*. I admit that offences are not to be charged in fuch a manner as will confound the evidence : but in cafes where it is neceffary that feveral defendants fhould be indicted jointly, and the evidence is complicated, it may be feparated for each particular defendant, as was done in the cafe before Mr. Juftice *Yates* at Hereford, in the trial of Mr. Powell's murderers. The fourth objection would be well founded, if the legal judgment on each count was different ; it would be like a misjoinder in civil actions. But in this cafe the judgment on all the counts is precifely the fame ; a mifdemeanor is charged in each. Moft probably the charges were meant to meet the fame facts : but if it were not fo, I think they may be joined in the fame indictment.

ASHHURST, J.—As to the firft objection : cafes which happened before the paffing of the 30th *Geo.* II. cap. 24, do not apply to this. For that ftatute created an offence which did not exift before, and I think it includes the prefent. The Legiflature faw that all men were not equally prudent, and this ftatute was paffed to protect the weaker part of mankind. The words of it are very general, " all perfons who knowingly by falfe pretences fhall obtain from any perfon money, goods, &c. with intent to cheat or defraud, &c." and we have no power to reftrain their operation. With refpect to the fecond objection ; it feems that the charge is as certain as the nature of the thing would admit. The third objection would have been much ftronger, if the charge had been laid as feveral ; for if they all acted together, and fhared in the fame tranfaction, it could not have been faid that one received the whole fum. Neither is there any foundation for the laft objection. Perhaps each count related to the fame fraud, though it is charged differently. But if it were not fo, I do not know any rule of law which prevents the joinder of two mifdemeanors in the fame indictment.

BULLER, J.—The first objection is the one deserving the most consideration. The principles of the common law have been truly stated. To make an offence indictable at common law, it must be public in it's nature. And the distinction, which has been taken in the case of using false weights and measures, shews it more clearly than any other. If a person sell by false weights, though only to one person, it is an indictable offence : but if without false weights he sell to many persons a less quantity than he pretends to do, it is not indictable. But though the common law, as applicable to this subject, is as stated by the counsel, it is in this case necessary to consider both the statutes 33 _Hen._ VIII. cap. 1, and the 30 _Geo._ II. cap. 24. By the former of those the offence consists in obtaining money or goods by _false tokens_ ; and unless some token be used, the case does not come within that act. Now suppose a token had been produced in this case, and that the defendants, after telling their story to the prosecutor, had said, " If you have any doubt, here is the Colonel's gorget ;" I think it would have fallen within the statute of 33 _Hen._ VIII. If it would, then let us consider what effect the 30 _Geo._ II. cap. 24. has on the case. The Legislature thought that the former statute was too limited ; and therefore the 30 _Geo._ II. cap. 24. was passed, which enacts that all persons, who shall obtain money from others by _false pretences_ with intent to cheat or defraud such persons, shall _be deemed offenders against the public peace._ The statute therefore clearly extends to cases which were not the subject of an indictment at common law. The ingredients of this offence are the obtaining money by false pretences, and with an intent to defraud. Barely asking another for a sum of money is not sufficient, but some pretence must be used, and that pretence false ; and the intent is necessary to constitute the crime. If the intent be made out, and the false pretence used, in order to effect it, it brings the case within this statute. Very few cases on this Act of Parliament have been brought before this Court : but there was an indictment on this statute against Count Villeneuve, tried at Chester in the year 1778, which I have had occasion to mention here several times, and which I have never heard doubted or contradicted. That indictment was tried while I sat with Moreton, C. J. on the bench of Chester, of whom all who remember him will bear testimony with me that he was a very able judge, and peculiarly cautious in criminal cases. The facts of that case were shortly these : the defendant applied to Sir T. Broughton, telling him that he was intrusted by the Duke de Lauzun to take some horses

from

from Ireland to London, and that he had been detained so long by contrary winds that his money was spent; Sir T. Broughton was induced by this representation to advance some money to him; afterwards it turned out that the prisoner never had been employed by the Duke de Lauzun, and his whole story was a fiction. On that case the prisoner was convicted, and sentenced to hard labour on the Thames. Now that case goes the full length of deciding this. As to three other objections, they admit of very easy answers. With respect to the objection that the charge is too general: in this stage of the proceeding, the Court must take it that the representation was made by the defendants in the same manner that it is charged in the indictment. And if that, though general, was sufficient to answer the defendant's purpose, we cannot say that it was too general. We are not to suppose that the Colonel's name was mentioned; and the prosecutor could not state it with greater particularity than the defendants used. The third objection is that this is not a joint offence: but, as this is the case of a misdemeanor, the case in Burrow, 984, is a decisive answer to it; there Lord Mansfield said, "it is a strange thing if the king cannot call a man to account for a breach of the peace, because he broke two heads instead of one." The present was, I think, a joint offence; it was a joint representation to answer one and the same purpose; neither is the proof several; it relates to one transaction. This is not like the case of a conspiracy, where the whole story must be taken up in detached pieces at different times to charge the different actors. But here it is one entire act, which they were all carrying on in concert together. If however any authority were necessary, a case happened about a year ago which is stronger than the present. Three persons were indicted on the Black-Act for shooting at the prosecutor; they were all charged with the single act, and the indictment was held by all the Judges of England to be sufficient. As to the remaining objection: that is founded on a point which once embarrassed me a great deal. Some years have elapsed since I looked into it, but I believe I can state pretty accurately how it stands. In misdemeanors the case in Burrow shews that it is no objection to an indictment that it contains several charges. The case of felonies admits of a different consideration; but even in such cases it is no objection in this stage of the prosecution. On the face of an indictment every count imports to be for a different offence, and is charged as at different times. And it does not appear on the record whether the offences are or are

not

not diſtinct. But if it appear before the defendant has pleaded, or the Jury are charged, that he is to be tried for ſeparate offences, it has been the practice of the Judges to quaſh the indictments, left it ſhould confound the priſoner in his defence, or prejudice him in his challenge of the Jury; for he might object to a juryman's trying one of the offences, though he might have no reaſon to do ſo in the other. But theſe are only matters of prudence and diſcretion. If the judge, who tries the priſoner, does not diſcover it in time, I think he may put the proſecutor to make his election on which charge he will proceed. I did it at the laſt Seſſions at the Old Bailey, and hope that, in exerciſing that diſcretion, I did not infringe on any rule of law or juſtice. But if the caſe has gone to the length of a verdict, it is no objection in arreſt of judgment. If it were, it would overturn every indictment which contains ſeveral counts. So where the evidence affects ſeveral priſoners differently, I have, as was done by Mr. J. Yates at Hereford, ſelected the evidence as applicable to each, and left their caſes ſeparately to the Jury. And in a caſe which happened before me on the laſt Spring Aſſizes at Exeter, where two priſoners were indicted for murder, and evidence given which preſſed very hard on one priſoner, but was not admiſſible againſt the other, I thought it the foundeſt way of adminiſtering juſtice to ſum up the evidence, and take the verdict againſt each ſeparately. But all theſe are mere matters of diſcretion only, which Judges exerciſe in order to give a priſoner a fair trial: for when a verdict is given, they are not the ſubject of any objection to the record.

GROSE, J.—My brother *Buller* has given a deciſive anſwer to the firſt objection. The ſtatute created a new offence; for it declares that all perſons obtaining money by falſe pretences, with an intent to cheat, ſhall be deemed offenders *againſt law* and the public peace. That particular offence is made an offence againſt law, whether it was ſo or not before. And I am clearly of opinion that this caſe comes within the Act of Parliament. As to the ſecond objection; it muſt be taken after verdict that the offence was proved as it was laid in the indictment; and if ſo, it could not have been charged in any other way. It is perfectly immaterial whether the name of the Colonel at Bath was or was not mentioned, ſince the defendants obtained the proſecutor's money by this repreſentation. With reſpect to the defendants being charged jointly; every crime which may be in its nature joint may be ſo laid. Here it is ſtated that all the defendants committed this offence, by all joining in the ſame plan:

plan: they were all jointly concerned in defrauding the profecutor of his money. And the offence being joint in its nature, it could not be laid with fo much propriety in any other manner. On the laft objection, I am clearly of opinion that it is no objection in arreft of judgment that the indictment charges feveral offences. The different counts in the indictment always ftate the offences as feparate: and if this objection were to prevail, every indictment which contains two counts muft be bad. It is no objection even in the cafe of felonies; ftill lefs is it fo in mifdemeanours.

Judgment affirmed.

REX v. *Inhabitants of* GWENOP.

George Treverton and family were removed from Penryn to Gwenop; and the Seffions, upon appeal, confirmed the Order of Removal.

C A S E.

George Treverton was a married man, and had a family, and had been drawn to ferve in the militia within the faid county in 1778, and was duly fworn and ferved his full three years in actual fervice in the faid militia; and at the end of that time was difcharged. His occupation was that of a hufbandman, working at daily wages for the fupport of himfelf and family: his refidence had been for fome years laft paft in Penryn, and he had never been chargeable thereto; and his laft legal fettlement was in Gwenop. He therefore infifted that, having ferved the faid three years in the militia, he was entitled to the privilege and benefit granted to militia-men under the act of the 26 *Geo.* III. cap. 107, and the other ftatutes in that cafe made, and was therefore irremoveable; but the Seffions confidered that his was not a trade within the meaning of the ftatutes.

ASHHURST, J.—This cafe feems to be extremely clear both on the words and the meaning of the Act of Parliament. The firft Act of Parliament on this fubject is the 22. *Geo.* II. cap. 44, which is confined to mariners and foldiers: and the preamble of it ftates that mariners and foldiers of different trades, and apprentices who had not ferved their time, were prohibited from fetting up their trades in corporate towns, &c. either by reafon of bye-laws therein
made;

made; or of the 5th Eliz. cap. 4. Now that was the inconvenience intended to be remedied; for which purpose it was enacted, that all such mariners and soldiers might set up their trades in any town, notwithstanding those disabilities. This therefore was a proper indulgence given to those persons who were taken out of their business in order to enter into his Majesty's service. And it is observable, that the statute 26 *Geo.* III. cap. 107, upon which this question arises has an express reference to the former one; and therefore we must suppose that the Legislature had in view the same inconveniences which were intended to be remedied by the 22 *Geo.* II. And this latter act says, that every person having served in the militia, &c. may set up any trade as freely and with the same provisions, and under the same regulations, as any mariner or soldier could do by virtue of the 22d *Geo.* II. And that *no such* militia-man shall be liable to be removed, &c. This act being made in *pari materia* with the 22 *Geo.* II. and expressly referring to it, may be considered as incorporated with it; and that relates to *persons in trade,* but not to common labourers, who would not suffer the same inconveniencies as the former, for they might easily find employment wherever they might happen to be.

BULLER, J.—If the Legislature had used any words giving these privileges generally to all militia-men, I should not have been inclined to confine the operation of them; being of opinion, that it would be the wisest law that could be made on this subject, that no person should be removed till he is actually chargeable. But as the Legislature has not said so, we cannot make the law. The first argument is, that every militia-man, who has actually served and is married, is entitled to two privileges: but that is doing great violence to the words; for then we must suppose that two-thirds of this clause in the act have no meaning. But in considering the description of the persons intended to be benefited, every part of the clause must be attended to. For the privilege given in the first part of the section is, that such a militia-man may set up any trade in any town, &c. as freely, and with the same provisions, and under the same regulations, as any mariner or soldier can do by virtue of the 22 *Geo.* II. entituled, "An Act to enable such officers, &c. *to exercise trades:*" then this statute goes on to say that *no such* militia-man shall be liable to be removed out of *such* town. The word " such" is material in both these places. The first means *such* persons as have served, are married, and have set up trades; the other refers to the town where they are to exercise the trades. I agree that a militia-man

who

who has ferved, &c. cannot be removed before he has fet up the trade, if he go there for that purpofe ; for he, who is privileged *morando*, is privileged *eundo*. This queftion therefore is extremely clear on this Act of the 26 *Geo* III. cap. 107. But if it be coupled with the 22 *Geo.* II. cap. 44. no doubt whatever can be entertained about it ; for that is exprefsly confined to perfons exercifing trades. The object of that Act was to protect foldiers &c. againft the 5th of *Eliz.* cap. 4, and certain bye-laws in particular towns: but a labourer is not a trader within the ftatute of *Elizabeth*. The argument drawn from the 24th *Geo.* III. bears againft the point for which it was mentioned : for if the words of this ftatute 26th *Geo.* III. be doubtful, reference muft be made to the 24th *Geo.* III. cap. 6, as they are made in *pari materiâ*; and by that it appears, that the foldiers, &c. are only irremoveable *during the time they exercife any trades*.

GROSE, J.----It is infifted, that a labourer is entitled to the privilege of being irremoveable until he become chargeable, if he has ferved in the militia and is a married man. But if we read the titles and preambles of the three ftatutes, which are made in *pari materiâ*, there can be no doubt in this queftion. For they were paffed to enable perfons, who have ferved their country, to fet up trades, which they could not do without incurring the penalties of the 5th of *Eliz* cap. 4, and of bye-laws in certain towns. And my conftruction of this laft act, which has an exprefs reference to the 22d *Geo.* III. cap. 44, is that all militia-men who have actually ferved, and are married, may exercife any trade in any town notwithftanding thofe bye-laws, and the 5th of *Elizabeth*. If this were not the intention of the Legiflature, they would have faid that, " all militia-men who have ferved and are married, going into any town, &c. fhall be irremoveable." But thofe are not the words of the ftatute. Therefore I have no doubt but this pauper was removeable, and that the order of feffions muft be confirmed.

Order of Seffions confirmed.

The

The KING v. the Inhabitants of HAMSTALL RIDWARE.

CASE.

Ann Cradock, being settled at Rudgley, was bound as a parish-apprentice to Susannah Cotton, of the same place; who assigned her to S. Walker, of Hamstall Ridware, with whom she resided there under the indenture more than 40 days, till the time of his death, when she was removed by order of two Justices from Hamstall Ridware to Rudgley. The indenture was assented to by two Justices of the Peace by signing the same *separately*; but the two Justices *did not assent to or sign the same at the same time*, or in the presence of each other. The sessions, on appeal, quashed the order.

LORD KENYON, C. J.---Perhaps the rule, requiring the concurrence of two Magistrates at the same time, may be sometimes attended with inconvenience. But the rule has been long settled to be, that the concurrence of Justices together is not necessary where the act to be done is merely *ministerial*; but they must confer together and form a joint opinion, where the act is of a *judicial* nature. It has been held (whether rightly so or not we are not now to enquire) that the allowance of a poor-rate is an act merely *ministerial*; and, that being once established, the consequence results that the two magistrates need not meet when they allow the rate. The words indeed of the section on which this question arises are nearly similar to those used in the first, under which the poor-rate is to be allowed: but when the nature of this case is considered, it appears to be one of the most serious subjects that fall within the decisions of the Justices. For they are empowered by this Act of Parliament to take children out of the arms of their parents, and to bind them out as apprentices till they are 21 years of age. The law has made them the guardians for those children, who have no others to take care of them. And who ought to judge of the fitness of the persons, to whom the poor children are thus to be apprenticed? Not the overseers——they are frequently obscure people, and perhaps in managing the business of the parish are not always attentive to the feelings of parents. But the Legislature intended that the Magistrates should have a check and control over the parish officers in this instance; and in my mind they are called upon

to

to examine, with the moſt minute and anxious attention, the ſituations of the maſters, to whom the apprentices are to be bound, and to exerciſe their judgment ſolemnly and ſoberly before they allow or diſallow the act of the pariſh-officers; for which purpoſe it is neceſſary that they ſhould confer together.

ASHHURST, J.—The act of the Juſtices in this caſe is in its nature an act of judgment. They are the guardians of the morals of the people, and ought to take care that the apprentices are not placed with maſters who may corrupt their morals. The Juſtices therefore ſhould enquire particularly whether or not they ought to allow the binding by the pariſh-officers; and I think they would be guilty of a breach of duty, if they implicitly gave their aſſent without examining into the circumſtances of the caſe.

BULLER, J.—It is not eaſily to be reconciled with any principle of common ſenſe to ſay that an act, which is merely *miniſterial, muſt be done with the conſent of two Juſtices.* And I much doubt whether the perſons who brought in the act, (43 *Eliz.* cap. 2.) requiring the conſent of two Magiſtrates to the allowance of a poor-rate, intended that the act of allowing it ſhould be only miniſterial; for it ſeems abſurd to require the aſſent of two Juſtices, and yet not to give them the power of withholding it, if they ſee occaſion. But the Legiſlature has not given them any authority to exerciſe their judgment upon that ſubject; and therefore this Court has ſaid, on the conſtruction of that ſtatute, that their allowance of the rate is merely miniſterial. But the act of aſſenting to the binding of pariſh-apprentices is purely *judicial*; for, on appeal, the Juſtices at the Seſſions are not only to conſider the propriety of binding out the apprentice, but alſo whether the maſter be bound to take him.

GROSE, J.—This act is peculiarly of a judicial nature; for the Magiſtrates are oppointed the guardians of thoſe who have no other guardians. They ſhould therefore exerciſe their judgment in this caſe with great deliberation.

Order of Seſſions quaſhed.

The

The KING *v. the Inhabitants of* ALLENDALE.

Drifdale and wife were removed by order of two Juftices from Lambley to Allendale, in Northumberland; Seffions on appeal confirmed the order.

C A S E.

In February, 1786, the pauper, John Drifdale, being *then an unmarried man*, not having child or children, was hired for a year to ferve Thomas Benfon, at Allendale, from May-day, 1786, to May-day, 1787, as a hind. It is the cuftom in that country to hire married men, as hinds, be-caufe their wives are bound to perform certain fervices for the mafter in time of harveft; and when the wife of a hind dies, he muft hire a female fervant to perform fuch fervices. It was in the contemplation of both the mafter and the fer-vant, and perfectly underftood by them, at the time of hiring, that the pauper would marry before he entered upon his fervice. After fuch hiring, and before the commence-ment of the fervice, he married his wife, the other pauper, *and entered upon his fervice a married man,* and ferved out the whole year a married man at Allendale.

BULLER, J.----Neither the cuftom of the country, nor the agreement between the parties, went to compel this pauper to marry before he entered upon his fervice; he was at li-berty to do fo or not as he pleafed. The cuftom of the country only amounts to this, that part of the fervice is to be performed by a female: it is therefore indifferent to the mafter whether the fervant be married or not, becaufe, if he be fingle, he muft hire fome female to perform thofe fervices. As to the cafe put at the bar, of a contract at an unreafonable diftance of time before the fervice is to com-mence, that would be ftrong evidence of fraud. So if this pauper had been under an agreement to marry, and the mafter had told him that he fhould not marry for a month in order to evade the ftatute, that alfo might be confidered as fraudulent. But there is no pretence to fay that there is any fraud in this cafe.

Both orders affirmed.

The

The KING, v. JOHN CLAPP.

The overseers of Sowton in Devon, apprenticed a pauper, with consent of two Justices, to the defendant. The defendant appealed to the Sessions, who confirmed the act of the Justices, subject to the opinion of the Court.

CASE:

The pauper was bound to the defendant, who resided in the parish of Pishoe, and occupied an estate in the parish of Sowton, of the value of 20l. *per ann.* upon which there was no house, but which was divided from the defendant's dwelling-house by the highway. The apprentice was tendered with the indenture to the defendant in the highway adjoining to the estate in Sowton.

LORD KENYON, C. J.—It is highly fit that this question should not remain any longer undecided. I remember a much older case than either of those mentioned at the bar, in which this question was discussed, but not decided. The question arises on the 5th section of the 43 *Eliz.* cap. 2. The general purview of that statute was to make a provision for the maintenance of the poor; and the first clause, in mentioning those who are to contribute to such maintenance, describes two sorts of persons, namely, *inhabitants* and *occupiers of lands, &c.* Amongst other provisions for the poor, the 5th section gives power to the parish-officers, with the assent of two Magistrates, to bind poor children apprentices *where they shall see convenient.* It is true, indeed, that those words cannot be taken so generally as they purport, because they cannot compel mere strangers, who stand in no relation to the parish, to take such apprentices. But I think that the context of the statute furnishes the means of circumscribing the general extent of those words: and that context I take from the first clause, which imposes other burdens of the same nature on *occupiers of lands, &c.* as well as inhabitants. The general object of the act was to compel all those, who had any property in the parish, to contribute their due proportion towards the maintenance of the poor; and the receiving apprentices is one mode of contributing to their general relief. In construing these words, I see no reason for confining the power of binding on the *inhabitants* of the parish; they ought to be extended to persons

fons *occupying lands in the parish, though residing out of it.*
Then it is faid that if this conſtruction be put upon the
ſtatute, the party may be doubly charged; in the pariſh in
which he lives in reſpect of his inhabitancy; in that, in
which he has lands, in reſpect of his occupation of them.
But if he find himſelf aggrieved, he may appeal to the Seſſions; and we muſt take it for granted that the Juſtices will
do what is right. They are to adapt the charge to the ſize
of the property which the perſon charged poſſeſſes: and theſe
are incidental charges which fall on him in reſpect of that
property. I remember it was argued in a former caſe on
this ſubject that, if this conſtruction of the ſtatute were
to prevail, ſome pariſhes would diſburthen themſelves of
many of their poor by apprenticing out their poor children
to perſons living out of the pariſh: but the anſwer to any
ſuch argument is, that at the time when the 43 *Eliz.* was
paſſed, the ſtatute 13 & 14 *Car.* II. was not in exiſtence.
However the ground of my deciſion here is, that this is one
of the modes provided for the maintenance of the poor in
this ſtatute, which impoſes the duty in reſpect of the property.

Order of Seſſions confirmed.

The KING v. the Inhabitants of LIVERPOOL.

Two Juſtices removed Samuel Littlemore, his wife, and
four children, from Liverpool, in the county Palatine of
Lancaſter, to Stourton in the county Palatine of Cheſter.
The Seſſions, on appeal, reverſed that order, ſubject to the
opinion of this Court.

C A S E.

The pauper, Samuel Littlemore, was originally ſettled in
Stourton, and about 16 years ago came to reſide in Liverpool; and while he reſided there, he was elected ſexton by
the proprietors of the ſeats in the church or chapel of St.
James's at a veſtry there held in the preſence of the church-
wardens, being recommended by the then miniſter to that
office; and executed that office ſix years, lodging all the
while in the pariſh of Liverpool. The boundary between
Walton and Liverpool is in the chapel yard of St. James's;
the church, and part of the church-yard, ſtands in the pariſh of Walton, and the other part of the church-yard is in
the

the parish of Liverpool: but not any corpse was ever buried in that part of the church-yard which lies in the parish of Liverpool, whilst the pauper executed the office, though corpses have been buried there since. The inhabitants of Liverpool, seat-holders and others, constantly attend the church of St. James's, in proportion of fifty to one of any other parish or place.

LORD KENYON, C. J.—There is no doubt but that part of the office of sexton consists in digging graves: this is different from that of the sacrist, which is an office scarcely known since the Reformation, except in some of the cathedrals; whose duty it is to take care of the sacred vestments. And it is as clear that the office of sexton is a public office within the meaning of the 3d of *W. & M.* cap. 11. § 6. In this case the church-yard lies in two parishes, and the sexton gained a settlement in that in which he resided.

Per Curiam,   Order of Sessions confirmed.

The KING *v. the Inhabitants of* WITTON *cum* TWAM-BROOKES.

A motion was made for a rule to set aside an order of Sessions, on the following

CASE.

The pauper's father rented a tenement of 16 l. a year in Witton, Chester, and resided upon it above a year, when the pauper was about six years old. He then went to Middlewick, where he did no act to gain a settlement, and two years after ran away from his family; and the pauper's mother, taking the pauper with her to Congleton, died in half a year, when the pauper was left in the care of one Jane Brookes, with whom he lived at Congleton, and worked at the silk mills there. The overseers of the poor of Witton paid the whole or a part of his maintenance for four years to Jane Brookes, after which period the pauper supported himself till the age of 16; at which time he got 3s. 9d. per week, and boarded himself where he liked. During the time he lived pauper at Congleton, he saw his father twice at the distance of about four years, at which times his father did not give him any thing (except a pair of breeches, and

two-

two-pence-halfpenny, and afterwards three halfpence). At 18 or 19 years of age, the pauper went from Congleton to Sheffield, and hired himself for four years, by which hiring, however, he gained no settlement. He heard that his father had been to enquire after him at Congleton, and that he then lived at Dunham, to which place the pauper went to see him, and was at that time 23 years of age, and married. It appeared that the father had made such enquiry as abovementioned after the pauper from his daughter (the pauper's sister) with intent as he said to give him a suit of cloaths, as he had done less for the pauper than any of his children. It appeared that the father had married a second wife, and held a tenement in Dunham of 11 l. a year, and had lived upon it eight years when his son went to see him there as above; upon which visit he staid only one hour, and never saw his father at any time but as above. Upon the above facts the Justices at the Chester Sessions were of opinion that the settlement of the pauper George Hewit was at Witton, that place appearing to them the last settlement the pauper's father had whilst the pauper remained a part of his family: and they confirmed an order of two Justices, by which the pauper, and his wife, and family, were removed from Stockport to Witton.

It was argued in support of the order of Sessions, that the pauper was emancipated, because his father had no domicile, of which the pauper could be a member, after he was 8 years of age.

LORD KENYON, C. J.—It was never conceived in any case that a son, who was only 16 years of age, and who had not gained any settlement in his own right, was not part of his father's family. The cases of emancipation have always been decided on the circumstances either of the son's being 21, or married, or having gained a settlement in his own right, or (as in the case of the soldier) having contracted a relation which was inconsistent with the idea of his being in a subordinate situation in his father's family.

BULLER, J.—Here the pauper remained under the power of his father the whole time.

Per curiam. Rule absolute; order of Sessions quashed.

The KING, *v.* T. CARLYON, *Clerk, and Another.*

Upon an appeal to the Quarter-Sessions of Cornwall, against a rate for the poor, they confirmed the rate, subject to the opinion of the COURT.

C A S E,

The appellants were the proprietors of the tithe-sheaf of the parish of Paul, and also of one-tenth of all fish taken within the parish : and that they and their tenants were rated as follows :

	£.	s.	d.
The Rev. Thomas Carlyon and Mrs. Veale, the rectorial tithe of pilchards - -	0	19	10⅝
Edward Paddy (who was a tenant to the appellants) for the tithe of the hook-fish, and all other fish, except pilchards and herrings, in the village of Newlyn, which lies in the parish of Paul - - - - - -	0	5	3¼
Benjamin Harry, Richard Wright and Co. who were also tenants of the appellants for the tithe of hook-fish, and all other fish (except pilchards and herrings) in Mousehole, also within the said parish - - -	0	2	4
John Glasson (who was also tenant to the appellants) for the tithe of sheaf - -	0	5	10

The question was the rateability of this property; and it having been always rated in this parish, and being a property *yielding a certain annual profit*, the Sessions were of opinion that it was rateable.

LORD KENYON, C. J.—This question is decided by the express terms of the Act of Parliament ; which after mentioning parsons and vicars, in the number of the persons who are to contribute to the relief of the poor, enumerates (among other things) *tithes impropriate*, and *propriations of tithes*, in respect of which the rate is to be made. And indeed the spirit of the law coincides with the words of this statute. For the Legislature intended that, when rates are made for the relief of the poor, every person should contribute according to the benefit which he receives within the parish. Here the parties receive a certain benefit arising from the tithe of fish in this parish, and run no risk whatever. Then it is said that only property, which is *visible*, should be rated: but I think that is carrying the rule of exemption too far; for oblations and other offerings, which constitute the rectorial or vicarial dues, are rateable.

BULLER, J.—Supposing the fishermen are not rateable, for the fish caught, the case of *Rowls v. Gells*, Cowp. 451, governs this. For though the owner of lead mines is not liable to be rated for them, yet his lessee, who runs no risk, is rateable in respect of the profits arising from *lot* and *cope*. So here the persons entitled to the tithe of fish run no risk, and their profit is certain: therefore, for that certain profit I think they are liable to contribute to the poor-rates.

Order of Sessions confirmed.

The KING v. WEBSTER.

This was an application for an information against the defendant, who was a Justice of the Peace for Devon, for having improperly convicted a person for killing a hare; which conviction was afterwards quashed at the Sessions.

Without going into the merits, it was contended against the rule, that the party convicted, before he applied for an information, should have made an exculpatory affidavit, denying the fact of which he had been charged.

LORD KENYON, C. J.—The question is not whether the doors of justice shall be stopped, but whether justice shall be approached by this particular avenue. If the defendant has acted improperly, however guilty the party applying might be of the charge which was imputed to him, there are other ways open to him for redress. But we cannot interfere in this particular manner, according to the established rules of the Court, without an affidavit, from the party complaining, that he is innocent of the fact with which he was charged. I remember an application of this sort made many years ago against Sir John Fielding, for having issued a warrant against one Bernard, upon a charge against him [not upon oath] by the Duke of Marlborough for sending threatening letters to extort money from the Duke. But the information was denied for want of such an exculpatory affidavit from Bernard.

ASHHURST, J.—said the Court had frequently required exculpatory affidavits from persons who applied for informations

mations for libels, and had refused to interfere because they were not made. Those cases, he thought, could not be distinguished from the present on principle, because the Court did not interfere on account of the individuals concerned, but for a breach of the public peace.

Rule discharged.

The KING v. the Inhabitants of UFTON.

John Henwood, his wife, and three children, were removed from Ufton, Berks, to Mortimer, Southampton; and the Sessions discharged the order of removal, subject to the opinion of the Court on the following

CASE.

John Henwood, the pauper, originally settled at Ufton, came to reside with his father John Henwood, about 23 years ago, on a cottage and premises at Mortimer, Hants, which his father had occupied several years. By indenture or deed of feoffment, dated 10th October 1766, with livery of seisin indorsed, and duly executed, *in consideration of natural love and affection, and of* 10 l. *to him paid* by the pauper, John Henwood, the father, granted, enfeoffed, and confirmed, the said cottage, &c. to the pauper in fee. About three years and a quarter afterwards, the pauper obtained from the parish of Ufton a certificate dated 1st January 1770, duly signed, certified, and allowed, acknowledging that he and his wife and family were inhabitants legally settled in Ufton. And the pauper afterwards occasionally received relief from Ufton during his residence in the cottage at Mortimer. The father of the pauper lived with the pauper upon the premises till his death, which happened about eight years ago. The pauper was his eldest son and heir at law, and continued to reside upon the premises until the year 1788. The pauper by lease and release dated 15th and 16th February, 1788, conveyed the same premises to John Stert for 50 l. which sum appeared upon evidence to be a satisfaction for a debt due for necessaries provided by Stert for the pauper and his family, and for money lent. The pauper being afterwards turned out of possession by Stert, to whom, after the sale, he had become a tenant, returned to Ufton, and was removed to Mortimer.

T 2

It

It was argued in support of the Order of Sessions, 1st, That this was a purchase for money within the 9th *Geo.* I. cap. 7. and, therefore gave no settlement; 2dly, That the certificate given by Ufton to the pauper, was conclusive against the parish granting it.

LORD KENYON, C. J.—There is nothing in either of the points made at the bar; the first of which has been settled these forty years, and the other near a century past (Fo. 257). In *Rex v. Marwood,* it was contended that *purchase* under the 9th *Geo.* I. cap. 7. was to be understood as contradistinguished from *descent*; as in a former case, *Rex v. Sawbridgeworth,* upon the subject. But the Court exploded that idea; and said that the Legislature only intended to prevent persons, who made small purchases for *pecuniary* considerations, from gaining a settlement; but that donations from a father to his child did not come within the statute. Now in this case we are bound to take notice that this conveyance was in consideration of *natural love and affection* as well as 10l. And we cannot suppose that 10l. was the real value of the estate, for there are circumstances in the case to shew the contrary: the case itself states that it was afterwards sold for 50l. Perhaps the 10l. was taken, because the father had some other child, upon whom he wished to bestow something arising out of this estate, and he took this mode of doing it. This, being a donation from a father to a son, is clearly not a purchase within the 9th *Geo.* I. cap. 7, notwithstanding part of the consideration was in money. On the other point, not the smallest doubt can be entertained: for though the certificate was conclusive at the time, it was afterwards done away by the pauper's residence on his own property at Mortimer.

Order of Sessions quashed.

BALL *v.* HERBERT.

This was an action of trespass for breaking and entering the plaintiff's close, being part of an artificial bank adjoining to the river Ouze, in Norfolk, and treading down the grass with men and horses, and towing certain barges.

Plea, that the port of Lynn hath been immemorially a common and public port, and that the river Ouze hath been immemorially a public King's highway and navigable river; that this close hath been immemorially part of the banks of and adjoining the said highway and navigable river.

The

The general queſtion was, whether, at common law, the public have a right to tow veſſels on the banks of either ſide of a navigable river?

LORD KENYON, C. J.—I remember when the caſe of *Peirſe* v. *Lord Fauconberg* was ſent here from the Court of Chancery, it was the current opinion of Weſtminſter Hall that the right of towing depended upon uſage, without which it could not exiſt. It has been ſaid that this right now in queſtion is of great importance to the navigation through ſeveral counties; now if this navigation has been carried on for a ſeries of years, and this right of towing conſtantly exerciſed, there would be abundant uſage on which it might be ſupported. But that is abandoned, and the defendant reſorts to the common law right. Now common law rights are either to be found in the opinions of lawyers, delivered as axioms, or to be collected from the univerſal and immemorial uſage throughout the country. That the right now in queſtion is not to be collected from the unanimous current of authorities, is manifeſt. Very little is to be found in the books upon the ſubject, the whole of which, down to his time, Lord Hale has collected; and after commenting upon it, he ſeems to have formed an opinion againſt the right: for he ſays that, where private intereſts are involved in the queſtion, they ſhall not be infringed without a ſatisfaction being made to the parties injured. But on what ground can a common law right ſtand, if ſatisfaction is to be made for the enjoyment of it, and that ſatisfaction not aſcertained: it muſt reſolve itſelf into an agreement between the parties, and cannot be conſidered as a right to uſe the banks *indefinitely*. And ſome of the paſſages in Lord *Hale*, which ſeem to favour the common law right, are rather applicable to banks of the ſea, and to ports; and it is part of the King's prerogative to create ports, which was lately exerciſed at Liverpool. Then is this bottomed on immemorial uſage: the right is not claimed on one ſide or the other as is moſt convenient, but on both ſides of the river. But that is directly contrary to common experience; for if we look at any of the great public rivers, we ſhall find that it is not uſed, although it would be highly convenient to the perſons uſing the navigations. On the contrary the navigators are obliged at ſeveral places to paſs from one ſide of the Thames to the other with great inconvenience and delay; that is the caſe by the Duke of Montague's gardens between Richmond and Kew, and in various other parts. Such is the right on that river, the *quantum* of which is aſcertained by the uſage. That there is ſuch a cuſtom on moſt

of

of the navigable rivers no person doubts, but still the right is founded solely *on the custom*; but here the claim is set up without any custom at all. The authorities which have been mentioned are very few. The case in Lord Raymond, 725, though before an eminent Judge, was only a *nisi prius* decision. It is a short note taken by Lord Raymond, when he was very young: not even the name of the case is given; and it does not appear what the case was, or how the question arose: I rather think the principal question there was whether, when a right of passage was ascertained, and that was founderous, the party entitled might not go on the adjoining land. However, at most it is only an opinion delivered at *nisi prius*; opposed to which is that of Lord Ch. J. Willes in the case cited. And Lord Hardwicke's opinion was against the right, as is evident from the manner in which he sent the case of *Peirse* v. *Lord Fauconberg*, into this Court, which was very fully considered. Therefore on these authorities, on the silence in the books respecting this common law right, and on account of the extreme inconvenience, to which individuals having lands adjoining the public rivers would be subject, I cannot bring my mind to say that the defendant's justification can be supported. Perhaps small evidence of usage before a Jury would establish a right by custom on the ground of public convenience: but the right here claimed extends to every bank of every navigable river throughout the kingdom.

ASHHURST, J.—I am of opinion, first, that no such *general* right exists as that claimed; and secondly, if *any qualified* right could be supported, the defendant's plea is not adapted to it. As to the first: it seems extraordinary (if there be any such right) that it is not defined with greater certainty in any of our law books. For it is a right that in its nature must, if it existed, be subject to some restrictions; as that it should be exercised only on one, and that the most convenient, side of the river: for it would in many instances be a very oppressive right if it could be claimed *on both sides*, and yet the defendant's claim would go to establish a right on both sides. The instances which have been mentioned where the right of towing has been given by several Acts of Parliament also negative the idea of general right; for we are not to suppose that rights should, from time to time, have been given by the Legislature which existed before; and it is no answer to say that such provisions were inserted *ex abundanti cautelâ*. And the reason assigned by the defendant's counsel why such a right was given by the 24th *Geo*. II. cap. 8, namely, because that part of the river was not navigable before, is not satisfactory; for when once a river becomes navigable, or, in other words, when it is made a common highway for all the king's subjects, that right would immediately attach. On the general ground therefore I think no general right of towing exists. But then it was contended that a right might be supported on making a reasonable compensation to the owner of the land. Lord Hale touches this right very tenderly; for he says that it does not exist without making a reasonable satisfaction. But it is not necessary to enter into that question here; because, if it were a right *sub modo*, it ought to have been so claimed in pleading. And even if such a right existed, the party should either pay or tender a reasonable satisfaction in order to give him that right. For it would be to no purpose to give the owner merely a right of action to recover that compensation, when it is to be enforced against strangers passing by, whom the owner cannot know, and who, perhaps, may be foreigners.

BULLER, J.—The defendant's plea on this record rests wholly on a general common law right; in deciding which it is not necessary to go into the question, which has been made, respecting the mode of pleading. This being claimed as a common law right, it can only be proved to exist by one of the ways mentioned by my Lord. As to the general usage throughout the kingdom, of which the Court is obliged to take notice, that clearly does not exist. Then the question is, whether in our books, or on records, that right is established for which the defendant contends. The case in Lord Raymond is a very loose and inaccurate note. Another authority cited is the passage in Bracton, and quoted by Callis: that plainly appears to have been taken from Justinian, and is only part of the civil law; and whether or not that has been adopted by the common law, is to be seen by looking into our books; and there it is not to be found. Callis compares a navigable river to an highway; but no two cases can be more distinct. In the latter case, if the way be founderous and out of repair, the public have a right to go on the adjoining land: but if a river should happen to be choaked up with mud, that would not give the public a right to cut another passage through the adjoining lands. Therefore I am of opinion that no common law right of towing exists. But I wish not to be precluded by this determination from giving an opinion on the question, which has been made on the pleadings, whenever it shall arise in future. At present I cannot agree with
what

what has been said on that head. This is not like the case of toll thorough. The distinction, which has been made between toll thorough and toll traverse, is not where the question arises on a defence merely, but where the right itself of taking toll has come in question. And the distinction taken is, that the party, who claims toll thorough, must shew a consideration for it, because it is against common right. Then if the defendant is right in saying that by the common law he has a right to go on the banks of navigable rivers, he need not shew any consideration, and the owner of the land would not be entitled to any satisfaction till after the defendant had used the towing-path. Customs, which are consistent, may be pleaded against each other. And the party pleading a general custom need not shew the modification of it, which is not inconsistent with the right claimed by him. The case of *Kenchin* v. *Knight*, is strong to this point: there the defendant pleaded a custom to put swine upon a common; to which the plaintiff replied that he could only put in such swine as were rung, without traversing the custom set up in the plea: and the replication was held good on demurrer, because the customs were not inconsistent. Now here, if every subject has a right to tow on the banks, making a reasonable satisfaction, it is not necessary for the party to plead such satisfaction, because that claim arises afterwards. And if it were otherwise, it would be attended with manifest inconvenience; because, the sum not being ascertained, it would be a perpetual dispute between the owners of the barges and the land-owners how much should be paid, which would be destructive of the right of the public, and the navigation would be stopped till the quantum was ascertained. I have said thus much on the subject lest I should be precluded from considering the question, whenever it should arise: but in the present case I am of opinion against the common law right. In addition to the observations made on the cases cited, I think that the instances of the three great rivers alluded to are very strong against the right. From what passed in the case of *Vernon* v. *Prior*, it seems as if Lord Ch. J. Willes entertained a wish that the public should have this right, and yet he could find no legal ground on which to support it; for the application to parliament in 1748, is said to have been made with his approbation. On the river Trent there have been some claims of this sort of a more recent date not unworthy notice. The persons passing there with barges endeavoured to set up this right, in consequence of which several actions were brought against the barge-owners, who, on being advised
vised

vifed that they could not support the right, fuffered judgement to go by default. But they ftill continued their towing, on which actions were again brought againft fixty or feventy perfons at the fame time, and then they abandoned their claim. The ftate of the banks of the Thames alfo affords a ftrong argument againft this common law-right; for if it exifts, all the houfes built on thofe banks muft be confidered as nuifances.

GROSE, J.---I perfectly agree in the general pofition, that there is not any *general* common law-right of towing.

Judgment for the defendant.

NOBLE *v.* DURELL *and others.*

The Jury chofen by the Court-Leet for the town of Southampton, feized upon a quantity of butter belonging to the plaintiff, becaufe it contained lefs than 18 ounces to the pound; whereas by the cuftom of that town every pound of butter expofed to fale in the markets, ought to be of the weight of 18 ounces. This was an action of trefpafs for fo feizing the plaintiff's butter, which the defendants juftified and pleaded the cuftom aforefaid. The queftion, therefore to be tried was, whether this cuftom was good.

LORD KENYON, C. J.---In deciding this queftion, I wifh not to be underftood to fay that a cuftom may not prevail that butter fhall be fold in *lumps*, or *yards*, containing any given number of ounces: but the queftion now before the Court is, whether a cuftom in Southampton, that a *pound* fhall contain 18 ounces, can be fupported in law. To fay that it can, would be to violate all the rules of language, as long as the Acts of Parliament which have been cited are to regulate this fubject. This has engaged the attention of the Legiflature for five centuries, and they have thought it of the utmoft importance that there fhould be one ftandard of weights and meafures throughout the kingdom. But it is faid, that there is no objection on the fcore of reafon and convenience why this rule fhould not be relaxed in a particular town; becaufe, when the exception is once eftablifhed, the inhabitants of that town will fquare their notions accordingly. But it is material to confider whether the exception to the rule will be confined to butter only: if this cuftom can be eftablifhed, it may alfo be extended to hops in Kent, or to any other commodity in any other part of the kingdom; and thus the greateft confufion will be introduced

duced on a subject that ought to be particularly plain. So one measure might prevail at Pool, another at Dartmouth, &c. and thus foreign merchants would never know on what terms they were treating. It might be as well contended that a custom could prevail in a particular place, that a less number of days than 7 should constitute a week, or that a less space of ground than an acre should be called an acre. It was then objected that, even supposing that the statute of *Hen.* VII. applied universally, the old customs should prevail till the weights and measures were sent down from the Exchequer, which was directed to be done by that act; and that the plaintiff should have replied that in point of fact they were sent to Southampton. But the Legislature did not say that, till that was done, the old customs should prevail. And we cannot suppose that that, which the Legislature directed, was not done. The statute of 13 & 14 *Car.* II. cap. 26, takes it for granted that a pound shall consist of 16 ounces, and that the weights and measures had been sent to the different parts of the kingdom. There are two kinds of weights; one containing 12 ounces of a certain denomination, the other 16 ounces of another denomination; and it appears that butter has always been sold by the latter. Then it was said, that customs may prevail against common law: but they are such *consuetudines* as are reasonable and beneficial; but this is the reverse of both; for all mankind have concurred in agreeing, that for their mutual convenience they should be regulated by one uniform standard.

ASHHURST, J.—The only ground on which this custom can be supported, is a supposition that the Legislature did not intend to interfere with the customs of any particular place. But that is totally unfounded; for the Legislature supposed that, at the times when the several acts passed, different weights and measures prevailed in different towns; to remedy which inconvenience they passed those acts. And in none of them is there any reservation of any ancient customs; but they are applicable to every place, directing that in future there shall be but one weight and measure throughout the kingdom.

BULLER, J.—This case does not interfere with the question alluded to in the argument, whether a custom to sell butter in *lumps* of any particular weight is good or not. That question will remain, notwithstanding this decision, as it did before: and I have never seen any thing in the Acts of Parliament requiring persons not to sell more or less than a pound. But the question here is, whether, when a person

is

is felling butter under the specific denomination of a *pound*, he shall be compellable to sell more than a pound. Butter is directed to be sold by Avoirdupois weight, where a pound consists of sixteen ounces. Then how can a person, who professes to sell a pound of butter, be compellable to sell more than a pound?—I am of opinion that the custom cannot be supported.

GROSE, J.—Of the same opinion.

Judgment for the plaintiff.

REX *v. inhabitants of* ACKLEY.

CASE.

The pauper, on Saturday the 13th of October, 1787, being three days after Old Michaelmas Day, was hired to T. Clarke, of Ackley, in the county of Oxford, to serve until the next Michaelmas. He accordingly continued in such service till Saturday the 11th of October, 1788, being the day after Old Michaelmas Day, which (it being Leap Year) happened on a Friday, and was paid his wages and went away. As this was a service of 365 Days, the Court of Sessions thought it gained him a settlement in Ackley, and confirmed the order of removal, by which he and his wife were removed from Bicester to Ackley.

BY THE COURT,—Here was no hiring for a year: it is stated that the pauper, three days after Michaelmas, contracted to serve till the Michaelmas following; this was therefore a hiring for two days short of a year. And though this Court has been extremely indulgent in determining that *services*, which have been in point of fact less than a year, shall be sufficient to confer a settlement, as where the pauper has been absent with leave, &c. yet they have been always strict in regard to the contract of *hiring*.

Order of Sessions reversed.

REX

REX v. *the* JUSTICES *of* YORKSHIRE.

This was a rule to shew cause why a *mandamus* should not issue, directing the defendants to hear an appeal of the inhabitants of Gate Helmsley, against an order of two Justices, for the removal of a pauper from Strensall to Gate Helmsley The order was made on the 26th of November, and executed on the 28th. The appellants attended the next Quarter Sessions, held on the 13th of January, and moved for leave *to lodge the appeal and to respite the hearing* to the then *next* Quarter Sessions. The following entry was made by the Sessions: " Forasmuch as it appears to this Court that there has been sufficient time since the removal of the paupers for the appellants to give notice and come prepared to try this appeal at this Sessions, and no cause shewn why they did not proceed accordingly, it is ordered that *the motion for lodging the same, and respiting the hearing to the next Quarter Sessions, be rejected.*"

In support of the rule it was contended, that it was not discretionary in the Justices at the Sessions to permit the parties to appeal; the statute is compulsory on them, and so also is the statute 9 *Geo.* I. for adjourning the hearing. And though it was perhaps irregular to make the motion to respite the hearing before the appeal was entered, yet at any rate the Justices were not warranted in refusing to receive the appeal.

BY THE COURT.—The Justices have not acted wrong; for the motion was in effect to adjourn the appeal. And it was evidently the intention of the parties not to enter the appeal, unless the Court would adjourn it. The Justices are to judge of the reasonableness of the time; and in some counties they establish a rule regulating the time of notice. Here it appears that the order of removal was executed on the 28th of November, so that there was sufficient time for the appellants to give notice, and to come prepared to try it; and the Justices, who are to judge of this, thought so.

Rule discharged.

The

The TRIAL *of* JACINTHO PHARARO, ANTHONI MURRI-
NI, *and* STEPHEN APOLOGIE, *for the murder of* JO-
SEPHI, *a Sardinian.*

OLD BAILEY, *April* 16, 1790.

Jacintho Phararo, Anthoni Murrini, and Stephen Apologie were indicted for that they, in the 14th of March laft,
at the parifh of Bedfont, feloniously, wilfully and of their
malice aforethought, did make an affault on one Jofephi,
then and there being; and that he the faid Jacintho Phararo
with a certain knife, in and upon the neck of the faid Jofephi, feloniously, wilfully, and of his malice aforethought
did cut, giving him in and upon the neck one mortal wound,
of which he then and there inftantly died; and the Jurors
further charge, that they the faid Anthony Murrini, and
Stephen Apologie were prefent, aiding, abetting, comforting, affifting, and maintaining him the faid Jacintho Phararo
to do and commit the faid murder.

Mr. MAZZINGI *was fworn Interpreter.*

Frederico Solari. I am a Genoefe failor. My father keeps
a public houfe: I landed at Gofport: we were all together in
one fhip. I fhipped myfelf at Genoa, in the fame fhip with
the three prifoners and the deceafed, Jofephi; he fhipped
himfelf in the ifland of Sardinia: we were four days at qua-
rentine, and from thence we came into the harbour of Portfmouth, to wait for orders. After I was difcharged, I
lodged with the three prifoners and the deceafed, in one
lodging; we lodged there about fix days.

Ques. Do you know whether thefe people had any property at that time?

Solari. They received with me: I received two guineas
and a half, and they received one guinea and a half: I ftaid
there about fix days.

Ques. Had Jofephi any property?

Solari. He had nothing; he received may be about a
guinea.

Quef. Had he any more property?

Solari. He had property: he received from the captain that came from his friends three joes and a half,
double joes, which go for three pounds ten; he changed
one of them in Gofport for three pounds ten; if they are
worth

worth more I cannot say. He spent about half a joe in his lodging; he bought a pair of black stockings, a hat and a pair of buckles. They set out on Wednesday, after dinner, to come to London, about three o'clock; I do not recollect the day of the month. They asked me if I would like to see them on the London road? which I said I would: we staid in the lodging four or five days, and my money was almost gone, and I came up by the coach; they set off to walk.

Ques. Did they all four set off together?

Solari. Yes.

Ques. How long after was it before you heard of this affair?

Solari. I was in London from one Thursday to the next Thursday, when they took me. I was afterwards at Bedfont, and saw the body. It was the body that was in company with these prisoners. Before they shewed me the person, I said he was wounded in two places in his hand; and he had a silver relick which when I left him, he used to wear about him; it was round his neck, and used to come before his breast. He valued it more than his life; I heard him say so thousands of times on board; several of the ship's company heard him say the same.

Court. Ask them if they would ask this witness any questions.

Prisoners. We wish to ask whether the pair of metal buckles that were found upon one of the prisoners, the deceased did not give to him at Gosport?

Solari. I was in a public house; the three went with the deceased to buy a pair of buckles; if the deceased gave him the buckles; I did not see it.

Stephen Hudson. I keep the White Lion, at Staines. On the 13th of March last, about four in the afternoon, the three prisoners came to my house; the man on the right hand, pitted with the small-pox, he could talk a little English, and I could understand him: he asked me if the four could have a lodging? I looked at him, and said they might; and they walked in all four together, and sat down in the box; they called for a pot of beer; a pot of beer was fetched; they then asked for some tobacco; I said I did not sell it, but would send for some; the deceased man pulled out his purse, and gave that man a shilling, and he gave it to the boy; that man said a shilling's-worth.

Ques. Did you observe the purse?

Hudson. To my knowledge, as far as I saw, I judged it to be a kind of a greasy dirty leather purse; but I never had it

in

in my hand; the boy fetched a shilling's-worth of tobacco, and brought it to them; they filled each of them a pipe, and began smoaking a little while, while they drank their pot of beer; by that time they asked what they could have for supper? They asked for a barber; and I sent my boy with them all four together, to Mr. John Lamb, to be shaved. They returned in about a quarter of an hour, and came and sat down in the same place.

Quest. When did they leave your house?

Hudson. On Sunday morning, just at four o'clock; that is, the next morning, the 14th; they got up and waked me; I got up and let them out; and just as I let them out, the clock struck four.

Quest. Are you sure that the body you saw was the body of the fourth man that was at your house?

Hudson. I am very clear it was. He paid every thing at my house, I received no money from any body else but from him.

John Lamb. I live at Stains: I am a barber. The four men came to my house on Saturday the 13th of March. I am sure these are three of the men; there were four in company; I shaved them all myself. I heard one was the person that was murdered, and I went out of curiosity; and saw it was the body of one of the persons that was at my shop. He took his money out of a black leather purse; but particulars I could not tell; he was the pay-master for all of them. I had no doubt on the view of the body, that it was the body of the fourth person; and I am sure that these three persons were in company with him.

Court to Interpreter. Explain to the prisoners this evidence.

Prisoners. It is very true: we gave him a shilling.

William Henley. I am a labouring man at Bedfont, about three miles and a half from Stains. On the 14th, about a quarter before six, I saw three men pass; I am not sure of the three; but the man on the left hand walked in the middle; they walked ten or a dozen yards at a distance. There were no more than three. The man I mean is Phararo. About a quarter before six, they were coming from London.

Prisoner Phararo. The reason I was behind, was, I had a sore foot.

Court to Henley. Do you know the place where the body was afterwards found?

Henley. Yes.

Quest.

Quef. Was the place where you faw this man, further from Staines, more on the way to London?

Henley. It was found nearer Staines; it might be about three hundred yards from where I faw them.

Prifoner Murrini. We parted from the deceafed about eight o'clock in the morning, as well as we can recollect, near a bridge.

Richard Foot. I am a labouring man: I live at Bedfont: I found a body about five o'clock on Sunday afternoon. I faw the appearance of a body dragged along out of the high-road, about one hundred and twenty yards along a wheat-field; it perfectly ploughed up the way; there was a great large quantity of blood, where he had been laid down under a hedge; the ditch was not deep enough to bury him; and they took him up from there, to carry him to the place to bury him; the blood was in the high-way; there was no blood in the path where the body had been dragged, only the print of one man's foot: I fuppofe the quantity of blood where they laid him down under the hedge, was as big round as my hat.

Court. Did there appear much trampling in the blood?

Foot. No, only one man's foot, by what I could difcern; there was not a drop of blood all along the track.

Quef. What was the appearance of the place where the body was depofited? Was there any blood?

Foot. None at all: the body was buried in fand four or five inches deep, in fand which had been carried out of the high-road; they afterwards pulled off the grafs off the bank, and fhook a-top of him, and then the boughs and bufhes covered it.

Court. The body was covered with fand and grafs and branches?

Foot. Yes; where they ftood underneath the hedge, it feemed as if the traces of foot-fteps had been fcratched out, that you could not fee the appearance of a man's foot, nor a horfe's foot, nor fheep's foot, nor any thing in the world; that was the place juft under the hedge where they ftood.

Quef. Was there any appearance of the ground having been harrowed up in the field?

Foot. No, not along the track where they dragged him.

Court to Hudfon. What fized man was the deceafed: was he a large man?

Hudfon. No, but a fhortifh man.

Quef. How was the body?

Foot. It was laid as ftrait as ever you faw; his throat was cut; his left fhoulder, on the bone, was cut all to mummy;

he

he was ftruck over the head, and had three cuts over the chin, before ever they cut his wind-pipe ; his wind-pipe was cut quite through.   The body was quite dead.

Court to Interpreter.   Tell them, on the Sunday afternoon, about five o'clock, he faw the body ; that it appeared to be dragged over a wheat-field, about one hundred and twenty yards on the highway.

Prifoners.   We are very forry for the poor departed foul, but we know nothing about him.

Prifoner Phararo.   It is no reafon why, becaufe the man was found murdered, and becaufe he was a foreigner, and we are foreigners, that we fhould be accufed ; it is moft likely that the man that is an evidence againft us, killed the man.

————*Bannifter.*   I live at Bedfont.   I faw the body juft as it was taken out of the ditch ; it was Sunday evening I think, to the beft of my recolle&ion ; it was a quarter after five ; I have the remainder of the clothes that were left upon it ; the fhoes were loft, and the breeches or trowfers, or what it was, were loft, and the hat was loft ; thefe are the clothes that were over the body that was murdered.   Thefe two combs were found on the body that was killed, and two-pence halfpenny and a buckle.

Patrick Sheen.   I live in Great Horfley-down : I know the three prifoners ; they came to Horfley-down New-ftairs to me, on Sunday, between nine and ten in the morning : the fhort man, Murrini, afked me to drink a pot of beer ; and I told him I had no money ; and he faid he would pay for the pot of beer, as plain as I can fpeak to you now ; they were all three in company ; I took them to the lodging ; they called for a pot of beer ; they gave me a fhilling to get them fome meat ; that fhort man fhewed me his fhip he faid he was going in ; I faw no more of them that night : but on Monday morning that fhort man came to me, and afked me to fhew him a goldfmith's fhop, to fell fome gold ; they were all three in company together ; I took them to Tooley-ftreet, to a man whofe name I cannot tell ; he weighed the piece, but he could not underftand what the value of it was ; and he gave me a bit of a dire&ion to carry it to Mr. Smith, and he gave me fix-pence for my trouble.

Interpreter.   My Lord, the prifoner Murrini fays the man muft be miftaken in point of the hour, becaufe a little after they came to London, they met with a cobler, who fhewed them the way to Horfley-down ; and before they reached there it was paft one.

VOL. I.   U   *Court*

Court to Sheen. Recollect yourself as well as you can, as to the time?

Sheen. It was between nine and ten, as nigh as I can recollect.

John Smith. I am a silversmith and salesman: on Monday (I think it was the 15th of March) in the forenoon, the last witness brought me a piece of foreign gold; it is a doubloon, seventeen penny-weights, nine grains; it is worth three pounds fifteen an ounce, which is three pounds five and a penny, the real worth of it; I gave him three pounds four shillings for it: Murrini was with him; it was one of those two little men; I think it is the man; I cannot be positive.

Robert Dawson. I am a headborough; and I attend the Public-Office in East-Smithfield: I received information from Bow-street, on Monday the 15th, from the Magistrates; in consequence of which I went down to the public houses kept by foreigners, and gave such information as I thought necessary; nothing transpired till the Thursday following; then I received information that three persons answering the description I had given, were seen to come to Union stairs, Wapping, and that they were pursued; that two of them had made their escape, but the third was in custody of the people at Wapping: I went down in company with Mayne, another officer, and apprehended the middle prisoner, Apologie; he was the person I found in custody; before that I had apprehended Solari; and he on that day was gone to Bedfont to view the body.

Court. Do you know when Solari came to town of your knowledge?

Dawson. No; he told us he came to town on the Monday before: I had given description of the three people; I had it in writing from the Magistrates in Bow-street; and he being a foreigner, and had come from Gosport, the people I had spoke to, apprehended him: on searching the prisoner Apologie, we found on him a pair of trowsers that were very bloody.

Court. Were they making part of his dress?

Dawson. Yes; they were what he then wore; we took them from him, and locked him up; secured him; and then went down the river in a boat, in search of the other two prisoners; we chased them on board several ships, and over from one ship to another, in the tiers as they lay: and they got away from us on the south side of the water, and got into a boat, and were rowed in that boat from that side of the water over to Union-stairs again, to the tier of ships;

and

and they got on board a Spanish ship; we found them on board the ship, and seized hold of them; and, after some resistance, we secured them, and handcuffed them; we got them into the boat, and then proceeded to search them; I searched the prisoner on the right hand, that is, Pharara; and in his left hand waistcoat pocket, I found this purse; it appears to be a skin: (*like a dirty leather purse*); and this knife, which appeared then to have blood upon it very fresh: (*a large clasp knife*): I likewise found this paper in his pocket, which appears to be an account from the captain; and in his right hand waistcoat pocket, I found these two strings of beads (*Roman Catholic beads*): I found nothing else upon him at that time; Mayne searched the other two when we came up to the King's-Arms in East-Smithfield, a house in which are lock-up rooms appropriated for the use of the office; we searched him again there, and found nothing more at that time upon him; I put some irons upon the two prisoners on the right hand, leaving Anthoni Murrini with a pair of hand-cuffs only, and then I took him (Murrini) to point out the house they lodged at: he took me to the sign of the Black Bull at the back of St. John's church, Southwark; and in a two pair of stairs room (the landlady said that the prisoner and two others lodged there; the prisoner was present; the prisoner took me to that room as his room;) on searching the room, I found a quantity of wearing apparel; and when we came down into the tap-room, I desired he would inform me of the different articles, and the persons to which they belonged; some he claimed as his own; he picked out this pair of trowsers, having belonged to Phararo; I brought him over again to the King's-Arms, and there I brought the prisoners into a room all together, and let them claim their property; and Phararo claimed these trowsers; my reason for that was, that these trowsers were very bloody.

Prisoner Phararo. It is paint.

Dawson. Nothing else appeared on the search; the witness, Solari, had not then arrived from Bedfont; but I charged them on suspicion. About half past nine, the same Friday night, Solari returned from Bedfont; and I found this hat on the head of Murrini.

Prisoner Murrini. We were all three apprehended together, but if he swears that we attempted to run away, he swears false, for the moment we saw the boat coming along-side the vessel, we made no resistance.

Peter Mayne. I am an officer belonging to justice. I went with Dawson in pursuit of these men; after a chace

of

of some time on the river, from one tier to another, we pursued them on board of a Spanish ship, laying off Union-stairs; there we apprehended the prisoners, after some struggle; and round the neck of Murrini I found a relique, a Madona. I took these trowsers from the middle prisoner, Apologie, which appeared to me to be bloody.

Court to Solari. Look at that hat?

Solari. This is the hat the deceased wore; I went with him to the shop to buy it; the gentleman put a bill in the middle; I asked him for what? He said, we must not sell any hats without; I took the bill off; I said, I suppose it is of no service now? Says he, you may throw it any where; it left a black mark; and I said, that black mark is as good as the bill. These are the buckles, that he had on the whole voyage, and that he came on board in. I cannot say any thing to those plated buckles, because I was not with him when he bought them; but I am sure the other buckles are the buckles that he wore on board, and that he came on board in; when he set off he had a pair of new buckles on. That is the purse that belonged to the deceased; I know it, because he always had a goe of tobacco in it; nobody else had such a purse; it is made of ram-skin. And that is the relique the man had about his neck the whole voyage; and when I left him in company with these three, he had it on; nobody else had one on board; I am sure of it; he said it would keep him from all danger some time in action. These are the pair of trowsers that belonged to the middle prisoner, Apologie.

Court. Ask the prisoners, one by one, what they have to say, and whether they have any witnesses to call; tell them they now stand for their lives; and the consequence will be, that death must follow the verdict of the Jury, if it be against them.

The Interpreter delivered the Prisoner Phararo's Defence.

They left the deceased at a bridge near London; the man on the left hand spoke to a man, desiring to conduct him to the water side, and they did not reach London till between eleven and twelve; the moment they arrived near the water side they got into a house, and afterwards went about to find a ship, and after they were on board a ship, that man and others came on board and seized them; the old man who was a witness here, the last but one, offered to find them a ship, saying that he knew a vessel that wanted sailors; after this conversation they went to church, and coming from church they pulled out a foreign piece of coin, which
they

they defired might be fold; they gave it to the old-man; they went to feveral places, and could not get this coin changed, but at laft did change it the next morning; and after changing it, the old man kept three fhillings; and he flattered them every day that he fhould be able to get them a fhip; he lived upon them; and when he found they had no more money, he abfconded; he fays, he will now explain to you how he came by this hat, and things belonging to the deceafed; they changed cloaths.

Prifoner Apologie's Defence.

I have nothing to fay more than the other.

Prifoner Murrini's Defence.

The deceafed was a paffenger on board the veffel; and the Captain had promifed to take him to Malaga; when the veffel was near Malaga, whether the Captain thought he had a favourable wind or not, he told us he could not go to Malaga; and wanting hands on board the veffel, the Captain told this paffenger if he would take on himfelf the office of cook, the cook fhould act as failor, and he would fave his expences. The deceafed anfwered him that he was not capable: then the deceafed called me upon deck, and begged me to affift him, and he would recompence me when he came to England; and likewife intreated me to lend him a pair of fmall clothes, upon which I lent him a pair of fmall clothes; and the evidence Solari was prefent at the time I gave him the pair of breeches; during the voyage, I never drank my fhare of the wine, but the deceafed and Solari drank my wine: we made our voyage fafe into the port at Gofport; we landed together: when we landed, and were difcharged from the fhip, the Captain did not pay us our due: we lived on credit from the Sunday to the Monday, when the Captain paid our wages: the deceafed had no money as well as us, for we all four together, from the Saturday to the Monday, we lived and lodged at a public-houfe on credit: the Captain gave the deceafed three doubloons and a half; the deceafed out of this purchafed a coat, a pair of fhoes, and two pair of ftockings, out of that money; and we remained in Gofport three or four days: on our leaving Gofport, the landlord told us it would be better to leave our clothes and things, and to fend them by the waggon; and before we departed, we changed our clothes again; and we configned to the waggoner, whoever he was, two facks, and two bags, for which the waggoner gave a receipt; and afterwards the landlord faid, I may as well
make

make one bill, one sack belonging to Solari, and two
sacks belonging to you: this man said, he would sew this
receipt of the waggoner's into some part of his coat; and
they all four set out together; and on the road he found he
had forgot the paper; and he said, Go on, my lads, I have
forgot the receipt of the waggoner's, and I will go back
and fetch it. We waited a little distance from Gosport, and
saw him coming; then we pursued our journey, thinking
he was behind: Solari overtook us, and said, I am informed
it will be better for us to go to London in the stage, which
will cost twelve shillings each. Upon which I said, We
have very little money, and the twelve shillings I shall want;
I will walk; upon which the deceased said, If you want to
ride, I have money, I will pay for you all three; afterwards
the deceased said, We may as well walk, we will see the
country, and we will see several villages; and here is a
doubloon which will serve to pay our expences to London;
but at that time the deceased did not give it us: having
thus agreed, we parted with Solari, and pursued our journey, and I took Solari's hat by mistake: we slept that night
five miles beyond Gosport, or thereabouts. I now come to
speak of the relique: he had promised me on board, that he
would give me a part, or some remnant of this relique; but
after having walked eight or nine miles on the road, the deceased said, Antonio, I will make you a present of this relique: we proceeded on our journey; he paid our share;
and the deceased said, as I have promised you this doubloon,
you shall have it: and at last we arrived to this fatal spot
about twelve o'clock; and being wearied and tired, and
having a sore foot, I desired to stop there to refresh, which
we all did: the moment we arrived, we had a pot of beer,
and asked the landlord where we could get ourselves shaved?
Upon which the landlord's son conducted us to a little barber's shop: the deceased, with the two other prisoners, were
shaved; and the man seemed unwilling to shave him for the
money: and the deceased said, Oh, get yourself shaved; I
will pay for it. We then returned, and desired the landlord
to provide something for supper; for one paid one day, and
one another: at night, while we were at supper, we entered
into conversation about a hat, as saying that the hat that
the man had bought, was too narrow in the crown; he
asked us to change it, accordingly we changed hats; that
night we slept together; we desired the landlord of the house
to call us early in the morning, at four o'clock: and we
went out, thinking it was five; we got up, and found it
was four; after we were dressed, and ready to depart, the

land-

landlord gave me two great coats that we had; and we had a glass of Geneva, for which we paid fifteen-pence: after we left the house, we continued in company together till we came to the bridge; and when we came to the bridge, the deceased told us, I find the other man has turned back to go to Gosport, I have a good mind to do the same; I will turn back too: on the bridge, we did not walk together, but at a distance from each other: but I do not know which way he took; but he said to me, good bye, I have taken it into my head I will give you a guinea a-piece; and to Apologie for some services he has done, I will give a guinea; and he gave us his purse, and parted: we proceeded towards London, after parting with the man; and at a small village near London, we looked at the clock, and it was then eleven o'clock. We frequently asked when we found ourselves near London (as well as we could make ourselves understood) our way to the shipping: but at last I said, let us at once take somebody to conduct us where we want to go, and a man shewed us to a poor cobler, who promised to conduct us; and when we came a little off this side of the bridge, we leaned for about half an hour on the foot of the bridge, without knowing which way to take; and I said, I wish I could find out where some of the ambassadors live; we might go to them to ask for a passage; thus we went towards the bridge: after we had walked over the bridge, we were going on a very long street, where we met the old man; he came up to us, and said, My lads, I suppose you are sailors; we said, Yes. He said, Do you want a birth? We said Yes.—Looking at the water-side, he shewed us a vessel; and told us, if you want to go on board a vessel, I will speak to the Captain to-morrow morning; then we thought we would not go to the ambassadors; and we asked the man to get us something to eat and drink, after finding ourselves hungry; and we told him as we had no more money, we wished to have that piece of gold coin disposed of; the landlord told us he did not know the coin, and could not change it; and the same day we went to church to make our devotions; and the landlord offered to lend us a guinea on the coin till the next morning. Apologie made objection; says he, to morrow you will go, and I want a part; either sell it, or have no money at all: the next morning we applied about the vessel; and the man told us he had not spoke to the Captain as yet; and every day he put us off from morning to night, from morning to night: afterwards he went with us to a silver-smith's shop, and changed that piece of coin.

LORD

LORD KENYON. — Gentlemen of the Jury, you have paid a very anxious attention to all the enquiry that has been made in the course of this case : that period of the cause is now arrived, when it becomes my duty to call your attention to the evidence that has been given ; and, gentlemen, undoubtedly you find yourselves in a very anxious situation ; for it is impossible, as men carrying about you the feelings of human nature, that you should not : for your verdict is to pass on the lives of three of your fellow creatures : but besides the importance of the case to the parties, it also must be important on the side of public justice ; for it is of the last importance to society, that those guilty of enormities against the lives of society should not go away unpunished for such crimes. It is not necessary, therefore, for Jurys to steel their minds against compassion ; God forbid ! every indulgence is to be made to the prisoners : but still you have a duty which you owe to your country, and that must be discharged with steadfastness, with firmness, and with fortitude ; like men who feel they have such a public duty imposed on them, which the country expects, and has a right to expect, they should discharge. Gentlemen, it is not necessary, in order to bring home the criminality in this or any such case, that there should be eye-witnesses of the fact of the commission of the crime : circumstances, pregnant circumstances, combined together, may make out a case to every man's satisfaction ; and sometimes various circumstances, brought together from a variety of witnesses, and all meeting together in one centre, may make it out more satisfactorily than the evidence of one witness, fallible as all mankind are, stating the facts that he saw : therefore, with these observations, I will state the material parts of the evidence, and you will judge as well as you can : if you can find there is any discrimination in the case of the different prisoners, you will apply only to that man that which belongs to him in the testimony given ; and not blend together, and confound in one common mass of iniquity (supposing iniquity belongs to the prisoners) other particulars than those which apply to each. (*Here the learned Judge summed up the evidence, and then added*) This is the evidence against the prisoners, in support of the prosecution : and against this there is no evidence produced on the behalf of the prisoners : they being called upon to make their defence, have satisfied themselves by delivering that which you heard repeated by the interpreter ; and they rest on the supposed difficulty of proof on the side of the prosecution : suggesting this, that the murder committed

mitted may have been committed by the first witness, the other Genoese sailor, namely Solari. Now, Gentlemen, with respect to that, certainly there is no evidence of it, nor any circumstance to induce the least suspicion in the world that he had any thing to do with it: now, upon the review of this evidence, there are some things which are most perfectly clear, and which are not, nor can be, controverted; namely, that this man has lost his life, that he lost his life by the hand of violence: for it is not here possibly to be presumed, no force of imagination can be equal to the presumption, that this man would put himself to death: the act of violence was committed, by the blood which appeared in the highway, at a considerable distance from where the dead corpse was afterwards found deposited; and the appearance of the field over which it was dragged leaves no doubt but that, by the act of man, that body had been removed; therefore you have here what is called the *corpus criminis*; the existence of the crime is beyond all doubt: but that being proved ever so clearly, it does not follow, as a necessary consequence, that that crime is to be imputed to any particular individual, or to any body of men; that one is to learn from the circumstances. Now, as to the time at which it was committed; it certainly was on the Sunday; it was on that day when the unhappy man had in company of these three men, about five in the morning, left the public-house at Staines; they then left it apparently, as the landlord tells you, to proceed on their journey to London: about six that morning, these three men are found near four miles from Staines, the fourth man not making part of the company; and the body was about three hundred yards further advanced on the road to London. Gentlemen, that is the important crisis of time in this cause: what became of that man who had set out with them, (and whose body was found dead that same morning, not above three hundred yards from the place) at the time they were met by the other witness, is undoubtedly, to say no more of it, an important circumstance: the weight which belongs to it, it is for you in your judgments to give it: you will draw from it that fair, necessary result, which your minds must be impelled one way or the other to draw; for if you are not impelled to draw conclusions unfavourable to the prisoners, you will not conjecture merely; but it is not necessary that the hand only which gave the blow should be considered as the murderer; because, if more people are concerned, aiding, abetting, and comforting, they all of them contribute to fortify the mind of the man who

gives

gives the blow; all of them are included in the same degree of guilt; all of them in the eye of the law, and of common sense and morality too, all of them are undoubtedly murderers. Gentlemen, if you could in this case discriminate one of the prisoners at the bar from the other, you would be glad to do it, because it is on the merciful side. There are other circumstances which it is for you to judge, it is for me only to present them to your judgement, how they affect either of the prisoners; for on each of them you will recollect some part of that property which appears to have belonged to the deceased, and some part of that property so marked as to induce at least suspicion of guilt, was in the custody of the prisoners; the bloody trowsers on one, the hat on another, the relique on another; this I think is the whole of the case: with you, Gentlemen, are the issues of life and death, with respect to these three men. I only recall to your recollection, that though the situation you are placed in is undoubtedly an anxious one, and distressing to feeling minds; yet it is a situation, in which by the constitution of the country you are placed: you have a great debt of humanity and justice to discharge, both with respect to the prisoners, and with respect to your country: no society can exist, no man is safe, if those who are plainly guilty elude the pursuit of punishment: you are not to thirst after blood, and to follow a man to his death, on slight suspicions, nor otherwise than on strong and pregnant circumstances; and if in your opinion, on those circumstances, though there were no witnesses present, yet if there are strong and pregnant circumstances which leave no doubt on your minds to whom to impute this murder (which undoubtedly was committed by somebody), then you will discharge your duty by saying they are guilty: but if, after deliberating on the whole of the case, you are not satisfied, then you will be glad to find the prisoners not guilty.

Prisoner Murrini. The blood on our trowsers was in consequence of having killed two pigs the day before we came on shore.

JACINTHO PHARARO,		
ANTHONI MURRINI,	}	Guilty.
STEPHEN APOLOGIE,		

Mr. RECORDER immediately passed sentence to be executed on the Monday following, and afterwards to be dissected and anatomised; which was executed accordingly.

An

An Argument in Defence of the Legality of impreffing for the Sea-Service, by Sir MICHAEL FOSTER, *then Recorder of Briftol, afterwards one of the Judges of the King's Bench.*

The Cafe of ALEXANDER BROADFOOT.

At the gaol delivery held for the city and county of the city of Briftol, Auguſt 30, 1743, Alexander Broadfoot was indiĉed for the murder of Cornelius Calahan, a failor belonging to his majefty's fhip the Mortar floop.

The cafe was thus: captain Hanway, commander of the Mortar floop, had a warrant from the lords of the admiralty, grounded on an order of his majefty in council, impowering him to imprefs, or caufe to be impreffed, feamen for his majefty's fervice. The warrant exprefsly direĉeth, " That " the captain fhall not intruſt any perfon with the execution " of it, but a commiffion officer; and fhall infert the name " and office of the perfon intruſted on the back of the war- " rant."

The lieutenant of the Mortar floop (the only commiffion officer on board befides the captain), was deputed by him to imprefs according to the tenor of the warrant.

On the 25th of April laſt, captain Hanway being at anchor in Kingroad, within the port and county of Briftol, ordered the fhip's boat down the channel in order to prefs as they fhould fee opportunity. But the lieutenant ſtaid in Kingroad on board with the captain.

Towards evening the boat came up with a merchant-man, the Bremen factor, homeward-bound, and fome of the crew went on board in order to prefs; who being informed that one or two of the Bremen's men were concealed in the hold, Calahan, with three others of the boats crew, went thither in fearch of them. Whereupon Broadfoot, one of the Bremen's men (who had before provided himfelf with a blunderbufs and piftols for his defence againſt the prefs-gang), called out and afked them what they came for: he was anfwered by fome of the prefs-gang, " We come for you and " your comrades." Whereupon he cried out, " Keep back, " I have a blunderbufs loaded with fwan-fhot." Upon this the others ſtopped, but did not retire. He then cried out, " Where is your lieutenant?" and being anfwered, " He " is not far off," immediately fired among them. By this

fhoꞇ

shot Calahan was killed on the spot, and one or two more of the press-gang wounded.

The case being thus, the Recorder, Mr. serjeant [afterwards judge] Foster, was of opinion, that the boat's crew having been sent out with a *general order to impress as they should see opportunity*, and having, in pursuance of that order, boarded the vessel without a proper officer, expressly against the terms of the captain's warrant, every thing they did was to be looked upon as an attempt upon the liberty of the persons concerned, without any legal warrant : and he accordingly directed the jury to find Broadfoot guilty of manslaughter. But this being a case of great expectation, and uncommon pains having been taken to possess people with an opinion that pressing for the sea-service is a violation of Magna Charta, and a very high invasion of the liberty of the subject, the recorder thought proper to deliver his opinion touching the legality of pressing for the sea-service, provided the persons impressed are proper objects of the law, and those employed in that service come armed with a proper warrant for that purpose.

The RECORDER's [FOSTER's] *Argument.*

This question, touching the legality of pressing mariners for the public service, is a point of very great and national importance. On one hand, a very useful body of men seem to be put under hardships inconsistent with the temper and genius of a free government. On the other, the necessity of the case seemeth to entitle the public to the service of this body of men, whenever the safety of the whole calleth for it.

Before I speak directly to the point, it will be necessary to throw out of the case every thing which does not enter into the merits of the present question.

We are not, at present, concerned to enquire, whether persons may be legally pressed into the land-service, nor whether land-men may be legally pressed into the sea-service. The present question, I say, is not whether people may be taken from their lawful occupations at home, and sent against their wills into a remote and dangerous service ; into a service that they are utterly unacquainted with, and possibly unfit for. No, the only question at present is, whether mariners, persons who have freely chosen a sea-faring life, persons whose education and employment have fitted
them

them for the fervice, and inured them to it, whether fuch
perfons may not be legally preffed into the fervice of the
crown, whenever the public fafety requireth it, *Ne quid de-
trimenti Refpublica capiat?*

For my part I think they may. I think the Crown hath
a right to command the fervice of thefe people, whenever
the public fafety calleth for it. The fame right that it hath
to require the perfonal fervice of every man able to bear
arms in cafe of a fudden invafion or formidable infurrection.
The right in both cafes is founded on one and the fame principle, the neceffity of the cafe, in order to the prefervation
of the whole.

It would be time very ill-fpent to go about to prove that
this nation can never be long in a ftate of fafety, our coaft
defended, and our trade protected, without a naval force
equal to all the emergencies that may happen. And how
can we be fecure of fuch a force? The keeping up the fame
naval force in time of peace, which will be abfolutely neceffary for our fecurity in time of war, would be an abfurd,
a fruitlefs, and a ruinous expence.

The only courfe then left is, for the crown to employ,
upon emergent occafions, the mariners bred up in the merchants fervice.

By this means the trade of the nation becometh a nurfery
for her navy; and the merchant, while he is increafing the
wealth of the kingdom, is at the fame time training up the
mariner for its defence.

And as for the mariner himfelf, he, when taken into the
fervice of the crown, only changeth mafters for a time: his
fervice and employment continue the very fame, with this
advantage, that the dangers of the fea and enemy are not fo
great in the fervice of the crown, as in that of the merchant.

I am very fenfible of the hardfhip the failor fuffereth from
an imprefs in fome particular cafes, efpecially if preffed
homeward-bound after a long voyage. But the merchants
who hear me, know that an imprefs on outward-bound veffels would be attended with much greater inconveniencies to
the trade of the kingdom; and yet that too is fometimes
neceffary. But where two evils prefent, a wife adminiftration, if there be room for an option, will choofe the
leaft.

War itfelf is a great evil, but it is chofen to avoid a
greater. The practice of preffing is one of the mifchiefs war
bringeth with it. But it is a maxim in law, and good policy too, that all private mifchiefs muft be borne with patience

ence for preventing a national calamity. And as no greater calamity can befall us than to be weak and defenceless at sea in a time of war, so I do not know that the wisdom of the nation hath hitherto found out any method of manning our navy, less inconvenient than pressing, and at the same time equally sure and effectual.

The expedient of a voluntary register, which was attempted in king William's time, had no effect.

And some late schemes I have seen appear to me more inconvenient to the mariner, and more inconsistent with the principles of liberty, than the practice of pressing: and, what is still worse, they are, in my opinion, totally impracticable.

Thus much I thought proper to say upon the foot of reason and public utility, before I come to speak directly to the point of law: which I shall now do.

According to my present apprehension (and I have taken some pains to inform myself,) the right of impressing mariners for the public service, is a prerogative inherent in the crown, *grounded upon common-law, and recognized by many acts of parliament*.

A general immemorial usage, not inconsistent with any statute, especially if it be the result of evident necessity, and withal tendeth to the public safety, is, I apprehend, part of the common law of England. If not, I am at a loss to know what is meant by common law, in contradistinction to statute-law. And therefore it is a great mistake in this case, as indeed it would be in any other, to conclude that there is no law, because perhaps there may be no statute that expressly and in terms impowereth the crown to press. For the rights of the crown, and the liberties of the subject too, stand principally upon the foot of common law; though both have been in many cases confirmed, explained, or ascertained by particular statutes.

As to the point of usage in the matter of pressing, I have met with a multitude of commissions and mandatory writs to that purpose, conceived in various forms; and from time to time directed to different officers, as the nature of the service required.

It would be tedious for me to cite one half of them; but I will endeavour to range them under some general heads, and then cite a few.

Some are for pressing ships.
Others for pressing mariners.
And others for pressing ships and mariners.

In

In some, the parties to whom they are directed are required to make a general imprefs upon certain great and emergent occafions.

In others, they are confined to a certain number of fhips and mariners for fpecial fervices.

And in others, they are ftill further confined to certain places on the coaft.

Some commiffioners, particularly thofe conferring the admiralty jurifdiction and the rights of admiralty, warrant an imprefs as often as there fhall be occafion.

Others impower commanders of fleets or fquadrons intended for certain expeditions, to prefs for that particular fervice.

And others impower mafters of particular fhips to prefs for manning their refpective veffels.

This general view will be fufficient to let us into the nature of thefe precedents. And though the affair of preffing fhips is not now before me, yet I could not well avoid mentioning it; becaufe many of the precedents I have met with and muft cite, go as well to that, as to the bufmefs of preffing mariners. And taken together, they ferve to fhew the power the crown hath conftantly exercifed over the whole naval force of the kingdom, as well fhipping as mariners, whenever the public fervice required it.

This however muft be obferved, that no man ferved the crown in either cafe at his own expence, mafters and mariners received full wages, and owners were conftantly paid a full freight. But whether the pay in either cafe commenced from the time of preffing, or from the time of actual entry into the fervice, is not fo clear.

There is in Cotton's Records a note of a petition of the Commons, and the King's anfwer upon this fubject, in the 47 *Ed.* III. which inclineth me to think the latter was the cafe. The petition as abridged by Cotton is thus: " That " mafters of fhips may be paid the wages of them and their " mariners from the day of their being appointed to ferve " the king." The anfwer is, " That taking of fhips fhall " not be but for neceffity, and payment fhall be reafonable " as heretofore."

In the fame parliament an attempt was made to obtain for owners of fhips an allowance for wear and tear in the king's fervice.

The petition is thus abridged, " The mafters of fhips require an allowance for the tackling of their fhips worn by " the King's fervice."

The

The anfwer is, " Such allowance hath been heretofore
" made."

In the 2d *Ric.* II, an attempt of the like kind was made
and with the like fuccefs. The petition is, " That owners
" of fhips taken up for the King's fervice, for their loffes in
" the fame may be confidered; and that mariners may have
" the like wages, as archers have." The anfwer is, " It
" fhall be as hath been ufed.

Thefe petitions, though ftyled in the Record the petitions
of the Commons as having probably begun in that houfe,
were really the acts of both Houfes; otherwife they could
not have been offered to the King in a parliamentary way.
For the antient method of paffing bills was, that the matter
of the bill was tendered to the Crown for the Royal Affent
by both Houfes in form of petitions. And according to
the anfwers from the throne they paffed into laws or were
rejected.

I cannot but obferve, that when we fee every branch of
the Legiflature fpeaking of the fubject of preffing in the
manner they do in thefe petitions and anfwers, it is not eafy
to conceive that the legality of the practice was then quef-
tioned. 'Tis plain at leaft, that it was in thofe early times
treated in parliament as antient and well-known ufage.

I come now to the commiffions and mandatory writs I
fpoke of. I will cite a few from Rymer's Fœdera, out of a
great number of the like kind which may be met with in that
valuable collection of publick records.

William Barret commander of the fhip Julian had a commiffion 29 *Ed.* III. to make choice of and take up in the
counties of Kent, Effex, Surrey, and Suffex, as well within
liberties as without, 36 mariners, and put them on board
his fhip, in order to proceed with the Prince of Wales on an
expedition to Gafcony.

The like commiffions were given at the fame time to the
commanders of feven other fhips for manning their refpective veffels for the fame fervice.

There is a commiffion to John Orewell one of the King's
Serjeants at arms to arreft and take up 60 able mariners in
the Thames and Medway and parts adjacent, as well within
liberties as without, and to caufe them to be at Sandwich
within 15 days for the King's fervice.

John Elingham, a ferjeant at arms, is impowered 15 *Ric.*
II. to arreft and take up in the counties of Somerfet, Briftol,
Devon and Cornwall, and in South Wales, as well within
liberties as without, fo many fhips, barges, and other veffels,

and

and alfo mariners fufficient for manning them, as fhould be found fufficient for an expedition to Ireland under the King's uncle the Duke of Gloucefter. And all fheriffs, mayors, bailiffs, mafters of fhips and mariners are required to be affifting to him in that fervice.

In the fame year the like commiffions iffued to two other Serjeants at Arms for the fame fervice, in Wales, Ireland, Lancafhire, and Chefhire.

John Kingfton commander of the fhip Katherine is commiffioned by himfelf or deputies to arreft and take up, as well within liberties as without, as many mariners as fhould be neceffary for manning his fhip, and to put them on board for the King's fervice. And all fheriffs, mayors, &c. are required to be affifting to him in that fervice.

Commiffions went at the fame time to fix commanders of other veffels for manning their refpective veffels in the fame manner, and for the fame fervice.

A mandatory writ iffued (21 H. VI.) directed to Thomas Colledge, ferjeant at arms, and to Ralph Ingolfby, and to the cuftomers of the port of Sandwich, and of every port from thence to Southampton, requiring them to arreft and take up for the King's fervice all and fingular fhips, barges, and other veffels capable of tranfporting men or horfes, of what burden foever; and alfo all mafters and mariners that could be found in any of the ports mentioned before, and to put the faid mafters and mariners on board the faid veffels for an expedition to the dutchy of Aquitain; any Royal Letters of Licenfe thentofore granted to any perfon or perfons, or any other matter notwithftanding: and all fheriffs, mayors, and other officers, are required to be affifting to them in that fervice.

At the fame time the like writs iffued to the cuftomers and other officers of almoft all the port-towns in the kingdom.

There is a commiffion 14 *Ed.* IV. to the mafter and purfer of the Mary Grace impowering them to arreft and take up, as well within liberties as without, wherefoever they could be found, as many mariners as fhould be fufficient for manning their veffel, and to put them on board at the King's wages and for his fervice.

At the fame time the like commiffions iffued to four other mafters for manning their refpective fhips in the fame manner.

The like commiffions to mafters of fix veffels.

The like to eleven mafters in the fame form.

I will now mention a few precedents of another fort; which, becaufe they relate in great meafure to one and the fame fervice, I will place together, to avoid as much as poffible a needlefs repetition in matters of form.

Thefe are either fpecial commiffions for commanding fleets or fquadrons intended for certain expeditions mentioned in the commiffions; or the general commiffions conferring the whole Admiralty Jurifdiction with the rights of Admiralty, whether to one perfon under the Style of High Admiral or to two under the character of Admirals of the North and Weft. Which latter was the ufual manner of conferring the Admiralty Jurifdiction before the office of Lord High Admiral of England came much in ufe.

As to the fpecial commiffions, 5 *Hen.* V. Sir William Bardolph was appointed admiral of a fleet then intended to be fitted out; his commiffion impowereth him among other things to make choice of and take up for the King's fervice a fufficient number of mariners and others, and to put them on board the fleet, and to punifh and chaftife fuch mariners who fhould be difobedient or refractory in that refpect.

The Lord Willoughby de Broke was appointed 5 *Hen.* VII. commander in chief of the fleet and army then intended for an expedition to France; he hath the fame powers with regard to the manning the fleet as Sir William Bardolph had.

Sir Robert Poyntz is appointed 8 *Hen.* VII. to command the fleet in the abfence of the Lord Willoughby, and hath the fame powers with regard to the manning the fleet.

Sir Martin Frobifher had a commiffion, 31 *Eliz.* which, after reciting that the command of a fmall fquadron intended againft the Spaniards in the Weft Indies had been given to him, goeth on thus: " We therefore let you, to wit, that we
" have authorized and appointed, and do by thefe prefents
" give full power and authority to the faid Sir Martin Fro-
" bifher, or to his fufficient deputy or deputies wherefoever
" he fhall have need, to prefs and take up for our fervice to
" the furniture of fuch fhips as fhall be committed to his
" charge in any place upon our coafts of England or Ireland,
" any mariners, foldiers, gunners or other needful artificers."
And then requireth all Juftices and other officers to be affifting to him in the premifes.

I would not be underftood to fay, that all commanders of fleets or fquadrons for fpecial fervices have had the fame powers as thofe I have mentioned. The truth is, the greater number of thefe fpecial commiffions, which I have
met

met with, and thofe too of the lateft date, are filent as to that point.

I come now to the general commiffions conferring the whole Admiralty Jurifdiction and the Rights of Admiralty.

And thofe I have met with, though I apprehend they all agree in fubftance with regard to the prefent queftion, yet differ a little in point of form.

In the 10th *Ed.* III. and in the 12th of the fame reign, the Admirals (for at that time there were two, one for the North, the other for the Weft) are impowered to make choice of, as well within liberties as without, able-bodied men fit for the fervice, and to put them on board the fleet. The word *eligendi* made ufe of in thefe commiffions, is the word ufed to the fame purpofe about that time in all the commiffions for preffing for the land-fervice, which was then likewife practifed. You have the word in relation to the land-fervice in the ftatute of the 18 *Ed.* III. " Men at arms, " hoblers, and archers chofen to go into the King's fervice " out of the realm, fhall be at the King's wages from the " day they depart out of the counties where they were chofen " 'till their return."

In the 50th *Ed.* III. the Admirals commiffions with regard to this matter ran thus : " Nec non naves & naviculas " guerinas, quot neceffariæ, cujufcunque portagii fuerint " quoties neceffa fuerit, congregandi : & marinarios & alios " pro navibus & naviculis illis neceffarios eligendi, capi- " endi, & in eifdem ponendi, & hujufmodi marinarios qui " rebelles & contrarientes fuerint in hac parte, debite com- " pefcendi & caftigandi : & ad omnia alia quæ ad officium " Admiralli pertinent IN HAC PARTE faciendi & exer- " cendi ; prout de jure & fecundum legem maritimam fuerit " faciendum."

And all Sheriffs, Mayors, Bailiffs, Minifters, Owners of Ships, Mafters and Mariners are required to be aiding and affifting to them in the premifes.

The Admirals Commiffions run exactly in the fame form.

So doth Thomas of Lancafter's Commiffion of High Admiral.

So doth the Earl of Warwick's Commiffion of High Admiral.

And fo doth the Duke of Richmond's, 17 *Hen.* VIII.

The Lord Seymour's Commiffion of High Admiral expreffeth the matter a little differently ; the words are, " Ac

X 2   " ad

" ad nautas & marinarios & alios pro omnibus & singulis
" navibus, conducendum & gubernandum neceffarios, eli-
" gendum, capiendum & apprehendendum, atque eofdem in
" dictis navibus & naviculis ponendum & retinendum.

In the fame year the Lord Seymour had another commiffion in fuller terms, with all the Jurifdictions and Rights of Admiralty particularly enumerated and fet forth at large; the words with regard to the prefent matter are, " Et
" infuper tam naves & naviculas guerinas quam quafcunque
" alias naves & naviculas feu vafa quaecunque, pro quibuf-
" cunque viagiis, feu negotiis noftris vel expeditione eorun-
" dem; nec non navigeros, five pilotas ac navium magif-
" tros, nautas, naucleros, vibreleatores, feu bombartioree
" ac marinarios & alias perfonas quafcunque, pro navibus,
" naviculis feu vafibus hujufmodi aptos & idoneos, de tem-
" pore in tempus quoties neceffe fuerit, ubicunque locorum
" infra regna & dominia noftra praedicta tam infra libertates
" quam extra, congregandum, deligendum, retinendum, ca-
" piendum, arreftandum, deputandum & affignandum abfque
" interruptione feu impedimento per quemcunque in contra-
" rium, fiendo; cum plena Jurifdictione & poteftate ad exe-
" quendum omnia & fingula quae in hac parte per magnum
" Admirallum noftrum & praefectum generalem claffis &
" marium, jure fieri debent, poffint, vel folent."

The Earl of Warwick had a Commiffion 3. Ed. VI. of High Admiral in the fame form.

And fo had the Duke of Buckingham, 16. Jac. I.

And now, when I confider thefe precedents not fetched from dark, remote, and unfettled times, but running uniformly through a courfe of many ages, all, as I conceive, fpeaking to the fame purpofe, though in different forms of expreffion; fome for making choice of, others, and thofe the much greater number, and of the lateft date, for making choice of and taking up, or for arrefting, preffing, and taking up, mariners, and putting them on board for the publick fervice: when I confider thefe precedents with the practice down to the prefent time, I cannot conceive otherwife of the point in queftion, than that the Crown hath been always in poffeffion of the prerogative of preffing mariners for the publick fervice. Which prerogative hath been carried into execution, as well by virtue of fpecial commiffions iffued as the exigency of affairs required, as by the perfons who from time to time have been intrufted with the whole Admiralty Jurifdiction.

And indeed, the words touching the manning the fleet, impowering the Admirals to do and execute all other matters and things touching that fervice *which belong to the office*

of.

of *Admiral* seem to imply, either that those powers were deemed to be inherent in the office, or that they had been constantly by express words in the commissions annexed to it.

To this purpose I will mention a very remarkable transaction in the Parliament of the 7th and 8th of *Hen*. IV.

Complaint was made in Parliament that the sea-service had been greatly neglected, and that depredations were daily committed. To remedy this evil, a very extraordinary expedient was offered, to which the necessity of the King's affairs obliged him, *for the present,* to submit. It was, that the naval force of the kingdom should, for a time, be put under the direction of the merchants themselves.

Accordingly, an act passed that the merchants should have the keeping of the seas from the 1st of May, 1406, to Michaelmas, 1407. And to defray the expence of this service they were to be entitled, by Writs of Privy Seal, to certain duties mentioned in the record, as I find it abridged by Cotton.

Among other provisions touching this matter, it was enacted that the merchants should name two persons, one for the North and the other for the South, who, by commission, should have the like powers as other Admirals have had.

In pursuance of this act, Nicholas Blackbourn was named by the merchants for the North, and Richard Cliderow for the South.

One might reasonably hope that no powers deemed illegal or oppressive, no powers hurtful to trade, or grievous to the mariners, should be inserted in the commissions of Admirals nominated by the merchants. But it happeneth that Blackbourn's commission is extant, and runneth in the very words of those I have cited from the 50th of *Ed*.III. to the 17th of *Hen*. VIII.

You have it in Rymer (8. 439). It reciteth the Act of Parliament, and that Blackbourn had been nominated by the merchants for the North; and then goeth on in the usual form, impowering him to make choice of, take up, and put on board, such mariners and others as shall be found necessary for the service, and to punish and chastise such as shall be disobedient and refractory in that behalf.

The commission was to continue as long as the merchants should have the keeping of the seas, which indeed was not long. For before that Parliament rose, this novelty came to an end: the merchants were eased of a service they were found to be very unequal to, their Admirals commissions

dropped

dropped, and the whole direction of the marine returned to its proper channel.

I think it may safely be inferred from this record that in the judgment of those times, and in a concern of the merchants themselves, the practice of manning the navy by the methods mentioned in these commissions, was esteemed to be necessary for the service, and a branch of admiral jurisdiction.

I come now to the statutes which speak of this matter.

And I do admit that I know of no statute now in force, which directly, and in express terms, impowereth the Crown to impress mariners into the service. And admitting that the prerogative is grounded on immemorial usage, I know of no necessity for any such statute. For let it be remembered, that a prerogative grounded upon general immemorial usage not inconsistent with any statute, not repugnant to the publick utility, is as much part of the law of England, as statute law. You will be pleased to carry this observation too along with you, that the statutes which mention pressing as a practice then subsisting and not disallowed, are at least an evidence of the usage if they go no further. I mean if they do not amount to a tacit approbation of it.

For it is hard to conceive, that the Legislature should frequently mention a practice utterly illegal, and repugnant to the principles of the Constitution as subsisting, without some mark of disapprobation.

The first statute I have met with is that of the 2 R. 2, cap. 4. It is an act against Mariners deserting the service; not to be met with in the latter editions of the Statutes at Large, which give us only the title of this Act, with a note that is altered by the 18th *Hen.* VI. and 5 *Eliz.*

It is however still in force, and as such is inserted by Rastal in his Abridgment under title " Mariner, No 1." My worthy friend Mr. Cay hath likewise inserted it in his Abridgment, under title " Seamen, No 1." I will give you the words of the Act as far as concerneth this point, as I find it in an edition of the Statutes at Large, ending with the last year of *Hen.*VII. " *Item*, because that divers ma-
" riners after they be arrested and retained for the King's
" service upon the sea, in defence of the realm, and thereof
" have received their wages, do flee out of the said service
" without licence of the Admirals or their Lieutenants.——
" it is ordained and established that all those mariners which
" from henceforth shall do in such manner——shall be holden
" to restore to our said Sovereign Lord the King the double
" of that they have taken for wages, and nevertheless shall
" have

" have one year's imprisonment, without being delivered by
"mainprise, bail, or by any other way."

The Act then goeth on to direct how fugitive mariners
shall be apprehended and dealt with; and concludeth with
this clause, " The like punishment shall be made of Ser-
" jeants of Arms, Masters of Ships, and all others that shall
" be attainted before the Admiral or his Lieutenant afore-
" said, that they have any thing taken of the said mariners
" for to suffer them to go at large out of the said service,
" after they have been arrested for the same service."

You will be pleased to observe that the word *arrest* twice
used in this Act, is made use of in the precedents I cited
of the 1st and 15th of this very reign, and in most of those
of latter date: it is likewise used in ten other commissions in
the same reign touching this very service, all likewise directed
for execution to Serjeants at Arms, which for brevity's sake
I have omitted.

So that if it be asked who are the persons subjected to the
penalties of this Act, it must be answered, mariners arrested
and taken into the service by virtue of commissions from
the Crown, in case of their desertion, and Serjeants at
Arms, masters of ships, and others executing such commissions, who for lucre shall suffer them to go at large after
such arrests.

Mariners indeed were not subject to the penalties of this
Act, unless they had received wages. But might not a mariner so arrested have reasonably said, I was compelled
against law into the service; I did my duty while I continued in it, and dearly earned the wages I received?
Might not a mariner have said this, and much more, upon
a supposition of the illegality of an impress? Certainly he
might. But you see mariners, though taken into the service by compulsion, are by this Act made liable to pecuniary and corporal punishment too in case of desertion.
This doth more than imply the legality of such compulsion.

It may possibly be objected that the word *retained* is used
in the Act, and that a retainer implieth a mutual contract
for some service to be done. It may, when it standeth
alone, have received that sense in modern language, but in
strict propriety it meaneth nothing more than the taking a
person into some service; and is in truth the Act only of the
person retaining or taking. And therefore when I see the
word *retained*, connected with one which hath no other
meaning in the English tongue than what carrieth with it
the idea of compulsion, I cannot conceive that the Legislature,

lature, speaking of persons *arrested* and *maintained*, should mean no other than persons taken into the service with their own consent.

That there was a practise then subsisting of taking mariners into the service by compulsion, cannot be denied: the Parliament could not be ignorant of it. Is it possible then to imagine, that they could use a word which manifestly signifieth compulsion, and yet mean nothing more than a mutual contract? Besides, it cannot be conceived that Serjeants at Arms, who, as I before observed, were the persons about that time usually employed in the service of pressing, could be expresfly, and by name, subjected to the penalties of the Act, if no mariners but such as voluntarily entered into the service, were comprehended in it.

The next Act is that of the 2d and 3d *Ph.* and *Mar.* which layeth a penalty on watermen plying between Gravesend and Windsor, who, to speak in the language of the Act, " in " the time of pressing by commission for the service of the " Crown upon the sea, do willingly and obstinately with- " draw, hide, and convey themselves into secret places and " out-corners; and after such time of pressing is over-passed, " return to their employments."

This provision, 'tis true, extendeth only to watermen on the Thames, and may be considered as one of the many wholesome regulations those persons are brought under by this Act. And it is mentioned in that light in an Act passed in the late Queen's time. But, at the same time, it sheweth that commissions for pressing were then in use. And, in my opinion, it likewise supposeth the legality and utility of such commissions, and that these people are the objects of them. Otherwise why are they subjected even to the slightest punishment, for absconding at the time of the execution of those commissions.

The Acts which come next to be considered are some made since the Revolution; a most auspicious period! when the principles of Liberty were well understood, and most gloriously asserted.

These are the 7th and 8th of King *William*, the 2nd, 3d, 4th, and 5th of the late Queen.

The first is intituled, "An Act for the Increase and Encouragement of Seamen."

It enacteth, among other things, that licenses may be given by his Majesty, or the Lord High Admiral, or Commissioners of Admiralty to any landmen willing to enter into the merchants service: which shall be a protection to them against being impressed for the space of two years.

Pro-

Provided such landmen bring two credible perfons to
vouch for them.   But if any perfon fhall vouch for any one
as a landman, who fhall afterwards appear to have been a
feaman, he fhall forfeit twenty pounds.

The 2d and 3d of the late queen is intituled " An act for
" the Increafe and better encouragement of Navigation and
" Security of the Coal Trade."   To thefe ends it impowereth parifh officers to bind out poor boys to fea in the
merchants' fervice: and enacted that boys, fo bound out,
fhall not be compelled, or *impreffed*, or permitted to enter
into the fervice of the Crown at fea 'till they attain their
age of eighteen; and that certificates of fuch binding fhall
be tranfmitted by the collectors of the refpective ports to
the Admiralty; and that thereupon protections fhall be
made for fuch apprentices without fee or reward.

And for encouraging other perfons to bind themfelves
apprentices in the merchants' fervice, it further enacteth,
that perfons fo binding themfelves fhall not be compelled
or impreffed into the fervice of the Crown for three years
from the time of fuch binding; and that upon certificates
of fuch binding, from the collectors of the refpective ports,
the Admiralty fhall grant protections without fee or reward.

And, for encouraging the coal-trade, it further enacteth,
that, during the war, there fhall be allowed to every veffel
employed in that trade, befides the mafter, mate, and carpenter, one able feaman for every one hundred ton of
the veffel, not exceeding three hundred ton, free from impreffing.

The 4th and 5th of the late Queen reciteth that claufe in
the Act of the 2d and 3d, which exempted voluntary apprentices for three years; and faith, " Whereas fuch ex-
" emption for three years, which was intended for the en-
" couragement of landmen to bind themfelves, hath been
" manifeftly abufed for the exempting and protecting of
" feamen from the fervice, to the great hindrance and preju-
" dice of her Majefty's fea-fervice;" therefore be it enacted
" and declared, that no perfon or perfons, of the age of
" eighteen years, fhall have any exemption or protection
" from her Majefty's fea-fervice, who fhall have been in
" any fea-fervice before the time they fo bound themfelves,
" any law or ftatute to the contrary notwithftanding." See
alfo 1 *Annæ*, Seff. 1. cap. 16. § 2. 6. *Annæ*, cap. 31. § 2.
13 *Geo.* II. cap. 17. § 1, 2, 3, and cap. 28. § 5.

Let us now take a fhort view of thefe Acts,

Perfons

Perfons under certain fpecial qualifications are exempted from being impreffed.

To that end, in one cafe, licences are to be granted by his Majefty, or from the Admiralty, but under proper caution to prevent abufes.

In other cafes, certificates are to be returned from the chief officers of the ports, and protections thereupon granted without fee or reward.

And, in every cafe, thefe exemptions, as they are confined to perfons under certain limited qualifications, fo are they limited too in point of time, and withal given by way of encouragement. And, laftly, the extending the benefit, even of a temporary exemption beyond the original intent of the Legiflature, is declared to be an abufe, and an abufe tending to the great hindrance and prejudice of her Majefty's fea-fervice.

Do not thefe things inconteftibly prefuppofe the expediency, the neceffity, and the legality of an imprefs in general? If they do not, one muft entertain an opinion of the Legiflature acting and fpeaking in this manner, which it will not be decent for me to mention in this place.

For the very notion of an exemption when granted by ftatute to particular perfons, and this too by way of encouragement, implieth, that without fuch exemption the parties entitled to the benefit of it would by law be liable to the duty or burden which is the fubject-matter of that exemption : otherwife the ftatute doth nothing, it operateth upon nothing, if no legal duty or burden be removed by it. And confequently the granting exemptions to feamen under certain limited qualifications, and for a limited time only, fuppofeth that all feamen in general, without fuch exemption, were by law liable to the duty or burden which is the fubject-matter of that exemption.

And the many provifions the Legiflature hath made to prevent abufes with regard to thefe exemptions, attended with a plain, full, and exprefs declaration, that fuch abufes, namely, the extending the benefit of exemptions beyond the intent of the Legiflature, tend to the great hindrance and prejudice of the fea-fervice, imply, that the duty or burden, which is the object of all this care and caution, is expedient and neceffary to the fervice.

And this burden is plainly an imprefs in time of war.

Which from the authorities I have cited appeareth to me to be grounded on common and ftatute-law. In other words, upon a general immemorial ufage, allowed, approved, and recognized by many acts of Parliament.

Againft

Againſt what I have ſaid, it hath been objected, that the practice of preſſing is inconſiſtent with the liberty of the ſubject, and a breach of *Magna Charta*.

I readily admit that an impreſs is a reſtraint upon the natural liberty of thoſe who are liable to it.   But it muſt likewiſe be admitted, on the other hand, that every reſtraint upon natural liberty is not *eo nomine* illegal, or at all inconſiſtent with the principles of civil liberty.   And if the reſtraint, be it to what degree ſoever, appeareth to be neceſſary to the good and welfare of the whole, and to be warranted by ſtatute-law, as well as immemorial uſage, it cannot be complained of otherwiſe than as a private miſchief; which as I ſaid at the beginning muſt, under all Governments whatſoever, be ſubmitted to, for avoiding a public inconvenience.

As to *Magna Charta*, it is not pretended that the practice of preſſing mariners for the public ſervice is condemned by expreſs words in that ſtatute.   And if it be warranted by common and ſtatute-law, it cannot be ſhewn to be illegal by any conſequences drawn from *Magna Charta*.   In like manner as preſſing for the land ſervice could not be deemed illegal, or inconſiſtent with the principles of our conſtitution, while there were temporary acts (as there were many in the late war) to warrant it.

Beſides, we know that *Magna Charta* hath been expreſsly and by name confirmed by many acts of Parliament, my Lord Coke ſaith 32.   And yet the practice of preſſing mariners ſtill continued through all ages, and was never, that I know of, once mentioned in any of thoſe acts as illegal, or a violation of the great charter.

In a ſimilar caſe, I mean the practice of preſſing ſoldiers for foreign ſervice, there are ſtatutes of an early date (1 Ed. III. 5, 25 Ed. III. 8.) which, I conceive, were intended againſt it; though it was practiſed long afterwards. But thoſe acts extend only to the caſe of preſſing for the land-ſervice, not a word do I find in them touching the ſea-ſervice.   One reaſon of the difference, among others, may be that the land-ſervice was thought to be ſufficiently provided for in ordinary caſes by the military tenures: and extraordinary caſes, caſes of neceſſity, ſuch as that of a foreign invaſion, were expreſsly excepted.   In thoſe caſes, ſaith the 1 Ed. III. " it ſhall be done as in times paſt;" which we know was by commiſſions of array.   Whereas no competent proviſion was made by law for the ordinary ſea-ſervice. There were no naval ſervices due to the Crown, except thoſe of the Cinque Ports, and a very few others; which all together were too inconſiderable to be mentioned, and
                                                                    bore

bore no fort of proportion to the common exigencies of the public in time of war.

But there is another objection which deferveth to be confidered. It is, that temporary acts have from time to time been made authorizing the preffing mariners for the fea-service. From whence it is argued, that the Legiflature, which is fuppofed to do nothing in vain, would not have given thofe powers for a time, if the King, by his prærogative, could have provided for the fervice without the aid of fuch temporary acts.

The gentleman who had the care of publifhing Lord Chief Juftice Hale's Hiftory of the Pleas of the Crown, referreth to feveral temporary acts made in the late Queen's time, authorifing, as he fuppofeth, the preffing of foldiers and mariners. I have looked into all thofe acts. They are folely for preffing foldiers and marines. Not a fingle word that concerneth the preffing of mariners do I find in any one of them.

There was indeed an act made in that reign (4 & 5 Annæ, c. 19.) for compelling mariners into the fervice by methods which it was then thought the prerogative alone could not warrant. To that end it authorized and required Juftices of the Peace, and other Magiftrates, to caufe privy fearches to be made, from time to time, for mariners, who, as the act expreffeth it, " did lie hid, withdraw, and conceal them- " felves," and to deliver them when apprehended to conductors for the fervice of the Crown. And conftables and other officers were, by warrants from the Magiftrates, to make privy fearches by night, and were impowered to enter houfes, and open doors, in execution of fuch warrants; and were required to give an account of their proceedings, from time to time, to the Magiftrates, on oath; and, in cafe of negligence or remiffnefs in the premifes, were fubjected to pecuniary punifhments. This is the fubftance of the firft nine fections of the act; which fections continuing in force only 'till the firft of March, 1706, are not printed in the later editions of the Statutes at large.

But it cannot, I conceive, be inferred from the new powers given by this act, that an imprefs by commiffion from the Crown, or by Admiralty-warrants, which was practifed at that very time, was illegal. All that can be inferred is, that the ordinary methods then in ufe were found ineffectual: and therefore the Legiflature had for that time recourfe to an extraordinary one, for compelling into the fervice thofe who could not be come at by the ordinary methods; thofe, who, in the language of the act, " lay hid, " withdrew

"withdrew, and concealed themfelves." And to that end, civil Magiftrates and civil Officers are required and authorized to do what, in the judgment of the Legiflature without the aid of that act, they could not have done, or at leaft were not compellable to do.

And whoever readeth and confidereth the 17th and 18th fections of this Act, which I have already cited to another purpofe, will hardly conceive, that That Parliament had any doubts concerning the legality of an imprefs by the ordinary methods of Law.

Indeed, the temporary Acts of the 16th and 17th *Car. I.* come directly to the point. They authorized an imprefs by Admiralty-warrants for a limited time. And had temporary Acts of that kind been frequent, or had the practice of preffing been difcontinued from the time of Charles the Firft, unlefs when revived by fubfequent temporary Acts, I think what hath been faid upon the root of antient precedents could, after all, have had very little weight. For I freely declare, that antient precedents alone, unlefs fupported by modern practice, weigh very little with me in queftions of this nature, I mean, in queftions touching the prerogative. But we all know that the practice of preffing by Admiralty-warrants hath continued now near a century, fince the expiration of thofe Acts of King Charles the Firft, without one ftatute of the like kind to authorize it.

Thefe Acts of King Charles the Firft do indeed fhew that the prerogative of preffing mariners into the public fervice was at that time doubted of. And whoever confidereth the peculiar circumftances of that time, when the prerogative had in too many inftances been carried to great lengths, and when the nation was at the very eve of a civil war upon the fubject of liberty and prerogative, and confidereth withal that a naval force muft in all events, as things then ftood, be provided; whoever I fay confidereth thefe things will not wonder that the prerogative of preffing mariners fhould at that very critical time be called in queftion; or that, in order to procure an univerfal fubmiffion to a meafure neceffary at that time, the authority of Parliament fhould be called in, in aid of the prerogative.

There was a temporary Act made in this very feffion for preffing for the land-fervice. It reciteth, that a rebellion was on foot in Ireland; and then declareth, almoft in the words of 1 *Ed.* III. before cited, " that by Law no man is com-" pellable to go out of his county to ferve as a foldier, ex-" cept in cafe of neceffity of fudden coming of ftrange ene-" mies

" mies into the kingdom, or except he was bound thereto by
" tenure."

It is worth obferving, that no fuch declaration, faving the
rights of the fubject, is to be found in any of the Acts of this
feffion for preffing mariners. And the different penning of
thefe Acts made in the fame feffion, and touching cafes of fo
fimilar a nature, ftrongly intimateth, that the point was not,
even at that critical time, thought equally clear in the one
cafe as in the other. The fame obfervation occurreth with
regard to the different penning of all the Acts of the late
Queen for preffing foldiers and marines, and of that for
preffing mariners; the former declare that it was neceffary at
that time of war, that foldiers and marines fhould be raifed
by the methods prefcribed in the Acts, " by common con-
" fent and grant in Parliament." Thefe are the words of the
Act, and they are the very words made ufe of to the fame
purpofe in the 25th *Ed.* III. already cited. The latter without any fuch declaration barely impowereth and requireth
magiftrates and other peace-officers to make fearch for and
apprehend mariners, who then lay hid, withdrew, and concealed themfelves, and to fend them into the fervice.

Lord Chief Juftice Hale, in his Hiftory of the Pleas of the
Crown, fpeaking of the legality of preffing, which he indeed
feemeth to doubt of, faith, " He that looketh upon the Acts
" enabling preffing foldiers and mariners for foreign fervice
" upon or beyond the fea, namely, 17 *Car.* c. 12. 25, 26.
" may think thofe times made fome doubt of it. But of this,"
faith he; " I deliver no opinion."

That learned man, you fee, carrieth the inference from
thefe temporary Acts no further than to render the matter
doubtful, and fo he leaveth it. But had he lived to fee the
practice of preffing mariners continue near a century longer,
and efpecially had he feen this practice treated by the Legiflature in the manner the Acts made fince the Revolution treat
it, I think what was then but matter of doubt would have
now appeared to him in a different light. I confefs it doth
fo to me. For rights of every kind, which ftand upon the
foot of ufage, gradually receive new ftrength in point of
light and evidence from the continuance of that ufage; as it
implieth the tacit confent and approbation of every fuccef-
five age in which the ufage hath prevailed. But when the
prerogative hath not only this tacit approbation of all ages,
the prefent as well as the former, on its fide, but is recognized or evidently prefuppofed by many Acts of Parliament,
as in the prefent cafe I think it is, I fee no legal objection
that can be made to it.

I make

I make no apology for the length of my argument, becaufe I hope the importance of the queftion will be thought a fufficient excufe for me in that refpect. For it is no more nor lefs than, whether the only effectual method yet found out for manning our navy in time of war, for raifing that number of mariners " which the Legiflature from time to time " declare to be neceffary" for defending our coaft and protecting our trade, whether this method be legal or no? This I fay is the queftion. And therefore I could not fatisfy myfelf without entering as far into the merits of it as I could.

And I have delivered my opinion upon it without any referve.

KING's BENCH, HILARY TERM, 29 GEO. III.

LEMAN *againft* GOULTY *and Another*.

This was a rule calling on the plaintiff and the Rev. G. Sandby, D. D. vicar-general of the epifcopal court of Norwich, to fhew caufe why a writ of prohibition fhould not iffue to prohibit that Court from holding further plea of the matters between the parties.

The defendants, who were churchwardens of St. Andrew's, Norwich, were cited on the 26th of March, 1788, in the Bifhop's Court, to exhibit, on oath, a true account of all fums of money which they had received, and paid, in the execution of their office, from Eafter 1787 to that time. At a fubfequent Court, held the 29th of April following, they gave in their accounts verified by oath. On the 18th of June objections were taken to two articles of the account; one of 6l. 11s. 6d. for lettering and gilding the pew doors; and the other 6l. 10s. charged as paid to the chief conftable, and not relating to the office of church-warden; which were difallowed. Then they were admonifhed to pay 12l. 1s. as the balance of their accounts, and 13s. 4d as cofts; and for not appearing at a fubfequent Court on the 23d of October 1788, and obeying the monition, the judge pronounced them contumacious, and excommunicated them. At a Court held on the firft of Auguft 1788, it was alleged, that the plaintiff was prefent at a veftry meeting of the parifhioners of St. Andrew's on the 12th of March 1788, when the Church-wardens' accounts were produced and allowed, and that the Plaintiff and the reft of the parifhrioners had fince paid the fums rated on them; and that the fum charged to have been paid to the conftable was an annual fum,

fum, which the Church-wardens for the time being appeared to have regularly paid. The fuggeftion ftated, that it appeared to the judge of the Spiritual Court, by the account delivered in by the Defendants on the 29th of April, that it had been allowed and approved at the veftry meeting.

LORD KENYON, Ch. J.—When the Churchwardens had delivered in their account, they had done every thing which the Spiritual Court had a power of enforcing. There was then an end of the jurifdiction of that Court; it was *functus officio*. The general grounds of a prohibition to the Ecclefiaftical Courts are either a defect of jurifdiction, or a defect in the mode of trial. If any fact be pleaded in the Court below, and the parties are at iffue, that Court has no jurifdiction to try it, becaufe it cannot proceed according to the rules of the common law; and in fuch cafe a prohibition lies. Or where the Spiritual Court has no original jurifdiction, a prohibition may be granted after fentence. But where it has jurifdiction, and gives a wrong judgment, it is the fubject matter of appeal, and not of prohibition. This doctrine was laid down in the cafe of *Symes* v. *Symes*, 2 *Burr*. 813. Now in this cafe, with refpect to the compelling of a production of the church-wardens' accounts, the Spiritual Court had exclufive jurifdiction: but there their authority ceafed; and every thing which they did afterwards was an excefs of jurifdiction, for which a prohibition ought to be granted.

ASHHURST, J.—It feems that the Spiritual Court have exceeded their jurifdiction, and therefore a prohibition fhould be granted. They had a right to compel the churchwardens to deliver in their account, but when that was done, they could take no further cognizance of the matter.

BULLER, J.—This is a motion for a prohibition after fentence; in which cafe we cannot go out of the proceedings, to fee whether the Spiritual Court had any jurifdiction. But I think it does appear on the face of thefe proceedings, that the Court below had no authority to give the fentence which they have given; and upon that ground a prohibition ought to be granted. If the Ecclefiaftical Judge give a wrong fentence on the merits, where he has jurifdiction, that is only the fubject matter of appeal, and not of a prohibition. But where it appears on their own proceeding that they had no jurifdiction, there a prohibition is the proper remedy.

GROSE, J.—Of the fame opinion.

                                        Rule abfolute.

THE
LAWYER'S
AND
MAGISTRATE'S MAGAZINE.
For JUNE, 1790.

Adjudged Cafes in the Courts at Weftminfter in Eafter Term, 1790.

Rex v. Joseph Scott, *Cl. and another.*

THE Seffions of Salop, upon an appeal againft a rate to the poor, charged upon two fchool-houfes at New-port, confirmed the rate fubject to the opinion of the Court.

CASE.

W. Adams having conveyed in fee a free-fchool and two houfes in Newport for the refidence of a mafter, and ufher, with a confiderable eftate at Knighton in the county of Stafford, for the fupport of the fame, and vefted the fame in the Haberdafhers Company in London as truftees, a private Act of Parliament was paffed in the 12th *Car.* II. entituled " An Act for the incorporation of the Mafter and Wardens of the Company of Haberdafhers, London, to be Governors of the Free-School and Alms-Houfes in Newport in the County of Salop, of the foundation of W. Adams, and for fettling Lands and Poffeffions on them for the Maintenance thereof, and other charitable Ufes;" which was confirmed and perpetuated by the 13 *Car.* II. By the Act of 12 *Car.* II, after reciting that W. Adams, had, out of a fincere intention for public good, at his own expence, erected the faid fchool-houfes for the mafter and ufher, and four alms-houfes in Newport, and for other pious and charitable purpofes, (among other things) it was enacted " That the manor and grange of Knighton, with the appurtenances, and all other lands and hereditaments, fettled and conveyed by Adams to the Governors and their fucceffors for the purpofes aforefaid, be, and at all times hereafter fhall be, *freed, difcharged, and acquitted of and from the payment of all and every manner of taxes, affeffments, or charges, civil or military, whatfoever;* hereafter to be laid and impofed by authority of Parliament, or otherwife; and the faid manors, meffuages, lands, tenements, and premifes, and the owners and occupiers thereof, or any of them, fhall not at any time hereafter be rated, taxed, or affeffed, to pay any fum or fums of money, or be otherwife charged in any way whatfoever, for or in refpect of the faid manors, lands, and hereditaments, or any of them, for or towards any manner of *public tax, affeffment, or charge, whatfoever;* any ftatute, law, or ordinance, to the contrary thereof in any wife notwithftanding." The appellants, having proved this act, and that the two houfes had been previoufly conveyed by Adams to, and vefted in, the faid Governors for the purpofes aforefaid, and that the premifes had not been rated or paid to the relief of the poor of the parifh in the memory of any perfon living, infifted that they were exempted by the faid ftatute, and were not liable to the payment of the poor's rate: but the Seffion adjudged that they were not exempted, and confirmed the rate.

LORD KENYON, Ch. J.----Thefe lands having been given for eleemofynary purpofes, the Legiflature feem to have intended to exempt them from all public taxes whatfoever. And it is immaterial to the parifh whether thefe lands be exempted from the poor's rate or not; fince if they be not exempt, greater contributions muft be raifed. If a conftruction of this Act of Parliament, manifeftly erroneous, had hitherto prevailed, we fhould have been bound to correct it: though indeed, had the words of the ftatute been very doubtful, the contemporary and fubfequent uniform ufage would have great weight. But without reforting to the ufage in this cafe, the words of this ftatute are very clear and pofitive; for they fpeak of all *publick taxes* whatfoever. The whole argument refolves itself into this, whether in the idea of the Legiflature at the time of paffing this Act of Parliament, the *poor's tax* was a *publick tax?* The Acts of Parliament, which have been referred to in the argument, do do not prove the point for which they were mentioned. But the other Acts of Parliament, respecting the poor, are decisive of this question. The statute of 3 *Will.* and *Mary,* cap. 11, § 6, speaking of the means by which a settlement may be gained, says, " that if any person shall be charged with and pay his share towards the *publick taxes or levies* of the said parish, he shall be adjudged to have a legal settlement in the same." Now on the construction of this statute, it never was doubted but that a payment towards the *poor's rate* was sufficient to give the party a settlement. I am therefore clearly of opinion, that the exemption which has hitherto prevailed, ought to continue in future.

The three other Judges concurred.

Order of Sessions, confirming the rate, quashed.

The KING v. *the Inhabitants of* HOLY TRINITY, *in the* MINORIES.

Two Justices removed Frances Whitfield, wife of Joshua Whitfield, (a patient in Guy's Hospital), with her three children, from Bermondsey to Holy Trinity. The Sessions confirmed the order.

C A S E.

Joshua Whitfield, the pauper, by indenture, dated the 24th of June, 1762, was bound apprentice to John Grimes, of Tower-Hill, London, taylor, (being a place neither within the parish of the appellants or respondents), to serve for seven years. He served his master about six years of the term ; when his master declined business, and informed the pauper that he wished him to get another master for his good. The pauper then went home to his father, who lived in St. Olave, Southwark, with whom he staid three or four weeks; and if the pauper could have got a service in that time, he would have taken it; but not meeting with any, he returned to Grimes, who thereupon told him that he heard Mr. Edwards (who was also a taylor, and lived in Holy Trinity) wanted a man; and told him to go to Edwards, and make an agreement with him for his (the pauper's) good; and that he understood Edwards would take him for twelve months. The pauper accordingly went to

Ed-

Edwards, and entered into an agreement in writing, under seal, with him, covenanting to serve him for twelve calendar months, from the 11th of July, 1768, in his business of a taylor; and Edwards thereby agreed to instruct him in that business, and find him in victuals, drink, and lodging, and at the end of the term, to pay him 12l. in consideration of his service. The agreement was not stamped. The pauper was 19 years of age when he left Grimes; and the indentures were not assigned, or cancelled: but after the pauper had served Edwards two months, Grimes gave him up his indentures; and he continued to serve and board with Edwards to the end of the term agreed, and then received his wages, and applied them to his own use. The question was, whether he gained a settlement by his service with Edwards in Holy Trinity?

LORD KENYON, Ch. J.—It is extremely clear that, while the indentures of apprenticeship continue in force, the apprentice is not *sui juris*, and cannot gain a settlement as a servant. But it has been settled as long ago as the beginning of the late reign, in *Rex v. St. George, Hanover Square*, that the apprentice need not continue in the actual service of the first master during the whole term, but that if he be assigned over by the first master, or continue with his privity and consent in the service of another person, he may gain a settlement by serving the second master forty days. The cases, which have been decided upon this subject, have been determined on nice distinctions: but still those distinctions ought to be adhered to, as they have settled the boundaries on this point. The one is the case of *The King against the inhabitants of Fremington*, where it was held that the apprentice gained a settlement by serving the second master with the *consent of the first*. The case on the other side is that of *Rex v. St. Luke's, Middlesex*, where a *general licence given by the master to the apprentice to serve whom he would*, without any consent to serve any person *in particular*, was held insufficient to enable the apprentice to gain a settlement by serving such second master. Now this case falls within the principle of the former of those: for the apprentice went not only with the consent, but with the express recommendation of the first master, to serve the second, and he went there to follow the same trade which his first master had exercised. It has been said that this case must be governed by that of *Rex v. Sandford*; but there is a solid distinction between that case and the present. For there the master gave up the indentures previous to the pauper's entering into the second service: but here the indentures were not given up till

till more than 40 days had elapsed after the apprentice had served the second master; and that is sufficient to give him a settlement in that parish.   Supposing this question were to arise in another shape, and that the pauper were prosecuted for exercising his trade without having served an apprenticeship according to the statute, there is no doubt but that the service with the second master would be deemed a service under the indentures previous to the time of their being delivered up.

BULLER, J.----The pauper could gain no settlement by living as an hired servant with Edwards, because the indentures of apprenticeship still existed: and the only question is, whether the master did *expressly consent* to that service or not.   For all the cases shew that *mere knowledge* is not sufficient; knowledge does not imply consent.   Now here was an express consent and recommendation of the first master to serve the second, and then the case comes precisely within that of *Rex* v. *Fremington.*   If indeed the apprentice had not gone into Edwards's service, he would not have gained a settlement by serving any other person, because a general licence to serve whom the apprentice chooses, is not sufficient. By going into the service of any other person, the apprentice would have gone without the express consent of the first master, and therefore might have been recalled by such master; but he could not have been recalled by the first master from the service of Edwards, because of the express consent to serve Edwards.   This is distinguishable from the case of *Rex* v. *the Inhabitants of Sandford;* for there the master had given up the indentures, and he had no longer any power over the servant: but here the indentures were in force during the first two months of the pauper's service with Edwards.

GROSE, J.---It is necessary to adhere to the adjudged cases; and I think that this case must be governed by that of *Rex* v. *Fremington.*   And that case also shews that the service with the second master need not be *for the benefit of the first.*   With respect to the case of *Rex* v. *Sandford;* the proper answer has been already given, and the distinction between that case and the present is sufficiently clear.   In this case the indentures were not given up till after forty days service with the second master, which was sufficient to give the apprentice a settlement by serving Edwards with the consent of the first master; and the circumstance of the indentures not being given up till that time rather shews, that the first master intended that the service should continue during that time under the Indentures.   Both orders confirmed.

REX

REX v. *the Inhabitants of* SAMBORN.

Two Justices removed W. Wheyam, from Samborn to Tamworth. Sessions, on appeal, quashed the order.

CASE.

In 1706, a certificate was given by the parish of Tamworth to the hamlet of Samborn, acknowledging H. Wheyam, the grandfather of the pauper, to be an inhabitant legally settled in their parish. T. Wheyam, the father of the pauper, was born at Samborn, under this certificate from Tamworth. W. Wheyam, the present pauper, never gained any settlement for himself; but his settlement depends on the settlement of his father, T. Wheyam. In 1736, a certificate of the pauper's father, T. Wheyam, was given to the parish of Tardebigge; in which T. Allcock and R. Boulton, of Samborn, *churchwarden and overseer of the poor of the parish of Great Coughton*, Warwick, acknowledged T. Wheyam, and E. his wife, to be *inhabitants legally settled at Samborn, in their said parish of Great Coughton*; and promised to receive them *into the said parish* whenever they should become chargeable; and to provide for them as their inhabitants legally *settled within the parish of Great Coughton.* This certificate was properly attested and allowed by two Justices of Warwickshire. The hamlet of Samborn does now, and did at the time of the date of the certificate of 1736, maintain its own poor separately from the parish of Great Coughton; and has, and at that time had, a churchwarden and an overseer of their own, separate from the parish of Great Coughton. T. Allcock and R. Boulton, who signed the certificate of 1736, were churchwardens and overseers of the poor of the *hamlet* of *Samborn*, at the time of granting the certificate.

It was now argued against the order of Sessions; 1st, That the certificate given with the pauper's father was not binding on the hamlet of Samborn, the overseers having styled themselves to be the officers of the *parish at large*; whereas the Certificate Act, 8 and 9 *Will.* III. cap. 30, requires the certificate to be signed by the officers of the parish, *township*, or *place*, and Samborn was, in fact, so far as respects the maintenance of the poor, totally independent of the parish at large,

large.   2dly, The Seffions ought not to have admitted evidence to contradict the certificate, which ftated the perfons granting it to be overfeers of the parifh at large.

LORD KENYON.   I cannot form any doubt in my own mind in this cafe.   The Certificate Act requires that the certificate fhall be figned by the churchwardens and overfeers of the parifh, townfhip, or place, granting the certificate; and it is exprefsly ftated in the concluding part of this cafe that the certificate in queftion was fo figned.

BULLER, J.——The evidence does not *contradict*, but it *explains*, the certificate.

Order of Seffions confirmed.

BENWELL v. BLACK.

The defendant brought a writ of error upon a judgement againft him; and the plaintiff brought another action on the judgement, and recovered, and fued out execution.

The queftion was, Whether he could fue out execution on the fecond judgement, before the writ of error was determined?

LORD KENYON, Ch. J.——There are two ways by which a plaintiff may reap the benefit of his judgement; either by a writ of execution, or by another action. The former is the more regular, as well as the leaft expenfive, mode: but it is admitted that in this cafe the plaintiff is not entitled to that: then we ought not to determine that that which is the moft oppreffive mode of obtaining the effect of the judgment, fhould be the moft favoured; and it would be permitting the plaintiff to do that indirectly which cannot be done directly. We are therefore of opinion, that the plaintiff is not entitled to fue out execution on the fecond judgment, as he could not have taken out execution on the firft.

But as this point had never been fettled before, the Court made the

Rule abfolute, to fet afide the execution.

GWIN-

GWINNET v. PHILLIPS, and others.

This was an action of debt on the 11th Geo. II. cap. 19.
§ 3. to recover double the value of the goods, which were
removed by the defendants to avoid a diftrefs for rent. The
declaration ftated that 57l. was in arrear for rent. It was
proved at the trial, that the notice of diftrefs alleged that
55l. was due; but the plaintiff was ready to fhew, by the
tenant's own admiffion, that 57l. was due : it was objected
that the plaintiff was bound by the notice of diftrefs, and the
plaintiff was nonfuited.

This was a rule to fhew caufe why the non-fuit fhould
not be fet afide, on the ground that the fum mentioned in
the notice was immaterial.

LORD KENYON, Ch. J.—There is no doubt but that if
the plaintiff profefs to fet out his title, he muft fet it out
correctly. So where a contract is to be ftated in a declaration, unlefs it be truly ftated, the plaintiff cannot recover.
But it is now faid, that *in every cafe* the facts alleged by a
plaintiff muft be ftrictly proved, otherwife he muft be non-
fuited. And therefore in an action of covenant for rent for
100l. if the plaintiff proved only 56l. he muft fail. But the
rule can never be carried to fuch an extent. I have heard
both in and out of Courts that the doctrine in *Briftow v.
Wright*, muft be confined to *contracts*. Good fenfe will reconcile all the authorities. If the plaintiff allege any thing
which forms a conftituent part of his title, he muft fet it
out correctly, as was held in *Savage, qui tam*, v. *Smith*.
There the ground of the execution was the judgement; and
though the plaintiff were not bound to have ftated the
judgment, yet being fet out, it ought to have been proved.
But here it was impertient to ftate what the rent was; the
defendants incurred a penalty under this Act of Parliament,
in fraudulently removing the goods which were fubject to
the diftrefs. Whether 5l. or any other fum, were in arrear, was perfectly immaterial; the damages were not to be
meafured by the quantity of rent, but by the value of the
goods removed. And the notice of diftrefs might have been
abandoned; for a party may diftrain for rent, and avow for
fealty.

ASHHURST, J.—If, in a cafe in which a fum of money is a
conftituent part of the plaintiff's demand, it be competent
to

to him to prove a smaller sum than that alleged in the declaration, (and such rule holds where the rent itself is the very ground of the action) *à fortiori*, was it competent to this plaintiff to state any sum as due for rent, since the rent was merely matter of inducement ? The gift of this action is the fraudulent removal of the goods from the premises in order to defeat the distress: it was therefore immaterial to the defendants whether one sum or another were due for rent ; for in either case they are guilty of a tort.

BULLER, J.—If in setting out the demise in this case, the plaintiff had stated a sum as reserved for rent different from that mentioned in the lease, this case would be governed by that of *Bristow* v. *Wright*. But this Court has repeatedly said that that case was not an authority beyond the cases of contracts ; for a contract is entire in its nature, and must be proved as laid. Perhaps the rule laid down in *Bristow* v. *Wright*, will be found to extend to *all cases of records, and written contracts* ; because when the plaintiff is under the necessity of stating a judgment or a record, he must state it truly ; for if he do not, the answer to the action is, that that which is proved is not the same as that which is declared on. But in this case the variance does not consist in any part of the contract, but in an averment of matter subsequent to the contract. The averment was merely a matter of inducement to the action ; and such averments need not be precisely proved.

Rule absolute.

JARMAN v. WOLLORTON, *Assignee of* DOVEY, *a Bankrupt.*

The bankrupt's wife, previous to her marriage, assigned to the plaintiff, as trustee under her marriage-settlement, her stock in trade, &c. for her separate use and disposal, to the intent she might carry on her separate trade, together with her other effects, at the apartments then in her occupation. After the marriage, the goods and effects were removed to the husband's house, where the wife still carried on her trade in a separate apartment there. There was no schedule of the effects annexed to the deed of settlement, but the trustee kept an inventory of the furniture, and some of the effects in question.

Upon the husband's bankruptcy, an action of trover was brought by the trustee against the assignees to recover the

stock

stock in trade and furniture, so settled to the wife's separate use.

Some doubts arose upon the evidence, whether the wife carried on the business strictly for her own separate use; but the Jury found that it was *not carried on separately*, and brought in their verdict for the defendant as to the stock in trade, and for the plaintiff for the furniture.

The defendant now moved for a new trial, on the ground that the trust-deed could not protect the furniture, especially as it was not particularly described and scheduled in the deed; and also because the assignees were entitled to keep the possession by the statute 21 *Ja.* I. cap. 19.

LORD KENYON, Ch. J.—How far it would have been wise to have determined originally that the actual possession should be considered as decisive evidence of all property, is a question now too late to be discussed. Because as far back as the year-books 37 *Hen.* VI. 30, a gradual was limited to *A.* for life, and afterwards to *B.* In modern times the courts, proceeding upon the same principle, have said that personal property may be carved out in the same manner, and possession given to one for life, and then over. Now in this case, before the bankrupt's marriage, a formal settlement was made of all the wife's property, with the consent of both parties. It is true indeed that there was no enumeration of the articles of which her property consisted; and though that circumstance was mentioned, with many others, by Lord Mansfield in *Cadogan* v. *Kennet*, it does not follow that he would have been of a different opinion if that circumstance had not existed in that case. And I do not see what difference it could make; for a schedule conveys no information to the rest of the world, if it were annexed to the settlement, its existence would only be known to the parties interested in it; and therefore such a transaction as this would be equally open to fraud, if there had been a schedule of this furniture as it is now. But the Jury have, by their verdict, negatived fraud; and to be sure there was no ground even to impute it to the transaction. And at the trial, the furniture claimed as the wife's property was fairly identified. Neither do I think that this case is affected by the 21 *Jac.* I. the words of that statute furnish an answer to the defendant's argument; for they are, "that if any person shall become bankrupt, and at such time shall, by the consent of the true owner, have in his *possession*, *order*, *and disposition*, any goods whereof he shall be the reputed owner, and take upon him the *sale*, *alteration*, *or disposition*, as owner, the commissioner, may sell."

BUL-

BULLER, J.—As it strikes me at present, I think the verdict bears rather hard upon the wife respecting the stock in trade. For the weight of evidence is, I think, against the defendants upon that point, and there is no pretence to say that there was fraud in any part of the case. This motion has been made on two grounds; first, that there was no inventory, or any specific account, of the furniture annexed to the deed, so as to identify the wife's property; and, secondly, that the defendants are entitled to these goods under the 21 *Jac.* I. cap. 19. With respect to the latter point, it is sufficient to say that the husband had not the *order and disposition* of this property *with the consent of the real owner.* The trustee was the legal owner; and he gave no consent for such purpose: and the wife's possession, in the manner proved at the trial, is no evidence of fraud; for she was the agent for the trustee. The objection arising from the want of a schedule annexed has no weight; if a schedule were necessary, here was an inventory which will sufficiently answer the purpose. But I think it is unnecessary, considering the nature of the property; it was not always to remain in the same state; the very object of the settlement was, that the wife should sell the goods and purchase others, in order to make a profit of them. In the case of *Haselinton* v. *Gill,* 24 *Geo.* III. some of the goods taken in execution were not those mentioned in the settlement, but stock bought by the wife with the profits of the sale of the milk. That case is an authority for the present throughout.

Rule discharged.

CASTLE v. BURDETT, and others.

This was an action of trespass tried at the Kent Assizes before *Gould,* J. in which the defendants, being excise officers, had seized a quantity of tobacco under the 23 *Geo.* III. cap. 70. The Act says, no writ shall be sued out against any person acting in execution of that statute, until *one calendar month next after notice* in writing, shall have been delivered to him. In this case the notice was served April 28th, and the writ sued out on the 28th of May, and the learned Judge being of opinion that the writ was sued out a day too soon, the plaintiff was non-suited.

Now upon an application to set aside the non-suit, and for a new trial,

THE

THE COURT said, That where a computation is to be made *from* an Act done, the day when such act was done is to be included, according to the rule laid down in the *King* v. *Adderly*, Doug. 446, and the cases there cited.

Rule absolute.

REX *v.* JAMES BEESTON.

The parishioners of *Drayton in Hales*, Salop, at a special public meeting, consented that the church-wardens and over-seers, or the major part of them, should contract with Wil-liam Atherton for maintaining and employing the poor of that parish. In consequence of which the three church-wardens, and two of the overseers, did contract with Atherton for that purpose; but the defendant, who was one of the overseers, refused to join, though he had the requisite sum of the parish money in his hands at the time.

This was a rule to shew cause why a mandamus should not issue against the said overseer, commanding him to pay the sum required. The question was, whether it was ne-cessary that all the church-wardens and overseers should concur in making this contract, or whether the majority of them did not bind the rest, the 9 *Geo.* I. cap. 7, § 4, on which this contract was made, enabling *the church-wardens and overseers of the poor of any parish, with the consent of the major part of the parishioners*, or inhabitants in vestry assembled, to contract.

LORD KENYON, Ch. J.—The construction contended for, namely, that the concurrence of all the overseers is ne-cessary, must have prevailed, if the Legislature had in ex-press terms required it: but as it would be attended with manifest inconvenience, the argument *ab inconvenienti* ought to have great weight in this case where the Legislature have not so required it. A contract has been entered into, in which the parish at large is concerned, and which the Act of Parliament has enabled the parish officers, with the con-currence of the parish, to enter into; and the question is, whether one obstinate man, in opposition to all the rest of the parish, in an act in which they are more interested than he is, shall be able to defeat their purpose. I do not mean to say that the church-wardens and overseers are technically a corporation; but as far as concerns the regulation of the poor of the parish, they stand in *pari ratione*. And in the

in

inftance of corporations, the act of the majority binds the whole; fo much fo, that the Court will compel the perfon who has the cuftody of the corporate feal, to affix it to any act according to the vote of the majority, though againft the confent of fuch perfon; as was done in the cafe of *Wadham College, Cowp.* 377. However, I do not go on the ground of this fimilitude; but the foundation of my opinion is this: the ftat. 43 *Eliz.* cap. 2, has directed that the general acts to be done by the church-wardens and overfeers refpecting the poor, fhall be done by the majority of them; and I think that the fpirit of that ftatute pervades all the fubfequent acts refpecting the government of the poor. The ftatute in queftion I confider as engrafted on the 43 *Eliz.* qualifying the particular act, but referring, for the execution of it, to the manner pointed out by that ftatute. Befides, in common underftanding, what is required to be done by the church-wardens and overfeers, is fatisfied by being done by a *majority*. And indeed if we were to determine otherwife, the inconvenience would be fo great as to make it neceffary for the Legiflature to interfere, and pafs another law. This is very different from the cafe of truftees in fettlements, who are generally chofen by the different branches of the family, in which cafe it is neceffary that they fhould all concur in every act, in order that each may protect the intereft which he was appointed to guard. With refpect to the cafe cited from 3 *Mod.* 371, that perhaps was determined on the ground that the church-wardens were to be confidered as an integral part: though indeed if that were *res integra*, I fhould be inclined to make a contrary determination, becaufe the 43 *Eliz.* enacts that the church-wardens, with certain other perfons, fhall be called overfeers of the poor. On the whole then, as our opinion does not contradict the words of the 9 *Geo.* I. but is conformable to the meaning of it, this rule muft be made abfolute.

BULLER, J. concurred, and faid, the general ufage under another claufe of this Act, ever fince it paffed, fhews what the general underftanding has been of the intention of the Legiflature upon this point. The 8th fection, fpeaking of the time of notice to be given of appeals from orders of removal, fays that no appeal fhall be proceeded on, unlefs reafonable notice be given by the church-wardens and overfeers of the parifh appealing unto the church-wardens and overfeers of the other parifh. But it never was imagined that a notice given only by three church-wardens and overfeers was infufficient; the contrary opinion has always been held.

held.   The ufage therefore fhews what is meant by the general terms " church-wardens and overfeers."

Rule abfolute.

STURDY *and Another, Affignees of* BLAKISTON, *a Bankrupt, againft* ARNAUD.

September 27, 1788, the defendant gave the bankrupt a bond before his bankruptcy, conditioned to pay him 100 l. a year by quarterly payments, upon which this action was brought.   The defendant pleaded that at the time of commencing this action, only four quarterly payments were due; that on the 29th of September, 1788, and before this action was brought, and alfo before the bankruptcy, the defendant had lent 200 l. bearing interest, to the bankrupt and another, on their promiffory note, payable on demand; that the bankrupt, before his bankruptcy, agreed, and *by a writing under his hand*, of the fame date, *authorifed and empowered the defendant to retain out of the annuity*, as the fame fhould become due, the 200 l. and interest; which 200 l. and the interest, still remain due in arrear and unpaid, otherwise than by retaining the fame out of the annuity fo due; and that the arrears of that annuity are ftill infufficient to fatisfy the fame.   The plaintiffs replied the bankruptcy of Blakiston after the above authority given, and the affignment of his effects to the plaintiffs before either of the quarterly payments of the annuity became due.   To this there was a demurrer and joinder.

LORD KENYON, Ch. J—The doctrine of lien and of set-off, bears no relation to the question now before us: and indeed I fhould be forry for the plaintiffs themfelves, if the law were with them, fince their conduct is fo unconfcientious that if the defendant were to apply to a court of equity for relief, that court would not only give fuch relief, but would alfo decree the plaintiffs to pay the cofts both in law and equity; on the fame principle on which Sir Thomas Moore, when Lord Chancellor, proceeded, when he first gave relief againft the penalty of the bond, the obligee in that cafe having paid the fum mentioned in the condition after, though not on, the day.   This is an action brought on a bond, which was made for fecuring the payment of an annuity at certain times in the year; and

be-

before the time of the firſt inſtalment, the obligor lent to
the obligee 200l. in order to ſecure the re-payment of
which, he entered into this agreement, ſtated in the plea,
by which he was authoriſed to retain the payments of the
annuity from time to time, till the 200l. and intereſt,
ſhould be paid. But in anſwer to this it is ſaid, that theſe
payments did not become due till after the bankruptcy of
the obligee, and that therefore they cannot be retained
againſt his aſſignees. Now in juſtice and conſcience it is
impoſſible to raiſe any doubt; neither is there any doubt in
point of law; for the condition of the bond has not been
broken, and conſequently no action can be maintained upon
it. It cannot be ſaid that the condition has been broken,
when it appears that payment has been made according to
the terms of it. For though this is not a formal plea of
ſolvit ad diem, yet it is equivalent to it. But it is ſaid that
this cannot be ſo conſidered, becauſe the aſſignees had a
right to thoſe payments which became due after the bankruptcy: but they have only that property to which the bankrupt is entitled, and they muſt take it ſubject to his equity;
and here thoſe payments were anticipated.

ASHHURST, J.—The defence ſtated in the plea does not
contradict the annuity bond; on the contrary, it is perfectly
conſiſtent with it, and proceeds on the ſuppoſition of there
being ſuch a bond. The plea affirms the bond, and ſpe-
cifies the mode by which the money lent to the obligee
was to be repaid, namely, by retaining the payments ſecured by the annuity bond. And it was competent to the
bankrupt to enter into ſuch an agreement before his bankruptcy.

BULLER, J.—This caſe does not want the aſſiſtance of an
Act of Parliament, or of a court of equity. There is indeed an old caſe which ſaid that payment *before* the day
would not diſcharge the bond. But, in the firſt place, that
caſe has been frequently over-ruled; and, if it were ſtill law,
it would not govern this caſe; becauſe it has been held that
the obligor may plead it as payment *at* the day, and this
would be evidence of ſuch payment.

Judgment for the defendant.

MILNER *and Others, against* MILNES *and Others.*

This was an action of trespass for seizing a boat belonging to the plaintiffs, and converting it to the use of the defendants; to which there was a plea *in bar* that Mary Murgatroyd, one of the plaintiffs, at the time of exhibiting the plaintiff's bill, was covert with R. Medd, her husband, now living. To this plea there was a general demurrer.

In support of the plea, it was contended that though the defendants might have pleaded the coverture in *abatement,* it might also be pleaded *in bar*, and *Audley's* case, *Moore* 25. *Thomson* and *Kitchin*, 11 *Mod.* 177. 3 *Bulstr.* 164. *Powes* v. *Marshal. Sid.* 172. *Blackbourn* v. *Greaves*, 2 *Lev.* 107. 2 *Raym.* 1237, were cited.

LORD KENYON, Ch. J.—We have looked into the cases which were cited in the argument; and though there is no precise precedent in point, we are of opinion, on a review of all the authorities, that this plea in bar cannot be supported. It is extremely clear on the one hand, that the marriage gives to the husband all the personal estate which the wife has in possession: it is also clear on the other hand, that where a *chose in action* of the wife is to be reduced into possession, and it is necessary to bring an action for that purpose, it must be brought in the names of both the husband and wife. And it was absolutely necessary that the wife should be a party to the present action. The defendant, by his plea, imputes to one of the plaintiffs a personal defect: now in general we find that personal disabilities must be pleaded in abatement. It is laid down as a general position in *Com. Dig. Tit. Pleader*, 2 *A.* 1, that coverture in a woman, when either plaintiff or defendant, must be pleaded in abatement: and though no authority is referred to in support of it, yet the opinion alone of so able a lawyer is of great authority. It is true that there is a precedent in the old entries, where the coverture of the plaintiff is pleaded *in bar:* but that is reprobated in 2 *Lutw.* 1641, where it is said that all the other precedents are of pleas *in abatement.* My brother *Buller* has also met with a case in the Year-books 39 *E.* 3. 32 *b*, which shews that this matter should have been pleaded in abatement. As to the case cited from 1 *Sid.* 172, it is true that two of the Judges gave the opinion which was stated by the defendant's counsel: but the other two Judges, namely *Twisden* and *Wyndham*, names of great authority, were of a different opinion, and held that the husband and wife ought to have joined in that action. We are therefore of opinion on the authority of the case in the Year Books, as well as on that of Lord Ch. B. *Comyns*, and on the reason of the thing, that the coverture should have been pleaded in abatement. There is indeed the inconvenience, which was stated at the bar, that the husband may bring error if he please: but that does not conclude this question. With respect to the inconvenience of the shortness of time which the defendant has to plead in abatement, where such a plea is not merely dilatory, but goes to the merits of the cause, the Court will allow him a longer time than the four days to offer such a plea; left the justice of the cause should be precluded, in the same manner that they will permit a rehder after a special imparlance.

Judgment for the plaintiffs.

RADFORD, *qui tam*, against M'INTOSH.

THIS was an action on the statute 27 Geo. III. cap. 26. The first count in the declaration stated, that after the first of August, 1785, mentioned in a certain Act, &c. made in the 25th year of the present reign, entituled "An Act," &c. (25 Geo. III. cap. 51), and also after the 1st of August, 1787, and within six calendar months before the commencement of this suit, to wit, on the 18th of November, 1789, at Driffield in the county of York, the defendant, then and there being a person letting horses to hire for the purpose of travelling post by the mile, and from stage to stage, and *being duly licensed* according to the form of the statute in such case made and provided, to wit, at, &c. did let divers, to wit, two horses to hire by the mile or stage, to be used in travelling post in Great Britain, that is to say, from Driffield to Bridlington Quay, in the county aforesaid, the same being a great distance, and then ascertained, to wit, 15 miles; and did, upon such letting to hire, then and there receive to and for the use of the plaintiff, who sues as aforesaid *(the said plaintiff being then and there the farmer or renter of rates and duties in that respect granted by the first-mentioned Act of Parliament)*, according to the form of the statute in such case made and provided, of and from the person hiring the said horses a large sum of money, to wit, 1 $d.\frac{1}{4}$ per mile, for each of the said horses, for each mile the said horses were hired to go, to wit, 15 miles, amounting in the whole to a large fum of money, to wit, the fum of 3*s*. 9*d*. yet the defendant, not regarding the ftatutes, &c. after he had received the faid fum of money as and for the rates and duties as aforefaid, to wit, on &c. at &c. was guilty of *making falfe accounts* in refpeɛt to the faid rates and duties, that is to fay, *in that he did not*, at any time in the weekly account kept by him for that week, wherein he fo received the faid money as laft aforefaid, under and by virtue of the ftatute in fuch cafe made and provided, *account for the faid fum of money fo received by him as laft aforefaid*, but wholly negleɛted and omitted fo to do, and after the receipt of the fame, to wit, on &c. at &c. attended, delivered in, and paffed, his faid account, wherein the faid fum of money ought to have been inferted as aforefaid, in purfuance of the faid ftatutes in that cafe made and provided, the faid fum of money not being accounted for therein; and the defendant did not at any time account for the fame; *with intent to defraud the plaintiff*, who fues as aforefaid, of the faid rate or duty impofed by the faid firft-mentioned aɛt, and by him the defendant received as laft aforefaid, cor:trary to the form of the ftatute, &c.

The fifth count was nearly fimilar to the firft; except that it ftated that the defendant had let divers, to wit, *eight* horfes, &c.

BULLER, J. before whom the caufe was tried at the York Affizes, ftated to the Court, that a licence to let poft-horfes was produced in evidence, granted by the plaintiff to the defendant; but it did not appear on the inftrument whether this licence was granted by the plaintiff in the charaɛter of *collector* of the duties, or of *farmer-general*. But at the bottom of it was a memorandum, fignifying that application muft be made to the *farmer-general* of the duties to renew this licence annually; and on this piece of paper feveral entries were made by the defendant. It was alfo proved that the defendant had, on feveral occafions, accounted with the plaintiff for the duties colleɛted under this aɛt, but had omitted in this inftance the fums ftated in the firft and fifth counts, though inftead of having let *eight* horfes, as alleged in the fifth count, he had only let *five*. No grant of the duties to the plaintiff was produced either from the Lords of the Treafury, or from the Commiffioners of the Stamp-Duties, who had only a *general* commiffion under the Great Seal, granted to them before the paffing of this Aɛt of Parliament. It was firft objeɛted on the part of the defendant

that

that the plaintiff who fued as farmer-general, had not proved himfelf to be fo, becaufe a legal appointment could only be made either by the Lords of the Treafury, or by the Commiffioners of the Stamp-Duties duly and fpecially empowered by them ; and, 2dly, that the evidence on the fifth count did not correfpond with the declaration; for it was ftated that the defendant had let to hire *eight* horfes, whereas the plaintiff only proved a letting of *five* ; and this being a contract of hire, it ought to have been fet out correctly. A verdict was taken for the plaintiff for two penalties, on the firft and fifth counts ; with liberty to the defendant to move to enter a nonfuit, if the firft objection were well founded ; or to enter a verdict for the defendant on the fifth count, if he were right on the fecond objection.

LORD KENYON, Ch. J.—In penal actions on the 2 & 3 *Ed*. VI cap. 13, § 2, which enables the owners of tithes to recover double the value, in cafe they are withdrawn, it has always been held fufficient proof againft the defendant that the party fuing is in the act of receiving the tithes from him. So in this cafe, the defendant had admitted that the plaintiff ftood in the relation of farmer-general to the duties, by accounting with him as fuch.

BULLER, J.—It appears that the defendant has treated with the plaintiff in the character of a farmer-general. Then this comes within the clafs of cafes mentioned by my Lord, and other inftances of actions for non-refidence, where it is fufficient to prove the defendant in poffeffion of the church, without proving prefentation, inftitution, and induction : as was held in *Bevan, qui tam,* v. *Williams,* E. 16 *Geo*. III.

And the Rule was difcharged.

A motion was then made to arreft the judgment ; becaufe no offence within the Act of Parliament was ftated in the declaration, becaufe the defendant is charged with having made falfe accounts, *in not inferting in the account the fum of money received by him* ; whereas the Act of Parliament only requires that the account fhall contain the number of horfes, and of miles, and the names of the drivers.

BY THE COURT. Judgment muft be arrefted on this objection. The ftatute 25 *Geo*. III. only requires the poftmafters, in making up their accounts, to infert therein the number of horfes let, and the number of miles, but does not require the amount of the duties received, to be fpecified. There is indeed a fchedule mentioned in the twelfth fection, but no penalty is given by that claufe ; and the fubfequent fection, which creates the penalty, does not require that the fums received fhould be inferted in the account, but only

Z 2

the materials which furnish the amount of the sums. It may be true, therefore, that the defendant has neglected to do that which is imputed to him, and yet have complied with all the requisites of the Act. Whether or not it would have been sufficient to state generally that the defendant had been guilty of delivering in a false account, without specifying in what particular instance it was so, we give no opinion, though perhaps such a general allegation might not be sufficient even after verdict: but the plaintiff in this case, after having alleged generally that the defendant had been guilty of making false accounts, proceeded to state in what the falsity of the account consisted; and, as that particular charge did not constitute any offence within the Act of Parliament, the plaintiff could not avail himself of the general allegation, even if it were sufficiently descriptive of an offence.

Rule absolute.

N. B. In a similar Case, where it was objected that it was not proved that the defendant was licensed, because the licence itself was not produced, and the plaintiff was non-suited, on a motion to set aside that non-suit,

BULLER, J. said, that he was convinced that there was no weight in the objection; that it was not necessary to prove a licence having been granted in fact, for that other evidence would be sufficient against the defendant, as that he had written up over his door " licensed to let post-horses."

REX v. the Marquiss of STAFFORD, and T. GIFFARD, Esq.

This was an application for a mandamus requiring the Lords of the Manor of Stowe Heath, in Staffordshire, to present to the Ordinary the nomination of W. Morton, Clerk, to be stipendiary Priest and Curate of the Chapel of Willenhall, in the said Manor, in order that he might obtain a licence from the ordinary

The affidavit stated the usage to be, that the minister ought to be nominated and appointed by the inhabitants of Willenhall, having lands of inheritance within the town, and presented and allowed by the Lord of the Manor of Stowe Heath. That it appeared from an ancient roll of the manor, dated in the 6th year of James I. that certain proceedings had been held before the commissioners of charitable uses; and that it had been consented and agreed that

cer-

certain copyhold lands therein mentioned fhould be let towards the reparation of the chapel and the maintenance of a ftipendiary prieft, for the faying of divine fervice, miniftering the facraments, &c. who fhould be from time to time chofen and appointed by the inhabitants of Willenhall having lands there, and prefented and allowed by the Lord of the Manor of Stowe Heath; and that the perfon fo appointed fhould conform to the Ecclefiaftical government, and refide on the curacy; and on complaint to the Lord of the Manor by the inhabitants, of his non-refidence, infufficiency, negligence, or any other mifdemeanor, the Lord of the Manor fhould give him half a year's notice to reform, and, if he did not reform, fhould prefent and allow another curate, &c. to be nominated and appointed by the inhabitants, &c. as aforefaid.   That on the death of the late incumbent, in December, 1781, William Moreton and A. Haden were the candidates; and in order to determine the election, a poll was fuggefted by the defendants; that Moreton had 67 votes, and Haden 29, on which the former was nominated and appointed by a majority, by a proper inftrument; but that the defendants refufed to allow his nomination, and prefent him to the Ordinary.   The affidavits in anfwer ftated, that this was originally a free and private chapel, built by, and belonging to, the Lords of the Manor of Stowe Heath: and is purely a donative, without the admiffion, inftitution, or induction, of or by the Ordinary, or any other Ecclefiaftical authority; and has not been augmented by Queen Anne's bounty. That the immediate predeceffor of the laft incumbent, who was appointed in 1720, was conftituted and allowed to be minifter by the defendants' anceftors by a deed, by which, after reciting that " the major part of the inhabitants of Willenhall, having lands there, had *(as much as they might or could)* elected and nominated E. Holbrooke, and had defired them (the defendants' anceftors) to allow him, &c." they prefented, and Holbrooke entered upon and performed the office, without any other inftrument.   [A fimilar appointment of the late incumbent in 1744 was alfo ftated. And with refpect to the late election, it was ftated that 43 of Moreton's electors were not refident in the town of Willenhall, but in adjoining diftricts within the hamlet of Willenhall; and that only four who voted for Haden were liable to that objection].   That the defendants had approved of Haden's nomination, and allowed and prefented him.   And that Moreton was a man of indecent and immoral life; that within the laft three years he had been repeatedly and notorioufly toriously guilty of drunkenness, swearing, gaming, lewd conversation, and other immoralities; and that he had not only neglected his duty as a minister, but had been actually in a state of ebriety whilst in the performance of divine service.

Erskine and *Leycester*, shewed cause against this rule in last Michaelmas Term; insisting, 1st, That the defendants did not act merely ministerially in allowing the nomination by the freeholders, but that they had a right to approve or reject the person so nominated; 2dly, That this benefice was purely a donative; and though the defendants, who were the patrons, could not arbitrarily reject the person nominated by the resiant freeholders, yet that they might reject him for any cause, which would be a sufficient ground to warrant a bishop in rejecting a person presented to him in the case of a presentative benefice. And that it sufficiently appeared by the affidavits in answer to this application, that Moreton was of such an immoral character as would have justified a bishop in refusing to admit him; and 3dly, That Moreton had another specific legal remedy, by *quare impedit*, which was a complete answer to an application for a *mandamus*.

BY THE COURT. It will be too much to determine whether the defendants have a right to approve or reject *on affidavits*. And if the defendants are to be considered as trustees, in executing that trust they are to exercise a proper discretion, and to judge whether the party were or were not *idoneus*, as a bishop may do in the case of a presentative, and may absolutely reject the nominee on account of his being illiterate, which question of fitness cannot be tried by a jury, but of which he is the sole judge. But as Mr. Moreton has been rejected on account of immorality and indecent conduct, that question may be properly determined by a jury of his country, to whom he has a right to appeal on the truth of the facts alleged against him. If however those facts are true, the defendants may return them upon the record. But as to the argument that Moreton has a remedy by *quare impedit*, the Court were inclined to think it would not lie, and were about to make the rule absolute, but afterwards ordered this point to be again argued;—after which, on a future day, the Court gave judgment.

LORD KENYON, Ch. J.—It appears from the ancient roll, referred to in the affidavits, that certain proceedings had been had before the commissioners of charitable uses, respecting the lands appropriated to the maintenance of the curate; and therefore it seems as if the inhabitants have

only

only an *equitable right*; if so, this Court cannot interfere at all; or if the inhabitants have a *legal right*, such right may be asserted in a *quare impedit*. Therefore *quácunque viâ datâ* this rule must be discharged. Perhaps the better remedy will be, an information in the Court of Chancery in the name of the Attorney General. Supposing this had been a legal right, there is one case (in addition to those cited) which my brother *Ashhurst* has found in *Rast.* 506, *b*, which shews that a *quare impedit* will lie by the persons having the right of nomination against him who has the presentation, and who obstructs the right. As to the case cited from 2 *Burr.* 1043, that was a *mandamus to be restored* to the curacy; there a *quare impedit* would not have lain, and the party applied for the only specific remedy to make him curate *de facto*.

ASHHURST, J. of the same opinion.

BULLER, J.—This determination will not interfere with any of the adjudged cases. For it appears to me on these affidavits, that this is a *trust*, and therefore that the remedy is in a court of equity. A party applying for a *mandamus*, must make out a *legal* right; though if he shew such legal right, and there be also a remedy in equity, that is no answer to an application for a *mandamus*; for when the Court refuse to grant a *mandamus*, because there is another specific remedy, they mean only a *specific remedy at law*.

GROSE, J.—This Court will grant a *mandamus*, where the party applying has no other specific legal remedy, or if such other remedy be obsolete. But here the party applying has no legal right; or if he have, it may be asserted in another legal mode.

Rule discharged.

REX v. MEIN.

This was an application for a *quo warranto* against the defendant, to shew by what authority he claimed to be portreeve of the borough of Fowey, in Cornwall; the relator produced an affidavit of the Recorder, stating Fowey to be an ancient borough, sending members to parliament since the 13th of *Elizabeth*, and that the portreeve is the returning officer. That, by the constitution of the borough, such persons only have a right to vote at elections as are Prince's tenants, duly admitted upon the court-rolls of the borough and manor of Fowey, in right of the freehold estates within

the

the borough, and who have done their fealty, and in such inhabitants of the borough only as pay scot and lot. That the Prince of Wales, as Duke of Cornwall, is lord of the borough and manor. The affidavit then impeached the titles of fifty persons, as having been improperly admitted at the last Court, held on the 26th of November, 1789; they having been admitted before any homage was sworn, and *without any presentment being made of their titles*; and because the steward had sworn-in 20 of those newly-admitted persons, together with the defendant, Thomas Mein, (who had before been admitted) upon the homage, for the purpose of presenting the defendant to be portreeve of the borough, which they accordingly did; and he was sworn-in immediately. In answer to which the defendant filed another affidavit, setting forth the method of electing the portreeve; and denying the custom of admitting tenants to be as stated in the relator's affidavit: and setting forth three instances of admissions from the court-rolls, the only instances to be found for 150 years back, to the contrary.

It was contended, *inter alia*, against the rule, that the affidavit in support of it having omitted to state in whom the right of election to this office was, the prosecutor could not resort to the affidavit on the other side to supply this omission.

LORD KENYON, Ch. J.—If the matter had rested on the relator's affidavit alone, I should have been clearly of opinion that the information could not go: but upon conference with my brothers, I find that it is not unusual to have recourse to the affidavits against the rule in order to come (if possible) at the whole truth of the transaction. And I agree that in so doing we must not garble any sentence referred to, so as to give it a different meaning from that which it naturally imports when taken altogether; but still we are not bound to take the whole of it to be true, but merely to refer to it as evidence of certain facts. Now the relator's affidavit had omitted to state in whom the right of election was to the office of portreeve, which chasm is filled up by the defendant's affidavit, disclosing the method of election. Then the next question is, whether such an office as that of portreeve is of magnitude sufficient for the Court to take notice of by way of information in the nature of *quo warranto*. Of that I cannot entertain a doubt. A portreeve, *ex vi termini*, implies a public peace officer, and he is here cloathed with that very important constitutional office of returning officer; that is perfectly sufficient to bring him within the scope of this information. But then

then it is objected that the titles of electors cannot be impeached through the medium of the elected; and the case in *Cowper*, 507, has been relied on: but there the electors were members of a corporation, whose titles might have been questioned in quo warranto informations; and there too Lord *Mansfield* laid considerable stress on the voters having been in the possession of their franchises for twelve years. At all events that rule cannot be extended to cases where the titles of those electors cannot be impeached at all; in such cases, of necessity their titles must be attacked by discussing the validity of the election made by them, in a proceeding against the person elected. Such is the case of a Coroner, who is elected by the freeholders of the county. Upon an information of this sort, the titles of the several freeholders who voted for him must come in discussion, and yet no such information lies against them for exercising a right incidental to the freehold. So in the case of a Steward of a Court-Leet. The same answer occurs here; it is a case of equal necessity. What sort of information could be framed against persons of the description of the Prince's tenants? They have an incidental power of electing the portreeve in the same manner as the freeholders of the county have with respect to the Coroner; and they are no more than freeholders. Lastly, it is objected that the evidence of the defendant outweighs that of the relator; now admitting it to be so, that has never been held to be an answer to an application of this kind. Where there is evidence on both sides, the Jury are the constitutional judges on which side the balance inclines; all that we are to look to is that a fair doubt is raised, and that the parties applying come with clean hands, and in proper time.

AsHHURST, J.—I entirely concur; and indeed I should have been of opinion that an information would have lain against the defendant to try his title to the office of portreeve, even if he had not been stated to be the returning officer.

Rule absolute.

COOKE

COOKE v. OXLEY.

This was a rule to fhew caufe why judgment fhould not be arrefted, on the ground that there was no confideration for the defendant's promife, in the following

CASE.

The defendant propofed to the plaintiff that the former fhould fell and deliver to the latter, 266 hogfheads of to-bacco at a certain price; whereupon the plaintiff defired the defendant to give him time to agree to, or diffent from, the propofal till the hour of four in the afternoon of that day, to which the defendant agreed; and thereupon the defendant propofed to the plaintiff to fell and deliver the fame upon the terms aforefaid, *if the plaintiff would agree to purchafe them upon the terms aforefaid, and would give notice thereof to the defendant before the hour of four in the afternoon of that day.* The plaintiff averred that he did agree to purchafe the fame upon the terms aforefaid, and did give notice thereof to the defendant before the hour of four in the af-ternoon of that day; he alfo averred that he requefted the defendant *to deliver* to him the faid hogfheads, and offered to pay to the defendant the faid price for the fame, yet that the defendant did not. &c.

At the trial a verdict had been taken for the plaintiff.

LORD KENYON, Ch. J.—Nothing can be clearer than that at the time of entering into this contract, the engage-ment was all on one fide; the other party was not bound; it was therefore *nudum pactum.*

BULLER, J.—It is impoffible to fupport this declaration in any point of view. In order to fuftain a promife, there muft be either a damage to the plaintiff, or an advantage to the defendant; but here was neither when the contract was firft made. Then as to the fubfequent time, the promife can only be fupported on the ground of a new contract made at four o'clock; but there is no pretence for that. It has been argued that this muft be taken to be a complete fale from the time when the condition was complied with: but it was not complied with, for it is not ftated that the defendant did agree at four o'clock to the terms of the fale; or even that the goods were kept till that time.

GROSE,

GROSE, J.—The agreement was not binding on the plaintiff before 4 o'clock; and it is not stated that the parties came to any subsequent agreement; there is, therefore no consideration for the promise.

Rule absolute.

DAY v. HANKS.

In an action on the case for disturbing the plaintiff in his right of common, the declaration contained two counts, for disturbances in two distinct commons; as to the first of which, the defendant suffered judgment to go by default: and upon the second he took issue, and upon trial obtained a verdict.

The plaintiff afterwards obtained a rule *nisi* for the *postea* to be delivered to him, and for the Master to tax his costs thereon.

And THE COURT were clearly of opinion that the plaintiff was not entitled to the costs of the trial; but, whether the defendant was entitled to such costs, they said would more properly come under consideration upon a review of the Master's taxation: they therefore directed that the *postea* should be lodged in the hands of the Master, that he might tax the plaintiff his costs on the judgment by default, and tax the defendant his costs on the verdict obtained on the second count.

A rule was now obtained for the defendant to shew cause why the Master's taxation of costs accordingly should not be set aside: and it was argued in support of the rule, that as the plaintiff is entitled to judgment on one count, the defendant cannot have judgment for his costs on the other; for then there would be two judgments, one for one party, and the other for the other party, on the same record.

BY THE COURT. There will be no incongruity in this case on the record. If the Court see two separate causes of action on the same record, on one of which the plaintiff succeeds, and the other is found for the defendant, they are bound to give two distinct judgments. So in an action for an assault and battery against two defendants, if one suffer judgment by default, and the other justify and obtain a verdict, there must be two separate judgments on the record. Here the plaintiff will have judgment up to the whole extent to which he is entitled, by having judgment for his costs on the first count, as to which the defendant made default:

fault: and as to the other count, which contains a separate cause of action, and which has been found for the defendant, he is equally intitled to have judgment for his costs incurred by the trial of that issue.

Rule discharged.

CROSS v. SALTER.

At the Exeter Affizes an action upon the case was tried before Baron *Hotham*, brought by the plaintiff, who claimed a pew in his parish church, and complained that the defendant interrupted him in the enjoyment of it. Plea, the general issue. The plaintiff called witnesses, who proved that he, and those whose estate he claimed, had sat in the pew between 50 and 60 years past, from the time that it was first built for one Richard Cross; and that before that time there were long benches on the spot, on which the singers used to sit. He also produced a sentence in the Consistorial Court of Exeter, dated January 26, 1787; and also the proceedings upon appeal to the Court of Arches, and the sentence thereon in the same year; and the final sentence of the Court of Delegates. The libel in the Consistorial Court was exhibited by the present plaintiff against the defendant and his wife; wherein the proponent alleged that Richard Cross, of Halberton, from whom he claimed, had, about the year 1736, built, at his own expence, the pew in question, *in right of a certain messuage called Rowridge*, situate in Halberton, and had peaceably enjoyed the same, and repaired it at his own expence; and he complained against Salter's disturbance of his *interest*, *right*, and *property* therein several times during the year 1785: that Court sentenced " That J. Cross (the plaintiff), had fully proved the purpose of his said libel, &c. and that nothing effectual on the part of the defendants had been alleged or proved to the contrary, &c. wherefore it was *decreed that the pew in question did belong to the said plaintiff, as owner of a certain messuage called Rowridge*, in the said parish of Halberton; that the defendant and his wife had intruded themselves into it, and thereby disturbed the plaintiff's right; and it admonished the defendants to quit the same, and not to disturb the plaintiff in his right of sitting in the said pew; it also condemned the defendants in costs." Upon an appeal to the Court of Arches from this sentence, that Court reversed the former sentence, and retained the principal cause; and by interlocutory

cutory decree *admonished the defendant and his wife not to fit in the said pew,* and condemned them in costs. From this second sentence, the defendant Salter and his wife appealed to the Delegates, on the ground that the Court of Arches had done wrong in retaining the principal cause, and in admonishing them *not to fit in the pew,* and condemning them in costs; that Court, on July the 6, 1789, dismissed the appeal with costs, and remitted the cause to the arches.

The defendant's counsel rested the defence upon the ground that the sentence of reversal in the Court of Arches, (confirmed by the sentence of the Court of Delegates,) having a concurrent jurisdiction upon this question with the courts of common law, was conclusive against the claim of *right* set up by the plaintiff, and on which this action was founded; and the learned Judge being of that opinion, nonsuited the plaintiff.

A rule having been obtained to shew cause why the nonsuit should not be set aside, it was now argued, in support of the rule, that, as against a wrong-doer the plaintiff had proved his case by proving possession; besides which, the possession of 50 years was strong evidence either of a prescriptive right, or of a faculty.

LORD KENYON, Ch. J. expressed a doubt, on the authority of *Kenrick v. Taylor,* 1 *Wils.* 326, whether possession alone was not sufficient against a wrong doer; and took time to consider of the case; but on a subsequent day his Lordship said the Court had looked into the proceedings in the Ecclesiastical Courts, which they were of opinion were not *conclusive* evidence; but what weight they would have on a trial, was not for their consideration.

Rule absolute.

REX *v.* JAMES HAIGH *and another.*

The defendants being overseers of a parish in Yorkshire were indicted before *Buller* J. at the Assizes for disobeying an order of a Justice for the payment of a weekly sum to one Mary Gray, for the maintenance of her bastard child; and it was argued on the part of the defendants that the were not bound to obey the order as the mother refused to go herself into the workhouse, alledging that she asked relief for the child only; though the stat. 9 *Geo.* I. Cap 7, §. 4. enacts that " in case any poor person in any parish where such house
shall

shall be so purchased shall refuse to be lodged, kept, or maintained, in such house, such poor person or persons so refusing shall be put out of the book where the names of the persons who ought to receive collection are registered, and shall not be entitled to ask or receive collection or relief from the churchwardens and overseers, &c."

At the trial a verdict was taken against the defendants, subject to the opinion of this Court.

LORD KENYON, Ch. J. The only question is, for whom was the relief asked? For such person only is, according to the terms of this act of parliament, to be sent to the workhouse. It is stated that the *child* only wanted relief; the application was indeed made by the mother, but it was not on her own account, but for her child only who was of too tender an age to apply herself. This is therefore very distinguishable from the case of *Rex* v. *Carlisle*, *Doug.* 317, where the relief was asked both for the parent and the child. It would be extremely hard, and contrary to the spirit and words of this act of parliament, if, when all the children of a family (except one) were capable of supporting themselves, and that one were unable either from the want of reason or of the use of its limbs to maintain itself, and were under the necessity of receiving relief, the whole family were to be sent to the work-house. Such a law would not only be repugnant to all ideas of mercy and humanity, but would also be prejudicial to the interest of the parish, who would in some measure be deprived of the benefit of the labour of such of the family as were able to work; for they could earn much more out of the work-house than in it.

Per Curiam,   Judgment for the prosecutor.

SMITH v. MULLER.

At the trial of this action there was a *reference of all matters in dispute between the parties in the cause, and the costs of the cause were to abide the event and determination of the award.* The arbitrator awarded and found these special facts; that the plaintiff sued out the writ on the 14th of November 1788, returnable the 20th November, when special bail was put in; that the declaration was filed in Hilary-term, 1789, entitled as of that term, stating the defendant to be indebted to the plaintiff for use and occupation before the 1st January, 1789, and upon other counts; that 1*l.* 11*s.* 6*d.* became due at Christmas,

mas, 1788, for a quarter's rent; that the defendant paid into Court all the rent due at Michaelmas 1788, and the plaintiff's other demands; that at Christmas, 1788, he tendered the rent which became due at that time, which was refused: and that the sum of 1*l.* 11*s.* 6*d.* was the whole sum remaining due from the defendant to the plaintiff, after the payment of the money into Court.

The question was, whether the declaration could include the rent which became due subsequent to Michaelmas term?

BY THE COURT.—We are clearly of opinion that the declaration should have been entituled of Michaelmas term; and that on application for that purpose they would have ordered it to be amended accordingly. The defendant therefore is not liable to the costs.

BULLER, J. added, that notwithstanding the difference between a reference " of all matters in dispute between the parties in the cause," and " of all matters in dispute in the cause between the parties," was now clearly and fully understood by the practicers of the Court, yet that the distinction was too refined for the general understanding of mankind; and therefore he thought it would be better to amend the terms of the reference thus: to make the former a reference " of all matters in difference between the parties," omitting the other words " in the cause;" and the latter a reference of " all matters in difference in the cause," omitting " between the parties." With respect to this particular case, it is the clear and undoubted practice of the Court that the declaration should have been delivered as *of* the term when the writ was returnable. According to the ancient practice the declaration was actually delivered in the same term; it was only in ease of the plaintiff that the time of actual delivery was enlarged; but still it must be considered as delivered *nunc pro tunc.* As to the practice of declaring, by the bye, that goes on a different ground: a declaration by the bye is not on the original writ: but the party being in Court in one action, a plaintiff may declare against him in another within two terms. Neither does any difficulty arise from the practise of pleading in abatement; for under such circumstances as the present the defendant might have entered a special imparlance, if necessary, or he might have filed the plea in abatement as of the Michaelmas term. Then as to the last case put at the bar of the action against two defendants, such a case cannot exist on one writ. For if both defendants are served before the return of the writ, and one of them do not appear in the same term, he must plead as of the

the term when he ought to have appeared; and if he be not served before the return of the writ, the plaintiff must sue out another writ.

Rule discharged.

LITTLER v. HOLLAND.

The plaintiff covenanted to build two houses for the defendant for 500l. on or before the 1st of april, 1788. An action was brought for the payment of the 500l. at the Stafford Assizes, when it appeared that the work was not completed on the first of April, 1788; but that the parties by a parol agreement, after the date of these articles, enlarged the time; and that the whole work was finished before the expiration of that enlarged time. On an objection taken by the defendant's Counsel that this did not prove the allegation in the declaration, which stated that the houses were built by the 1st of April, according to the agreement, the plaintiff was nonsuited.

LORD KENYON, Ch. J.—This point is so clear, that I am not inclined to grant a rule to shew cause. The declaration charges that the parties had stipulated by deed to perform a specific thing on a certain day : then if the plaintiff, who sues on that contract, be not bound to prove it as laid, the defendant has no notice of that which he had called upon to answer. I remember an action being brought many years ago by Mr. Garrick, or one of the managers of the theatres, against Barry for not performing his contract; it appeared on the trial that the manager had given the defendant a *parol* licence to be absent; but as the articles, on which the action was founded, required such a licence to be *in writing*, this Court held that it could not be dispensed with, and that the parol agreement was no answer to the plaintiff's action; though perhaps the defendant had another remedy in a court of equity.

BY THE COURT,   Rule refused.

ELIZABETH CHAPMAN, *verſus* WILLIAM SHAW,
*Attorney at Law. Action of Damages for a Breach of pro-
miſe of Marriage; before* LORD KENYON, *in the* COURT
of KING'S BENCH *May* 22, 1790.

Counſel for the plaintiff.

Mr. MINGAY,

Mr. GARROW.

For the Defendant.

Mr. ERSKINE,

Mr. LAW.

Mr. MINGAY,

I am Counſel for Miſs Chapman; ſhe is the daughter of
a very reſpectable tradeſman; you will find by the evidence which I ſhall produce to you, that the defendant
uſed every little art and addreſs by which men too often
get poſſeſſion of the affections of the other ſex. He
from time to time, viſited the family, and repeatedly
promiſed to marry this lady. You will find by his letters, and by the evidence of a great number of perſons, he
pretended it was impoſſible for him to enjoy any happineſs in this world without marrying her; and in this
manner he got complete poſſeſſion of her affections; he
kept up this intimacy with her until the very time that he
was married to another lady; he repeatedly ſaid that he
would marry her, although contrary to the inclinations
of his family; and, immediately after, to her utter ſurpriſe,
the plaintiff found that he had married a young lady in
Yorkſhire; what fortune induced him to this marriage, I
know not, although I ſhall be able to give general evidence of his ſituation and circumſtances. It is not poſſible
to aggravate a caſe of this kind by any obſervations I can
make. There cannot be a more unjuſt, a more unmanly
conduct, than for a man to ſeduce a woman's affections by
every little art and ſtratagem, when at the ſame time he has

no serious intentions of marrying her, and I trust you will mark it by your verdict. I shall call witnesses, and prove my case, and then you, Gentlemen of the Jury, will give to this young lady such a satisfaction in damages, as the nature of the case seems to require.

Mrs. MARY CHAPMAN, *sworn*.

The plaintiff is my daughter. From the latter end of August, 1787, to the latter end of July, 1789, Mr. Shaw paid his addresses to her; during all that time she resided in my family. During that time, except about ten weeks, when he was in the country, he was every day at our house; he was received with approbation by my husband and the rest of the family; he was traited as a suitor to my daughter; he entered into a conversation with me respecting his intentions towards my daughter about the latter end of July, 1788; says he, " Mrs. Chapman, I and Miss Chapman have agreed to be married." I answered——"Well——I approve of it." I then turned about to him, thinking that he was going to say something more upon the subject. He looked a little *shy*, and said, " I thought, Madam, it was best to acquaint you with it." This was all the conversation that passed at that time in the parlour. Mr. Shaw then went up stairs, and I followed to the room where my daughter had her musick, and where she slept; " My dear," said he, addressing himself to my daughter, " I have acquainted your mother at last." " What did you say?" said she. " I have told your mother," said he, " that you and I have agreed to be married."——I turned into the other room, where my husband and I slept. I thought I would not interrupt them. About an hour after that he went away. I do not know that I had any conversation with my daughter, on this subject, that night. The next day was Sunday, when Mr. Shaw was again at our house——he was at our house every day; he said he would communicate every thing to Miss Chapman, and open to her all his future hopes and prospects in life; he took leave, very kindly, of all my family when he went into the country for the vacation. I think I saw him again about the middle of October following. Mr. Shaw and my daughter were extremely fond of one another. After his return from the country, he said, " Miss Chapman, I'll bring your brother-in-law to see you;" meaning his own brother. He turned about to me, in the presence of my daughter, and said, " Mrs. Chapman, I'll bring my brother to see you." I said, " Sir, I shall be very glad to see

fee him, and be proud of his company." In a fhort time
after this, he brought Mr. John Shaw to my houfe.   Mr.
Shaw, the defendant, had chambers, and I was prefent at a
converfation in my houfe, when he faid " Mifs Chapman,
will you go and fee how you like my chambers?" This was
in the month of May, 1788.   " Pray," faid he, " go and
fee whether they will do for us."   He was at this time in
pofleflion of the chambers.   He then turned about to me,
and faid, " Mrs. Chapman, won't you go and fee my
chambers?" I anfwered him, " I have no notion of ladies
going to fee gentlemen's chambers."   After his return, in
the month of October, he continued for fome time to pay
his attention to my daughter.   He married in October,
1789, at the diftance of a year.   I never faw any alteration
in his behaviour.   I know no reafon that my daughter gave
him to break off his connexion.   I did not fufpect any more
than the firft moment he was in her company.   I had not
the leaft fufpicion that he was courting another lady, until
about two months before he was married.   He married
a Mifs Wright.   My daughter is twenty-three years of age;
Mr. Shaw is about twenty-four or twenty five years of age,
and is an Attorney.   On the 16th of December, Mr. Shaw
fent for me to Mr. Brown's; faid he, " Mrs. Chapman, I acquainted you with the affair between Mifs Chapman and me."
" Certainly you did," faid I.   " You told me that you and
Mifs Chapman had agreed to be married."   I then upbraided
him with every thing I could think of, and afked him how
he could do what he had done; he faid he was very forry
for it; he was very forry he was married, for that Mifs
Chapman was a very virtuous young lady, and of ftrict integrity; he had no fault to find with her, nor with any belonging to her; he then had on a ring with fome of my
daughter's hair in it; he faid, he knew he had acted very
cruelly to her; he was very willing to make her a recompence.   He faid he had no fortune with his wife, but about
an hundred pounds.   This converfation paffed in the prefence of Mr. Brown.   Mr. Brown faid, " Mr. Shaw, you
would have had a devilifh deal more with Mifs Chapman."
He faid he wifhed he had known; that he had got no property of his own.   I afked him what recompence he could
make her.   He faid, he would make her a yearly recompence.   I upbraided him with the injuftice and unmanlinefs
of the whole of his conduct.

   Crofs-examined by Mr. Erfkine.   My hufband is a chair-
maker.   I have eight children; three of whom are daughters.

In
re daught

In the month of July, 1788, my son was fellow-clerk with the defendant; he introduced him first into our house. He said, " Mother, I shall have a gentleman or two, and hope you will make a little entertainment." I said, I would. After Mr. Shaw had visited at our house for some time, I observed him pay a particular attention to my daughter. I knew perfectly well who he was: he was clerk at the office of Mr. Sharples; he was out of his clerkship. In July, 1788, he said he was a man of no fortune. I never asked him what fortune he had, during the twenty-three months courtship which he paid to my daughter. I never advised my daughter to discourage his addresses: I knew his family, that it was a very respectable one; and he said, he was the twelfth brother. Having a knowledge of his family, I did not think there was any necessity in writing to his father or brother. I had a mind the young people should do as they pleased. As I said before, Mr. Shaw introduced his brother to us, one evening, about six o'clock. I believe he drank tea; and my husband shook hands with him. The defendant was under this brother's protection. I received him as I would have done any other gentleman. When the defendant went into the country, he wrote directly to my daughter. It was before he went into the country, that he introduced his brother. I was not at all surprised, when he desired my daughter to go and see his chambers, because I then looked upon him as much my daughter's husband, as if he had actually been married to her. After Mr. Shaw was married, he sent for me. He said, Miss Chapman was a lady of great virtue and integrity; that he was very sorry he was married; and was willing to make any reparation in his power to my daughter. He had only a small property with his wife. He had only an hundred pounds, and no property of his own.

The defendant went every where, where we visited: he visited with us at Mr. Neal's, and all our acquaintance. We have married three of our family already. We gave each of them a portion of several hundred pounds; and this daughter would have got the same. After Mr. Shaw discontinued his visits to my daughter, *she was out of her mind two months.* She kept her bed, and never slept for *seven days.* She was ill twice; and this illness was manifestly occasioned by Mr. Shaw's breaking off his visits. In expectation of marriage, I laid out 30l. with a linen-draper, and 12l. for silk with another.

Richard

Richard Chapman sworn.

I am brother to the plaintiff. I knew of Mr. Shaw's vifits to my fifter. The conduct of the defendant was fuch as left me no-doubt but that he had gained her fincere affections. One day, he was counting how many months it would be to July, when he fhould go to the country; " And when I return," faid he to my fifter' " we fhall be married, Liz."

Crofs-examined. They were to be privately married in November. I do not know from whom I underftood this. I have heard it fince the action was commenced.

Mr. Chapman sworn.

I am the elder brother of the plaintiff. I know Mr. Shaw, and have feen him frequently at our houfe. I always received him as a perfon paying his addreffes to my fifter; and he was fo received by all the family. There appeared to me to be a great attachment between them. She was ill, in confequence of his difcontinuing his vifits, and was attended by a medical perfon. Mr. Shaw was acquainted in our family for eighteen or twenty months. He told me, he was a clerk, *for improvement, for eighteen fhillings a week!* My brother was clerk with Mr. Sharples. I do not know that Mr. Shaw was fellow-clerk with my brother. He never ftated, in my hearing, his intention of marrying my fifter. I remember this young man's brother coming to our houfe; he was there moft of the evening. I do not know that there was a word faid by this young man, that he was going to be a hufband to my fifter. I cannot fay that he was at our houfe in the fummer of 1789, but know that he was there one evening between eleven and twelve at night. My fifter made a complaint of it to me.

Crofs-examined. The defendant is an attorney, and lives in Thanet place. He was in our houfe in 1789, about a fortnight before he went into the country. In the months of January and February, 1789, he was in London and never vifited us: he then lived in New-Inn. I never fent to fee what was become of him; and, as far as I know, my fifter never called or fent to him.

Mr. Turney Sworn.

I am an apothecary, and attended Mifs Chapman for fome months in the year 1789, when fhe was very ill. Her mind was difordered: her diforder was the effect of an unhappy mind.

LORD

LORD KENYON. I must undoubtedly take it for granted that the plaintiff was ill in consequence of her great attachment to the defendant.

Mr. Erskine. I wonder to what extent the mysterious science of medicine will arrive at last. I believe they will follow it by and by to the next world.

Charles Chapman sworn.

I am brother to the plaintiff; I know Mr. Shaw the defendant; during the latter period of his visits at our house, he did business for himself; he was agent for his two brothers, and he did business for another gentleman whom I knew.

DEFENCE.

Mr Erskine, Counsel on the part of the defendant, then addressed the Jury.

Gentlemen,

What is passing before us in this Court at present, is a miniature of what is passing in the world at large; (as scenes in private life something resemble those which are acted in publick) I shall endeavour to defend my client against this family compact. I will preface what I am about to say to you, with an observation which I give you my word of honour is a sincere one. There is no man living, who feels more regard than I do for the honour of WOMEN; or who enters more ardently into their distresses: there is no man living who more pathetically laments seduction; or would more willingly hold up to public detestation their seducers. No man respects private life more, or thinks higher of the peace, happiness, and prosperity of families who are engaged in the lower, but I think in the most useful walks of life; namely, those who are engaged in trade. And therefore, I am ever ready to allow that any tradesman who has sustained an injury, has a right to be heard and to be attended to by a Jury of his country. I am only sorry to remark, that the conduct of these witnesses does not much credit to that purity, honour, and fairness of dealing, which are often found in these walks of life. You have before you the defendant, Mr. Shaw, who is a young man just coming into the world, endeavouring to provide for himself, and to forward his fortune. Gentlemen of the Jury, many of your connexions may probably be in the same situation. The youngest of twelve children, thrust out into the world to struggle against all the vicissitudes of fortune, and to

hold

hold out against all her vanities and caprices. My client was sent out into the wide world to seek his maintenance at the age of nineteen. For a short time he was clerk to an attorney, and in the same office with one of the brothers of the present plaintiff, who first introduced him into his family. Mr. Chapman, although he is the father of this family, and the head of this house, has not been summoned as a witness in this cause. In cases of this sort women are better witnesses than men, and Mrs. Chapman has conducted herself better than her husband could have done; women concern themselves more with these little attentions which are paid to their sex by men; and therefore, they are more competent witnesses. But when you come to a serious connexion, the husband most undoubtedly must be consulted : because, by the law of England, you must obtain the consent of the lady's father.

Mr. Mingay. The lady is of age.

Mr. Erskine. She may be of age; but if there had been any serious intention of a marriage, the father would certainly have been acquainted with it. You will observe, Gentlemen, that during the period of *twenty-two months,* Mr. Shaw visited at the house of Mr. Chapman, paying those attentions to his daughter which young men, at that time of life, usually pay to the young women whose company they keep. And although the parents knew he was a clerk at eighteen shillings a week, the mother tells you she never warned her daughter against forming an attachment to him, although, as he had no fortune, she must have seen that this marriage would never have produced any desirable effect. But it seems to be a principle with this family to dispose of their daughters in marriage as soon as they can, and how they can; it would be better for them to desist from this mode. People ought never to join themselves in marriage without having the means of a comfortable support; for no proverb is truer than this (and there is a great deal of truth in most proverbs), " When poverty comes in at one door, love goes out at another." This is a very innocent and a very virtuous young woman. And if she has been unhappy, she is yet more happy than she would have been if she had married Mr. Shaw. The first time was the 7th of July, 1788, when, according to the evidence of the mother, the defendant expressed an intention to marry her daughter. I ask you, Gentlemen, for I know your honour and justice will make you extremely attentive; did she mention the conversation that passed between the defendant and her to her husband? Has she stated her husband ever signified

nified his approbation to my client that he fhould marry his daughter? She has concealed this part of the ftory which this young man told her, that he had no property, and de—fired her to communicate this to her hufband, to acquaint him that unlefs it would be convenient for him to give his daughter a fortune, it would be impoffible to carry on this engagement. And from that time, not a fyllable paffed which conveyed an inclination or defire on the part of the parents to carry this marriage into effect. This was in July, 1788. He went into the country; and what corre—fpondence has been produced from him in his abfence? They have been able to produce *one* letter from this *ardent* lover, during the abfence of three months. This young woman was fuppofed to have had fuch an affection for the defendant, as to have turned her brain. If fo, when he returned to London, I fhould think he would have been a little reprimanded by his lover, for neglecting to correfpond with her. He returned to town in the end of the year 1788. Between two and three months in the fpring of the fame year, he is living in New-Inn; he is never once at the houfe; he is never vifited by her; he is never inquired after by the parents, although in the month of July before, it was announced to the mother by the defendant, that his marriage was to be carried into effect in the month of No—vember; then, faid my client, I fhall be married to Liz. It was a great pity Mr. Neale was not prefent at this conver—fation, which paffed at the houfe of the parents before he went away. No! he could not get him to the houfe. Mr. Shaw faw the folly and danger of the connexion, and the ruin that it would bring on both him and this young lady. Mr. Shaw had unfortunately deftroyed a letter written by Mifs Chapman to him, acknowledging that this connexion ought to be deftroyed and put an end to by abfence, or in any fhape. Here is a meeting at the houfe of Mr. Neale; this young gentleman, one of the brothers of the plaintiff, is prefent at this converfation, and fwears that Mr. Shaw faid he would marry Liz in November. Mr. Shaw comes back in November: Did Mr. Chapman ever put Mr. Shaw in mind of his promife? Had Mr. Chapman no regard for the honour of his fifter? Had he no regard for the refpect due to his family? Did he never fay to his mother, What is become of Shaw? He has returned, and yet has never per—formed his engagement? I afked the mother and all the three fons, for this action is carried on at the family ex—pence, and with family witneffes, and no one would fwear this man is fixed with this breach of promife; but this is not

not all; no perfon who attends, in the fmalleſt degree, to the manner in which this bufinefs has been conducted, but muſt fee that this is a caufe trumped up againſt a young man, who is obliged to marry againſt his own will, who would have much rather married this young woman, but was prevented, becaufe there was no property on either fide.

Gentlemen, if any of you had a fon, and had no property to give him, and who was to work his fortune through the world, and ſhould form an attachment to any tradefman's daughter, would you not expect, from the fairnefs and honeſty of people of this defcription, to have had fome communication on the fubject? Would you not have expected fomething to this effect? Your fon has vifited my daughter; a new connection has fprung up between them: is it for the advantage of either or both? Common honour, common honeſty, called for fuch a communication. I ſhould confider it as a confpiracy againſt me, if any family were to permit a fon of mine to form an attachment to one of their daughters, and never communicate it to me. If, in confequence of fuch an acquaintance, he ſhould form an injudicious connexion, I ſhould confider it as a confpiracy, if not made acquainted with it. By the law of England, a father who has a fon under age, is intitled to ratify the contract of marriage, and if performed without the confent of the father, it is no engagement. It is evident that this family, I do not fay wickedly, but foolishly, fuffered my child to go on in forming an attachment to their daughter, without either directly or indirectly communicating it to any branch of my child's family.

This is not all; you are defired to believe, by Mrs. Chapman, that the defendant faid to her, I will bring my brother, Mr. Shaw, to vifit you. The defendant was to introduce his brother as a brother-in-law; as a man who was to be received with open arms, and taken into the affections of this family. She tells you, ſhe addreffed Mr. Shaw as ſhe would any one of you. He remained from fix or feven in the evening, until twelve o'clock at night; the father prefent, the mother prefent, all the brothers prefent, the man himfelf prefent, who promifed to marry the young lady, when he returned in November; and yet not a fyllable is faid on the fubject.

When the defendant comes back in November, 1788, he was to be married privately firſt.—Why?—They tell you he was of age, and ſhe was of age; why then a *private* marriage? Was it to conceal it from his own family before
his

his parents and his numerous brothers could come and enter their proteſt againſt a connexion which would involve both the parties in ruin? This is the true ſituation of the buſineſs; but you will obſerve further, one of the brothers ſays, they were to have been married *privately*. Why, when he came to town, was not this taken notice of? There is not a ſyllable of evidence in the cauſe, of his ever having been called on to carry this marriage into effect. Mr. Shaw's affections were undoubtedly fixed on Miſs Chapman, but he had no fortune. Did Mr. Chapman ever offer him a fortune with his daughter? Mrs. Chapman knows that ſhe concealed a part of the converſation between her and the defendant, who deſired her to aſk her huſband what he would give, and yet this man, Mr. Chapman, is kept in the back ground; why was he not ſworn, ſince he could have thrown light upon the ſubject? Then comes the apothecary in Macbeth, ſhaking his head, with a portentous air, and whirling his fingers about like ſome conjuror. When phyſicians cannot find any diſorder in the body, they ſay there muſt be ſome diſorder in the mind; the greateſt phyſicians that adorn the world and ſcience, when they go out of the path of experimental philoſophy and truth, only make aſſes of themſelves in the face of the public, and will make every man laugh at them, who becomes acquainted with their preſumption aad ridiculous folly.

Gentlemen, you may give the plaintiff a verdict of ſixty or ſeventy pounds; you may caſt my client into priſon; you may make another family unhappy, for there is another unfortunate woman; and if there has been any crime committed, ſhe has not partaken in it.

Gentlemen, the defendant ſtands in the ſame ſituation in which I am afraid we have all, at one time or other ſtood; we have caſt our affections into a quarter where fortune has not caſt her ſmiles. The law undoubtedly has put the whip into your hands, and feeling like diſcreet, honourable men, like men of humanity and juſtice, I am ſure you will make a proper and moderate uſe of it.

LORD KENYON's *Charge to the Jury.*

Gentlemen of the Jury,

This cauſe lies in a very narrow compaſs. There are two points in it. Firſt, Whether the promiſe ſtated by the plaintiff, and made to her, has been broken? and Secondly, What are the damages? If any perſon who enters into this en-

engagement, is reputed to be of fober life and converfation, but who turns out, on a fair inquiry, to be a woman whofe character is ftained, the promife, although made to her, will not bind the other party in point of law. If a lady is chafte and virtuous at the time of making the promife, but, before the performance of it, acquires a different character, there is in this cafe likewife an end of it: but nothing of this kind appears in the prefent cafe; and the learned Counfel for the defendant feems to admit that the verdict muft be for the plaintiff, and undoubtedly it muft; and then the queftion arifes refpecting damages. And, Gentlemen, it is fcarcely neceffary to mention, that you ought always to have refpect to the fituation in life of the perfon who is to pay thefe damages. The conduct of the defendant during this bufinefs does not appear to me marked with any peculiar delinquency. Too often, indeed, an improper intimacy, by the inattention of parents, has happened; the daughters have been feduced; but fortunately, in this cafe, nothing of that fort has occurred. It was a pleafing dream; but the defendant was at laft awaked from it, from a view of his own fituation: this, however, does not juftify him in breaking his promife, but prefents him to you in a fituation more favourable. His fituation in life is certainly very narrow; he is living upon the fmall earnings arifing from the profeffion to which he has been bred up; he is now connected with another woman. Whether he is the father of a family or not, I do not know; but he is the hufband of a wife; and you will undoubtedly advert to that fituation. I do not fay, always, that a man who cannot pay in his purfe, fhall not be called upon to pay in his perfon. However, the defendant does not appear to you in that criminal fituation in which feveral others have been placed.

Gentlemen, You are now acquainted with all the circumftances of this cafe. The confequence of large damages will not be productive of much benefit to the plaintiff; at the fame time, they may crufh the defendant. You are the fole and only conftitutional judges of what the damages fhall be. You will attend to the fituation of the parties, and, I am fure, will do fubftantial juftice.

Verdict for the plaintiff, Twenty Pounds.

SESSIONS CASE determined in the COURT OF KING's BENCH, subsequent to the Publication of the last Edition of BURN's JUSTICE.

REX *v.* THOMAS FORREST, *and Others.*

C A S E.

An appeal was made to the Quarter Sessions of Middlesex by John Abrahams, and two other persons, on behalf of themselves and the rest of the parishioners of St. Pancras, against a warrant of appointment, made by four justices, of Thomas Forrest, John Powell, and one Jones, to be overseers of the poor of that parish: and a special case was reserved for the opinion of the Court. The appellants exhibited their petition and appeal, setting forth that the parishioners of St. Pancras had always been accustomed to assemble in open vestry on Tuesday in Easter week, in pursuance of a notice given, for the purpose of returning proper persons to the Magistrates of the division, to be by them appointed to the offices of church-wardens, overseers, and constables. That there being three divisions with a separate overseer for each, and two or more persons having always been nominated for each division, the parishioners had always proceeded to make their election by voting; and on a return being made by the vestry-clerk of the proceedings to the magistrates, they had invariably appointed such persons as had the majority of votes. That on Tuesday in last Easter week, a number of parishioners attended, and six persons were put in nomination for the office of overseer for the ensuing year: that there appeared for one Hall 136; for Young 118; for Forest 94; and for Powell 79 votes: yet Jacob Leroux, Esq. an acting magistrate in that parish, who attended the vestry and voted, without waiting for the return, signed a warrant, appointing the said Forest and Powell, together with one Jones, overseers for the ensuing year; and then sent such warrant to three other justices, that they might sign it, who separately signed the same at their respective houses. That the appointment so made in favour of the persons in the minority being in direct opposition

position

position to the usual custom in the parish, and without any cause, inasmuch as Hall and Young were in every respect eligible to the office; and the warrant being also illegally signed, the petitioners conceived themselves aggrieved.

On hearing the appeal, it was objected by the respondents that no such appeal from parishioners, not included in the appointment, lay: which objection was over-ruled. It was admitted by the respondents that the warrant was signed by one of the justices, and then sent by him to the three other justices, who *separately signed* the same at their respective houses; and that no two of them had signed it in the presence of each other. Whereupon the Court of Sessions vacated the order of the said justices.

On a rule to shew cause why the order of Sessions should not be quashed,

Fielding and *Garrow*, against the order of Sessions, abandoned the question relative to the usage which was stated in the case, because it was in direct opposition to the 43d. *Eliz.* cap. 2. but made two objections to the order of Sessions. 1st, That nobody but the person who was appointed overseer could appeal under the 43d. *Eliz.* cap. 2. That no other line could be drawn, otherwise every parishioner might appeal, and even upon separate grounds; but it never could have been the intention of the Legislature to open such a door to litigation. 2dly, The appointment was good, notwithstanding all the Magistrates did not sign it together. In the case of an order of removal, where the Justices are to examine into the facts, and make an adjudication with respect to the settlement of the party to be removed, it is necessary that they should act together, because they form a Court of Judicature and pronounce a judgment: but that is different from the present case, where the signing of the appointment is a mere ministerial act. No examination of witnesses takes place; and they merely approve of the nomination of the parishioners; which may be done as well when they are acting separately as when they are together.

LORD KENYON, Ch. J.—The clause in the 43d *Eliz.* is conceived in the most general terms. It enacts that, " if *any person* shall find himself aggrieved, &c. he may appeal, &c." A case may reasonably be imagined to exist in which the parishioners would feel themselves aggrieved by the appointment of overseers, when we recollect the enormous sums of money which are received for the relief of the poor; as, for instance, if the Magistrates were to appoint persons who were insolvent. As to the other question: perhaps at this

time

time of day no great inconvenience would follow from permitting the appointment to be made by a single magistrate. But we are to decide this question on the statute 43d *Eliz.* cap. 2. the first section of which expressly declares, that the overseers shall be nominated by two or more justices of the peace, *whereof one shall be of the quorum.* Now those words are very material in the decision of a question arising upon this statute. For though in modern times all the Justices in the commission (except one) are of the *quorum,* yet at the time when that act passed, some persons were selected on account of their superior knowledge, and appointed to be of the *quorum.* However, I do not wish to decide on that sort of argument. But it is admitted that in the case of orders of removal, they must act together, and for this reason, that they should assist each other, and that the result of their conference should be the ground of their determination. Now I cannot distinguish this case from that. This is not merely a *ministerial* act : if it were, like signing a rate, that might perhaps vary the question : but it is a *judicial* act, wherein the Justices are to exercise a discretion. And, in order to make this a good appointment, the Justices should have acted together. With respect to the usage which is stated in the case, no question can be entertained about it ; because as the statute 43 *Eliz.* commenced in the time of legal memory, no usage can prevail to oppose it.

ASHHURST, J.— The Justices in appointing overseers do not act ministerially ; the statute has vested a discretion in them, and they should act together. And, it being a matter of discretion, they should confer together for the purpose of a communication on the subject matter on which they are to determine : but this cannot be done when they are not together, and when no conference can take place. On the other point, I agree with my Lord.

GROSE, J.— The usage which has been attempted to be set up in this case, is contrary to the statute. Neither can any doubt be entertained on the question relative to the appeal. As to the other point, I agree that the Justices should be together when they sign the appointment. This is not a mere ministerial act ; if it were, the Justices would have nothing more to do than to confirm the appointment presented to them by the parishioners : but they are to exercise a discretion upon the subject. And the general rule is, that, when an Act of Parliament requires the concurrence of two magistrates they should both act together. This point has been determined not only in the case of orders of removal, but

but in orders of baftardy alfo, in *Billings* v. *Prim* and another, in the Court of Common Pleas.

Rule difcharged.

CROWN CASES.

WILLIAM MORRIS'S CASE.

At the Old Bailey in July Seffion, 1787, George Horne was indicted on the ftatutes of 12 *Anne*, cap. 7, and 2 *Geo* II. cap. 25, for ftealing two Bank Notes in the dwelling-houfe of Stephen Sullivan, Efq. the *property* of the faid Stephen Sullivan; and William Morris ftood charged in the fame indictment on the ftatutes of 3 *Will.* and *Mary*, cap. 9, § 4, and 5 *Anne*, cap. 31, § 5, for receiving the faid Notes, the *property and chattels* of the faid Stephen Sullivan, he the faid William Morris well knowing the faid *notes and chattels* to have been felonioufly ftolen. There was another count, charging William Morris as an acceffary after the fact, at common law, with harbouring and maintaining the principal felon.

The prifoners were found guilty on all the counts, (except that which charged Morris as an acceffary at common law) on very clear and fatisfactory evidence; but the Counfel for William Morris fubmitting two objections in his favour to the Court, they were extremely well argued both for the prifoner and for the Crown; and the Court referved the cafe for the opinion of the TWELVE JUDGES.

On the 14th of November following all the JUDGES, except Lord MANSFIELD and Lord Chief Baron EYRE, affembled at Serjeants-Inn-Hall, and the cafe was again argued by Mr. Knowlys on behalf of the prifoner.

Firft Objection: There is a fatal variance in the indictment, between the count againft the principal, and the count againft the acceffary. The firft charges the things ftolen to be the *property* of Stephen Sullivan, and the fecond charges them to be the *notes, property,* and *chattels* of Stephen Sullivan. There cannot be an acceffary for receiving ftolen goods, unlefs the goods ftolen are of fuch a kind as are legally included within the meaning of the words "*goods*
and

and chattels;" for no other kind of goods can be the subject of larceny. The word *property* is not synonymous with *goods or chattels*; for a man may have a property in many things which, in respect of the vileness of their nature, are not the subject of theft, as mastiffs, blood-hounds, cats, monkeys, &c. So also, if they respect the realty, as a box in which charters are contained, although the box may be of great value, and, if stolen without the charters in it, would have been the subject of an indictment of larceny. The framer of the indictment therefore having confined the subject of it by a certain *description*, it shall not be now permitted to define the thing stolen more strictly in the charge against the accessary than they have done in the charge against the principal: being called *property* as to the *principal*, it cannot be construed *chattels* as to the *accessary*.

Second objection: The receiving of Bank Notes, knowing them to have been stolen, is not felony, either by the common law, or by the statutes on which the charge against the accessary is founded. The receiving of stolen goods was, at common law, a misdemeanor only; and a man could not be guilty as an accessary after the fact, except by receiving the felon himself. But it is enacted by the statutes of the 3 *Will.* and *Mary*, cap. 9, § 4; and 5 *Anne*, cap. 31. § 5: " That whoever shall buy or receive any *goods or chattels* that shall be feloniously taken or stolen from any other person, knowing the same to be stolen, shall be taken and deemed an accessary to such felony after the fact, and shall incur the same punishment as an accessary to the felony after the felony committed." The question therefore is, Whether *Bank Notes* can be considered as *Goods and Chattels* within the meaning of these statutes? Bank Notes were not, at common law, the subject of larceny; for although that offence is defined to be the felonious taking and carrying away the goods and chattels of another, yet it has always been confined to the mere personal goods and chattels of another, which do not extend to every species of personal property of which a man may become possessed. The words *bona et catalla* do not, of their proper nature, extend to charters, or to any evidences concerning the freehold or inheritance, or to obligations, or to deeds, or to other specialties; and therefore it is said by Lord Dyer, that an action of trover will not lie for a bond, nor can the value of it be demanded by the name of goods or chattels. Among this species of property, which were not the subjects of larceny, because they were not comprehended within the legal idea of goods and chattels, were Bank Notes, and every other description of of property which is within the denomination of a *chose in action*. But it is enacted by the statute 2 *Geo.* II. cap. 25, § 3: " That if any person, or persons shall steal or take by robbery any Exchequer Orders, Exchequer Bills, *Bank Notes*, Bonds, Bills of Exchange, &c. notwithstanding any of the said particulars, are termed in law a *chose in action*, he shall be deemed guilty of felony, of the same nature, and in the same degree, as it would have been if the offender had stolen any *other goods* of the like value with the money due on such orders, bills, bonds, notes, &c. or secured thereby." This statute undoubtedly makes Bank Notes so far goods and chattels, as to make them the subject of larceny, but no further; it does not say that the receivers of stolen Bank Notes shall be considered as accessaries after the fact, or that Bank Notes shall be considered as goods and chattels, to all intents and purposes whatsoever. As to the provision, that such persons who shall steal them shall be punished " in the same manner as if they had stolen *other goods* of the like value," the word " goods," in this part of the Act, is not used in the strict, legal, and technical sense of the term, but is only put as an instance, and used in the general and colloquial acceptation of the word, as synonymous to " *property*" in general. If any doubt could be entertained on this subject, the opinion of LORD MANSFIELD, in the case of *Miller* v. *Race*, long subsequent to the passing of the Act, would certainly remove it; for his Lordship expressly declares, that Bank Notes do not resemble, and therefore ought not to be compared, to *goods*, securities, documents, and other chattels; but are to be treated as money, or cash; and it has been uniformly held, that money cannot be included within the meaning of the words " goods and chattels." In Davidson's case, at Carlisle assizes, 1766, a man was indicted for receiving money, knowing it to have been stolen; and Mr. Justice *Bathurst* was clearly of opinion, that money was not within the statutes 3 *Will.* and *Mary*, cap. 9, or 5 *Anne*, cap. 31. In the case of *Woolcomb* v. *Woolcomb*, it was held by Lord Chancellor KING, that the ready money and bonds of a testator do not pass by the word " *goods*." Mr. Justice *Foster* also says, that *money* is not within the 10 and 11 *Will.* III. cap. 23, which makes it a capital offence to steal any *goods*, *wares*, and *merchandizes*, to the value of five shillings, from a shop or warehouse. But even admitting that Bank Notes were now taken to be goods and chattels by virtue of the 2 *Geo.* III. cap. 25, to all intents and purposes whatsoever, yet it would be impossible to include the receivers of them under the 3 *Will.* and *Mary*, cap. 9, and 5 *Anne*, cap. 31, because " *Bank Notes*" could not be at that time in the contemplation of the Legiſlature as goods and chattels. All bonds, bills, notes, and other ſecurities were then *choſes in action*, and could not be included, by any conſtruction, within the meaning of the words " *goods and chattels*; for thoſe words can only refer to the receipt of ſuch things as were goods and chattels at the time the Acts were paſſed. The ſtatute of the 31 *Eliz.* cap. 12, takes away clergy from acceſſaries after the fact in horſeſtealing; but it has been held that the ſtatute only extends to ſuch offenders as were acceſſaries at the time the Act was made, *viz.* acceſſaries at the common law, and therefore a man knowingly receiving a ſtolen horſe, if he did not alſo receive the felon, was not within the Act. It is true, that ſuch an offender may now be puniſhed as a receiver of ſtolen goods under the 5 *Anne*, cap. 31.

After the argument was cloſed, the auditors were ordered to withdraw, and the JUDGES conferred among themſelves upon the ſubject.

Mr Baron PERRYN, in January Seſſion, 1788, after ſtating the particulars of the caſe, delivered the reſult of their conference to the following effect: This caſe was reſerved in July Seſſion laſt by Mr. *Roſe*, and referred to the conſideration of the Judges, on two grounds. Firſt, On a variance between the count againſt the principal, wherein the notes are charged to be the *property* of Stephen Sullivan, and the count againſt the acceſſary, wherein they are charged to be the *property and chattels* of Stephen Sullivan. Secondly, That the receiving the Bank Notes is not within any Act of Parliament which makes receivers acceſſaries after the fact. On the firſt day of laſt Michaelmas Term, the JUDGES, on a conference had by them, directed Counſel to be heard on theſe objections; and on the 14th of November the caſe was argued before TEN JUDGES with great ability, and very much at large, by Mr. *Knowlys*. The JUDGES have ſince conſidered of thoſe arguments; and, with reſpect to the firſt objection, they are unanimouſly of opinion, that the word " *chattels*," in the count againſt the acceſſary, may be rejected as ſurpluſage. The ſubject of the ſecond objection has occaſioned a difference of ſentiment among the JUDGES; but a majority of them are of opinion, in which opinion I concur, that *Cayle's Caſe*, 8 *Co.* 33, *Channel v. Ramſhottom*, *Yelv.* 68, and particularly *Miller v. Race*, 1 *Bur.* 457, are in point; and that " *Bank Notes*" are not " *goods and chattels*" within the meaning of the ſtatutes of the 3 *Will.* and *Mary*, cap. 9, and 5 *Anne*, cap. 31, and the judgment againſt
William

William Morris, the prisoner at the bar, must be consequently be arrested.

The prisoner was accordingly discharged.

BALLIE'S CASE.

This was a case reserved, at the Old-Bailey, September, 1785, by Mr. SERJEANT ADAIR, *Recorder*, for the opinion of the TWELVE JUDGES.

The prisoner had been apprehended on the statute 23 *Geo.* III. cap. 88, by which it is enacted, "That if any person shall be found in or upon any dwelling-house, warehouse, coach-house, stable, or out-house; or in any inclosed yard, or garden, or area, belonging to any house, with intent to steal any goods or chattels, he shall be deemed A ROGUE AND A VAGABOND, within the meaning of the statute of 17 *Geo.* II. cap. 5, usually called *the Vagrant Act*;" and having been committed to the House of Correction till the then next ensuing Session, the Justices, on examination of the circumstances, had adjudged him to be A ROGUE AND A VAGABOND within the meaning of the Act; and ordered him to be detained in the House of Correction for six months, by virtue of 17 *Geo.* II. cap. 5. § 9. Before the six months had expired, the prisoner made his escape; but he was again apprehended, and at an adjournment-day of the same Session, he was committed by a warrant of two Justices, under the 4th section of the Vagrant Act, as an INCORRIGIBLE ROGUE, and ordered to be detained in the same House of Correction for two years. Before this term of imprisonment had expired, he again broke gaol, and was again apprehended, on another clause of the statute 23 *Geo.* III. cap. 28, by which it is enacted, "That any person having upon him any picklock key, crow, jack, bit, or other implement, with an intent feloniously to break and enter into any dwelling house, warehouse, coach-house, stable, or outhouse; or shall have upon him any pistol, hanger, cutlass, bludgeon, or other offensive weapon, with intent feloniously to assault any person, shall be deemed A ROGUE AND A VAGABOND, as aforesaid."

Under these circumstances, the prisoner was now indicted on the statute 17 *Geo.* II. cap. 5, § 9, by which it is enacted, that if any person committed as an INCORRIGIBLE ROGUE shall break out or make his escape, or shall offend again *in*

like

like manner, he shall be guilty of FELONY, and be transported for seven years.

The indictment accordingly *stated*, that the prisoner had been committed by a Justice, and convicted by the Sessions, as A ROGUE AND VAGABOND under the 23 *Geo.* III. cap. 88, and having been committed for six months, had escaped, &c. That afterwards he had been convicted for that escape, and committed as AN INCORRIGIBLE ROGUE, and again broke gaol before the expiration of the time, &c. And then it charged, that the said George Baillie, on such a day, did offend again *in like manner* as A ROGUE AND VAGABOND, in having upon him a certain offensive weapon called a pistol, with intent feloniously to assault some person or persons, against the peace, &c.

The records of his former convictions were produced, his identity, and the fact of his having the pistol for felonious purposes, was fully proved, and he was found guilty; but the judgment was respited, and the case referred to the consideration of the JUDGES, on the two following questions.

First, Whether the offence for which the prisoner was convicted, being created by the statute 23 *Geo.* III. cap. 88, could be maintained under an indictment on the statute of 17 *Geo.* II. cap. 5.

Secondly, Whether the words " shall offend again *in like manner*," in the statute of 17 *Geo.* II. cap. 5, do not refer to such offences only as bring the offender under the description of AN INCORRIGIBLE ROGUE? and if so, Whether the present indictment is good in charging the prisoner with having offended *in like manner* as A ROGUE AND VAGABOND, instead of having offended *in like manner* as AN INCORRIGIBLE ROGUE?

Mr. Justice GOULD, in February Session, 1786, after stating the proceedings above-mentioned, delivered the opinion of the JUDGES to the following effect:

This case was reserved by Mr. RECORDER, upon two objections raised by the Counsel for the prisoner. On the first day of last Hilary Term, the JUDGES assembled to consider of this case; and they are unanimously of opinion, That there is no foundation in law for either of the objections.

As to the first objection, The title of an Act of Parliament, although it is not considered as any part of the Act, yet it may serve to explain the intent and meaning of the Legislature; and the title of the 23 *Geo.* III. cap. 88, is

" Ab

" An Act to extend the provisions of an Act [setting out the title of the 17 Geo. II. cap. 5,] to cases not therein mentioned." It enacts, that every person under the circumstances in which the prisoner is described in the indictment to have been found, shall be deemed a rogue and vagabond within the meaning of the 17 Geo. II. cap. 5. The JUDGES are therefore of opinion, That the 23 Geo. III. cap. 88, is to have the same operation as if the offences described in it had been originally inserted in the Vagrant Act, in continuation of the offences therein described; and that it is in every respect to be considered as incorporate into, and making a part of, that Act.

As to the second objection,—The JUDGES, upon weighing the several provisions of the 17 Geo. II. cap. 5, as far as they apply to the case of the prisoner, are of opinion, That the indictment is right both in form and substance. The statute divides offences into three classes. *First*, IDLE AND DISORDERLY PERSONS, who on conviction by one witness, before one Justice, may be committed to the House of Correction, not exceeding one month. *Secondly*, ROGUES AND VAGABONDS, who are to be examined by the Magistrate, and publickly whipped, or ordered to be sent to the House of Correction till the next Session, or for any less time, as such Justice shall think proper. *Thirdly*, INCORRIGIBLE ROGUES, who it seems must be committed till the next Session, and cannot be punished by the Magistrate.

It appears that the prisoner escaped from his commitment as a rogue and vagabond, upon which escape he immediately became an incorrigible rogue; and on being brought before the Session, he was so adjudged, and sentenced to be detained in the House of Correction for two years, and afterwards made his escape. These facts are introduced into the indictment; and it then goes on to state the offence which he had committed against the statute 23 Geo. III. cap. 88; and concludes by averring, in the words of the 17 Geo. II. cap. 5, that he had " offended again *in like manner.*"

The statute of 23 Geo. III. cap. 88, declares, that the persons therein described shall be considered as rogues and vagabonds, within the meaning of the 17 Geo. II. cap. 5. It is enacted by the 17 Geo. II. cap. 5. § 4, " That all *rogues and vagabonds* who shall break or escape out of any House of Correction before the expiration of the term for which they were committed; and all persons who, after having been punished as *rogues and vagabonds,* and discharged, shall again commit *any of the said offences,* shall be deemed *incorrig rigible rogues."* The Act then goes on, in § 9, to authorife the Juftices in Seffion to detain fuch *rogue and vagabond* in the Houfe of Correction for any time not exceeding fix months; and fuch *incorrigible rogue* for any time not lefs than fix months, nor exceeding two years; and then follows the claufe on which the prefent queftion arifes: " And if fuch *incorrigible rogue,* fo ordered by the Seffions to be detained in the Houfe of Correction, fhall break out or make his efcape, *or* fhall offend again in like manner, he fhall be guilty of felony, and be tranfported for feven years." The context of this claufe of the Act, which adopts the words, " *in like manner,"* refers to the next antecedent words, " *fhall break out or make his efcape*;" recourfe therefore muft be had to the other parts of the Act, to find out what the Legiflature by thefe words means: and the JUDGES are of opinion, That the words " *in like manner"* muft neceffarily refer to the offences defcribed in the fourth fection beforementioned.

What then is the fituation of the prifoner? He is committed to the Houfe of Correction for fix months as a *rogue and vagabond:* by breaking gaol he is guilty of a new act of vagrancy, and is adjudged and committed for two years as an *incorrigible rogue:* from this imprifonment he again makes his efcape before the two years are expired; and commits another act of vagrancy as *a rogue and vagabond,* againft the 23 *Geo.* III. cap. 88. By this efcape he becomes *an incorrigible rogue* a fecond time; and he afterwards offends again " *in like manner"* as a rogue and vagabond. All thefe facts are difclofed in the indictment. No technical terms or words of art are made neceffary to the defcription of this offence. The law therefore muft draw the inference from the words, *viz.* that by having offended again in like manner as a *rogue and vagabond,* he becomes *an incorrigible rogue* a fecond time, and thereby incurs the guilt of felony; and it is therefore the unanimous opinion of the JUDGES, That the indictment is proper; and that the prifoner is in the predicament which the Legiflature has faid fhall be punifhed with tranfportation.

He was accordingly ordered to be tranfported for the term of feven years.

LOCK-

LOCKHART'S CASE.

Old Bailey, June Seffion, 1785. The prifoner was indicted for ftealing a number of diamonds and pearls, the property of Ewen Baily, Efq. in the dwelling-houfe of Narciffa Mafcall.

He had made a full confeffion of the fact, by which it was difcovered that part of the property had been difpofed of to a Mr. Grant, and the Counfel for the profecution called Mr. Grant as a witnefs to identify the property.

The confeffion had been obtained by fuch promifes of favour as rendered it admiffible evidence; and it was therefore contended, that as the difcovery of Mr. Grant refulted from the illegal confeffion which had been obtained from the prifoner, he, Mr. Grant, was not competent witnefs.

But the COURT faid, that the law was clearly fettled, that although a confeffion improperly obtained cannot be given in evidence, yet it can never go the rejection of the evidence of other witneffes, which are got at in confequence of fuch a confeffion.

AICKLES'S CASE.

Old Bailey, September Seffion, 1785.

John Henry Aickles had been convicted in January Seffion, 1784, of fimple grand larceny; and in the July Seffion following, received judgment of tranfportation *to America* for feven years: but, in confequence of ftrong interceffion in his favour, he afterwards received his Majefty's pardon, " on condition of tranfporting himfelf *beyond the feas* for the fame term of years, within fourteen days from the day of his *difcharge*, and of giving fecurity to the fatifaction of the RECORDER fo to do." He gave the fecurity required, and a warrant was accordingly iffued by the RECORDER, directed to the Keeper of Newgate, authorifing his difcharge; but as there was a number of civil detainers againft him, his difcharge was neceffarily delayed until they were fuperfeded. On the 26th of May following, he was apprehended at Iflington; and was now put to the bar on AN INDICTMENT for

" re-

" returning from transportation, and being found at large without *any lawful cause*, before the expiration of the term of seven years, for which he was sentenced to be transported."

Under these circumstances, it was held incumbent on the prosecutor to prove the precise day on which the prisoner was *discharged*; and for this purpose Mr. Newman, Clerk of the Papers of the prison, produced a daily book, which he kept, containing entries of the names of all the debtors and criminals who are brought into the prison, and the times when they are discharged; but it appeared that those entries were not made from Mr. Newman's own knowledge of the facts, but that he generally made them from the information of the turnkeys and frequently from the turnkey's indorsements on the back of the warrants, which warrants were afterwards regularly filed.

It was contended by the prisoner's Counsel, that these were not original entries of the facts, and therefore that the turnkey himself, by whom Aickles was discharged, or the original minute from which the entry of his discharge had been made, should be produced, because they alone were the best evidence upon this subject, and it was in the prosecutor's power to produce them. It was compared to the production of a tradesman's ledger, in order to prove the delivery of goods, instead of producing the original memorandum or day-book from which the ledger had been posted; and it was argued, that no credit could be given to entries made intirely from hearsay and information, and therefore they ought not to be received as evidence.

The COURT, however, were clearly of opinion, That the contents of this book might be given in evidence. It is a book very different in its nature from the books or memorandums of a tradesman. It appears to have been the constant and well established practice of the keepers of a publick prison to register the discharge of prisoners in such a book as the one produced, and in the manner which the witness has described. The clerk of the Papers is a public officer in the prison; and the law reposes such a confidence in public officers, that it *presumes* they will discharge their several trusts with accuracy and fidelity; and therefore whatever acts they do in discharge of their publick duty, may be given in evidence, and shall be taken to be *true*, under such a degree of caution as the nature and circumstances of each case may appear to require, except the *falsity* of them can be made to appear; for every presumption may be repelled by contrary evidence. In the present case, Mr. Newman

has

has no private interest whatsoever in this book, to induce him to make factitious entries in it. He is a public officer, recording a public transaction. Any person may undoubtedly falsify the entries if he can; but unless the truth of the entry as to the present fact can be impeached, it is admissible evidence.

The entry was accordingly read; and it proved that the prisoner was discharged from Newgate, by virtue of Mr. RECORDER's warrant for that purpose, on the 14th of March, 1785.

The fact of the prisoner's having been found at large before the term of his transportation had expired, being clearly proved, the question was, Whether he was at large *without lawful cause?* And it was submitted to the Court upon the authority of *the King* v. *Max. Miller,* and *Patrick Madan's Case,* that having *literally* complied with the condition of the King's pardon, by giving security to the satisfaction of THE RECORDER to transport himself beyond the seas, and having in consequence thereof been legally discharged from Newgate by virtue of THE RECORDER's warrant, that discharge was *a lawful cause* for his being at large, notwithstanding he had forfeited the recognizance of himself and his bail, by breaking the other part of the condition, in not transporting himself within *the fourteen days.*

The COURT appeared to differ in their opinion upon this point; and it was thought a proper question for the consideration of THE JUDGES, in case the Jury should find the prisoner guilty. On further evidence, however, it appeared that he had at the time of his discharge a real determination to quit the kingdom within the time, but that he had been prevented from carrying it into effect by unaffected poverty, distress, and ill-health; and the Court being of opinion, That these impediments, if true, amounted to a *lawful excuse,* the Jury found a verdict, NOT GUILTY.

The KING *against* AICKLES.

At the Old Bailey in February Session, 1787, John Henry Aickles was indicted before Mr. Justice *Grose,* for forging a certain promissory note for the payment of money, with intent to defraud Robert Harvey Gedge.

There was also a second count, for uttering it knowing it to be forged, with the like intention. The form of the note was as follows:

" £ 25

"£.25 10s 0d.   London, Dec. 18, 1786.
" Three months after date, I promise to pay to Henry
Byron, Esq. or order, twenty-five pounds ten shillings, for
value received.
          " No 4, Argyle-Street,
              Oxford road.   " JOHN MASON."

Henry Byron, the payee of the note, went to the shop of
Mr. Gedge, a linen-draper in Leicester-fields, and having
looked out several pieces of goods to the amount of twenty
guineas, he presented the note above described, in payment.
Mr. Gedge asked Byron, who John Mason, the drawer of
it, was. Byron answered, " He is a gentleman of considerable fortune, with whom I am concerned in the profits
of a coal-mine; and he lives at Nᵒ 4, Argyle-street, Oxford road." Mr. Gedge, however, refused to take the note
until he had enquired into its validity; and Byron very readily left the note with him, unindorsed, for that purpose, desiring that he would not send the goods until he was perfectly satisfied. Mr. Gedge accordingly sent his servant to
Nᵒ 4, Argyle street, where he was introduced to the prisoner as Mr. Mason. The prisoner, on being shewn the
note, said that the name John Mason was his hand-writing,
and that it would be punctually paid when due; but before
Mr. Gedge had parted either with the note or with the
goods, Mr. Byron was apprehended for defrauding a hosier,
and Mr. Aickles for having returned from transportation before his time. The prisoner had taken the house in Argyle-
street, about a month before he was apprehended in the
name of John Mason; and had signed a written agreement in that name with his landlord, who had enquired
his character in that name at a coffee-house in Round-
court in the Strand. He was also known by the name of
John Mason where he had before lodged; and he alleged in
his defence, that John Mason was his real name, but that he
had been known for three years by the fictitious name of
John Henry Aickles; and he had re-assumed his real name for
the purpose of avoiding the detection to which the longer
use of his fictitious name would unavoidably have exposed
him.

It was contended by a gentleman at the bar, in behalf of
the prisoner, that these facts did not amount to the crime of
forgery, for that the law required the act, to be done in the
name of another person.

The

The Jury found the prisoner guilty; and they added, that they believed the name of *Mason* was assumed for the purpose of negotiating the note in confederacy with *Henry Byron*, but that the name he was best known by was *John Henry Aickles*.

The judgment, however, was respited, and the case referred to the consideration of the TWELVE JUDGES.

Mr. Justice ASHHURST, in May Session, 1788, said, "The JUDGES have been consulted upon the law of this case; and they are of opinion, That *under the particular circumstances which occurred in evidence*, the indictment is not maintainable, and therefore the judgment must be staid."

The prisoner, having been tried in the former part of the Session for returning from transportation, and acquitted, was remanded under his original sentence.

MAJOR SEMPLE'S CASE.

At the Old Bailey, in July Session, 1786, J. G. Semple was put to the bar, to be arraigned on an indictment of larceny.

The indictment stated, " That James George Harrold, otherwise Semple, otherwise Kennedy, *labourer*, one chaise, called a post-chaise, of the value of fifty pounds, the goods and chattels of John Lycett, feloniously did steal, take, and carry away, &c."

Before the prisoner had pleaded, it was moved to quash the indictment on the ground of informality; the *addition* being placed after the *alias dictus*, and not after the first name.

The COURT, upon the authority of *Staundford*, *Hale*, and *Hawkins' Pleas of the Crown*, directed the indictment to be quashed, and the prisoner to be detained till the next Session.

At the ensuing Session the prisoner was again indicted for the same offence, before Mr. Serjeant ADAIR, *Recorder*, present Mr. Justice *Gould*, and Mr. *Rose*, D. R.

The following facts appeared in evidence: —The prosecutor, Mr. Lycett, was a coachmaker, who let out carriages to hire. The prisoner was a gentleman who lodged in the neighbourhood, and had frequently hired chaises from the prosecutor, as the occasion required, and for which he had always paid with great punctuality. On the first of September, 1785, the prisoner hired a post-chaise of the prosecutor, faying that he fhould want it for three weeks or a month, as he was going a tour round the North . It was agreed that the prifoner fhould pay at the rate of five fhillings a day during the time that he kept the chaife; and a price of fifty guineas was talked about in cafe he fhould determine to purchafe the chaife on his return to London, but no pofitive agreement took place between them on the fubject of the purchafe. In a few days afterwards the prifoner fetched the chaife from Mr. Lycett's with his own horfes; and it was in evidence, that he was driven in it from London to the Crown and Cufhion at Uxbridge, where he ordered a pair of horfes, and went from thence to the Duke of Portland's, and returned. He took frefh horfes at the Crown and Cufhion, but where he went with the chaife afterwards, did not appear. The fact was he never returned it to Mr. Lycett; nor could any tidings be obtained of him till twelve months afterwards, when he was accidentally apprehended by the activity of Mr. Feltham, in Fleet-ftreet, upon a fufpicion of having, under falfe pretences, defrauded him of a quantity of ladies hats.

The Counfel for the prifoner fubmitted to the Court, that admitting the whole of the evidence to be true, the offence did not amount to felony; and they endeavoured to diftinguifh it from *the King* v. *Pares*, and *Aickles' Cafe*, inafmuch as in thofe cafes the parties had never obtained the legal poffeffion of the property delivered to them; but that in the prefent cafe the prifoner had obtained the chaife upon a contract, which it was not proved that he had broken; for the chaife was not hired for any definite length of time, or to go to any certain place; and the mere underftanding that it was for three weeks or a month, for the purpofe of making a tour round the North, made no part of the contract. He had hired it for fuch a length of time as he fhould pleafe to keep it, at a certain ftipulated price for each day; and it being delivered to him upon thefe terms, he had the entire poffeffion of it in himfelf, and was anfwerable in damages for its detention, or for any injury which might happen to it during his abfence. But fuppofing the contract fhould be thought not to extend beyond the three weeks or a month, it is clear that during that time he had at leaft the legal poffeffion; and then no intention to convert it wrongfully to his own ufe arifing afterward, whether from neceffity or difhonefty, will make the withholding it felony; for the *animus furandi* muft exift at the time the property is firft obtained. In all the leading cafes upon this fubject of conftructive felony, there has always been fome evidence of a

tortious

tortious *converfion*; but in this cafe it has not been proved that the prifoner has difpofed of the chaife: it may be at this very moment in his poffeffion, for any thing that appears to the contrary, and a converfion cannot be inferred from his having neglected to return it.

THE COURT—The Court is bound by the determination of former cafes. It is now fettled that the queftion of intention is for the confideration of the Jury; and in the prefent cafe if they fhould be of opinion that the original hiring of the chaife was felonious, it will fall precifely within the principle of *Pares' Cafe*, and the other decifions which the JUDGES have made upon the fubject of conftructive felony. If there was a *bonâ fide* hiring of the chaife, to pay fo much for every day for the ufe of it, and a real intention of returning it, a fubfequent converfion of it cannot be felony, whether the time for which it was hired be limited or indefinite; for by the *bonâ fide* contract, and fubfequent delivery, the prifoner would have acquired the lawful poffeffion of it; and therefore, although he afterwards abufed that truft and that poffeffion, felony could not enfue, becaufe the original taking was lawful. But, on the other hand, if the hiring was only a pretence made ufe of to get the chaife out of the poffeffion of the owner, without any intention to reftore it, or to pay for it; in that cafe, the law fuppofes the poffeffion ftill to refide with the owner, though the property itfelf is gone out of his hands, and then the fubfequent converfion will be felony. The cafe of *the King* v. *Pares*, was very folemnly debated at Ld. Ch. Juftice *De Grey's* houfe; and the unanimous opinion of the JUDGES was at laft, That the direction given to the Jury by the learned Judge who tried the prifoner was right. The moft important part of the argument turned upon the confideration, Whether the delivery of the horfe to *Pares* had in law divefted the owner either of his property or the poffeffion of it? The queftion left with the Jury was, Whether the contract was meant fairly? or, Whether it was a mere colour and pretence? The Jury found, that it was a mere colour and pretence: and upon that finding, the JUDGES determined the taking to be felony; becaufe it is an eftablifhed principle of law, that the poffeffion of property cannot be obtained through the medium of a fraud. But it has been attempted to diftinguifh the prefent cafe from *the King* v. *Pares*.——FIRST That the hiring in this cafe was indefinite, but that in *the King* v. *Pares*, it was certain and limited. The time cannot be material in queftions of this nature. *Pares* hired the horfe in the morning, under pretence of going to Sutton in Surrey,

Surrey, and to return in the evening; but as the hiring was
found to be felonious, the law of the case muſt have been
the ſame, although it had appeared that the hiring was for
two days, a week, a month, or any other given time; nay,
if the time had been left entirely unlimited. The circumſtance of the time being long or unſettled, may indeed render the proof of guilt more difficult, but cannot alter the
law of the caſe.—SECONDLY, It is ſaid, that this caſe differs from *the King* v. *Pares*, becauſe it was proved that *Pares*
had ſold the horſe, and therefore had converted it to his
own uſe; but that in the preſent caſe no proof has been
given that the priſoner has ſold or otherwiſe converted the
chaiſe. Proof of actual converſion certainly is not neceſſary,
but the Jury muſt judge of it from the circumſtances of the
caſe. If the priſoner, at any time before the proſecution
was commenced, had offered to reſtore the chaiſe to the
owner, or to pay him for it, ſuch a conduct would have
been evidence of an honeſt intention when he originally
hired it, and would have reprobated the idea of a fraudulent
deſign. But he hires the chaiſe for a month, and a year
paſſes, and neither the chaiſe nor the man are heard of till
he is taken. There is no evidence even at this moment
that the chaiſe is forthcoming, nor does any one pretend to
know where it is. This therefore raiſes a preſumption a-
gainſt the priſoner, which it is incumbent on him to repel;
and if he cannot, it will be for the conſideration of the Jury,
under all the circumſtances of the caſe, whether they think
he has *feloniouſly* diſpoſed of it, or otherwiſe converted it to
his own uſe. In their determination of this point, they
muſt recur to the time of the original hiring, and to the nature and meaning of the contract then made between the
parties. If they think the *re-delivery* of the chaiſe formed
any part of the contract, the *non-delivery* of it muſt neceſ-
ſarily form a part of their conſideration. They will then
conſider whether the *non-delivery* is ſufficient evidence to ſatisfy their conſciences that he has converted it to his own
uſe. Theſe two conſiderations will naturally lead to a third,
viz. Whether the property thus converted was originally
obtained with a felonious deſign? which will carry them
back to the inſtant of time that he obtained poſſeſſion of it:
and if they ſhould find the original hiring was felonious,
the moſt ingenious ſubtlety cannot diſtinguiſh this caſe from
that of *the King* v. *Pares*. There is a caſe in *Kelynge* of a
perſon who took a lodging in a houſe, and afterwards at
night, while the people were at prayers, robbed them. The
Jury found that the intention of taking the lodging was

to

to commit the felony; and the JUDGES determined that this was *burglary*. There was also a case determined very lately by the JUDGES, A man ordered a pair of candlesticks from a silversmith to be sent to his lodgings. They were sent to his lodgings with a bill of parcels; but he contrived to send the servant back, and to keep the goods; and this was held to be felony, although they were delivered, with the bill of parcels, under an expectation of being paid the money: for the Jury found it a pretence to purchase, with intention to steal.

The question of original intention was left with the Jury; and they found the prisoner *Guilty*. A motion was made in arrest of judgment; but he received sentence of transportation for seven years.

TRAPSHAW'S CASE.

At the Old Bailey in August Session, 1786, William Trapshaw was convicted of breaking and entering the dwelling-house of James Linnel, in the day-time, Frances his wife being therein, and stealing several articles of wearing apparel, value 7s. and 4d. the property of the said James Linnel: but the judgment was respited, and a question submitted to the consideration of the TWELVE JUDGES, Whether, under the following circumstances, the room broke open by the prisoner was laid in the indictment to be the dwelling-house of James Linnel?

The house was situated in the Temple-Mews, and belonged to the Earl of Radnor, who let *the whole* of it out in lodgings. It was inhabited by three families, and had only one outer door, which was common to all the inmates. James Linnel rented the ground-floor, and a single room up one pair of stairs. It was the parlour-door on the ground-floor that was broke open, and the things mentioned in the indictment were taken from that room.

The JUDGES assembled at Lord *Loughborough's* Chambers on the first day of Hilary Term, to consider this case; and at the Old Bailey, in the February Session following, Mr. Justice *Gould* publicly declared their opinion.

Mr. JUSTICE GOULD—.The indictment upon which this question arises, is founded on the second part of that clause of the statute 3 and 4 *Will*. and *Mary*, cap. 9, § 1, which enacts, " That all and every person or persons that shall at any time *rob* any other person, or shall feloniously take away any goods or chattels being in any dwelling-house, the owner or any other person being therein, and put in fear; OR *shall rob any dwelling-house in the day-time, any person being therein;* OR shall comfort, aid, abet, assist, counsel, hire, or command any person or persons to commit any of the said offences; OR to break any dwelling-house, shop, or ware-house thereunto belonging, or therewith used in the day-time, *and feloniously take away any money, goods, or chattels of the value of five shillings* or upwards, therein being, although no person shall be within such dwelling-house, shop, or warehouse; OR shall counsel, hire, or command any person to commit any burglary, shall not have the benefit of his or their clergy." The word *rob*, in a legal construction, always includes the idea of *force and violence*; and although this part of the statute does not expresly signify that *breaking and entering* the house is necessary to constitute the crime, yet it has always been held upon this statute, as well as upon other Acts of Parliament penned in the same manner, that those ingredients are *ex vi termini* included in, and implied by, the word ROB. It is therefore essential to consider what degree of breaking and entering is necessary; and it is settled in a variety of determinations upon the statutes relating to this subject, that the breaking must be of a *dwelling-house,* in the same way as would be necessary to constitute the crime of burglary upon the rules of the common law; the only difference between the two offences being, that burglary must be committed in a dwelling-house in the night-time, and this offence must be committed in a dwelling-house by day. The next consideration therefore is, what shall be considered as a dwelling-house within the meaning of this Act of Parliament. In Mich. Term, 1773, a case on a conviction of burglary was determined by the JUDGES, the circumstances of which were analogous to the present case. The owner of the house had let *the whole* of it to different lodgers. The prosecutor rented a room on the first floor, a shop and a parlour on the ground-floor, and a cellar underneath the shop, at 12l. 10s. a year. The owner took back the cellar to keep lumber in, for which he allowed the prosecutor a rebate out of his rent of 10s. a year. The entrance was into a passage by a door from the street, and on the side of the passage one door opened into the shop, and another into the parlour; and beyond the parlour was the stair-case, which led to the upper apartments. The shop and parlour doors were broke open; and the JUDGES determined that these rooms were properly laid to be

the

the dwelling-houfe of the profecutor; for it could not be called the manfion of the owner, as he did not inhabit any part of it, but only rented the cellar for the purpofes before mentioned. And the number of houfes, efpecially in the metropolis, which are in a fimilar fituation, muft have been left entirely unprotected againft burglary, had it been determined that the apartments of lodgers were not their dwelling-houfes, when the owner has, as it were, abandoned the dwelling himfelf, and left the whole houfe to their enjoyment and poffeffion. In February Seffion, 1781, the cafe of *the King* v. *Carrol* for burglary, was referved by Mr. *Recorder*. The houfe belonged to one Nafh, who had let *the whole* of it in feparate tenements. The profecutor, as tenant at will to Nafh, rented a fleeping-room up one pair of ftairs, and a work-fhop in the garret. The door of this work-fhop was broke open; and the queftion was, Whether it could be confidered as the manfion of the profecutor? According to my note of this cafe, the JUDGES were unanimoufly of opinion in the affirmative; and they relied upon *the King* v. *Rogers* as a cafe in point. I have indeed feen a memorandum of the fame cafe by Mr. Juftice *Buller*, in which he takes notice, that only TEN of the TWELVE JUDGES were of this opinion; and from the known accuracy of that learned Judge, I muft prefume the fact was as he ftated it: but I have no recollection that either *he* or Mr. Baron *Eyre* diffented at the time from the opinion of the other JUDGES. In the prefent cafe, however, all the JUDGES are of opinion, That the two determinations which I have recited are precifely in point; and that the prefent indictment properly charges the room broke open, to be the dwelling-houfe of James Linnel. The reafon of this opinion becomes evident the moment it is ftated. The owner of the houfe is, if I may fo exprefs myfelf, THE LORD of it; but having relinquifhed every part of it to the habitation of others, it cannot with any propriety be confidered as *his* manfion or dwelling-houfe. The entierity which refides with him is fplit into feveral poffeffions; and every feparate apartment, being in a diftinct and feveral occupation, is the diftinct manfion-houfe of its refpective poffeffor.

The prifoner accordingly received fentence of death.

WILLIAM WYNNE'S CASE.

At the Old Bailey in April Seſſion, 1786, William Wynne was indicted before Mr. Baron *Eyre*, for ſtealing a deal-box, containing a quantity of wearing apparel and two bonds, the property of Francis Welden, Eſq.

The priſoner was a hackney-coachman, and was called from his ſtand to convey the proſecutor from Oſborn's Hotel in the Adelphi, to No 9, Orchard-ſtreet, Portman-ſquare. Among ſeveral trunks and packages which were put into the coach, was the box mentioned in the indictment. On arriving at the houſe in Orchard-ſtreet, the proſecutor took all the articles out of the coach, except this box, which remained under one of the ſeats. The priſoner received his fare and drove away. A few minutes after he was gone the box was miſſed, and every poſſible means were uſed that day to diſcover the coach; but without ſucceſs. Hand-bills were diſperſed the enſuing morning, and advertiſements inſerted in the public prints, offering a reward to any perſon who ſhould bring home the box. Two days afterwards two perſons called at the proſecutor's houſe in Orchard-ſtreet, and deſired to ſpeak with the Gentleman who had loſt the box; but he not happening to be at home, they left the number of the coach in which it had been left, and the nick-name of the coachman. The very next morning, as the proſecutor was going along Holborn, he diſcovered both the coach and coachman waiting at a door for his fare. The priſoner, on perceiving him, immediately ſaid, " Sir, I and my wife were at your houſe this very day with the box, but I did not leave it, becauſe no perſon was at home to pay the three guineas you offered for finding it; and wanting money very much, I have carried it to one Michael Mitchel, a Jew, who lives at No 5, New Caſtle-ſtreet, Whitechapel." The proſecutor and the priſoner went together immediately to the Jew's houſe. The Jew produced the box, but on examination it was found uncorded, with the haſps forced off; and two bonds, with the papers out of ſeveral pocket-books were miſſing. The priſoner acknowledged that he had uncorded the box, and looked at ſome of the things, but denied having taken any of them away. He alſo acknowledged having borrowed eight ſhillings of the Jew's wife when he left the box that morning

ing

ing in her custody. The prisoner accused the Jew of having burned the bonds. The Jew retorted the same charge upon the prisoner.

The learned Judge observed, that as it appeared the prisoner had not originally taken possession of the property himself, but that it had been thrown upon him by the negligence of the prosecutor, in leaving it behind him in the coach, no felonious intention could be supposed to exist in his mind at the moment the property was first acquired; and although the subsequent circumstance of his keeping it till it was advertised, was a breach of moral duty, it could not of itself be legally considered as a criminal conversion. He therefore directed the Jury, that if they thought the prisoner had detained the box merely in the hope and expectation that a reward would be offered for its restoration, and that he meant then to return it to its right owner, they ought to acquit him; but that, on the other hand, if they were in their consciences perfectly satisfied that he had uncorded the box, not merely from natural though idle curiosity, but with an intention to embezzle any part of its contents, it would become a matter of legal consideration, whether a person so guilty should not be reached as a felon?

The Jury found the prisoner *Guilty*; but the judgment was respited, and the case submitted to the opinion of the TWELVE JUDGES.

In the July Session following, the prisoner was put to the bar, and informed by the RECORDER, that his case had been considered by the JUDGES, and that they approved of the verdict the Jury had given.

He received sentence of transportation for seven years.

JOHN SEARS'S CASE.

At the Old Bailey in January Session, 1789, John Sears was indicted before Mr. Justice *Ashhurst*, for *stealing* a parcel of callico, and other things, the property of Sarah Dixon. The prosecutrix hired the prisoner, who was a hackney-coachman, to drive her from her house in Manchester Buildings, to a linen-draper's in Oxford-Road, where she purchased the articles named in the indictment. They were tied up in a parcel, and put into the coach. The prisoner drove back to Manchester Buildings, and the prosecutrix, on getting out of the coach, ordered him to give the parcel to her servant; but he neglected so to do, and drove *expeditiously*

C c 2

tioufly away. The things were advertifed, and a reward offered to any perfon who fhould reftore them; but without effect. A few days afterwards the profecutrix met the prifoner; but he denied all knowledge of her perfon, or of the things, or of his ever having had fuch a fare. The goods, however, were traced to the prifoner's poffeffion, and the parcel had been opened. The prifoner on his defence acknowledged that he had driven the profecutrix from Manchefter-Buildings to the linen-draper's and back again, but he denied that fhe ever defired him to deliver the parcel to her fervant. Upon this evidence he was convicted of FELONY, and received fentence of imprifonment for fix months by virtue of the ftatutes of 5 *Anne*, cap. 6, and 19 *Geo.* III. cap. 74, § 3.

REX *v.* JOHN PATCH.

At the Old Bailey in February Seffion, 1782, John Patch was indicted before Mr. Juftice *Gould*, prefent Mr Baron *Perryn*, and Mr. Juftice *Buller*, for ftealing a filver watch, a fteel chain, a gold feal, two pieces of foreign coin, and feven fhillings in money, the property of Jeremiah Bumftead.

The profecutor depofed, that the prifoner, and two other perfons who made their efcape, had joined company with him in the ftreet, and after walking a fhort fpace one of them ftooped down and picked up a purfe, which upon infpection contained a ring, and a receipt for 147l. purporting to be the receipt of a jeweller for " a rich brilliant diamond " ring." The prifoner propofed that they fhould go into fome public-houfe, to confider in what manner their refpective portions of this prize were to be divided, and accordingly they all four of them went into an ale-houfe on Saffron-hill. Various modes of diftribution were fuggefted: at length the prifoner afked the profecutor, if it would be agreeable to him to take the ring into his own poffeffion, and to depofit his money and his watch as a fecurity to return it upon receiving his portion of its value. The profecutor affented to this propofal; and figned a written agreement, " That when the prifoner, or either of the other two men " returned the watch and money, and *feventy pounds*, he " would re-deliver to them the purfe and the ring." The profecutor accordingly laid the watch and money mentioned in the indictment upon the table, and received the ring. The prifoner beckoned the profecutor out of the room, upon

a pretence

a pretence of speaking to him in private; and during this interval the other two men marched off with the property. The abrupt manner in which they went away suggested to the profecutor that he had been defrauded, and he fecured the prifoner. The ring was valued at ten fhillings.

It was objected by the prifoner's Counfel, that, as the profecutor had parted voluntarily with the poffeffion of his property, it was a fraud only, and not a felony; but the COURT, upon the authority of *the King v. Pares*, p. 392. *infr.* referred it to the Jury to confider, Whether the whole tranfaction was not an artful and preconcerted fcheme in the three men, felonioufly to obtain the profecutor's watch and money?

The Jury found the prifoner guilty; and he was fentenced to raife gravel three years on the river Thames.

HUMPHREY MOORE's CASE.

This was a cafe referved for the opinion of the TWELVE JUDGES by *James Adair*, Efq; RECORDER, at the old Bailey, in April Seffion, 1784, upon the trial of an indictment for ftealing Twenty Guineas, and four pieces of foreign gold coin called Doubloons, the property of John Field, in the dwelling-houfe of John Brown.

The material circumftances of this cafe, as they appeared in evidence, were as follow: The profecutor John Field, a foldier, juft returned from the war in America, was walking along James-ftreet, Covent-Garden, when a ftranger joined company with him. As they walked in friendly converfation with each other down Long-Acre, the ftranger fuddenly ftopped, and picked up a purfe which was lying at a door. After they had proceeded about forty yards, "Come," fays the ftranger, "we will go and drink a pot of porter, and fee what we have picked up." The profecutor was perfuaded to comply; and they accordingly went into a private room in an adjacent public-houfe, where the ftranger pulled out the purfe, and from one end of it produced a receipt, figned "*W. Smith*," for 210l. for one brilliant diamond clufter-ring, and from the other end he pulled out the ring itfelf. A converfation enfued upon the fubject of their good fortune, during which time the prifoner Humphry Moore entered the room; and, being fhewed the ring, he praifed the beauty of its luftre, and offered to fettle the divifion of its value. Upon the ftranger lamenting that he had no money, the prifoner afked the profecutor if *he* had any. The profecutor replied,

replied, that he had *forty* or *fifty pounds* at home. "That sum will just do," said the prisoner. A coach was immediately called, and all three were driven to the prosecutor's lodgings at Chelsea. The prosecutor and the stranger went into the house together, leaving the prisoner at the door. The prosecutor took his money from his bureau, put it into his pocket, and returned with the stranger to a public-house in the Five Fields, Chelsea, kept by John Brown, where they again met the prisoner, who said, "I will give you your share of the ring, if you will be content till to-morrow." The prosecutor put down Twenty Guineas and four Doubloons, which the stranger took up, and in return gave the prosecutor the ring; desiring that he would meet him at the same place on the next morning at nine o'clock, and promising that he would then return the Twenty Guineas and the four Doubloons to the prosecutor, and also One Hundred Guineas for his share of the ring. The prisoner and the stranger went away together. The prosecutor attended the next morning pursuant to the appointment, but neither of the parties came. The ring was of a very trifling value.

It was left with the Jury to consider, Whether the prisoner and the other man were not in concert together; and they were of opinion, that the prisoner was confederating with the person unknown for the purpose of obtaining the money by means of the ring, and did therefore aid and assist the person unknown in obtaining the Twenty Guineas and the four Doubloons from the prosecutor. They accordingly found him guilty of stealing, but not in the dwelling-house, subject to the opinion of the TWELVE JUDGES, whether it was felony.

On the first day of Michaelmas Term 1784, all the Judges, except Lord *Mansfield*, assembled at Lord *Loughborough's* Chambers, to consult upon this case; and in the December Session following Mr. Justice *Willes* delivered their opinion at the Old Bailey to the following effect: All the JUDGES agreed, That, in considering the nature of larceny, it was necessary to attend to the distinction between the parting with the possession and the parting with the property only; that in the first case it is felony, and in the last case it is not. Upon the circumstances of the present case two of the Judges were of opinion, that the Doubloons were to be considered as money, and that the whole was a loan on the security of the ring, which the prosecutor believed to be of much greater value than the money he advanced on it, and therefore that the possession as well as the property was parted with: but nine of the Judges were clearly of opinion, that it was felony;

for

for they thought the Twenty Guineas and the four Doubloons were only deposited in the nature of a pledge till the half of the supposed value of the ring was paid to the prosecutor, and therefore he had parted with the property only, and not with the possession; and they could not distinguish this case from *the King v. Patch*, tried in this Court before Mr. Justice *Gould*, in February Session, 1782, and *the King* v. *Pares*, in September Session 1779. The majority of the Judges therefore were of opinion, That this case had been properly left to the Jury; and that the prisoner was guilty of felony.

The prisoner was accordingly transported.

REX v. DAVIS.

The following case, on *the black Act*, was reserved by Mr. Baron PERRYN, at Hereford Summer Assizes, 1788, for the opinion of the TWELVE JUDGES.

The words of the statute are, " That if any person or persons shall *wilfully* and *maliciously* shoot at any person in any dwelling-house, or other place, every person so offending shall be deemed guilty of felony, and suffer death without the benefit of clergy."

The Indictment stated, " that James Davis, being an ill-designing and disorderly person, of a wicked and malicious disposition, &c. &c. with a certain pistol, loaded with gun-powder and a leaden bullet, which he the said James Davis in his right-hand had and held, he the said James Davis did *unlawfully, maliciously,* and *feloniously* shoot at one ——. &c.

The Question was, Whether the indictment could by any possible construction, or implication, be supported, the drawers of it having neglected to pursue the very words of the statute, by leaving out the word " *wilfully*," and inserting only that the offence was committed " unlawfully, maliciously, and feloniously ?"

The Judges assembled at Lord *Kenyon's* house on 22d February, 1789, to consider this question, and the point was very much debated. —Some of the JUDGES thought that the word *wilful* was implied in the word *malicious* ; but a great majority were clearly of opinion, that as the Legislature had by the special penning of the Act, used both the words " *wilfully*" and " *maliciously*," they must be understood as a description of the offence; and that the omission, in the present indictment, was fatal to its validity.

The prisoner, at the ensuing Assizes, was ordered to be discharged.

JOHN

JOHN PARE'S CASE.

This case was reserved by Mr. Justice *Ashhurst* at the Old Bailey in September Session, 1779.

The prisoner was indicted for stealing a black mare, the property of Samuel Finch. It appeared in evidence, that Samuel Finch was a livery-stable-keeper; and that the prisoner had hired the mare of him to go to Sutton in Surrey and back again, saying he lodged at Nº 25 in King-street, and should return about eight o'clock the same evening. He did not return; and it was proved that he had sold the mare on the very day he had hired her, to one William Holls, in Smithfield-market; and that he had no lodging at the place to which he had given the prosecutor directions.

The Jury found that the facts above stated were true; and also that the prisoner had hired the mare with a fraudulent view, and intention of selling her immediately.

The question was referred to the JUDGES, Whether the delivery of the mare by the prosecutor to the prisoner, had so far changed the possession of the property, as to render the subsequent conversion of the mare a mere breach of trust, or whether the conversion was felonious?

The JUDGES were unanimously of opinion, That the question, as to the original intention of the prisoner in hiring the mare, had been properly left to the Jury; and as they had found, that his view in so doing was fraudulent, the parting with the *property* had not changed the nature of the *possession*, but that it remained unaltered in the prosecutor at the time of the conversion, and that the prisoner was therefore guilty of felony.

THE

THE

LAWYER'S

AND

MAGISTRATE'S MAGAZINE.

For JULY, 1790.

The Trial of RENWICK WILLIAMS, before Mr. JUSTICE BULLER, at the Old Bailey, July 8, 1790.

CLERK *of the arraigns.*—Renwick Williams, hold up your hand. You ſtand indicted by the name of Renwick Williams, for that you, on the 18th of January laſt, with force and arms, at the pariſh of St. James, Weſtminſter, in the King's highway, in a certain public ſtreet there, called St. James's ſtreet, unlawfully, wilfully, maliciouſly, and feloniouſly, did make an aſſault on Ann Porter, ſpinſter, with an intent to tear, ſpoil, cut, and deface her garments and cloaths, and the ſame day with force and arms in the ſame public ſtreet, wilfully, maliciouſly, and feloniouſly did tear, ſpoil, cut, and deface her garments, to wit; one ſilk cloak, value 10s. one ſilk gown, value 10s. a pair of ſtays, value 5s. a ſilk petticoat, value 5s. one other petticoat, value 5s. a linen petticoat, value 5s. and a ſhift, value 5s. her property, part of the apparel which ſhe had on her perſon, againſt the form of the ſtatute, and againſt the King's peace, &c.

Counſel for the Proſecution.
Mr. PIGOTT, Mr. SHEPHERD.

Counſel for the Priſoner.
Mr. KNOWLYS.

Ann

Ann Porter sworn.

Mr. Shepherd. I believe, Madam, you live in St. James's Street?

Miss Porter. Yes, Sir.　On the Queen's birth-night, I went to the Palace; I left the palace about a quarter past eleven, and came from thence towards my father's house.

Q. Who was with you?

A. My sister and Mrs. Mead.

Q. Did you, on that evening, see the prisoner at the bar?

A. Yes, Sir, but not till I was at my own door.

Q. Did you perceive any thing remarkable in the conduct of your sister, or the lady who was with you, before you came to your own door?

A. Yes, Sir; my sister desired me to make haste, and we went as fast as we could; she said something else, but I did not distinguish the words.　My sister went first to the door, Mrs. Mead followed her, and I was the last; my sister went first to ring the bell.

Q. Did any thing happen to you at the door of your father's house?

A. Yes; just as I was passing the corner of the rails, I felt a violent blow on my hip; I turned round to see from whom it proceeded, and I saw that man stoop down.

Q. That man?

A. Yes, Sir, that man.

Q. Before I ask you any other question about what passed that time, you say it was that man?

A. Yes, Sir.

Q. Had you ever seen him before?

A. Yes, three or four times.

Q. When you had seen him before, had he said any thing to you?

A. Yes; he had.

Q. Did you know him as an acquaintance?

A. I know no more of him than walking in the middle of the day, he insulted me and my sisters with very gross and indelicate language; he walked behind me and muttered.

Q. I do not ask you to repeat what he said to you; but in what manner did he speak, and what sort of language?

A. Very gross, and very abusive.

Q. Had that happened to you more than once?

A. Yes, Sir, three or four times.

Q. At the times when he accosted you in that way, had you any opportunities of observing his person?

A. Yes, Sir, because it was in the day time.

Q. When

Q. When you was standing at the door of your father's house, and received this blow, and turned round and saw the man stooping down, did you at that time recognize that man to be the same that had spoken to you?

A. It struck me immediately to be the same man; I knew him the moment.

Q. How long did he continue at your father's door after he gave you this blow?

A. I cannot say, Sir; he did not run away: I was very much shocked at the sight of him; I endeavoured to pass on the side of the door; I felt a very strange sensation, and I fancy he must have passed at the same time I did; he stood opposite to me and stared in my face; he walked up to the top of the steps on the opposite side of the door I was of, and stood as close to me as he possibly could.

Q. Had you then a full and complete opportunity of observing his face?

A. Yes, perfectly.

Q. Look at him; have you any doubt of that being the person that struck you the blow?

A. No, Sir, I have not the smallest doubt; I could not have been positive, but I saw him three or four times before; I suffered so much from the insults I received, that it is impossible I could be mistaken; I could never forget him.

Q. In what manner were your cloaths cut?

A. They are here, Sir.

Q. Did they appear to be cut with a sharp instrument?

A. Yes, a very sharp one.

Q. How long after this circumstance had happened to you did you next see the prisoner?

A. Not till Sunday evening as I was walking in the park, the 13th of June, with my mother and all my sisters; Mr. Coleman was with me, and his brother with my mother and sisters.

Q. Did you see the prisoner?

A. Yes; we were in the Mall, and he passed me very close.

Q. Did he meet you, or pass you?

A. He met me, and passed me very close; I was struck with his appearance; I knew him the moment I saw him; I was very much agitated, and Mr. Coleman asked me the reason. I knew him the moment I saw him; I turned round to look at him, and he was turning back to look at me.

Q. When was the next time you saw him?

A. At

A. At my own house that evening; Mr. Coleman brought him.

Q. Did you recognize him when he came into your house?

A. I was in such a state, I was almost insensible.

Q. Have you had since that time an opportunity of seeing him more than once, and of recollecting whether he is or is not the man?

A. I wanted no recollection; I knew him the moment I saw him; I knew him the next day at Bow-street.

Q. When you saw him at Bow-street, was he pointed out to you, or did you know him as soon as you saw him?

A. I knew him the moment I saw him.

Mr. Knowlys, Prisoner's Counsel.—I do not wish to ask you any questions to confuse you; I assure you there is no man in this Court that feels more sincerely for the pain that has been occasioned to you by some person or other, than I do; I must ask you a few questions that are necessary to my duty.—You say you live in St. James's Street?

A. Yes.

Q. You say only with one sister and Mrs. Mead, you went to the ball room?

A. Yes, Sir.

Q. As you were coming home, how far was you from St. James's, before your sister spoke to you, telling you to run?

A. A few doors up the street.

Q. You say you did not hear what your sister said, when she desired you to run?

A. I did not.

Q. I take it, that it flurried you a little?

A. I was not agitated then; I ran fast; I thought she had some motive.

Q. Did you run as fast as you were able to run?

A. I ran particularly fast.

Q. You were at that time, ladies unprotected by any gentleman?

A. Yes.

Q. Have you any recollection at the time, whether the door was open, and your sister and Mrs. Mead had got in before this happened?

A. No, Sir, the door was not open till after.

Q. I think you describe that you felt a pretty violent blow, very violent indeed?

A. Very much so.

Q. Be

Q. Before you felt this violent blow you had not seen the person whom you supposed to be the prisoner?

A. No.

Q. I take it then you was a good deal alarmed and turned round to see from whence it came: did not the blow give you a very sudden alarm and flutter?

A. Yes, it did.

Q. How close was the person to the house, at the time you turned round?

A. He was close to the rails, and as close to me as he could be.

Q. In the middle of the street; I take it there was a great deal of light?

A. Our house is surrounded with lights.

Q. Were you at all able to observe the dress he was in at that time?

A. I know he had a light coat on, which fell across his shoulders; I believe he had another coat under that.

Q. Can you be accurate as to the time when this matter happened?

A. It was exactly a quarter past eleven: my father and two friends were come to fetch us: I was rather anxious as the Queen retired so early, and Mrs. Mead desired me to look at my watch, which I did; that was while we were in the Ball-room, the instant we quitted the gallery; and I do not think it was above five minutes before we got to our door.

Q. All the other times you had seen him, it was in the day time?

A. No; once I saw him at Ranelagh, at night, while we were waiting for a coach. (*The cloaths produced.*) This is the gown I had on.

Q. Was that rent in the gown the effect of the blow you received?

A. Yes.

Q. You can put that in a wearable state without much difficulty?

A. No, Sir. (*The shift produced which was cut.*)

Mr. Shepherd. Q. Your person was hurt, as well as your cloathes were cut?

A. Yes, Sir.

Q. Was it with a sharp instrument?

A. I did not see the instrument, but it must be a sharp instrument.

Q. Was the street light enough to distinguish every person's face who stood as near to you as the prisoner did?

A. Yes,

A. Yes, it was quite light enough.

Sarah Porter sworn.

Mr. Piggot. Will you please to look at the prisoner at the bar; did you ever see him before the 18th of January?

A. Yes.

Q. Were you acquainted with him?

A. No.

Q. Where then have you seen him?

A. In the street at different times; he has followed me, and talked to me.

Q. Were your sisters with you at the time?

A. Yes; my eldest sister, and one of the others.

Q. In what manner, I do not mean to be particular, did he accost you?

A. In walking close behind me with his head quite leaning over my shoulder, and talking the most dreadful language that can be imagined.

Q. The most gross, shocking language?

A. Dreadful.

Q. Have you ever heard any other sort of language from him?

A. No.

Q. How many times might you have seen him in this manner before the 18th of January?

A. Four times he spoke. I observed him particularly, and perfectly know his person.

Q. Did you see the prisoner at the bar on the 18th of January?

A. Yes; at the bottom of St. James's street; at about half an hour past eleven; it was a quarter past eleven when we left the ball; he was standing with his back towards me; he was looking down the street.

Q. Are you sure it was him?

A. Oh, I am certain it was him; I knew him before I came up to him; some chairmen were passing by, who said, By your leave! upon which he started round, stared in my face and looked again, and said Oh, oh! and instantly gave me a violent blow on my head, the back part of my head.

Q. Upon that, what did you do?

A. I requested my sister to run; I said, Nancy, for God's sake make haste, do not you see the wretch is behind us? a name we always distinguished him by.

Q. There was another lady with you, I understand; did you all run?

A. Yes,

A. Yes, as faft as we could; I ran firft to ring at the door; while I was ringing at the door, I turned round to fee if he was coming, and I faw him run paft acrofs the ftable-yard; he was clofe to my fifter, and he ftooped down; I was terrified, and I called out again; the words were half uttered, when he rufhed between Mrs. Mead and me, and I faw him ftrike with the greateft violence, and I heard the filk rent; his hand was fhut, I obferved particularly.

Q. Was the man whom you faw ftrike in confequence of which you heard the gown rent, the fame man who had fpoke to you in the ftreet four times before?

A. Yes, I am confident of it, and there was no other man near; I faw him perfectly; I have no doubt in the world; I am as clear as I am of any thing.

Q. Was there fufficient light to enable you to difcover his perfon?

A. The ftreet was very much illuminated.

Q. What ftate did you find your fifter in?

A. My fifter followed me in; I ran as faft as I could, and I turned round, and he was on the threfhold of the door; our paffage was very light, which gave me particular opportunity of feeing him perfectly.

Q. When did you next fee him?

A. I faw him the week before he was apprehended, go down St. James's-ftreet; I was fitting at work at the front window, and my fifter was ftanding at the other; I was fo exceffively terrified, that I faid, Good God, Nancy, look over the way! and fhe immediately faid, There is the Wretch that wounded me. We fent two men after him, but they unfortunately followed another man.

Q. When you went to Bow-ftreet, did any body point him out of the crowd, or did you yourfelf felect him?

A. Sir Sampfon Wright defired me to look round, and I pointed him out directly: he was ftanding indifferently among the crowd, and I pointed him out.

Q. Upon looking at the prifoner at the bar, have you the fmalleft doubt that the prifoner is the perfon?

A. If I had any fhadow of doubt, I would not have fworn to him; but I am certain of it.

Mr. Knowlys. Q. I believe you know, in point of fact, that there is another indictment againft the prifoner, at your fifter's profecution, for cutting her, is there not?

A. Yes.

Rebecca Porter fworn.

Mr. Shepherd. Q. You are the fifter of the two laft witneffes?

A. Yes.

Q. You

Q. You were not with your fifters at the Ball-room on the 18th of January?

A. No. I was not.

Q. Did you ever fee the prifoner at the bar before?

A. Yes, I have feen him feveral times.

Q Did you ever fee him any time when he was with your fifter?

A. I faw him once when I was with my fifter Ann.

Q Did you ever fee him accoft your fifter?

A. Yes, he accofted us both that time.

Q. I do not afk you to exprefs it, but what fort of converfation, what fort of language did he make ufe of?

A. The moft horrible I ever heard in my life.

Q. Are you fure that the fame perfon who accofted your fifter Ann is the prifoner at the bar?

A. Yes, I am fure of it; I have not the leaft doubt, Sir.

Martha Porter fworn.

Mr. Piggot. Look at the prifoner at the bar; did you ever fee that man before?

A. Yes, Sir, feveral times; the firft time I ever faw him, my fifter Ann was with me; he accofted her.

Q. In what manner did he accoft her? I do not wifh you to ftate the words he ufed.

A. In the moft horrid manner poffible.

Q Then you heard the words he ufed?

A. Yes, Sir, and very dreadful words they were.

Q Have you any doubt that is the man that ftands there?

A. No, Sir, I am pofitive that is the man?

Q. Did you fee him at Bow-ftreet, at the time he was apprehended?

A. Yes, I did.

Q. And you are pofitive that is the man?

A. Yes, Sir, I am very pofitive.

John Coleman fworn.

Mr. Shepherd. Q. Do you remember being with Mifs Porter on the 13th of June laft, in St James's Park, in the evening?

A. Yes; I perceived her very much agitated, and fhe told me the Wretch had juft paffed her; fhe pointed him out to me.

Q Was that the perfon fhe pointed out to you?

A. That was the perfon; I followed him, and he walked exceedingly faft; I followed him out of the Park, and out of Spring-Garden-Gate; he walked as low as the Admiralty;

ralty; he paffed down the Admiralty paffage; then he perceived I was following him; he looked up at a houfe, and
then turned round and faw me: I am very fure he faw I was
following him; he walked to the bottom of this paffage,
and walked up Spring Gardens again; then he went along
Cockfpur-Street, into Pall-Mall.

_2._ At what diftance might you follow him?

_A._ I fuppofe a number of times it was not a yard, fometimes four or five yards; he went up St. James's-Street; then
I overtook a gentleman, an acquaintance of mine, and he
went with me, and we went up to the top of St. James's-
Street, he croffed over by the White-Horfe-Cellar, and went
down by the Duke of Devonfhire's wall; then he went into
Bolton-Street, and knocked at a door, and went in; in
about five minutes he came out; I immediately followed
him; he went down St. James's-Street again, and knocked
at the door of a china-fhop; I was at the ftep of the door,
the fame time that he was; a man fervant came down to the
door; he afked fome queftion, I do not know what; the
fervant was going to fhut the door, I prevented him from
fhutting the door; the prifoner was then in hearing, and I
afked the fervant, who opened the door, whether he knew
the perfon who knocked at the door juft now; he faid no,
he did not know him: I then followed him up St. James's-
Street and Bond-ftreet. I did every thing that laid in my
power to infult him, by walking behind him, walking before him, looking at him very full in the face, making a
noife behind him; he would not take any infult; he never
faid a word; I followed him behind, and I behaved in
this kind of way, (peeping over his fhoulders, and making
a clapping with my hands), and I was going to knock him
down once or twice; he croffed Oxford-Road, and went into
Vere-Street; he knocked at a door there which had a bill
againft the fhutter; it was a fhop, and a bill againft the door;
I do not recollect what was the bill; I there fpoke to him,
I was leaning on the rails; in a very impertinent manner I
told him, Sir, this is an empty houfe: he faid no, it was
not, for he knew the people very well, their names were
Pearce, and he knocked again, but nobody came to the
door; from thence he went into South-Molton-Street, he
knocked at the door of Mr. Smith. I was behind him, very
clofe indeed. I afked Mr. Smith to fee the prifoner; Mr.
Smith introduced me to the prifoner in the dark in the front
parlour, he defired I would walk into the parlour; I began
to make an apology for my rude behaviour to this gentleman, and I told him, I thought it very odd he did not take

any notice of my manner of proceeding: I told him, I had come to a resolution to know his address, and would give him mine; he said he thought it was very proper that I should assign some reason for my wishing to know his address; I did not know what reason to assign; I was a little agitated; I did not like to say, Sir, you are supposed to be this Monster; and I told him at last that he had insulted some ladies that I was very intimate with, who had pointed him out to me, and as far as lay in my power I would have satisfaction for that insult; he said, Good God! I never insulted any ladies in my life; I told him I was not sure he was the man, but he must favour the ladies with a sight of him; Mr. Smith said, that I talked very fair, and that he thought it was very proper to give his address to me: Mr. Smith wrote my address, and then the prisoner's " Mr. Williams, No 52, Jermyn-Street." I said, Williams, Williams, I have some recollection of you; I think I know you: he said, I know you too, and he asked if I was not introduced at a ball in Bond-Street to which he belonged; I told him no, but I recollect being introduced to a little assembly that he had belonged to; I said, It is very odd I should follow you so long and not know you before; he said, It is very odd I should not know you; we went contrary ways; I went up South-Molton-Street, and he went down South-Molton-Street.

Q. Did you go to No 52, Jermyn-Street?

A. No, I did not; I walked down Bond-Street, and I considered within myself that I had acted very improperly in letting him go; I overtook him in Piccadilly near the top of St. James's-Street; he said to me, We meet again! I said, We do meet again: walking down St. James's-Street, I said, Good God! Williams, I do not think you are the person I took you for; if you will give the Ladies an opportunity of seeing you this evening, it will be better: he said, It is late; I said, It is late, but it is not far from here where the Ladies live: we walked down St. James's-Street, nearly opposite Mr. Porter's door*; I then asked him to cross the way; we were crossing over the way together; nobody was with me but the prisoner, and my brother was crossing the way with the two Miss Porters; we went up to Mr. Porter's door; I desired the prisoner to walk in; he looked at the house and said, Good God! this is Mr. Porter's. I said, Yes; I introduced the Gentleman to the Ladies in the parlour, and two of the Miss Porters immediately fainted

* Mr. Porter keeps the House called Pero's Bagnio, in St. James's-Street.

away:

away: that was Mifs Sarah Porter and Mifs Ann Porter, exclaiming, " Oh, my God! Coleman, that is the wretch."

Q. Did you fay any thing when you introduced him?

A. No, Sir.

Q. Before they exclaimed in this way, and fainted away, had you particularly pointed him out as the man, or had you only introduced him into the parlour?

A. No, I defired him to walk in.

Q. How did the prifoner conduct himfelf at the time they fainted away?

A. He did not conduct himfelf in any particular way; I thought he poffeffed very great refolution in cafe he was the guilty man.

Q. Did he fay or do any thing when the Mifs Porters cried out, That is the wretch?

A. He faid, The Ladies behaviour is extremely odd; he faid, Good God! they do not take me for the perfon about whom there has been fo many publications? I anfwered, It really is fo, Sir; I do not recollect he made any anfwer to it.

Q. How long did he ftay there?

A. He was there an hour; Mifs Porter thought proper to fend for fome ladies; I heard him fay once or twice that the ladies were prejudiced.

Court. Q. What anfwer did he give; or did he give any when you faid it really was fo?

A. I do not think he faid any thing; I cannot fay; I did not make any particular obfervation.

Crofs-examined by Mr. Knowlys. When you gave your reafons for wanting his addrefs, he gave you an addrefs where he was to be found?

A. Yes.

Q. When he got to Mifs Porter's he was not at all embarraffed?

A. Not in the leaft.

Patrick Macmanus fworn.

Mr. Pigot. Q. Did you ever fee the prifoner at the bar?

A. Yes.

Q. Where did he lodge?

A. In Bury-Street, Jermyn-Street.

Q. At what houfe?

A. At the George public-houfe.

Q. What lodging had he there?

A. It was a room where there were two beds, and a little room parted off, and in that there was another bed, but there was no way in but through the two-bedded room.

Q. What fort of a public-houfe?

A. I believe they are good people.

Q. Did you fearch his lodging?

A. Yes, in the lodging I found thefe two articles in a box, which I underftood had been opened the day before by fomebody elfe.

Q. Did you find any cloaths?

A. They are here; a coat, a hat, and a pair of fhort boots. I fhewed him thefe cloaths found at his lodgings, and he faid they were his; the coat is lapelled; I have feen him myfelf in this coat before.

Mr. Knowlys. *Q.* You fay that the lodging was not a dear one; the people were good?

A. As good as any that keep a public houfe.

Q. That is a clofe-bodied coat?

A. Yes.

Q. Is it a coat to wear over another?

A. No, I think not.

Jury. It is not a furtout coat, certainly.

Court. What number was it?

A. I do not know the number.

Q. Did you ever hear the prifoner fay he lodged there?

A. I did.

Mr. Knowlys. On fearching the lodging of the prifoner did you find any cutting inftruments?

A. No, Sir.

Court. I want to know whether the direction he gave, N° 52, Jermyn-Street, might apply to the houfe in Bury-Street. Where did the mother live?

A. In Duke-Street, which goes out of Jermyn-Street.

Q. Whether a direction, N° 52, Jermyn ftreet, might carry a man to that houfe in Bury-ftreet, which goes out of Jermyn-ftreet, in order to fearch for any perfon they wanted?

A. I fhould not look for it in Bury-Street.

Court. Macmanus's evidence is perfectly irrelevant to the cafe, as to this circumftance, whether the refidence of the prifoner does or does not correfpond with the card given to Coleman.

Court to Coleman. Was that addrefs which the prifoner gave you in writing, one that he wrote down after you afked for his addrefs, or had be it ready written before?

A. Mr. Smith wrote it.

Q. By his direction?

A. Yes,

A. Yes, my Lord.

Mr. *Tomkins,* Surgeon, *sworn.*

Mr. Shepherd. Q. I believe you attended Mifs Ann Porter after fhe was hurt?

A. I did.

Q. From the nature of the wound which fhe had, muft it have been made with a fharp inftrument?

A. A very fharp inftrument.

Q. Did you examine the cloaths?

A. I did; I examined the gown, which was confiderably cut, and the petticoat too; I am not fure whether I faw the fhift; I believe I did not.

Q. Did it appear to be done with the fame inftrument, and at the fame time?

A. Certainly.

Q. How deep was the wound?

A. The firft part of the wound was only through the fkin, the middle part was at leaft three or four inches deep, and then it run about three inches more through the fkin only. The whole length of the wound was, I believe, between nine or ten inches.

Mr. Knowlys. Q. Whether a cut with a fharp inftrument, merely to cut the cloaths, would have wounded fo deep as that?

A. That I do not know; it muft have been with great violence; part of the blow was below the bow of the ftays; if not, it would probably have pierced even the abdomen.

Mr. Knowlys to Macmanus. You called at his mother's houfe?

A. Yes.

Q. Was not it the corner of Duke-Street, and Jermyn-Street?

A. Yes.

Q. Was it No. 52?

A. I do not know; it is a perfumer's fhop.

Court. In which ftreet was the door of the mother's houfe?

A. I went in at Jermyn-Street; I do not know whether there was any other door or not.

Prifoner's Defence.

My Lord, and Gentlemen of the Jury, I ftand here an objea deferving your moft ferious attention and compaffion; from confcious innocence of the very fhocking accufations made againft me, I cannot but hope that juft and really liberal

beral minds will have reason to commiserate my situation, and must feel me deserving pity and compassion. I admit in justice that I should have experienced the hardships I have suffered in the process of the law against me, till my innocence could be proved; but while I revere the law of my country, which presumes every man to be innocent till proved guilty, yet I must reprobate the cruelty with which the Public Prints have abounded, in the most scandalous paragraphs, containing malicious exaggerations of the charges preferred so much to my prejudice, that I already lie under premature conviction, by an almost universal voice. I chearfully resign my case into the hands of this tribunal, and which, I trust, will not suffer the fate of a fellow-creature to be determined by popular prejudice. I rest my case to the decision of an English Jury; and, in hopes of being able to establish my innocence in your opinion, I most seriously appeal to the Great Author of Truth, that I have the strongest affection for the happiness and comfort of the superior part of this creation, the fair sex, to whom I have, in every circumstance that occurred in my life, endeavoured to render assistance and protection. I have nothing, my Lord and Gentlemen, further to say, but that, however strange and aggravated this case may appear to you, I solemnly, and with the utmost sincerity, declare to you all, that this prosecution of me is founded in a dreadful mistake, which I hope the evidence I shall bring will prove to your satisfaction.

WITNESSES FOR THE PRISONER.

Amarvel Mitchell sworn. (The witness being a foreigner, an interpreter was sworn.)

Mr. Knowlys. Q. What business are you, and where do you live?

A. A flower-maker, in Dover-Street, Piccadilly.

Q. Do you know the prisoner?

A. Yes. Between eight and nine months he worked with me.

Q. Was he at work with you on the Queen's birth-day, the 18th of January?

A. Yes. He worked from nine in the morning till one; he returned at half after two, and worked till twelve at night; and then after that he supped with me, and staid till half after twelve; we usually only worked till nine o'clock; on that day we worked till twelve; we supped at twelve.

Q. Are you, or are you not sure, that the prisoner was at work all that time, from half past two till twelve, when you went to supper?

A. Yes.

A. Yes.

Q. At what time did the prifoner quit your houfe?

A. At half paft twelve at midnight.

Q. If he was abfent any fpace of time, muft you have obferved it?

A. I fhould certainly have perceived it, and taken notice of it.

Q. How many perfons were there employed in the houfe with you?

A. Myfelf, my fifter, two work-women, and the prifoner; the work-women lodged at the houfe.

Q. What character is the prifoner?

A. I can give him the beft character a man can have.

Q. Did he behave with civility and good nature to the young ladies that worked with him in the houfe?

A. Always perfectly well; no reproach at all to the man; there were two people that were at work that day, did abfent themfelves two or three times, one went out at eleven, and the women went out at half after.

Mr. Pigott. *Q.* How long have you been in this country?

A. Almoft four years.

Q. Have you the whole of the houfe in Dover-Street, Piccadilly?

A. Only the ground-floor.

Q. How long have you known the prifoner?

A. I do not exactly recollect when he firft came to me; it was either in November or December: he offered himfelf to me to work.

Q. Nobody introduced him?

A. No.

Q. You took him in that way.—What does your family on this ground-floor confift of?

A. Myfelf, my fifter, and two work-women?

Q. Who are the people that work at thefe artificial flowers?

A. Three women.

Q. Does any man work at this artificial flower-work, except the prifoner, at your houfe?

A. I have one man to cut out the flowers; that was the man that went out at eleven o'clock the fame night; the other went at half an hour after.

Q. Then there is no other man who worked at the trade but the prifoner, the other three being women.—At what hour in the evening did they generally leave the work?

A. At nine.

Q. How

Q. How many times in the year may you have worked till twelve at night.

A. We were very full of bufinefs for about a fortnight before this; commiffions from Ireland; and the prifoner always worked extra hours with the reft.

Q. Do you mean to fay that every evening for fourteen days before this you worked till twelve at night?

A. I cannot fay every day for the preceding fortnight, but every day for the laft nine days.

Q. What day of the week was the Queen's birth-day?

A. On Monday.

Q. What time did you go home that day?

A. I returned home about fix in the evening.

Q. What time did you go ou.?

A. About three o'clock.

Q. Had you no curiofity after fix o'clock to go out that evening?

A. I could not, for a commiffion from Ireland demanded my attendance at home.

Q. Then, having this extraordinary work, how came you to indulge your curiofity in going till fix o'clock?

A. The extraordinary order came to me after I came home at fix in the evening; it was an order for a lady's gown, which preffed me particularly.

Q. Then that was the reafon for working till twelve at night?

A. Yes; becaufe it was a work that was to be finifhed; and I promifed to do it againft the next morning, for which reafon I kept the prifoner fo late.

Q. For whom was that gown?

A. For Mrs. Abington.

Q. Who brought it?

A. Mr. Jerfo: he is a Frenchman.

Q. What is he?

A. He is a merchant of modes.

Q. Where does he live?

A. I think it is in Caftle-Street, Leicefter-Fields.

Q. When was this gown to be got ready?

A. There was no determined time, but as foon as poffible. I delivered it between ten and eleven the next morning.

Q. Had none of your working people gone out, led by the attractions of the day, in the courfe of the day?

A. The three Englifh women went out, becaufe I was not apprifed of this order.

Q. Then the three Englifh women did not affift in this

A. I

A. I gave them leave, at one o'clock, to leave work for that day, and to come the next morning.

Q. What time did the three English women come home?

A. They did not come back that day.

Q. Who then did work at this gown, after the order came in, till twelve at night?

A. The prisoner, my sister, and two work-women who lodge in the house.

Q. Where did the prisoner dine that day?

A. I do not know.

Q. Did the prisoner usually eat in your house?

A. Whenever I employed him beyond nine in the evening, he then used to sup with me; but never except there was extraordinary work, and I wished to have his assistance.

Q. Did the prisoner then work constantly at this work in your house?

A. The prisoner never came to my house but to work only.

Q. Did he constantly work at your house?

A. During the eight or nine months that he worked with me, he never absented himself, and I do not recollect giving him leave above once or twice.

Q. What were the whole number of hours in the day which the prisoner during this eight or nine months worked constantly at this flower-work?

A. From about nine in the morning, till after one in the afternoon; and after dinner-time till nine at night.

Q. Then during all these eight or nine months, from nine in the morning till half past one, and again from two till past nine, the prisoner at the bar never was in the streets?

A. No, only with the exception of one or two times that I gave him leave to be absent, he never was in the streets, unless it was on commissions which I had given him.

Q. Did you use often to send him out on errands?

A. Not above once or twice in all that time, as I believe.

Q. What time at night did the prisoner quit you?

A. Half after twelve at night.

Q. Did not you look at your watch just at the moment the prisoner was going away?

A. I cannot say I looked at the watch.

Q. Did you look at the clock?

A. I did not.

Q. Then how durst you swear positively that it was half past twelve at night when the prisoner quitted you?

A. I

A. I only know by the maid looking at the clock, and saying that it agreed with the watchman going the hour.

Q. Then at that moment that the prisoner was going out, the maid said she looked at the clock, and that the clock agreed with the watchman, who then cried half past twelve?

A. The maid looked at the clock, hearing the watchman cry the half hour, and told me how well the clock went, agreeing with the watchman.

Q. Where stands this clock?

A. In the parlour, which you must go through to go out of the house.

Q. Where was you?

A. In my workshop.

Q. What is the distance between the parlour and the workshop?

A. A little court between the two rooms, in one of which I was seated, in one of which the prisoner was.

Q. Who let the prisoner out at the door?

A. Molly.

Q. Was it Molly that made the observation on the time?

A. Yes.

Q. Where did she make the observation?

A. I cannot exactly recollect; it was not to me, but to my sister, and my sister reported it to me.

Q. Then you did not hear this girl make the observation at all?

A. No.

Q. When did your sister first tell you that this observation had been made by Molly?

A. It was some time afterwards; not at that time, nor that day.

Court. How long afterwards?

A. About a fortnight or three weeks from this time; this maid lived no longer with me, and we called upon her to know if she recollected any thing.

Q. Do you cook your victuals in your own house?

A. Yes.

Q. What had you for supper that night?

A. I do not recollect.

Q. When did you next see the prisoner after that again?

A. He came back to work the next morning.

Q. Do you mean at his usual hour?

A. He came early the next morning.

Q. How long after the birth-day did he continue to work with you?

A. Till

A. Till the King's birth-day, the 4th of June.

Q. Who was that Irish order from, that you spoke of?

A. From a Mr. Crowe, in Ireland; he was here in person when he gave that order; there is the written order.

Q. When did you first recollect that all this happened on the Queen's birth-day?

A. The prisoner sent to me to know if I could recollect those circumstances of that day.

Q. Have you ever in the course of your life walked out with the prisoner?

A. Never, unless by chance about our business.

Q. Was you at home last night?

A. Yes; but I walked out with a friend, and returned about six in the evening to tea.

Q. Does the witness know Lord William Gordon's house in Piccadily.

A. Yes, I have been there.

Q. Did you happen to pass that house last night, or where did you walk last night?

A. I did not pass by that house yesterday: I came from Marybone through Grosvenor-Square, Berkley-Square. I recollect now that I did not go out after the time I returned to tea in the evening. I went through Bond-street, and so strait up to Marybone, then down the fields to the Turnpike, then to Berkley-Square, Grosvenor-Square, and home. I now recollect I went out afterwards to settle a bill in Jermyn-street with a carpenter. I did not find him at home; I then went to Duke-Street, where I met an acquaintance, and conversed with him a short time, and from thence I returned directly home.

Q. Then that was the whole of your walk the second time?

A. Yes.

Q. Then you was not in the Green-Park?

A. I was not.

Q. And all the rest that you have sworn to day is just as true as the last, that you was not in the Green-Park yesterday evening?

A. Just as true.

Q. Then, not being in the Green-Park, I need hardly ask you whether you accosted any ladies in the Green-Park yesterday evening?

A. No, I did not address any ladies in the Green-Park.

Q. Or near Lord William Gordon's house * ?

* These questions were suggested by the circumstance of a Lady in Court thinking the witness was a person who behaved rudely to her the evening before in the Green-Park, but as she was not afterwards examined, it is presumed she discovered her mistake.

A. I

A. I was not near that way.

Mr. Knowlys, Is not the Queen's birth day a very particular day for you to notice in the course of your business?

A. Yes.

Q. Have you the least doubt in your own mind that the facts that you relate took place on the Queen's birth-day last?

A. I am firmly persuaded of that.

Q. What is the name of your friend that you took with you?

A. Mr. Jerso: he is not here; he is at my house, to take care of it in my absence.

Court. Let that witness not go out of Court.

Miss Reine Mitchell sworn.

Mr. Knowlys *Q.* Was the prisoner employed, in January, by your brother in his business?

A. He has worked there for about eight or nine months.

Q. How long was he at work there on the Queen's birthday?

A. He staid till half past twelve; for he supped with us.

Q. Was he absent any part of the day from your house?

A. He absented himself only at dinner-time, as usual. He came soon after, and worked with me all the day. He did not go out from the time he returned from dinner till half after twelve.

Q. What was his behaviour to you and the ladies who worked there; was it good-natured or not?

A. I cannot but give him the best of characters in that respect ever since the time he worked with us.

Q. Are you perfectly sure he did not quit the house from the time he returned from dinner till half after twelve?

A. I am.

Cross-examined by Mr. Shepherd.

Q. Was it a customary thing to work as late as this at your brother's house?

A. It is not.

Q. Had they worked often as late as that about that time?

A. For about three weeks we were very much pressed to work, and had been busy particularly that day.

Q. But the whole of the three last weeks you had worked late, was you not working to complete an Irish order?

A. We had a great deal of work for Ireland.

Q. Then you was as much hurried that day as you had been for three weeks before?

A. The same.

Q. Had

Q. Had you the fame reafon for working late that day as you had before?

A. About fix o'clock there came an order from Mrs. Abington.

Q. When did the other two women go away?

A. They went away about half paft eleven: they did not work on Mrs. Abington's order.

Q. When had you promifed Mrs. Abington's order to be done?

A. At eight o'clock the next day we promifed it, but we could not finifh it till between nine and ten.

Q. What were the names of thefe women?

A. There were two worked, but one was a man and the other a woman, a young girl the daughter of a taylor; one went away at half paft ten and the other at paft eleven; the man went away at eleven, and the girl at half paft ten.

Q. Who came with Mrs. Abington's order?

A. Mr. Jerfo. I was there, and I think my brother was there; he did not give the order to me particularly, I think it was to my brother.

Q. Did Mr. Jerfo point out the fort of work to you, or did he fay what fort of work it was?

A. He came to us and fhewed us a pattern that we fuppofe he had from Mrs. Abington; he drew a pattern and brought it himfelf in the evening.

Q. Was your brother out that day, or was he hard at work?

A. He was not out all the evening from fix o'clock when he returned, when we fet to this work.

Q. About what time did Jerfo come?

A. About fix o'clock.

Q. Was your brother at home when Jerfo came?

A. He was there and received the order with me.

Q. Name the names of all thofe that were prefent when Williams went away that night?

A. My brother, myfelf, two women that lodged in the houfe, and a man who came in to fetch work that night before the prifoner left the houfe.

Q. When Williams went away who let him out?

A. One of the maids.

Q. Which of them?

A. We call her Mary; but we do not know her other name?

Q. Did the prifoner work as late as this at any time after that day?

A. He

A. He has worked some other days since that, but I cannot recollect on what days.

Q. What makes you think it was so late as half past twelve?

A. Because the maid came in and said, that when she opened the door the watchman went half past twelve, and she made a remark that the clock went extremely right, for it agreed with the watchman.

Q. Do you mean that the maid stated that at that time?

A. I do not recollect that the maid mentioned the circumstance at that time, but since that time she came and told us of it, and made the remark voluntarily; we sent to the maid to know if she could recollect the circumstance, and then it was that the maid stated the fact about the watchman and the clock.

Q. How long ago was it?

A. Since the prisoner was apprehended.

Q. Did that maid usually let the prisoner out at the door when he went away, if he staid late?

A. She did that night; but it is not customary for her alone to do it. Sometimes her, and sometimes other people.

Q. Did you ever talk with this maid about these circumstances, till after the prisoner was apprehended?

A. Never, it was impossible for her to do it; she did not know any thing about it.

Q. So that she had no other reason to observe any thing that happened that night more than any other night of the working days?

A. No; all this I have heard since he was apprehended.

Court. Did your brother carry on a large trade?

A. Very largely for a great many ladies.

Q. Does he keep any books?

A. Yes.

Q. Do you know who was made debtor for Mrs. Abington's gown; was it Mrs. Abington or Jerfo?

A. Mr. Jerfo.

Q. Are the books here?

A. No, it was delivered to Mr. Jerfo, and he stands in the book.

Court. Let an officer go with Mr. Mitchell for his books, and call on Jerfo and bring him.

Catherine Alman sworn.

Mr. Knowlys. Q. Did you live in January last with Mr. Mitchell?

A. Yes, I live in the houfe.

Q. Was the prifoner at work on the Queen's birth day?

A. He was.

Q. How late did you work?

A. Till near one; I was not out during the courfe of the day.

Q. How long was the prifoner at the bar at work that day?

A. Till half paft twelve; he was abfent from one till two, that was his ufual time of being abfent.

Q. Now from two, till half paft twelve, are you able to fay whether he was abfent or not?

A. He was not.

Q. Are you fure of that?

A. Pofitively fure of it.

Q. How do you know it was half paft twelve?

A. Becaufe my fifter related to me in coming along, that when fhe had opened the door it was half paft twelve.

Q. From the opportunity you have had of judging of his character, do you think him an ill-natured man, or a good-natured man?

A. A very good-natured man, and a man that is very fober and attentive.

Crofs-examined by Mr. Piggott.

Q. It was not ufual to work fo late?

A. No; nine o'clock is the ufual time.

Q. Was the prifoner quite conftant at his work?

A. Quite conftant. He worked the ufual hours.

Q. How long have you lived there?

A. Three years.

Q. The prifoner fupped this night at the houfe, I think you fay?

A. Yes.

Q. And your fifter let him out?

A. Yes.

Q. Only fince the prifoner was apprehended, did your fifter tell this circumftance, that fhe heard the watchman call half paft twelve?

A. No, Sir, I recollect her coming into the room where we had fupped, and fhe faid to me it is half paft twelve, and I am afraid it will be too late for Williams to get into his lodgings.

Q. Then your fifter had fome anxiety for Mr. Williams?

A. No further than he mentioned in the courfe of the evening he was afraid the door would be fhut; on the morn-

ing

ing afterwards he related that the clock struck one when he went into bed. Her fear was such as any body would entertain for a person being out, and shut out, that is not used to be out late?

Q. Will you take upon you, upon your oath, to say that the prisoner ever since that staid one night till about that hour?

A O yes, Sir, he has staid several nights, and later than that if possible; but that day having worked particularly, I am perfectly sure to that day.

Q. How long have you and your sister been acquainted with Williams?

A. Ever since October last.

Q. Did you ever happen to visit him at his lodgings?

A. No, Sir, never. He lodged when he came to our house at Mr. Williams's, in Duke's-Court; there he lodged on the Queen's birth-day.

Q. Where was you when your sister came in and made this observation about the watchman?

A. I was in the workshop, where we had been supping.

Q. Who was with you.

A. Mr. Mitchell, and Miss Mitchell, and another gentleman, when my sister came in and made this observation; she spoke to me in English, therefore they might not know what she said.

Q. The common conversation of the family is in French, is it not?

A. Yes, unless we talk by ourselves.

Q. Had not you been conversing on that evening and all that day in French?

A. Yes; but my sister generally spoke to me in English whenever she spoke to me; not one time in a hundred, I can say, that she spoke French, because she could not speak French then so well.

Q. Why you told me you had been speaking French the whole evening?

A. Certainly, Sir, because whenever we all spoke we spoke in French?

Q. But this observation was in English?

A. Yes, it was.

Q. Now, Miss Alman, recollect yourself upon your oath, when did your sister make this observation to you?

A. After she shut the door, she came strait from the shop door into the back shop where I was, and related the same I now tell you.

Q. When did you first recollect this observation of your fifter?

A. Never till fince I heard that Mr. Williams was taken up; one obfervation and another brought them all to my memory; I had no occafion to recollect it before.

Q. But then you did recollect this obfervation on the watchman?

A. Yes.

Q. Who worked on Mrs. Abington's gown that night?

A. My fifter, Mr. Williams, and Mr. Mitchell.

Mary Alman fworn.

Mr. Knowlys. Where do you live?

A. I lived in January laft at Mr. Mitchell's, with my fifter.

Q. Do you know whether the prifoner lived, or was at Mr. Mitchell's houfe on the Queen's birth-day?

A. Yes, I do; he worked there all day.

Q. Can you fay how long he ftaid on that day?

A. Till half paft twelve at night.

Q. How do you know that it was fo late as half paft twelve when he quitted the houfe?

A. Becaufe I looked at the clock, and I heard the watchman go as I let him out.

Q. If he had been abfent half an hour, or an hour, muft you have obferved it?

A. Yes, I muft, becaufe I had been fitting with him the whole time.

Crofs-examined by Mr. Shepherd.

Q. Had you lived there a fortnight before this time?

A. Yes; a fortnight or a month.

Q. During that time, had the prifoner ftaid fo long after his working-hours at any time?

A. Yes, fometimes he did, but not very late; I look upon that to be the lateft night he ever ftaid.

Q. You let Mr. Williams out?

A. Yes.

Q. How came you to look at the clock?

A. He afked me what o'clock it was, and I looked at it to tell him.

Q. Pray was he going through the fame room as you was?

A. Yes.

Q. Had you a candle?

A. Yes.

Vol. I. *Q.* Why

Q. Why could not he look himfelf?

A. He told me to look, and I looked; and I let him out and came back again into the fhop.

Q. Did you tell your fifter when fhe applied to you to re-collect thefe circumftances, that you had looked at the clock to tell Mr. Williams what o'clock it was?

A. Yes.

Q. How many times had you worked late during the time you had been there?

A. We had not worked late before, while I was there.

Q. How came you to be in a hurry?

A. About this drefs.

Q. And fo they fet you about this drefs, who had never worked before?

Mr. Knowlys. If I underftand your fituation right, you were the perfon employed to do the houfhold work?

A. Yes, I was.

Mr. Shepherd. How long had you known Williams before?

A. I do not know how long, only while I lived at Mr. Mitchell's.

Q. Had you any particular anxiety about his conduct that night?

A. No, Sir.

Q. You had not faid that you was afraid he would be too late at his lodgings?

A. No.

Mr. Knowlys. Had he expreffed that fear to you?

A. He had.

Frances Bowfield fworn.

Q. Was you at work at Mr. Mitchell's on the Queen's birth-bay?

A. Yes.

Q. Was the prifoner there on that day?

A. Yes.

Q. Was he at work?

A. Yes.

Q. Till what time did you work there yourfelf?

A. Till half an hour paft eleven.

Q. Are you fure it was half paft eleven?

A. Yes.

Q. How do you know?

A. Becaufe I afked the watchman when I went home, and he faid it was half an hour paft eleven.

Q. Where is your home?

A. In

A. In Coventry-Court; one end of it comes into Coventry-Street, and the other into the Haymarket.

Q. Had you observed the prisoner working there that day?

A. Yes.

Q. Were you working in the same room with him?

A. Yes.

Q. Was he at Mr. Mitchell's, in the same room, when you left it?

A. Yes.

Q. Had he been working from dinner time?

A. Qes.

Q. Did you leave him there?

A. Yes.

Q. Was the cloth laid when you left them?

A. It was going to be laid; it was not laid.

Typhone Fournier sworn.

Mr. Knowlys. Did you work for Mr. Mitchell in January last?

A. Yes.

Q. Do you recollect the Queen's birth-day, and was you at work then?

A. Yes.

Q. Do you know the prisoner, whether he worked at Mr. Mitchell's house that day?

A. Yes.

Q. How long did you work at Mr. Mitchell's house that day?

A. Till eleven o'clock.

Q. Did you see the the prisoner there, and how long was he there while you was at work?

A. I left him at work there.

Mitchell returned with the books, and Mr. Jerso.

———— Jerso sworn.

Mr. Knowlys. *Q.* You had dealings with Mr. Mitchell?

A. Yes.

Q. Did you call upon him on the Queen's birth day?

A. Yes.

Q. Did you give him any order then, and what order?

A. Yes, an order for a trimming for Mrs. Abington.

Q. Are you sure that order was given on the Queen's birth-day?

A. Yes.

A. Yes, I am sure of it; I drew the pattern at Mr. Mitchell's house that very day.

Q. What made you recollect it?

A. I remember it, because the streets were quite illuminated.

Q. What time was it?

A. It was later than seven. I carried the pattern about seven, and I brought the order to Mr. Mitchell after; it was very near eight when I gave the order.

Q. Did they begin to work upon it directly?

A. I do not know; I went away immediately when I gave the order; I did not look at the work, I said it was necessary to have four yards the next morning about twelve, and the remainder in the afternoon; but the next morning I received eight yards about nine or ten.

Q. Did you see Mitchell himself?

A. No, he was out when I drew the pattern; it was about seven.

Q. When you went the second time, which was about eight did you see him then?

A. I do not recollect at all whether he was at home when I came back; I cannot say whether he was or was not.

Q. Then you do not recollect whether you saw Mitchell at all about this?

A. No, I do not know whether I gave the order to Mr. Mitchell or Miss Mitchell, but whomsoever I did give it to it was about eight at night.

Court. Are you sure of the quantity?

A. It was eight yards.

Q. Look at your own book; explain to us what the entry means?

A. When I carried the trimming to Mrs. Abington, she said she wanted only six yards, and I was obliged to keep the other two yards, and she took it two months after.

Q. Did not she want this for the Queen's birth-day?

A. No, the next day.

Q. What is the whole sum charged in your book?

A. Eighteen shillings a yard, for six yards 5l. 8s.

Court. You dealt with him for a great many other articles, did you not?

A. Yes.

Mr. Piggott. Q. Do you live at the house?

A. No, I married a sister of Mr. Mitchell's, and the prisoner has come two or three times to my house.

Sarah

Sarah Brady sworn.

I worked in Mr. Mitchell's house; I have known the prisoner six months.

Mr. Knowlys. Q. What has been his character for good-nature?

A. Very good-natured.

Q. Did you ever perceive any instance of a spiteful disposition?

A. No; quite the contrary.

Sophia Cameron sworn.

I have known the prisoner eight years; but I have worked with him five months.

Q. During all the time you have known him, what has been his character for good-nature?

A. Truly good-natured.

Q. Did you ever see any thing of him spiteful or ill-tempered?

A. Quite the reverse.

——— Terry sworn.

I am in the Navy-Office; I have known the prisoner from about Michaelmas, 1786, to the present time.

Q. What character has he borne for humanity and good-nature all the time?

A. The most amiable character for good-nature, amiable behaviour, and politeness.

Q. How long has he quitted Mr. Gallini?

A. I believe he quitted him before I knew him; he used to come to help his sister to make flowers; he had no other business that I know of; I believe he used to assist Mr. Gallini in teaching at some boarding-schools.

Thomas Williams sworn.

I deal in china, in St. James's-street; the prisoner is no relation; I have known him near six years.

Mr. Knowlys. Q. During that time, what has been his character for good-nature?

A. Very good natured; he liked the ladies too well; and I was astonished when I heard he was the man; I thought his character very good.

Sarah

Sarah Seward sworn.

I live at the feven dials; I have known him four years.

Q. What has been his character for humanity and good-nature?

A. His character—when I firſt knew that young man, I was exceedingly ill: I never knew him any thing but an honeſt young man; and his behaviour to me was manly, and a credit to any man, for he faved my life.

The prifoner likewife called nine other witneſſes, who all gave him a very good character for humanity and good-nature.

CHARGE.

Mr. JUSTICE BULLER.—Gentlemen of the Jury, to imagine or fuppofe that any body in this crowded audience, ſhould not have heard of the great many very ſerious and atrocious injuries which have been done to ladies in the neighbourhood of this place, would be abfurd: the prifoner, in his defence, has taken it for granted, that every body here muſt have heard what outrages either have been committed, or at leaſt are fuppofed to have been ſo; and therefore he has very rightly addreſſed himfelf in his defence, not only to your paſſions and your feelings, but to your juſtice; for he has told you that popular prejudice has prevailed much againſt him; and therefore he requeſted from your juſtice; that you will hear and confider his cafe with patience and attention, before you pronounce your opinions on him: it is but common juſtice you ſhould do ſo, for popular prejudice often injures, but it never ferves the caufe of juſtice; and therefore I am fure that you in the opinions which you may form on this cafe, will totally lay afide every thing that you may have heard before you came into this Court, and confider the cafe coolly and difpaſſionately on the evidence that has been given: in this, as well as in all criminal cafes, indeed I ſhould fay criminal and civil, you will have only to confider what are the truths of the faƈts that are alledged; and in order to bring the cafe to as narrow a compafs as I can, for your own confideration, I will tell you what appear to me to be the material points for you to difcufs: if after confidering the whole of the cafe, you ſhould be of opinion that the faƈts are made out againſt the prifoner, ſtill I ſhall referve his cafe for the confideration of all the Judges of England, on two grounds; firſt, becaufe this undoubtedly is the firſt profecution that has ever taken place on the ſtatute on which he was indiƈted; and therefore, though

though I cannot profeſs to entertain the ſmalleſt doubt in my own mind, what is the ſure conſtruction of that Act of Parliament; yet being a new caſe, I think it is right that the opinion of all the Judges of England ſhould be known: another point in which, in caſe of conviction, I ſhall ſave the caſe for the opinion of the Judges is, that at preſent I do entertain ſome doubts about the form and ſufficiency of the indictment *; but theſe are queſtions which it is not neceſſary now to agitate. The ſtatute is an act paſſed in the 6th of *Geo.* I. the words of the act are " That if any perſon ſhall wilfully and maliciouſly aſſault another in the publick ſtreets or high ways with intent to tear, ſpoil, cut, tear, burn, or deface, and ſhall tear, ſpoil, cut, burn or deface the garments or cloaths of ſuch perſon, every perſon ſo offending being thereof convicted, ſhall be adjudged to be convicted of felony:" now on this ſtatute you obſerve, Gentlemen, that it is neceſſary that the aſſault ſhould be committed in the ſtreets or highways, that it ſhould be made wilfully and maliciouſly, and alſo with intent to cut or ſpoil the cloaths, and it likewiſe requires that the cloaths ſhould in fact be ſo cut or ſpoiled; now before I ſtate to you the particulars that have been given in evidence, perhaps one might aſſume it as pretty clear that ſome perſon did aſſault Ann Porter, who is the perſon that ſtood forward as the proſecutrix, in the ſtreet, and did give her a blow, which not only cut her cloathes, but cut her perſon alſo; then the two points that are moſt material for your conſideration are, firſt, whether that perſon, be he whom he might that made the aſſault on her, did it wilfully and maliciouſly with an intent to cut her cloaths; becauſe I take it to be very clear that where the intent is a material ingredient in the conſtitution of the crime, that intent is a matter of fact, and not a matter of law; an intent, therefore, being matter of fact, muſt be brought before the Jury. Gentlemen, the next queſtion for your conſideration will be, (if you ſhall be ſatisfied that the perſon, be he whom he might, that thus accoſted Miſs Porter, and gave her the blow ſhe deſcribed, did it with intent to cut her cloaths, as well as to cut her perſon,) whether that man was the priſoner at the bar. Theſe I think are the two leading points for your conſideration. Ann Porter tells you, &c. *Here the learned Judge ſummed up the evidence on the part of the proſecution; and then added,*) Gentlemen, this is the whole of the evidence, on

---

* *The doubt reſpecting the indictment is ſuppoſed to be, that the* cutting *is not expreſsly ſtated to be at the* preciſe time *that the aſſault was made.* the

the part of the prosecution: first, you find that the four young ladies have all sworn very positively to the person of the prisoner; you will naturally examine what opportunities they had of knowing the prisoner; and whether they were likely to be mistaken; as I mentioned to you in summing up the evidence, they had seen the prisoner several times before, and in the day-time; and the manner in which they had seen him, certainly called upon them to pay particular attention to his person; and those who were at the Ball-room, swear equally positive that he was the man; they saw him that night, and they have seen him three times since; and upon no occasion did they entertain the smallest doubt; but when they saw him in St. James's Park, in consequence of what they said he was apprehended, then the said most positively that he was the person, and challenged him like-wise at their house.

Gentlemen, there are two or three other circumstances that are necessary to be taken into consideration with respect to the fact whether they are accurate or mistaken as to his person; first, what it was that passed when the prisoner or the man, whoever it was, met them at the bottom of St. James's-Street, the sister says the prisoner turned round and stared at her, and made use of this expression, Oh, ho! and im-mediately gave her a violent blow on the back of the head; now be the man whom he might, the person that stopt and looked at Miss Sarah Porter at that time, and afterwards gave the wound to Miss Ann Porter, made use of that ex-pression: what is to be collected from it? Is it the expression of a man who was a total stranger and had never seen their faces before? Is it the expression that an intimate friend or acquaintance would use, or is it more likely to be the ex-pression of some man who had seen them before, and be-tween whom something or other had passed that was not so agreeable? The man who had formerly insulted them, might use such an expression. But why should any man do it that had never seen her before; that he was an ac-quaintance of theirs there is no reason or pretence for sup-posing; but they say they have seen him often before; if the man had never seen either of them before, the expression does seem to be very unaccountable. The next thing, Gen-tlemen, to be considered, is the conduct of the prisoner himself when challenged in St. James's Park? Coleman pursued him in consequence of what Ann Porter had said, the prisoner walked on pretty fast, and he led him from place to place at pretty considerable distances; did he or did he not perceive he was pursued by Coleman? If you imagine

gine he did not, it takes off a great deal from the weight of
the evidence; but Coleman tells you he is pofitive, fo early
as when they got down to the Admiralty, the prifoner muft
perceive he was purfued by him, how comes it then that
nothing is faid by the prifoner, that he fhould go from place
to place till he goes to one place where he ftaid about five
minutes, and Coleman had endeavoured to affront him in
every way; and notwithftanding that, the prifoner takes no
notice of it. The next thing that arifes is, what paffed when
they went down St. James's-Street; he tells you the prifoner,
when they croffed the way, faid, This is Mr. Porter's!
Now I do not fee how this affords any inference either way;
becaufe if the prifoner had lived in London and faw Coleman crofs, he might ufe fuch an expreffion, and mean nothing; however, the prifoner is conducted into the parlour,
and what paffed there will be alfo material for your confideration; for, according to the evidence of Mr. Coleman,
a more diftrefsful or melancholy fcene could hardly be exhibited; two young ladies fell into fits, and fainted away; one
exclaimed, That was the Wretch! What is the prifoner's behaviour at that time? Why his obfervation to Coleman is,
" The ladies behaviour is extremely odd! They do not take
me for the perfon advertifed!" he is told pointedly, " Yes,
they do." Now in that fcene, fhould you expect from an
innocent man that he fhould preferve a total filence, or endeavour to give fome explanation of himfelf, or refer to
fomebody to give fome account of him? but Coleman fays
he does not recollect any anfwer that he gave; if he gave
no anfwer, it will be for you to fay what inference is to be
drawn from a man being totally filent when he faw fuch a
fcene of diftrefs, and was told he was charged as doing this
injury: did he appear embarraffed? No, fays Coleman, he
did not; he faid the ladies were under prejudices; but did
he fhew any fenfe of guilt or innocence? What is his general
deportment? Why, fays he, that I cannot tell; it depends
on people's nerves and feelings; fome men may be bafhful;
others very confident and impudent; but when he faw thefe
two young ladies, his applying the circumftances of it to himfelf, by faying, They do not fufpect I am the perfon advertifed;
and being told they did, he fays nothing, or fomething fo
immaterial, that Coleman cannot recollect any one word he
faid: thefe are circumftances arifing from the prifoner's conduct, that undoubtedly give great credit to the pofitive oaths
of the four Mifs Porters, who have fworn moft decidedly
as to his perfon; they, you obferve, fpeak of him at different times; they fpeak of him as having a moft perfect
knon-

knowledge of his perfon before this fact happened ; they are
equally fure of him at the time the fact did happen, and also
at the three periods when they faw him afterwards. Now,
let us fee how the evidence correfponds, and, comparing one
time with another, could they, or is it probable that they
might, be miftaken as to this being the perfon whom they
had feen four times previous to the day or the night when
this injury was done to Mifs Ann Porter? They had feen
him by day ; they had obferved his perfon ; they had agreed
the moment they faw him again, in faying it was the fame
man. If they are accurate in that refpect, and have proved
to your fatisfaction, that the perfon they faw four times before, was the fame perfon they faw three times after, their
evidence goes the length of fhewing that this man was the
perfon whom they had feen at the four different periods that
they fpeak of previous to the time of the injury. The ftreet
was very light ; the houfe was very light ; they had full opportunities of feeing his perfon, becaufe he was clofe to them,
and they fwear that they knew him immediately ; this
ftrongly imports that the man, whoever he was, was not
unknown to them. Gentlemen, fo ftands the evidence on
the cafe on the part of the profecution. For the prifoner,
you have had a great number of witneffes called, feven of
whom are for the purpofe of proving that this prifoner could
not be the man, but that the Mifs Porters are miftaken ; becaufe the prifoner, on that night when the offence was committed, was in another place, namely, at Mr. Mitchell's
houfe : and Mr. Mitchell himfelf tells you, &c. (repeating
Mitchell's evidence). This feems to be obvious from the evidence of Mitchell, that he never recollected, or, in fact,
knew many of the circumftances which he has defcribed to
you, till within a fortnight or three weeks from this time ;
to be fure this is a very loofe way of making up his mind as
to the recollection of a fact which had paffed at the diftance
of pretty nearly fix months. You will find, as I ftate to
you the other evidence, that there are many circumftances
in which this witnefs is contradicted, and in which the
other witneffes have contradicted themfelves ; but what effect
that ought to have, or may have on your minds, is for you
alone to decide. It is not in every little circumftance, in
which witneffes differ who fpeak of the fame tranfaction, that
by differing they deftroy the credit of each other ; but
the queftion is, whether the facts in which you find they
differ, are fo material, and fo pointed, fo much within the
knowledge of each witnefs, that if they told you the truth,
and fpoke accurately on what paffed they could not vary

fo

o much. (*Here his Lordſhip ſummed up the reſt of the evidence on the part of the priſoner.*)—Gentlemen, this is the whole of the evidence. It is for you to ſay whether you give any, and what credit to this alibi; and whether it is proved in a manner that ſatisfies you, that the four Miſs Porters, confirmed as they are by the circumſtances, are miſtaken as to the priſoner. In the firſt place, it is natural to examine, what was there on the night of the Queen's birth-day that called on theſe people to take particular notice of what paſſed then, more than any other night? It is admitted by them, one and all, that they never thought about it, nor converſed about it, till after the priſoner was taken; but that ſeems to me not to diſcredit them. Why ſhould they do it? for, according to their own account, there was nothing to call them to it. After the priſoner was taken up, they endeavoured to refreſh their memories, and bring to their recollection what paſſed on this particular day. Now, in doing that, they certainly varied very much in the accounts they have given; and, at laſt, is there any thing that calls on them peculiarly to fix on the Queen's birth-day as the night when the priſoner remained at Mitchell's houſe till half paſt twelve, and ſupped with them? Was it a peculiar thing that the priſoner ſupped with Mitchell? Mitchell tells you no; that was not ſo; becauſe whenever he ſtaid there after the uſual hour of work, he uſed to ſup there. What is there then that calls upon them to fix with any degree of certainty in the month of July, whether the night in which the priſoner ſupped with Mitchell, and ſtaid till half paſt twelve, was on the 18th of January, or any other day? That he might have ſupped there ſome night, may be very true; that in the courſe of that day Mr. Jerſo was there, and did give an order for Mrs. Abington's gown, might be very true; but it does not follow from thence, that this was the night in which the priſoner ſupped there; and when we bring the caſe to that point, to be ſure the very contradictions that are in the teſtimony, are extremely material, particularly in endeavouring to fix the time; Mitchell and his ſiſter have no other line to go by, but what one ſervant tells them another ſervant told her; and theſe two ſiſters directly contradicting one another. Gentlemen, it is for you to ſay which ſide you give credit to; if you believe the witneſſes, on the part of the priſoner, and that he continued in Mitchell's houſe, from two or three that afternoon, till half after twelve, he could not be the perſon that committed this injury; and of courſe you will acquit him: if, on the other hand, you are ſatisfied from

th

the teſtimony, the very poſitive teſtimony, of the four Miſs Porters, that he was the man, and that they knew his perſon ſo well before, that they could not be miſtaken; if you ſee from his conduct, at the time he was brought back, and in the moment he ſpoke to Miſs Sarah Porter, that he was the man; if you believe this evidence, when put together, you muſt give the effect to it, and pronounce that the priſoner was the man: if you are of that opinion, the only queſtion that remains then is, what was his intent? If his intent was to cut both the cloaths and the perſon, I cannot ſay I entertain the ſmalleſt difficulty myſelf, but that the caſe will fall directly within the Act of Parliament. Many caſes may be figured, in which cloaths may be cut, and yet it would not be an offence within this ſtatute; for if the object was clearly different, and in the courſe of a ſcuffle the cloaths were cut, I ſhould ſay it was not within this ſtatute; firſt, becauſe it was not part of the original deſign it does not come within the words " wilfully and maliciouſly aſſaulting, with intent to cut;" and in the next place, becauſe it appears that the object was different; but if the intention was to do both, as it ſeems to me, the queſtion could admit of no doubt: and there is a third caſe, which would be equally clear as to the conſtruction of the Act; that is, ſuppoſing that the priſoner meant to cut her perſon; whether in that deſign he did not alſo intend to cut her cloaths: in conſidering that queſtion, it is material to attend to the manner in which he accoſted Miſs Porter, the inſtrument he uſed, and the place to which he aimed the blow; the inſtrument muſt have been very long, and very ſharp; and the witneſſes ſay the cloaths are extremely torn; it is not like a pointed inſtrument, calculated to injure the perſon only, but it has rent her cloaths; and if he made the blow in ſuch a way that he could not ſtrike her perſon, without cutting her cloaths, then the queſtion will be, whether he who intends the end, does not alſo intend the means; ſo it goes on the queſtion, as intention: therefore I can only leave the caſe, on both points, for your conſideration; it is for you alone to diſcuſs, and pronounce the priſoner, GUILTY or INNOCENT; as you ſhall judge the truth of the caſe to be.

The Jury immediately pronounced a verdict, GUILTY.

Court. Let the ſentence be reſpited till December Seſſions; and all the witneſſes, who are bound over on the other proſecutions, their recognizance muſt be reſpited till that time.

The

The profecution of RENWICK WILLIAMS, upon the ftat. 6 Geo. I. cap. 23, § 11, which makes it felony to affault any perfon with intent to cut or fpoil his CLOATHS, when his obvious purpofe was to cut and wound the PERSON; being founded on the authority of the following Cafe, a full ftatement of that Cafe cannot be unacceptable to our readers, efpecially as a difference of opinion is fuppofed to exift among the Judges upon the propriety of *Williams's* profecution on this ftatute.

Cafe of ARUNDEL COKE, Efq.

Arundel Coke, Efq. of Bury St. Edmunds, was indicted at the Suffolk Affizes, before Lord Chief Juftice *Pratt*, March 13, 1721, together with John Woodburne, upon the *Coventry Act*, 22, 23 *Ch.* II. for affaulting and flitting the nofe of Edward Crifpe, Gent. with an *intent him to maim and disfigure.*

It appeared on the trial, that Coke who was brother-in-law to Crifpe, and was intituled to an eftate upon his death, procured Woodburne to murder him, and himfelf lay in wait, aiding and abetting: and that Mr. Crifpe was terribly wounded with a hedge-bill, his noftril cut through, and left for dead; but he afterwards recovered. Coke had the effrontery to reft his defence upon this point, that the affault was not with an intent to disfigure, but with an intent to murder. The proceedings upon which we fhall give at large, as they occurred on the trial.

Mr. Coke. My Lord, I am very fenfible that a point of law may arife on the ftatute whereon I am indicted.

Ld. Ch. Juftice. Whereon?

Coke. With refpect to my intention.

Ld. Ch. Juftice. Your intention is matter of fact, and muft be tried by the Jury, whether your intent was to maim and disfigure; this doth not feem to me to be a point of law; if there be any point of law that fhall arife, you fhall have Counfel to fpeak to it; but whether you flit Mr. Crifpe's nofe, with an intention to disfigure him, is a matter of fact.

Coke. My intent was to kill Mr. Crifpe, and not to maim or disfigure him.

Ld Ch. Juftice. But that is the queftion the Jury are to try, Whether you did not of malice flit his nofe, with an
in-

intent to disfigure him. If the Jury do not find that you so
did, you must be acquitted on this indictment. Supposing
your design was to kill, yet your design might be likewise to
maim; and this the Jury must try; this is a matter of fact
for their consideration.

Coke. This is a very penal statute, and I am unable to
plead my own cause; I beg your Lordship to assign me
counsel.

Ld. Ch. Justice. If any point of law doth arise upon the
statute, you shall have counsel; but as yet there is nothing
but matter of fact; whether the fact proved doth support the
charge in the indictment; or, in other words, whether the
evidence be sufficient to make good the charge; this must be
left to the Jury; I will state the fact to them, and they are
on their oaths to give in their verdict.

Coke. This is a very penal statute, and I cannot argue it
for myself; I hope your Lordship will assign me counsel;
this is the first indictment that ever was upon this statute.

Ld. Ch Justice. What do the King's Counsel say to it?

Serj. Selby. After so full an answer as your Lordship has
given, I think it but vain to say any thing; I always thought
that no matter of law could arise upon this fact and indictment; for Woodburne did the fact of malice forethought,
by lying in wait, and with an intention to maim; Mr.
Coke was aiding, abetting, and privy to the fact: therefore,
though it was an intent to kill, it must be to maim also;
he could not intend to kill him with such an instrument,
without intending to maim him first; and therefore, if there
were two intentions and but one executed, there is no pretence to say, that what was executed was not intended. Mr.
Coke says, there never was any indictment before upon this
statute; if not, it must be because no man before ever thought
of being guilty of so horrid an action.

Ld. Ch. Justice. If any point in law doth arise, you shall
have counsel; but the fact must be agreed and stated, before the law can come in debate. You say, your intent
was only to murder; but that is not yet agreed or found to
be fact: it is the point now in trial, whether you did it not
with an intention to maim or disfigure; and according as
that intention shall appear to the Jury, so will they either
acquit or convict you; therefore if you have any thing more
to say I desire you to go on.

Coke. I submit to your Lordship's judgment.

Ld. Ch. Justice. Gentlemen of the Jury, this is an indictment of the prisoners at the bar, John Woodburne and
Arundel Coke, for felony, by lying in wait, and purposely
and

and malicioufly flitting the nofe of Edward Crifpe, with
intention, in fo doing, to maim or disfigure the faid Edward Crifpe.   John Woodburne is indicted for the principal
actor, or the perfon who did the fact; and Arundel Coke is
indicted for being prefent, aiding and abetting. This indictment is founded on a ftatute made in the two and twentieth year of King Charles the fecond, intituled, " *An act
to prevent malicious maiming and wounding*;" whereby it is
enacted, That if any perfon or perfons, from and after the
twenty-fourth day of June, in the year of our Lord 1671,
on purpofe, and of malice forethought, and by lying in
wait, fhould unlawfully cut out, or difable the tongue, put
out an eye, flit the nofe, cut off a nofe or lip, or difable any
limb or member of any fubject of his majefty, with intention in fo doing to maim or disfigure, in any the manners
beforementioned, fuch his majefty's fubject, that then, and
in every fuch cafe, the perfon or perfons fo offending, their
counfellors, aiders, and abettors (knowing of, and privy to
the offence, as aforefaid,) fhall be, and are thereby declared
to be felons, and fhall fuffer as in cafes of felony, without
benefit of the clergy.   Now the queftion on this indictment
is, whether John Woodbourne did on purpofe, and of malice forethought, and by lying in wait, unlawfully flit the
nofe of Edward Crifpe, with an intention to maim or disfigure him therein? And, whether Arundel Coke was felonioufly prefent at the fact, aiding and abetting Woodbourne
in the commiffion and perpetration of it? To make out this
matter, feveral witneffes have been called; the firft witnefs
was Edward Crifpe himfelf, who informs you, that Arundel
Coke married his fifter, and Mr. Brown, Coke's fifter; and
that laft New-years-day they were invited to fup at Mr.
Coke's; and that before fupper Mr. Coke propofed to go
to Mrs. Monke's; and that after fupper, about ten o'clock
at night, Mr. Coke called Mr. Crifpe out of the parlour to
go to this Mrs. Monke's; and that when they had walked
three or four turns before the houfe where Mrs. Monke dwelt,
Coke ftood ftill, and made a noife like a hollowing, which made
Mr. Crifpe afraid, being dark, fo he made toward the wall;
but in a quarter of a minute's time a man came and knocked
him down: who that man was, nor what was then further
done to him, he could not then tell, becaufe by the blow
he loft his fenfes for fome time; but afterwards he got up
again, and returned to Mr. Coke's houfe from whence he
came, but in a fad condition, much wounded and bloody,
where Mr. Sturgeon the furgeon came to him, from whom
you have the particulars of his cafe. He fays, that Coke
was clofe by him when he was knocked down; but did not
hear

hear Coke say any thing. He also says, that upon his death one hundred pounds *per annum* wou'd have gone to Coke's wife, as one of his sisters and co-heir.

The next witness is Mr. Brown, who married Coke's sister; and he says, that he, his wife and daughter were invited to sup at Mr. Coke's the evening of New-years-day; that he came about six o'clock, and found Mr. Coke and Mr. Crispe drinking a glass of wine in the parlour before supper; that he sate down and drank with them till supper; that after supper they three came into the parlour again, and some time after Coke went out of the room, and then came back again, and called Mr. Crispe out of the room, who followed him; that Coke returned again in about ten minutes, and seemed to be out of breath, as if he had been walking faster than ordinary; that Coke's house is distant from the churchyard about twice the length of the shire-house; that Coke, after he came in, drank a glass of wine; and that Brown asked Coke what was become of Mr. Crispe; and that Coke said, he believed he was gone home in the dark; and that in about two or three minutes after Mr. Crispe came in much wounded and bloody; and that it was about half an hour between the time of Mr. Crispe's going out and returning again.

Mr. Sturgeon the surgeon swears, that being sent for, he came to Mr. Crispe about eleven o'clock that night; that he had lost a good deal of blood, and was very much wounded; and that in the whole he had received seven distinct wounds, which he apprehends were by so many several blows. He hath given you a particular description of the several wounds; the second wound is that which is alledged to be within this statute. He tells you, that this wound divided the right side of the nostril; and that though the edge of the nose was cut through, yet it was cut through in another place; the nose was slit; there was cut from without into the nostril; indeed the slit was not very great, for he sewed it up with one stitch; but he is sure that a slit there was, and you have seen Mr. Crispe's nose. Now the slitting of the nose is one of the particular facts mentioned in the statute.

Mr. Willet the constable swears, that he was with Woodburne after his commitment, and that he told him, he was concerned in the wounding Mr. Crispe; that he had been there waiting for that purpose; and that when Coke whistled to him, he went up and made the assault upon Mr. Crispe with an hook or bill, that was new ground for that purpose, and directed him where to find it at his house, which he accordingly did, and brought it to Woodburne, who said that was the hook; and the hook hath been now produced before you; and you have seen it.

The next witness is Mr. Wetherell the gaoler, who swears, that the day after Coke was committed to his custody, Coke sent him up into his chamber, and told him, that he and Woodburne had had a design to murder Mr. Crispe, and had attempted it several times, and desired him to go and secure Woodburne, which he accordingly did. He hath given you an account how and in what manner he secured him; and he swears moreover, that Coke told him several times that he had a design to murder Crispe, and that he employed Woodburne, and delivered Crispe into his hands; that Woodburne did it with an hook, and that he bid Woodburne to cut his windpipe? and that if Woodburne had not been a cow-hearted dog, he would have soon done, and secured Crispe from telling tales. Wetherell likewise swears, that Coke told him, that he called Crispe out of his house, went into the churchyard with him, and there delivered him into Woodburne's hands; and he farther swears, as to Woodburne, that Woodburne owned that he and Coke had lain in wait several times, and at several places, to murder Mr. Crispe; and as to this particular fact, he gave him this account, that he struck him a blow with his hook, and that not quite striking him down, he gave him a second blow; and that as Crispe was falling, he cried out, God damn him; and that then it grieved him to kill a man with an oath in his mouth.

Robert Moon swears, That when he heard what was befallen Mr. Crispe, he said, that he knew the person that did the fact, or him who employed the person; and the reason was, because about three years and a half before Mr. Coke sent for him, and told him, that he wished Mr. Crispe out of the world, and that somebody would knock him on the head; and that when he asked him what advantage that would be to him? he replied, a very good estate; and afterwards told him, he did not value ten or twenty guineas to knock him in the head: this made Moon reflect upon himself, and was concerned that he should have such an opinion of him, and thereon told him, that he would not kill the greatest villain in the world for ten such towns as Bury.

John Carter swears, that on Friday before New-year's-day last, Coke sent Woodburne to him, to tell him that his master Coke wanted to speak with him; that thereon he went to his house, and was ordered to come up to him in his chamber, which he did; and there Coke first enquired, whether he could help him to a good strong horse? And then told him, that he heard he had lost much of his business, he had no iron, nor coal; and that he had a thing in agitation that would make a man of him as long as he lived; and thereon asked him, whether he could keep a secret, and one of the biggest secrets in the world? And upon his telling him that he could, he asked him whether he could cut five or six mens heads off without scruple of conscience? And when he told him that that was too much for a man's conscience to bear, he told him, there were those above, meaning the South-Sea gentlemen, who had done ten times worse, ruined families, and beggared gentlemen; and that to cut mens heads off was but a trifle to them. That hereon Carter told him, he believed he spoke only in joke, and by way of merriment; but Coke asked him, whether he thought he sent for him only by way of joke? And then asked him, whether he could cut off one man's head without scruple of conscience? And when Carter told him, no; then Coke told him, if he could not cut off a man's head, and lay it down on the table before him, he was not for his turn; and then gave him a glass of brandy, and bid him consider of it for a day or two, and if he could cut off a man's head without scruple of conscience, he should have plenty of gold and silver, and any thing else he should ask: whereto Carter replying, that he needed no consideration, he could not do it: then he bid him send Woodburne to him, which he did.

In all this discourse between Carter and Coke, I do not find that Crispe was the person named on whom this outrage should be committed: but Carter, who is a tenant of a house of Mr. Crispe's, says, that Coke told him he heard the house was out of repair: that it would be his after Mr. Crispe; and asked him, whether he would not like it better for Coke to keep it in repair, as he had done before, whilst he was Crispe's steward?

This is the substance of the evidence given against the prisoners at the bar, to prove that they maliciously, and by lying in wait, have slit Mr. Crispe's nose, with an intent to disfigure him therein.

Woodburne doth not deny the general fact, that is, the designed lying in wait to assault Mr. Crispe, nor the cutting or knocking him down with his hook; his confession is not evidence against Coke, but it is against himself; and you hear what he hath owned; that last barley-harvest Coke sent for him to mend his copper, and then ordered him to meet him at another place, which was accordingly done; where

Coke

Coke told him, That he had a thing for him to do, but it was not to be done prefently; and if he would do it, he fhould want for nothing. And when he afked him, what it was? He faid, To fet Crifpe afide, that is, to kill him; and Coke gave him eighteen pence. That then he told him, he could not do it; that Coke folicited him feveral times afterwards to murder Crifpe; the particulars whereof I do not enumerate, becaufe they principally relate to Coke, againft whom it is not evidence; but yet they fo far relate to Woodburne, as to fhew his knowledge and deliberation in this matter; therefore to come to the day whereon this fact was done, Woodburne faith, That about eight or nine in the morning, Coke fent for him, and told him, that that day they fhould have the faireft opportunity to kill Mr. Crifpe; and it was agreed between them, that Woodburne fhould be in the church-yard, at Mr. Morrice's porch, about eight o'clock in the evening. He accordingly went with his hedge-hook, or bill, which hath been here produced. Coke came out to him twice by himfelf, and the third time, a little after ten o'clock, Coke and Crifpe came out together; and then Coke whiftled, which was the fignal between them; and thereon Woodburne came up, and owns, that with his hook he cut and knocked down Crifpe, and that though he never heard Crifpe fwear before, yet that now, as Crifpe was falling, he fwore God damn him; whereon he gave him thofe feveral other wounds and blows that Crifpe received; and then reflecting on what he had done, immediately went to his own houfe, where he was about to take a rope to hang himfelf:

By this defence of Woodburne, you fee that he doth not deny the affaulting and wounding of Mr. Crifpe; but that what he chiefly infifts on is, that what he did was by the folicitation and procurement of Mr. Coke; which is no juftification or excufe. However, he hath called two witneffes, Ann and Sarah Woodburne, his two daughters, to prove that Coke did frequently fend for their father, and often came to him at his own houfe, and would be in private conference together, which probably was about this matter; but if it were, this only confirms what Woodburne infifts on, that he was folicited and hired by Coke to do this fact; which, as I faid, will neither juftify nor excufe him; for no man is to obey the unlawful commands, or hearken to the illegal advices, of any other perfon whatfoever.

As for Mr. Coke, that which he principally puts his defence upon, is, that his intent was to kill and murder Mr. Crifpe, but not to maim him, or to flit his nofe, or to disfigure him

in

in so doing; and therefore, though in pursuance and execution of the attempt to murder Mr. Crispe, they slit his nose, or might thereby disfigure him, yet that not being their intention and design, he is to be acquitted on this indictment, wherein the intent of the party is one of the principal ingredients to make him guilty.

That this attempt on Mr. Crispe was designed, malicious, and by laying in wait, the evidence is very strong; there hath been also very strong evidence given, that the nose of Mr. Crispe was slit by Woodburne, and that Coke was present on the same design with Woodburne.

But the thing chiefly insisted on is, that the slitting of Mr. Crispe's nose was not with an intention in so doing to maim or disfigure him; and if it were not with that intent, then the prisoners will not be guilty upon this indictment.

Now, Gentlemen, what the intent of these persons was in slitting Mr. Crispe's nose, you are to try; this is a matter of fact for your consideration and determination: it is the same in other felonies, where the intent of the party makes the crime. Burglary is breaking open an house in the night-time, with an intent to commit a felony; though no felony be committed, yet if there was an intent to do it, it is burglary; which intent is to be tried by the Jury. Larceny, or theft, is taking away another man's goods, with an intent to steal; if it were without such an intent, it would only be a trespass, and no larceny; but whether it were or were not with such an intent, is a matter of fact to be inquired into and determined by the Jury. Nay, the intent is so necessary in all felonies, that a person who hath no intent or design, as a madman, lunatick, infant, &c. cannot commit felony for that very reason; because he cannot have any intent or design in his actions. So that in this case you are to try no other matter than what is tried in other felonies, viz. the intent of the party.

Now how is the intent of the party discovered in other cases? By the facts themselves, by the precedent, concomitant, and subsequent circumstances of the facts, by the manner of doing, and the like.

There are some cases where an unlawful or felonious intent to do one act may be carried over to another act, done in prosecution thereof; and such other act will be felony, because done in prosecution of an unlawful or felonious intent: as, if a man shoots at a wild fowl, wherein no man hath any property, and by such shooting happens unawares to kill a man; this homicide is not felony, but only a misadventure or chance-medley, because it was an accident that hap-

happened in the doing of a lawful act: but if this man had shot a tame fowl, wherein another had property, but not with intention to steal it, and by such shooting had accidentally killed a man, he should then have been guilty of manslaughter, because done in prosecution of an unlawful action, viz. committing a trespass on another's property: but if he had had an intention of stealing this tame fowl, then such accidental killing of a man would have been murder, because done in prosecution of a felonious intent, viz. an intent to steal. So a man of malice intends to burn one house, in execution thereof he happens to burn another house; this is a malicious and felonious burning of this other house, because sprung out of a malicious and felonious intent. The like may be instanced where poison is intended to be given to one person, and another takes and eats it, and thereby dies. And other cases there are of the like nature, where acts done in prosecution of felonious intents participate of the nature of their original from whence they spring.

But now the indictment on this statute is for a certain particular intent; for purposely, maliciously, and by lying in wait, flitting Mr. Crispe's nose, with an intention in so doing to maim or disfigure: and you are to consider, whether the ingredients necessary to make this a felony within the statute, have been proved to your satisfaction. The facts necessary to be proved on this indictment are, that on purpose, and of malice forethought, and by lying in wait, they unlawfully flit the nose of Mr. Crispe, with intention in so doing to maim or disfigure. As to the fact of flitting the nose, that is directly and positively sworn: there can be no doubt but that it was an unlawful flitting. Then the next thing for your consideration will be, whether this unlawful flitting was on purpose, of malice forethought, and by lying in wait. As to this, a great deal of evidence hath been given; and what passed before, and at the time of the fact, will guide you herein. And if on a review of the evidence, you shall be of opinion, that this unlawful flitting of the nose was on purpose, of malice fore-thought, and by lying in wait; then the next question will be, whether this was an intention to disfigure? Facts do in some measure explain themselves; and the circumstances preceding and accompanying those facts, and the manner of doing them, do many times more fully explain and declare the intent of the party. The prisoner, Mr. Coke, insists, that their intention was to murder, and not to maim; and that if they did maim or flit the nose, it was with an intention to kill, and

not

not with an intention to maim or disfigure. On the other side, it is infifted on by the King's Counfel, that though the ultimate intention might be to murder, yet there might be alfo an intention to maim and disfigure, and though the one did not take effect, yet the other might : an intention to kill, doth not exclude an intention to maim and disfigure. The inftrument made ufe of in this attempt was a bill, or hedging-hook, which in its own nature is proper for cutting and maiming; and where it doth cut or maim, doth necelfarily, and by confequence disfigure. The attempt intended on Mr. Crifpe was immediately to his perfon, to do him a perfonal injury. Befides, the manner of doing and perpetrating this fact is proper to be confidered; that it was done by violence, and in the dark, where the affailant could not well make any diftinction of blows; but knocked and cut on any part of Mr. Crifpe's body where he could, till he had funk him down, and done to him whatever elfe he pleafed. And if the intention was to murder, you are to confider, whether the means made ufe of, in order to effect and accomplifh that murder, and the confequences of thofe means, were not in the intention and defign of the party; and whether every blow and cut, and the confequences thereof, were not intended, as well as the end for which it is alledg'd thofe blows and cuts were given.

All thefe feveral things, which I have mentioned, are proper for your confideration: you will add to them your own obfervations; and if, upon the whole, you are fatisfied from the evidence, that Woodburne did on purpofe, and of malice fore-thought, and by lying in wait, unlawfully flit the nofe of Edward Crifpe, with intention, in fo doing, to maim or disfigure; and that Arundel Coke was felonioufly prefent at the commiffion of this fact, and aiding and abetting therein, then you will find them Guilty : but if this hath not been proved to your fatisfaction, then you are to acquit them, and find them Not Guilty.

Then the Jury brought in their Verdict GUILTY.

When Coke was brought up for judgement on the following day, he addreffed the Court as follows :

Though your Lordfhip did not think it proper yefterday to affign me Counfel, yet I hope your Lordfhip will now give me leave to fpeak for myfelf; efpecially fince I am the firft unhappy inftance of indictment on this ftatute; no indictment, as far as it appears by the Law-Books, was ever yet founded on this ftatute, and therefore ought to be very well weighed; efpecially in the firft inftance to which it appears to have been ever applied. It is a very penal ftatute, and

and confequently by the known rule of law not to be carried beyond the exprefs letter of it; confequently no crime, of what nature or magnitude foever, can fall within the purview of it, but fuch as is identically the fame in every circumftance with that defcribed by the words of the ftatute itfelf.

The crime defcribed by the ftatute is the unlawful cutting out, or difabling the tongue, putting out an eye, flitting the nofe, cutting off a nofe or lip, or difabling any limb or member, attended with thefe particular circumftances:

First, on purpofe, and of malice forethought.

Secondly, by lying in wait.

Thirdly, with intention in fo doing to maim or disfigure in any of the manners before mentioned in the ftatute.

Thefe circumftances muft all concur to conftitute that particular crime defcribed by the ftatute; and where any of them are wanting, of what magnitude foever the offence may be, it is not the offence which the ftatute has fpecified.

If the firft circumftance be wanting, no man can fay that any offence, though attended with the other two, can fall within the ftatute; this is fufficiently plain of itfelf.

As to the fecond; A. and B. of malice forethought, appoint and meet to fight a duel; A. in the rencounter runs B. into the eye, and puts it out; no body has ever imagined this to be within the ftatute, becaufe the circumftance of lying in wait is here wanting.

As to the third; fuppofe A. lies in wait to rob B., B. refifts, and in the fcuffle is wounded, as the ftatute defcribes, but gets off. This is a cafe which very frequently happens, yet no one ever thought it to be within the ftatute, nor was any one ever indicted for this upon it: the only reafon of which muft be, becaufe the intention was to rob and not to maim and disfigure the perfon.

In my cafe, if it be taken upon the evidence of Mr. Crifpe, nothing more appears than the affault itfelf: if my confeffion be read, the lying in wait, and the malice forethought will be proved; but then it will be likewife proved, that I had no other intention but to kill, and had no other part, but by giving orders to Woodburne for that purpofe; and my confeffion muft be taken together.

Nor is it an objection to fay, that the crime which is proved by the evidence is much worfe than that which is defcribed by the ftatute; for if it is worfe, then it cannot be the fame. Even in cafes of crimes by the common law, if upon an indictment for a crime of an inferior nature, the

evi-

evidence proves the fact, attended with circumstances which bring it within the description of a crime of superior nature, the person indicted must be acquitted. At Summer Assizes at Dorchester, Anno 1712, a woman was indicted before Mr. Justice Eyre, for the murder of another woman; upon this evidence it appeared, that the person murdered was her mistress, which made the crime petty-treason. The Judge directed this matter to be specially found, and upon conference with all the Judges, it was held, she ought to be acquitted upon this indictment, as she accordingly was; and was afterwards indicted for petty-treason, and convicted and executed thereupon.

When a new offence has been created by statute, or an old one made more penal, the utmost strictness has always been used to comply with the letter of the statute, whatever inconveniencies might result from such a restraint.

As for example:

By the statute of the 39 Eliz. cap. 15, Clergy is taken away from any person or persons who shall be convicted of taking any money, goods or chattels out of any dwelling-house, &c. in the day-time, to the value of five shillings. One Evans and one Finch were indicted on this statute, 1 Crola 473 Evans and Finch's case: the case was thus upon the evidence, that Evans, by a ladder, climbed to the upper-window of one Audley's house, and took out thereof forty pounds; and that Finch stood upon the ladder, in view of Evans, and saw Evans in the chamber, and was assisting and helping to the committing of the robbery, and took part of the money: upon a special verdict it was adjudged, that because Finch did not actually enter the chamber, and take the money, though what he did amounted to a taking by construction of law, and was such a taking as made him a felon; yet the very letter of all penal statutes must be pursued, and therefore he, id est, Finch had his Clergy, and Evans was hanged.

Numerous cases might be put of this kind of nicety in the construction of penal statutes.

To mention but one more: by the statute of 1 Edw. VI. cap. 12, clergy is taken away from such persons as shall be convicted for the felonious stealing of horses, geldings, or mares.—So scrupulously did the Judges adhere to the letter of this law, that there was forced to be another statute made, viz. 2 & 3 Edw. VI. cap. 33, to enact, that a person convicted for feloniously stealing one horse, should be ousted of his clergy in the same manner as if he had stole two.

Nor

Nor is it in this cafe enough to fay, the Jury are judges of all this: for as the evidence now appears, and is admitted, it is matter of law, how far this evidence thus admitted on all hands is fufficient to fupport this indictment. If it were in a civil cafe, the party might demur to the evidence. But if he is not allowed that liberty in criminal cafes, it is upon the common notion, that the Judges are the prifoner's counfel; and are obliged to determine all the matters in law arifing upon the evidence, as much as if the perfons had demurred to that evidence.

And, as in this cafe, the prifoner admits the evidence given to be true, and infifts upon it, that it doth not fupport the indictment; and therefore has a right to have the opinion of the Judges thereupon, as much as if the evidence were ftated at length upon the record (as it muft be in the cafe of a demurrer to evidence), and nothing ought to be left to the Jury, but under the Judges directions as to point of law.

In all thefe cafes therefore, my Lord, it has been ufual to allow the fact to be fpecially found; which gives the prifoner the advantage he might have had by the demurrer to the evidence.

Serj. Selby.—My Lord, I do agree with the prifoner at the bar, that this is a very penal ftatute, and that thefe facts muft be made out to bring his cafe within the letter of the Act, *viz.* an intention or purpofe, of malice forethought, to maim or disfigure in fuch a manner as the ftatute defcribes; a lying in wait for that purpofe; a maiming, or disfiguring accordingly; and an abetting and being privy to thefe facts: thefe are all facts which the Jury only could determine, either by pofitive, prefumptive, or circumftantial evidence; for no man's thoughts or intentions can be otherwife proved than by his actions. My Lord Chief Juftice hath left the whole evidence of thefe facts to the Jury, who by their verdict have found all thefe facts as laid in the indictment, againft which nobody can now open his mouth: we apprehend therefore that no matter of law hath arifen, and that what hath been infifted on by the prifoner is befide his cafe, and needs no anfwer.

Serj. Branthwait.—My Lord, the Jury have found him Guilty. I apprehend nothing can properly be alleged now by Mr. Coke that is contrary to the verdict: if there is any fault in the indictment, we are ready to anfwer any objections he fhall make againft it. That he does not pretend to. What is now offered by him is againft the verdict, and contrary to what is found by the Jury. I beg
your

your Lordship's leave to give an anfwer to the objections he is pleafed to make againft the verdict, however improperly and out of time made, for the fatisfaction of himfelf, and of the perfons here prefent. I agree, a penal Act fhall not be conftrued by equity, or carried farther than the words or letter of the Act, as the cafes mentioned by him to prove, but affirm, that this prefent cafe is within the words and meaning of the Act: for though the ultimate intent of Mr. Cope might be to murder Mr. Crifpe (as by him is alleged in excufe of himfelf) all the means made ufe of to effect that intent were alfo on purpofe, and fuch blows could not be given by an inftrument, without an intent to maim and disfigure. They were given by one lying in wait on purpofe; and the fact and manner of doing the fame fufficiently prove, and are a certain and neceffary indication of the intent. The defendants might have an intent to cut off, or flit the nofe; put out an eye, or difmember; and an intent alfo to kill and deftroy; one intent did take effect, the other not. The defendants ought not to anfwer for what was not done, but ought to anfwer for what was done; which was the flitting of Mr Crifpe's nofe, on purpofe to maim and disfigure him, by one lying in wait; which is all that is required by the Act.

As to the objection; that if *A.* and *B.* go together to fight a duel, if *A.* flit the nofe of *B.* this is not within the Act; the reafon is, becaufe there is no lying in wait.

As to the cafe of *A.* lying in wait to rob *B,* I with great fubmiffion do fay, that if *A.* lie in wait to rob *B.* and to effect that purpofe with the greater eafe, *A.* on purpofe difmembers *B.* or puts out his eyes, or does any other fact prohibited by the Act; though *A.* be hindered from robbing *B.* he is within the Act of Parliament; for the intent and purpofe to rob will be no excufe to one that fhall commit the facts prohibited by the Act.

As to the cafe of Evans and Finch, *Cr. Car.* 473, on 39 *El.* which takes away the Clergy from him that enters and fteals: Finch was not within the ftatute, and had his Clergy; for the exprefs words of the ftatute take away the Clergy from him that enters the houfe, which Finch did not. As to the indictment of a fervant for murder, in killing her miftrefs; it is plain, that it is a crime of a higher degree than murder, it is an offence of another fpecies, it is petit-treafon, and not murder.

The fame anfwer may be given to the other cafes mentioned, where the words of an Act of Parliament are exprefs. No cafe fhall be conftrued within a penal Act, but what is

within

within the words: but as to the present case, the Jury have
found every fact that the Act of Parliament requires, that
an unlawful assault was made on Mr. Crispe by the prisoners; that his nose was slit on purpose to maim and disfigure
him, by lying in wait. And all these facts were proved by plain,
clear, and I believe convincing evidence to every person that
heard the trial.   I am sure the prisoners cannot complain
of any hardship done them ; the prosecution was carried on
for the sake of justice, for the safety of his Majesty's subjects.   This being the first instance of a crime so heinous,
cruel, barbarous, and inhuman, that has been committed
since the making the Act of Parliament, it is hoped by this
prosecution a second will never be committed; for which
reason, I pray your Lordship's judgment for the King against
the prisoners.

Mr. Raby.——My Lord, I did expect at this time I should
have heard, from this unhappy gentleman, something in
arrest of judgment; something to shew that this indictment
and record, now before your Lordship in judgment, had
been insufficient, and such as your Lordship could not have
proceeded upon to give judgment against the prisoners: but
I do not perceive any thing has been objected to this indictment or record; and therefore since nothing appears, or
is objected, they must be taken to be sufficient, and such as
your Lordship ought by law to give judgment upon against
the prisoners now at the bar.

But this gentleman has been pleased to take notice of the
Act of Parliament on which this prosecution is founded : he
has also made some mention of the facts which have been
given in evidence against him ; and cited some cases (as I
apprehend) to shew, that penal statutes, and criminal Acts
of Parliament, ought not in construction to be carried beyond the letter and words of the Act.   This which he has
offered (as I take it) is now meant to shew (or at least that
he apprehends) that from the evidence given, it has not fully
appeared he is guilty of the offence with which he stands
charged within the strict words and meaning of this Act
of Parliament: and for this end he has been pleased to make
some observations from the words of the statute, what things
he apprehends to be necessary to bring him within the com-
pass of this Act, *viz.*   That such wound or maiming, as is
described by the statute, ought to be,

1. On purpose, and of malice forethought.
2. By lying in wait.
3. With an intention to disfigure.

All

All thefe have been already admitted to him; and he will fee every one of thefe circumftances not only taken notice of by us in our obfervations upon the evidence, but alfo more fully by your Lordfhip, before the Jury gave their verdict.

But with what intent this fact was done, whether of malice forethought, by lying in wait, and with intent to disfigure, are circumftances only to be collected from the evidence and the facts themfelves; of which neither we nor the Court can determine; but can only be enquired of, and determined by the Jury; and therefore, though it would be a full anfwer to what is now objected, to fay, that the Jury have confidered of the evidence, have determined upon it, and found you guilty of the indictment, with all thofe circumftances which the prifoner objects are neceffary to bring the offence within the ftatute; though this, I fay, might be anfwer; yet for the juftice of this proceeding, and to fatisfy the prifoner in his own objections, and that they fhould not pafs unanfwered, your Lordfhip will permit me to take notice of the cafes cited, and alfo to recollect the evidence, fo far as the prifoner has made it neceffary to repeat it.

I confefs, it is with concern I mention it again; for I would not do any thing which might add to the weight of thofe afflictions which this unhappy gentleman is under, had not he himfelf made it neceffary to take farther notice of it.

As to the cafes cited, only two of them which he mentions are cited to be adjudged; that at Dorchefter by Mr. Juftice *Eyre*, that a woman was indicted for murder, and upon evidence it appeared to be a different offence, viz. petit-treafon, for fhe had killed her miftrefs; and that thereupon Mr. Juftice Eyre caufed her to be indicted for petit-treafon, and fhe was convicted. Certainly, my Lord, that judgment was right, and very juft; for when it appeared upon evidence that fhe was guilty of a diftinct and different offence than that of which fhe ftood indicted, could any thing be more juft, than to caufe her to be indicted for that offence of which, upon the nature of the evidence, fhe appeared to be guilty. The fecond cafe cited of Evans and Finch (which is reported in *Cro. Car.*) is no more than this: Evans was hanged; Finch had his Clergy, and was only burnt in the hand; and with great reafon: for the ftatute, 39 *Eliz.* which takes away Clergy, takes the Clergy only from him that enters; and therefore to have taken the Clergy

from

from Finch, who did not enter, had been unjuft and unreafon-able. And as to what is mentioned of the ftatute 2 & 3 *Ed.* VI. cap. 33, made in explanation of the ftatute which took Clergy from him who ftole horfes, and to take Clergy from him who ftole only one horfe, there is fuch an Act of Parliament; but this Act and the cafes cited, only fhew that regard has always been had not to extend penal ftatutes beyond the words of them. But before thefe cafes were mentioned (and indeed had they never been cited) this rule of conftruction had been allowed to the prifoner; for all the particulars now infifted on by the prifoner were before taken notice of by the Court, as circumftances neceffary to make out the offence againft the prifoner: nor has one of thofe circumftances paffed without obfervation; but the Court did with great juftice before declare thofe circumftances to be neceffary ingredients to prove this offence. And as to the other cafes, they are to the fame purpofe, and not cited as cafes adjudged; and therefore I need not take further notice of them. But certainly no inferences can be drawn from the cafes cited, or any the leaft colour to fay, thofe cafes prove that the prifoner is not guilty of the offence he ftands charged with, and of which he is convicted.

I am forry he has given this occafion to mention again the fact which has been proved, from whence it appears that the Jury have given an impartial and juft verdict.

It cannot be forgot, that this was confulted and premeditated for three years and more, before it was put in execution; and therefore it was certainly purpofed and of malice forethought; alfo that it was by lying in wait. Certainly this unhappy gentleman cannot have forgot the fignal he gave: and to what purpofe was that fignal, if none was in waiting to hear it? And that this was with an intent to disfigure, muft be fubmitted upon the fact and the evidence. A man ufes a weapon fit to maim and disfigure, he cuts another on the face and does disfigure him, fhall he afterwards be at liberty to fay, it was not his intent fo to do? How dangerous that would be is obvious to every one; this Act would then be eafily eluded, if it fhould be fufficient, if it fhould avail an offender, who has maimed and disfigured another, to fay, Prove that I intended it; it would be eafy then to be out of the reach of this Act of Parliament; indeed if that prevailed, none would be within it, it would be an eafy repeal of this law. It is objected, his intent was to kill: he that intends the end, certainly intends the means, especially thofe means which he ufes; and

the

the means used were cutting Mr. Crispe on the face, and disfiguring him; and the weapon is such, that, by cutting him on the face with that weapon, could less be intended or expected? And if the intent does not appear from this fact, sure it never can from any: the intent of a man's mind cannot appear but from the act which proceeds from his mind.

It is said, this is the first indictment on this statute: I believe there have not been many; for this is an offence so barbarous, that I must agree it is such as seldom happens, and that by the general laws of our country there was not a punishment provided equal to this offence: for our laws (as the laws of most nations also do) provide against offences which most frequently happen: but this is an attempt so barbarous, that it was scarcely imagined any man could be so base and wicked as to attempt any thing like it, until it happened in the case of Sir John Coventry; and then such an abhorrence was shewn by the Parliament, that this law was made to punish it, and to prevent the like for the future: and as this is the like offence, it ought in justice to have the like punishment.

I shall add no more, but pray your Lordship's judgment.

Mr. Lee.——My Lord, the observations made at the Bar being after a verdict, and therefore out of time, I shall not trouble your Lordship with a repetition of the facts that have been proved, further than the prisoner has made it necessary for me to mention some particulars, in order to make the answers to what he hath insisted on the more clear and plain.

I believe it has been truly said by the prisoner, that the present prosecution is the first instance of any proceedings on this statute, and I hope it will be the last; because it is to be hoped there never will be found any other person so wicked, as to give occasion for a prosecution on this statute.

I believe likewise, that the true design of making this statute was to subject persons to death, who intended to maim only, where the maiming was in such manner as is mentioned in the statute; but I can't think that it does from thence follow, that a person who intends to murder, and only maims, is not within this statute; for though it should be taken that there was an intention to murder, yet from the fact done, from the manner of doing it, and from the weapon made use of, it seems apparent that the prisoner intended to maim; and the Jury have now found that he did so intend.

As to the cafes which the prifoner has cited, I beg leave to confider each of them, and offer fuch anfwers to them as now occur.

The firft cafe he has been pleafed to cite, is thus put:

A. and *B.* of malice forethought, appoint to meet and fight a duel; *A* in the rencounter, runs *B.* into the eye, and puts it out: the prifoner fays fuch a cafe would not be within this ftatute.

I agree it would not, becaufe this cafe has not the circumftances which the ftatute requires; for in the cafe thus put there is no lying in wait, which is a circumftance required by the ftatute.

It is faid, that if *A.* lies in wait to rob *B.*, *B.* refifts, and in the fcuffle is maimed in the manner defcribed by the ftatute, that fuch maiming would not be punifhable by this ftatute; but I don't obferve any cafe is cited to prove this affertion: and I am, with fubmiffion to your Lordfhip, inclined to think, that if there is a lying in wait, with malice forethought, with intent to rob, and in profecuting this intent, the robbers fhould affault and maim in the manner defcribed by the ftatute, that fuch maiming would be within this ftatute.

It is faid, that though the intent to murder makes the offence worfe than if the intent had been only to maim, yet fuch intent proves it not to be the fame offence which is mentioned in the ftatute: and if a man be indicted of an offence of an inferior nature, and upon the evidence it appears that he is guilty of an offence of a fuperior nature, the perfon indicted muft be acquitted; and to prove this, a cafe is cited, which is faid to have been before Mr. Juftice *Eyre* at Dorchefter Affizes. The cafe, as put, is this: a woman is indicted for the murder of another woman: on the evidence it appeared, that the perfon murdered was her miftrefs, which made the crime petit-treafon: this was found fpecially, and upon conference with the Judges, they were of opinion, that the woman ought to be acquitted on this indictment.

Admitting this cafe to have been adjudged, I apprehend it does not affect the prefent cafe.

The law has diftinguifhed crimes under different denominations; and as offences are ranked under different fpecies, fo the indictment muft be fuited to that fort of crime whereof the party is guilty; and therefore proving a perfon guilty of a fact, known in the law by the name of petit-treafon, does not prove him guilty of an indictment for murder; murder being an offence which the law has diftinguifhed from

from petit-treason, and to which it has assigned a different punishment.

But in the present case, that offence which is charged in the indictment is proved in every circumstance, and the facts proved do constitute that crime which is made felony without Clergy by the statute. The statute requires lying in wait, it requires malice forethought; it requires slitting the nose, &c. with intent to maim, &c. The indictment charges these facts, the witnesses have proved those facts to the satisfaction of a Jury, who have found the defendant guilty of the charge as laid.

The prisoner says farther, that this is a very penal statute, and that penal statutes are always taken with the utmost strictness; and, to prove this, cites a case adjudged on statute 39 *Eliz.* by which statute Clergy is taken away from any person or persons who shall be convicted of taking away money, &c. in any dwelling-house, &c. in the day-time, to the value of five shillings: and to prove the same matter, an instance is likewise put of the construction on the statute, 1 *Eliz.* cap. 12, which takes away Clergy from such persons as shall be convicted of feloniously stealing horses, &c. The case in the statute 39 *Eliz.* is the case of Evans and Finch, *Cro. Car.* 473, in which case Finch had his Clergy, because he did not actually enter the chamber and take the money. The construction on *Edw.* VI. was, that Clergy was not taken away from a person who feloniously stole one horse.

But I apprehend neither of these cases come up to the case now before your Lordship. As to the case of Evans and Finch, which was a case upon the statute 39 *Eliz.* by that statute a person is ousted of Clergy who takes away money to the value of five shillings in any dwelling-house, &c. Finch did not enter into the house, for he only stood on the ladder; and therefore he was not within the words of that statute, which spoke only of persons who took away goods in an house, &c.

As to the construction upon the statute 1 *Edw.* VI. it is plain that the felonious stealing one horse could not be within an Act of Parliament which took away Clergy only from such persons as feloniously stole horses. The reason therefore of these cases was, that the facts proved did not bring the persons accused within the words of the statute.

But it is not so in the case now before your Lordship; for the prisoner is found guilty of a fact, which is within the words of the statute upon which he is indicted; and
every

every circumstance required to make him guilty of the felony mentioned in the statute has been very fully proved.

My Lord, I am very sensible that the objections taken at the bar, being after verdict, did not require these particular answers; but this being a case wherein life is concerned, I hope the impropriety will be excused.

Ld. Ch. Justice. — I do agree with the prisoner, that this is a penal law, and not to be extended by equity: that he that is guilty within this statute, must be guilty of all the circumstances within it; and if any of the circumstances prescribed by the statute be wanting, he is not guilty. And therefore in all those cases put by you, if any of the circumstances prescribed by the statute be wanting in any one of them, such case is out of the statute. But whether all the circumstances required by the statute did not concur in your case, was a matter of fact which the Jury, who are the proper judges, have tried; and on such trial they have found them all to concur. You seem to argue upon a supposition of this fact to be otherwise than the Jury have found it. The Jury have found you guilty of all the circumstances within the statute. There was no matter of law in this case, but matter of fact; whether on purpose, and of malice forethought, and by lying in wait, the nose of Mr. Crispe was not slit, with intention, in so doing, to maim or disfigure; and whether you were not feloniously present, aiding, and abetting. The Jury had the whole evidence before them; they considered of the whole matter, of the preparation and lying in wait to do the fact; of the fact itself; of the means and instrument made use of to do it; of the manner of doing it; and of all the other circumstances and particulars relating to the fact: and, on the whole, after they had withdrawn, and considered amongst themselves for some time, they have found you guilty within the terms and circumstances of the statute; so that though all the cases put by you should be very good law, yet they do not any wise affect yours, because you are actually found guilty of the crime itself.

He then received judgment of death, and was executed, together with Woodburne, March 31, 1722, at Bury St. Edmund's.

Adjudged Cafes in the Court of King's-Bench,
         in Eafter Term, 1790.

CURTIS v. VERNON Executor of PALMER.

This was a cafe on promifes by the teftator. Plea, 1ft.
That Palmer died inteftate, and the defendant never poffeffed
any of his goods, but as executor of his own wrongs, that
adminiftration was granted to Palmer's widow ; and the defendant delivered over to the adminiftratrix all the effects belonging to the inteftate which came to his hands*.   2dly,
That the defendant recovered 5000l. on a bond in this
Court in the inteftate's lifetime ; that no goods or effects of
the inteftate ever came into defendant's poffeffion, except
goods of the value of 794l. 13s. 9d. which are not fufficient
to fatisfy his faid debts ; and that the adminiftratrix, as fuch,
affented to his retaining thofe goods in fatisfaction of his
debt.

To thefe two pleas there was a general demurrer, and a joinder in demurrer, which were argued much at large, and the
Court took time to confider the queftion.

LORD KENYON, Ch. J next day faid, 'we have looked
into the authorities which were cited on the part of the defendant (*Whitehead* v. *Sampfon, Freem.* 265 ; 2 *Show.* 373 ;
Baker v. *Berefford,* 1 *Sid.* 76 : 2 *Ventr.* 180 ; *Williamfon* v.
Norwich, Sty. 337 ; 1 *Rol. Abr.* 923. L. pl. 12 ; and *Vaughan* v.
Brown, 2 *Str.* 1106 ; *Andr.* 328.) ; but they do not eftablifh
the propofitions for which they were adduced, namely, that
if, *after Action* brought, and *before* plea pleaded, the executor
take out letters of adminiftration, he may plead a retainer for
his own debt.   The cafe in 1 *Sid.* 76, is reported in a con-
fufed manner ; but it concludes with faying " that an executor *de fon tort* cannot pay himfelf."   Now that goes the
length of deciding the prefent cafe.   And indeed the cafes
cited from *Freem. Mod.* and *Strange,* all prove the fame point,
that an executor *de fon tort* cannot retain for his own debt.
They alfo take the diftinction between fuch an executor *de
fon tort* after legalifing his own wrong by taking out letters of

---

* *This happened after the action was brought.*

                                                    adminiftration

administration.   The case in *Strange* shews this matter very clearly; where the Court said it would be extremely hard, that if a person, entitled to administration, is opposed in the ecclesiastical court, and does any acts *pendente lite* to make himself executor *de son tort*, those acts should not be purged by his afterwards obtaining letters of administration.   And they added, that the granting administration legalises those acts which were notorious at the time.   With respect to the first point of this case, the opinion of Lord Ch. J. *Holt* in *Salk.* 313. is decisive; where he says, "if *H.* get the goods of an intestate into his hands, and administration be granted afterwards, yet he remains chargeable as a wrongful executor, *unless he deliver the goods over to the administrator before the action is brought*, and then he may plead *plene administravit*."   From all the authorities it is clear, first, that an executor *de son tort* must deliver over the goods of the intestate to the rightful administrator *before* an action is brought against him; and 2dly, that, though he be a creditor of a superior nature, he cannot retain in satisfaction of his own debt.   Therefore we are of opinion that both these pleas are bad; and consequently that there must be

Judgment for the plaintiffs.

DYER *qui tam against* HAINSWORTH *and Another.*

   This was an information against the defendants for packing, exporting, and pressing together worsted and yarn made of wool, upon the statute 28 *Geo.* 3. c. 38. intituled, "An act to explain, amend, and reduce into one act of parliament, several laws now in being for preventing the exportation of live sheep, rams, and lambs, wool, woolfels, mortlings, shortlings, yarn, and worsted, crnels, coverlids, waddings, and other manufactures, or pretended manufactures made of wool, slightly wrought up or otherwise put together, *so as the same may be reduced to and made use of as wool again*, mattrasses, or beds stuffed with combed wool, or wool fit for combing, fuller's earth, fulling clay, and tobacco pipe clay, from this kingdom, and from the isles of Jersey, Guernsey, Alderney, Sark, and Man, into foreign parts, and for rendering more effectual an act passed in the 23d *Hen.* VIII. intituled "An Act for the winding of wool.

G g 2

The

The firſt Count ſtated, that the defendants unlawfully exported and conveyed, and cauſed to be exported and conveyed, out of the kingdom of Great Britain, into a certain place out of the kingdom of Great Britain, and out of the iſles of Jerſey, Guernſey, Alderney, Sark, and Man, and each of them, that is to ſay, into a place called Bilboa in Spain, divers, to wit, 2000 pounds weight *of yarn made of wool* of the growth of the kingdom of Great Britain, in contempt, &c. and againſt the form of the ſtatute, &c. whereby and by force of the ſaid ſtatutes the defendants have forfeited to the plaintiff who proſecutes, &c. 300l. being three ſhillings for every pound weight of the ſaid yarn exported and conveyed as aforeſaid. The 2d count was for exporting *worſted made of wool.* The 3d for preſſing together with ſcrews into a certain wrapper, made of canvas, *yarn* made of wool. The 4th for preſſing *worſted* made of wool in the ſame manner ; the 5th count was for preſſing together 2000 pounds weight of *yarn made of wool*: and the 6th, for preſſing together 2000 pounds weight of *worſted* made of wool. The 74th ſection of the ſtatute enacts, that all informations grounded on it ſhall be tried by a *Jury to be ſummoned out of any other County* than that where the facts were committed. The facts were committed in the county of *York*, but a *venire facias* was iſſued accordingly into Weſtmoreland, and the information was tried at *Appleby* before Baron *Thomſon*, at the laſt ſummer aſſizes, where *Hainſworth* was found guilty.

Now on his being brought up for judgment in this Court, ſeveral objections were taken. 1ſt. That the defendants ought to have been tried in Yorkſhire, *though by a Jury of a different county*, the ſtatute 21ſt Ja. I. c. iv. requiring that all informations on penal ſtatutes ſhould be tried where the offence is committed, and not elſewhere.

2dly. That the 5th Count on which the verdict is taken, does not ſtate the offence deſcribed in the Act of Parliament, the words of the 9th ſect. ſtatute being, " that every perſon who ſhall tranſport, &c. any wool whatſoever of the growth of the kingdom, or any woolfels, mortlings, ſhortlings, yarn, or worſted made of wool, woolflocks, cruels, coverlids, waddings, or other manufactures, or pretended manufactures, made of wool ſlightly wrought up, or otherwiſe put together, *ſo as the ſame may be reduced to and made uſe of as wool again,* or mattraſſes or beds ſtuffed with combed wool, or wool fit for combing or carding, ſhall forfeit 3s. for every pound weight ; and ſhall alſo ſuffer ſolitary impriſonment in the common gaol of the county where he is convicted for three months."

months." The 30th and 31ft fections extend the punifhments to perfons preffing together any wool whatfoever, or any yarn made of wool, or other the woollen or worfted articles by the act prohibited from being exported. Which laft words relate to *all the preceding terms* in the claufe; and it ought therefore to have been averred in the information, that the yarn in queftion was capable of being afterwards made ufe of as wool; which in fact it is fo fpun and twifted as to be incapable of.

3dly. No judgment can be given by this court, becaufe the ftatute (fect 31) fays, *the Court and Juftices before whom fuch perfons fhall be tried and convicted,* fhall have power and authority to punifh any fuch offenders accordingly.

BY THE COURT. As to the firft and 3d objections, we have no doubt. The trial was properly had in *Weftmoreland.* And certainly where the proceedings originate in an inferior Court, judgment muft be given there; but where the proceedings are commenced here, and the record is fent down to be tried below, the defendant is not properly convicted till the record is returned here; the court of *nifi prius* is merely an emanation from this court, and the proceedings muft be returned here before judgment can be given. Befides, in this cafe the imprifonment is not difcretionary; the ftatute is imperative. The meaning of that claufe is, that the Court *fhall inflict fuch punifhment,* and they thereby have power and authority fo to do.

But they took time to confider of the fecond objection; and now

Lord Kenyon, C. J. faid, We firft entertained confiderable doubt on the fecond objection; but we are now of opinion that the conftruction contended for by the profecutor is the right one, namely, that the words, *fo that the fame may be reduced to and made ufe of as wool again,* were not intended by the Legiflature to apply to *all* the articles enumerated, but muft be confined to the latter words, *coverlids, waddings,* and *other manufactures or pretended manufactures."*

LEE

Lee v. Carlton.

Declaration was filed on the 22d of April; and on Monday the 26th of April, the defendant filed a plea in abatement. As 4 days only are allowed to plead in abatement, the plaintiff signed judgment; to set aside which a rule was now obtained to shew cause. Against this rule it was argued, on the authority of a note in *Jennings v. Webb* (1 Term Rep. 278) that Sunday should be considered as one of the four days, and this plea was therefore filed too late.

BULLER, J.—If the last of four days happen on a Sunday, the defendant may plead in abatement the next day; otherwise, as no plea can be filed on a Sunday, the time would be limited to three days in such cases. The note referred to in *Jennings v. Webb* meant that Sunday should only be considered as one of the days when it was not the last; for in some instances when any act is to be done by the party in a limited number of days, as in the case of a motion in arrest of judgment, the party has four law days, when the Court is actually sitting, in which to do it; and in those cases Sunday is not one, though it be an intervening day.

Rule absolute.

ABSTRACT of an Act made in the 30th Year of his present Majesty, to alter, explain, and amend an Act, made in the 28th Year of the Reign of His present Majesty, intituled, " An Act for limiting the Number of Persons to be carried on the outside of Stage Coaches, or other Carriages," and for regulating the Conduct of the Drivers and Guards thereof.

Whereas the regulations and penalties established and inflicted by the said act (28 *Geo.* III. c. 57) have proved insufficient to answer the good purposes thereby intended:

Be it enacted, that, from and after the 29th of September, 1790, if the driver of any coach, chaise, or other carriage of the like sort, drawn by three or more horses, and going or travelling for hire, shall permit or suffer more than one person
son

fon on the coach box, befides himfelf, and four perfons on the roof; and if fuch coach, chaife, or other carriage, fhall be drawn by lefs than three horfes, more than one perfon on the coach-box, and three perfons on the roof, (except the driver of fuch coach, chaife, or other carriage, drawn by lefs than three horfes, which fhall not go or travel a greater diftance than twenty-five miles from the Poft Office in the City of London; and who fhall not carry more than one perfon on the coach box, and four perfons on the roof, at one and the fame time), to go and be conveyed by any fuch coach, chaife, or carriage, refpectively; every fuch driver fhall pay to the Collector of the Tolls, at every turnpike gate through which fuch carriage fhall pafs, the fum of five fhillings for each and every perfon above the number, fo as above limited and allowed to be conveyed, which every fuch collector is hereby authorized to afk, demand, and receive; and if any fuch paffenger or paffengers, beyond the number fo limited as aforefaid, fhall be fet down, or taken up, whereby the faid payment of the faid fum of five fhillings may be evaded, then and in every fuch cafe the driver of fuch carriage fo offending, and being convicted on fuch offence, either by his own confeffion, the view of a juftice, or the oath of one witnefs before any juftice of the peace, where fuch offence fhall be committed, fhall, for every fuch offence, be committed to the common gaol, or houfe of correction, where fuch offence fhall have been committed; there to remain, without bail or mainprize, for any time not exceeding one calendar month, nor lefs than fourteen days, at the difcretion of the juftice or juftices by whom fuch offender fhall be convicted.

And be it further enacted, that the faid fum of five fhillings fhall be collected, and recovered in like manner as the turnpike Tolls at the gate where fuch payment by this act directed to be made, are authorized to be collected, and recovered.

And be it further enacted, that from and after the faid 29th of September, there fhall be painted on the outfide of each of the doors of every fuch ftage coach, or other carriage, (the coaches carrying the mail, under the direction of the Poft-mafters General, excepted) in large and legible characters, the chriftian and furname of the proprietor, or of one of the proprietors, of fuch coach or other carriage; and in cafe of there being more than one proprietor of fuch coach or other carriage, and any one of them fhall refide within the cities of London or Weftminfter, or the limits of the bills of mortality, then and in

fuch

such case the name of such last-mentioned proprietor shall be the name to be put upon such carriage, as above directed.

And be it further enacted, that if the coachman, or person having the care of any stage coach, or other such carriage, shall permit or suffer any other person to drive the same, without the consent of the passengers within such coach, or other carriage, or shall quit the box without reasonable occasion, or for a longer space of time than such occasion may require; or shall, by furiously driving, or by any negligence or misconduct, overturn the carriage, or in any manner endanger the persons or property of the passengers, or the property of the owners or proprietors of such carriage; every such coachman so offending, shall, for every such offence, forfeit and pay any sum not exceeding five pounds, nor less than forty shillings.

And be it further enacted, that if any such person going or travelling as a guard to any stage coach, or other such carriage, shall fire off the arms he is entrusted with, either while the coach or carriage is going on the road, or going through, or standing in any town, otherwise than for the defence of such coach or other carriage, every such person shall, for every such offence, forfeit and pay the sum of twenty shillings.

And be it further enacted, that the penalties by the said Act inflicted on peace officers, neglecting to execute warrants, shall extend to like refusals in pursuance of this Act; and that the penalties and forfeitures inflicted by this Act shall be recovered and applied in the same manner, as by the said Act is directed respecting the penalties thereby inflicted; and that the forms of proceedings relative to the several matters contained in this Act shall be the same as those in the said Act, with such Additions or variations only as may adapt them to the particular circumstances of the case; and that no objection shall be taken, on account of want of form only.

CROWN

CROWN CASES.

Rex v. Mason.

In the King's Bench, June 1, 1788.

At the Quarter Sessions at Worcester, Thomas Mason had been convicted on the statute 30 *Geo.* II. cap. 24, and received sentence of transportation for seven years. The indictment consisted of two counts. The first charged, that Thomas Mason, on the 13th of June, 1777, " unlawfully, knowingly, and designedly, did obtain from one Robert Schofield divers sums of money; that is to say, the sum of two guineas, of the value of two pounds two shillings of the lawful money of Great Britain, of the proper monies of the said Robert Schofield, by false pretences, with an intent then and there to cheat and defraud the said Robert Schofield of the same." The second charged, that the said Thomas Mason, on the 21st of July, 1777, " unlawfully, knowingly, and designedly did obtain from the said Robert Schofield the sum of four pounds fourteen shillings and sixpence, of lawful money of Great Britain, of the proper monies of the said Robert Schofield, with intent then and there to defraud the said Robert Schofield of the same, to the great damage, &c." and so concluding, " against the form of the statute in such case made and provided."

This indictment was removed by Writ of Error into the Court of King's Bench; and two errors were assigned. First, That it does not appear in the first count what the particular and specific *false pretences* were by which Thomas Mason obtained the money of Robert Schofield. Secondly, That the second count does not state by what particular means or pretences, or on what particular account, the said Thomas Mason obtained the 4l. 14s. 6d. with intent to defraud Robert Schofield.

Marryat, for the defendant.—To the first count these three objections may be made. First, the offence imputed to the defendant is not specified with sufficient particularity. Secondly, The charge is repugnant. Thirdly, It does not conclude either against the peace, or against the form of the statute.

First, The offence is not specified with sufficient particularity. Without having recourse to Lord Coke's definition of the kind of certainty which is required in law proceedings,

ceedings, it is sufficient to refer to the rule which Lord Chief Justice *De Grey* laid down in Mr. *Horne's* case, *Cowp.* 682, " That the charge must contain such a description of the crime that the defendant may know what crime it is which he is called upon to answer, that the Jury may appear to be warranted in their conclusion of *guilty* or *not guilty* upon the premises delivered to them; and that the Court may see such a definite crime that they may apply the punishment which the law prescribes." " This," continues his Lordship, " I take to be what is meant by the different degrees of certainty mentioned in the books; and it consists of two parts, the matter to be charged, and the manner of charging it. As to the matter to be charged, whatever circumstances are necessary to constitute the crime imputed, must be set out, and all beyond are surplusage;" Now the first count of the present indictment does not specify the sort of pretence by which the money is supposed to have been obtained: the pretence is of the very essence of the crime, and constitutes the offence. The defendant therefore should have had notice of this, in order to prepare for his defence; and if the pretence had been stated, he might have been able to have proved, that he never made such a misrepresentation as was imputed to him, besides, it is the usual form of the precedents of indictments to state the pretence. In civil actions, a declaration, stating that the defendant by divers false pretences and misrepresentations, had occasioned an injury to the plaintiff, or had deprived him of a sum of money, would be adjudged insufficient. So would a declaration in *assumpsit*, stating that the defendant was indebted to the plaintiff for divers sums of money for divers valuable considerations; then if these objections would vitiate a declaration, *à fortiori* they will apply to an indictment where greater certainty is required. In such an indictment as the present, certainty is peculiarly necessary, because it has been determined that there are various kinds of pretences which are not within the meaning of the statute; and it cannot be contended that all these determinations were previous to the passing of the Act; for in *the King v. Wheatley*, 1 Geo. III. where the *defendant* had been convicted of selling malt liquor by short measure, the judgment was arrested on an objection similar to the present. In *the King v. Munoz*, where the defendant had been convicted for procuring a promissory note by *false tokens* under the statute 33 *Hen.* VIII. cap. 1, the judgment was arrested, because the indictment did not specify the tokens; and here *false pretences* are equally uncertain.

lng's cafe, and *Popplewell's cafe*, convictions on the statute of 6 and 7 *Will.* III. cap. 11, were quashed, because the oaths and curses were not set forth. An indictment also has been quashed, as being too general, charging that the defendant *male et negligenter fe geffit* in execution of the office of Constable. So in rescue it is necessary to state for what offence the party was in custody. It is no answer in this case to say, that the indictment pursues the words of the statute; for that answer was attempted to be given in the case of *Davy v. Baker*, 4 *Burr.* 241, and over-ruled:—That was in an action on the statute 2 *Geo.* II. cap. 24, for preventing bribery at elections; and the judgment was arrested, because the declaration only stated that the defendant did receive a gift or reward, without specifying what he received as a reward.

Secondly; The charge is repugnant. It states that the defendant obtained *divers fums* of money, TO WIT, *the fum* of two guineas. The fum alone is repugnant to divers fums; and if it be rejected as surplusage, it is equally fatal, because then it does not specify what fums he did obtain. And if this count were to be adjudged sufficient, without particularizing either the fums which the defendant obtained, or the pretences by which he obtained them, it would be equally sufficient to state that he had obtained *divers goods*, without specifying what those goods were.

Thirdly, This count does not conclude either against the peace, or against the form of the statute. The former of these is a sufficient objection to this count, for every indictment ought to aver the offence to have been committed against the peace. It is equally necessary that every indictment on a statute should conclude *contra formam ftatuti*. The judgment upon the present record is, *transportation*, which is a punishment not known to the common law; and therefore, if warranted at all, must be so by statute. But it is said in 2 *Hawk. P. C.* cap. 25, § 116, " that a judgment by statute shall never be given on an indictment at common law, as every indictment which does not conclude *contra formam ftatuti*, shall be taken to be; and therefore, if an indictment do not so conclude, and the offence indicted be only prohibited by statute, and not by common law, it is wholly insufficient, and no judgment at all can be given upon it." It must be observed, that this is not an application to quash an indictment, which depends on the discretion of the Court; but this indictment comes before the Court by Writ of Error, and if the Court see that the indictment is defective, they are bound to reverse the judgment.

As

As to the second count it was objected, that it was manifestly defective, inasmuch as it did not contain a charge of any crime either against the common law or statute law.

Mr. Caldecot, for the Crown.—In answer to the objection, that the charge in the first count is too general and uncertain, because it does not give the defendant sufficient notice to prepare his defence; it cannot be denied that the use of this general form of indictment is, in many instances, established law; as in those of a common scold, where it is not necessary to specify any instance. So in charging the offence of keeping a bawdy house, it is said in *Hawkins* cap. 25, that it is needless to set forth any circumstances. The like for keeping a gaming-house, or for conspiracies. So in all cases of barratry; and *Hawkins* says, " It is enough to charge that the offender is a common barrator, without shewing any of the particular facts; for barratry is an offence of a complicated nature, consisting in the repetition of divers acts in disturbance of the common peace, all of which it would be too prolix to enumerate in the indictment." If then in a crime so defined, it is only necessary to state in the indictment that the defendant is a barrator, where the modes in which a person may illegally move and promote suits are certainly infinite, it is equally unnecessary in the present instance to state more than that the defendant obtained the money by false pretences; for upon the principle of notice, it is in itself much more likely that a defendant should know the particular acts of fraud and deceit which he has practised against the prosecutor, which is the present case, than where the prosecutor is at liberty to range through the transactions of a defendant's whole life, which is the case in a charge of barratry. It is admitted that all the cases cited were before the 30 *Geo.* II. cap. 24, except that of *Rex* v. *Wheatley*, and that case was determined on the ground that it was not an indictable offence. Besides, this general form of indictment on this statute has obtained so long in practice, that it ought to be considered as established law. And it has been held by this Court in many cases, and particularly in those on the game laws, that printed forms, such as those in *Burn*, shew the general sense and understanding of the profession. This form of indictment is continued in the latest edition of *The Crown Circuit Companion*, which, though not a book of authority, affords historical evidence of the use of this form at the Old Bailey; and in point of fact it is well known that many persons have been transported for this offence under this form of indictment. At all events, there is no ground for the objection in this indictment;

dictment; for it states the sums of money of which the prosecutor was defrauded, and the times when the fraud was committed. To this it is objected, that the charge is repugnant; because it is stated that the defendant obtained *divers sums* of money, that is to say, *the sum* of two guineas. But it is sufficient if one charge be stated under the *videlicet.* With respect to the second count, it is good, as charging the defendant with an offence at common law, namely, for cheating.

BULLER, J.—Several objections have been made on the part of the defendant; but the material one, on which I found my judgment is, that the indictment does not state what the false pretences were. The question is not a new one; for I remember a case when I was at the bar, though the name of it does not occur to me now, and I argued it on the analogy to the case in *Strange* for obtaining a note by false tokens, which entirely governs this. That was a case on the statute 33 *Hen.* VIII. cap. I., which makes it an offence to obtain money or goods by false tokens. The statute 30 *Geo.* II. cap. 24, only enlarges the description of the offence in the statute of *Hen.* VIII. Both statutes are made in *pari materiâ*; and whatever has been determined in the construction of one of them, is a found rule of construction for the other. The judgment was arrested in the case in *Strange*, because the indictment did not specify the *false tokens:* then by the same reason an indictment on the 30 *Geo.* II. cap. 24, which speaks of *false pretences*, must state what the false pretences are, otherwise the indictment is bad: there is no distinction between the two cases; the same objection which held in the one, must also prevail in the other. With respect to the form of the indictment; I am clear that the precedents have not been universally in the same form as the prosecutor's Counsel has stated, for it was otherwise in the first indictment on this statute which I ever tried; the indictment did state what the false pretences were. The other objections seem to have great weight in them; but it is not necessary to consider them in this case, because I am of opinion that the first objection is fatal, and that the judgment must be reversed.

GROSE, J.—I am of opinion, with my brother *Buller*, that the objection, that the pretences are not specified, is decisive, and for the reasons mentioned by the defendant's Counsel; that the defendant may know what he is to defend, and the Court may see what punishment they are to inflict. These reasons apply to all offences. The cases, mentioned at the bar, of a scold, of barratry, and keeping
a gaming-

a gaming-house, differ materially from this: they consist of several facts; this of a single one. This is a charge for a precise crime, and therefore it must be alledged. With respect to any practice to the contrary, founded on any faulty precedent, if such a practice has prevailed, it is time that it should be rectified. But such practice cannot always have obtained; for I recollect having tried several defendants on indictments which stated what the false pretences were. Therefore, without going further into the case, I am clearly of opinion that the indictment cannot be supported.

THE COURT reversed the judgment, and ordered that the defendant should be set at liberty.

JOHN BROWN'S CASE.

John Brown was tried and convicted, before Mr. Justice Gould, for the wilful murder of John Moncaster.

It was argued on the trial by the prisoner's Counsel, that the offence was only *manslaughter*, and the learned Judge concurring in that opinion, had so directed the Jury; but they thought fit to find the prisoner guilty of *murder*, and persisted in their verdict. Sentence of death was accordingly passed upon him; but he was reprieved from execution until *the evidence* which had been given against him was submitted to the consideration of the TWELVE JUDGES; and on the first day of the ensuing Michaelmas Term, the case was stated at Serjeant's-Inn-Hall, to the following effect:

CASE.

The prisoner was a common soldier, in a regiment of foot, commanded by Captain Peter Hunter, and was, at the time mentioned in the indictment, on a recruiting party at Sandgate. In this character he had behaved during the course of five years with great propriety as a soldier, and with good nature and humanity as a man. On the 26th of June, 1776, he went with several of his comrades into a public-house in Sandgate, kept by one Meggison, to drink. This was between one and two o'clock in the morning. A quarrel arose soon after between the soldiers and a number of freshmen who were in the house. They went out into the street, and a violent affray ensued, which occasioned a great tumult of men, women, and children. Between two and three o'clock o'clock one of the soldiers was seen stripped, and a party of five or six came up, fell upon him, and beat him cruelly. A woman called out from a window, " You rogues, you will murder the man." The prisoner, who had before, with his sword in the scabbard, driven a part of the mob down the street, returned; when feeing his comrade thus used, he drew his sword, which he brandished in the air, and defiring the mob to stand clear, said, " There it is, I'll sweep the street." The mob preffed in upon them, and he struck at them with the flat fide feveral times. The mob then fled, and he purfued one of them down the street to a place called *the Swell*. The foldier who was stripped got up, and ran into a paffage to fave himfelf. The prifoner returned, and asked if they had murdered his comrade. The people came back and affaulted him feveral times, and then ran from him. He fometimes brandifhed his fword, and then struck fire with the blade of it upon the stones of the street, calling out to the people to keep off. At this time the deceafed, who had a blue jacket on, and might be miftaken for a keelman, was going along about five yards from the foldier; but, before he paffed, the foldier went to him, and struck him on the head with his fword. The deceafed ran fome paces and fell down, rofe again, ran a few paces further out of the prifoner's fight, fell down again, and immediately expired. The mob ran into the paffages near the Swell. The foldier faid he had been badly ufed; and it was the opinion of two witneffes, that " if he had not drawn his fword, they would both of them have been murdered."

The Judges were of opinion this was only manflaughter.

REX v. SNOW.

The following cafe was fubmitted to the confideration of the TWELVE JUDGES, at Serjeant's-Inn-Hall, on the firft day of Michaelmas Term, 1776, by Mr. Juftice *Willes*.

At the preceding Summer Affizes for Northampton, William Snow was indicted for the murder of Thomas Palmer. It was queftionable from the evidence, whether the crime amounted to murder, or to manflaughter; and Mr. Serjeant *Vaughan*, at the requeft of the learned Judge, came into Court, and argued the point of law in favour of the prifoner, with great ability. The Jury however thought that there appeared to be an *implied malice* in the prifoner's behaviour,

haviour, and they accordingly found him guilty of murder. But the judgment was respited, in order to take the opinion of the JUDGES, Whether this conviction was warranted by the circumstances of the case?

CASE.

William Snow was a shoe-maker; and Thomas Palmer a labouring man. They lived in the same neighbourhood; and at no great distance from each other. On the afternoon of the day mentioned in the indictment, the prisoner, very much intoxicated by liquor, passed accidentally by the house of the deceased's mother, while he was thatching an adjacent barn. They entered into conversation; but on the prisoner's abusing the mother and sister of the deceased, very high words arose on both sides, and they placed themselves in a posture to fight. The mother of the deceased hearing them quarrel, came out of her house, threw water over the prisoner, hit him in the face with her hand, and prevented them from boxing. The prisoner went into his own house, and in a few minutes came out again, and set himself down upon a bench before his garden gate, at a small distance from the door of his house, with a shoe-maker's knife in his hand, with which he was cutting the heel of a woman's shoe. The deceased having finished his thatching, was returning in his way home by the prisoner's house. On passing the prisoner as he sat on the bench, the deceased called out to him, "Are not you an aggravating rascal?" The prisoner replied, "What will you be, when you are got from your master's feet?" On which the deceased seized the prisoner by the collar, and dragging him off the bench, they both rolled down into the cartway. While they were struggling and fighting, the prisoner underneath and the deceased upon him, the deceased cried out, "You rogue, what do you do with that knife in your hand?" and made an attempt to secure it: but the prisoner kept striking about, and held the deceased so hard that he could not disengage himself. The deceased however made a vigorous effort, by which means he drew the prisoner from the ground, and during this struggle, the prisoner gave a blow; on which the deceased immediately exclaimed, "The rogue has stabbed me to the heart; I am a dead man!" and expired. Upon inspection, it appeared that he had received three wounds; one very small on his right breast; another on the left thigh, two inches deep, and half an inch wide; and the mortal wound on his left breast.

The

The Judges, after great argument and confideration, determined, That the offence was manflaughter only.

LAVEY AND PARKER's CASE.

At the Old Bailey in December Seffion, 1776, William Lavey and Elizabeth Parker were indicted before Mr. Baron *Hotham*, on the 8th and 9th *Will*. III. cap. 26, § 4, for felonioufly and traitoroufly colouring with a wafh, and materials producing the colour of filver, one round blank of bafe metal, of a fit fize and figure to be coined into counterfeit milled money, refembling the filver coin of this kingdom called a fixpence.

The Jury found the prifoners guilty upon very clear and fatisfactory evidence; but it appeared that the colour of filver was produced by melting a fmall portion of good filver with a large portion of bafe metal, and throwing it, after it had been cut into round blanks, into *aqua fortis*, which draws to the furface whatever filver there is in the compofition, and makes it affume the colour and appearance of real filver. A doubt therefore arofe, Whether this was " colouring with a wafh and materials," within the meaning of the ftatute? or, Whether the legiflature did not intend fuch a colouring only, as is produced by a fuperficial application?

Upon this doubt the queftion was referred to the confideration of the Judges. The words of the act are, " that whofoever fhall colour, gild, cafe over with gold or filver, or with any wafh, *or materials producing the colour of gold or filver*, any coin refembling any of the current coins of this kingdom, or any round blanks of bafe metal, or of coarfe gold, or coarfe filver, of a fit fize and figure to be coined into counterfeit milled money, refembling any of the gold or filver coin of this kingdom fhall be guilty of high treafon." And they were unanimoufly of opinion, That this procefs of extracting the latent filver from the body to the furface of the bafe metal by the power of *aqua fortis*, was a colouring within the words, " materials producing the colour of filver."

JAMES BOLLAND'S CASE.

At the Old Bailey in February Seffion, 1772, James Bolland was tried before James Eyre, Efq. RECORDER, prefent Mr. Juftice Nares, for forging on the back of a promiffory note, for the payment of money, drawn by one Thomas Bradfhaw, and indorfed by one Samuel Pritchard, a certain indorfement in the name of *James Banks*, with intent to defraud Francis-Lewis Cardeneaux.—The note was in the words and figures following:

"*L.* 100.   *London*, 12 *October* 1771.
" Two months after date, I promife to pay to Mr. Samuel Pritchard, or order, one hundred pounds, value received,
" *Charles-ftreet, Covent Garden.*   T. BRADSHAW."

He alfo ftood charged for uttering and publifhing as true the faid forged indorfement of the name of *James Banks*, knowing the fame to be forged, with the like intention.

The Jury found the prifoner guilty of uttering and publifhing the bill, knowing it to be forged; but the Court refpited the judgment; and it was fubmitted to the confideration of the TWELVE JUDGES, Whether, under all the circumftances of the cafe, Bolland had been guilty of forgery within the meaning of the ftatute of 2 *Geo.* II. cap. 25.

The following circumftances appeared in evidence:

Money tranfactions of a very complicated nature, and to a very large amount, fubfifted between Bolland and one Pritchard. Bolland had arrefted him for 2,600 l. and obtained a judgment for 1,498 l. 15 s. A Mr. Jeffon had difcounted for Bolland a bill upon Pritchard of 52 l. 10 s. but neither Pritchard nor Bolland being able to take it up when it became due, it remained unpaid in the hands of Jeffon. In the month of October, 1771, Bolland, Jeffon, and a Mr. Lilburne, met at the George and Vulture Tavern in Cornhill, in a public room. Jeffon afked Bolland when he would fettle the note of fifty guineas: Bolland immediately produced the prefent note for 100l. drawn by Bradfhaw, payable to Pritchard, and indorfed " *James Bolland*," and afked Jeffon to difcount it. Jeffon, upon obferving Bolland's indorfement, told him, that as his name was on the back of it, it, he could not negotiate it; that he knew Bradshaw, and considered him as a good man; but that he did not chuse to put his (Jesson's) name on the same paper with Bolland's. Bolland replied, " I can take off my name." Immediately Mr. Lilburne took up one of the table-knives, with intention to erase all the name; but when he had erased all but the initial *B*, for he began at the last letter of the name, Bolland said, " Don't scratch it all out, for it may disfigure it, or cancel it by scratching a hole in it; I will think of some other name that begins with a *B* ;" and he immediately filled it up with " *anks*," which made the name *Banks*. When this was done, he returned the note to Jesson, who put it into his pocket, saying, " I shall give it to a particular friend of mine, and he will undoubtedly ask me who Banks is." To this Bolland replied, " Banks is a publican or victualler, and lives near or in Rathbone Place."

The ensuing day, Jesson applied to Mr. Cardeneaux, to get this bill discounted. Cardeneaux took the bill, and promised to give Jesson the money for it on the Friday following. Jesson having some money to make up, applied to Cardeneaux on the Thursday, and borrowed 15 l. 16 s. on the credit of the bill. On the Saturday morning, Bolland applied to Jesson, and insisted on having the bill returned, or the amount of it paid to him. Jesson and Bolland went to a coffee-house, and sent for Cardeneaux. He came, and Jesson introduced him to Bolland, as the owner of the bill. Cardeneaux enquired of Bolland who Pritchard the payee, and Banks the indorser of the bill were. Bolland said, " Pritchard is a man extremely well known ; he is a dealer in horses, and a man of great property. Banks also is a man of property ; he deals largely in wines and spirits, and lives in Rathbone-Place." Cardeneaux told Bolland that it was not convenient to him to give the whole in cash ; upon which Bolland produced another bill of 10 l. 10 s. and Cardeneaux gave him his note for 50 l. and a draught upon his banker for 44 l. 5 s. which, with the 15 l. 16 s. he had paid before to Jesson, and 9 s. discount, made up the 110 l. 10 s. for both the bills.

Cardeneaux never desired Bolland to indorse the bills ; because Jesson had told him when he gave him the 100 l. bill, that it was better *his* name should not appear upon it, he having been formerly a Sheriff's Officer ; and that the bill would not pass properly at the Bankers with his name on it.

Before the bill came due, both the drawer Bradshaw and the payee Pritchard became bankrupts. Upon these events,

Cardeneaux applied to Jesson for a direction to Bolland; and having got it, he said to Bolland, "That bill I discounted for you will not be paid." Bolland, with an air of astonishment, said, "What bill! I never discounted a bill with you, Sir. You mistake me. My name is *James Bolland.* I never saw you in my life; and you have no bill with my indorsement on it." And when Cardeneaux insinuated that he was acquainted with his having altered the name, he treated the idea of its being a forgery with the most supercilious contempt.

When the bill became due, Bolland refused to pay it, and Cardeneaux put it into the hands of a Mr. Morris, in order to obtain the money.

While things remained in this situation, Mr. Levi, an Attorney, two of whose clients Bolland had deceived, got intelligence from Pritchard of the alteration of the name of "*Bollana*" to that of "*Banks*," and he applied to Cardeneaux to prosecute, to which Cardeneaux consented. To obtain the note, Levi, by the desire of Cardeneaux, gave Mr. Morris an undertaking to deliver up, or to be accountable to him for the bill. Levi apprehended Bolland, and on his being committed by Sir John Fielding, deposited the note with Sir John's Clerk, who produced it at the trial.

After Bolland's commitment, a person brought the note to Mr. Cardeneaux, in the name of *James Banks,* and he gave him a receipt, the form of which the person brought with him, in the name of *James Banks*, containing a promise to deliver up the bill on demand; the bill being then in the custody of the Magistrate. But it did not appear that there ever was in fact such a person existing as *James Banks of Rathbone-Place.*

The opinion of the Judges upon this case was never publicly communicated. The principal doubt seems to have been, Whether forgery can be committed in the name of a person who never had existence?

Bolland was executed at Tyburn on the 18th of May, 1772.

CATHERINE

CATHERINE GRAHAM'S CASE.

At the Old Bailey in February Seſſion, 1772, three men, of the names of Jennings, Birch, and Smith, were tried as principals in ſimple grand larceny, before Sir *James Eyre*, Recorder; preſent Mr. Baron *Smythe*, Mr. Juſtice *Aſhhurſt*, and Mr. Juſtice *Nares*.

The indictment contained two counts; the firſt of which charged the priſoners above-named with ſtealing *two bank-notes*; and the ſecond charged them with ſtealing *a pocket-book* and other things, the property of James Madden, privately from his perſon.

In the ſame indictment one Catherine Graham was charged as an acceſſary after the fact, at common law, for harbouring and maintaining the principal felons, "ſhe well knowing that the ſaid Jennings, Birch, and Smith, had committed *the felony aforeſaid*." She alſo ſtood charged with receiving the ſaid goods, well knowing them to have been ſtolen.

Birch was acquitted of the whole charge. Jennings and Smith were found guilty of ſtealing, but not privately from the perſon. Catherine Graham was found guilty of concealing and harbouring the principals.

Sir James Eyre ſuggeſted a doubt as to the propriety of the conviction of the acceſſary. The indictment charged the principals with *two diſtinct felonies*; and the acceſſary with harbouring thoſe principals, well knowing they had committed *the felony aforeſaid*. It was therefore uncertain to which of the felonies this charge referred.

THE COURT concurring in this doubt, the judgment was reſpited, and the queſtion ſubmitted to the conſideration of the TWELVE JUDGES. In the June Seſſion following, the judgment was ordered to be arreſted; and the priſoner Catherine Graham was diſcharged.

REX v. AICKLES.

At the Old Bailey, 1784, John Henry Aickles was tried before Mr. Justice *Heath*, present Mr. Justice *Ashhurst*, for stealing a Bill of Exchange, value 100 l. the property of Samuel Edwards.

CASE.

Mr. Edwards wishing to get his own note of hand discounted, had made application to several persons in the discounting line of business for that purpose. A few days afterwards, the prisoner, a total stranger to Mr. Edwards, left an address at his lodgings while he was from home, " Mr. H. N° 21, Great Pultney-street, from six to seven in the evening, or from eleven 'till twelve in the morning." In consequence of this address, Mr. Edwards the next morning called upon the prisoner in Pultney-street; and a conversation upon the subject of money transactions taking place between them, the prisoner told Mr. Edwards that he was in the discounting line, and would, whenever he chose, discount a bill for him at the usual premium of 2½ *per cent. agency*, provided it was drawn upon and accepted by a person of known credit and responsibility. About three weeks after this interview, Mr. Edwards again called upon the prisoner; but not finding him at home, he the next day sent his clerk Mr. Croxall to enquire whether he would discount a bill of 100l. accepted by Mr. Wells, of Cornhill; and requesting that he would call in the City, that he might be fully satisfied of its validity. The prisoner returned with Mr. Croxall to the house of Mr. Richard Wells, in Cornhill; where he was shewn into a room to Mr. Edwards, who asked him the terms upon which he would discount a bill for 100l. provided he approved of it. The prisoner replied, " Two and a half *per cent. agency*, exclusive of the legal interest for two months." Mr. Edwards immediately delivered the bill described in the indictment into the hands of the prisoner, and referred him to Mr. Richard Wells, the acceptor of it, who was there present, to satisfy himself that it was a genuine acceptance. Mr. Wells said the acceptance was his hand-writing. The prisoner addressing himself to

Mr.

Mr. Edwards said, " Sir, if you will go with me to the West end of the town, to Pultney-street, I will give you the cash." Mr. Edwards replied, " I cannot conveniently go with you myself, but Mr. Croxall shall attend you, and pay you the 25s. agency, and the discount, on receiving the hundred pounds." On their departure, Mr. Edwards whispered his clerk not to leave the prisoner without receiving the money, nor to lose sight of him; promising to follow them in half an hour. The prisoner and Mr Croxall accordingly proceeded together to the prisoner's lodgings in Pultney-street. When they arrived, the prisoner shewed Mr. Croxall into the parlour, and desired him to wait while he fetched the money; saying, " It is only about three streets off, and I shall be back again in a quarter of an hour." Mr. Croxall however followed him down Pultney-street, but in turning the corner of Brewer-street lost sight of him. He walked backwards and forwards in the street for a length of time, in hope of seeing him return; but without success. During this interval Mr. Edwards, who had previously called at the prisoner's lodgings, came up to Croxall, and they returned together to the prisoner's lodgings, where they waited three days and three nights in a vain expectation of the prisoner's return. On the Saturday following, however, Mr. Edwards apprehended him at the house of a lady in Margaret-street, where he had dined. He expressed his sorrow for what had happened; made several apologies for his misconduct; and promised to return the bill; but he was carried before a Magistrate, who committed him *" on suspicion of being a common cheat."* It was proved that the bill had been seen a few days before the trial, in a state of negotiation, in the hands of a Mr. Smith, and that a *subpœna duces tecum* had been served upon him; but he did not appear, nor was the bill produced in evidence.

The Counsel for the prisoner submitted two points to the consideration of the Court: 1st, That the bill itself ought to have been produced in evidence. 2dly, That the facts, admitting them to be true, do not amount to felony.

To the second point, they argued, that, To satisfy the definition of larceny, as it appears in the works of the most distinguished writers upon Crown Law, the *property* must be taken from the *possession* of another. The taking of the *property* itself, after it is once separated from the legal possession of its original proprietor, can never become a subject of larceny. There is a distinction between those actions which are committed *animo furandi,* and those which are the consequence

sequence of *artful contrivance*; and this is the great difference between *felony* and *fraud*. The criterion of a *felonious intention* is where the act of taking is accompanied by such circumstances as plainly import it to have been by *constraint*, and *against the inclination* of the owner. But where the mind of the owner is beguiled by the means of some deceitful practice, and under the influence of that deceit he consents, foolishly perhaps, but *voluntarily*, to part with his property, it is evidence of a *fraudulent intention*; but whether in this case the *possession* accompanies the *delivery* or not, it will be impossible to build upon such a foundation the notion of larceny, which requires that the goods shall be obtained against the owner's consent.

The COURT left the case with the Jury to consider, *first*, Whether they thought the prisoner had a preconcerted design to get the note into his possession, with an intent to steal it? And, *secondly*, Whether the prosecutor intended to part with the note to the prisoner, without having the money paid before he parted with it; They found the affirmative of the first question, and the negative of the second; and concluded that the prisoner was therefore GUILTY.

The judgment was respited, and the following questions referred to the consideration of the TWELVE JUDGES.

First, Whether as the bill in question had not been produced, the parole testimony which had been given concerning it was legally received?

Secondly, Whether the prisoner was guilty of FELONY, under all the circumstances of this case?

The JUDGES were unanimously of opinion, That the parole testimony had been properly received; and as the Jury had found a pre-concerted design in the prisoner to steal the note, he had been legally convicted of felony, and he received sentence of transportation accordingly.

THE

THE
LAWYER'S
AND
MAGISTRATE'S MAGAZINE.

For AUGUST 1790.

—————————————

Adjudged Cafes in the Courts at Weftminfter in the late Term.

—————————————

BUTCHER'S COMPANY *v.* MOREY.

IN the year 1750, the Butchers within the City of London and fuburbs thereof, and within two miles of the fame, were incorporated by Letters Patent, with full power and authority to appoint, from time to time, fuch reafonable ordinances, decrees, orders, and conftitutions, which to them, or the major part of them, fhould feem to be good, wholefome, profitable, honeft, and neceffary, for the good order and government of the Mafter, Wardens, &c. and of *all other perfons* for the time being, exercifing or ufing the faid art or myftery of butchers, or *expofing flefh to fale* within the City of London, and for declaring in what manner the faid Mafter, &c. and *all perfons ufing the art, &c.* or *expofing flefh to fale* within the faid City, and within two miles thereof, in their offices, fervants, and trades fhould behave, bear, and ufe themfelves for the public good and common benefit of the faid Mafter, &c. and in all cafes and things whatfoever, touching or in what manner foever concerning the art or myftery, &c. and as
often

often as they should make, constitute, &c. such institutions, ordinances, orders, and constitutions, should make, limit, and provide, such pains, penalties, and punishments, by imprisonment of the body, or by fines and forfeiture, or by either of them, against and upon *all offenders* against such laws, as to the said Master and Wardens, &c. should seem necessary. In consequence of which a bye-law was duly made as follows: " Whereas the Lord's day was by Christians to be kept holy, it was ordained that *no person* then using, or who should thereafter use the said art, and should dwell within the said city, or within two miles of the same, should keep open any shop, or *offer to sale* any fresh meat upon the said day: and that *every such person* who should offend, contrary to any part of that ordinance, should forfeit and pay to the said Master, &c. for the first time 20*s.* for the second time 40*s.* and for every time afterwards 3*l.*"

An action had been brought against the defendant, who exercised the trade of a butcher in *Mint-Street, Southwark*, being within two miles of the City, for divers penalties incurred under this bye-law, for selling meat on the Lord's day. At the trial a verdict was found for the plaintiffs.

Now, upon a rule to shew cause why judgment should not be arrested, the question came before the Court, whether the Corporation so constituted without the authority of Parliament, could make bye-laws, binding upon persons *not* members of the Company, which the defendant was not?

LORD LOUGHBOROUGH.—I can see no good ground of objection to this bye-law itself, nor to the subject matter of it. It is a regulation made in affirmance of the general statute law of the kingdom, 29 *Ch.* II. cap. 7, which prohibits buying and selling on the Lord's day. The Butcher's Company have affixed a penalty on persons exercising the trade of butchers, who shall sell meat on that day, and have increased the penalty in proportion to the first, second, and third offence. The objection raised is, that the authority by which these regulations are made, is defective, because, it is contended, it can only extend to those persons who are members of the Company. It is also said, that though large corporations, and those which are established for the general purposes of local government have a right to bind by their laws all persons within the limits of their jurisdiction, yet that a private particular corporation like the Butcher's Company, can have no right to affect any person but their own members. But no case was cited which supports this position. I agree, that strangers and they who

are

are not concerned in the trade, for the regulation of which
the Company was eſtabliſhed, cannot be bound by the laws
of that Company : if this bye-law had inflicted a penalty on
the *buyers* of meat, I ſhould hold it to be clearly bad,
becauſe they are perfect ſtrangers.   It is an object of public
policy that the exerciſe of certain trades ſhould be under the
regulations of particular bodies ; charters have various effects according to the ſubjects of them.   Some are granted
with excluſive rights to particular perſons : others contain
rules which only affect certain members.   On principles of
general policy the object of the law is, that by means of
charters of this kind, the power of carrying on trade, of
making up goods, of expoſing them to ſale, and the like,
ſhould belong to the local government of particular diſtricts.
For theſe purpoſes, certain reſtraints are impoſed, ſince every
regulation is more or leſs a reſtraint.   Now if in the preſent
inſtance, the Butcher's Company had no power to regulate
their own trade, ſo as to make laws binding on perſons
who exerciſe that trade, as well thoſe who were not members of the Company, as thoſe who were ; the conſequence
would be, that the beneficial purpoſe of the charter would
be entirely defeated, and the only perſons injured by the reſtraint would be the members themſelves.   For then all
other perſons might carry on the trade without controul,
while the members of the Company would be excluded, and
the whole buſineſs of ſupplying meat on *Sundays*, would
fall into the hands of the butchers not of the Company.
But this would be contrary to the intent of the charter.
I think this caſe caſe comes within the principle of the *Exeter*
caſe, (*Pierce* v. *Bartrum, Cowp.* 269, where a bye-law to
prevent butchers ſlaughtering within the City, was held to
bind the defendant, though not a member of the Corporation) ; and therefore the judgement ought not to be arreſted.

GOULD, J.——The only difference between this and the
Exeter caſe is, that there the regulations were confined to the
City of *Exeter*, but here the limits extend beyond the
boundaries of the City of *London*.   But where a charter is
granted to a Company in affirmance of an Act of Parliament, made for the purpoſe of common decency and piety,
it is fit that the limits of the charter ſhould be as extenſive
as the miſchief to be remedied.   If the charter were confined to the City itſelf, perſons who pay no regard to the
law might eaſily go out of the limits preſcribed, and buy
meat ; by which means the purpoſe of the charter would be
de-

defeated. I therefore think these are reasonable limits, and see no reason to object to the validity of the bye-law.

HEATH, J.—I am of the same opinion. The bye-law seems to me to be a good one, and within the authority given by the charter to the Company. Nor is it contrary to the case in 1 *Bulſtr.* 11. where it is said, the bye-law had been good, if made to suppreſs any general inconvenience. And that case may be well reconciled with 2 *Ventr.* 33. which was on a queſtion, whether a bye-law of the Univerſity of *Oxford* was good, which reſtrained all perſons, townſmen as well as ſtudents, from walking in the ſtreets after nine o'clock at night: a prohibition was granted, and one of the Judges obſerved, that though it might be proper to reſtrain ſcholars of the Univerſity from being in the ſtreets after that hour, yet there was no reaſon why the townſmen ſhould be under the ſame reſtraint. Now this agrees with the doctrine in *Bulſtrode*, for ſo far from ſuppreſſing a general inconvenience, it would be highly inconvenient, if the inhabitants of a town were prevented from walking in the ſtreets after nine o'clock, whatever may be the caſe in regard to the ſtudents of an Univerſity.

WILSON, J.—I am of the ſame opinion. I think it a good bye-law, and that no objection can be made to the ſubject-matter of it. The ſame prohibition is eſtabliſhed all *England* over by Act of Parliament. But it was ſaid, that the charter could give no ſuch power to the Company. If this be true, the King had no right to grant ſuch a charter, which expreſsly gives a power to bind not only members of the Company, but likewiſe all perſons exerciſing the trade in *London*, and within two miles round. The queſtion then is, whether the King could give this power; for the object of its exertion is admitted to be a proper one. Now is there any authority denying the King to have the right? It is allowed that general corporations have ſuch a power by their charters. But by what authority? Who could give them that power but the King? Then if the King can grant a power of this kind to general corporations, what ſhall prevent him from granting it to particular and private corporations?

Rule diſcharged.

MILLS

MILLS v. AURIOL.

This was an action of covenant against a bankrupt for a quarter's rent accrued subsequent to the assignment of his lease to the assignees of the bankruptcy.

To the defendant's plea, that before any part of the money in the declaration mentioned, became due and payable, he became bankrupt, and the lease in question, together with other effects, was duly assigned and set over to the assignees of the said bankruptcy, there was a general demurrer; which was argued much at large, the short question being, whether, the lease, and all the bankrupt's interest, being vested in the assignees under the commission, he is discharged from an express covenant?

LORD LOUGHBOROUGH.—There is no degree of doubt but that the law is established, that an action of *covenant* may be brought on a covenant to pay rent, though the lessee be not in possession of the land, and after acceptance of rent from the assignee by the lessor. This is by privity of contract: but the distinction is clear between *debt* and covenant. Then when the term is taken under the assignment of commissioners of bankrupt, the question is, whether it is not by the act of the bankrupt himself? It is taken from him because he has contracted debts, and instead of any single creditor suing out a *fieri facias*, the common law execution, there being many creditors they join in taking out a commission of bankruptcy, which is in the nature of a statute execution. By this the property is vested in the assignees, but not so absolutely as in the vendee by a sale under a *fieri facias* made by the Sheriff; because if the effects were sufficient without it, the term would remain to the lessee. Covenant they may well be brought against him. Though he is out of possession, yet he is placed in that situation by his own act. I am therefore of opinion that the judgment ought to be for the plaintiff.

WILSON, J.—The plea of the defendant is not supported by any adjudged case. It has never yet been decided that an action of covenant would not lie upon a covenant by a lessee which runs with the land, and which was entered into before, but broken after the bankruptcy of the covenantor. I entertained no doubt on this question, except what arose from the hints thrown out by some of the Judges of the Court of King's Bench, whenever the question has come

come before them, on account of the dictum of Mr. Justice *Yates*, in *Mayor* v. *Steward*, (1 *Bur.* 2439), that as the bankrupt is divested of his whole estate, and rendered incapable of performing the covenants, it would be a hardship upon him if he should still remain liable to it, when he is disabled by the Act of Parliament from performing it. But this opinion was clearly extra-judicial, for under the circumstances of that case, the Court held the plea to be bad. In *Wadham* v. *Marlow*, (*Cooke's* B. L. 518), Lord *Mansfield* spoke of the opinion of Mr. Justice Yates as deserving great weight, though it was extra-judicial. But in that case it was not stated that the plaintiff had accepted rent from the assignee as his tenant, and it was contended that debt as well as covenant would lie against the lessee, because the lessor had done no act to shew his assent to the assignment. But the Court decided, on the ground that the plaintiff had virtually assented to the assignment, every man's assent being implied to an Act of Parliament, and not on the ground that an action of debt would not lie. And in *Ludford* v. *Barber*, the Court gave judgement for the defendant, because the covenant declared upon had never been entered into by him with the plaintiff. Thus the question stands with respect to judicial decisions. The several statutes relating to bankrupts, prior to the 4 *Anne*, cap. 17, left the bankrupt not only liable to all contingent debts, but to the remainder of the debts which his effects had been unable to satisfy. The hardship was the same, for the bankrupt was deprived of his all, and yet left without any protection against his creditors. The statutes previous to that time, meant to give an execution for the equal benefit of all the creditors, and if they were not fully satisfied by it, to leave them for what was unsatisfied, to every remedy against the bankrupt which they had before. Neither that statute, nor the now existing statutes upon the subject, extend to this case. The 34 *Hen.* VIII. cap. 4, directs that the Lord *Chancellor* and other great officers shall have power to sell and dispose of the lands and goods of bankrupts in as full a manner as the bankrupt himself might have done. Subsequent statutes have empowered the assignees to make the same disposition. The intent of these several statutes was, that the act of the assignees should do no more than the act of the bankrupt himself. I therefore do not see how the maxim " *In jure non remota sed proxima spectantur*," is applicable. The Act of Parliament only assigns the interest of the bankrupt in the land, but does not destroy the privity of contract between lessor and lessee. An action of cove-

nant

nant remains after the estate is gone ; but, generally speaking, when the land is gone, the action of debt is also gone, debt being maintainable because the land is debtor.   Covenant is founded on a privity collateral to the land.   A covenant of this kind is mixed, it is partly personal and partly dependant on the land, it binds both the person and the land. This brings the case within the principle of *Mayor v. Steward.*

Judgement for the Plaintiff.

ARTHRINGTON *and* HERDCASTLE *v. the* BISHOP *of* CHESTER *and* JACKSON, *Clerk.*

. This was a question reserved at the York Assizes for the opinion of the Court, whether the right of presentation to *the perpetual Curacy* of the Church of *Coverham,* in the diocese of Chester was in the plaintiffs, or belonged to the King who had then lately presented the defendant *Jackson* to the same.   On the trial at the Assizes, a verdict was found for the plaintiffs.

C A S E.

In the reign of *Hen.* III. the rectory of Coverham was appropriated to the abbey of Coverham, and from that time to the time of the dissolution of the abbey, the parish church of Coverham was served either by some of the monks, or by some person whom they employed, there *not appearing to have ever been a vicarage endowed.*

Upon the dissolution of the abbey, 27 *Hen.* VIII. the same with all its members and appurtenances came to the Crown, and continued in the Crown till *Ed.* VI. by letters patent granted the same to John Ward for 21 years, reserving a rent of 20*l.*   In this grant there is the following exception : " Exceptis tamen semper nobis heredibus et suc- " cessoribus nostris omnino reservatis, omnibus boscis et " suboscis, de in et super præmissis crescentibus et existen- " tibus, ac advocat vicariæ ecclesiæ de Coverham præ- " dictæ habendum et tenendum."

Queen Elizabeth, by letters patent in the 14th year of her reign, after reciting the above grant of *Ed.* VI. in consideration of 853*l.* 12*s.* granted to Thomas Allen and Thomas Freeman a reversion of the same, together with the

whole

whole rectory of Coverham with the appurtenances, and also the rectory of Iford, to have and to hold the said rectories of Coverham and Iford in as full and ample a manner as any abbot of Coverham, or the former owners of the rectory of Iford had enjoyed the same.

" Exceptis tamen semper et extrà presentem concessionem " nostram nobis heredibus et successoribus nostris omnino " reservatis omnibus campanis, et toto plumbo, de in et " super premissis existentibus præter plumbeas gutturas, et " plumbum in fenestris eorundem premissorum ac etiam om- " nibus advocationibus rectoriarium vicariarium et ecclesia- " rum premissis seu eorum alicui spectantium seu pertinen- " tium nobis heredibus et successoribus nostris simili modo " exceptis et reservatis."

During the time of the rectory of Coverham remained in the Crown, an annual pension of 5l. 6s. 8d. was paid by the Crown to the person who was Chaplain and Curate for the time being of the parish church of Coverham.

There was a vicarage at Iford at the time of the above grant of Queen Elizabeth to Allen and Freeman.

In 1642, Thomas Dickinson was licensed to serve the curacy of Coverham, on the presentation of William Hardcastle and Thomas Horner, impropriators.

In 1691, Thomas Oddie was licensed to serve the curacy of Coverham, but it did not appear on whose nomination.

Between the years 1691 and 1708, John Turner was licensed to serve the curacy of Coverham.

In 1708, the said John Turner was instituted to the rectory and vicarage of Coverham, on the presentation of Queen *Anne,* patron *per lapsum temporis.*

In 1727, on the supposed death of the said John Turner, Humphry Dickinson was instituted to the vicarage of Coverham on the presentation of King *George* II. patrone *pleno jure.* That Turner afterwards appeared and claimed the church, upon which Dickinson gave it up.

In 1737, while the said Turner was in possession of the church, Christopher Lonsdale was nominated to the curacy of Coverham by Thomas Hardcastle and Richard Geldart impropriators.

By a process in the Consistory Court of Chester, the said Turner was dispossessed, and in 1739 the said Lonsdale was licensed to the curacy of Coverham, which he enjoyed till his death in 1789.

LORD LOUGHBOROUGH.——In this case, it is stated, that after the dissolution of religious houses the abbey of Coverham was demised by *Ed.* VI. to one Ward for 21 years, and

that

that in the grant, after the demise of the rectory, there is an exception of all woods, underwoods, and a demise of the advowson of the vicarage of the church of Coverham: that the reversion expectant on that term for years was sold by Queen *Elizabeth* to Allen and Freeman. The letters patent of *Eliz.* are set forth, which begin by reciting the former demise, and then the Queen grants the reversion of the rectory, with the appurtenances as before specified in the patent and the demise for years. After this, there is a grant of the whole rectory, with a very ample description and all general words of grant, which concludes with granting it to Allen and Freeman in as full a manner as it was possessed by any abbot of Coverham. This undoubtedly grants expressly more than was contained in the terms of the demise to Ward, because it directly grants the woods and underwoods which were excepted out of the demise to Ward. It then mentions a grant of the rectory of Iford, in the county of Sussex; and at the close there is an exception of all advowsons of the rectories, vicarages, and churches belonging to the premises. The case goes on to state, that there was a vicarage belonging to the rectory of Iford, but none to the rectory of Coverham; but during the time the rectory of Coverham remained in the Crown, an annual stipend of 5*l.* 6*s.* 8*d.* was paid by the Crown to the Curate. It is then stated, that Thomas Dickenson was admitted to the curacy in 1642, on the nomination of the grantees; that in 1691, one Oddie was licensed by the diocesan to serve the curacy; that afterwards one Turner was licensed in the same manner, and that the same Turner, in 1703, was instituted to the rectory and vicarage of Coverham, on the presentation of Queen *Anne* by lapse. The case next states, that in 1727, on the supposed death of Turner, one Dickenson was instituted to the vicarage of Coverham, on the presentation of King *George* I. *pleno jure*, that afterwards Turner, who was not dead, nor had made any avoidance of the living, appeared, and claimed the church, upon which Dickenson gave it up: that in 1737, one Lonsdale was nominated to the curacy by the impropriators, while Turner was in possession, who was afterwards dispossessed by process in the Consistory Court of Chester; and that by the death of Lonsdale there is now an avoidance.

On this case the question for the determination of the Court is, what passed by the grant of Queen *Elizabeth*, to the persons under whom the present parties claim? For if all the interest in the rectory passed, the curacy which is incident to the rectory, (I rather call it incident than appurtenant) undoubtedly paffed along with it. It is contended on the part of the plaintiffs, that on the true conftruction of the grant, no exception can be intended of the curacy; and that if fuch exception had been inferted in the grant, it would have been void, as repugnant to the grant itfelf, becaufe the rector of a rectory impropriate, where there is no vicarage endowed, and no perpetual curacy, is obliged by law to find a curate to ferve the church, and give him a reafonable allowance. He may make the beft terms he can; but that it is the duty of the bifhop by ecclefiaftical cenfures, to compel the performance of the duty for the fake of the church. That queftion would lead pretty far; but it is immaterial to enter into the confideration of it, if on a thorough view of the grant, together with the facts of the cafe, there is no reafon to fay that the curacy was excepted. *That* to us appears to be the true conftruction, and confirmed by the ufage. The grant of *Elizabeth* begins, as I before ftated, with a recital of the demife to Ward; but it would not be juft to conclude that it meant to give no more. It is manifeft that Ward had not all which the grantees afterwards had, becaufe there is an exprefs refervation in the demife to him of a part which they enjoyed. He was to have the profits of the rectory, paying a rent of 20l. *per annum* during the term; but the tranfaction with Allen and Freeman was for an abfolute fale at a large price paid. The grant does not ftop fhort; it was neceffary to recite the term, becaufe it was a grant in fee, and the purchafer under the Crown acquired a right during the remainder of the term to the rent. It therefore begins with giving to the grantees the reverfion after the term for years, and goes on in explicit and diftinct words, granting this and all other commodities and emoluments whatever belonging to the rectory parcel of the poffeffions of the abbot of Coverham; it mentions exprefsly the woods, underwoods, and trees, and clofes a very long recital of the particulars with the words " in as ample a manner and form as any abbot of the abbey of Coverham had poffeffed and enjoyed the fame." The general exception which follows, was to prevent dilapidations, which were at that time very common, to the deftruction of churches. In the exception of the vicarage it is perfectly clear that the nomination to the curacy is not in terms included. Yet it is argued, that in a grant of the crown which is to be favourably conftrued, the Court would extend the meaning to a refervation of the nomination to the curacy, if the words of the grant could juftify that extenfion to be made. But the words of this grant

grant hardly juftify fuch an extenfion.   If there had been an exception of the advowfon of a vicarage fpecifically named in the grant of the rectory of Coverham, the argument would have had this ground to ftand upon, namely, that fomething muft be meant to be excepted, that as in reality (there being no vicarage at Coverham) the only nomination which could be made, was to the curacy, it muft be implied that the curacy was meant, though improperly defcribed as a vicarage.   But that is not the cafe.   The words in the grant are general and fufficiently anfwered, if there be a vicarage belonging to either of the livings.   Now to one of the livings, to Iford, there is a vicarage belonging.   That fully fatisfies the words of the exception.   They are not nugatory words, and it is not *neceffary* in the conftruction of them that there fhould be an intention in the grant, to make any exception whatever relative to the rectory of Coverham.   Befides this, there are fubfequent words in the grant, which I think go pretty far to fhew that this could not be the intention.   For there is a provifion on the part of the Crown, to indemnify the purchafers from all burthens, charges, and rents which might be iffuing out of the object of the grant, and a particular exemption from the payment of a penfion of 4*s. per annum*, payable out of the rectory of Iford to the vicar.   Now the nomination to that vicarage being intended to be referved to the Crown in the general mention which is made of all burthens iffuing out of the things granted, the payment of this annual ftipend to the vicar of Iford is particularly noticed.   But there is no exemption from the payment of any allowance to be made to the curate.   The effect therefore of the grant would be, according to the argument, to make the grantee of the rectory fubject in the law to payment of the curate without giving him the power of nomination; and we fhould intend a refervation fevering the nomination to the curacy from the fund, out of which the provifion for the curate muft come.   This would be certainly contary to good policy, and productive of mifchief, by making it queftionable who was to maintain the curate, and leaving the Ecclefiaftical Court deftitute of means to compel fuch maintenance, by fequeftering the profits of the living.   The curate alfo would be left without having any refort to the perfon by whom he was nominated, for a provifion for his fubfiftence.   It is too much therefore to contend, as the defendant does in this cafe, without fpecial words, that a refervation fhould be made by intendment out of the general

words

words of the grant, when there is no part of the subject matter, nor any thing in the nature of the case, which would tend to induce such an intendment, and when reason and policy are against it. If this intendment were to hold, then the question would arise, which was argued with a great deal of force, but which it is not necessary now to enter into, whether such a reservation could be made? The usage, it is said, stands very loosely on behalf of the impropriators. But it is certainly in their favour. The first nomination, of which there is an account, was made by the impropriators. How the next person was appointed does not appear. The nomination of Turner which followed, which is the first exercise of the right of the Crown, is stated to have been by lapse, from which it is to be presumed, that the Crown had no original right to nominate. The next presentation of Dickenson in 1727, is still less in favour of the right of the Crown, because it was clearly made, on complete mis-information. There was no vacancy, no avoidance; and Turner had still the title to the living. It must have been made on a supposition either that he was dead, or that there was an avoidance by some other means. It was a presentation granted by the Crown in a case, which neither intitled the Crown, nor any one else. Turner appeared, and Dickenson gave up the church to him, and he resumed the possession. While Turner was so in possession, the impropriators nominated Lonsdale, and on a suit in the Consistory Court, the Bishop of Chester affirmed their right to nominate, and Turner was in consequence dispossessed, which would not have been, if the right had been in the Crown. All therefore that we know of the enjoyment of the right of nomination to this curacy, from the time of the grant down to the present time, is, as far as it goes, in favour of the plaintiffs, and there is no instance of a clear right of nomination on the part of the Crown. It is for these reasons we are of opinion that there ought to be

Judgment for the plaintiffs.

STUDD

STUDD v. ACTON.

This was an action on the case on the stat. 23 *Hen*. VI. cap. 9, against a sheriff for refusing to take bail on an attachment out of Chancery.   The declaration in substance was as follows : Nathaniel Lee Acton, Esq. late Sheriff of the county of Suffolk, was attached to answer to James Studd, in a plea of trespass on the case, and thereupon the said James complains : for that whereas by a certain Act made in the 23d year of the reign of King Henry VI. it was amongst other things enacted, that all Sheriffs should let out of prison all manner of persons by them or any of them arrested, or being in their custody, by force of any writ, bill, or warrant, in any action personal, or by cause of indictment of trespass, upon reasonable sureties.   And whereas one John Revett prosecuted out of the Court of Chancery, a certain writ of *attachment*, directed to the Sheriff of Suffolk, by which said writ the King commanded the said Sheriff to attach the said James and Elizabeth his wife, and one James Reilly and Elizabeth Cotton, so as to have them before the same lord the King in his Court of Chancery in eight days after St. Hilary ; which said writ the said John Revet delivered to the said Nathaniel Lee, in due form of law to be executed ; by virtue of which said writ, the said Nathaniel Lee, so being such Sheriff as aforesaid, took and arrested the said James Studd and Elizabeth his wife : and the said James Studd, immediately after the taking and arresting of them, they the said James and Elizabeth his wife, tendered to the said Nathaniel Lee reasonable sureties of sufficient persons, for the appearance of them the said James and Elizabeth his wife, according to the command of the said writ.   Nevertheless the said Nathaniel Lee, not regarding the said statute, but wrongfully intending unjustly to injure, aggrieve, and oppress the said James Studd, and to put him to great trouble and expence in this behalf, absolutely refused to accept of any bail or sureties for them, carried them to the common gaol in the said county, and them then and there kept and detained prisoners, for the space of 10 days, against the form of the statute in such case made and provided ; wherefore the said James Studd saith, he is injured and hath sustained damages to the value of 1000*l*.

The question now came to be argued upon a demurrer, whether the Sheriff is bound to take bail upon an attachment
out

out of *Chancery*—and it was contended in support of the demurrer, that the statute of *Hen.* VI. is confined to process from the courts of common law, and does not extend to proceedings issuing out of a Court of Equity.

LORD LOUGHBOROUGH.—We have taken this case into full consideration, and have conferred with the other Judges on the subject, and the result is, that we are all of opinion that the action as laid cannot be maintained. It being the case of process issuing out of the Court of Chancery, we think that it does not come within the statute 23 *Hen.* VI. cap. 9, which directs that the Sheriffs shall let all persons out of prison by them arrested, or being in their custody " by force of any writ, bill, or warrant in any action personal," which words are confined to actions at law. A subsequent statute, 13 *Car.* II. stat. 2, cap. 2, which was made on the same subject, is distinctly confined to actions in the King's Bench and Common Pleas, and it does not appear to have been the intent of the Legislature to interfere with the process of a Court of Equity. It is extremely clear that the usage has been for the Sheriff to take a bail-bond in 40*l.* on an attachment, and it is so laid down *Darby* v. *Lawson, Eq. Ca. Abr* 351. But it does not appear that he is obliged to take it by the statute. The first process in the Court of Chancery is a *subpœna*, and if the party does not appear, then an attachment of contempt issues. If on this attachment he cannot be taken, and the Sheriff returns *non est inventus*, they go on to a second attachment, and if the party be not taken on that, the next process is a commission of rebellion. On this the Commissioners ought in all cases immediately to bring the party up into Court. There is an inaccuracy therefore of expression in *Harrison's Chanc. Prac.* where it is said that the Commissioners ought to take bail, and not keep the party lingering in prison in their houses. They certainly have no right to keep the person arrested in prison : their duty is to bring him up without delay, to the Court of Chancery. There are cases indeed where they may not take bail. But in the present case, if the Sheriff has done wrong, it is for that Court to interfere, out of which the process came. I do not mean to say, that there are no cases of this kind, where it would be right for the Sheriff to take bail ; but the question for us to determine is, Whether he is bound to do it by the statute? And for the reasons I have stated, we are all of opinion that he is not bound to do it, and therefore there must be

Judgement for the defendant.

CROWN

CROWN CASES.

STONE'S CASE.

Old Bailey July Seffions, 1784. This was an indictment on the ftatute 10 and 11 *Will*. III. cap. 23, for privately ftealing a watch, the property of Sir Robert Hefkett, in the fhop of John Alcock.

Sir Robert Hefkett had fent his watch to his watchmaker, Mr. Alcock, for the purpofe of being repaired, and it hung in the fhew-Glafs in Mr. Alcock's fhop at the time it was ftolen.

The COURT faid, that the meaning of the act of parliament upon which the capital part of the indictment was founded, had always been reftrained to fuch goods only, as are expofed to fale in fhops: and did not extend to mere *repofitories* for goods, although they might appear in the nature of *fhops*; and that as Mr. Alcock's fhop was not, with refpect to this watch, *a place of fale*, but a mere *repofitory*, the prifoner ought to be acquitted of the capital part of the charge. The Jury accordingly found him guilty of the fimple larceny only, and he was tranfported for feven years.

GEORGE DRUMMOND'S CASE.

At the Old Bailey in September Seffion, 1784, George Drummond was indicted before Mr. Baron *Eyre*, prefent Mr. Juftice *Gould*, for robbing the earl of Claremont of a gold watch, chain, feals, and trinkets.

During the trial, the prifoner's Counfel informed the Court, that a young man of the name of Edwards, very much refembling the perfon of the prifoner, had been recently executed for a highway robbery, and that immediately previous to the awful moment of his fate, he had communicated *fomething* to the Rev. Mr. Villette, the Chaplain in Ordinary of the Prifon, touching the commiffion of the identical robbery then under confideration. He therefore fubmitted to the Court, that as Mr. Villette's knowledge upon this fubject had proceeded from *the folemn declaration of a dying man*, it was admiffible evidence in favour of the prifoner.

THE COURT.—It would be inconfiftent with the rules of evidence, which are rules of Juftice, to examine a witnefs to the declaration of a perfon dying under the circumftances defcribed. The principle upon which this fpecies of evidence

is

is received, is, that the mind, impreffed with the awful idea of approaching diffolution, acts under a fanction equally powerful with that which it is prefumed to feel by a folemn appeal to God upon oath. The *declarations* therefore of a perfon dying under fuch circumftances, are confidered as equivalent to the *evidence* of the living witnefs upon oath. But to examine a witnefs to the declarations of an attainted convict, would be carrying the rule of evidence beyond its poffible extent, even if the perfon were alive; for as an attainted convict, he could not have been admitted to give teftimony upon oath, and the dying declarations of fuch a perfon cannot, confiftently with the principles of juftice, be confidered as better evidence than his teftimony on oath would have been if he had been alive. The fact, however, that a man refembling the perfon of the prifoner was executed, may be given in evidence, provided it is confined within fuch time as to make it probable that he was the perfon who committed this robbery.

The prifoner's Counfel did not venture to call any witnefs to eftablifh that fact; and the Jury found the prifoner guilty

ELIZABETH THOMPSON'S CASE.

At the Old Bailey September Seffion, 1784, Elizabeth Thompfon and Mary Macdaniel were indicted on the 12 *Anne*, cap. 7, for ftealing 7 guineas, the monies of Thomas Clifford, in the dwelling-houfe of the faid Mary Macdaniel.

The ftatute recites, " Forafmuch as divers wicked and ill-difpofed *fervants* and other perfons are encouraged to commit robberies in houfes, by the privilege of demanding the benefit of their Clergy;" and therefore enacts, " That all and every perfon or perfons that fhall felonioufly fteal any money, goods or chattels, wares or merchandizes, of the value of forty fhillings or more, being in any dwelling-houfe or out-houfe thereunto belonging, although fuch houfe or out-houfe be not actually broken by fuch offender, and although the owner of fuch goods, or any other perfon or perfon, be or be not in fuch houfe or out-houfe, or fhall affift or aid any perfon or perfons to commit any fuch offence, fhall be debarred from the benefit of Clergy.

It appeared in evidence, that the houfe in which the *larceny* was committed, was in fact the houfe of Mary Macdaniel; and the COURT held, that the meaning of the Legiflature did not extend to the cafe of a perfon ftealing in his own houfe.

KING'S

KING'S BENCH, Sittings after TRINITY TERM, 1790.

HENRY CECIL, *Esq. against the* Rev. WILLIAM SNEYD, *for Criminal Converfation with plaintiff's Wife.*

This was an action of damages againſt the defendant for having ſeduced and debauched the plaintiff's wife. The damages were laid at TEN THOUSAND POUNDS.

Mr. BOWER, *Counſel for the plaintiff,* ſtated that Mr. Cecil is a gentleman of high rank and family, and preſumptive heir to the Earl of Exeter, alſo a member of Parliament. Thirteen or fourteen years ago, he married Miſs Vernon, his preſent wife, then a young lady, the only daughter and heireſs of Mr. Vernon, in Worceſterſhire, a gentleman alſo of very large fortune.

From the year of their marriage, 1776, until the time when the injury was done by Mr. Sneyd, no two perſons could live in a ſtate of greater affection or greater harmony than Mr. and Mrs. Cecil; he had not the ſmalleſt ſuſpicion of her infidelity, and treated her with the moſt tender affection.

In the year 1780, the defendant came to the pariſh of Hanbury, in which Mr. Cecil reſided, in the character of Curate; he was the ſon of a reſpectable gentleman, the younger ſon of a family in Staffordſhire. Under this deſcription he was likely to be treated with attention and politeneſs; he was accordingly introduced into the family, and often dined with the plaintiff; and being in a poor ſtate of health, when the weather was bad he was conſtantly accommodated with a bed in the plaintiff's houſe, and was treated in every reſpect as a gentleman, and as a proper gueſt to viſit in his houſe; but it ſhould ſeem that ſome intimacy had ſubſiſted, for ſome time prior to 1789, between Mr. Sneyd and Mrs. Cecil, from the facts which I am about to ſtate.

About the middle of June laſt, Mrs. Cecil prevailed upon her huſband to go on a party of pleaſure to Birmingham, which is about 18 or 20 miles diſtant from Mr. Cecil's houſe; it was intimated to Mr. Cecil by his Lady, that the diſtance was too great to go with their own horſes, and therefore that it would be better to take poſt-horſes.—Mr. Cecil

Cecil complied with the requeſt.—He, Mrs. Cecil, and Mr. Edward Sneyd, the defendant's brother, ſet out for Birmingham;—Mr. Cecil returned back to Hanbury alone, in the evening, and Mrs. Cecil was to have followed him, in company with Mr. Edward Sneyd.

When Mrs. Cecil had remained out much longer than her huſband expected, he began to be anxious about her, but had no idea of what was going forward; and as ſhe did not return, he made what enquiries he could, but could not find her out; and this enquiry was made more difficult, by Mrs. Cecil and Mr. Sneyd aſſuming fictitious names.

The moment that Mr. Cecil had diſcovered that his wife had eloped, he left his houſe, and has never ſince returned to his friends, and now reſides ſomewhere beyond the ſeas.

Mr. Sneyd and Mrs. Cecil were afterwards diſcovered to be at an hotel at Exeter, under the name of *Mr. and Mrs. Benſon,* and then at an obſcure village in Devonſhire, where they lived three or four months in lodgings; they then quitted that place, and came to London, where they now reſide;—in ſeparate lodgings, indeed—but viſit each other every day.

You, Gentlemen of the Jury, will feel the nature of this ſort of injury. You ſee the ſituation of the parties, and the rank of Mr. Cecil, and the neceſſity of his taking care that no ſpurious iſſue be impoſed on his family. You will attend to the evidence which I ſhall now lay before you, and give ſuch a compenſation in damages, as ſubſtantial juſtice requires.

EVIDENCE FOR THE PLAINTIFF.

William Wells ſworn.

Mr. Wells. This is a true copy of the regiſter of the marriage of Mr. and Mrs. Cecil. They were married on the 23d of May, 1776, at St. George's, Hanover-Square.

William Janſey ſworn.

William Janſey. I lived as butler with the plaintiff, near four years and a half.

Q. During that time, had you any opportunity of obſerving how he treated his wife?

A. I always thought he was a very good huſband; they appeared to live very happily together, and he treated her with tenderneſs and affection.

Q. Did you know Mr. Sneyd, the defendant?

A. I

A. I did; he was the Curate of Hanbury. He was Curate there when I came to Mr. Cecil, and continued until the month of June, 1789.

Q. Did he vifit in your mafter's family?

A. Yes, Sir, frequently.

Q. Did he ever ftay all night at your mafter's houfe?

A. Sometimes he did; he was fometimes there at fupper; and in bad weather he flept there frequently.

Q. Do you remember your mafter and miftrefs going to Birmingham?

A. I remember Mr. and Mrs. Cecil going to Birmingham in June, 1789.

Q. When did Mr. Sneyd leave Hanbury?

A. About the end of May, or the beginning of June, 1789.

Q. How far is Birmingham from your mafter's houfe?

A. About eighteen or twenty miles.

Q. When did your mafter return from Birmingham?

A. He came home the fame night, but Mrs. Cecil did not come home with him.

Crofs-examined by Mr. Erfkine.

Q. At what time did you ever obferve, in the time from the month of June, 1785, when you came into this fervice, until May, 1789, when Mr. Sneyd left Hanbury, any affiduity of Mr. Sneyd towards Mrs. Cecil, or of Mrs. Cecil towards him?

A. They were frequently walking out together; they were fond of fifhing.

Q. Your mafter knew this of courfe?

A. I fuppofe fo. Mr. Cecil was fometimes with them; but they were often together by themfelves.

Q. Mr. Cecil knew that Mr. Sneyd and Mrs. Cecil went on thofe fifhing parties together? he knew they were fecreted a good deal together, and ufed to be in private?

A. He knew they ufed to walk out together in the fields;— I do not believe that he knew they ufed to be in private together.

Q. Did not the plaintiff know that Mr. Sneyd and Mrs. Cecil ufed to be often together; and was it not the conftant courfe for two years?

A. They were very often alone.

Q. Do you remember Mr. Cecil's going away and leaving his houfe?

A. I do.

Q. Do

Q. Do you recollect what passed there before his leaving the house?

A. I do not.

Q. Had not Mr. Sneyd left Hanbury, and gone to Birmingham, in the month of May, 1789?

A. I believe it was in May or in June.

Q. Do you remember his being delirious in a fever?

A. I do.

Q. When was that?

A. About a week before he left Hanbury.

Q. Has he recovered from that delirium?

A. I know not; I have seen him since, and he looked well—I never saw him look better than when I saw him last.

Q. What did you mean? You said, first that this gentleman was delirious in a fever; then I asked you, whether he was recovered? You said you did not know; and then you said, you knew he was well, with the greatest unconcern in the world---Look to the Jury, Sir---You say you never saw him look better?

A. By his look, and his face, and his fresh colour, he seemed to be well.

Q. Did you happen to know, from your master, the conversation that took place between the unhappy gentleman and him, previous to the time of his leaving his house?

A. I do not.

Q. Has Mr. Cecil never told you that he had no suspicion, and that he did not know any thing of any infidelity in his wife, until this gentleman himself (the defendant) told him of the situation he was in with his wife, which was the cause of his leaving Hanbury?

A. I do not know.

Q. Do you mean to swear, Sir, that you never heard this circumstance mentioned in your presence; that the first time your master heard of any attachment between your mistress and Mr. Sneyd, was when he came to Mr. Sneyd's sick-bed, and when he told him of it with tears in his eyes?

A. I was not in the room.

LORD KENYON.----Did you ever hear your master say any thing about it?

A. I never did; I have heard it from the servants.

Mr. Erskine. Do you know where Mr. Sneyd went when he left Hanbury.

A. He went into his father's carriage.

Q. Did he go to Birmingham?

                                        A. He

A. He went the Birmingham road.

Q. What state of health was he in at the time he went away?

A. He seemed a little better.

Q. Was not his complaint at that time a fever and delirium?

A. I believe so.

Q. Was Mr. Cecil present when Mr. Sneyd went into his father's carriage at Hanbury-Hall, in the month of May?

A. Yes, Sir, my master was present.

Q. I ask you upon your oath, Sir, whether you have any reason to believe, either directly or indirectly, that Mr. Sneyd, before he left Hanbury-Hall, planned the scheme of Mr. and Mrs. Cecil, and Mr. Edward Sneyd's coming to Birmingham on the 20th of June?

A. I have no reason to know or believe, this was a plan contrived by Mr. Sneyd for the purpose of getting this lady from her husband.

LORD KENYON.--Have you any reason to think that this was a scheme formed by Mr. William Sneyd?

A. I have not, my Lord; I cannot swear more than I have said.

Mr. Erskine. You say, you recollect your master and mistress, and Mr. Edward Sneyd going to Birmingham in a party in June last; now, upon your oath, Sir, were they not going on a visit to Mr. Sneyd?

A. I cannot tell.

Q. Were they not going to Birmingham?

A. They were.

Q. How came Mr. Edward Sneyd to accompany them to Birmingham?

A. He had been some time in the house.

Q. Was not the adultery of this woman, Mrs. Cecil, notorious in the husband's family at the time they set out for Birmingham?

Mr. Bower. I submit to your Lordship that this is not evidence.

LORD KENYON.----I think this question may be asked: Whether it was not matter of notoriety that she was false to her husband's bed?

Mr. Erskine. Was it not notorious in your master's family, at that time, that this adultery had been committed, and that it had been discovered to your master?

A. I have heard that it was discovered to my master.

Q. Then you have reason to believe, from the common report of the family, that the adultery of this lady was known to her husband?

A.]

A. I believe it was.

Mr. Bower. I submit to your Lordship, that this is nothing like evidence.

Mr. Erskine. It is my duty to try if I can, consistently with the rules of evidence, get at this fact, not only that it was notorious in the family, but also that this notoriety was accompanied with the discovery of it to the husband.

LORD KENYON.---If you can, obtain an actual discovery of it.

Mr. Erskine. Have you no reason to believe that Mr. Cecil did know of it before he went to Birmingham?

LORD KENYON.--Did you ever hear it spoken of in your master's presence?

A. I did not.

Mr. Erskine. Did you discover no alteration in your master's appearance before he went to Birmingham?

A. He appeared the same; he did not seem to be ill-affected with any thing.

Mr. Erskine, to the Witness. Now I ask you, Sir, if, since it was notorious to the family that your mistress had been guilty of adultery, how happened it that you did not mention it to your master; particularly, since you discovered by his appearance that he did not know it? Was it like the fidelity of a servant, not to communicate such an affair to his master?

A. I made no mention of it to my master.

Q. How many servants has Mr. Cecil?

A. Three or four and twenty.

Q. Now, Sir, I ask you, whether these servants did not know and speak of it as a fact, and whether it did not engross every part of their conversation?

A. They did not all speak of it, because they were not all in the house.

Q. Then you had no reason to know that the husband, Mr. Cecil, set out for Birmingham, to indulge his wife with a sight of this gentleman, to take her final leave of him?

A. I do not know that he did that; but I know they were going to Birmingham.

Q. Are any of the servants here that went that journey?

A. No, Sir.

Ann Vinican, examined by Mr. Bower.

Mrs. Vinican. I and my husband are servants to Mr. Thompson, who keeps the hotel in the Church-yard at Exeter.

Q. De

Q. Do you remember any perfons coming to your houfe, who called themfelves *Mr. and Mrs. Benfon,* but whom you knew fince to be *Mr. Sneyd and Mrs. Cecil?*

A. Perfectly well.

Q. Do you recollect in what cloaths Mr. Sneyd came?

A. He came in a pepper and falt-coloured coat; about the middle of June laft year.

Q. Did you know Mrs. Cecil?

A. Yes, Sir, perfectly well; I know fhe came to my mafter's houfe, and went by the name of Mrs. Benfon.

Q. How long did they remain at your mafter's houfe?

A. Three or four days.

Q. Now, during the time that they were at your mafter's houfe, did they fleep in different bed-chambers, or in the fame?

A. In the fame, and in one bed:---I left them in the room together, with the candle burning; ---they defired me to leave it, and faid they would put it out.

Q. Did you make the bed in the morning?

A. Sir, I did.

Q. Had it the appearance of two perfons having flept in it?

A. There was no other bed in the houfe made for Mr. Sneyd.

DEFENCE.

Mr. Erfkine. May it pleafe your Lordfhip, and you, Gentlemen of the Jury.

I am the Counfel for this unfortunate defendant, who, not being himfelf in a fituation capable to give me any inftructions, I am obliged to rife up, altogether uninftructed, in his defence, having nothing but this little piece of paper that ftates the pleadings in my hand.

I moft heartily concur in the obfervations which have been made by my learned friend on the fubject of adultery.

Either as it concerns religion, or morals, or wife policy, it is the bufinefs and duty of juries to check it; and I do affure you, my Lord, I do not mean any flattery; but I fay, that there is no man who has a higher refpect and veneration than I have for the manner in which your Lordfhip has always confidered thefe caufes when they have come into Court before you; and I think it unqueftionably my duty here, while I am defending an unhappy man, not to ftrike at the happinefs of fociety, by advancing any thing which can leffen the fanction of nuptial obligation, in which the happinefs of mankind is fo much involved. Indeed this caufe is an awful monument, that Virtue is its own reward;

and

and that Vices and Errors bring their own punishment along with them.   It is an awful monument, that the rules of Religion and Morality, and the various restraints they impose on our behaviour, instead of being impositions and restraints of harsh and powerful task-masters, operate as acts of parental benevolence and affection, and that every thing which we are commanded to do, tends ultimately to our good.

This unhappy gentleman has felt it.   He was a very young man, and fell into the snare of this woman, from whom the plaintiff will be relieved by your verdict.

This cause is only the fore-runner to that divorce which he will be entitled to receive by the proceedings of Parliament; for I do not mean to charge Mr. Cecil, either directly or indirectly, with having connived at this criminal intercourse which took place between this unhappy gentleman and the plaintiff's wife, or to charge him with any immoral or indecent conduct whatever.

This injured husband is entitled, by your verdict, to be released from those obligations which must be very distressing to him.

Gentlemen, you have no evidence here of that which is the great sting in these cases.   You have no evidence before you of the seduction.   It appeared in evidence, indeed, that this young Curate constantly walked out in different parts with a woman who might be considered as a matron.   She was possessed of no personal beauty or attractions; but who, from the rank and dignity which she held in the country, as wife of Mr. Cecil, had an opportunity of drawing into her snare an unfortunate young man, who possessed an handsome person, which happened to attract her attention.

Gentlemen, when the defendant recollected the situation to which he was reduced, it pierced his mind.   He fell into a delirium; and it is a fact absolutely notorious, that no person in the family dreamed of any thing like a criminal intercourse between these parties, until it was confessed by this unhappy young man, in the hour of sickness, who was desirous to make some sort of atonement to the person whom he had injured, and to obtain his forgiveness.   He was not the aggressor—but was drawn in by the allurements of this lady.

Gentleman, can you conceive, that for a month before, the adultery of this woman was notorious in a family where there were so many servants, and that the husband should be the only man who was ignorant of it? Although one servant might conceal it for fear, and another from want of fidelity to his master; yet it is contrary to all experience to suppose, that in a family, consisting of so many domestics, no person should be inspired with so much honour, with so much allegiance and fidelity to the injured master as to inform him of his wife's baseness. Why did none of them approach the husband?---Because they knew he was already acquainted with it.

I do not mean to tax Mr. Cecil with being that unconcerned man which he was described to be by one of his domestics. It is not true that he appeared always with the same face.

He was disposed at one time to do an act which would have tied him to this woman for ever. She fell down on her knees, and implored her husband to allow her once more to go and see this defendant, to take her final leave of him, and to give up his embraces for ever; and that she would then return to her duty. Our first parent turned towards Eve, and the plaintiff, following his example, was willing to forgive his weaker half.

This lady set out to find this miserable creature the defendant---a person lying in his bed---The moment she found him, she put a white coat upon him, clapped a false tail to his hair, and carried him off without delay, to Thompson's Hotel at Exeter?

Gentlemen, my learned friend has conducted this cause very honourably :---I am sure he will not contradict me in what I am about to say, because he knows it as well as I do, and therefore will not oblige me to call witnesses to prove it : we both know that the defendant is one of many children; that his father has very little property, and is unable to pay large damages. The defendant himself is a Curate, without any preferment whatever; and if you were to give a verdict for damages any thing like that which a man of fortune would be obliged to pay, he would be utterly undone and ruined; and now he is left an awful monument---deprived of his reason, lost in his health, and miserable in the extreme.

I hope, Gentlemen, you will remember one thing---that in this case there is no evidence of seduction. The defendant felt for the honour of his friend, as well as for his own situation.

Gentlemen, I shall trouble you with no more observations on this subject---This unfortunate defendant is entirely at your mercy---and I am sure you will do that which is right between both parties.

LORD KENYON.

Gentlemen of the Jury,

I have too often had an opportunity of ſtating to Juries the opinion which I entertain of crimes of this ſort. The puniſhment of them is part of that public duty which the law has repoſed in you---I ſhall only, at preſent, ſtate to you who the parties are.

The plaintiff is a Gentleman of very large property, and the preſumptive heir of one of the largeſt fortunes in the kingdom. His wife alſo was a Lady of great fortune.

The ſituation of this young man, the defendant, has been intimated to you.

This is a ſubject entirely for your conſideration : you will not put him into a ſituation that will make him a priſoner for life.

The jury found a verdict for the plaintiff, Damages, ONE THOUSAND POUNDS.

KING'S BENCH Sittings after TRINITY TERM, 1790.

HOOKER BARTTELOT, *Eſq. againſt* SAMUEL HAWKER, *Eſq. for Criminal Converſation with the Plaintiff's Wife.*

This was an action of damages againſt the defendant, for having debauched and ſeduced the plaintiff's Wife. The damages were laid at 5,000.

Counſel for the plaintiff.

MR. ERSKINE *and* MR. SHEPHERD.

For the Defendant.

MR. BOWER *and* MR. BALDWIN.

Mr. Erſkine opened his addreſs to the Jury with an apology for appearing now for the *proſecution* in a cauſe of a ſimilar nature to that laſt tried (*Cecil againſt Sneyd*), in which he had undertaken the *defence* ; and ſaid, I flatter myſelf,
Gen-

Gentlemen, that I may, without any inconfiftency, call your ferious attention to this cafe ; for you might have obferved, where my profeffional duty called me to defend an unfortunate man in the former caufe, I have neither attempted to infult the Court, nor difgrace myfelf, in the defence of my client, by fpeaking lightly of the ferious confiderations of a Court of Juftice ; but every man who attends to the prefent cafe, muft be fenfible that a moft grievous injury has been fuftained by the plaintiff.

Mr. Barttelot is a gentleman of family and fortune, who married in 1783, and lived with his wife in the greateft affection, until the time fhe was debauched by Mr. Hawker, a gay military man, and an officer of dragoons.

Having ingratiated himfelf into this lady's affection, and ufed every art to debauch her, he at laft unfortunately fucceeded.

The defence that is to be fet up this day, is one of a very artful defcription, and I muft therefore folicit you to treat it with the contempt it merits.

My learned friend the counfel for the defendant, will have an opportunity of producing articles of feparation ; of difagreements and differences that happened between Mr. and Mrs. Barttelot ; and I fhall not, perhaps, be able to prove any act of adultery antecedent to thefe articles of feparation : and then, moft likely, I fhall hear this defence from my learned friend :---" Why bring any complaint into a Court of Juftice? Why has the hufband fuffered ?---This is not an action to punifh the immorality of the offence, but to recover a recompence to the hufband for the lofs of the affection and company of his wife.---What has her hufband loft from being deprived of the comfort and fociety of a woman from whom, previous to any act of adultery, he had voluntarily feparated himfelf?"

And I have no doubt, in fuch a cafe, if this defence is eftablifhed, but it will go ftrongly to the mitigation of damages, although it would not be lefs heinous in the eye of God ; yet, *quoad* the hufband, it will leffen the damages. But if, on the contrary, I fhall be able to prove the previous adultery to you, as I am inftructed I fhall, this defence will redound, with a ten-fold force, upon themfelves.

I need not tell thofe who have come to that time of life at which you have arrived, that it is impoffible for a man and a woman to live in peace, tranquility, and conjugal affection with each other, where the mind of the woman is alienated by a paffion for another perfon. From the moment any third perfon has been able to infufe an attachment into the breaſt of a woman, there is an end of that affection and attention to her huſband, which alone can create reciprocity in affection; there is an end of every thing which conſtitutes the peace and happineſs of domeſtic life.

This caſe differs very much from the other which you have tried this morning: there the injured huſband may be ſeparated from his wife; he may marry again, and have a progeny to delight him, and to inherit the great eſtate to which he was born: in this caſe, the unhappy huſband, after ſeeing his wife debauched, muſt alſo have the mortification to ſee a baſtard iſſuing from her body very ſoon after the ſeparation took place, and all this proceeding from the ſeduction of the defendant; and, what is ſtill worſe, this baſtard may poſſibly ſucceed to the plaintiff's eſtate.

LORD KENYON.---Mr. Erſkine, will this action lie where there have been articles of ſeparation?

Mr. Erſkine.---Yes, my Lord, I think it will.

LORD KENYON.---I doubt that exceedingly. I never heard of ſuch an action: and I doubt on principles. It does not abate the immorality of the action; it ſtill leaves that.

Mr. Erſkine.------Gentlemen of the Jury, I felt this doubt; and, I confeſs, the damages muſt in a manner ſink from under me, if the acquaintance between the huſband and wife was at an end by the articles of ſeparation, previous to any act of adultery committed by the defendant. But, I hope, my Lord will reſerve that point to me, how far the action can be maintained, if the adultery is proved prior to theſe articles.

I ſhall be able to ſatisfy you, that from the period of the marriage, up to the time when Mrs. Bartelot became acquainted with this gentleman, the greateſt affection and domeſtic comfort ſubſiſted between her and her huſband. From the moment ſhe became acquainted with the defendant, or at leaſt ſoon after, thoſe differences aroſe; that coldneſs, that alienation of affection ſucceeded, which ended in their ſeparation. Immediately after this, Mrs. Bartelot fell into the hands of the defendant, who has lived with her, and has a child by her. Your judgment, Gentlemen, in ſuch a caſe, will direct you to exemplary damages.

LORD KENYON.------Mr. Baldwin, did you ever know an action like this?

Mr. Baldwin------No, my Lord, I never knew ſuch an action brought.

LORD KENYON.------I have a ſtrong opinion it will not lie.

Mr.

Mr. Erskine.——Your Lordship fees it would be very hard on this gentleman, as it would deprive him of a divorce.

LORD KENYON.—Many persons may be in a situation that may deprive them of divorces. What Parliament might do in this case, God only knows; they generally require a verdict at law; but if he *could not* have an action, I think they would stop short of justice, if they did not dispense with it.

EVIDENCE FOR THE PLAINTIFF.

The marriage of Mr. and Mrs. Barttelot, on the 18th of January, 1783, was proved by John Horton, Mrs. Barttelot's brother.

Cross-examined by Mr. Bower.

Q. Do you know how they lived together; I believe they did not live in great affection?

A. They were always quarrelling, some time after their marriage. Within a month they often quarrelled together; and within two months after their marriage, the family was obliged to be called in to compose their differences; their tempers were so different, and so ill-suited to each other.

Q. They were, therefore, a very unhappy couple?

A. Quite so.

Mary Rothe sworn.

Q. Mrs. Rothe, do you know Mr. and Mrs. Barttelot?

A. Yes, Sir; they came to live at my house in July, 1785, at Ashford, in Kent, and stayed five weeks.

Q. How did they behave to each other?

A. At first when they came, they behaved extremely well.

Q. Did you know Captain Hawker?

A. I did. I have seen Captain Hawker and Mrs. Barttelot together?

Q. Did you ever observe any thing particular between them?

A. I have seen them behave in a manner which I looked upon to be very indecent. I saw Mr. Hawker put his hand on Mrs. Barttelot's leg, in a very indecent way.

Q. Were her cloaths up?

A. Yes, Sir, they were higher than the calf of the leg; and Mr. Hawker put his hand very indecently.

Q. Did you communicate this to Mr. Barttelot?

A. No, Sir, not then.

Q. Did you make any other observations on their conduct?

A. I

A. I thought this was very unbecoming in any woman, particularly in a married woman.

Q. Did Mr. Barttelot behave in an affectionate manner to his wife?

A. Always, Sir.

John Barbic sworn.

Q. Mr. Barbic, I believe you live near Canterbury. Do you remember Mr. and Mrs. Barttelot coming to live at your house in the year 1785?

A. I do, Sir, it was some time in the month of August.

Q. Do you remember Captain Hawker visiting them?

A. Very well.

Q. After they had been there some time, did you make any observations on the conduct of Mrs. Barttelot and Mr. Hawker?

A. I entertained some suspicion of an intimacy between them.

Q. During the time that Mr. and Mrs. Barttelot lodged at your house, do you remember his going to London for a few days about some business?

A. I do.

Q. During the time that Mr. Barttelot was in London, do you recollect any circumstance relating to Capt. Hawker and Mrs. Barttelot?

A. I heard a man's voice in Mrs. Barttelot's bed-chamber about one o'clock in the morning.

Q. Now, how did Mr. Barttelot behave to his wife?

A. He seemed to me to behave to her with a great deal of tenderness.

Q. Do you remember Mrs. Barttelot going away?

A. I remember very well she went away with the maid-servant, during the absence of Mr. Barttelot.

Q. Do you remember Mr. Barttelot's returning?

A. I do. About one or two days after.

Mrs. Barbic sworn.

Q. Do you remember Mr. and Mrs. Barttelot lodging at your house?

A. Yes, Sir, I do.

Q. How did this gentleman behave to his wife?

A. So far as I saw, he always treated her with tenderness and affection.

Q. Do you remember the time of their having been visited by Captain Hawker?

A. I do.

Q. Did

Q. Did you obferve any thing particular in his behaviour towards this lady?

A. I did.

Q. What did you obferve in particular?

A. I obferved a familiarity between them.

Q. Do you remember Mr. Barttelot's going to London for two or three days, and leaving Mrs. Barttelot at home?

A. Yes, I do.

Q. Do you remember any perfon being in her bed-chamber in the night?

A. I do.

Q. Who was that perfon?

A. Captain Hawker.

Q. Have you any doubt about it?

A. I have no doubt of it; I faw him go up ftairs about twelve o'clock at night; he loitered about the door for a great while, until eleven or twelve o'clock at night, and then went up ftairs.

Q. Will you fwear pofitively that he was in Mrs. Barttelot's bed-chamber?

A. I will, and that he remained there until the next day, when I faw him come down again.

Mr. Barbic called again.

Q. Is that the perfon whofe voice you heard in the room with Mrs. Barttelot?

A. Yes, Sir, it was.

Q. to Mrs. Barbic, How long did he remain in Mrs. Barttelot's bed-chamber?

A. He remained there all night, and the next day until three o'clock in the afternoon:---the fervants were then difpofed all in different ways, and this gentleman came down.

Q. He had been in the bed-chamber with the lady then?

A. I heard him in the bed-chamber, and he was there all night. I told Mrs. Barttelot of it next day.

The Rev. Mr. Bond fworn.

Q. Do you know Mr. and Mrs. Barttelot?

A. I do; I had an opportunity of feeing them very frequently.

Q. Upon thofe occafions, how did Mr. Barttelot behave to his wife?

A. With the greateft tendernefs. They feemed to live very happily together.

DE-

DEFENCE.

Mr. *Bower.*—May it pleafe your Lordships, and you, Gentlemen of the Jury! I muft agree with my learned friend, Mr. Erfkine, that the queftion which you have to try, is not, Whether the defendant has been guilty of an immorality? but, Whether this breach of morality has been attended with any injury to the plaintiff?

To fay, whether adultery ought to be encouraged or difcouraged, is a queftion which will admit of no doubt; and, about which, I truft, every man in this Court is fully agreed: but in no cafe that comes before a Court is it more neceffary to attend to the fituation of the parties, than in thofe cafes where there is a charge of feduction. In the prefent cafe, the plaintiff has no ground of complaint; becaufe, from the commencement of their marriage, they were miferable. They were compofed of materials fo utterly difcordant, that from the very hour the connexion took place, they found themfelves in mifery and in ruin.

The lady's own brother proved, that within two months of their marriage, they were a moft miferable and wretched couple; and it is in vain to remove this impreffion, by calling three witneffes, who faw them only at particular times, and had no opportunity of obferving their hiftory.

I fhould not be the man to excufe the defendant, if he had been the original feducer: if he had corrupted this lady's mind; had alienated her affections from her hufband, and had been the mifchievous inftrument of difturbing his domeftic peace and tranquillity. But I fhall prove to you, by the Lady's father, that in the fpace of one month after this marriage, there was fuch ill treatment, and fuch quarrels between the parties, that he, on a vifit from his fon-in-law and daughter, fpent almoft a whole night in reconciling the quarrels, which within that fhort fpace had arifen between them. He will prove to you, that the family was a fcene of perfect wretchednefs.

Gentlemen, you will obferve that it has not been attempted to be proved to you, that Mr. Bartelot ever knew of the improper intercourfe that fubfifted between his wife and Mr. Hawker at Afhford, in 1785, and therefore it was not in confequence of this that the feparation took place, but in confequence of that perpetual ftate of mifery which had fubfifted between them, previous to that acquaintance with Mr. Hawker, and from the time of the marriage.

And

And to get rid of that load of misery, at a time when he was not conscious of any infidelity in his wife, he consented, in 1786, to articles of separation, and to leave her at liberty to act as she pleased.

In these articles it was mutually agreed between the parties, that she, Sophia, should from thenceforth live separate and apart from him, the plaintiff, at such place or places, and with such person or persons as she pleased; and that she be free from and without, molestation or hindrance by him, or any other person in or through him, in any manner, or on any account or pretence whatever; and that he the said Mr. Barttelor, his heirs and executors, should not molest or trouble, institute or prosecute, or cause to be instituted or prosecuted, any suit or suits, action or actions, in any Court or Courts whatsoever, against the said Sophia, " or against " those with whom the said Sophia should live and cohabit; " and if any such action or actions, suit or suits, should be " commenced or instituted, then, in every such case and " cases, this shall be pleaded specially in bar, and shall be " considered as full recompence and satisfaction for every " such action or actions."

This man, therefore, without any suspicion of his wife's infidelity, voluntarily entered into articles of separation, which were extremely desirable on both sides.

The defendant, instead of being a man of fortune, as was stated by my learned friend, is only one of ten children, the son of a clergyman, and has only a lieutenancy in the army to support him.

How can you say, Gentlemen, that the husband's peace has been destroyed by this man?

From the situation of the parties, you must see that no injury has been done; which is the question you are to try, and not whether the defendant has been guilty of an immoral action.

Under these circumstances, I submit that nominal damages will answer the justice of this case.

Doctor Horton sworn.

Q. Doctor, had you an opportunity of seeing the terms on which these parties lived?

A. Soon after they were married, they lived on very indifferent terms.

Q. Did it appear to you, Sir, to be a marriage of inclination?

A. I do not think there was much inclination in it.

Q. Did

Q. Did they continue to live unhappy from the time of their marriage to their feparation?

A. Very much fo, indeed.

Q. Do you remember any particular behaviour from Mr. Bartelot towards his wife?

A. I do, Sir. About five weeks after the marriage, they had been quarrelling about going into a hackney-coach, and at night I had great difficulty to reconcile them; I was an hour and more in attempting it.

Crofs-examined by Mr. Erfkine.

Q. You are the father of this lady. Did you ftate to Mr. Bartelot your daughter's difinclination to him?

A. No, Sir, I did not.

Q. I would wifh, Sir, to know the conduct of this gentleman towards your daughter, immediately after the marriage; what was it?

A. They lived very unhappily together.

Q. Did fhe bring him a fortune?

A. No, fhe did not; I fuppofe he married her for affection.

Q. From what you know of your daughter, have you any reafon to fuppofe that fhe would fall into this fort of conduct, without the feduction of fomebody?

A. No, Sir; I certainly have not.

Q. Had you any reafon to believe fhe was ever guilty with any other perfon than Mr. Hawker?

A. I had no reafon, nor any thing like it, to believe fhe was ever criminal with any other perfon.

Q. I fhould be glad to know what was the nature of thofe difputes that took place between this gentleman and his lady?

A. There were many quarrels between them; but the firft that I recollect, was one night about getting into a hackney-coach; there were four of us there. He faid he would rather walk home.

Q. Now, then, what did the lady fay?

A. She entreated him to come into the coach, and fo did thofe who were with her, and he then came, and fhe reproached him for being fo rude and ungentleman-like, and for doing all this before fome of her beft friends.----Here the difpute ended.

Q. To be fure this was very rude and obftinate, not to come into the hackney-coach; but was there any thing to occafion a feparation from bed and board?

A. No;

A. No; but there was a continuance of thefe quarrels.

Q. This, then, was the firſt remarkable inſtance that occurred?

A. This was one of the moſt prominent diſputes that made their appearance in the family. They were married in January, and this happened in February.

Mr. Bower.---I think, Sir, you ſaid they lived very unhappily from the time of their marriage, to the time of their ſeparation?

A. Exceedingly ſo, indeed.

Q. Had they any children?

A. No children.

Mr. Erſkine.---Do you not know, Sir, that your daughter had a child?

A. I know, from being told, that ſhe had a child by Mr. Hawker; but I never ſaw it.

Q. I wiſh you would give us an inſtance of thoſe harmonious jangles that took place between your daughter and ſon-in law?

LORD KENYON.---I am afraid theſe quarrels proceed very often from very ſmall things, and put the parties in a very ridiculous ſituation.

Witneſs.---In the middle of the night I heard a ſtamping and ſwearing. I then got up, and reproached my ſon-in-law very much, for his indecent behaviour in my houſe; my daughter ſaid ſhe was afraid of him. After a good deal of altercation, I, with difficulty, got them to bed again.

Andrew Scott ſworn.

Q. Do you know the defendant, Mr. Hawker, Sir.

A. I do; he is a Lieutenant in a Regiment of Dragoons, and his father is a Clergyman.

Q. Has he any thing to ſupport him but his pay?

A. Nothing.

MR. ERSKINE.

May it pleaſe your Lordſhip, and you, Gentlemen of the Jury,

I can by no means ſubſcribe to a great deal which I have heard from the learned Counſel for the defendant.

I do admit, that as Divines or Moraliſts, or as Adminiſtrators of Criminal Juſtice, you are not to decide as againſt men acting againſt the Law of God and of Morality: but I ſay, where the conduct of the defendant, even in a civil ſuit, is connected with the intereſts of ſociety, and the preſervation of the peace of mankind, that it be-

becomes a matter of confequence infinitely ferious; and he who has invaded the rights of individuals, being more pernicious than others, by having fet a bad example to fociety, fo he deferves a more fevere punifhment.

It has been faid, that my client does not come into a Court of Juftice, under circumftances to claim the compaffion of a Jury; and that the defendant being one of ten children, and the fon of a Clergyman without property, ought therefore to go free.

God forbid, Gentlemen, that a man who has nothing but his commiffion in the army, might commit heinous crimes, and then be permitted to plead his poverty; he might then break into your houfe——he might violate your wife, and might deflower your daughter:——he might do every act to which the law attaches a punifhment, if he had only to plead his poverty, and then to be fet free from all the confequences of his villainy.

My learned friend fays, that the hufband has loft nothing—— Has he not? If this woman brings forth children, they muft inherit his fortune.

But, Gentlemen, my friend is anxious to convince you that the plaintiff has fuftained no lofs, becaufe there were fome bickerings between him and his wife: becaufe people are not angels, does it follow from thence that there is no comfort belonging to that fituation?

Becaufe a man may have fome paltry difputes with a woman with whom he lives, does it from thence follow, that they have no affection and regard for each other? May not he bring back her wandering imaginations by conftant attention to her, although fhe does not love her hufband, who ought to be the object of her affections? May they not acquire a mutual attachment, by the children that might be produced?——You have heard fhe had a child by this man.——She might have borne children that might have been pledges of their affection—that might have been a bond of union, and all thefe quarrels ended.

The defendant, taking advantage of the hufband's abfence, took that opportunity of debauching the plaintiff's wife.

Gentlemen, I cannot fuppofe that men of your decent manners——I cannot fuppofe that men of your moral behaviour——I cannot fuppofe that men of your religious education, can countenance a conduct of this fort, either as public or private men.

I have

I have another observation to make to you; and it is this: though you must be satisfied there was an act of adultery, yet no man commits crimes in the face of the public, as he enters into contracts.

You must collect the evidence circumstantially. People do not commit adultery, and invite others to be witnesses to the scene. But mark the evidence: the defendant lounges about the door—waits for the opportunity—conceals his person from observation——and at last gets into the bed-chamber of a married lady, and remains there all night. Now, are you to presume—my learned friend, with a great deal of good sense, has made no such observation—are you to presume *they sat up all night*—that a man who came here for the purpose of adultery, which is evident from what followed, went into her bed-chamber for this purpose of sitting up all night? Common sense rejects the idea.

I have only one observation more to make. The father had not an opportunity of telling you how long Captain Hawker was introduced to his daughter. You find them acquainted in the year 1785. How can you tell but that these quarrels were first occasioned by his seduction; and that all these differences might have been put an end to by children?

There is nothing more serious than the preservation of morality; it is essential to the very being of a nation; for when there is a want of morals, there is an end of every thing that is great and honourable among men, and damages is here the only punishment.

I trust, Gentlemen, because some disputes subsisted between Mr. and Mrs. Barttelot, you will not think that the husband has lost nothing; but will give him a verdict in damages suited to the circumstances of his case.

LORD KENYON.

Gentlemen of the Jury,

You have tried two causes of this sort this morning.

The most likely way to preserve men in the road of their duty is, by implanting in their breast sentiments of religion and virtue. When this fails, the next resource is punishment; and in causes of this kind, it depends upon Juries not to let men go from this Court, without smarting for the injuries they have done to their neighbours, and for the wretched state to which they reduce the private peace of families.

That the relation of husband and wife subsisted between Mr. and Mrs. Barttelot has been proved.

There

There are two questions in this case for your consideration.

First----Whether the defendant has been guilty of the charge which has been imputed to him? And,

Secondly----If you find him guilty, what damages are to be given.

Now, it has been very properly said, that in offences of this kind, and in general, persons who are guilty do not summon witnesses to see their guilt. You must prove it as well as you can from circumstances; and if they are cogent and convincing, you must give them the same force as if you had been eye or ear witnesses.

In order to prove this party guilty, the first witness stated instances of extreme indelicacy between these persons. The other witnesses have carried the case further; for Mr. and Mrs. Barbie proved that they heard, at an improper hour of the night, the voice of a man in Mrs. Barttelot's bed-chamber. Mrs. Barbie says,--That the defendant went up stairs about *eleven or twelve o'clock at night*; he passed her briskly, and she did not distinguish him; but in the morning she saw him come down. But it is said, she was not in the room--- nor was it necessary; he could have no business there, but the purpose which this cause imputes to him.

Gentlemen, it is for you to deliberate on that; and if you are led to believe, that this act was done at that time, as, I confess, it seems so to me, the conclusion follows of course.

The next point is ———The *damages* you will give. And, certainly, it is no apology to say, " I am poor:" and it would be reading a very bad lesson to tell young officers, or any other persons, " On account of your poverty you may commit offences up to any extent; you may invade the dearest rights of mankind, and your poverty shall be spread before you as a shield."

There are some circumstances to extenuate, and others to aggravate this offence. It is an aggravation to defile the bed of a married man, as he is deprived of the comfort and conversation of his wife. To be sure, it is often pressed, and not improperly, that the offence is not so aggravated, where there were no children. Although this be so, yet it is equally a breach of religion and morality.

An act of adultery has been proved in the year 1785. In the *following* year, articles of separation took place.

Gentlemen, it is entirely with you to say--First, Whether he is guilty?—And then, if he is—What damages are to be given to the injured party?

The

The Foreman of the Jury afked, Whether Mrs. Barttelot's child, by Mr. Hawker, muft inherit the eftate of Mr. Barttelot.

LORD KENYON faid, This muft depend on circumftances.

The Jury then gave their verdict for the plaintiff, with Seven Hundred Pounds damages.

STATUTES paffed in the laft Seffions of Parliament.

An Act to impower Juftices, and other Perfons, to vifit Parifh Workhoufes or Poorhoufes, and examine and certify the State and Condition of the Poor therein to the Quarter Seffions.

Whereas the laws now in being for the regulating parifh workhoufes, have been found deficient, when the poor in fuch houfes are afflicted with contagious difeafes, in which cafes particular attention to their lodging, diet, cloathing, bedding, and medicines, is requifite; be it enacted, That after the 29th day of September, 1790, it fhall and may be lawful for any of his Majefty's Juftices of the Peace, or any Phyfician, Surgeon, or Apothecary, for that purpofe authorized by warrant under the hand and feal of any fuch Juftice or Juftices, or for the officiating Clergyman of the parifh or place, duly authorized, as aforefaid, at all times, in the day time, to vifit any parifh workhoufe, or houfe provided for the maintenance of the poor of any parifh or place, within the county, riding, liberty, or divifion, wherein fuch Juftice or Juftices fhall be refident and have jurifdiction, to examine into the ftate and condition of the poor people therein, and the food, cloathing, and bedding of fuch poor people, and the ftate and condition of fuch houfe or houfes; and if upon any fuch vifitation the faid Juftice or Juftices, or perfons authorized aforefaid, fhall find any occafion of complaint, fuch Juftice or Juftices, or perfons authorized as aforefaid, fhall, if he or they fhall think fit, certify the ftate and condition of fuch workhoufe or poorhoufe, and the ftate of the poor therein, and of their food, cloathing, and bedding, to the next Quarter Seffions of the Peace to be held

held for such county, riding, liberty, or division, wherein such workhouse or poor house shall be situate, under his or their hands and seals respectively; and such Justice or Justices, or persons aforesaid, shall cause the Overseers of the Poor, or Master or Governor of the said workhouse or poorhouse to be summoned to appear at the same Sessions, to answer such complaint; and the Justices assembled at such Quarter Sessions, on hearing the parties on any such complaint, shall and may make such orders and regulations for the removing of any cause of complaint contained in such certificate as aforesaid, as to them shall seem meet; and all the parties concerned shall, and they are hereby required to abide by and perform such orders and regulations as shall be so made by the Justices at the said Sessions.

Provided always, and be it further enacted, That in case any Justice or Justices of the Peace, or persons duly authorized by warrant as aforesaid, shall, upon any such visitation, find any of the poor afflicted with any contagious or infectious disease, or in want of immediate medical or other assistance, or of sufficient and proper food, or requiring separation or removal from the other poor in the said house, then and in such case or cases, if such visitation shall be made by a Justice of the Peace, he is hereby directed and required to apply to one or more other Justice or Justices of the Peace, in the county, riding, liberty, or division, and certify to him or them the state and condition of the poor in such parish workhouse or poorhouse; or if such visitation shall be made by the persons duly authorized as aforesaid, they are hereby required to apply to two or more Justices of the Peace in such county, riding, liberty, or division; and thereupon the said Justices shall and may, and they are hereby authorized to make such order for the immediate procuring medical or other assistance, or of sufficient and proper food, or for the separation or removal of such poor as shall be afflicted with any contagious or infectious disease, in such manner as they the said Justices, under their hands and seals, shall think proper to direct, until the next Quarter Sessions of the Peace, to be held in and for the said county, riding, liberty, or division, wherein such house shall be situate; at which Quarter Sessions of the Peace the said two Justices are to certify the same, under their hands and seals respectively, to the Justices assembled at such Quarter Sessions, who are hereby authorized and required to make such order for the further relief of the poor in such parish workhouse or poorhouse, as to the Justices assembled at such Quarter Sessions shall seem meet and proper;

pet; and the charges and expences of relieving such poor shall be, and is hereby directed to be paid out of the poor's rate of such parish in such manner as the said Justices assembled at such Quarter Sessions shall direct.

Provided always, that nothing herein contained shall extend to any poorhouse or workhouse in any district or districts which have been, or may be hereafter incorporated or regulated by any special Act or Acts of Parliament.

An Act to explain and amend an Act, passed in the Twentieth Year of the Reign of His present Majesty, touching the Election for Knights of the Shire to serve in parliament for that Part of Great Britain called England.

Whereas an Act was passed in the twentieth year of the reign of His present Majesty, (cap. 17), intituled " An Act to remove Difficulties relative to County Elections," it is enacted, that no person shall vote for Knights of the Shire in respect of any messuages, lands, or tenements, which have not, for six months next before such election, been charged towards the Land Tax, in the name of the person or persons who shall claim to vote at such election for or in respect of the same, or in the name of his or their tenant actually occupying the same as a tenant of the owner or landlord thereof: and whereas the form of assessment prescribed by the said Act, and thereunto annexed, denotes that the names, both of the proprietor and of the occupier, ought to be specified; and doubts have arisen, whether, if such form be not strictly pursued, the suffrage of the person claiming to vote be admissible.   Be it therefore enacted, That nothing in the said Act contained shall prevent any person from voting at any election of Knights of a Shire, or at any election of a burgess for the Borough of Cricklade, for or in respect of any messuages, lands, or tenements, which have been charged or assessed, for six calendar months next before such election, towards some aid granted or to be granted to his Majesty, his heirs or successors, by a land-tax, in the name of the person claiming to vote, or for or in respect of any messuages, lands, or tenements, to which the person so claiming to vote shall have become entitled by descent, marriage, marriage-settlement, devise, promotion to any benefice in a church, or promotion to any office, within twelve calendar months next before such election, and which meſſuages, lands, or tenements, ſhall have been within two years next before ſuch election charged or aſſeſſed to the land-tax, in the name of the perſon or perſons by or through whom ſuch perſon ſo claiming to vote, ſhall derive his title to ſuch meſſuages, lands, or tenements, or of ſome predeceſſor of ſuch perſon ſo claiming to vote, although the name of the tenant or tenants actually occupying ſuch meſſuages, lands, or tenements, ſhall not be inſerted in ſuch aſſeſſment, according to the ~~form of aſſeſſment~~ to the ſaid firſt recited Act annexed.

And be it further enacted, that nothing in the ſaid Acts ſhall prevent any perſon from voting at any ſuch election of Knights of any Shire, or of Burgeſſes for the ſaid Borough of Cricklade, for or in reſpect of any meſſuages, lands, or tenements, which have been charged or aſſeſſed, for ſix calendar months next before ſuch election, towards ſome aid granted, or to be granted to his Majeſty, his heirs or ſucceſſors, by a land-tax, in the name of a tenant or tenants actually occupying the ſame at the time of ſuch aſſeſſment being made, although the name of the perſon ſo claiming to vote, or the perſon or perſons by or through whom ſuch perſon ſo claiming to vote derives his title, or of the predeceſſor of the perſon claiming to vote, ſhall not be inſerted in the aſſeſſment, according to the form of the aſſeſſment to the ſaid firſt recited Act annexed.

An Act for diſcontinuing the judgment which has been required by Law to be given againſt Women convicted of certain Crimes, and ſubſtituting another Judgment in lieu thereof.

Whereas it is expedient that the judgment which has been required by law to be given and awarded againſt any woman or women in the caſes of high-treaſon, or of petit-treaſon, ſhould be no longer continued: be it enacted, that after the 5th day of June, 1790, the judgment to be given and awarded againſt any woman or women convicted of high treaſon, or of petit-treaſon, ſhall not be, that ſuch woman or women ſhall be ſeverally drawn to the place of exe-

execution, and be there burned to death; but that such woman or women being so convicted as aforesaid, shall be severally drawn to the place of execution, and be there hanged by the neck until she or they be severally dead; any law or usage to the contrary thereof in anywise notwithstanding.

And be it further enacted, that if any woman or women shall be convicted of the crime of petit-treason, such woman or women shall be subject and liable to such further pains and penalties as are particularly specified and declared with respect to persons convicted of wilful murder, in an Act passed in the 25th year of King George II. (intituled, "An Act for preventing the Crime of Murder"); and the Court before whom any such woman or women shall be convicted, shall pass sentence at such time, and shall give such orders with respect to the time of execution; the disposal of the convict's body after execution, and all such other matters and things as are directed to be given by the said Act, with respect to persons convicted of wilful murder.

And be it further enacted, That whenever any woman shall be convicted of the crime of high-treason, or of the crime of petit-treason, or of abetting, procuring, or counselling any petit-treason, and judgment shall be given thereon, according to the directions of this act, then, and in every such case, such woman, being so attainted of such crimes respectively, shall be subject and liable to such and the like forfeitures, and corruption of blood, as they severally would have been in case they had been severally attainted of the like crimes before the passing of this Act.

An Act for repealing the Duties upon Licences for retailing Wine and Sweets, and upon Licences for retailing distilled Spirituous Liquors; and for granting other Duties in Lieu thereof.

Whereas by an Act, made in the 9th year of Q. Anne, cap. 23, it was enacted that there should be, for every piece of vellum, parchment, or paper, on which should be written any licence for retailing of wine, the sum of four shillings: and whereas, by another act made, 30 Geo. II. cap. 19, it was enacted, that there should be paid, for every licence for retailing of wine, to be granted to any person who should not take out either

ther a licence for retailing of fpirituous liquors, or a licence
for retailing of beer, over and above all other rates and
duties, an additional ftamp duty of five pounds; for every
licence for retailing of wine, to be granted to any perfon
who fhould take out a licence for retailing beer, but fhould
not take out a licence for retailing of fpirituous liquors,
over and above all other rates and duties, an additional
ftamp duty of four pounds; and for every licence for retailing of wine, to be granted to any perfon who fhould
alfo take out a licence for retailing of fpirituous liquors,
over and above all other rates and duties, an additional
ftamp duty of forty fhillings; and it was by the faid Act
provided, that, in all cafes where a duty of five pounds was
therein before directed to be paid on a licence for retailing
wine, a duty of three pounds fix fhillings and eight-pence,
and no more, fhould be paid for a licence to retail wine in
Scotland; and that in all cafes where a duty of four pounds
was therein before directed to be paid for fuch licence, a
duty of two pounds thirteen fhillings and four-pence, and
no more, fhould be paid for a licence to retail wine in
Scotland; and that in all cafes where a duty of two pounds
was therein before directed to be paid for every fuch licence,
a duty of one pound fix fhillings and eight-pence, and no
more, fhould be paid for a licence to retail wine in Scotland: and it was by the faid Act enacted, that no perfon
whatfoever, unlefs he fhould be authorized in the manner
therein prefcribed, fhould fell by retail, (that is) by the
pint, quart, pottle, or gallon, or by any other greater or lefs
retail meafure, or in bottles in any lefs quantity than fhould
be equal to the meafure of the cafk or veffel in which the
fame fhould have been, or might lawfully be imported, any
kind of wine or wines, or any liquor called or reputed wine,
upon pain to forfeit for every fuch offence the fum of one
hundred pounds: and whereas, by a claufe in another Act
made 31 Geo. II. cap. 31, it was enacted, that no perfon
whatfoever, unlefs he fhould be authorized by having taken
out the licence to fell wine by retail, fhould fell or utter
by any retail meafure, or in bottles in any quantity lefs than
twenty-five gallons, any kind of liquor made in Great Britain by infufion, fermentation, or otherwife, from foreign
fruit or fugar, or from Britifh fruit or fugar, or from fruit
or fugar mixed with any other ingredients, commonly called
fweets or made wines, or any kind of liquor made in Great
Britain, and known by the name of fweets or made wines
of whatfoever materials, or in whatfoever manner the fame
might be made, upon pain to forfeit for every fuch offence
one

one hundred pounds: and whereas by another Act, made in the 26th *Geo.* III. cap. 74, " for granting to his Majesty additional Duties upon Sweets," reciting, that it was then expedient that separate licences should be granted to the venders of foreign wines imported, and to the venders of sweets or British made wines, it was enacted, that it should be lawful for his Majesty's Commissioners of Stamps, to grant any licence for selling of sweets or British made wines by any retail measure, to any person applying for the same (although such person or persons should not have a spirituous liquor or ale-licence), with a stamp of two pounds and four shillings; and all persons selling British-made wines only under such licences, should be freed and discharged from any penalty for selling wine under licences not stamped as by the said Acts were directed: and whereas by another Act, made in the 28th *Geo.* III. cap. 37, " to prevent the Sale of Sweets for Consumption in the Houses of Retailers thereof, who shall not have Licences to sell Beer or Ale," reciting so much of the said Act made in the 26th year of his present Majesty as is hereinbefore recited; and that it was expedient to restrain the selling British wines for consumption in the houses of retailers thereof to such persons only as should have obtained as well a licence for selling beer and ale, as a licence for the sale of British-made wines, it was enacted, that no person should, by virtue of any licence for the sale of British-made wines or sweets, be intituled to sell such wines or sweets, for consumption in his or her own house, unless such person should also have obtained a licence for selling beer and ale: and whereas it is apprehended, that if the said recited duties were repealed, and other duties imposed in lieu thereof upon licences to be granted, by the Commissioners, Collectors, and Supervisors of EXCISE, in England and Scotland respectively, to persons retailing foreign wine, or British-made wines or sweets, such last-mentioned duties would be more conveniently and effectually managed and collected: BE IT THEREFORE ENACTED, that after the 10th day of October, 1790, the said recited duties, under the management of the said Commissioners of STAMPS, by the said Acts imposed upon any such licence as aforesaid, shall cease and determine.

And whereas, by another Act made in the 26th *Geo.* II. cap. 8, it was enacted, that no person should presume to retail any distilled spirituous liquors, or strong waters, without first taking out a licence for that purpose for which he should pay the sum of twenty shillings: and whereas, by another Act made in the 24th *Geo.* II. cap. 40, it was enacted,

enacted, that there should be paid unto his Majesty, an additional duty of twenty shillings per annum for every licence that should be taken out by any person or persons for the retailing spirituous liquors: and whereas, by three several other Acts of Parliament, made in the 19th Geo. III. cap. 25; 21 Geo. III. cap. 17; 22 Geo. III. cap. 66; three several additional duties of five pounds per Centum became charged upon the produce of the said several duties: and whereas, by another Act made in the 27th Geo. III. cap. 30, it was enacted, that there should be paid the several sums upon all licences, by all persons who should retail any distilled spirituous liquors; and whereas it is expedient to repeal the said recited duties by the said several Acts, and, in lieu thereof, to impose other duties on licences to be taken out by persons who shall retail distilled spirituous liquors, according to the directions of this act; be it therefore further enacted by the authority aforesaid, that, from and after the 10th day of October, 1790, the said recited duties, by the said several Acts imposed, for or in respect of the licences therein mentioned, shall cease and determine.

Provided always nevertheless, that nothing herein-before contained shall extend to any arrears of the said respectively recited duties which may remain unpaid, or to any fine, penalty, or forfeiture relating thereto respectively, which shall have been before incurred.

And be it further enacted, that from and after the said 10th day of October, 1790, all licences which before shall have been granted by the said Commissioners of Stamps, to any person whatsoever, to sell wine by retail, or to sell by retail British-made wines or sweets, and which shall be then unexpired; and also all licences which, before the said 10th day of October, 1790, shall have been granted by the said Commissioners of Excise, or by the Collectors and Supervisors of Excise, or by their appointment, to any person whatsoever, to retail distilled spirituous liquors, and which shall be then unexpired, shall, on the said 10th day of October, 1790, become and be null and void, to all intents and purposes whatsoever; any thing in the said licences expressed, or in any Acts of Parliament contained to the contrary thereof in any wise notwithstanding.

And be it further enacted, that every person whose licence for retailing of wine, sweets, or spirituous liquors, shall become null and void by virtue of this Act, shall, on his, her, or their taking out a licence of the same kind as the licence so become null and void for the year ending on the 10th day of October, 1790, under and by virtue of

this

this Act, be allowed to deduct out of the money by this Act directed to be paid for such last-mentioned licence, a rateable proportion according to the sum of money by him paid for such licence so become void, and the portion of time for which such licence was granted to be in force which shall be unexpired at the time of such licence so becoming null and void.

And be it further enacted by the authority aforesaid, that, from and after the said 10th day of October, 1790, all and every person, before he shall retail any foreign wine, or any British-made wines or sweets, or any distilled spirituous liquors or strong waters, shall take out such licence herein-after mentioned, as the case may require, authorizing such person to retail foreign wine, sweets, or distilled spirituous liquors, as the case may require; which licences respectively shall be granted in manner herein-after mentioned; that is to say, if any such licence shall be taken out within the limits of the chief office of Excise in London, the same shall be granted under the hands and seals of two or more of the Commissioners of Excise in England for the time being, or of such persons as they the said Commissioners of Excise, or the major part of them for the time being, shall from time to time appoint for that purpose; but if any such licence shall be taken out in any part of the kingdom of England not within the said limits, the same shall be granted under the respective hands and seals of the several Collectors and Supervisors of Excise within their respective collections and districts; and in case any such licence shall be taken out within the limits of the City of Edinburgh, the same shall be granted under the hands and seals of two or more of the Commissioners of Excise in Scotland for the time being; or if any such licence shall be taken out in that part of Great Britain called Scotland, out of the said limits of the City of Edinburgh, then the same shall be granted under the respective hands and seals of the several Collectors and Supervisors of Excise in Scotland, within their respective collections and districts; and the said Commissioners of Excise in England and Scotland respectively, or any two or more of them respectively, and the persons to be appointed by the said Commissioners of Excise in England, or the major part of them, and also all such Collectors and Supervisors are hereby respectively authorized and required to grant such licences to the persons who shall apply for the same, on the person or persons applying for the same first paying for such licences the several sums of money following; that is to say,

For

For every licence which shall be granted to authorize any person to retail foreign wine in England, and who shall not have an excise licence for retailing distilled spirituous liquors or strong waters, or a licence for retailing of beer, ale, or other exciseable liquors, the sum of 5l. 4s.

For every licence which shall be granted to authorize any person to retail foreign wine in England, and who shall take out a licence for retailing beer, ale, and other exciseable liquors, but shall not have an excise licence for retailing of distilled spirituous liquors or strong waters, the sum of 4l. 4s.

For every licence which shall be granted to authorize any person or persons to retail foreign wine in England, and who shall also have an excise licence for retailing distilled spirituous liquors or strong waters, the sum of 2l. 4s.

For every licence which shall be granted to authorize any person or persons to retail British-made wines or sweets, either in England or Scotland, the sum of 2l. 4s.

For every licence which shall be granted to authorize any person or persons to retail foreign wine in Scotland, and who shall not have an excise licence for retailing distilled spirituous liquors or strong waters, or a licence for retailing of beer, ale, or other exciseable liquors, the sum of 3l. 6s. 8d.

For every licence which shall be granted to authorize any person or persons to retail foreign wine in Scotland, and who shall take out a licence for retailing beer, ale, or other exciseable liquors, but shall not have an excise licence for retailing distilled spirituous liquors or strong waters, the sum of 2l. 13s. 4d.

For every licence which shall be granted to authorize any person or persons to retail foreign wine in Scotland, and who shall also have an excise licence for retailing distilled spirituous liquors or strong waters, the sum of 1l. 6s. 8d.

And for every licence which shall be granted to authorize any person or persons to retail distilled spirituous liquors or strong waters in any part of Great Britain, the sum of 4l. 14s. if the dwelling-house in which such person shall reside, or retail such distilled spirituous liquors or strong waters, at the time of taking out such licence, shall not, together with the offices, courts, yards, and gardens therewith occupied, be rated, under the authority of an Act made in the 19th year of the reign of his present Majesty, " for imposing Duties on inhabited Houses," at a rent of 15l. per Annum, or upwards.

If such dwelling-house shall, together with the offices, &c. therewith occupied, be rated as aforesaid at 15l. per annum, or or upwards, and under 20l. then such person shall take out a licence as aforesaid, and pay for the same the sum of 5l. 2s.

If such dwelling-house shall, together with the offices, &c. therewith occupied, be rated as aforesaid at 20l. per annum, or upwards, and under 25l. then such person shall take out a licence as aforesaid, and pay for the same the sum of 5l. 10s.

If such dwelling-house shall, together with the offices, &c. therewith occupied, be rated as aforesaid at 25l. per annum, or upwards, and under 30l. then such person shall take out a licence as aforesaid, and pay for the same the sum of 5l. 18s.

If such dwelling-house shall, together with the offices, &c. therewith occupied, be rated as aforesaid at 30l. per annum, or upwards, and under 40l. then such person shall take out a licence as aforesaid, and pay for the same the sum of 6l. 6s.

If such dwelling house shall, together with the offices, &c. therewith occupied, be rated as aforesaid at 40l. per annum, or upwards, and under 50l. then such person shall take out a licence as aforesaid, and pay for the same the sum of 6l. 14s.

And if such dwelling-house shall, together with the offices, &c. therewith occupied, be rated as aforesaid at 50l. per annum, or upwards, then such person shall take out a licence as aforesaid, and pay for the same the sum of 7l. 2s.

And be it further enacted, that the said several sums of money by this Act directed to be paid for such licences respectively, shall be paid as hereinafter; that is to say, such thereof as shall be taken out within the limits of the chief Office of Excise in London, shall be paid at the chief Office of Excise in London; and such thereof as shall be taken out within the limits of the City of Edinburgh, shall be paid at the chief Office of Excise in Edinburgh; and such thereof as shall be taken out in any part of Great Britain, not within the said respective limits, shall be paid to the respective Collectors of Excise granting such respective licences.

And be it further enacted, that all licences to be granted under and by virtue of this Act, shall remain and continue in force until and upon the 10th day of October next ensuing the time of the granting thereof, and no longer; provided always nevertheless, that where any licence shall be first granted between the 5th day of April and the 10th day of October in any year, there shall be charged only a rateable proportion of the money herein-before directed to be paid for or in respect of such licence, according to the time for which such licence shall be granted.

And

And be it further enacted, that no person shall retail any foreign wine, or any British-made wines or sweets, or any distilled spirituous liquors or strong waters, after the expiration of such his, her, or their licence, unless such person or persons shall take out a fresh licence for the like purpose, in the manner herein-before directed, 10 days at least before the expiration of such former licence, and so in like manner renew every such licence from year to year; and if any person or persons shall retail any foreign wine, or any British-made wines or sweets, or any distilled spirituous liquors or strong waters, without first taking out a licence authorising him, her, or them so to do, and renewing the same as is herein-before in that behalf directed, he, she, or they shall, for every such offence, forfeit the sum of 50l.

And be it further enacted by the authority aforesaid, that upon the death of any person so licensed, or upon the removal of any person or persons so licensed from the entered house or premises in which such his, her, or their licence shall authorize him, her, or them to retail foreign-wine, or to retail British-made wines or sweets, or to retail distilled spirituous liquors or strong waters, it shall and may be lawful to and for the Commissioners of Excise in England and Scotland respectively for the time being, or any one or more of them, and to and for the several Collectors and Supervisors of Excise in England and Scotland respectively, within their respective collections and districts, to authorise and impower the executors or administrators, or the wife or child of such deceased person, or the assignee or assigns of any such person so removing, who shall be possessed of such house or premises, in like manner to retail foreign wine, or to retail British-made wine, or to retail distilled spirituous liquors, as the case may require, in the same entered house or premises where such person, by virtue of such licence, carried on such trade, during the residue of the term for which such licence was originally granted, without taking out a new licence during the residue of the said term: provided always, that persons trading in partnership, and in one house or shop only, shall not be obliged to take out more than one licence in any one year, either for retailing foreign wine, or for retailing British-made wines, or for retailing distilled spirituous liquors, as the case may be; and that no one licence, which shall be granted by virtue of this Act, shall authorize any person to retail foreign wine, or to retail British-made wines, or to retail distilled spirituous liquors in any other house, or place, than that in which he shall
re-

retail foreign wine, or retail British-made wines, or distilled spirituous liquors, as the case may require, at the time of granting such licence, and whereof entry in writing shall be made at the Office of Excise in the name of such person at the time of granting such licence.

Provided always, that nothing herein contained shall in any wise be prejudicial to the privileges of the two Universities.

Provided also, that nothing herein-before contained shall be prejudicial to the commonalty of the Vintners of the City of London, or to any other city or town corporate, but that they may use and enjoy such liberties and privileges as they have heretofore lawfully used and enjoyed: provided also, that no person who shall be admitted to the freedom of the said Company of Vintners of the City of London by redemption only, shall be exempted from the obligation of taking out a licence for retailing foreign wine, but that the freemen only of the said company, who shall have been already admitted to their freedom, or who shall be admitted to their freedom in right of patrimony or apprenticeship, shall be intitled to such exemption.

Provided also, that nothing herein-before contained shall debar the Mayor or Burgesses of the Borough of St. Alban's in the County of Hereford, or their successors, from enjoying all such liberties to them heretofore granted by several letters patent, by Queen Elizabeth and King James I. for licensing of three several wine taverns within the borough aforesaid, for and towards the maintenance of the free-school there.

Provided always nevertheless, that no licence to retail foreign wine, or to retail British-made wines or sweets, or to retail distilled spirituous liquors, shall be granted to any person or persons whatsoever, save and except to such persons only to whom a licence to retail foreign wine, or to retail British-made wines, or to retail distilled spirituous liquors respectively, might lawfully be granted by the several Acts of Parliament in force immediately before the passing of this Act.

And be it further enacted, that all and every person who shall sell, or expose to sale, any foreign wine, in any less quantity than shall be equal to the measure or quantity in which the same shall have been or may be lawfully imported by way of merchandize, shall be deemed and taken to be a retailer or retailers of foreign wine within the meaning of this Act; and if any foreign wine shall at any time be sold,

or expofed to fale, by any perfon whatfoever, in any quantity lefs than the meafure in which the fame fhall have
been or might have been lawfully imported by way of merchandize, fuch felling, or expofing to fale, fhall be deemed
to be a retailing of foreign wine, within the meaning of
this Act; and every perfon who fhall fell, or expofe to fale,
any Britifh-made wine, in the quantity of twenty-five gallons, or under, fhall be deemed and taken to be a retailer
of Britifh-made wines or fweets, within the meaning of this
Act; and if any Britifh-made wine fhall at any time be
fold, or expofed to fale, by any perfon whatfoever in any
quantity lefs than twenty-five gallons, fuch felling, offering, or expofing to fale, fhall be deemed and taken to be a
retailing of Britifh-made wines within the meaning of this
Act; and all and every perfon who fhall fell, expofe to fale,
any brandy, rum, arrack, ufquebaugh, geneva, aquavitæ,
or any other diftilled fpirituous liquors or ftrong waters, unmixed or mixed with themfelves or any other ingredients,
in any lefs quantity than two gallons, fhall be deemed and
taken to be a retailer of diftilled fpirituous liquors and ftrong
waters within the meaning of this Act; and if any diftilled
fpirituous liquors or ftrong waters, unmixed or mixed with
themfelves, or any other ingredients, fhall at any time be
fold, offered, or expofed to fale, by any perfon or perfons
whatfoever in any quantity lefs than two gallons, fuch felling, offering, or expofing to fale, fhall be deemed and taken
to be a retailing of diftilled fpirituous liquors and ftrong waters within the meaning of this Act.

And be it further enacted, that all fines, penalties and
forfeitures impofed by this Act fhall be fued for, recovered,
or mitigated, by fuch methods as any fine, penalty, or forfeiture may be fued for, or mitigated, by any law or laws
of excife, or by action or debt, bill, plaint, or information,
in any of his Majefty's Courts of Record at Weftminfter,
or in the Court of Exchequer in Scotland, refpectively;
and that one moiety of every fuch fine, penalty, or forfeiture,
fhall be to his Majefty, his heirs, and fucceffors, and the
other moiety to him or them who fhall inform, difcover, or
fue for the fame.

And be it further enacted by the authority aforefaid, that,
from and after the faid 10th day of October, 1790, the faid
feveral Acts made in the 9th year of the reign of her faid
late Majefty Queen Anne, in the 30th and 31ft years of the
reign of his faid late Majefty King George II. and in the
20th year of the reign of his prefent Majefty, fo far as the
fame give any power or authority to the faid Commiffioners
of

of Stamps, or any of them, to grant licences to fell wine by retail, or to fell by retail British-made wines or fweets; and alfo that the faid feveral Acts, made in the 16th and 24th years of the reign of his faid late Majefty King *George* II. and in the 27th year of the reign of his faid prefent Majefty, fo far as the fame gave any power or authority to the Commiffioners of Excife in England and Scotland refpectively, or any of them, or to the Collectors and Supervifors of Excife in England and Scotland refpectively, to grant licences to retail diftilled fpirituous liquors or ftrong waters, fhall be, and the fame are hereby repealed.

And be it further enacted by the authority aforefaid, that all the powers, rules, exceptions, matters, and things, which in or by any Act or Acts of Parliament relating to the retailing of foreign wine, or British-made wines or fweets, or diftilled fpirituous liquors, or to licences to retail the fame refpectively, in force immediately before the paffing of this Act, are contained, provided, fettled, or eftablifhed, for raifing, levying, collecting, paying, recovering, adjudging, mitigating, afcertaining, enforcing, or fecuring the rates or duties by law impofed for or in refpect of fuch licences, and for preventing, detecting, and punifhing frauds relating thereto, or for the regulating of the faid liquors refpectively, and not being exprefsly repealed, or controuled by this Act, or not being repugnant to any of the matters in this Act contained, fhall be and continue in full force, and be duly obferved, and put in execution throughout Great Britain, in and for the managing, raifing, collecting, recovering, mitigating, fecuring, the faid feveral duties by this Act impofed, and for preventing, detecting and punifhing frauds relating thereto, and for regulating the retailing of the faid liquors refpectively, fo far as the fame are applicable thereunto refpectively, as fully and effectually, to all intents and purpofes, as if all and every the faid powers, provifions, matters, and things, had been exprefsly inferted and re-enacted in this Act.

And be it further enacted by the authority aforefaid, that all and every the powers, directions, rules, penalties, forfeitures, claufes, matters, and things, which in and by an Act made in the 12th year of the reign of King *Charles* II. cap. 24, or by any other law now in force relating to the revenue of Excife, are provided and eftablifhed, for managing, raifing, or recovering the duties thereby granted, or any of them (other than in fuch cafes for which other penalties or provifions are made and prefcribed by this Act) shall be put in execution as fully and effectually, to all intents and purposes, as if all and every the said powers, matters, and things, were particularly repeated and re-enacted in this present Act.

An Act for converting certain Annuities, to be attended with the Benefit of Survivorship in Classes, established by an Act of the last Session of Parliament, into certain Annuities for an absolute Term of Years; and for enabling the Commissioners of the Treasury to nominate Lives for the Shares so converted.

Whereas, in pursuance of an Act made and passed in the last Session of Parliament, (intituled, "An Act for raising a certain Sum of Money by Way of Annuities, to be attended with the Benefit of Survivorship in Classes"), several persons who had become contributors towards raising the sum of 1 million 2,500l. have actually advanced and paid to the Cashiers of the Bank of England the full sums contributed: and whereas the several contributors, for every 100l. 5s. advanced, are at liberty to name the life of some one person, on or before the 10th day of October, 1790, and by virtue thereof will become intitled from the said 10th day of October, 1790, for and during the life of the nominee who shall be appointed, to an annuity, to be attended with the benefit of survivorship in classes, in manner in the said Act mentioned: and whereas the several contributors, or some of them, are or may be willing and desirous to have such respective interests converted into certain annuities for an absolute term of years herein-after mentioned; be it enacted, that all and every person or persons who may be entitled to any life-annuity or annuities, with benefit of survivorship as in the said Act is granted, and who shall be possessed of any certificate, made out by the Cashier of the Bank of England, in pursuance of the said Act, may, on or before the 20th day of September, 1790, carry the said certificate to the Auditor of the Exchequer, to be exchanged for other certificates to be made out by the said Auditor, in the manner herein-after mentioned; and shall and may, by writing on the back of every such certificate, elect to have his interest in any such life-annuity with benefit of survivorship,

vorſhip, converted into annuities for ſuch certain and abſolute term or terms of years as herein is mentioned; and the ſaid Auditor is hereby required, on the receipt of any ſuch certificate, after computing the intereſt to become due thereon on the 10th day of October, 1790, to give a receipt for the ſame, expreſſing the principal ſum or ſums of money contained in ſuch certificate or certificates, and the ſaid intereſt, and cauſe the ſaid certificate to be filed in his office; and the ſaid Auditor ſhall, in lieu thereof, cauſe to be made out a diſtinct certificate in reſpect of every entire ſum of 100l. 5s. to the Bank of England, for the amount of the principal ſums contained in the certificates for which no fee ſhall be taken, nor ſtamp paid; and the perſon or perſons who ſhall be poſſeſſed of any ſuch laſt-mentioned certificate ſhall, upon delivery thereof to the ſaid Bank, be intitled to an annuity, at and after the rate of 4l. 5s. *per annum*, for and upon every entire ſum of 100l. 5s. which ſhall be expreſſed in ſuch laſt-mentioned certificate, to commence from the 10th day of October, 1790, and to continue for a certain term of 69 years and one quarter of a year, and then to ceaſe; which ſhall be paid half-yearly, (that is to ſay), on the 5th day of April and the 10th day of October in every year during the ſaid term, the firſt payment thereon to be due for half a year on the 5th day of April, 1791, and ſo ſhall continue; and in every ſuch caſe, the right and benefit which might ariſe to ſuch contributor, or his aſſigns, by virtue of the ſaid Act, to any annuity, with benefit of ſurvivorſhip, ſhall ceaſe, determine, and ſhall be deemed to be merged and extinguiſhed in the ſaid certain and abſolute term of years by this Act granted.

And be it further enacted, that in the office of the Accountant General of the Bank of England, a book ſhall be kept, in which the names of every perſon who ſhall have delivered certificates to be made out by the ſaid Auditor in purſuance of this Act, and the principal ſums contained therein, ſhall be fairly entered, which book or books the ſaid perſons, their ſucceſſors, and aſſigns reſpectively, and all perſons who ſhall continue to have an intereſt in ſuch life-annuity, with benefit of ſurvivorſhip as aforeſaid, ſhall from time to time, reſort to and inſpect, without any fee or charge.

And be it further enacted, that the perſons to whoſe credit ſuch principal ſums ſhall be ſo placed, their ſucceſſors, and aſſigns, ſhall and may have power to aſſign and transfer the ſame, or any part thereof, to any perſons whatever, in the books of the Bank of England, and ſuch ſums ſhall

carry

carry an annuity after the rate of 4*l*. 5*s*. *per ann.* in refpect of every fum of 100*l*. 5*s*. for the certain term of 69 years and one quarter of a year, and then to ceafe, and fhall be taken and deemed to be ftock transferable, according to the true intent and meaning of this Act.

And be it further enacted, that all annuities for the term of 69 years and one quarter of a year, by this Act granted, fhall be paid, and be transferable at the Bank of England, and that fuch perfons, their fucceffors, and affigns, converting any life-annuities, with benefit of furvivorfhip, into annuities for the faid term of years, fhall have good and fure interefts and eftates therein, according to the feveral provifions in this Act contained; and that the faid feveral annuities fhall be free from all taxes, charges, and impofitions whatfoever.

Provided always, that the feveral contributors who fhall have had the intereft, to become due on the faid 10th day of October, 1790, computed by the Cafhier of the Bank of England, purfuant to the Act of the laft Seffion, be intitled to receive at the Exchequer, fuch intereft after the rate in the faid Act mentioned.

And be it further enacted, that all perfons who fhall be entitled to any of the annuities hereby granted, fhall be poffeffed thereof, as of a perfonal eftate, which fhall not be defcendible to heirs, nor liable to any foreign attachment by the cuftom of London, or otherwife; any law, ftatute, or cuftom to the contrary notwithftanding.

And be it further enacted, that books fhall be kept, wherein all affeffments or transfers, in refpect of the faid annuities, fhall be entered and regiftered; which entry fhall be figned by the parties making fuch transfers, or by their refpective attornies, thereunto authorized, in writing under their hand and feal, to be attefted by two or more credible witneffes, and that no other method of affigning and transferring the faid annuities, fhall be good or available in law.

Provided always, that all perfons poffeffed of any fhare or intereft in the faid ftock of annuities, or any eftate or intereft therein, may bequeath the fame by will in writing, attefted by two or more credible witneffes, but that no payment fhall be made upon any fuch bequeft until fo much of the faid will as relates to fuch fhare, be entered in the faid office; and that in default of fuch transfer or devife, fuch fhare, eftate, or intereft in the faid ftock of annuities, fhall go to the executors, adminiftrators, fucceffors, and affigns; and that no ftamp-duties whatever fhall be charged on any of of the said transfers; any law or statute to the contrary not-withstanding.

And be it further enacted, that the said Auditor of the Exchequer shall, immediately after the 20th day of September, 1790, certify to the Commissioners of his majesty's Treasury the number of certificates which shall be filed as aforesaid in the Office of the said Auditor; and also the number of such shares of and in the life-annuities, with benefit of survivorship, which shall have been converted into annuities for such terms of years as aforesaid depending thereon; and the said Commissioners of the Treasury shall and may, for and in respect of each and every such sum of 100l. 5s. contained in such certificates, be at liberty to name, in the manner herein directed, the life of some one person, at any time or times on or before the 10th of October, 1790, in the manner hereinafter directed; during which life and lives there shall be reserved at the said receipt of Exchequer, to the use of the publick, at the respective days of payment in the said Act mentioned, such and the like annuity and annuities respectively, with the like benefit of survivorship in classes, as any contributor or contributors in the same classes respectively would be intitled unto by the said Act in respect of an equal number of shares thereof, and which annuity or annuities so reserved at the said receipt to the use of the publick, shall from time to time, as they respectively grow due and arise, be carried to and made part of the consolidated fund towards satisfying and replacing the annuities at and after the rate of 4l. 5s. granted under this Act, and charged thereon as aforesaid.

And be it further enacted, that the said Commissioners of His Majesty's Treasury shall, out of the several degrees of persons hereinafter mentioned, select so many nominees as shall be necessary to carry into execution this present Act; (that is to say) Peers of Great Britain, or of Ireland, or the children or grand-children of such Peers respectively; or Baronets of England or Scotland, or Lords of Manors in England or Wales, or persons named in the Commission of the Peace for any County in England or Wales, or their children; or who are or shall be spiritual persons, promoted to any Bishoprick, Deanry, Archdeaconry, Prebend, or other Dignity in any Cathedral, or other Church, or beneficed with any Parsonage, vicarage, or donative in England, or a Fellowship in any College or Hall of either of the Universities of Oxford or Cambridge; or are or shall be for the time being Governors of the Charter-House, the Foundling-Hospital, or Christ's Hospital; or such persons

who are duly regiſtered in the Books of the Amicable Society for Inſurance on Lives in Serjeant's Inn, and whoſe
names, places of abode, and ages reſpectively, ſhall be fully
ſet forth in ſuch regiſter; and all and every ſuch perſon and
perſons reſpectively, who ſhall be appointed nominees by
the ſaid Commiſſioners of the Treaſury, at any time or
times on or before the 10th day of October, 1790, out of
the orders, degrees, or ſocieties of perſons abovementioned,
ſhall be deemed and adjudged to be nominees, during
whoſe lives reſpectively there ſhall be reſerved, for the uſe
of the publick, annuities to be attended with benefit of ſurvivorſhip, at and after the reſpective rates, and at the times
in the ſaid Act mentioned, as fully and effectually as if ſuch
nominees had been appointed under and by virtue of the ſaid
former Act.

    Provided always, that the ſaid Commiſſioners of the trea-
ſury ſhall deliver to the ſaid Auditor a true copy of the regiſter of the birth or baptiſm of every ſuch nominee, and
alſo a certificate of the ſame, under the hands of the Miniſter of the pariſh or place where ſuch regiſter ſhall be
kept, or of the Churchwardens or Overſeers, or other principal inhabitants, of ſuch pariſh or place, or any two of
them, thereby certifying the ſame to be a true copy of ſuch
regiſter; and alſo a certificate under the hands of the Miniſter of the pariſh or place where ſuch nominee ſhall reſide, or of the Churchwardens or Overſeers, or other principal inhabitants of ſuch pariſh or place, or any three or
more of them, thereby certifying the name, ſurname, and
place of abode, of ſuch nominee; and in caſe any ſuch nominee ſhall be regiſtered in the books of the ſaid Amicable
Society, then the ſaid Commiſſioners of the Treaſury ſhall
alſo deliver to the ſaid Auditor a certificate, under the hands
of two or more of the Directors, certifying the name, place
of abode, and age, of every ſuch nominee, together with ſuch
other apt deſcriptions to aſcertain the perſon of every ſuch
nominee as may appear in the books of the ſaid Society or
Company; and which copies and certificates aforeſaid the
reſpective Miniſters, Officers, Directors, or Governors, or
other perſons aforeſaid, are hereby reſpectively required and
enjoined, upon application in writing, to deliver to the
ſaid Commiſſioners of the Treaſury, or to the perſon or
perſons to be appointed by them, at ſuch times reſpectively
as the ſaid Commiſſioners of the Treaſury, or any three of
them, ſhall direct; and any appointment in writing, under
the hands and ſeals of the ſaid Commiſſioners of the Treaſury, of nominees by virtue of this Act, ſhall be a ſufficient

cient warrant to the proper officers for admitting every such person to be a nominee in the proper class, according to the directions of the said Act.

And be it further enacted by the authority aforesaid, that the said Commissioners of the Treasury for the time being shall, half-yearly, during the continuance of any life or lives so nominated and appointed as aforesaid, transmit to the several parishes and places in Great Britain, where any such nominees shall reside, a list of all the nominees appointed under this Act residing in such parish or place; and also to the Directors of the said Society a list of all such nominees registered in the said Society; and the respective Ministers, Officers, or other persons aforesaid, of the respective places to which such lists shall be transmitted, and the Directors or Governors of the said Society respectively, shall, half-yearly (that is to say) before the 5th day of April, and the 10th day of October, in each year, on such days and times respectively as the said Commissioners of the Treasury shall direct, return to the said Commissioners a certificate, under the hands of such Ministers, Officers, or other persons, or of any two of them, or under the hands of such Directors, or any two of them respectively, thereby certifying the lives of all and every nominees appointed by the said Commissioners of the Treasury which shall then subsist; and also the deaths of such nominees which shall have come to their knowledge respectively, or of the removal of such nominees, or any of them, from such parish or place, as the case may require: and the certificates certifying the lives of the said nominees, being filed at the Office of the Auditor of the said Exchequer, shall be a sufficient warrant for setting apart and reserving at the said receipt, to the use of the publick, the half-yearly payments which shall arise or grow due, or shall have arisen and grown due, in respect of the said nominees so certified, according to the true intent and meaning of this Act, and which certificates shall not be chargeable with any stamp-duty.

Provided always, and be it further enacted by the authority aforesaid, that if, at the time when any half-yearly payment shall become due, to any such nominee or nominees in his Majesty's land forces, or navy, it shall be lawful to produce to the said Auditor, for the purposes aforesaid, a certificate of the lives or deaths of such nominees, under the hands of the respective officers commanding the regiments or corps, where such nominees shall serve or have served, or under the hands of two or more of the Commissioners of the Admiralty or Navy for the time being, as the

case

case may require; and in case any such nominee or nominees shall be resident at either of the said Universities, or at any school, then, and in such case, it shall be lawful to produce the like certificate, under the hand of the principal Rector, Warden, or master of the College, Hall, or School aforesaid, in which such nominees shall be respectively resident; which certificates shall be likewise a sufficient warrant for setting apart and reserving the said half-yearly payments.

And be it further enacted, that the said Auditor of the Exchequer shall, immediately after the 20th day of September, 1790, certify to the Commissioners of the Treasury, or the Lord-High-Treasurer for the time being, the name and number of persons which shall have been then appointed to be nominees, under the said Act; and the said Commissioners shall, in the appointment of nominees on the part of the publick, distribute the number of nominees among the several classes of the tontine, in the same proportion in which the number of nominees appointed by the several contributors, and the number of shares depending on the lives of such nominees, shall appear to have been distributed among the said classes respectively.

And be it further enacted by the authority aforesaid, that the names of all persons of any of the descriptions hereinbefore enumerated, whose respective ages and places of abode shall be ascertained by the Commissioners of the Treasury, at any time on or before the 20th day of September, 1790, shall be distributed into six classes, corresponding to the several classes directed by the said Act of the last Session of Parliament, and written or printed on distinct pieces of paper, being rolled up in the same manner; and shall be put into six boxes, according to the six several classes, in the presence of the said Commissioners of the Treasury, and also the Deputy Governor of the Bank, be publickly drawn in their order, until a sufficient number of names in each class shall be drawn out of the said boxes, to fill up the proportion of nominees to be appointed on the part of the publick, according to the provisions of this Act.

And be it further enacted, that no fee or gratuity shall be taken for paying the said annities, or for any transfer, upon pain that any person offending, shall forfeit the sum of 20l.

ALPHABETICAL TABLE of CASES.

END OF VOL I.

CPSIA information can be obtained
at www.ICGtesting.com
Printed in the USA
BVHW081441260819
556817BV00017B/2230/P

9 781318 556984